Fourth Edition

Teaching and Learning Elementary and Middle School Mathematics

Linda Jensen Sheffield
Northern Kentucky University
Douglas E. Cruikshank
Linfield College

JOHN WILEY & SONS, INC.
New York • Chichester • Weinheim • Brisbane • Singapore • Toronto

Library of Congress Cataloging-in-Publication Data
Sheffield, Linda Jensen
    Teaching and learning elementary and middle school mathematics /
Linda Jensen Sheffield, Douglas E. Cruikshank. — 4th ed.
      p. cm.
    Cruikshank's name appears first on earlier eds.
    Includes index.
    ISBN 0-471-36546-7
    1. Mathematics—Study and teaching (Elementary) 2. Mathematics—
Study and teaching (Middle school)   I. Cruikshank, Douglas E.,
II. Title.
QA135.5.C778   2000
510′.71′2—dc21
                                                            99-17762
                                                            CIP

Photo credits: Pages 1, 15, 35, 63, 151, 191, 331, 381 and 449 courtesy of Douglas Cruikshank; pages 81, 117, 229, 261, 303, and 421 courtesy of W. M. Sheffield.

Printed in the United States of America

10 9 8 7 6 5 4 3 2 1

ISBN: 0-471-36546-7

Preface

This fourth edition of *Teaching and Learning Elementary and Middle School Mathematics* is designed to assist you as you teach mathematical concepts and skills to elementary and middle school students, grades kindergarten through eight. Our focus is on the future; children with strong mathematical foundations will be better equipped for the world they face in the years ahead. No one can predict all of the changes that will take place as the years pass, but we do know that it will be insufficient to teach elementary and middle school students merely to compute or to solve the problems of today. The mathematical foundations are laid when children actively construct or invent mathematics, develop sound concepts and skillful applications of mathematics, discuss and write about their work, and solve a variety of problems. Students must be able to think mathematically, logically, visually, and creatively. Calculators and computers will be welcome tools in the learning process.

Purpose

The purpose of this text is to help you understand and carry out the teacher's role in elementary and middle school mathematics instruction. To this end, we have:

- drawn research from a variety of sources
- reviewed and included recommendations from documents intended to guide reform in school mathematics such as those published by the National Council of Teachers of Mathematics (NCTM), including the draft of *Principles and Standards for School Mathematics* (1998), *Curriculum and Evaluation Standards for School Mathematics* (1989), *Professional Standards for Teaching Mathematics* (1991), and *Assessment Standards for School Mathematics* (1995)
- employed experiences gained from children and teachers. All of these experiences have been carefully applied using numerous activities and models to illustrate how to teach mathematics concepts and principles effectively in your classroom.

New to This Edition

We have expanded and strengthened the fourth edition of this text by:

1. Incorporating recommendations suggested in *Principles and Standards for School Mathematics: Discussion Draft* (1998).
2. Expanding the presentation of the constructivist view of learning, including a list of descriptors for constructivist teachers.
3. Reporting the results of the Third International Mathematics and Science Study (TIMSS) and updates of the National Assessment of Educational Progress (NAEP), including the Internet addresses of the detailed reports. In addition, we have provided examples of the TIMSS test items used during that study and the Internet address that provides the entire set of released test items for all testing levels.
4. Updating the Math Program section of each chapter to represent the broad approaches to teaching mathematics.
5. Providing a complete illustrative description of open-ended problems, a discussion of their characteristics, and an explanation of how they may be assessed.
6. Discussing gender issues in teaching and learning mathematics, including suggestions for maintaining gender equity in the classroom.
7. Including expanded sections on graphing calculators, probability, statistics, graphing, and elementary and middle-level algebra, and a new section on fractal geometry.
8. Providing introductory questions at the beginning of each chapter to guide the reader and discussion questions at the end of each chapter for further reflection.
9. Suggesting Internet sites as additional resources and introducing children's literature to enrich mathematical learning.
10. Updating information on special learners, especially the mathematically promising.

11. Including a series of icons to denote references to children's literature, calculators, computers, writing, and videos.

Text Features

The features that made the early editions of this text distinctive have been maintained:

1. Focus on the future.
2. Use of current research on how children learn specific mathematical topics.
3. Consideration of children's different learning styles and of special learners, including the mathematically promising.
4. Integration of computers and calculators as tools in the teaching of each content strand.
5. Focus on problem creation and problem solution, teaching children to use their own higher-level thinking processes, including mental calculation and estimation.
6. Presentation of numerous activities in each chapter using physical models for concept and skill development.
7. Display of pages from elementary and middle school mathematics programs and the discussion of their instructional uses.
8. Inclusion of probability, statistics, and graphing—all of which have been emphasized recently due to the influence of personal computers.
9. Presentation of reference lists in each chapter that direct the reader to recent research material in each content area.
10. Suggestions and problems that serve as the basis for journal entries that open each chapter.
11. Presentation of a number of appendixes, including an expanded selection of blackline masters for frequently used instructional materials and addresses of publishers of software and commercially prepared manipulative materials.

We hope you will use many of the activities we have presented. Teachers who discover the joy of actively participating in the learning of mathematics are more enthusiastic and confident when teaching, and their interactions with children are richer and more exciting. You are encouraged to add to the collection of activities in this text, modify others for your particular students, and share activities and experiences with other teachers.

We anticipate that you will be the finest teachers ever to assist children in learning. We need more skillful, knowledgeable, and compassionate teachers. If this textbook can, in any way, help prepare, direct, and encourage you in nurturing the growth of young people as they learn mathematics, then our purpose in writing this book will be fulfilled.

Acknowledgments

We would like to thank the many students we worked with as we were preparing this manuscript for their invaluable feedback on activities and the mathematics they were learning. A special thanks to students in McMinnville, Oregon, and Powell County and Ft. Thomas, Kentucky, for their help and inspiration. Thanks to the preservice and in-service teachers we have worked with over the last 30 years of college teaching. We could not have produced this book without all your feedback and suggestions.

We would like to express our sincere appreciation to the reviewers of this fourth edition. Their suggestions as well as those of reviewers of the first, second, and third editions made this a much stronger textbook. Reviewers of the fourth edition were Betty K. Hathaway, University of Arkansas at Little Rock; Victoria Boller LaBerge, Northern Illinois University; Barbara J. Lehman, East Central University; and Kay Reinke, Oklahoma State University. Reviewers of the first edition include Lucy Dechene, Fitchburg State College; Jon Engelhardt, Arizona State University; Boyd Holtan, West Virginia University; Charles Lamb, University of Texas at Austin; Walter Secada, University of Wisconsin-Madison; Richard Shumway, Ohio State University; and Alan Zollman, University of Kentucky. Reviewers of the second edition were Jerry Becker, Southern Illinois University at Carbondale; Joan C. Carson, University of Mississippi; Anne G. Dorsey, University of Cincinnati; Louis Fillinger, Fort Hays State University; Hiram D. Johnston, Georgia State University; William L. Merrill, Central Michigan University; and Helene J. Sherman, University of Missouri–St. Louis. Reviewers of the third edition were Lucy Dechene, Fitchburg State College; Anne G. Dorsey, University of Cincinnati; Jon Engelhardt, Arizona State University; Hiram D. Johnston, Georgia State University; Barbara Lehman, Mississippi State University; and Dorothy Spithmann, Dakota State College.

Finally, our families and friends deserve much credit for their understanding and support. We are deeply grateful to Bill, Dan, Linda, Lori, and Julie.

Contents

Chapter 1

Preparing to Teach Mathematics

My Math Journal

Before you begin this book, we want you to think about the topic you are about to study. Take a few minutes to write down your answer to the question below. We hope you will feel free to write in the space provided or make or purchase a small book to use for this writing activity that will continue throughout this text. After you have read the first chapter, add other comments to your answer. Continue to add comments as the term progresses. At the end of the term, look back at your comments and see if your thoughts about mathematics have changed.

What is mathematics?

As you read the following pages, consider these guiding questions:

1. What is mathematics and what does it mean to know mathematics?
2. What forces shape mathematics curriculum, instruction, and assessment at the national, state, and local levels?
3. What are common themes that run through each chapter in this text?
4. How does assessment effect mathematics programs?
5. What aspects of the teaching process should you consider as you begin working with students?

You are about to start on a very important journey. This journey will be an investigation of how you can be successful in your role as an elementary or middle school teacher of mathematics. We hope that by the end of the journey you will have gained confidence as a person and as a teacher and that you will be ready to share the joy and excitement that emerges from sound mathematics instruction. This is not a journey during which you will be asked to sit back and relax; rather, you will be challenged to develop new confidence in your own mathematical ability, to attack intriguing mathematical problems, to look inward at yourself as an individual and as a teacher, and to set personal goals for your elementary or middle school teaching. This textbook is intended to provide assistance and offer direction on your journey. We realize, however, that the most effective test of your mathematics teaching ability will be your own teaching experiences. You will be supported by your teachers, supervisors, fellow students, and, of course, by your students, who will appreciate your methods of teaching.

How do individuals prepare to teach mathematics? At first glance, the natural question, "How will I teach mathematics?" appears to be one that will never be satisfactorily answered. The beginning of the journey to answer this question is found here in Chapter 1. Two important topics are examined to give you a foundation for your investigation of how to teach mathematics:

1. Philosophical considerations.
2. Influences on the school mathematics curriculum.

Philosophical Considerations

You have taken mathematics courses to prepare yourself for teaching. It is common to have taken such courses, perhaps for several years, and yet never have been introduced to the nature of mathematics and what it means to know mathematics. Yet knowing something about the nature of mathematics and what it means to know mathematics is considered fundamental by the Mathematical Sciences Education Board of the National Research Council (1990, p. 9). This Board has pointed out that "To

realize a new vision of school mathematics will require public acceptance of a realistic philosophy of mathematics that reflects both mathematical practice and pedagogical experience."

The notion of a new vision of school mathematics comes from several sources that will be discussed in this and the next chapter. It refers to a new way to think about how children learn mathematics and how the subject may be effectively taught. You will be a part of an exciting period of new emphasis in school mathematics. Let us turn to two questions that will serve as a philosophical basis for school mathematics in the future.

What Is Mathematics?

Mathematics is particularly well defined by the National Research Council in its publication *Everybody Counts:*

> As a practical matter, mathematics is a science of pattern and order. Its domain is not molecules or cells, but numbers, chance, form, algorithms, and change. As a science of abstract objects, mathematics relies on logic rather than on observation as its standard of truth, yet employs observation, simulation, and even experimentation as means of discovering truth. (1989, p. 31)

The idea of patterns is key to the nature of mathematics. Children observe patterns long before entering school; they bring with them the ability to discover and recognize patterns. Elementary and middle school children are introduced to patterns in counting, addition tables, geometry, fractions, and decimals. Students understand mathematics because they are able to discern patterns in physical models, pictures, and symbols (see Figure 1–1). Number and geometric patterns exhibit a regularity that is consistent and makes sense to young learners. Thinking of mathematics as the science of patterns and order helps you as a teacher when you begin to teach children mathematics. By raising awareness of patterns, you will assist children in looking for and developing patterns in their study of mathematics.

What Does It Mean to Know Mathematics?

What it means to know mathematics emerges from the nature of mathematics. Thus, to know mathematics means to know patterns and relationships among patterns. The National Research Council expands on this notion. The learner needs

> . . . to be able to discern patterns in complex and obscure contexts; to understand and transform relations among patterns; to classify, encode, and describe patterns; to read and write in the language of patterns; and to employ knowledge of patterns for various practical purposes. (1990, p. 12)

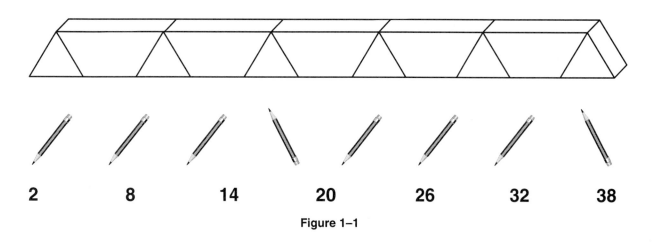

Figure 1–1

Students must have the opportunity to study, discover, and invent patterns of many different types while in the process of learning and eventually knowing mathematics. This suggests that the process of knowing mathematics involves active mental activity that is an outgrowth of many types of experiences. As a teacher, you have a responsibility to help students in their quest to know patterns and relationships among patterns.

Implications of These Philosophical Considerations

By developing a philosophical basis for mathematics education we hope to illustrate how the new vision of school mathematics will influence the teaching of mathematics to elementary and middle school students. Classifying mathematics as a science suggests that mathematics is actively explored through experimentation, discovery, manipulation, and discussion, and that calculators and computers can be used as tools of mathematics. This view contrasts with the view that mathematics is only a paper and pencil exercise that relies on rules, formulas, and memory.

Thinking of mathematics as a search for patterns suggests that the content of a mathematics program should include patterns of many types, including those discovered in the study of numbers, geometry, measurement, and algebra, topics usually considered in contemporary mathematics programs. Problem situations, problem solving, and problem posing are provided as ways to search for patterns. This view contrasts with the view that elementary and middle school mathematics programs should focus only on arithmetic—rules and algorithms.

Your philosophical beliefs about mathematics will serve you as you engage in teaching. You will be able to envision a broader mathematics curriculum, one that includes more than just arithmetic. You will feel comfortable about encouraging students to introduce problems

from their own experiences. You will see merit in the use of modern technology in teaching. You will be convincing as you discuss your beliefs with parents and colleagues. In short, you will have a strong rationale for the new vision of school mathematics.

Influences on the School Mathematics Curriculum

Many forces influence the mathematics content taught in elementary and middle schools. Some have greater influence than others, and the influence shifts as times change. Nevertheless, all of the forces interact with one another. Among the most influential forces are professional organizations, mathematics textbooks, assessment procedures, and state governmental bodies.

Professional Organizations

The mathematics education community in this country has strong, active membership in several professional organizations. Among those organizations are the Mathematical Association of America (MAA), National Council of Teachers of Mathematics (NCTM), School Science and Mathematics Association (SSMA), Research Council on Mathematics Learning (RCML), and Psychology of Mathematics Education (PME). In addition, individual state mathematics organizations play an important role by supporting sound programs of mathematics in their states.

The National Council of Teachers of Mathematics is perhaps best known to elementary and middle school teachers. Its members assume leadership roles at the national, state, and local levels of mathematics education, providing a structure through which sound mathematics programs may be created. The NCTM develops position papers based on the work of its many national committees. The NCTM disseminates information to teachers and administrators through its publications. Pamphlets, yearbooks, small books, and journals provide readers with up-to-date information about teaching mathematics.

The NCTM web site, http://www.nctm.org/, provides up-to-date information about the organization and its activities. Elementary and middle school teachers find many teaching ideas for classroom use in *Teaching Children Mathematics,* published nine times a year; and *Mathematics Teaching in the Middle School,* published seven times a year.

The NCTM and its affiliated state organizations hold outstanding conferences throughout the school year. Each year, there is one national meeting, and there are numerous regional conferences. These conferences are highlighted by hundreds of sessions and workshops that show teachers effective ways to present mathematics.

The leadership provided by the NCTM helps influence the direction of the school mathematics curriculum. In 1989 NCTM published the first of three documents that were to transform mathematics education in the United States. It was the *Curriculum and Evaluation Standards for School Mathematics.* Two additional documents followed: *Professional Standards for Teaching Mathematics* (1991) and *Assessment Standards for School Mathematics* (1995). After a decade of application and discussion, the standards have been rewritten into a single document, *Principles and Standards for School Mathematics.* According to the NCTM (1998, p. 13): "The charge to the *Principles and Standards* Writing Group was to 'build on the foundations of the original NCTM *Standards* documents and to consolidate the classroom aspects of all three documents.' In addition, the Writing Group was charged to organize this document into four grade band sections, thereby allowing more detail and specificity for the grades."

Copies of or excerpts from *Principles and Standards for School Mathematics* are available to teachers throughout the world. An electronic version of the document may be found at http://standards-e.nctm.org. You will notice that the grade level designations are presented in four groupings (Pre-K–2, 3–5, 6–8, and 9–12) and that the standards for each grouping are spelled out. The examples for each grouping illustrate the meaning of the standards and suggest ways to meet them.

Because the final version of *Principles and Standards for School Mathematics* is unavailable at the time of this printing, the original *Standards* documents will be discussed, providing you with the foundation upon which *Principles and Standards for School Mathematics* is based. As you read these *Standards,* compare them to the latest version at the *Standards* website. Look at electronic examples (e-Examples) available on-line to view video vignettes, animations, interactive aplets, and other resources that will help you understand and implement the *Standards.*

Curriculum and Evaluation Standards for School Mathematics

This document consists of a set of standards for a K–12 mathematics curriculum. It also consists of a set of standards for evaluating both the curriculum and students' mathematical achievement. Accordingly, the NCTM (1989, p. v) noted that "The *Standards* is a document designed to establish a broad framework to guide reform in school mathematics in the next decade. In it a vision is given of what the mathematics curriculum should include in terms of content priority and emphasis." The *Standards* was a remarkable document in that it represented the thinking of a broad cross-section of the mathematics education community in the United States, including classroom teachers. It was also the first time that the NCTM recommended a broadly stated K–12 mathematics curriculum. The result was an expanded definition of mathematics instruction. The direction of mathematics education in the 1990s and beyond was greatly influenced by the message and recommendations contained in this document.

The *Standards* contained five general goals for all students, along with several implications:

... (1) that they learn to value mathematics, (2) that they become confident in their ability to do mathematics, (3) that they become mathematical problem solvers, (4) that they learn to communicate mathematically, and (5) that they learn to reason mathematically. These goals imply that students should be exposed to numerous and varied interrelated experiences that encourage them to value the mathematical enterprise, to develop mathematical habits of mind, and to understand and appreciate the role of mathematics in human affairs; that they should be encouraged to explore, to guess, and even to make and correct errors so that they gain confidence in their ability to solve complex problems; that they should read, write, and discuss mathematics; and that they should conjecture, test, and build arguments about a conjecture's validity. (1989, p. 5)

These goals are appropriate for you as an elementary or middle school teacher. Your enthusiasm for mathematics and your ability to teach mathematics effectively will depend, in part, on your thoughtful consideration of these goals and their implications as a personal challenge.

The curriculum standards presented in this document were divided into three levels: grades K–4, 5–8, and 9–12. The evaluation standards were presented in a fourth section. Twenty-six standards were presented in levels K–4 and 5–8 (see Table 1–1). Each standard was then discussed and illustrated with examples of how the standard might be realized in the classroom. You will find the standards included throughout this textbook.

The *Standards* clearly called for change in mathematics education. It suggested that in-

TABLE 1–1   Curriculum Standards

Grades K–4	Grades 5–8
1. Mathematics as Problem Solving	1. Mathematics as Problem Solving
2. Mathematics as Communication	2. Mathematics as Communication
3. Mathematics as Reasoning	3. Mathematics as Reasoning
4. Mathematical Connections	4. Mathematical Connections
5. Estimation	5. Number and Number Relationships
6. Number Sense and Numeration	6. Number Systems and Number Theory
7. Concepts of Whole Number Operations	7. Computation and Estimation
8. Whole Number Computation	8. Patterns and Functions
9. Geometry and Spatial Sense	9. Algebra
10. Measurement	10. Statistics
11. Statistics and Probability	11. Probability
12. Fractions and Decimals	12. Geometry
13. Patterns and Relationships	13. Measurement

NCTM, (1989), pp. 15, 65. Reprinted by permission.

creased attention be given to topics previously given little or cursory attention, such as developing the meanings of fractions, decimals, numbers, operations, and spatial sense; probability and statistics; and reasoning. It suggested that decreased attention be given to topics that previously dominated instruction, such as performing complex paper-and-pencil computations, memorizing rules and algorithms, and manipulating symbols. While not covering all of the areas of increased and decreased attention, these examples should give you a sense of the shift in direction recommended by the NCTM. You are encouraged to become familiar with the *Curriculum and Evaluation Standards for School Mathematics,* to use your knowledge of these standards to understand the direction taken in *Principles and Standards for School Mathematics,* and to establish yourself as a forward-looking teacher of mathematics. These standards may be found at the web site: http://www.enc.org/ reform-/journals/ENC2280/280dtoc1.htm and are presented in the chapters that follow.

Professional Standards for Teaching Mathematics. This document was designed to complement the *Curriculum and Evaluation Standards* discussed above. It set standards for teachers and administrators so they could provide the kind of instruction recommended by the *Curriculum and Evaluation Standards.* The professional standards for teaching mathematics involve four different aspects of professional responsibility: (1) teaching, (2) evaluation of teaching, (3) professional development of teachers, and (4) support and development of teachers and teaching. There are a total of 24 professional standards (see Table 1–2). Following the presentation of each standard, there is an elaboration of the standard followed by a vignette or an example that illustrates how the standard might be met. The professional teaching standards are included in Chapter 15.

Assessment Standards for School Mathematics. The *Assessment Standards* (1995) was designed to complement the *Curriculum and Evaluation Standards* and *Professional Standards for Teaching Mathematics.* This document carefully outlines and discusses in depth six standards to be used to judge procedures used to assess children's mathematical growth. The six assessment standards are listed in Chapter 15 in the section called Assessing, Recording, and Reporting Students' Progress.

According to the assessment document, ". . . new assessment strategies and practices need to be developed that will enable teachers and others to assess students' performance in a manner that reflects the NCTM's reform vision for school mathematics" (1995, p. 1). The assessment standards were designed to expand and complement the Evaluation Standards from the 1989 *Curriculum and Evaluation Standards.* It is noted that most assessment systems that are currently being used do not conform to current reform efforts in school mathematics. Thus, the assessment document stands to influence future mathematics assessment heavily.

Mathematics Textbooks

The mathematics textbook, commonly referred to as the "math text," has historically been very influential in determining the elementary and middle school mathematics curriculum. It establishes an important curricular framework. It provides a continuity from September to June and consistency from one level to another. The mathematical topics included in math texts have evolved

TABLE 1–2 Professional Standards for Teaching Mathematics

Standards for Teaching Mathematics	Standards for the Evaluation of the Teaching of Mathematics
Tasks	The Process of Evaluation
1. Worthwhile Mathematical Tasks Discourse	1. The Evaluation Cycle
2. Teacher's Role in Discourse	2. Teachers as Participants in Evaluation
3. Students' Role in Discourse	3. Sources of Information
4. Tools for Enhancing Discourse Environment	The Foci of Evaluation
5. Learning Environment Analysis	4. Mathematical Concepts, Procedures, and Connections
6. Analysis of Teaching and Learning	5. Mathematics as Problem Solving, Reasoning, and Communication
	6. Mathematical Disposition
	7. Assessing Students' Mathematical Understanding
	8. Learning Environment

Standards for the Professional Development of Teachers of Mathematics	Standards for the Support and Development of Mathematics Teachers and Teaching
1. Experiencing Good Mathematics Teaching	1. Responsibilities of Policymakers in Government, Business, and Industry
2. Knowing Mathematics and School Mathematics	2. Responsibilities of Schools
3. Knowing Students as Learners of Mathematics	3. Responsibilities of Colleges and Universities
4. Knowing Mathematical Pedagogy	4. Responsibilities of Professional Organizations
5. Developing as a Teacher of Mathematics	
6. The Teacher's Role in Professional Development	

NCTM (1991), pp. 19, 71, 123, 177. Reprinted by permission.

steadily for over a hundred years of textbook publication. The textbooks change when new trends emerge and are supported by teachers, mathematics leaders, parents, and administrators. Publishers respond to their customers. Recent textbooks reflect the recommendations of the NCTM *Standards.*

Well-designed textbooks in the hands of skillful teachers are powerful educational tools. With texts, teachers can diagnose and evaluate children's mathematical performance. They can assign exercises to reinforce concepts and skills already learned as well as to teach and reteach important mathematical concepts and skills that are new to the student.

Skillful teachers know that they must go beyond the pages of the textbook. Activities and projects must often replace pictures and symbols. Teaching styles that differ from the textbook presentation will be needed. Mathematical applications will require children's more active participation. The daily textbook routine should give way to other methods to allow mathematics to come alive in the minds of the children.

The National Research Council expressed the challenge faced by textbook publishers in light of recent research findings:

> New textbooks must be designed and written to reflect the important principles of mathematics curricula: genuine problems; calculators and computers; relevant applications; reading and writing about mathematics; and active strategies for learning. (1990, pp. 49–50)

You will need to be a discerning consumer of mathematics textbooks. You must decide if textbooks serve your instructional needs and you must decide how math textbooks best serve the needs of students. This is the art of teaching.

Assessment Procedures

Assessment procedures that influence mathematics curriculum in the United States vary from those that are national and international in scope to those at the state, local, and district levels. A discussion of each is presented below.

According to Forgione, "The Third International Mathematics and Science Study (TIMSS) is the largest, most comprehensive, and most rigorous international study of schools and student achievement ever conducted" (1997, p. 3). The TIMSS data were collected during the 1994–95 academic year. Involved were more than half a million students taking mathematics and science at three grade levels in 41 countries. In the United States, about 22,000 fourth and eighth grade students were involved and another 11,000 high school seniors were involved.

The TIMSS contained a variety of components: student assessments, questionnaires, curriculum analysis, performance assessments, videotape observations of mathematics instruction, and ethnographic case studies of key policy topics. The achievement data showed that

U.S. fourth graders scored slightly above average in mathematics when compared with students from the 26 countries in the TIMSS fourth grade assessment. U.S. eighth graders scored slightly below average in mathematics when compared with their peers in the 41 countries in their comparison group. U.S. twelfth graders scored significantly below average in mathematics when compared with their counterparts in 21 countries. The national media expressed disappointment in these results, for a country that had been challenged to be first in the world in mathematics by the year 2000. More important, however, was the opportunity to analyze the volumes of data that were generated by the study and to find areas on which to focus attention.

For example, Burrill noted that the TIMSS video study data of eighth grade students revealed that ". . . the goals of U.S. teachers were directed toward showing students how to do something—61 percent of the reported goals were skills oriented. In contrast, 75 percent of goals of Japanese teachers in the study were focused on helping students understand a mathematical concept" (1998, p. 3). Burrill then challenged U.S. teachers to consider their own approaches to teaching mathematics. TIMSS is a good example of how carefully collected assessment data may be used as a basis for a national discussion on mathematics goals, curriculum, and teaching approaches. For examples of questions that were asked and more detailed discussions of the findings see http://nces.ed.gov/timss.

Every school district assesses its students' mathematical learning at some time during the academic year. This assessment comes from the state and local goals established to guide the districts' mathematical instruction. The form of the assessment may vary among school districts. It may take the form of nationally standardized achievement tests or district or state examinations. It may take the form of performance-based assessment procedures. It may take the form of a combination of measures. Mathematical assessment may be embedded in broad curriculum assessment. Regardless of the form of assessment, the results provide local districts and communities with a measure of the students' accomplishments in mathematics. A summary of test results is commonly published in local newspapers. Considerable importance is accorded these results. Thus, many teachers set high expectations for achievement, whether by exam or other types of performance. In this way the mathematics curriculum is heavily influenced by assessment procedures.

If the current reform efforts in mathematics education are expected to be successful, changes in the way we currently assess students' mathematical growth will have to take place. A set of assessment reforms are spelled out in the document mentioned earlier, *Assessment Standards for School Mathematics* (NCTM, 1995).

The *Assessment Standards* is intended to be used to evaluate mathematical assessment programs. Alternative means of assessment will be expected of you as an elementary or middle school teacher. Those who carefully design assessment procedures do not intend that the procedures be used to determine the curriculum. Assessment procedures are developed to measure growth in students' understanding of mathematical concepts as well as thinking processes commonly found in elementary and middle school mathematics programs throughout the country. Assessment follows from the goals of the curriculum and determines if the instruction effectively meets those goals. As mathematics programs reflect the changes that are recommended by the NCTM *Curriculum and Evaluation Standards* and other forward-looking documents, the methods for assessment broaden to meet the expanding definition of mathematics instruction.

State Governmental Bodies

Influenced by numerous national reports on education and a public concerned with the quality of education, state legislative education committees and legislatures, state departments of education, and teacher certification offices have developed laws, policies, and regulations that have an impact on elementary and middle school mathematics curricula. There has been concern about the overall quality of education in this country. As a result, state and local study committees have made recommendations about how to improve the quality of education. As new statewide goals are established, curricular areas such as mathematics are being reviewed. Thus, revisions are being made to statewide mathematics curricula, in part to align them with the new standards.

Changes in mathematics curricula in various large states result in changes in textbooks and necessitate changes in assessment procedures. The forces that influence the curriculum are interrelated. The mathematics curriculum with which you will be involved has been affected by the forces mentioned above. The response you and your students have toward mathematics and the textbook will likely influence curricular change in the future.

Looking Ahead

Most of the remaining chapters of this book (Chapters 5 through 14) include the following sections:

a. NCTM *Standards*
b. Developing Concepts
c. Developing Skills
d. The Math Program
e. Estimating and Mental Calculating

f. Solving and Creating Problems
g. Grouping for Instruction
h. Communicating
i. Connecting
j. Assessing Learning of Mathematics
k. Something for Everyone

Each chapter includes a set of guiding questions, a set of activity/discussion questions, and a brief section, *Key Ideas,* that summarizes the chapter. We discuss how mathematical concepts are developed in Chapter 2, solving and creating problems and estimating and mental calculating in Chapter 3, and grouping for instruction in Chapter 15. Throughout the text you will find references to children's literature as it relates to mathematics instruction, suggestions for computer software, and appropriate Internet sites that can enhance your mathematics lessons. What follows is a brief discussion of the remaining sections.

NCTM Standards

The *Standards* was discussed earlier in this chapter. Each standard is presented in more detail at the beginning of the chapter that contains the content strand mentioned in the standard. As a result, you will be able to see the connection between a particular standard and suggestions for developing that content strand in the elementary or middle school classroom.

Developing Skills

Once mathematical concepts have been introduced, skills associated with those concepts may be taught. Skills include the basic facts and procedures that students apply as they calculate and solve problems. Many of the skills students use are memorized. For example, the basic addition facts, those from $0 + 0$ to $9 + 9$, are important when students perform mental and paper-and-pencil calculations.

Included with activities for developing skills are activities that employ calculators and computers. As mentioned above, these tools play an important role in the learning of elementary and middle school mathematics.

The type of understanding that comes from learning skills has been called "procedural understanding" (Hiebert & Lefevre, 1986) or "instrumental understanding" (Skemp, 1987). It is substantively different from conceptual understanding, which is discussed in Chapter 2. Hiebert (1986, p. 8) explained that "Conceptual knowledge, by our definition, must be learned meaningfully. Procedures, on the other hand, may or may not be learned with meaning. We propose that procedures that are learned with meaning are procedures that are linked to conceptual knowledge." He goes on to explain that procedures that have not been connected with conceptual knowledge are more easily forgotten and more difficult to reconstruct. We concur that when skills or procedures are taught, they should be associated whenever possible with their underlying concepts.

The Math Program

Chapters 3 through 15 contain, in each chapter, an illustration from a mathematics program or a textbook page that corresponds to the topic emphasized in that chapter. In presenting the program examples, we recognize the important role that print materials play in the instructional program; on the other hand, we have devoted the bulk of this textbook to the presentation of activities you can use to help children learn mathematics with or without a textbook. In the math program inserts, we illustrate a variety of programs to give you an idea of those that are currently available. We also take the opportunity to comment on the material illustrated, to show how the author recommends that it be used, and to offer additional suggestions when we feel that they are appropriate.

Communicating

Throughout the learning process, communication is crucial. The ways that teachers and students communicate affect the quality of learning. New emphasis is being given to the oral and written communication that occurs during the learning of mathematics. As students construct and invent mathematics, their discussions and writing are rich with explanations of their thinking processes. As students read and listen to the writings of those who include mathematics in their works, their imaginations and understanding are enhanced. Writing in mathematics and using literature in mathematics help students see how communication enhances understanding of their thoughts and those of others. A brief description of ways that children may communicate as they learn mathematics is included in each of the content chapters.

Connecting

The focus of connecting is to help show how mathematical ideas are related and to show how mathematics is related to daily life both in and out of the classroom. We believe that much of what this textbook presents shows how mathematical ideas are connected, and we take the opportunity in this section of each chapter to illustrate how mathematics is related to daily life. We show this relationship through examples of lessons that have been tried in a variety of classrooms.

Assessing Mathematics Learning

There are a number of reasons for assessing students' growth in understanding mathematics. Among the most important is to improve teaching and learning. Thus, teachers are able to determine where students currently are in their mathematics learning so that appropriate instruction may be planned. Currently, the most commonly used tools for assessing mathematics learning are the curriculum-embedded tests provided with basal textbook series and standardized achievement tests. The textbook tests provide diagnosis at the beginning of a chapter or section, evaluate the children's progress during and at the end of each chapter, and check their ability to recall concepts and skills from earlier chapters. Standardized tests that include sections designed to test mathematics achievement are commonly administered once per year to a group of children.

There are, however, alternative assessment techniques that overcome the shortcomings of textbook tests and standardized tests. Considerable attention has recently been focused on dynamic ways to assess growth in mathematics. These alternatives are an important part of the current mathematics reform movement. Among them are observation and questioning, performance-based assessment, diagnostic interviews, teacher-made assessment tasks, writing activities, and group problem solving. Along with the assessment techniques are procedures for collecting students' work such as individual student portfolios. These techniques have an important role in broad-based assessment programs. In each chapter, assessment procedures are discussed with regard to the content emphasis of the chap-

ter. A more detailed description of assessment procedures is included in Chapter 15.

Something for Everyone

All schools should provide elementary and middle school children with the most effective instruction possible. Teachers should consider the learning styles of their students when planning lessons. While children learn using all of their senses, some children depend more on a particular sense. **Visual learners** learn more readily by looking at pictures, illustrations, and objects; **auditory learners,** by listening and talking; and **kinesthetic learners,** by touching objects and moving about (see Figure 1–2). Visual learners should have plenty of pictures, illustrations, and physical models available. Auditory learners should be given clearly stated directions and explanations and should be encouraged to discuss their own knowledge and understanding. Kinesthetic learners should be provided with opportunities to move about and to touch and manipulate objects. Students with a tendency toward a systematic, logical approach will do well with the textbook. Students with a tendency toward a graphic approach will do well with a more active, pictorial, manipulative approach. Thus, while the daily mathematics program may be textbook-based, you must adjust your teaching to allow for the differences among your students. Each chapter discusses ways that you can help children with different learning styles master the content emphasized in the chapter.

There are other students with special needs, those who have unusual difficulty learning mathematics and those who have particular talents when it comes to mathematics.

a. **Visual Learners**   b. **Auditory Learners**   c. **Kinesthetic Learners**

Figure 1–2

Both groups require the teacher's attention. Chapter 15 further discusses the special needs of various children.

Teaching Considerations

Finally, we need to consider our interaction with the children with whom we work. Teaching is a tremendous challenge, and both teachers and students reap enormous personal rewards. Beliefs, upbringing, prejudices, values, self-concept, and personality affect an individual's teaching style. The approach a teacher takes to children, classroom organization, and disruptions is an extension of who that teacher is. Three aspects of teaching in general, as well as of teaching mathematics in particular, are **failure, management,** and **encouragement.** Each is briefly discussed below.

Failure.   Children, especially young children, seem to cope naturally with failure. Gaining an initial understanding of life, which includes learning about the environment and roles within the family and society, involves trial and error. Failure in this context is used as a springboard to future success. The healthy use of mistakes can provide a foundation for growth.

On the other hand, failure may be harmful to the child. When teachers or parents teach that failure should be avoided at all costs, children develop sophisticated mechanisms to avoid failure. Holt (1964) discussed many reactions or strategies that children develop to avoid failing. For instance, when a teacher asks a question, some children excitedly wave their hands even though they do not know the answer because they know that the teacher will call on the children who look apprehensive. Or, for example, a child begins to give a response and then closely observes the teacher for clues, usually nonverbal clues, that the response he or she has begun is correct. Teachers may feel that it is their duty to point out all mistakes. Holt and others appropriately warn of the consequences of such behavior. It is far healthier to look for children's strengths and assets. Teachers should not ignore incorrect mathematical concepts, but they should teach concepts without destroying children's egos.

Children need to feel secure. The following are several suggestions for developing children's abilities so that they may become confident learners. Teachers and parents should

1. Accept their own mistakes openly in front of students. Show students how failure is useful in learning and unimportant in determining one's overall worth.
2. Allow for failure and treat it as a natural part of the learning process. Let students make mistakes and learn from their mistakes. Avoid embarrassing them for making mistakes.
3. Provide opportunities for students to succeed. Develop their confidence through success to the extent that they will maintain confidence when they do not succeed.
4. Avoid blaming students who do not meet adult expectations. Expect high-quality performance, but keep in mind the capabilities of the youngsters.
5. Accept students as individuals worthy of respect. Believe that students deserve respect. Listen when they wish to share ideas and feelings. Respond in a warm manner.
6. Provide opportunities for students to make decisions that affect their lives within the school setting. Make sure the decisions are real and the students can and will abide by the logical consequences of their decisions.
7. Discuss failure with individuals and with the class group. Come to agreements about how failure will be dealt with. Live up to those agreements.

Management.   Management and discipline are of utmost concern to teachers and parents regardless of the age of the children. Many factors affect children's behaviors. Some of these factors are genetic, but most behaviors are learned in the home environment. Others result from the school experience and interaction with society at large. When children are brought together in a group, individual and group behavior should be channeled constructively. Even free play activities involving several individuals in parallel play should be managed so that children with overlapping interests avoid conflict. Cooperation and compromise should be introduced and nourished to the degree that children understand those concepts. Even though ego-centeredness is characteristic, respect for the rights of others should be fostered.

Themes commonly found in textbooks on classroom management include these teacher responsibilities: developing and maintaining a working environment, defining the rules for individual and group work, providing a quality educational program, being the educational leader in the classroom, involving students in decision making, being consistent, providing stability, monitoring and guiding activities, and treating misbehavior. You are urged to select one or more books on classroom management and to incorporate in your teaching style management techniques characterized by an ongoing respect for youngsters and their talents.

Encouragement.   Encouragement has been carefully studied. Self-evident as it may appear, encouragement is seldom recognized as a crucial factor in the growth and development of healthy young minds. Teachers and parents tend to discourage youngsters even while they profess the need for encouraging them. Discouragement emerges as one of the greatest single causes for failure.

Dinkmeyer and Dreikurs comment on the importance of encouragement in working with children:

> We, as educators, as parents, and as teachers, are in charge of the greatest treasure society possesses, the next generation. The urgent question which confronts us today is whether we will be able to guide them into becoming capable and responsible human beings or whether we will have to wait until youth itself claims its right to proper guidance and education. This question will be decided, in our opinion, by our ability to change from a punitive, retaliatory, and mistake-centered educational practice to one of encouragement for all those who have failed to find their way toward fulfillment. (1963, pp. 124–125)

As a result of their extensive work on the encouragement process, Dinkmeyer and Dreikurs (1963, p. 50) have delineated nine methods of encouragement:

1. Place value on children as they are.
2. Show faith in children to enable them to have faith in themselves.
3. Have faith in children's abilities; win their confidence while building their self-respect.
4. Recognize effort and a job well done.
5. Utilize the group to facilitate and enhance the development of the child.
6. Integrate the group so that children can be sure of their place in it.
7. Pace skills sequentially and psychologically to permit success.
8. Recognize and focus on strengths and assets.
9. Utilize the interests of children to energize instruction.

KEY IDEAS

A philosophical foundation incorporating the nature of mathematics and what it means to know mathematics is important for teaching the subject. Mathematics is the science of pattern and order. To know mathematics is to know patterns and relationships among patterns. Thus, the study of mathematics is an active investigation of many types of patterns.

Among the major influences on the mathematics curriculum are professional organizations, mathematics textbooks, assessment procedures, and state governmental bodies. The National Council of Teachers of Mathematics has published a set of standards for mathematics curricula, a set of standards for evaluation, and a set of standards for assessment. These are influential guidelines for contemporary mathematics instruction.

DISCUSSION QUESTIONS

1. You have written your own thoughts about the meaning of mathematics and you have read the section in this chapter that focuses on "What is mathematics?" Seek out three additional sources to answer the question. These might include a mathematics textbook, a teacher of mathematics, a dictionary, or another source. From this information construct a "new" answer to "What is mathematics?"

2. What are your views about mathematics as an educational subject? What mathematics is important? What mathematics should students learn? How much mathematics is enough? What role should technology (calculators and computers) and problem solving play in learning mathematics? How important is memory in learning mathematics? The responses that you make to these and other questions begin to spell out your philosophical basis for mathematics education.

3. Ask three teachers about what influences their mathematics curriculum. How broad are these influences? Compare your findings with others who have asked different teachers. Is there a pattern in the answers, perhaps by the teachers' grade levels or experience?

4. Investigate one of the three topics mentioned under Teaching Considerations near the end of the chapter—failure, management, and encouragement. What information can you find that supports the position in the text or an alternative position on the topic that you have chosen?

REFERENCES

Burrill, Gail, "TIMSS—What Can We Learn?" *NCTM News Bulletin.* Reston, VA: National Council of Teachers of Mathematics, March, 1998.

Carson, Joan C., and Ruby N. Bostick, *Math Instruction Using Media and Modality Strengths.* Springfield, IL: Charles C. Thomas, 1988.

Dinkmeyer, Don, and Rudolf Dreikurs, *Encouraging Children to Learn: The Encouragement Process,* Englewood Cliffs, NJ: Prentice Hall, 1963.

Forgione, Pascal D., Jr., "Commissioner's Statement" in U.S. Department of Education, National Center for Education Statistics, *Pursuing Excellence: A Study of U.S. Fourth-Grade Mathematics and Science Achievement in International Context,* NCES 97–255, Washington, DC: U.S. Government Printing Office, 1997.

Hiebert, James, and Patricia Lefevre, "Conceptual and Procedural Knowledge in Mathematics: An Introductory Analysis," in *Conceptual and Procedural Knowledge: The Case of Mathematics,* ed. Hiebert, James. Hillsdale, NJ: Lawrence Erlbaum Associates, 1986.

Holt, John, *How Children Fail.* New York: Pitman, 1964.

National Council of Teachers of Mathematics, *Assessment Standards for School Mathematics.* Reston, VA: NCTM, 1995.

————, *Curriculum and Evaluation Standards for School Mathematics.* Reston, VA: NCTM, 1989.

————, *Principles and Standards for School Mathematics: Discussion Draft*. Reston, VA: NCTM, 1998.

————, *Professional Standards for Teaching Mathematics*. Reston, VA: NCTM, 1991.

National Research Council, *Everybody Counts: A Report to the Nation on the Future of Mathematics Education*. Washington, DC: National Academy Press, 1989.

————, *Reshaping School Mathematics: A Philosophy and Framework for Curriculum*. Washington, DC: National Academy Press, 1990.

Skemp, Richard R., *The Psychology of Learning Mathematics*. Hillsdale, NJ: Lawrence Erlbaum Associates, 1987.

Standards 2000 Writing Group Leaders, "*Standards 2000* Draft Coming in Fall of '98," *NCTM News Bulletin*. Reston, VA: National Council of Teachers of Mathematics, April, 1998.

U.S. Department of Education, National Center for Education Statistics, *Pursuing Excellence: A Study of U.S. Eighth-Grade Mathematics and Science Teaching, Learning, Curriculum, and Achievement in International Context*, NCES 97–198, Washington, DC: U.S. Government Printing Office, 1996.

Web Sites

http://standards-e.nctm.org   Site for *Principles and Standards for School Mathematics*.

http://www.enc.org/reform/journals/ENC2280/280dtoc1.htm The original (1989) *Curriculum and Evaluation Standards for School Mathematics* is found at this site.

http://www.nctm.org/   The home page of the National Council of Teachers of Mathematics.

Chapter 2

Children and Mathematics

My Math Journal

Think back to your own experiences in elementary or middle school mathematics. What do you remember as your favorite parts of learning mathematics? Do you remember any teachers that really made you love mathematics? Did you have any bad experiences learning mathematics? Were there any teachers that made you dislike math? Tell about these memories in your journal.

As you read the following pages, consider these guiding questions:

1. What are the characteristics of constructivist teachers?
2. As children develop from infancy into the middle school years, what in their world prepares them to learn mathematics?
3. What is a concept? How do students form mathematical concepts and what conditions enhance that concept formation?
4. How can you as a teacher guide the learning of mathematics?

Elementary and middle school children are natural learners. Their potential and energy for learning are considerable. They are exposed to enormous amounts of information, much of it outside of school.

Mathematics touches many subjects that are popular among children. For example, children manipulate plastic toys of varying sizes to transform earth or space vehicles into heroic robots—an exercise in spatial visualization. These toys also demonstrate the notion of transformation, which is fundamental to the concept of an operation. Other aspects of children's lives affected by mathematics include correspondences between family members, meal portions, routes taken to and from school, time and television programming, pricing and the ability to purchase items at the store, and baking cookies using measured ingredients. These are but a few examples. The myriad ways that mathematics touches the experiences of children stretch the imagination.

Space, number, shape, puzzles, time, distance, and computers provide a rich milieu in which elementary and middle school children grow. A teacher enables children to understand mathematics by providing an instructional environment. In Chapter 2, we explore four topics that influence how children learn mathematics:

1. A constructivist view of learning
2. The children's world
3. Psychological considerations in teaching mathematics
4. Teaching children mathematics

A Constructivist View of Learning

From the literature on teaching mathematics to young children comes an approach that is influenced by **constructivism,** a theory about the nature of knowledge and the nature of learning. Constructivists believe that children gain knowledge by inventing it, that they construct knowledge for themselves. According to Piaget (1973, p. 20), ". . . to understand is to discover, or reconstruct by rediscovery, and such conditions must be complied with if in the future individuals are to be formed who are capable of production and creativity and not simply repetition." Based heavily on the work of Piaget, con-

structivism guides teachers to interact with children through questioning and discussion, skillfully responding to the children's ideas, and allowing children to discover relationships and predict future events. Children engage in manipulating physical models, playing games, and interacting with one another. Constructivist principles are being applied to teaching at all levels of learning. Eighth-grade students who use algebra tiles to discover the meaning of factoring polynomials have the opportunity to construct that knowledge through their manipulations, questions, and discussions, as do primary students who use a geoboard to discover the meaning of $\frac{1}{2}$.

A proponent of teaching based on the principle of constructivism, Kamii (1989, p. *x*), notes that "Encouraging children to construct knowledge from within is the diametric opposite of trying to impose isolated skills from the outside." The approach that Kamii (1989, p. 184) advocates contrasts with that of more traditional educators, who ". . . assume that the job of the teacher is to put knowledge into children's heads. They also assume that the proof of this transmission of knowledge is a high score on standardized tests. Both of these assumptions . . . are erroneous and outdated."

Kamii's work has been based, in part, on her work with primary teachers of grades 1–3. Besides stressing the importance of children creating their own mathematical relationships, Kamii emphasizes that word problems are an important part of teaching. Children are able to construct mathematical ideas from problems arising from their personal lives; first-grade children can solve verbal problems without formal instruction. This leads Kamii to note that

> If children add numerical quantities repeatedly, actively, in the context of everyday classroom occurrences, games, and problems that they understand, they *will* remember the results of these mental actions and *will* become able to read and write conventional mathematical signs. The focus of the teacher's concern should be on children's *thinking* rather than on their ability to *write* correct answers. (1985, p. 94)

Kamii suggests that the overriding aim of education is to develop moral and intellectual autonomy among learners. As a result, children should be encouraged to develop their own opinions and to judge when another opinion is better. Kamii notes that

> This is not to say that children do not learn from workbooks and transmission. They do, and they usually acquire the truth faster by being told than by constructing it themselves. But we must think of learning in a larger context than the memorization of sums and the ability to produce high test scores. In other words, we need to see autonomy as the ultimate aim of education. . . . (1985, p. 36)

Developing autonomy among learners requires teachers to be student centered and willing to forgo the tendency to direct students' every move. This would suggest that there is a continuum on which an individual teacher would find a level of comfort as she begins her teaching experience. At one end of the continuum is the student-centered teacher and at the other end, the content-centered teacher. Constructivist teaching would be associated with the former end of the continuum. Brooks and Brooks (1993, p. 10) noted:

> . . . when the classroom environment in which students spend so much of their day is organized so that student-to-student interaction is encouraged, cooperation is valued, assignments and materials are interdisciplinary, and students' freedom to chase their own ideas is abundant, students are more likely to take risks and approach assignments with a willingness to accept challenges to their current understandings. Such teacher role models and environmental conditions honor students as emerging thinkers.

We believe that you should consider using constructivist approaches as a teacher of elementary and middle school mathematics. Recent discussions and guidelines presented by the National Council of Teachers of Mathematics and the National Research Council are having a significant impact on school mathematics (see Chapter 1). They strongly support a shift away from a teaching model based on the transmission of knowledge and toward a model based on student-centered experiences. Thus, the opportunity to employ alternative teaching approaches, including constructivist approaches, is at hand. As you continue reading, you will find that many of the activities suggested in this textbook fit with constructivist teaching methods.

The following descriptors of constructivist teaching behaviors were set forth by Brooks and Brooks (1993, pp. 103–117) and are presented as guidelines for those interested in experimenting with this teaching approach. Perhaps you will be one of those teachers.

1. Constructivist teachers encourage and accept student autonomy and initiative.
2. Constructivist teachers use raw data and primary sources, along with manipulative, interactive, and physical materials.
3. When framing tasks, constructivist teachers use cognitive terminology such as *classify, analyze, predict,* and *create.*
4. Constructivist teachers allow student responses to drive lessons, shift instructional strategies, and alter content.
5. Constructivist teachers inquire about students' understanding of concepts before sharing their own understanding of those concepts.
6. Constructivist teachers encourage students to engage in dialogue, both with the teacher and with one another.
7. Constructivist teachers encourage student inquiry by asking thoughtful, open-ended questions and encouraging students to ask questions of each other.
8. Constructivist teachers seek elaboration of students' initial responses.
9. Constructivist teachers engage students in experiences that might engender contradictions to their initial hypotheses and then encourage discussion.
10. Constructivist teachers allow wait time after posing questions.
11. Constructivist teachers provide time for students to construct relationships and create metaphors.
12. Constructivist teachers nurture students' natural curiosity through frequent use of the learning cycle model.

If you decide to use these descriptors you would be well advised to read further and in more depth about their meaning. Brooks and Brooks (1993) is a good place to start. There are many other helpful resources in the literature.

You are encouraged to explore further how children learn mathematics. Only when teachers begin to understand the aspects and stages of mathematical learning will children receive the kind of instruction most appropriate to their individual learning styles. In addition, exploration will help you to understand why this textbook emphasizes manipulation of physical objects, multiple embodiments of mathematical ideas, active participation of learners, use of alternative teaching strategies, use of mathematical relationships, various kinds of communication, and formation of mathematical ideas according to the developmental characteristics of children.

The Children's World

As a teacher, you must know and understand the world from a child's perspective, how children view the world, and how children develop knowledge. In this section, we describe the ways in which children experience the world mathematically. Their learning of mathematics, now and in the future, is built upon this foundation.

Children Have Many Number Experiences

Number experiences are a part of children's lives from the moment they begin to communicate. Communication and physical movement include intensity of sound; varying duration of activity; exploration of space; embrace and separation; sequence of occurrences; and similarities and differences among humans, objects, places, and emotions. As youngsters record these relationships, they learn to quantify their world.

The lives of children are increasingly being affected by the computer. Today, children can skillfully draw and design using computer power. Their lines are straight and their angles are precise. Color, texture, and shading can be applied at the touch of a key. Children can prepare graphic animation with the assistance of clever software packages. Outlining and writing with word processors assist the thinking processes. Computers tease and baffle the imagination. Each year teachers are using these magnificent tools to an even greater extent.

Children begin their schooling with enthusiasm, energy, and a willingness to participate. They usually enjoy success in their early mathematical work because they have been exploring relationships for years. Mathematics is, after all, the study of patterns and relationships and how things are connected. Among the teacher's challenges will be increasing the likelihood of success by helping children see meaning and sense in their mathematics.

Children Are Active in Their World

Teachers and parents rarely have to instruct children on how to be active or how to play. School is one of the first places where children are asked to be passive and quiet. Some orderliness and conformity is necessary for significant learning to take place. But, at the same time, there must be opportunities for spontaneous response and divergent thinking.

Children should be physically involved in mathematics. Materials such as stacking blocks, pattern blocks, colored cubes, attribute blocks, puzzles, Cuisenaire rods, geoboards, sand, clay, water, various containers, computers and appropriate software, and calculators should be available in the school. These and other learning aids are introduced in later chapters of this book. Children use these materials for counting, developing patterns, creating, observing, constructing, discussing, and comparing. From the manipulations and observations come the abstractions of quantitative ideas and the communication of these ideas in pictorial and, later, symbolic form.

Children Observe Relationships in Their World

Children and adults make connections among objects that seem separate at first glance. Language is often closely tied with the expression of these relationships. Relationships may be simple. For example, because, again and again, an infant hears a certain sound and then receives attention, he begins to learn the relationship between his name and himself. Later it becomes apparent that other individuals have names. Distinguishing between a person's name and the name of the position that person holds in the family is more difficult. That is, Linda and Julie are names, whereas mommy and sister, although used as names, state family relationships. Eventually, children discover their relationships to grandparents, uncles, aunts, and cousins.

Seventh-grade students can readily differentiate between a rectangle and a parallelogram but may be confused as to how they are related. That is, it may not be apparent to them that all rectangles are parallelograms but not all parallelograms are rectangles. Some may firmly believe that rectangles and parallelograms share no common characteristics. Experience and discussion, then, help them to understand some less obvious relationships.

As children quantify their world, they become aware of arithmetical, spatial, logical, and collective relationships through their active participation with and their discussion about their natural environment. Physical models in the school classroom provide an effective basis for mathematical learning. Some relationships are obvious. Others are not, and it becomes necessary for teachers to provide experiences to link the more subtle relationships. Eventually mathematics makes sense, because the learners understand how most of what they have been learning is connected. Learning how things relate is sharply distinguished from learning by memorizing many disconnected facts. When things are related, mathematics is presented as possessing structure; when memory is stressed, structure is generally ignored.

Relationships can be expressed in visual form. In moving from purely concrete work using physical objects to more abstract work, visual representations can be employed effectively. For example, Figure 2–1 is a visual representation of the relationships in one family drawn by a five-year-old. This representation links the physical world to the abstract idea of family relations. Teachers should be aware of relationships and are encouraged to develop experiences and representations to further the learning of how things relate.

Children Learn Mathematics in Concert with Other Subjects

By the time children enter school, they are proficient at learning interrelated skills and concepts. Walking, talking, toilet habits, rote counting, and language are learned without being isolated from other life experiences. The packaging of bits and pieces of knowledge or the separation of skills from their applications creates an artificial environment alien to the unified world of all humans. Integrated experiences in school are important in providing a more natural and balanced setting for learning.

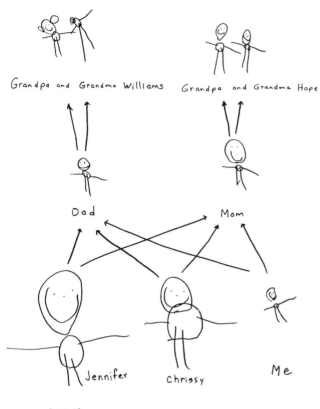

Figure 2–1

The skillful teacher is afforded the opportunity to integrate mathematics with other subjects and the world in general. The interrelatedness of mathematics with subjects such as art, language, literature, social studies, and science illustrates the close ties of all bodies of knowledge. Just as mathematics is embedded in other subjects, other subjects are embedded in mathematics. The educative process should bring many connected experiences to children in a lifelike environment. It is crucial that children see the connections.

There are few thinking skills unique to mathematics. Rather, most thinking skills transcend specific knowledge or a specific discipline. When developed in a setting of integrated learning, thinking skills provide the opportunity for children to learn how to learn. Observing, describing, conjecturing, questioning, judging, valuing, and communicating are skills of life. They are also the foundation upon which problem solving is built.

Children's Feelings Affect Their Ability to Learn

Children's feelings about themselves and their ability to succeed, as well as their feelings about others, home,

school subjects, and life affect their behavior. While there is not a direct causal link between children's feelings about mathematics and mathematics achievement and participation, their feelings about mathematics do appear to be important in their learning of mathematics. The impact of these feelings may vary by gender, or by cultural and ethnic background. Feelings about mathematics is only one of a number of factors that have an influence on mathematics learning.

Not all children will attack mathematics or anything else with the same energy and enthusiasm. Students should be exposed to the historical and cultural aspects of mathematics as well as its structure. Some students are interested in theoretical mathematics. Others are motivated by a historical approach. Still others are excited by the relationships between mathematics and art, mathematics and music, or mathematics and language. Applications of mathematics interest many children.

Much has been written about **math anxiety,** which can be described as reluctance to engage in, and fear of, mathematics-related activities. Individuals who exhibit such anxiety do not enjoy doing arithmetic, particularly in public. They agonize over mental arithmetic, apologize for their lack of skill, and avoid activities associated with mathematics. In short, they are dysfunctional in mathematics.

Most individuals with math anxiety are beyond elementary school age. Research shows that mathematics is liked and enjoyed by a majority of elementary students. We are unconvinced that large numbers of elementary school children suffer math anxiety.

However, we are convinced that many children have learned not to enjoy mathematics. These children have experienced considerable failure in their attempts to learn concepts and skills. They have been asked to learn certain mathematical ideas that they were not ready to learn; they have been moved through a curriculum, "learning" mathematics for which they did not have the prerequisites and struggling with new concepts that did not make any sense. They may have been pressured to memorize hundreds of unrelated basic addition and multiplication facts and subjected to timed tests in front of their peers. They believe that success in mathematics is knowing a certain "magical process" that results in correct answers. As a result, some children begin to dislike mathematics and do not want to do mathematics. Failure and humiliation are powerful forces that cause children to be reluctant to engage in mathematics. Dislike of mathematics and reluctance to participate in math activities is more prevalent in middle school, providing a challenge to teachers.

Gender and culture have been issues in mathematics education for many years. The full participation of all students in learning mathematics should be the goal for teachers. Female and minority students have

FoxTrot   by Bill Amend

Figure 2–2

the capability to engage successfully in mathematics when given the opportunity.

The insightful FOXTROT cartoon in Figure 2–2 illustrates three points related to gender issues: 1) low mathematics scores for boys are often attributed to not studying (here mom suggests that Jason did not study), and low scores for girls are often attributed to lack of ability; 2) boys' attitudes about girls are typically very negative as compared with girls' attitudes about boys, and here Jason exemplifies that negative attitude; and 3) girls tend to get better grades than boys in elementary school math.

Gender socialization has shaped the perceptions of girls and boys about their need to study mathematics and their ability to be successful in mathematics. Gender socialization is the process whereby girls and boys are taught their expected roles and behaviors by those around them. Girls learn, among other things, that math is unimportant in their future, that it is not "cool" to be good at math, and that because mom was not good at math they will not be good at math. Sometimes teachers reinforce these perceptions by calling on boys more than girls, asking different types of questions of boys (interpretive) and girls (factual), and waiting longer for boys to answer than for girls to answer. Some teachers praise girls for how their work appears and praise boys for the content of their work. Some teachers explain of boys how to solve problems but solve the problems for girls. Some teachers assign different classroom tasks on the basis of gender. All of these teacher behaviors are doing a disservice to the mathematics education of girls.

From his research, Geary (1994) reports that there is no mathematics gene that favors boys over girls and that there are essentially no gender differences in the most fundamental numerical skills found in humans, that is, a basic understanding of number, counting, and arithmetic. Further, Sadker and Sadker (1994, p. 13) noted that "In the early grades girls are ahead of or equal to boys in al-most every standardized measure of achievement and psychological well-being. By the time they graduate from high school or college, they have fallen back. Girls enter school ahead but leave behind." In a discussion of the meaning of gender equity in mathematics education, Fennema (1990, p. 5) states, "At the end of schooling, there should be no differences in what females and males have learned, nor should there be any gender differences in how students feel about themselves as learners of mathematics. Males and females should be equally willing to pursue mathematics-related careers and should be equally able to learn new mathematics as it is required. The definition of equity as the achievement of equal outcomes offers the greatest promise for achieving true justice."

Your responsibility to provide gender equity as a mathematics teacher can be enhanced by following these suggestions:

1. Believe that girls are as capable as boys in learning and doing mathematics. Expect girls to perform well. Your goal should be that all students, male and female, persist and work independently in mathematics.
2. Provide verbal and written feedback as part of the learning process. Provide time for questions and encourage the asking of questions. Work with a student until she can say "I've got it!"
3. Incorporate cooperative mathematics activities and limit competitive ones. Monitor the composition of small groups in your classroom so that all students learn to work cooperatively and have an opportunity to get the explanations and help that they need.
4. Provide students with many opportunities to see that math is as readily a girl's field as it is a boy's field. Convince boys as well as girls that girls doing well in math is cool. Encourage all students. Stress the importance and value of mathematics to all students.
5. Present female role models in math and science.

6. Respond to sexist, racist, and violent interactions among students.

7. Use physical models and hands-on activities. Begin class activities with little discussion, then discuss the activity with all students when it has been completed. If pupils begin working on an activity with little introduction from the teacher, everyone has access to the same experience. Discussion that follows after all students have completed an activity encourages more participation by girls.

8. Work to make math a gender-neutral activity by avoiding targeting a few students, usually boys, for particular attention; by avoiding becoming preoccupied with those students, usually boys, who make the most noise; and by running an orderly class and calling on everyone.

9. Use sex-equitable materials, for they will encourage gender-balanced knowledge of people in society, will develop more flexible attitudes and more accurate sex-role knowledge, and will encourage students to imitate role behaviors contained in the materials.

By the turn of the century, one of every three American students will be a minority. African Americans, Hispanics, and Native Americans constitute 90 percent of minorities in this country. According to the Mathematical Sciences Education Board (MSEB), minority students do not reach their full potential in their mathematics education and thus fail to go on to earn higher degrees in mathematics (1990, p. 4). This suggests that the mathematics education of minority students in elementary and middle school needs to be nurtured. Your high expectations for all students is crucial. Raising the awareness of students to the importance of mathematics in the workplace is imperative. The MSEB suggests what teachers can and should do to encourage the full participation of all students in mathematics learning:

1. Accept that the primary responsibility for revitalizing school mathematics rests with teachers.

2. Increase the level of student participation in class.

3. Create a classroom climate that is directed as well as friendly to all students.

4. Incorporate teaching strategies and new assessment tools that develop reasoning skills in all students.

5. Attend teacher institutes and summer programs that communicate strategies for teaching different types of students with varying learning styles and backgrounds.

6. Insist on the development of activities aimed at understanding the factors that influence minority achievement.

7. Become actively engaged in issues of teaching and learning.

8. Nurture the expectation that *all* students can and must be given the opportunity to learn mathematics.

9. Encourage parents to feel "at home" in the classroom and to play a significant role in their children's education.

10. Develop positive and productive school climates that facilitate students' learning of mathematics.

11. Provide opportunities for students to improve their self-esteem.

12. Work to assure that administrators follow national curriculum developments; join with them to institute a core curriculum for all students that is based on national standards (1990, p. 6).

These suggestions provide the foundation for strengthening the mathematics education of all students. As teachers, we should consider them periodically to remind us of our broad responsibility in the classroom.

Psychological Considerations in Teaching Mathematics

In the broadest sense, learning mathematics serves as both a means and an end. Learning mathematics is a means of developing logical and quantitative thinking abilities. The key word is *thinking*. Thinking children are liberated from the dull routine that sometimes characterizes school. Learning mathematics is an end when students have developed basic computational skills and can apply mathematics to their world; that is, when mathematics becomes functional in the lives of children. At least a part of a young person's environment can be explained by simple mathematical principles.

At every level, learning mathematics should be a natural outgrowth of the children's lives. Learning should be interesting for the students, should challenge their imagination, and should beget creative solutions in their art, dance, music, movement, and conversation. The discovery of mathematics should be devoid of boredom, meaninglessness, and coercion.

Logical and Psychological Approaches to Mathematics

Approaches to teaching mathematics have generally followed the logical structure of mathematics presented by most children's textbooks. Thus, counting is followed by adding at the pictorial and symbolic levels. Subtracting, multiplying, and dividing follow. Later or concurrently, children learn the properties of these operations. To augment learning computation, courses of study include patterns and relationships, spatial sense, probability, statistics, and simple measurement. Understanding is developed to the extent that children see meaning in what they are doing. Some children readily understand. Many others do not or cannot understand. The presentation of mathematics as an organized, logical structure does not ensure children's understanding.

To complement the logical structure of mathematics, teachers should weigh the psychological aspects of learning mathematics. Teachers who consider how children learn mathematics can provide activities that blend what is known about children and mathematics. For example, a teacher taking this approach would realize that the child's developing understanding of the concept of *number* involves classifying, relating, and ordering, along with discussion. The teacher would use objects and groups of objects to illustrate and enhance the learning of number, operation, and addition. Psychological considerations that help children learn mathematics are the focus of the next several pages.

Sources of Information about How Children Learn Mathematics

The study of how children learn mathematics is not new, but until relatively recently, little had been written that was directly applicable to classroom instruction. Useful works include those by Bruner (1977), Burger and Shaughnessy (1986), Copeland (1984), Ginsburg (1983), Kamii (1985, 1989, 1990), Piaget (1973), and Skemp (1987). These and other sources have been included in the bibliography at the end of Chapter 2. Much of what appears in the following chapters rests on the foundation provided by these authors.

The work of Piaget has greatly influenced the way teachers view cognitive development. Among the most well-known ideas associated with Piaget are those dealing with the evolution of thought through a series of four stages. Children move through the stages of cognitive development as a result of the interaction between internal forces (maturation) and external forces (environment). The first stage, **sensorimotor,** generally occurs in the first two years of life. Here, the child begins to imitate sounds and actions, and recognizes that objects still exist when they are out of sight. The second stage, **preoperational,** generally lasts from age 2 to age 7. Here, the child gains an initial use of language and the ability to think in symbolic terms. The third stage, **concrete operations,** generally lasts from age 7 to age 11. Here, physical objects provide the medium for learning. Children discover that objects can be changed or moved and still retain many of their characteristics, and that these changes can be reversed. The fourth stage, **formal operations,** may begin around age 11, although many adults never operate fully at the formal level. Here, students can think logically about abstract problems. The age ranges are only approximations, but all individuals progress through these stages in the order they are presented.

An important idea associated with Piaget's work and noted in the stage of concrete operations is **conservation.** Conservation of number means that the number of objects in a set does not change if the objects in the set are placed in different positions as in Figure 2–3. Conservation of quantity means that the amount of liquid poured from a tall, narrow container into a short, wide container remains constant. Conservation of length means that an object retains the same length if the object is moved. Until children are about seven years old, they do not conserve number. Again, seven is just a benchmark; children vary in their ability to conserve number. Teachers do not, nor should they, teach conservation, for the ability to conserve results from the development of logico-mathematical knowledge—the understanding of relationships.

Two additional and complementary processes that Piaget described are **assimilation** and **accommodation.** Assimilation is the process by which an individual takes in information. The information may come from any source, such as playing with blocks, watching a bird fly, or listening to an explanation. Assimilated information may cause individuals to adjust or modify their understanding of an idea or event; in such cases, the process of accommodation takes place. The adjustment or modification of an idea resulting in a new cognitive structure is the process of **equilibration.** It stems from an individual's need to reach equilibrium when perceptions are in conflict with new information. Equilibration has taken place once the new information is accommodated and the conflict has dissipated. In the process of learning, assimilation and accommodation are constantly taking place, resulting in the process of equilibration. You should recognize the importance of these processes in learning mathematics. Further mention is made of assimilation and accommodation during the discussion of how children form mathematical concepts.

Piaget's work has influenced the authors, and you will find references to his work throughout the book. Perhaps Piaget's most important idea is that children can and

Figure 2–3

should be involved in inventing mathematics. It is through experiences that children discover relationships and solve problems. The theory of constructivism, discussed earlier in this chapter, has emerged from the work of Piaget. That children should be guided to construct their own knowledge is a powerful notion in teaching mathematics.

Investigations on how children think mathematically have shown that young children in the preoperational stage use mental counting procedures to solve arithmetic problems. This has led to revised theories about number understanding (Resnick, 1983). Certain types of simple mathematical thinking can occur before the Piagetian stage of concrete operations. According to Carpenter (1986, p. 114), "Contrary to popular notions, young children are relatively successful at analyzing and solving simple word problems. Before receiving formal instruction in addition and subtraction, most young children invent informal modeling and counting strategies to solve basic addition and subtraction problems."

Mathematics education was particularly affected by Brownell, who set forth his **meaning theory** of arithmetic instruction in the 1935 yearbook of the National Council of Teachers of Mathematics. According to Brownell (1935, pp. 19, 31), "... this theory makes meaning, the fact that children shall see sense in what they learn, the central issue in arithmetic instruction." He went on to call for an "instructional reorganization" so that arithmetic would be "... less a challenge to the pupil's memory and more a challenge to his intelligence." Brownell supported his theories with his research throughout his professional career. One such study, *Meaningful vs. Mechanical Learning: A Study in Grade III Subtraction,* suggested that retention, transfer, and understanding are enhanced by teachers using a "meaning method" as opposed to a "mechanical method" of instruction (Brownell and Moser, 1949). In the ensuing years, general agreement has been reached among psychologists and educators that teaching with meaning or understanding tends to be richer and longer lasting than other teaching. It has also been suggested that when learning is seen as a function of personal meaning, teaching centers on the children and their interpretations of what is being taught. Thus, teaching the meaning of mathematics provides an extra incentive for the teacher to know how children learn mathematics.

How Children Form Mathematical Concepts

A **concept** is an idea or mental image. Words and symbols are used to describe or label concepts. For example, *potato* is a collection of sounds that brings to mind an image representing some generalized form of a garden vegetable. Exactly what image appears depends on the experiences, heritage, geographical location, and language of the listener. The symbol 5 represents a mental image of all groups containing ● ● ● ● ●, or five, things. Again, the precise image that appears depends on the background and experiences of the listener.

Concepts are learned. Virtually all children from the time of birth can learn concepts. Concept formation begins immediately. The language and symbols that name concepts lag behind concept formation but eventually emerge. As children grow and mature, language and symbols are introduced to name mental images already formed and are used later to teach new concepts. To learn a concept, children require a number of common experiences relating to the concept. Initially, a parent introduces potatoes to a child by spooning a white, strained substance into the child's mouth, perhaps exhorting the child to "Eat your potatoes." As this procedure continues for several months, the child begins to associate the word *potato* with the mushy substance. Obviously, the concept of potato is very limited at this time. Soon, mashed potatoes from the parent's plate may be introduced to the child with the same plea: "Eat your potatoes." Over time, potatoes prepared in many ways are given to the child and, finally, after two or three years, the child is informed that the vegetable the parent is washing, peeling, and cutting is a potato and can be prepared in numerous ways. The concept of potato begins to emerge as an accurate, generalized mental image.

Two aspects of this example have clear implications for teaching children. First, the concept of potato did not become *known* until potatoes had been seen, felt, smelled, and tasted in many ways; that is, until the child experienced potatoes in numerous guises. Each of these guises is an embodiment of potato. When several examples that appear different yet have something common about them (in this case, deriving from a single vegetable) are presented, we say that we are using the multiple embodiment principle. We are presenting the concept of potato in many embodiments and providing the opportunity for the child to discover the common element among them all. The multiple embodiment principle is discussed further in Chapter 5. When the child was able to discern the common property among the various ways in which potatoes were prepared, namely, each dish originated from a certain recognized vegetable, the concept of potato was formed. Second, the word *potato* had to occur in concert with or had to follow the experiencing of the vegetable. The sounds that make up the word *potato* were not helpful before the experience. Hearing only the word or a definition, the child would not have learned what a potato was.

The two processes just described provide the foundation for the learning of mathematics. Children who find the common property of several seemingly disconnected examples are **abstracting.** The abstraction that is made is a **concept.** Children learn their mathematics by abstracting concepts from experiences with physical models. The language is developed during or after concept formation, never before. Objects and events that are a part of children's lives and are easily observed are less abstract than objects and events that are not easily observed. Thus, dogs, automobiles, houses, toys, and mothers are less abstract than are color, height, number, time, and multiplication.

Skemp has stated two principles of learning mathematics that relate directly to the notion of concepts:

1. Concepts of a higher order than those which people already have cannot be communicated to them by a definition, but only by arranging for them to encounter a suitable collection of examples.
2. Since in mathematics these examples are almost invariably other concepts, it must first be ensured that these are already formed in the mind of the learner (1987, p. 18).

Children learn the meaning of number by experiencing number in many varied situations—through a suitable collection of examples. The suitable collection of examples represents the multiple embodiment principle mentioned a few paragraphs ago. Multiple embodiment is as appropriate for the concept of number as it is for the concept of potato. The same holds true for addition, subtraction, multiplication, division, fractions, geometry, measurement, operations on integers, variables, algebra, and so forth. The activities presented throughout the following pages are typical examples of activities for learning mathematical concepts.

In addition, developing mathematical concepts requires constantly providing experiences that build foundations on which to base further mathematical learning. Attempting to develop mathematical concepts on a foundation of previously memorized, vague notions results in frustration for both children and teacher. Skemp again notes that "... before we try to communicate a new concept, we have to find out what are its contributory concepts; and for each of these, we have to find out *its* contributory concepts, and so on, until we reach either primary concepts [derived from sensory and motor experiences] or experience which we can assume" (pp. 19–20).

Dealing with Concepts Once Formed

The concepts and experiences acquired by a person make up the knowledge that person possesses. As new experiences occur, they are fitted into a person's existing mental structure. This is the Piagetian process of assimilation. Depending on the familiarity of the experiences and the learning style of the learner, the experiences are received or rejected because of a person's mental structure or **schema.** The schema is a part of the mind used to build up the understanding of a topic. Thus, to increase or alter what is already known, the schema takes in new ideas and fits them with what is already known. For example, if children are still learning about potatoes and have experienced only strained, mashed, and boiled potatoes, the schema of *potato* may be limited. When french-fried potatoes are introduced, it may be difficult for children to immediately recognize the new food as potatoes. Although they are told that what they see, smell, feel, and taste are potatoes, children initially may not be convinced that they are experiencing potatoes. The schema of potato must be changed to accept potatoes in this new form. Once this change or accommodation has taken place, the schema has adjusted to accept french-fried potatoes as potatoes. French-fried potatoes are understood. Understanding a concept means an appropriate schema has accommodated that concept.

The idea of schema and how it functions provides a powerful tool for teaching mathematics. That a mental framework can be identified and developed means that mathematical relationships, patterns, and ideas can be understood rather than merely memorized; in the long run, children will have the ability to build up mathematical knowledge. When rules are memorized, children reach a point in their mathematical learning at which they are unable to remember the rules and are unable to continue learning. Understanding has long since vanished. As mathematics is introduced, its understanding is predicated on children's having already developed appropriate early schemas. The implications are clear. Teachers should provide mathematical experiences in a form that will ensure that the mathematics is understood. Such a foundation provides a basis for all later mathematical understanding.

Children's Thinking

The teacher's goal should be to provide experiences so that children can progress from a concrete, intuitive level of learning dependent on the teacher toward a more symbolic level of learning independent of the teacher. This is a life's work for both learner and teacher. **Intuitive thinking,** the process of knowing without conscious reasoning, is not a stage through which an individual passes on the way to abstract thinking. Even when an individual has reached the Piagetian stage of formal operations, intuitive thinking may be necessary to gain a preliminary understanding of a new concept. For a child yet unready for formal thinking, intuitive thinking is the primary source of learning. For a middle school student, intuitive thinking is very useful in problem solving and developing the "rules" for more complex operations.

Learning by intuitive thinking means learning by experimenting with physical models through experiencing ideas in various concrete ways, and by visualizing ideas. Because of intuitive thinking, a concept makes sense to a student before full understanding has taken place. For example, children who are constructing patterns using rods of two colors and who stumble on the pattern shown in Figure 2–4 are not learning much about the commutative property of addition, but they are certainly gaining an intuitive grasp of what the commutative property means. Later, when the commutative property of addition is presented, these children should be able to understand the property. The bulk of children's early learning takes place at the intuitive level. Teachers should encourage such thinking. **Reflective thinking** comes later. Reflective thinking means being able to reason with ideas without needing physical models. The processes of reflective thinking include reflecting, inventing, imagining, playing with ideas, problem solving, problem creating, theorizing, and generalizing.

Reflective thinking allows individuals to know how something is accomplished rather than merely being able to perform a task. Not only is it important for seven-year-old children to add two numbers such as 18 + 17, but it is also important that they be able to effectively explain how they accomplished the task. Likewise, a 13-year-old student needs to effectively explain to her cooperative group members why a six-point jump overnight in a common stock should be challenged.

Reflective thinking also allows individuals to alter or correct schemas. Individuals may consider their perception of an idea or process and compare it with a new interpretation of the same idea or process and thus alter the original schema. Piaget has noted that children develop the ability for some verbal thought with sufficient concrete representations by the age of 7 or 8. From 7 or 8 to 11, children can manipulate concrete ideas in their

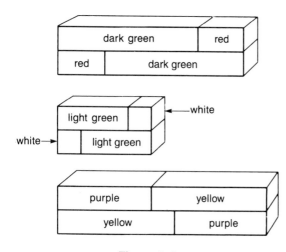

Figure 2–4

heads, but complete facility with reflective thinking comes later, as children approach adolescence. Many adults never perfect their ability to think reflectively.

Children's Communication of Mathematical Concepts

"Mathematics as Communication" is a common thread woven throughout all levels of the NCTM *Standards.* It was noted that "Communication plays an important role in helping children construct links between their informal, intuitive notions and the abstract language and symbolism of mathematics; it also plays a key role in helping children make important connections among physical, pictorial, graphic, symbolic, verbal, and mental representations of mathematical ideas" (1989, p. 26). As students mature, so does their ability to communicate. A middle school student's questions about concepts and skills or that student's writing about or discussing a problem provide the opportunity to broaden the thinking process. It is the middle school teacher's challenge to promote reading, writing, and communicating about problems to enhance mathematical understanding.

Children think quantitatively long before they engage in their first school activities. They have explored their personal space, and they begin to think about the **proximity** of objects, that is, they become aware that some objects are near to them while others are farther away. They notice that fingers are close to a hand or an arm, eyes are near the nose, and grandparents live far away (even if they live down the street).

Order is another spatial relationship about which children think. A child may have noticed the order of the cars on the toy train in the playpen or may be aware of the sequence of significant events. When the child cries, a parent appears, then holds and comforts the child.

Children classify objects as belonging together or not belonging together, for example, close family members versus neighbors and friends. They begin to judge objects as being few or many, big or small, tall or short, fast or slow. Obviously, they are not studying mathematics per se. The children are, however, thinking about their world quantitatively.

As children experience quantitative events and develop language to express these ideas, they are able to communicate with other people. They are developing the ability to classify objects and events more precisely. Although the language that emerges may not sound mathematical, it does represent the foundation on which the more exact language of mathematics is built. When children discriminate by *volume,* they may use the following words:

much	lots	some	empty
more	all	full	huge
less	little		

When discriminating by *size,* children may use the following words or phrases:

big	little	tall	bigger than
short	biggest	wide	smaller than
thin	fat	long	fatter than

When indicating *time,* children may use the following words or phrases:

before	now	spring	when the
after	later	winter	bell rings
yesterday	tomorrow	last summer	when it gets warmer

When discussing the *location* of objects, children may use the following words or phrases:

here	there	inside	on top of
up	down	outside	in the box
over	under	above	below

When describing *how many,* children may use counting strategies that they have developed through a variety of contexts. Recent investigations have provided fresh insights into how children develop the ability to count and how they use counting to solve simple problems. For example, Fuson and Hall reported that children acquire a variety of number word meanings by their use in sequential, counting, cardinal, measure, ordinal, and non-numerical contexts (1983, pp. 49–107). Counting is an important part of quantitative learning.

Children develop language in concert with their experiences. The experiences are crucial for the language to make sense. In the initial stages of mathematics learning, the quantitative experiences must be closely connected to the language that describes those experiences. Elementary and middle school students need physical experiences as models before they are exposed to the language from which the concepts are abstracted. A serious mistake occurs when addition is taught before the child can bridge the gap between the intuitive notion of addition (usually involving counting and manipulating objects) and the symbolic representation of addition.

The home provides early, extensive language development, but the teacher is responsible for providing school experiences and the concomitant language that allow for a natural combination of experience and language. A textbook or workbook alone cannot perform this function. Students must be physically active. Teachers enhance language development by frequent discussions with individuals, small groups, or the entire class about a particular activity or discovery. As a natural extension of growth in understanding mathematics and in language ability, the teacher or students may write experience stories to describe quantitative experiences. Older students may keep journal entries describing how they set about solving a problem or describing their thoughts about a particular aspect of mathematics.

Mathematics is an area of knowledge in which language often causes distortions and misunderstandings. The confusion most often occurs when unfamiliar language is presented before the experiences described by the language. Once introduced, the language may conjure up mental images that are distorted. Children may decide not to attempt to develop images and cease to listen, or they may simply memorize the verbal description and repeat it verbatim as a response to a stimulus. Language that is introduced by drawings, pictures, or diagrams is generally more helpful for children; however, the illustrations sometimes make little sense.

By way of contrast, the language may be introduced after children have experienced the ideas that the language describes. Thus, children using *state-operator-state machines* may discover that they can develop an understanding of the term *operation.* For example, consider a machine with an input, an operator, and an output. The machine accepts as inputs various attribute blocks. The rule for operating is to change the color of the incoming block (Figure 2–5). A red block placed in the input may be blue when it reaches the output; that is, after the operation has been carried out. A *join machine,* in which a group of objects is placed in the input, might cause children to join three objects to the input group, as in Figure 2–6. In such a case, the output would be the input group joined with the group described in the operation.

Many other machines can be devised to allow children to manipulate and discover the notion of operating or transforming and to help them understand the term *operation* when it is later applied to this transforming.

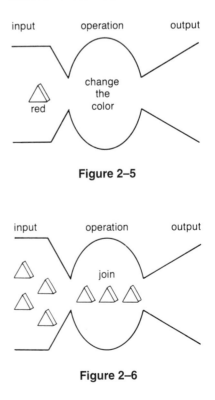

Figure 2–5

Figure 2–6

Weaver provided support for the use of change-of-state situations in introducing symbolic sentences (1982, pp. 60–66).

Language and symbols for language stand for abstractions; thus, it is by language and symbols that we communicate what has been abstracted. In order to be meaningfully communicated, the abstraction must have taken place. Unfortunately, students are often introduced to language and symbols before they are ready to make the appropriate abstractions. To abstract a concept, students must perform a variety of concrete operations. From these activities, which have a common structure, youngsters draw mental pictures, or images. The images of the elements common to the structures are the abstractions of concepts to be learned. Once concepts are understood, they can be verbalized and symbolized meaningfully.

Teaching Children Mathematics

The main purpose of this textbook is to provide some suggestions about how to help children develop mathematical concepts and skills. You have already learned some ways to be an effective elementary or middle school mathematics teacher. You have strengthened your mathematics background by taking courses. Your attitudes about mathematics will grow more positive as you gain more experience with mathematics and children. A psychological foundation for teaching mathematics should include teachers' attitudes about children, teaching style, and enhancing and guiding learning.

Teachers' Attitudes about Children

Much of this book focuses on children as learners of mathematics, but it is important also to look at just the children themselves. The teacher's beliefs about children will affect the children's performance in many academic cases, including mathematics.

The beliefs adults have about children, how children should be treated, and how children should be taught vary dramatically. Some believe that children must be left alone, to grow and develop with little interference from adults, and others believe that children must be closely watched and directed. Surely the optimum treatment of children includes some combination of laissez-faire and strict direction. The overall degree of teaching success depends more on what teachers believe about children than on how they organize to teach them, because teachers interact with children in ways that reflect their beliefs about children.

One example has been described in the research literature. When teachers believe children are low achiev-ers, the children tend to receive marks indicating low achievement. When teachers believe comparable children are high achievers, the children tend to receive marks indicating high achievement. Teachers are often unaware that they treat children according to their personal beliefs about the children. They do so through both verbal and nonverbal interaction. As beliefs about children become more positive, a greater amount of the children's potential can be realized (Rosenthal and Jacobson, 1968). Teachers need to be keenly aware of the children with whom they work. A well-articulated set of beliefs provides the basis on which to develop a sound style of teaching.

Teaching Style

Teaching means directing, channeling, providing, suggesting, expecting, and encouraging children. It also means managing a classroom of diverse individuals, some who are happy to be there and cooperative, and a few who are reluctant to be there and combative. Some people consider teaching an art; others consider teaching a science. It must surely be some of both. Skillful teaching is difficult and tiring, but it is rewarding, too. Although much direction is given to teachers in carefully designed guides to textbooks and workbooks, the teaching of mathematics is improved immeasurably if teachers

1. Enjoy teaching and appreciate mathematics.
2. Continue to learn mathematics in formal or informal settings.
3. Extend their teaching beyond the basal textbook.
4. Seek out and communicate with colleagues who are excited about and current in elementary mathematics.
5. Pay close attention to how children learn mathematics.

There are also numerous learning environments, and within them are many teaching-learning strategies. The learning environment consists of physical settings in which teaching and learning take place. Within the context of schooling, these physical settings are generally at or near the school building. Thus, the learning environment may be the physical organization of a classroom, the confines of the playground, a nature trail, an urban neighborhood, or an auditorium. Within the learning environment, a teacher's behavior toward a particular group of children is determined by that teacher's beliefs, experiences, education, and feelings. In developing teaching-learning strategies, the teacher should be aware that many alternatives exist.

Development of a particular strategy is the function of an individual teacher. Although it is recognized that there is no one best way to teach, if you teach in only one way (that is, using but one strategy continuously) you are not as likely to succeed over a period of time as you are if you use several approaches. Teachers should be aware of more than one way of teaching and learning. Variety makes teaching and learning more interesting and enjoyable. This is true of teaching mathematics as well as of teaching reading, science, or social studies.

Enhancing and Guiding Learning

It would be inappropriate to recommend a single approach to teaching elementary or middle school mathematics. Because of the various ways in which individuals learn and the different personalities of learners and teachers, teachers must vary their strategies and adapt them to their own specific needs and those of their students. The process of fitting instruction to children's differing needs and styles is discussed at some length in Chapter 15. It is appropriate at this juncture to consider a framework in which successful teaching can take place. Recent documents, mentioned in Chapter 1, have made strong statements about mathematics teaching.

Duckworth (1987, p. 64) remarks, "In most classrooms, it is the quick right answer that is appreciated. Knowledge of the answer ahead of time is, on the whole, more valued than ways of figuring it out." Duckworth continues, suggesting that

> If a child spends time exploring all the possibilities of a given notion, it may mean that she holds onto it longer, and moves onto the next stage less quickly; but by the time she does move on, she will have a far better foundation—the idea will serve her far better, will stand up in the face of surprises. (1987, p. 71)

We, too, want to encourage you to help all of your students understand mathematics. Based on the recommendations of the National Research Council (1989, 1990) and the National Council of Teachers of Mathematics (1991), as well as our own reading, study, and teaching experience, we have developed the following guidelines for forward-looking teachers. There are 10 principles to which we adhere in designing mathematics instruction. Each is discussed briefly in the list that follows:

1. *Provide developmental instruction.* Although most of the following principles help define developmental instruction, it is appropriate to keep your attention focused on this principle. Developmental instruction suggests that teachers should attend to the cognitive growth of their students. Learning how children think and the levels of their thinking is crucial to developmental instruction. In planning your teaching, keep the children foremost in your mind. You must continually assess the understanding and progress of the students.

2. *Engage the children in active learning.* Using physical models has been a cornerstone of successful mathematics instruction for a number of years. One part of constructing knowledge is exploring materials freely or in problem situations. Active learning may also mean engaging in cooperative learning projects or spirited exchanges of mathematical ideas. You will find many examples of activities in this textbook that are intended to suggest ideas for your teaching. You are challenged to develop activities of your own.

3. *Lead discussions and question children about their thinking.* Children should be encouraged to explain their thinking, offer opinions, and exchange thoughts with other students. The teacher plays an important role in this process. The types of questions you ask can lead you to discover what and how a child understands. Duckworth suggests various kinds of questions:

> What do you mean? How did you do that? Why do you say that? How does that fit with what she just said? I don't really get that; could you explain it another way? Could you give an example? How did you figure that? In every case, those questions are primarily a way for the interlocutor to try to understand what the other is understanding. Yet in every case, also, they engage the other's thoughts and take them a step further. (1987, p. 97)

The teacher seeks to discover what the students understand by carefully questioning the children, and sharing opinions with them. Students are able to share their thinking in writing as well as orally. Writing should be encouraged throughout the mathematics program.

4. *Employ calculators and computers.* Calculators provide children with a means to explore mathematics and enjoy the challenge of problem solving. Children at all levels should have calculators available as tools in the learning process as well as during examinations. Computers also serve as powerful tools in the learning process and provide children with opportunities to be problem solvers. *Logo* programming serves as a creative outlet for children in learning aspects of geometry. With the proliferation of sites on the Internet, students have many areas of mathematics to explore. A good example of such a site is The Math Forum that is housed at Swarthmore College. Its Student Center web address is: http://forum.swarthmore.edu/students/. At this location students may link to pages with problems of the week at their learning level, to specific pages of interest for elementary and middle level students, to a page where they can ask a mathematics question of "Dr. Math," and to several other intriguing pages.

5. *Utilize student-centered instruction.* The ideas, opinions, and interests of the children are focal points

around which instruction is centered. Word problems based on the children's environment help begin the guided learning process. State and local content goals for mathematics along with textbooks are necessary for a sound mathematics program. Coupled with the interests and curiosity of children, the content of mathematics becomes fertile ground for the intellectual growth of children.

6. *Develop children's mathematical power.* Children gain power in mathematics when they understand the concepts and procedures that they have constructed. Having power means that children can apply mathematics to tasks and problems because they understand what they are doing. Having power in mathematics also means that children are able to reconstruct concepts and procedures when they have been forgotten. Mathematical power provides children with the confidence to attack problems and to persist when challenges arise.

7. *Encourage higher-level thinking.* Children should be challenged with problems, puzzles, and patterns throughout their learning of mathematics. The place to start is with examples from the students' own experiences. Stories that incorporate problems can be intriguing and can stimulate considerable divergent thinking. Warm-up activities at the beginning of a mathematics lesson can lead to creative thinking. Encouraging children to pose problems will help the children think differently about problem solving.

8. *Provide opportunities for children to construct and communicate mathematics.* When children construct mathematics through their experiences and subsequent interactions with teachers and peers, they develop schemas that serve them well as they continue to learn mathematics. Their understanding of mathematics is powerful in the sense mentioned above. You have the opportunity to be a constructivist teacher for at least part of the time you teach mathematics. Be prepared for an explosion of ideas as children invent mathematics. Encourage them to share their findings both orally and in writing.

9. *Teach diagnostically.* As children learn mathematics, teachers need to constantly monitor their progress. Assessing children's work and assisting them in overcoming their misconceptions are major teaching responsibilities. The primary techniques for gathering information are observing children and discussing their thinking processes with them. You should be aware of the personal logic of students and ways to interpret their thinking. By discovering how children think you will be a more effective teacher.

10. *Introduce new techniques.* Throughout your teaching career, you will be invited to participate in workshops and conferences at which exciting ideas for teaching mathematics will be introduced. The presenters will be successful teachers and experts. Take advantage of these opportunities and employ those techniques that you believe will enrich your classroom. Read journals such as *Teaching Children Mathematics* and *Mathematics Teaching in the Middle School* to discover the trends and new directions in mathematics education. If you wish, accept the role of change agent.

In addition to these principles, there are other considerations to be taken into account. For example, the way in which students are organized for instruction is important. Johnson and Johnson (1987), in *Learning Together and Alone: Cooperative, Competitive, and Individualistic Learning,* develop a strong argument for providing cooperative learning experiences for children. Cooperating and sharing a common goal foster personal growth and identification. When cooperation is encouraged, competitive learning and individualistic learning are decreased. In many of the activities presented in this textbook, cooperative learning is suggested. A discussion of cooperative learning is included in Chapter 15, along with a presentation of other useful suggestions for teaching.

KEY IDEAS

The theory of constructivism holds that students should have the opportunity to invent mathematics. It is thought that when students construct knowledge through interaction with their environment and discussion, they build a strong foundation for understanding mathematics. Twelve descriptors of constructivist teaching behavior were presented.

A fundamental reason for learning mathematics is so that we can intelligently function in society. The environments in which children are born and grow provide many experiences that help establish a foundation for learning mathematics. The years before school are important in learning mathematics. Children are active learners. They observe and establish relationships among people and objects. These relationships become an important basis for learning mathematics, which is a study of patterns and relationships. Children learn mathematics in concert with other areas of knowledge. Children's attitudes about mathematics and their perceptions about themselves play a role in how they learn mathematics.

Psychological considerations in teaching mathematics include knowing about how children develop concepts in general and mathematical concepts in particular, what happens once a concept is learned, how to foster the thinking process, and the role of language. In teaching mathematics to children, teachers' attitudes about children affect the learning environment. There are many successful teaching styles.

As you read the remaining chapters of this textbook, we hope you will gain a sense of excitement and opportunity. The excitement of active, meaningful mathematics will be reflected in the attitudes and enthusiasm of the children you teach. The opportunity to enliven the classroom environment will provide both you and your students with many enjoyable hours of mathematical exploration.

DISCUSSION QUESTIONS

1. Expand your knowledge of constructivism by reading one of the books by Brooks and Brooks or Kamii or the article by Clements listed in the chapter references. Become comfortable is discussing the theory and how its application in teaching mathematics can enhance children's learning.

2. Discuss the difference between "understanding" a concept and "understanding" a skill, for example, understanding addition and understanding how to add.

3. Read Richard Skemp's article "Relational Understanding and Instrumental Understanding" (see References). After reading it, discuss the role of the teacher in developing conceptual understanding.

4. Consider the ten principles in designing mathematics instruction that begin on page 30. Read each one carefully and add a sentence or two of your own to each discussion.

5. ⌨ Go to The Math Forum Home Page on the Internet: http://www.forum.swarthmore.edu/. Click on the link to Key Issues in Math and look through the variety of issues presented. Pick one of interest and read about the issue and opinions that have been offered to address the issue. Write a response to one of the opinion pieces.

REFERENCES

Allardice, Barbara S., and Herbert P. Ginsburg, "Children's Psychological Difficulties in Mathematics," in *The Development of Mathematical Thinking,* ed. Herbert P. Ginsburg. New York: Academic Press, 1983.

American Association of University Women Report, *How Schools Shortchange Girls.* Washington, DC: AAUW Educational Foundation, 1992.

Baroody, Arthur J., and Herbert P. Ginsburg, "The Relationship Between Initial Meaningful and Mechanical Knowledge of Arithmetic," in *Conceptual and Procedural Knowledge: The Case of Mathematics,* ed. James Hiebert. Hillsdale, NJ: Lawrence Erlbaum Associates, 1986.

Brooks, Jacqueline Grennon, "Teachers and Students: Constructivists Forging New Connections," *Educational Leadership,* 47, no. 5 (February 1990), 68–71.

Brooks, Jacqueline Grennon, and Brooks, Martin G. *The Case for Constructivist Classrooms.* Alexandria, VA: Association for Supervision and Curriculum Development, 1993.

Brownell, William A., "Psychological Considerations in the Learning and the Teaching of Arithmetic," *The Teaching of Arithmetic.* National Council of Teachers of Mathematics, The Tenth Yearbook. New York: Bureau of Publications, Teachers College, Columbia University, 1935.

Brownell, William A., and H. E. Moser, *Meaningful vs. Mechanical Learning: A Study in Grade III Subtraction.* Duke University Research Studies in Education, no. 8. Durham, NC: Duke University Press, 1949.

Bruner, Jerome S., *The Process of Education.* Cambridge, MA: Harvard University Press, 1977.

Burger, William F., and J. Michael Shaughnessy, "Characterizing the Van Hiele Levels of Development in Geometry," *Journal of Research in Mathematics Education.* 17, no. 1 (January 1986), 31–48.

Carpenter, Thomas P., "Conceptual Knowledge as a Foundation for Procedural Knowledge," in *Conceptual and Procedural Knowledge: The Case of Mathematics,* ed. James Hiebert. Hillsdale, NJ: Lawrence Erlbaum Associates, 1986.

Clements, Douglas H., "(Mis?)Constructing Constructivism," *Teaching Children Mathematics,* 4, no. 4 (December 1997), 198–200.

Copeland, Richard W., *How Children Learn Mathematics.* Englewood Cliffs, NJ: Merrill/Prentice Hall, 1984.

Dienes, Zoltan P., "An Example of the Passage from the Concrete to the Manipulation of Formal Systems," in *Educational Studies in Mathematics,* vol. 3, ed. H. Freudenthal. Dordrect, Holland: R. Reidel, 1971, pp. 337–352.

Duckworth, Eleanor, *"The Having of Wonderful Ideas" and Other Essays in Teaching and Learning.* New York: Teachers College Press, 1987.

Fennema, Elizabeth, "Justice, Equity, and Mathematics Education," in *Mathematics and Gender,* eds. Fennema, Elizabeth, and Leder, Gilah C. New York: Teachers College Press, 1990.

Franklin, Margaret (director). *Add-Ventures for Girls: Building Math Confidence.* Newton, MA: Women's Educational Equity Act Publishing Center, 1990.

Fuson, Karen, and James W. Hall, "The Acquisition of Early Number Word Meanings: A Conceptual Analysis and Review," in *The Development of Mathematical Thinking,* ed. Herbert P. Ginsburg. New York: Academic Press, 1983.

Geary, David C. *Children's Mathematical Development: Research and Practical Applications.* Washington, DC: American Psychological Association, 1994.

Ginsburg, Herbert P., ed., *The Development of Mathematical Thinking.* New York: Academic Press, 1983.

Ginsburg, Herbert, and Sylvia Opper, *Piaget's Theory of Intellectual Development.* Englewood Cliffs, NJ: Prentice Hall, 1969.

Johnson, David W., and Roger T. Johnson, *Learning Together and Alone: Cooperative, Competitive, and Individualistic Learning.* Englewood Cliffs, NJ: Prentice Hall, 1987.

Kamii, Constance Kazoko, *Young Children Reinvent Arithmetic.* New York: Teachers College Press, 1985.

————, *Young Children Continue to Reinvent Arithmetic.* New York: Teachers College Press, 1989.

————, "Constructivism and Beginning Arithmetic (K–2)," in *Teaching and Learning in the 1990s,* ed. Thomas J. Cooney and Christian Hirsch. Reston, VA: National Council of Teachers of Mathematics, 1990.

Mathematical Sciences Education Board, *Making Mathematics Work for Minorities.* Washington, DC: MSEB, 1990.

Morse, Susan (ed.). *Separated by Sex: A Critical Look at Single-Sex Education for Girls.* Washington, DC: AAUW Educational Foundation, 1998.

National Council of Teachers of Mathematics, *Curriculum and Evaluation Standards for School Mathematics.* Reston, VA: NCTM, 1989.

————, *Professional Standards for Teaching Mathematics.* Reston, VA: NCTM, 1991.

National Research Council, *Everybody Counts: A Report to the Nation on the Future of Mathematics Education.* Washington, DC: National Academy Press, 1989.

————, *Reshaping School Mathematics: A Philosophy and Framework for Curriculum.* Washington, DC: National Academy Press, 1990.

Piaget, Jean, *The Child's Concept of Number.* New York: W. W. Norton, 1965.

————, *To Understand Is to Invent.* New York: Viking Press, 1973.

Resnick, Lauren B., "A Developmental Theory of Number Understanding," in *The Development of Mathematical Thinking,* ed. Herbert P. Ginsburg. New York: Academic Press, 1983.

Romberg, Thomas A., and Thomas P. Carpenter, "Research on Teaching and Learning Mathematics: Two Disciplines of Scientific Inquiry," in *Handbook of Research on Teaching,* ed. Merlin C. Wittrock. Englewood Cliffs, NJ: Merrill/Prentice Hall, 1986.

Roper, Ann. *Cooperative Problem Solving with Unifix Cubes.* Sunnyvale, CA: Creative Publications, 1990.

Rosenthal, R., and L. Jacobson, *Pygmalion in the Classroom: Teacher Expectation and Pupils' Intellectual Development.* New York: Holt, Rinehart & Winston, 1968.

Sadker, Myra, and David Sadker, *Failing at Fairness.* New York: Charles Scribner's Sons, 1994.

Sanders, J. (1994). *Gender-biased student/teacher interactions.* Gender Equity Project Workshop. City University of New York. New York, NY. Unpublished Manuscript.

Scada, Walter G., Fennema, Elizabeth, and Adajian, Lisa Byrd (eds.). *New Directions for Equity in Mathematics Education.* New York: Cambridge University Press, 1995.

Skemp, Richard R. "Relational Understanding and Instrumental Understanding," *Arithmetic Teacher,* 26, no. 3 (November 1978), 9–15.

Skemp, Richard R., *The Psychology of Learning Mathematics.* Hillsdale, NJ: Lawrence Erlbaum Associates, 1987.

Steffe, Leslie P., "Adaptive Mathematics Teaching," in Cooney, Thomas J., and Hirsch, Christian. *Teaching and Learning in the 1990s,* ed. Thomas J. Cooney and Christian Hirsch. Reston, VA: National Council of Teachers of Mathematics, 1990.

Suydam, Marilyn N., "Attitudes Toward Mathematics," *Arithmetic Teacher,* 32, no. 3 (November 1984), 12.

Tobias, Sheila, *Overcoming Math Anxiety.* New York: W. W. Norton, 1978.

Warren, Rebecca Lowe, and Thompson, Mary H. *The Scientist Within You: Women Scientists from Seven Continents.* Eugene, OR: ACI Publishing, 1995.

Weaver, J. Fred, "Interpretations of Number Operations and Symbolic Representations of Addition and Subtraction," in *Addition and Subtraction: A Cognitive Perspective,* ed. Thomas P. Carpenter, James M. Moser, and Thomas A. Romberg. Hillsdale, NJ: Lawrence Erlbaum Associates, 1982.

Yakel, Erna, et al., "The Importance of Social Interaction in Children's Construction of Mathematical Knowledge," in *Teaching and Learning in the 1990s;* ed. Thomas J. Cooney and Christian Hirsch. Reston, VA: National Council of Teachers of Mathematics, 1990.

Web Sites

http://forum.swarthmore.edu/students/   A dynamic site designed for students to engage in mathematics.

http://www.forum.swarthmore.edu/   The home page for The Math Forum housed at Swarthmore College.

Chapter 3

Solving and Creating Problems, Estimating, and Mental Calculating

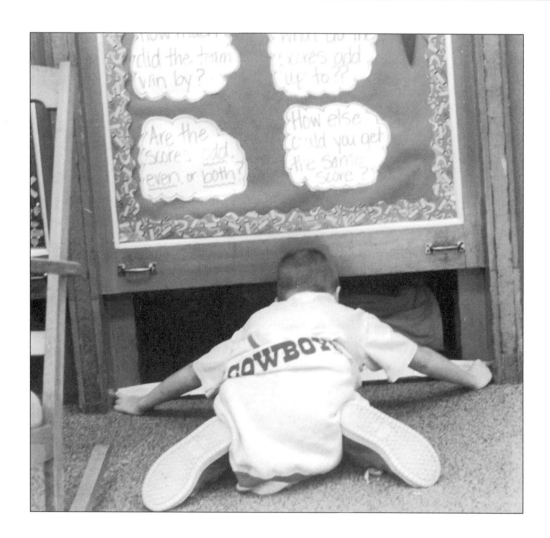

NCTM Standards

GRADES K–4

Standard 1: Mathematics As Problem Solving

In grades K–4, the study of mathematics should emphasize problem solving so that students can—

- Use problem-solving approaches to investigate and understand mathematical content;
- Formulate problems from everyday and mathematical situations;
- Develop and apply strategies to solve a wide variety of problems;
- Verify and interpret results with respect to the original problem;
- Acquire confidence in using mathematics meaningfully.

Standard 2: Mathematics As Communication

In grades K–4, the study of mathematics should include numerous opportunities for communication so that students can—

- Relate physical materials, pictures, and diagrams to mathematical ideas;
- Reflect on and clarify their thinking about mathematical ideas and situations;
- Relate their everyday language to mathematical language and symbols;
- Realize that representing, discussing, reading, writing, and listening to mathematics are a vital part of learning and using mathematics.

GRADES 5–8

Standard 1: Mathematics As Problem Solving

In grades 5–8, the mathematics curriculum should include numerous and varied experiences with problem solving as a method of inquiry and application so that students can—

- Use problem-solving approaches to investigate and understand mathematical content;
- Formulate problems from situations within and outside mathematics;
- Develop and apply a variety of strategies to solve problems, with emphasis on multistep and nonroutine problems;
- Verify and interpret results with respect to the original problem situation;
- Generalize solutions and strategies to new problem situations;
- Acquire confidence in using mathematics meaningfully.

Standard 2: Mathematics As Communication

In grades 5–8, the study of mathematics should include opportunities to communicate so that students can—

- Model situations using oral, written, concrete, pictorial, graphical, and algebraic methods;
- Reflect on and clarify their own thinking about mathematical ideas and situations;
- Develop common understandings of mathematical ideas, including the role of definitions;
- Use the skills of reading, listening, and viewing to interpret and evaluate mathematical ideas;
- Discuss mathematical ideas and make conjectures and convincing arguments;
- Appreciate the value of mathematical notation and its role in the development of mathematical ideas.

NCTM (1989), pp. 23, 26, 75, 78. Reprinted by permission.

My Math Journal

If everyone in your class shakes hands with everyone else, how many total handshakes would there be?

Try to find more than one way to solve this problem. We have given you a chart to help get you started, but there are several other ways to attack this problem. As you read the chapter, try other strategies to solve this problem. See if you can find other related problems in this chapter and use some of those ideas to solve or extend this problem. As you write out your work, be sure to look for patterns and explain all of your thinking.

Number of people	1	2	3	4	5	6...
Number of handshakes	0	1	3	6		

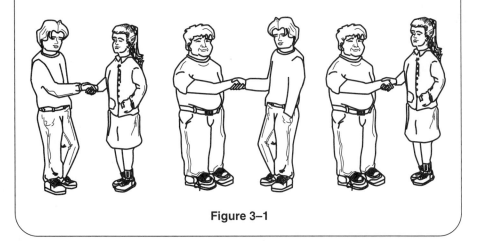

Figure 3–1

As you read the following pages, consider these guiding questions:

1. What is a problem, and what are some characteristics of good problem solvers?
2. What are your goals for students as learners of mathematics?
3. What are several heuristics and/or strategies that students might use to solve mathematical problems?
4. What are some of the influences on a child who is trying to solve and create problems?
5. What is the place of estimation in problem solving, and what are some strategies that students might use to become more proficient at estimating?
6. What is the role of mental calculation, and what strategies might you use to help students develop more skill with it? How do mental calculation and estimation differ?
7. What techniques might be used to assess students' knowledge and understanding of mathematics and how might the results of the assessment be used?

Every day, children and adults alike are faced with problems. A seven-year-old may be faced with the problem of saving enough money to buy a coveted baseball trading card, or a 13-year-old may have the problem of budgeting her time wisely to be sure there is enough time for homework, piano lessons, soccer games, and talking with her friends. She may need to determine the most important activity if she finds there is simply not enough time in a day to do everything. Frequently, when we solve our daily mathematical problems, we do not use paper and pencil or a calculator. Either we make an estimate, which will give us an approximate answer, or we calculate mentally to determine the exact answer. In this chapter, we will look at the importance of problem solving and the uses of estimation and mental calculation. These topics will be expanded further in the following chapters.

Problem Solving

Problem solving has long been recognized as one of the most important mathematical processes by the National Council of Teachers of Mathematics (NCTM). In 1980, the NCTM published *An Agenda for Action,* which consisted of a set of recommendations for elementary and secondary mathematics instruction in the 1980s. The first of eight recommendations was that "problem solving be the focus of school mathematics in the 1980s" (NCTM, 1980). When the NCTM published the *Curriculum and Evaluation Standards for School Mathematics* in 1989, problem solving was listed as one of the four strands that should receive increased attention at all grade levels from kindergarten through twelfth grade (NCTM, 1989). In *Principles and Standards for School Mathematics* (NCTM, 1998), problem solving is one of ten standards at all levels, Pre-K–12. Frequently, students need to define or create problems on which to work. Outside of school, problems are not generally spelled out for us in advance. We need to determine the problem before we can find a solution.

This emphasis on problem solving and problem creating raises some very important questions: What is a problem? What are problem solving and problem creating? What are some characteristics of good problem solvers and good problem creators? What influences a person trying to solve or create problems? What are some heuristics and strategies one should use when solving or creating problems? What types of grouping should be used for problem solving and problem creating? How should the processes and results of problem solving and problem creating be communicated? Answers to these questions will be explored in the remainder of this chapter and throughout this book, for it is important to make problem solving and problem creating integral parts of all the topics in a mathematics program, not separate topics to be investigated only at special times during the school year.

What Is a Problem?

A problem may be thought of as a perplexing question or situation. It should be a question or situation that does not suggest an immediate solution or even an immediate method of solution. For our purposes, a problem should involve some aspect of mathematics, but that does not mean that it must involve numbers. Some excellent mathematics problems involve spatial or logical reasoning but do not involve numbers. A good problem is one that interests the problem solver and one that the problem solver makes an attempt to work. Notice that this definition does not include many of the so-called word problems or story problems that are seen in many textbooks because the student generally has an immediate method for solving the problem and is frequently not interested in the outcome. This definition refers to those nonroutine problems for which the students do not have an immediate method of solution and those problems that arise commonly in everyday life for which there may be several methods of solution.

Traditionally, problems that have been used in elementary and middle school classrooms have had one right answer, and often one correct method of solution. Shimada, a Japanese researcher who has studied problem solving and higher-level thinking, refers to these as "complete" or "closed" problems. He has developed what he refers to as an "open-ended approach" where an "incomplete" problem is first presented to the students. Children are then encouraged to use many different approaches to solving the problem that may have a variety of correct responses (Becker and Shimada, 1997). Teachers are taught to use the many correct answers to help students construct new mathematical knowledge by combining students' knowledge, skills, and ways of thinking that have previously been learned. Throughout this book, you will find a variety of open-ended problems, and you should attempt to find your own unique methods of solution to as many as possible.

Solving and Creating Problems

We can think of our competencies or depth of understanding in mathematics as forming a continuum or hierarchy, as shown in Figure 3–2. At the bottom of the hierarchy is the elimination of mathematical *illiteracy*. Many people in the United States today seem almost proud of the fact that they do not understand or use mathematics. It is not uncommon to hear an adult say, "Oh, I always hated mathematics. I never was good at it." This attitude rubs off on students, who assume it must be all right not to be able to do mathematics. This is a very dangerous belief, however, as our world becomes ever more dependent on a mathematically and technologically literate society.

Just above illiteracy is the ability to do some computation with whole and rational numbers; students at this level are called *doers*. These students have memorized rules for addition, subtraction, multiplication, and division and generally do fairly well on tests of computation from the math text, as long as they simply have to repeat a process over and over again. Generally, however, they do not understand why they are performing an operation in a certain way.

Above the level of the doers is the student who can *compute* well with all types of rational numbers and who understands the structure of the number system and the concepts of the operations. However, we certainly cannot be satisfied with students who can merely compute, when any $5 calculator would be faster and more accurate than most of the best human calculators.

Beyond the ability to compute is the ability to apply mathematical concepts to solve everyday problems—to be a *consumer*. For our society to function, we must be able to use mathematics every day, both at work and at home. Students need to learn how to use mathematics in stores or in restaurants, when painting a house or balancing a checkbook, and in a multitude of other situations. They must use mathematics to be intelligent consumers in today's society. It is at this level that students are able to solve everyday problems that require more than one step. These problems require that students reason and plan a series of steps in order to solve routine exercises.

It is at the next level that students *solve* the problems mentioned above. These students are able to apply their knowledge of mathematics in new situations when the answer is not obvious and they have no preset rule to fall back on. They frequently use a method that they have not tried before or apply a method they have used to solve a completely different type of problem.

Beyond the ability to solve problems that someone else has suggested is the ability to create, define, or *pose* problems. This requires an ability to see important aspects of a situation and ask questions about it. Most of the mathematics known today has been discovered in the last 50 years, and new solutions would never have been found if someone had not suggested new problems on which to work. It is here that we begin to develop mathematical power. We realize that we control our ability to learn new mathematics by always questioning our results and by searching for new understanding.

At the top of the continuum is the *creation* of new mathematics. This requires first the creation of new questions upon which to work and then the discovery or invention of the mathematics to answer the questions. Even young children can discover or create mathematics

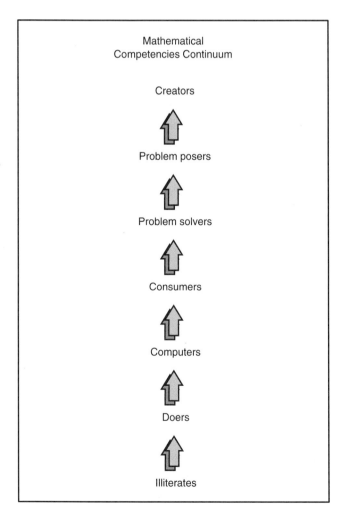

Figure 3–2

that is new to them, and they should be encouraged to do so. They will understand and remember the mathematics they have constructed for themselves much better than any of the mathematics we try to teach them.

Characteristics of Good Problem Solvers and Good Problem Creators

In *Problem Solving—A Basic Mathematics Goal: A Resource for Problem Solving,* the following are listed as traits that good problem solvers usually possess:

- Good estimation and analysis skills.
- Ability to perceive likenesses and differences.
- Reflective and creative thinking.
- Ability to visualize relationships.
- Strong understanding of concepts and terms.
- Ability to disregard irrelevant data.
- Capability to switch methods easily, but not impulsively.
- Ability to generalize on the basis of few examples.
- Ability to interpret quantitative data.
- Strong self-esteem.
- Low test anxiety. (Ohio Department of Education 1980, p. 13)

The ability to see relationships seems to be one of the main characteristics that separate expert problem solvers from novices. Students who are not good at solving problems tend to try to memorize rules and facts as unrelated bits of information. Good problem solvers look for the underlying structure and try to relate any new problem to information they already possess.

In creating new problems, good problem solvers use information they understand and problems they have already solved as jumping off points for new questions. They view mathematics as a topic to be explored, with rich new ideas waiting to be discovered or invented, rather than as a series of rules that they must memorize.

Good problem solvers may not be the fastest computers. They take time to think about the problem before they begin to write. They do not give up easily if a problem is difficult. They view the problem as a challenge and enjoy working on it. These are skills that all children can learn. If we give students time to think about what they are doing and let them experience the joy of solving a difficult problem, all students can become better problem solvers.

Influences on a Person Trying to Solve or Create Problems

The ability to solve and create problems and to construct new mathematics is closely related to the student's attitude toward mathematics, the student's beliefs about the nature of mathematics and about his or her ability to do mathematics, the student's knowledge of mathematics, and the neurological makeup of the student's brain. All of these components may change as the student gains more experience in the construction of mathematics. The arrows in the diagram in Figure 3–3 go both ways, indicating that as the student constructs mathematical knowledge, attitudes and beliefs about mathematics and the neurology of the brain change. In addition, attitudes, beliefs, and neurology affect the ways in which the student creates mathematics.

Students with strengths in areas affecting the learning of mathematics may have different brain patterns than students with weaknesses in these areas. For example, students who process information well visually have different brain processing patterns than those who do not. As students with weak visual skills practice visual tasks, their brain patterns change to more closely resemble those of strong visual processors. Attitudes toward mathematics may also be reflected in the physical makeup of the brain. Students who are afraid of mathematics may emit chemicals in the brain that inhibit the higher cognitive functions. On the other hand, a student who enjoys solving mathematical problems may emit chemicals in the brain that enhance learning.

Beliefs about mathematics that affect learning include the belief that mathematics is a series of unrelated facts to be memorized as opposed to the belief that mathematics is the study of patterns and relationships. Students with one belief will approach the learning and construction of mathematics much differently than students with the other. Students' beliefs about themselves also greatly affect their learning. A student who believes that he or she cannot do math will generally work to show that this is true, while a student who is confident of success will generally be much more successful. Again, the arrow goes both ways, showing that students who suc-

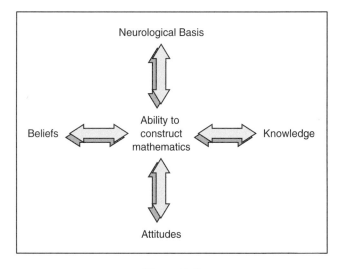

Figure 3–3

ceed at constructing mathematical concepts change both their beliefs about the nature of mathematics and their beliefs about themselves.

Attitudes toward mathematics affect the construction of mathematical knowledge in much the same way as beliefs. Students who hate or fear mathematics do not do as well as students who love it. Again, the arrow goes both ways, showing that students who do construct mathematics learn to enjoy it.

Background knowledge, of course, also affects a student's ability to construct new knowledge. Students need to develop fundamental concepts before they can build on that foundation to construct new information. Again, as students construct new knowledge, they naturally add to their store of knowledge. This knowledge is generally much longer lasting than anything they have tried to memorize by rote.

Heuristics or Strategies Used in Solving and Creating Problems

A *heuristic* is a general method of solving a problem. A heuristic that has proven to be useful for both the creation and the solution of problems is the model in Figure 3–4. Notice that this is not a linear model. Students can move from any point on the star to any other point.

Students may begin at the step that is represented by the point on the star labeled *Relate*. It is here that a student uses all available information that relates to the mathematical area on which he or she is working. For example, a student studying prime numbers may study the sieve of Eratosthenes, greatest common divisors or factors, least common multiples or denominators, composite numbers, even and odd numbers, and other number theory topics. After a student has investigated several related areas, he or she may create a new question on which to work. This question is then investigated, although the student may look at other relationships or create other questions to study during this process. After a thorough investigation, the solution or solutions are evaluated and promising solutions are reported to any interested individuals. These individuals may include classmates, younger students, professional mathematicians or mathematics educators

(through journals, the Internet, or conferences), interested parties in industry, and teachers. Results from any investigation should then be recycled to stimulate the creation of other questions to study.

Among the best-known general approaches to problem solving is that of Polya (1957). He outlined four steps in the problem-solving process: (1) **understand the problem,** (2) **devise a plan,** (3) **carry out the plan,** and (4) **look back.** The first step seems obvious, yet children are often frustrated because they do not understand what the problem asks. It is at this stage that students must restate the problem in their own words and reflect on the meaning of any questions in the problem. The second step suggests that reflection and planning will be rewarded later on. The third step requires children to apply one or more problem-solving skills. The fourth step calls for reviewing the process to make sure the problem is solved and there are no loose ends.

The skills that serve children as they tackle mathematical problems have been enumerated in many publications, some of which are listed at the end of the chapter. One exemplary program, "Problem Solving in Mathematics" (Lane County Mathematics Project, 1984), suggests these five skills:

1. **Guess and check.** Individuals using this skill make an educated guess and check the guess against the conditions of the problem. The result allows the problem solver to make a new, more refined guess. The process continues until a solution is reached. Here is an example.

   Problem: The Ridefun Toy Store sells only wagons and bicycles. On a particular day, it sold 12 items, with a total of 32 wheels. How many wagons and how many bicycles were sold that day?

   - *Understanding the problem.* Perhaps we can visualize the wagons and bicycles. The wagons each have 4 wheels; the bicycles, 2. A total of 12 items are sold on this day.
   - *Devising a plan.* We can draw pictures of wagons and bicycles and count the number of wheels. This will take a while. Perhaps we can guess a number of wagons, then find the number of bicycles by subtracting. Then, we can multiply the number of wagons by 4 and the number of bicycles by 2 and add together the products to find the total number of wheels.
   - *Carrying out the plan (guess and check).* We observe that 8 wagons alone have 32 wheels, so fewer than 8 wagons are purchased. Our first guess is 6 wagons and 6 bicycles (see Figure 3–5). We find that those 12 items produce 24 + 12, or 36, wheels. Because the total is too many wheels, we refine our guess to 5 wagons and 7 bicycles. Now we have 20 + 14, or 34, wheels. Finally, we guess 4 wagons and 8

Figure 3–4

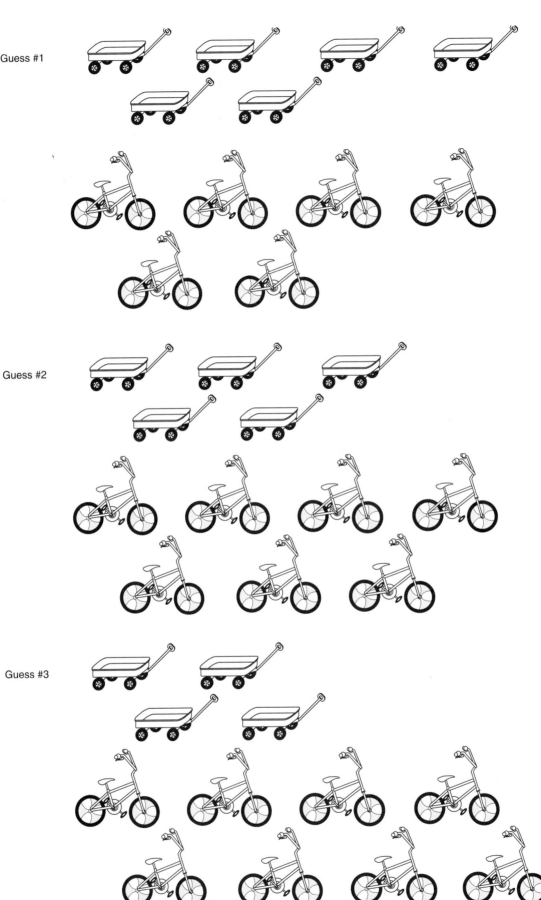

Figure 3–5

bicycles. Thus, we have 16 + 16, or 32, wheels, meeting the requirements of the problem.

- *Looking back.* We make sure our 4 wagons and 8 bicycles make a total of 12 items. And, because we know there are 32 wheels, we are satisfied with the results.

2. **Look for a pattern.** In some problems, we try to find patterns. These patterns may be visual, numerical, or sometimes both. Once a pattern is recognized, the problem will most likely be quickly solved.

   Problem: Numbers describe the triangular dot patterns shown below. What are the next three numbers that follow 15?

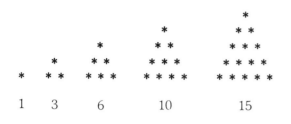

| 1 | 3 | 6 | 10 | 15 |

As we reflect on this problem using Polya's guidelines, we look for a pattern. We notice that each dot pattern has one more dot in its bottom row than the previous dot pattern: 1 has one dot in the bottom row; 3, two dots in the bottom row; 6, three dots in the bottom row; 10, four dots in the bottom row; and 15, five dots in the bottom row. We also notice that as we move up each triangle, each dot row has one less dot than the previous row. Using this pattern, the next triangle would have six dots in the bottom row, for 6 + 5 + 4 + 3 + 2 + 1, or 21, total dots. Next would be a triangle with seven dots in the bottom row, for 7 + 6 + 5 + 4 + 3 + 2 + 1, or 28, total dots. The final triangle would have eight dots in the bottom row, for 8 + 7 + 6 + 5 + 4 + 3 + 2 + 1, or 36, total dots.

3. **Make a systematic list.** This skill is used when it is necessary to describe all possibilities for an event. A list is developed systematically to decrease the chance of omitting an item.

   Problem: Using only quarters, dimes, nickels, and pennies, how many different ways can you pay for an item that costs $.25? Using Polya's framework for problem solving, we decide to list all the ways to produce $.25 with the coins given. Here is the list that we developed:

Quarters	Dimes	Nickels	Pennies	Total
1	0	0	0	$.25
0	2	1	0	.25
0	2	0	5	.25
0	1	3	0	.25
0	1	2	5	$.25
0	1	1	10	.25
0	1	0	15	.25
0	0	5	0	.25
0	0	4	5	.25
0	0	3	10	.25
0	0	2	15	.25
0	0	1	20	.25
0	0	0	25	.25

Notice that as we moved from left to right in the list, we started with the largest number of each coin we could use to produce $.25. (You may have thought of another equally effective way to make this list systematic.) As a result, we found 13 different ways to pay for an item that costs $.25.

4. **Make and use a drawing or model.** Some problems can be solved easily with a drawing or model. The drawing includes the conditions of the problem and allows the solver to see the solution.

   Problem: Adams School has 11 members on its volleyball team, 6 on the court and 5 substitutes. Whenever the team scores a point, the 5 substitutes jump up and give each other a "high five" to celebrate—that is, each substitute jumps up and slaps the upheld hand of each of the other substitutes. How many high fives are given for each point scored? After understanding the problem, we decide that drawing a representation of the substitutes will be helpful. Figure 3–6 shows circles to represent the five substitutes. The line drawn between each pair of

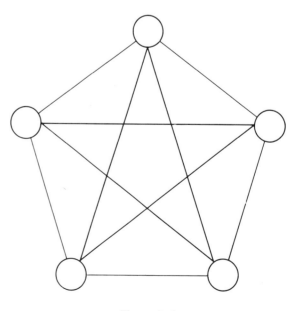

Figure 3–6

substitutes represents the hand slap between those two. When we count all the lines on the drawing, we find that there are 10 high fives for each point scored.

5. **Eliminate possibilities.** Using this skill allows the problem solver to reduce the number of possible responses that a problem may suggest. When possibilities are eliminated, the solution becomes more manageable.

Problem: Jill threw 4 darts at a dartboard target like the one shown in Figure 3–7. Each dart hit the target and none landed on a line.

Which of the scores below could Jill have earned?

| 14 | 23 | 26 | 8 | 16 |
| 34 | 19 | 32 | 6 | 30 |

As we thought about how this problem might be solved, it occurred to us to find the largest and smallest scores possible with 4 darts. If they all landed in the region worth 8 points we would have 32 points, the largest possible score; if they all landed in the region worth 2 points, we would have 8 points, the smallest possible score given that all the darts hit the target. We can now eliminate any score below 8 or above 32.

Next, we notice that all regions have even-numbered scores. Even scores mean that any combination of 4 scores will produce an even total. We can now eliminate the odd numbers. After eliminating the odd numbers, those below 8, and those above 32, we have 14, 26, 8, 16, 30, and 32. With a little checking, we find that Jill could have earned any of these scores.

The skills just discussed are but a sampling of the problem-solving skills you are likely to find as you further investigate problem solving. The skills fit well into Polya's general approach.

There are several other lists of problem-solving strategies, some of which are variations of these and some of which are a bit different. For example, you might see "make a table or chart," which would be similar to "make a systematic list," or you might see "use a simpler problem" or "use logical reasoning," which may be similar to "eliminate possibilities." Other useful problem-solving strategies include working backwards, acting out the problem, and changing your point of view.

Working backwards is useful when you know the desired outcome of a problem but are having difficulty getting started working toward it. You may be able to work to the beginning from the end more easily than working to the end from the beginning.

Problem: Hank is selling boxes of raspberries from his garden. The first person he meets buys half of his boxes. The next person buys 4 boxes of berries. When he meets a third person, he sells half of the remaining boxes. The next customer buys 7 boxes of berries. Hank now has only 1 box of berries left, and he gives this to his father for a fresh raspberry tart. How many boxes of berries did Hank have to begin with?

After understanding the problem, we may try the strategy of guess and check. It is very difficult to guess the original number of boxes, however, and this strategy may go on for quite some time before the answer is guessed. However, if we start at the end and work back to the beginning, the problem is fairly simple as shown in Figure 3–8. We know that at the end, Hank had 1 box left. If customer number 4 bought 7 boxes, he must have had 8 boxes left after the third customer. If the third customer bought half of his boxes, he must have had 16 boxes left after the second customer. The second customer bought 4 boxes, so he must have had 20 boxes left after the first customer. This was half of the original number. Therefore, Hank began with 40 boxes.

Acting out the problem is a fun strategy as well as a useful one. Children frequently need to work through the problem with their peers both to understand the problem better and to solve it.

Problem: Jack said to Andreas, "You are my father." Andreas said to Judy, "You are my mother." Judy said to Tyson, "You are my son." Tyson said to Jennifer, "You are my daughter." What is the relationship between Jack and Jennifer?

Students would probably have difficulty figuring out the relationship between Jack and Jennifer by just reading the problem. Some students may be able to figure out that the two are cousins by drawing a picture of the

Figure 3–7

Figure 3–8

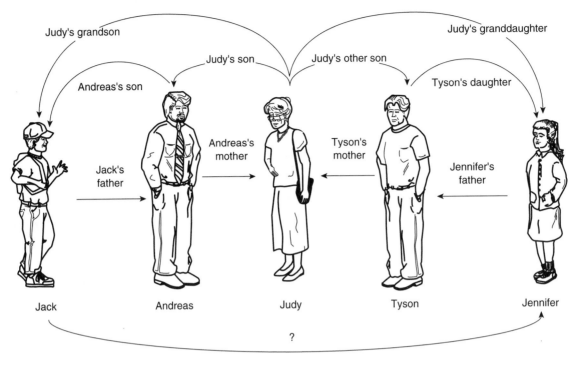

Figure 3–9

relationships as in Figure 3–9, but others may need to actually see children taking the roles of the people in the problem and discussing their relationships.

Changing your point of view is a useful strategy to use with some tricky problems. You might think you understand a problem when in fact you are reading into it conditions that do not exist. The following problem is a well-known example.

Problem: Connect all nine dots in the following diagram using only four line segments without lifting your pencil.

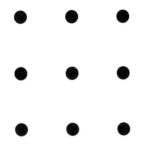

You might think that you are not allowed to break out of the restrictions of the 3-by-3 array. You have to change your point of view to realize that if you go beyond the array, you can connect the dots as follows.

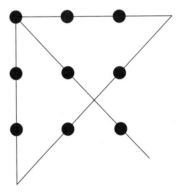

Open-Ended Problems.   As noted earlier, many problems lend themselves to a variety of solutions, and children should have numerous experiences with these. These problems are not designed to teach any specific problem-solving strategy, but rather give the students an opportunity to use a more open-ended heuristic such as the one in Figure 3–4. In this case, they relate the question to problems they have solved earlier and then create their own strategies, thus developing higher-level thinking skills. As they investigate the problem, students might use multiple representations such as tables, drawings, symbols, physical models and equations. Throughout the problem solving, students are asked to evaluate their solutions and to communicate their results with others.

A sample of one of these problems, with a variety of possible responses and related problems, follows. In a typical textbook problem, students might be asked to look at a series of odd numbers and determine the next numbers in the sequence. On a more difficult level, the teacher might ask the students to determine what the 100th number in the sequence would be. A more interesting way of looking at this problem would be to ask the students to do the following investigation.

Problem: Study the following diagram. Where would the number 289 appear if this sequence continues?

```
                       1
                    3     5
                 7     9     11
              13    15    17    19
           21    23    25    27    29
        31    33    35    37    39    41
     43    45    47    49    51    53    55
```

Different students might attack this in different ways such as the following:

1. One student might simply continue the pattern through the 17th row and notice that 289 is in the middle.
2. Another student might figure that 289 would be the 145th number in the sequence. Then, noting that Row One has one number, Row Two has two numbers, Row Three has three numbers, etc., and continuing this pattern, a student could discover the 145th number in the middle of Row 17.
3. Another student might notice that the numbers going down the left side of the triangle increase by 2 more each time. That is, they increase by 2, then 4, then 6, then 8, etc. Continuing this pattern, the student could find that the first number in Row 17 is 273 and the first number in Row 18 is 307.
4. A fourth student might notice that the middle number in each odd numbered row is the square of that number. Knowing that 289 is 17^2, this student might immediately notice that 289 is the middle number of Row 17.

These are only a few examples of what students can do with interesting, open-ended problems. Students who have been taught to play with problems, patterns, and connections approach mathematics very differently from students who have been taught that there is one right way to solve a problem, the teachers and the textbooks know what it is, and it is the students' job to listen and find out. On the other hand, students flourish and blossom when they are asked to explore problems in depth using a variety of approaches, looking for patterns, making and verifying hypotheses and generalizations, and connecting new knowledge to earlier learning.

As students work on open-ended problems, they should be encouraged to ask themselves a number of questions designed to help them dig more deeply into the problems. The following is a list of phrases or questions that are good to use when investigating problems. These questions help the students to investigate mathematics that is more complex, make more connections, create deeper understandings, evaluate their own reasoning, and give them interesting opportunities to communicate their findings.

1. Why?
2. Why not?
3. What if . . . ?
4. What if . . . not . . . ?
5. What patterns do I notice?
6. What predictions or generalizations can I make?
7. How is this like . . . ?
8. How is this different from . . . ?
9. Will that always work?
10. Will that ever work?
11. Can I do that another way? How many ways might I . . . ?
12. What is the largest? the smallest?
13. Convince me. Prove it. Show me.
14. Explore the converse or the inverse of the problem.
15. What other related problems might I explore?

Applying this list of questions to the problem given earlier might result in the following investigations:

1. Why is the number in the middle of each odd numbered row a square number?
2. Why are there not any even numbers on the triangle? Where would the even square numbers be if they were on the diagram?
3. What if I added the numbers on the triangle? What patterns would I notice?
4. What if I did not use odd numbers on the triangle? Would the same pattern be true for even numbers?
5. Is there a pattern to the sum of the numbers in each row? How many other patterns do I notice?
6. Can I generalize the sum of all rows through any row *N*?
7. How are patterns in this triangle similar to Pascal's triangle?
8. How are patterns in this triangle different from Pascal's triangle?
9. Will the *N*th row always have *N* numbers in it?
10. Will there ever be a square number on the triangle that is not in the middle of a row?

11. What is the smallest sum of a row that is also an even number? Is there a largest sum that is an even number?
12. Prove that the sum of the numbers in any row will always be the cube of the row number.
13. What is the first number in Row 10? Row 20? Row *N*?
14. How is this problem related to finding the sum of the first *N* counting numbers? the sum of any consecutive numbers? the sum of any consecutive odd numbers?

Open-ended problems cannot be scored simply correct or incorrect. A variety of assessment criteria must be used. These might include:

1. Depth of understanding—the extent to which mathematical concepts are explored and developed.
2. Fluency—the number of different correct answers, methods of solution, or new questions formulated.
3. Flexibility—the number of different categories of answers, methods, or questions.
4. Originality—solutions, methods, or questions that are unique and show insight.
5. Elaboration or elegance—quality of expression of thinking, including charts, graphs, drawings, models, and words.
6. Generalizations—patterns that are noted, hypothesized, and verified for larger categories.
7. Extensions—related questions that are asked and explored, especially those involving why and what if.

Many teachers use scoring rubrics or guidelines to evaluate students' work on open-ended problems. One sample of these will be presented later in the chapter.

As useful as they may be, there is more to teaching problem solving than teaching about heuristics and strategies. Schroeder and Lester (1989, p. 32) distinguish between three different approaches to teaching problem solving: (1) teaching about problem solving, (2) teaching for problem solving, and (3) teaching via problem solving. In teaching about problem solving, teachers help students learn strategies and heuristics such as those discussed here, and students are encouraged to be aware of these processes as they solve problems. In teaching for problem solving, teachers help students learn to solve problems so that they may use their problem-solving abilities outside of school. In teaching via problem solving, teachers help students realize that problem solving is not only the goal of learning mathematics but also the means to learn mathematics. In this way, students begin a mathematical topic with a problem to solve and learn mathematics through the solution of the problem. They construct their own knowledge of mathematics as they work through the problem. Throughout this book, we will present problem solving as a means to learn mathematics and as a goal and a topic to be learned in its own right. The most important of these, however, is as a means of learning mathematics, for in questioning answers and solving problems students become mathematically powerful.

Problem Solving in Projects

Presenting individual problems for students to solve is one valuable approach. Another is to challenge students by presenting a task or a project with one or more problems imbedded in it. These tasks or projects may take several days to complete. One such project designed by preservice teachers Errin Neufeld, Tonya Peters, and Dana Reimer for middle-level students is described below. It is intended for groups of 3 to 5 students.

Project Title: Parking at the MetroPlex Theater
Description of the Task: The new MetroPlex Theater is being built nearby and you have been hired to design its parking lot. There will be 5 theaters in the building. Two theaters will have 175 seats each and the other three will have 325 seats each. The theater will have only one entrance. A city ordinance states that for every 3 seats in a theater, one parking place must be provided. Also, for every 25 regular parking spaces, one handicapped space near the theater entrance must be provided. Your job is to design the most cost-efficient parking lot for the theater. Property for the parking lot sells at $12 per square foot and asphalt costs an additional $.90 per square foot. Keep in mind that your parking lot needs to be safe for vehicles and pedestrians, attractive to customers, have convenient access to the theater, and fit all of the above requirements.

Expected End Product: A drawing to scale of the entrance of the MetroPlex Theater and the entire parking lot, including a written description of how the problem was solved and a budget for the project.

Knowledge and Skills (from the NCTM Standards):
Calculation and Estimation: Students use mathematical calculations to figure the cost per square foot of property and asphalt that they will need and how many parking spots (regular and handicapped) they will need. Further, they will calculate the units for their scale drawing. *Geometry:* Students will determine the size and shape of the most efficient parking lot. *Measurement:* Students will use measuring tools as they draw their parking lot to scale. *Mathematical Problem Solving:* Students will use pictures, models, and diagrams when making the layout of their parking lot, as well as using basic problem solving strategies.

Scoring Criteria for the Project:

1. Attractive scale drawing
2. Carefully written description of work
3. Reasonable budget for the project

4. Appropriate number of parking spaces
5. Appropriate number and location of handicapped parking spaces
6. Safe parking lot
7. Attractive parking lot
8. Convenient access to the theater

Estimating

Another of the topics that will be presented throughout this book is that of estimation. Estimation may involve amount, length, weight, area, volume, or size. Computational estimation may involve using addition, subtraction, multiplication, or division of whole or rational numbers when an approximate answer is needed. Computational estimation involves many of the same skills as mental calculation, but is used when an exact answer is not needed.

Coburn (1989, p. 44) distinguishes between six categories of computation. Each category combines one of three methods of computation—mental, written, or calculator—and one of two reasons for computation—to calculate an exact sum, difference, product, or quotient, or to obtain an estimate. You should discuss with the children which of the methods of computation is appropriate for the type of problem on which you are working.

Estimation can assist children as they calculate using both paper and pencil and calculators. When estimation is applied, overall accuracy should improve. For example, a fifth-grader who is multiplying 38×27 should be able to determine that the answer will be close to but less than 40×30, or 1,200. If that student multiplies and gets 10,206 or 102.6, it should be apparent that an error was made. Estimating will not eliminate all errors, but it will help in many cases.

Just as there are strategies in problem solving, there are also strategies in estimating. Reys (1986) reports five such strategies from her research. They include the front-end strategy, clustering, rounding, compatible numbers, and special numbers. The **front-end strategy** has two steps: (1) perform the operation using only the most significant digits, and (2) adjust or refine the estimate by performing the operation on the remaining digits. For example, to estimate $193 + 428 + 253$, children should think that $1(\text{hundred}) + 4(\text{hundred}) + 2(\text{hundred}) = 7(\text{hundred})$, using the most significant digits first. Then, to adjust the estimate, they should think that 93 is about 100 and $28 + 53$ is about 75. The final estimate is $700 + 100 + 75$, or 875. The **clustering strategy** is used to estimate the sum of several numbers that cluster around a particular value. The strategy involves estimating the average of the numbers and then multiplying the average by how many numbers there are. For example, to estimate $23 + 28 + 22 + 25 + 29 + 27$, children can estimate

the average of the numbers as 25 and then multiply by 6. The result, 150, is a good estimate of the actual sum.

The **rounding strategy** may be used for any operation. The process involves rounding the numbers being used and then performing the operation. It is important to round carefully in order to provide the best estimate. For example, to estimate 43×57, children can round and then multiply 40×60 to give an estimate of 2,400. The 43 is rounded down, and the 57 is rounded up. If both numbers are rounded down, the result is an underestimate. If both numbers are rounded up, the result is an overestimate. In such cases, mental adjustments up or down should be made.

The **compatible numbers strategy** refers to looking for numbers that seem to fit together. For example, to estimate $2 + 8 + 5 + 2 + 3 + 9 + 4$, children can search for pairs of numbers whose sums are close to 5 and 10. Thus, $2 + 8 = 10$, $5 + 2 + 3 = 10$, 9 is close to 10, and 4 is near 5, so the estimated sum is $10 + 10 + 10 + 5$, or 35.

The **special numbers strategy** refers to seeking values that are easy to use in mental computation. This strategy is best used with fractions, decimals, and percentages. For example, to estimate $0.9 + 5.8$, children can think that $1 + 6 = 7$. Children should look for values near 1, 10, and 100 as part of the special numbers strategy.

To become competent estimators, children must be carefully taught the estimation strategies and must be given time to practice the strategies. Periodic checks should be made to confirm that students are remembering estimation strategies.

Weekly Estimations

We have suggested ways to incorporate estimation with each topic presented in this text. Another successful procedure is to have a special estimation activity once a week at the beginning of a math lesson. For example, using the same glass jar, one with a capacity of 250–450 milliliters, place a different type of material in the jar each week. Begin with larger objects, such as colored cubes, shell macaroni, marshmallows, individually wrapped candies, unshelled peanuts, and bottle caps. On estimation day, distribute slips of paper to the children and have each child write down his or her name and estimation of how many objects are in the jar. Make up a small certificate to award to the student or students with the closest estimate.

As time passes, decrease the size of the objects placed in the jar. For example, the following items work well: pennies, beans, buttons, various sizes of Cuisenaire rods, breakfast cereal, and paper clips. Toward the end of the school year, try rice and split peas. Every now and then, vary the type of estimation. For example, for three or four weeks, use different sizes of jars but use the same objects.

You might want to read stories or poems to the children that encourage estimation. If you have a jar full of jelly beans, the children might enjoy hearing *The Jelly Bean Contest* by Kathy Darling. The poem, "How Many, How Much," by Shel Silverstein is a good introduction to children making up their own estimation questions about things they may not have thought of before.

One week, put a golf ball in the jar with instructions to estimate the number of dimples on the ball (380 to 500, depending on the brand). Another week, tape the torn-off edges of several pages of computer paper along the chalkboard and have the children estimate the number of holes in the strip. Place a small box from some household product on a table and ask how many centimeter cubes it would take to fill the box (the volume of the box).

Gulley (1998) describes a highly motivating "estimate of the week" contest at a middle school in which she has been involved. In this case all students at the school are invited to participate in estimating objects such as the length of a piece of rope on the wall or ceiling, the area of the school, the volume of a sleeping bag stuff sack, the number of a particular kind of cereal in a box, the combined ages of the faculty, the mass of a pumpkin, the percent of pink paper to the total paper in a stack, and the time it takes to melt a punch bowl of solid ice at room temperature.

Keep looking for objects to challenge the estimation skills of your students. It will not be too difficult to provide something for each week of the year.

Mental Calculating

The skill of mental calculation not only helps students become better at computation, it also enhances the development of concepts in a number of different areas. Students who are good at mental computation have good number concepts, whether the numbers are whole numbers, integers, or other rational numbers. They understand the properties of numbers and operations, can switch from one form of a number to another, and generally can be quite flexible in their thinking. These are all skills we wish to develop in good problem solvers. Teaching mental calculation supports the curriculum for teaching via problem solving. A student who is a good mental calculator, when faced with the problem of finding 75 percent of 280, would not try to multiply 75×280 mentally. This student would probably recognize that 75 percent is 3/4, whose complement is 1/4, and would then find 1/4 of 280. After finding this answer, 70, the student could either multiply 70×3 to find 3/4 of 280, or subtract 70 from 280, since 3/4 is 1/4 less than 1. Perhaps the student will work the problem both ways to double check her answer. Students working in different groups might solve the problem using different methods

and then compare answers to determine that there are a number of correct methods of solution and that some might be more efficient than others. Students who have had experience with mental calculation find that this method is frequently faster and sometimes more accurate than using pencil and paper or even a calculator. It also may help build spatial visualization abilities since mental calculation skills frequently build upon skills with manipulative materials. Students who usually construct concepts using manipulatives may learn to use mental images of manipulatives to solve problems.

Reys lists several skills that should be included in a mental calculation curriculum:

- Development of, and proficiency with, efficient mental algorithms.
- Attention to place value (especially how certain mathematical operations affect the place value of an answer).
- Inclusion of, and a healthy respect for, the creation and use of alternative algorithms.
- Emphasis on thinking about an efficient solution strategy before attacking the problem.
- Attention to various types of numbers, including not only whole numbers but fractions, decimals, and percentages as well.
- Attention to oral mental computation as well as to visual presentation of problems. (1985, p. 46)

These skills for mental calculation will be presented in each chapter in the "Estimating and Mental Calculating" section.

Warm-Ups for a Math Lesson

We believe that nearly every math lesson should be preceded by some sort of brief activity to get the mind prepared for doing the mathematics of the day. When possible, this mental warm-up should match the content to be presented, thus anticipating what is to come. Try to use a warm-up that will introduce the concept that is to be developed in the day's lesson. If this is not possible, other warm-ups may work as well.

Warm-ups should last from 5 to 10 minutes. They should be fast-paced, involve all the students, and require thinking. Warm-ups may be problem-solving activities, mental arithmetic exercises, or short games.

We present three examples of warm-ups below, the first intended for first-grade students, the second intended for fourth-grade students, and the third intended for eighth-grade students.

Illustrative Warm-Up (Grade 1). Begin by making sure the students are quiet and ready. Then turn to the chalkboard and make three loops connected by lines, as in Figure 3–10a. Then write the numeral 5 in the top loop, make five tallies in the second loop, and draw five triangles in the third loop, as in Figure 3–10b.

Do this carefully so the children can observe what you are doing. Then move to a new space on the board and begin again, this time starting with the numeral 8, as in Figure 3–10c. Instead of completing the loops, turn and offer the chalk to a student you think may be able to fill in the second loop (tallies).

The student may ask, "Do you want me to go up there?" pointing to the board.

Nod. It will become clear that talking is unnecessary. The student goes to the board, makes eight tallies in the second loop, and gives the chalk back to you.

Then point to the third loop and offer the chalk to another student. This student knows what to do and draws eight triangles in the third loop. After that, the next two examples are completed rapidly. Time is up. Thank the class for being quiet during this game of silent math.

Illustrative Warm-Up (Grade 4). Before the activity starts, place five cards containing numerals and letters like those in Figure 3–11 above the chalkboard. Begin the lesson by saying, "As we start today, I am going to give you a signal, and I would like you to give me a letter of the alphabet." Clap three times then tap the top of a nearby table two times. Wait. In a moment, two hands shoot up. Call on Julie, who says, "The letter *h*."

Respond, "Sorry, not this time." Then call on Lori.

Lori suggests, "The letter is *m*." Walk over, shake her hand, and nod.

By this time, other hands are going up. Next, clap four times and tap the table four times. Most of the hands go up. The first student called on says the letter is *t*.

Give several other examples. All but two students easily identify the letters. Ask Margo to explain how the letters are identified.

"Well," Margo replies, "the number of claps tells which card the letter is on and the number of taps tells which position on the card is being used. Five claps mean card 5 and three taps mean the third position, or the letter *x*."

Then ask the students what value they think the letter *i* will have.

One student points out that if the letter is identified by two claps and four taps, the value could be 2×4, or 8. That is the value you want to use today, so agree. Then ask what the value of the word *cat* will be. Shortly, the answer 20 is given. Not all students catch on, but an explanation is saved for another day. Time is up.

Illustrative Warm-Up (Grade 8). The teacher begins by using the overhead projector to introduce the letter combinations shown in Figure 3–12. The information is derived from basic musical chord "inversions." To provide practice for the students, the teacher asks each student to write three three-letter words as "roots" and to write the first and second inversions of the words.

Several students are asked to share their inversions. Dan says that one of his root words is "top," the first inversion is "opt," and the second inversion is "pto." Sarah notes that Dan's first inversion is the word "opt" and suggests that there might be other root words with words in their inversions. The teacher asks if there are other students who found words in their inversions. Six students raise their hands and share their words. Then the teacher asks if anyone found a root word that produced words in both the first and second inversions. No one has found such a word and the students are challenged to find one. Within a minute, Darlene finds the word "ate" and its inversions, "tea" and "eat."

Once it is apparent to the teacher that the students understand how inversions work, she asks the students to see if they can find a "root" number whose first inversion

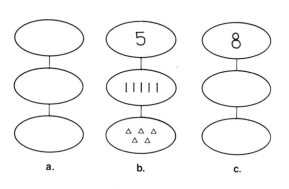

a.   b.   c.

Figure 3–10

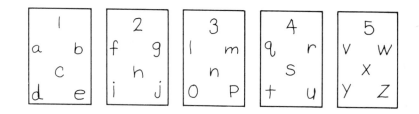

Figure 3–11

INVERSIONS		
Root	First Inversion	Second Inversion
ceg	egc	gce

Figure 3–12

is an even number and whose second inversion is divisible by five. The students are then asked to find a number whose first inversion is a palindrome and whose second inversion is an odd number. Then the students are asked to find the root number whose first inversion is greater than 500 and whose second inversion is less than 50. Finally, the students are asked to pose a number inversion problem for the rest of the class.

These three episodes represent just the tip of the iceberg. These activities can be reused and modified or extended. They can all be made more or less difficult. It will take a while to collect enough suitable warm-ups for a given grade level, but the effort is well worth it. The opportunity for mental activity should be taken advantage of. The references at the end of the chapter includes several sources of warm-up activities.

Grouping Students for Problem Solving, Estimating, and Mental Calculating

If you use problem solving as the means of instruction, you will find that students can learn to solve problems in many different types of learning groups. Solving a problem with one or two other students is often very effective. It gives the student a chance to discuss the problem and learn from others' mistakes and successes. Cooperative learning needs to be carefully planned, however. You cannot simply let the students work with their friends and hope for the best. If students have never worked in cooperative learning groups before, they will probably need some instruction on how best to work together. They need to learn that everyone should be actively involved in problem solving and that they cannot leave all the work to one person. Students must learn to be accepting and supportive of each other's ideas; telling one of the group members that he is stupid is counterproductive. It may help to assign roles in the group, such as an organizer, a checker, a relator, and a confidence builder, as suggested by Johnson and Johnson (1989, p. 242). Make sure that the children understand that they are each individually accountable for understanding and explaining the problem. Students then become peer coaches as they make sure that everyone in the group understands the problem. Cooperative learning is described in detail in Chapter 15.

Games and puzzles are a great way for children to solve problems and learn to enjoy mathematics at the same time. There are lots of good books that have problems and puzzles for children of all ages and several of these are listed in the references at the end of the chapter. You especially might want to look at the books by Adler, Anno, Burns, Fixx, and Gardner.

In addition to books, several videos and computer games give students a chance to enjoy challenging problem solving. Some of these are listed in the reference list and you and your students will find several others. Be sure to preview some of the videos from Learning Wave and some of the software from Sunburst and Broderbund. The Math Mystery videos are a great way for intermediate and middle grades students to use their mathematical problem solving and problem posing skills in a variety of settings.

Some problems may involve estimation and mental calculation. A group may be asked to make the best possible estimate of the number of jelly beans in a jar or to find as many ways as possible to add 289 and 345. When a question is open-ended, it allows for much more mathematical reasoning and creativity on the part of the students. Students may also be given a situation such as the jar full of jelly beans and asked to find both their own questions and the answers.

Roper (1990) has developed a series of books for exploring cooperative problem solving using a variety of manipulative materials such as unifix cubes, pattern blocks, tangrams, and attribute materials. Each problem is written on a set of four cards, which are dealt to four students. Each student keeps the card he or she was dealt and does not show it to anyone else. Students do, however, read their clues to each other. All four cards are essential to solving the problem. The students must work cooperatively to piece all the clues together and solve the problem.

Not all problem solving goes on in small groups. There are times when the teacher will want to present a problem to the entire class at once. Be careful when using problems with a number of children at once. These problems should have lots of correct answers or methods of solution, so that when one child finds an answer, the rest of the children can continue to work on the problem to discover other correct answers or methods.

When children work on problems individually, be sure to leave time for a discussion of the solutions. Children may need time to construct information for themselves without the distractions of others, but after a solution has been found, discussion with others opens up many other possibilities.

Communicating in Problem Solving

As students work together to solve problems, they are naturally communicating. This should be encouraged whenever possible. It changes your classroom from a setting with one teacher and 25 students to a setting with 26 teachers and 26 learners. Let students take turns solving problems with a partner where one is the speaker and the other the listener. The speaker should describe what she is thinking about at each stage of the problem solving. The listener should not interrupt, but may ask questions for clarification such as, "Is this what you mean . . . ?" or "Could you explain that in another way?" Do not limit yourself to oral communication, however.

Students should be encouraged to draw pictures or build models to demonstrate the solutions to problems whenever possible. Students of all ages benefit when they see how someone else has solved a problem. You might even challenge students occasionally to demonstrate their solutions without using words.

Problem solving is also an area in which students can use writing. Not only can they write out a description of how they went about solving a problem, they can write out word problems for other students to solve. These problems are very motivating for the other students. It is much more fun to solve problems written by your friends than to solve the ones in the book.

Be sure not to restrict problem solving to mathematics. The communication of mathematical learning enhances the language arts curriculum, strengthens reading skills, and is a necessary skill in science and social studies. Ask the students to be on the lookout for opportunities to express their mathematical problem-solving abilities in all of these areas. For example, students may keep a daily journal in which a discussion of the solutions of any new problems might be a prominent part. All of this should be included in a portfolio where the students keep a collection of their best work.

As children are writing in their daily journals or responding to oral questions, be sure that the phrases listed on page 47 for investigating open-ended problems are included frequently. Students should frequently discuss the patterns that they see and the reasons they occur. They should be asked to justify the statements that they make and should try to generalize the patterns that they notice.

Connecting Learning of Problem Solving, Estimating, and Mental Calculating

Ms. Greiner's fourth-grade class is planning a party for the kindergarten to celebrate Halloween. They are trying to estimate the amount of food, drink, and supplies that they will need. They have determined that each student will have two glasses of Witches' Brew and two black-cat cookies. They have a recipe for two gallons of punch and six dozen cookies. They also need to buy napkins that come in packages of 24 and cups that come in packages of 12. There will be 42 children and 2 teachers at the party. The class is divided into three groups, one for drinks, one for cookies, and one for supplies. They have a budget of $36 to work with. Each group has surveyed at least three different grocery stores to determine the best place to shop, and they are preparing to present their results to the class. They are keeping a journal on the processes that they are using.

Mr. Rodriguez's eighth-grade class is surveying the community to determine the level of support for a new recycling program. They have talked to the city council and two different waste-removal companies and have outlined three different possible recycling plans: a drop-off center, a curbside recycling program for paper and metal cans only, and a more complete curbside program that also includes glass and several types of plastic. They are organizing data for a presentation to the city council next month. They are hopeful that they will be able to implement the more complete curbside program if they have a convincing presentation. In addition, the students see that their study of mathematics has a practical application in their daily lives.

Assessing Learning of Problem Solving, Estimating, and Mental Calculating

The assessment of a student's ability to solve problems, estimate, and calculate mentally will require methods other than the traditional paper-and-pencil test. Although paper-and-pencil tests seem to be getting better at testing skills other than computation and rote memorization, there are better ways to determine if a student is competent at problem solving, estimating, or calculating mentally.

Charles, Lester, and O'Daffer (1987) discuss **holistic scoring** as one way to assess problem solving. Holistic scoring refers to assessing the solution to a problem by considering all the written evidence produced by the student in solving the problem. The focus of holistic scoring is the process the student used to reach a solution. This approach is different from the typical approach: first check the answer, then, if the answer is incorrect, try to figure out what the student did wrong. Holistic scoring helps the teacher assess the student's overall performance.

One type of holistic scoring is analytic scoring. With this approach, the teacher assigns a certain number of points to each aspect of the problem-solving process. An example

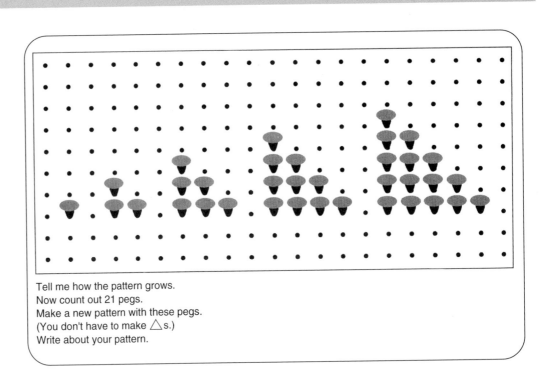

Tell me how the pattern grows.
Now count out 21 pegs.
Make a new pattern with these pegs.
(You don't have to make △s.)
Write about your pattern.

Figure 3–13 From Calvin Irons and Paul Trafton, *Growing with Mathematics,* San Francisco, CA: Mimosa, 1998, p. 274. Reprinted with permission.

Math Program

Figure 3–13 is an open-ended activity from the second-grade program, *Growing with Mathematics.* This problem introduces triangular numbers on a concrete level and encourages students to make their own observations about the pattern. Students are then asked to develop their own patterns and to write about them.

In this program, open-ended activities such as these are used to assess reasoning skills. Teachers use these to determine which strategies students use to solve a variety of problems. Note the emphasis on the development of reasoning from the concrete use of a pegboard to the pictorial representation of the pattern to the written work of the students. This use of concrete and pictorial materials as a bridge to mathematical language and symbols is one of the main features of the program from the primary level on. In addition, the program recommends that students' written work such as this be kept in individual portfolios that can be shared periodically with families to let them see the growth of children's understanding of concepts, basic skills, and problem solving. Other assessments in this program include an ongoing assessment checklist for each topic and paper-and-pencil assessment of concepts and skills.

Mathematical language and reasoning are also developed using *Mathtales* designed specifically for the program, a giant-sized *Discussion Book,* and investigations from *Mathematics from Many Cultures.* All of these encourage students to use their natural language and spatial visualization to see how mathematics relates to their everyday lives.

of an analytic scoring guide, or rubric, to guide the teacher in an assessment is one developed for use in Oregon (see Figure 3–14). The aspects of the problem-solving process that are scored with this scoring guide are (1) conceptual understanding, (2) processes and strategies, (3) communication, and (4) verification. Each of these aspects is defined in general and also specifically in each column of the scoring guide. For each aspect of the problem, the score may range from NE (no evidence) to 6 points depending on the criteria spelled out in the scoring guide and the judgment of the teacher. We will illustrate this scoring guide applied to a student's work on the following problem.

Problem: Ms. Newton's class is divided into the girls and the boys. Each group made 40 random spins with the circle spinner having four colors: red, blue, green, and yellow. They graphed their results below. Examine the graphs and draw the spinner the class most likely used. Be certain to explain why the spinner is divided the way it is.

One Possible Solution.   Using the total of 80 spins, calculate the percentage of each color from the combined results of the girls and boys. Thus, there were 20 of 80 spins or 25% that landed on blue; 42 of 80 spins or 52.5% on red; 10 of 80 spins or 12.5% on green; and 8 of 80 spins or 10% on yellow. Because of the relatively small number of total spins, it is reasonable to suggest that one-fourth of the spinner is blue, that one-half is red, that one-eighth is green, and that one-eighth is yellow.

Figure 3–15 is the solution to the problem by a student. The student has described her solution and included a table and an illustration. When her problem was assessed using the scoring guide, she received the following score: Conceptual Understanding—5; Processes and Strategies—5; Communication—5; and Verification—5. In Oregon she needed to score at least a 4 in each aspect of the process and needed the accuracy of the solution to be Essentially Correct or Precisely Correct to meet the state standard. For this problem, she easily met the standard.

Holistic scoring techniques provide alternative assessment tools for teachers who wish to collect information that is helpful both in designing problem-solving instruction for students and in helping students become aware of their own thinking processes. Students may use a problem-solving guide or checksheet that corresponds to the criteria on the scoring guide to help them develop improved skill in problem solving.

If students are keeping journals, one method of assessing their work would be to ask the students to record not only the methods of solution, but also how well they are doing at understanding concepts or mastering particular skills. Even young students are often quite capable of self-assessment and can fairly accurately judge their own strengths and weaknesses. You could collect three or four journals each day and keep your own log of the students' progress. Be sure you review everyone's journal at least once every two weeks.

Students working in groups can often do a peer assessment. They know which students are strong on particular skills, and they can help each other and you pinpoint weaknesses, as well as work to help each other strengthen those areas.

There is no substitute for direct observation in assessing some problem-solving, estimation, and mental-calculation skills. If you want to know if a student can mentally add two two-digit numbers or multiply a percent by a whole number, you need to give the student a problem and listen for a response. If you want to know if students are working well in cooperative learning groups, you need to sit in on the group and observe. Checklists and a teacher's journal help you remember what you have seen.

You might also want to enlist the aid of parents in this assessment. You could send home a note explaining that you are interested in assessing the student's ability to solve a problem involving making change or estimating volumes and ask parents to observe the students as they go to the store or cook and to question them on their understanding.

The skills you are assessing are as important as the assessment methods you use. In problem solving, you should be concerned with more than whether or not students get the correct answer. The processes they use and the strategies they attempt are also important. You should observe if students can work on problems independently or if they always seem to need help, if they give up before really trying or if they are persistent, if

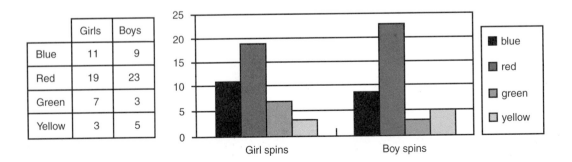

	Girls	Boys
Blue	11	9
Red	19	23
Green	7	3
Yellow	3	5

MATHEMATICS PROBLEM SOLVING OFFICIAL SCORING GUIDE

	ACCURACY _____ Precisely Correct _____	Essentially Correct (no additional instruction appears necessary) _____		Not Correct
	Conceptual Understanding	Processes & Strategies	Communication	Verification
	Showing an understanding of the mathematical concepts related to the task (the "what")	*Choosing strategies that can work, and then carrying out the strategies chosen (the "how")*	*Showing the reasoning (the "why") behind the process, using pictures, symbols, and/or vocabulary*	*In addition to solving the task, reviewing the work and defending the solution in relation to the task (the "defense")*
6				
5	A. The task is translated into thoroughly developed and/or complex mathematical concepts B. The task is enhanced through connections and/or extensions to other mathematical ideas	A. Pictures, models, diagrams, and/or symbols used to solve the task are thoroughly developed B. Complex mathematical processes/strategies are completed	A. The reasoning behind the process of solving the task is clearly displayed throughout and enhanced through the use of graphics and/or examples allowing the reader to move easily from one thought to another	A. The verification is clearly identified and thoroughly developed B. A different perspective used as a defense of their solution *may* enhance the "defense"
4	C. The task is translated into adequate mathematical concepts using relevent information and/or data from the task	C. Pictures, models, diagrams, and/or symbols are used to solve the task D. Reasonable mathematical processes/strategies are completed	B. The reasoning behind the process of solving the task is clearly displayed	C. The verification is identified, completed, and supports their solution
3	D. An understanding of some of the major concepts is displayed E. Fragments of the information and/or data presented in the task are used	E. Pictures, models, diagrams, and/or symbols may be only partially useful in solving the task F. Reasonable mathematical processes/strategies are partially completed (or partially recorded)	C. The reasoning behind the process is partially displayed with gaps that have to be inferred	D. The evidence of verification is partially completed (or partially recorded) or partially effective
2	F. The translation of the task is underdeveloped or sketchy G. Assumptions about the information and/or data may be flawed	G. Pictures, models, diagrams, and/or symbols used may partially detract from solving the task H. Processes/strategies are underdeveloped	D. The reasoning behind the process is partially flawed E. Communication explains the solution, but does not indicate a clear path to the solution	E. The process of checking the work is underdeveloped (e.g., focusing *only* on their solution or its reasonableness)
1	H. The task is translated into inappropriate concepts or uses inappropriate information I. The evidence of conceptual understanding is minimal	I. Pictures, models, diagrams, and/or symbols conflict with their solution J. Processes and strategies are ineffective or minimal	F. The display of the reasoning detracts from the work and may include irrelevant ideas	F. The process of checking the work is ineffective (e.g., verification is minimal, verification strategy is inappropriate)
NE	J. No evidence is provided	K. Strategies are not recorded	G. The communication is not provided	G. No evidence of a defense is provided

Figure 3–14   Reprinted by permission of Oregon Department of Education, 1998.

they will try more than one method of solution or if they quit if the first method does not work, and whether or not they check their answers.

In assessing estimation and mental calculation, look beyond the answer to determine if the students have a good understanding of the numeration system, if they can use a variety of techniques, if they can apply the principles and properties of operations, and whether or not they double check to determine whether answers are reasonable.

Total spins — (Boys and girls added together)

Blue - 20
Red - 42
green - 10
Yellow - 8

First I added the boys and the girls spins together to get the total. Then I divided the spinner into four equal parts of 20. (See dotted lines.) I left one part alone because blue had 20 total spins. I cut another part in half for the 10 green had. For the 8 yellow had, I brought the line from the bottom right up a little bit. So then I had 20 and 20 and 2 wich a total of 42 and Red had 42. So all I needed to do was take away the dotted line separating them.

To check I averaged

Blue 11 + 9 = 20 ÷ 2 = 10
19 + 23 = 42 ÷ 2 = 21
7 + 3 = 10 ÷ 2 = 5
3 + 5 = 8 ÷ 2 = 4

10/40 = 1/4 of the spinner
21/40 = about 1/2 " " "
5/40 = 1/8 of " "
4/40 = 1/10 of " "

(These match my spinner real close

Figure 3–15 Reprinted by permission of Oregon Department of Education, 1998

Something for Everyone

Problem solving is an excellent topic for all types of learners. Auditory learners do well in cooperative learning groups, in which they can discuss their ideas and listen to those of others. Tactile-kinesthetic learners do well using concrete materials and models to solve problems, and visual learners may draw sketches to illustrate their solutions. It helps all types of students to realize that there are lots of ways to solve problems and that they can use their areas of strength to attack a problem.

Auditory learners frequently enjoy mental calculation, but visual and tactile-kinesthetic learners may find it difficult. Be sure that problems are often presented visually as well as orally. Let the students use concrete materials when they are first developing the mental algorithms, for they may later manipulate these images in their heads.

Cooperative learning groups give students of all ability levels a chance to participate with others of varying abilities. Students who are good at paper-and-pencil computation, who may have been the shining stars in the classrooms of yesterday, will learn to appreciate students with other abilities in areas such as spatial reasoning or mental estimation and calculation. All students can learn to be accepting of differences and they will find there is much to be learned from those with different learning styles. Be sure to be flexible when setting up groups. There are times when you will want students of different abilities to work together, but be sure that there are also times when you have your top students together so that they may challenge each other. They need time to build on each other's strengths, to learn from each other, and to gain new and deeper insights into a variety of problems.

You should strive to use problems that can be worked on a variety of levels so that all students can be successful at some level, and talented students are challenged to perform at very high levels. Open-ended questions that ask students to solve the problem in a variety of different ways and to ask and solve related questions are very good for this purpose. Some excellent problems can be found on-line at a variety of sites. Several of these are listed in the references. Also, encourage students who enjoy competitions to join such competitions as MATHCOUNTS (http://thechalkboard.com/MC/) and the American Junior High School Mathematics Examination (http://www.unl.edu/amc/).

KEY IDEAS

In this chapter, a problem is defined as a perplexing question or situation that does not suggest an immediate method of solution. A problem should also interest the learner. Goals in problem solving include not only helping the students to become proficient problem solvers, but also helping them to pose problems and to create mathematics to solve those problems.

Characteristics of good problem solvers were listed and discussed, as were factors that influence a person who is constructing new mathematical concepts. Strategies for solving problems include guess and check, look for a pattern, make a systematic list, make and use a drawing or model, eliminate possibilities, work backwards, act it out, and take a different point of view.

Polya has outlined a four-step problem-solving heuristic: (1) understand the problem, (2) devise a plan, (3) carry out the plan, and (4) look back. Students may also use the following five-point heuristic: relate, create, investigate, evaluate, and communicate.

Estimation and mental calculation involve similar skills, but estimation is used when students want to find an approximate answer and mental calculation is used when an exact answer is required. Students should discuss when it is appropriate to use mental skills and when using paper and pencil or a calculator would be more efficient. Estimation strategies include the front-end strategy, the clustering strategy, the rounding strategy, the compatible numbers strategy, and the special numbers strategy.

Students should work in a number of different types of groups as they solve problems, estimate, and calculate mentally. Students should be encouraged to communicate their learning in these areas orally, in writing, and through pictures and models. Each of these areas poses a number of issues for the teacher to consider in assessment.

Problem solving, estimating, and calculating mentally will be explored more fully throughout the remainder of this book. As you read each chapter, ask yourself how you will encourage the students to use their problem-solving and mental skills in each area.

DISCUSSION QUESTIONS

1. Investigate the problem on p. 47, finding the location of the number 289. Choose one of the related problems that follows it, and solve that problem. Compare your results to those of another student in your class. Did you use the same strategies to solve the problem?

2. Make a list of occasions when estimation would be more important than exact computation. When would exact computation be more important than estimation? Make a tally chart of the number of times in a 48-hour period when you estimate, compute mentally, compute with paper and pencil, and compute with a calculator or computer. Compare your results with others in your class and discuss the implications for teaching children.

3. Choose three children to solve one "closed" and one "open" problem. You might use problems from this chapter or find good problems on the Internet or in any of the problem-solving books listed in the reference list. Observe the children as they work. What strategies did they use? Did they seem to follow Polya's four problem-solving steps? How do they compare on the criteria for evaluating open-ended problems listed on page 47? Share your results with the class.

4. ▢ Observe children using one of the problem-solving computer programs listed at the end of this chapter. How does their work on a computer compare to their work solving problems using paper and pencil?

5. ▢ Investigate whether your state has a state assessment program that includes the assessment of mathematical problem solving. If it does, what types of tests are given to the students at what grade levels? What criteria are used to judge student responses? If possible, review several of the items that are used along with their scoring rubrics (if they exist) and report your findings to the class. You might want to use the Internet to find examples from other states. Try http://www.enc.org/reform/ for a listing of state and national curriculum standards and frameworks.

REFERENCES

Adler, Irving, *Magic House of Numbers.* New York: John Day, 1974.

—————, *Math Puzzles.* New York: Franklin Watts, 1978.

Anno, Mitsumasa, *Anno's Math Games.* New York, NY: Philomel, 1982.

—————, *Anno's Math Games II.* New York, NY: Philomel, 1989.

—————, *Anno's Math Games III.* New York, NY: Philomel, 1991.

Becker, Jerry P., and Shigeru Shimada (eds.), *The Open-Ended Approach: A New Proposal for Teaching Mathematics.* Reston, VA: National Council of Teachers of Mathematics, 1997.

Brown, Stephen I., and Marion I. Walter, *The Art of Problem Posing.* Hillsdale, NJ: Lawrence Erlbaum Associates, 1983.

Burns, Marilyn, *The I Hate Mathematics Book.* Boston: Little, Brown, 1975.

—————, *The Book of Think.* Boston: Little, Brown, 1976.

—————, *Math for Smarty Pants.* Boston: Little, Brown, 1982.

California State Department of Education, *A Question of Thinking: A First Look at Students' Performance on Open-Ended Questions in Mathematics.* Sacramento, CA: Bureau of Publications, California State Department of Education, 1989.

Charles, Randall, and Frank Lester, *Teaching Problem Solving: What, Why & How.* Palo Alto, CA: Dale Seymour Publications, 1982.

Charles, Randall, Frank Lester, and Phares O'Daffer, *How to Evaluate Progress in Problem Solving.* Reston, VA: National Council of Teachers of Mathematics, 1987.

Coburn, Terence, "The Role of Computation in the Changing Mathematics Curriculum," in *New Directions for Elementary School Mathematics.* ed. Paul R. Trafton and Albert P. Shulte. Reston, VA: National Council of Teachers of Mathematics, 1989.

Darling, Kathy, *The Jelly Bean Contest.* Champaign, IL: Garrard, 1972.

Davidson, Neil, *Cooperative Learning in Mathematics.* New York, NY: Addison-Wesley, 1990.

Del Regato, John C., Mary E. Gilfeather, & Jane A. Schwarm, *Mathematics Pentathlon.* Indianapolis, IN: Pentathlon Institute, 1986. (Divisions I–IV, Grades K–7)

Fixx, James, *Solve It! A Perplexing Profusion of Puzzles.* Garden City, NY: Doubleday, 1978.

Gardner, Martin, *Aha! Insight.* San Francisco: Freeman, 1978.

—————, *Aha! Gotcha.* San Francisco: Freeman, 1982.

—————, *Puzzles from Other Worlds.* New York: Vintage, 1984.

Gulley, Wendy, "Estimate of the Week," *Mathematics Teaching in the Middle School,* 3, no. 5 (February 1998), 324–328.

Hope, J. A., L. Leutzinger, B. J. Reys, and R. E. Reys, *Mental Math in the Primary Grades.* Palo Alto, CA: Dale Seymour, 1988.

Hope, J. A., B. J. Reys, and R. E. Reys, *Mental Math in the Middle Grades.* Palo Alto, CA: Dale Seymour, 1987.

—————, *Mental Math in Junior High.* Palo Alto, CA: Dale Seymour, 1988.

Johnson, David W., and Roger T. Johnson, "Cooperative Learning in Mathematics Education," in *New Directions for Elementary School Mathematics,* ed. Paul R. Trafton and Albert P. Shulte. Reston, VA: National Council of Teachers of Mathematics, 1989.

Krulik, Stephen, and Jesse A. Rudnick, *Problem Solving: A Handbook for Elementary School Teachers.* Boston: Allyn & Bacon, 1988.

Kulm, Gerald (ed.), *Assessing Higher Order Thinking in Mathematics.* Washington, DC: American Association for the Advancement of Science, 1990.

Lane County Mathematics Project, *Problem Solving in Mathematics.* Palo Alto, CA: Dale Seymour, 1984.

Lenchner, G., *Creative Problem Solving in School Mathematics.* Boston: Houghton Mifflin, 1983.

McFadden, Scott, *Math Warm-Ups for Jr. High.* Palo Alto, CA: Dale Seymour, 1983.

Moses, Barbara, Elizabeth Bjork, and E. Paul Goldenberg, "Beyond Problem Solving: Problem Posing," in *Teaching and Learning Mathematics in the 1990s,* ed. Thomas J. Cooney and Christian R. Hirsch. Reston, VA: National Council of Teachers of Mathematics, 1990.

National Council of Teachers of Mathematics, *An Agenda for Action.* Reston, VA: National Council of Teachers of Mathematics, 1980.

—————, *Curriculum and Evaluation Standards for School Mathematics.* Reston, VA: NCTM, 1989.

—————, *Principles and Standards for School Mathematics.* Reston, VA: NCTM, 1998.

Ohio Department of Education, *Problem Solving . . . a Basic Mathematics Goal: A Resource for Problem Solving.* Columbus, OH: Ohio Department of Education, 1980.

—————, *Problem Solving . . . a Basic Mathematics Goal: Becoming a Better Problem Solver.* Columbus, OH: Ohio Department of Education, 1980.

Page, David A., and Kathryn Chval. *Maneuvers with Number Patterns: Student Lab Book.* White Plains, NY: Dale Seymour, 1995.

Polya, George, *How to Solve It.* Garden City, NY: Doubleday, 1957.

Reys, Barbara J., "Mental Computation," *Arithmetic Teacher,* 32, no. 6 (February 1985), 43–46.

—————, "Teaching Computational Estimation: Concepts and Strategies," in *Estimation and Mental Computation.* ed. Harold L. Schoen and Marilyn J. Qweng. Reston, VA: National Council of Teachers of Mathematics, 1986.

Reys, Barbara J., and Robert E. Reys, "Estimation—Direction from the *Standards,"* *Arithmetic Teacher,* 37, no. 7 (March 1990), 22–25.

Roper, A., *Cooperative Problem Solving.* Worth, IL: Creative Publications, 1990.

Rowan, Thomas E., and Josepha Robles. "Using Questions to Help Children Build Mathematical Power," *Teaching Children Mathematics,* 4, no. 9 (May 1998), 504–509.

Sachar, Louis, *More Sideways Arithmetic from Wayside School.* Jefferson City, MO: Scholastic, 1994.

Schroeder, Thomas L., and Frank K. Lester, Jr., "Developing Understanding in Mathematics via Problem Solving," in *New Directions for Elementary School Mathematics,* ed. Paul R. Trafton and Albert P. Shulte. Reston, VA: National Council of Teachers of Mathematics, 1989.

Silverstein, Shel, How Many, How Much? In *A Light in the Attic.* New York: Harper and Row, 1981.

Skinner, Penny, *What's Your Problem?* Portsmouth, NH: Heinemann, 1990.

Sowder, Judith T., "Mental Computation and Number Sense," *Arithmetic Teacher,* 37, no. 7 (March 1990), 18–20.

Stenmark, Jean, Virginia Thompson Kerr, and Ruth Cossey, *Family Math.* Berkeley, CA: Regents, University of California, 1986.

Stone, Janet I., *Hands-On Math: Manipulative Math for Young Children.* Glenview, IL: Scott, Foresman, 1990.

Van Delft, Pieter, and Jack Botermans. *Creative Puzzles of the World.* Berkeley, CA: Key Curriculum, 1995.

Whitney, Julie G., and Linda J. Sheffield, *Adventures in Science and Math: Integrated Activities for Young Children.* New Rochelle, NY: Cuisenaire, 1991.

Whitin, David J., and Sandra Wilde, *Read Any Good Math Lately?* Portsmouth, NH: Heinemann, 1992.

Williams, David E., *Creative Mathematics Teaching with Calculators: Explorations and Investigations.* Sunnyvale, CA: Stokes, 1992.

Yeager, David C., *Problem Solver Projects: Collaborative Group Activities.* Mountain View, CA: Creative Publications, 1996.

Technology

Annenberg/CPB, *Teaching Math: A Video Library,* K–4. Boston, MA: WGBH Educational Foundation, 1995.

—————, *Mathematics Assessment: A Video Library,* K–12. Boston, MA: WGBH Educational Foundation, 1995.

Broderbund, *Carmen Sandiego Math Detective.* Novato, CA: Broderbund. (Software).

—————, *Logical Journey of the Zoombinis.* Novato, CA: Broderbund. (Software).

Connell, David D., and Jim Thurman, *The Case of the Unnatural. Mathnet TM Casebook No. 1.* New York: Children's Television Workshop/Freeman, 1993. (Video and guidebook)

Davidson, *Math Blaster Jr.* Torrance, CA: Davidson, 1997. (Software)

Edmark, *Mighty Math Zoo Zillions.* Orlando, FL: Harcourt Brace, 1996. (Software)

—————, *Stanley's Sticker Stories Grades K–2.* Orlando, FL: Harcourt Brace, 1996. (Software)

Koetke, Walter, *Hot Dog Stand.* Pleasantville, NY: Sunburst. (Software).

Learning Wave, *Codebreakers.* Pleasantville, NY: Learning Wave. (CD-ROM and linked website).

—————, *Curriculum in a Box: Math Mysteries.* Pleasantville, NY: Learning Wave. (Series of four video kits: The Pizza Perfect Caper, The Manor House Mystery, The Phantom of the Bell Tower, Mr. Marfil's Last Will and Testament).

O'Brien, Thomas, *Puzzle Tanks.* Pleasantville, NY: Sunburst. (Software).

—————, *Teasers by Tobbs.* Pleasantville, NY: Sunburst. (Software).

Sunburst, *The Pond.* Pleasantville, NY: Sunburst. (Software).

Web Sites

http://thechalkboard.com/MC/   MATHCOUNTS

http://www.enc.org/reform/   State and National Curriculum Standards and Frameworks

http://www.forum.swarthmore.edu/   A great site for lesson plans, Ask Dr. Math, Problems for all ages.

http://www.nova.edu/Inter-Links/puzzles.html   Source of puzzles and brain teaser for all ages.

http://www.unl.edu/amc/   American Mathematics Competitions.

Chapter 4

Technology in Teaching and Learning Mathematics

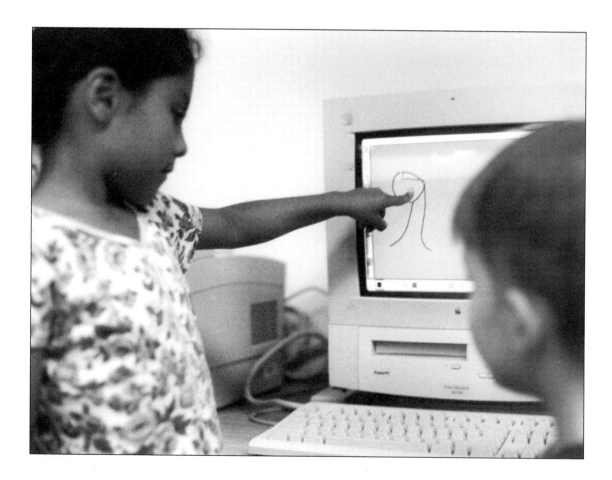

My Math Journal

Do you think students should be allowed to use calculators in their elementary and middle school mathematics classes? Should they be allowed to use them at any time, or only for special occasions? What are the effects of unlimited use of calculators?

As you read the following pages, consider these guiding questions:

1. What role should calculators play in the elementary and middle school mathematics programs?
2. If you were to recommend purchasing calculators for your classroom, what type would you suggest for grade 3, grade 5, and grade 7?
3. What are five different computer applications that would strengthen a mathematics program?
4. In a multimedia presentation related to mathematics what type of technology would be most useful?
5. How does a teacher judge the quality of software before she decides which software to purchase?

As we enter the twenty-first century, the differences between the industrial age of the early twentieth century and the information age of today are ever more apparent. We can no longer prepare children for the future by giving them only the "shopkeeper skills" of computing with whole numbers using paper and pencil. We must educate children for the future by teaching them to think, reason, and solve problems using as much technology as possible, always keeping in mind that the technology they will need to use in the future will be far more advanced than anything available today. We would be doing students a great disservice, however, if we did not let them use all that is available now. This means that we must encourage students of all ages to take full advantage of calculators, computers, and other technology.

The National Council of Teachers of Mathematics has recommended that

- Appropriate calculators should be available to all students at all times;
- A computer should be available in every classroom for demonstration purposes;
- Every student should have access to a computer for individual and group work;
- Students should learn to use the computer as a tool for processing information and performing calculations to investigate and solve problems. (1989, p. 8)

Having this technology available does not mean, as some have suggested, that students will no longer need to think to do mathematics. In fact, the availability of technology offers us the opportunity to emphasize the thinking, reasoning, and problem solving and to deemphasize the rote memorization that so often characterizes the teaching of basic facts and algorithms. Using a calculator or computer to assist with computation should be for a mathematician what using a word processor is for a writer. The technology does not do the thinking, but it frees the writer, or mathematician, to focus on the work that he or she is creating. Students should be afforded this same opportunity. What a waste of a student's years in elementary school if all we teach students is to perform

paper and pencil computations that could be done more accurately and efficiently on an $8 calculator!

It is important for teachers to know what children can do with calculators other than check homework and to know computer applications other than those that transfer drill sheets from a workbook to a computer screen. The following sections investigate some common misconceptions about technology and suggests some uses for it.

Calculators

When I hear parents today complaining that their children are using calculators, I am reminded of my grandfather complaining that my father was allowed to use paper and pencil when he did his mathematics in school. My grandfather learned to do all his mathematics mentally and scoffed at the idea of having to write down anything to do multiplication or long division. He was quite concerned that my father might need to do some arithmetic on the job and would find that he did not have a pencil or a piece of paper. Today, some parents worry that children might not have a calculator with them or that it might be too dark to use a light-activated calculator. Now, mathematics educators are realizing that my grandfather had the more urgent concern. As adults, we are called upon to do mathematics mentally much more frequently than we are to do calculations with paper and pencil. Mental computation and estimation and calculators and computers are used to do much of the computation work on the job. The need to do long paper-and-pencil computation is minimal and losing importance every day, while the need to mentally compute and estimate is growing in importance, and the optimal use of calculators and computers is essential.

Research has consistently shown that we do not need to worry that children will become dependent upon calculators and never learn their basic facts once they have a calculator available. From a review of several studies on the effects of calculator usage, Hembree and Dessart (1986) concluded that not only do calculators not harm children's knowledge and use of basic facts and algorithms, but that with proper use, they can improve the average student's basic skills with paper and pencil and can improve problem-solving skills. Further, Wheatley and Clements (1990, p. 22) suggested that learning opportunities can be presented by using calculators in problem situations. These learning opportunities, from a constructivist perspective, focus on meaning, assist students as they solve problems, and allow the learner to consider increasingly complex tasks. In addition, calculators can help improve a student's self-concept in mathematics and lessen math anxiety. It is time to stop worrying and to start using calculators.

How Should Calculators Be Used?

Calculators should be used as an everyday part of the mathematics curriculum. They should be used as instructional tools and as computational tools. Teachers should plan lessons that employ the calculator to assist students in developing their thinking abilities. Students should be encouraged to decide when a calculator would be useful and when it would be quicker and easier to solve problems mentally. Throughout this book we will suggest ways in which to use calculators. The following list will give you just a few ideas:

1. *To develop an understanding of the calculator.* Students need to be taught what the calculator does and what individual keys do. Introductory activities include opportunities for children to explore the calculator as they would any manipulative material, to see what they can discover about pushing the keys. Other activities include recognizing numerals, both from the keypad and from the display, and learning the keyboard numeral sequence. To help with the latter skill, a large keyboard may be placed on the floor for students to walk on, and a student can hop from one key to another as directed by the teacher or another student. Later, the keystroke sequence for keying a problem can be acted out on the large keypad. Teachers or students can use a calculator on the overhead projector that matches the individual calculators used by students at their desks to demonstrate certain procedures. Counting and skip counting on the calculator and other activities follow. As a part of these initial activities, the children should be encouraged to learn the vocabulary of the calculator and to discuss what they find as they work with the calculator and what they think is happening. It is important to focus on what buttons to push in order to obtain a desired result, the order of pushing buttons to achieve the desired result, ways to efficiently use the calculator, ways to use the calculator memory, whether the calculator follows the correct order of operations, and why different students get different answers when doing the same calculations (the nature of round-off error).

   Students in the middle grades will find the calculator to be a particularly useful tool as they work on problem solving and projects. For example, in Chapter 7, we discuss two activities in the Connections section. In the first, Mrs. Robinson's fifth-grade class plans a Thanksgiving dinner and then takes a trip to a local grocery store to price the food items needed for the dinner. A calculator helps the students determine the total cost of the food items. Perhaps the store that they visited had shopping carts with built-in calculators to assist shoppers. In the

second activity, Miss Collin's eighth-grade class is participating in a holiday extravaganza gift-buying simulation. Calculators help the students total the cost of items on the catalog order form and to balance their checkbooks.

To understand what the calculator does and how it works is to be able to use the calculator in its many appropriate applications.

2. *To develop number sense and place value concepts.* Students should frequently use calculators in conjunction with concrete materials in order to develop solid concepts of the numbers they are using. Understanding leads to number sense, the ability to recognize number relationships, the ability to determine if operations are reasonable, and the ability to interpret numbers used in daily life. For young children, this may mean using a calculator as they count a pile of pennies they have saved. As one child moves one penny at a time from one pile to another, another child can push + 1 on the calculator each time. The first child can then announce the number of pennies in the new pile as the second child pushes the equals sign on the calculator to check the total. Special notice should be taken when the number in the tens place changes as a result of adding 1. Ask the children to predict what number will show in the display if you begin at 19 and add 1.

   Applying number sense with the calculator means, in part, being able to determine quickly if a calculator result is reasonable. For example, when asked to find 6×189 the student might think that 189 is near 200 and 6×200 is 1,200. Thus, the result should be near 1,200, and because 189 is less than 200, the result will be less than 1,200. On the other hand, the student may think that because 189 is 11 less than 200, 6×189 will be 6×11 or 66 less than 6×200, that is, the result will be $1,200 - 66$. The final result, 1,134, may be computed on a calculator or mentally. This type of procedure and others are presented by Bobis (1991) in a discussion of number sense and calculators.

   Middle level students might use the calculator to help them determine if they are at least 1 million days old, 1 million hours old, 1 million minutes old, or 1 million seconds old. They could also use it to determine if 1 million ping pong balls or 1 million mathematics books would fit in their classroom. These activities help them develop a much better sense of the relative magnitudes of numbers than would filling in a worksheet that asks them which numeral is in the millions place in 23,456,741.

3. *To develop and recognize patterns.* Using a calculator takes much of the drudgery out of computations and allows students to perform computations that might be too time-consuming using only paper and

pencil. Third-graders might wish to explore what happens when numbers are multiplied by 9. As they multiply 9×1, 9×2, 9×3, etc., on a calculator, many patterns begin to emerge. They should notice that when multiplying by a one-digit number, the sum of the digits in the answer add to 9 and the ones digit decreases by one while the tens digit increases by one. They could probably also discover these patterns without a calculator, but what happens when the multiplier becomes larger than 10? Will the sum of the digits in the answer always be a multiple of 9? Will the pattern in the ones and tens places continue? With a calculator, children can explore patterns involving very large numbers and can focus on finding reasons for the patterns rather than on the computation itself. They can then go on to other patterns, such as those in multiples of 3, 5, 10, or 11. They may wish to record their findings on a hundreds chart and expand their search to include such topics as prime and composite numbers.

Many mathematical puzzle books offer other ideas for students to explore, especially in sections on mathematical magic, which give students ideas for fooling their friends and families using some of the structure of our numeration system.

An interesting exploration with the calculator was discussed by Zollman (1990). Zollman noted that subtracting various sequences of digits that follow certain *geometric* patterns results in the difference 198. Figure 4–1 illustrates three of these patterns.

Figure 4–1a illustrates the *rows* pattern. For example, $321 - 123$ results in 198. Likewise, $654 - 456$ and $987 - 789$ both result in 198. Figure 4–1b shows the *diagonals* pattern. For example, $951 - 753$ results in 198, as does $357 - 159$. Figure 4–1c shows the *right angles* pattern. For example, $785 - 587$ results in 198 and $624 - 426$ also results in 198. There are other combinations that follow these patterns and result in 198. There are other patterns, as well, such as the *crosses, squares, obtuse angles,* and *acute angles* patterns. Can you find them? Encourage the students to explore why these patterns exist.

4. *To develop concepts of operations.* A calculator is of no use if you do not know which operation to use to solve a given problem. Students can explore with a calculator to determine why addition and subtraction are inverse operations or why multiplication may be used instead of repeated addition. Second-graders may wish to determine the number of eggs stored in the cafeteria. One student may note that there are 15 cartons of eggs in the school refrigerator, each holding a dozen eggs, and may suggest that they add $12 + 12 + 12 \ldots 15$ times to determine the total number of eggs. Another student may suggest simply multiplying 12×15. Ask half of the students to find the answer using repeated addition while the other half use multiplication, and discuss the results. Ask the students to suggest several problems of this type and work them using both addition and multiplication to convince the students that the answers will always be the same.

Figure 4–1

Students in the middle grades might use a calculator that displays and computes with fractions in the $\frac{P}{Q}$ format. This can help them see that one does not add numerators and denominators together when adding fractions. They can then use concrete materials to explain what is happening on the calculator.

5. *To develop problem-solving and thinking abilities.* When children are given problem situations involving the calculator they have the chance to increase their skills in reasoning and in constructing mathematical relationships. Wheatley and Clements (1990) describe activities that facilitate these thinking processes. A description of one of these activities follows. This is an activity for two middle-level students using a nonscientific calculator. Some calculators cannot be used for this activity, and you should check the calculators available before starting the activity. One student picks a mystery number, such as 43, and enters 43 ÷ 43 =. This will result in a *1* in the calculator display. This programs the calculator with the constant function ÷ 43. Be sure to check the calculator you are using to determine whether this method works, or whether a different set of keystrokes is necessary. The calculator is given to the second student, who is instructed to "guess my number." The second student enters his or her guess and pushes the equals key. The second student will have successfully guessed the number when the calculator again displays a *1*. A series of guesses is shown below that eventually result in achieving the goal.

$$8 = 0.1860465$$
$$13 = 0.3023256$$
$$25 = 0.5813953$$
$$50 = 1.1627907$$
$$45 = 1.0465116$$
$$44 = 1.0232558$$
$$43 = 1$$

The mystery number is 43. The process students use to successfully determine the target number may initially involve random guessing, but soon students will recognize the relationship among the strings of digits. Eventually, the activity will take on greater meaning as understanding of division and decimal numeration is increased. Students who solve this problem are constructing meaning in a way that makes sense to them.

6. *To get a graphic picture of the data.* Middle school students should explore the uses of a graphing cal-

culator. With a prompt of "Y =" on the calculator, the students can discover what happens to the graph of the formula $y = mx + b$ as m or b changes. They can graph formulas that they have seen in other classes, such as force = mass × acceleration ($F = ma$), and study the effects of changing one of the variables, such as the mass or the acceleration. Again, this should accompany a concrete experiment to avoid trying to develop concepts in isolation. Few middle school students are able to develop a new concept on a completely abstract level, although we may be tempted to try to present concepts on an abstract level with the aid of a calculator.

Taylor and Nichols (1994) note, "Many graphing-calculator activities are appropriate for middle school students, enriching their understanding of, and appreciation for, mathematics." In their article, they present three problem solving activities that help develop understanding of variable and function, involving a distance-rate-time problem, a population problem, and a box problem. These activities are interesting and come from the student's experience. With the opportunity to develop skill with the graphing calculator, the students will attack the problem with enthusiasm and interest.

Depending upon the graphing calculator that you use, you may be able to display several different types of graphs from lists of data. These graphs may then be transferred to a computer and used in mathematics reports, projects, and other investigations. Explore the use of scatter plots, histograms, circle graphs, box-and-whiskers plots, and even pictographs, if these are possible on your calculators. As you do this, be sure to discuss with the students which types of graphs are appropriate for the data that you have. Although a calculator may be able to draw a pictograph, a circle graph, a histogram, and a line graph from the same lists of data, it is unlikely that all of these are appropriate.

7. *To solve problems where the computation might otherwise be prohibitive.* There are lots of examples of problems in everyday life that we would hesitate to solve if we did not have a calculator available. Young students might wish to plan a budget for their allowances. If they are trying to save enough money to buy a toy for $3.75 on an allowance of $.50 a week, first-graders might use a calculator to determine the number of weeks they will have to save. They might suggest subtracting $.50 from $3.75 until no money remains and then counting the number of times they subtracted. This might also be a good opportunity to discuss the use of division as repeated subtraction. Middle school students may be starting to think about saving money for an automobile and could use the calculator to determine

which of several banks or savings and loans are offering the best interest rate. Ask students to be on the lookout for problems in everyday life that you would use a calculator to solve. You might set up a store or bank in your classroom that the students would run with the aid of a calculator. One class of middle school students selected up to five stocks from the New York Stock Exchange listings and followed the performance of their stocks over a period of several weeks. The calculator was important in determining gains and losses during the activity.

8. *To improve mental computation and estimation skills.* Calculators should be used in conjunction with mental computation and estimation and not as a replacement for these skills. Students should get in the habit of estimating to determine whether an answer on the calculator makes sense. You might try playing a "target" game to help the students improve these skills. In this game, the leader puts a number sentence on the board such as $16 \times \underline{} = 4{,}562$. Each student then writes down his or her best estimate. After the estimate is recorded, the student is allowed to use the calculator only to multiply that estimate by 16. After this calculation is performed, the students are polled to determine the winner of the round. For example, if the best estimate is 300, the leader would write on the board $16 \times 300 = 4{,}800$. Students would then use this information in order to come up with a better estimate. Play continues for several rounds or until the answer is within 10 of the correct product. Older students may be encouraged to use decimals until the answer is less than 1 away from the correct product. Games such as this one help students develop their mental computation skills and can be adjusted to the level of the students. Younger children might play the game with addition and subtraction, rather than multiplication and division.

9. *For practice and skills development.* Some calculators will quiz students on their knowledge of numbers and operations. On these calculators, an equation or a question about place value will appear on the display for which students must supply the answer. These calculators give the students a chance to practice basic computation skills in much the same way as flash cards, only with a patient, nonjudgmental questioner, the calculator itself. Students often prefer this electronic type of practice to more traditional methods and may be willing to work longer on basic computation or place value skills in this fashion.

10. *To aid in spatial visualization and measurement concepts.* Some calculators contain a dynamic geometry program that enables the student to draw, measure, and manipulate geometric figures. On these calculators, students can explore such concepts as creating tessellations and lines of symmetry, measuring angles, sides and areas of polygons and exploring properties of similar and congruent geometric figures. Information may be transferred to a computer for printing or for further exploration. These calculators give students an opportunity to develop and extend the geometric and measurement concepts that they have developed with physical models.

11. *To aid in the collection and analysis of data.* Some calculators can be connected to Calculator-Based Laboratory Systems™ (CBLs) or Calculator-Based Rangers™ (CBRs). These systems allow students to collect data from experiments involving such things as motion, temperature, light, sound, pH, and force. Students use sensors and probes to collect data using a CBL or CBR that can then be analyzed further on the calculator. Such systems are very useful in science as well as mathematics classes.

12. *To investigate probability using simulations.* Some programmable calculators allow students to design experiments and write simple programs to simulate such things as tossing a coin or rolling a die. For older students, writing and using a simulation program not only allows them to collect and analyze sample data rapidly, but also gives them the opportunity to design and write simple programs, thus further developing logical reasoning skills.

For more ideas on any of these uses of calculators, consult some of the calculator books in the references at the end of the chapter.

What Types of Calculators Should Be Purchased?

This is a very difficult question and one upon which the "experts" disagree. The answer will depend on the level of the students with whom you are working and your budget. For many computations, a simple four-function calculator will be sufficient. If you choose this type of calculator, be sure to choose a brand that is light-activated; otherwise, the expense of batteries would soon amount to more than the cost of the calculator. You should look for a calculator that has memory and constant functions and a key for square roots. These can usually be found for under $5. The main drawback is that the operations will probably be done in the order in which they are entered into the calculator and not in correct mathematical order. This should be discussed with the students if you opt for this type of calculator. For about $8, you can purchase a four-function calculator from Texas Instruments that uses correct order of operations. For a few dollars more, you might want to consider buying calculators that have the built-in capacity to quiz students on their computation and place value concepts. You should also obtain a calculator for the overhead projector that matches the calculator the students are using so that you can demonstrate its use to all of the students simultaneously.

For students in the intermediate grades, you might consider purchasing a calculator that will operate on common fractions in the $\frac{P}{Q}$ form and that displays the result of division as an integral answer and a remainder as a decimal. There is also an overhead calculator to match this calculator. Middle school students should have access to a scientific calculator at the very least. You might also want to consider graphing calculators that make use of CBLs™ or CBRs™. For teaching geometry, consider getting an overhead calculator that makes use of dynamic geometry and, if possible, a classroom set of these for the students. They are versatile and provide for a number of applications commonly found in the middle school mathematics curriculum.

Computers

Computers are finding an ever more important place in society and they are commonplace in schools. Access to the Internet provides students with the opportunity to find rich sources of information and data. Whether they are looking for the art of Escher (http://www.auburn.edu/~churcwb/escher.html), or for biographies of women in science and mathematics (http://crux.astr.ua.edu/4000WS/4000WS.html), or for U.S. Census bureau statistics (http://www.census.gov/), students can quickly access the information from a classroom or resource room computer. With the proliferation of computers and the variety of uses to which they can be adapted, we must be careful to ensure that computers are used in ways that take appropriate advantage of their speed and power. The following are a few of the ways in which computers may be used in a mathematics class:

1. *As a tool for either student or teacher use.* The computer can help the teacher and the student with a variety of tasks. These include word processing, record keeping, constructing graphs and charts, preparing student presentations using applications such as *HyperStudio,* communicating, and finding information on the Internet. Teachers may use the tools to keep track of student progress and manage individualized assignments or to help with assessing or recording attendance. With the new emphasis on communication in mathematics, word processing makes it easier for students to write problems for other students to solve, to record how they solved a problem, or to keep a daily log of what they are learning in mathematics. Graphics and music programs even allow students to illustrate their work and set it to music. Students and teachers alike may use a data base to collect information to solve real-life problems. For example, students could collect census information about the class, and they could use the data to create

Figure 4–2

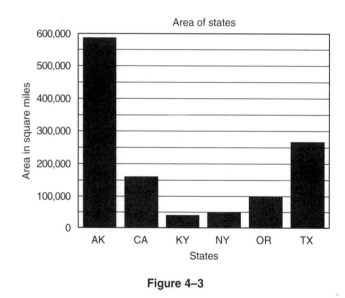

Figure 4–3

graphs and other displays to answer questions of interest. In addition, students could compare information such as the population and the area of selected states. Figure 4–2 is a computer-generated graph that shows the population of six states.

The data are entered into a computer-graphing application and the type of graph is selected. The computer generates the appropriate graph.

If another graph such as that shown in Figure 4–3 is produced, then a graphic comparison can be made between the two types of information displayed, population and area. Bay, Bledsoe, and Reys (1998) describe another computer-based activity, this time using the *Geometer's Sketchpad,* which was part of an eighth grade interdisciplinary unit on the United States. One focus of the project was to compare the relative sizes of the states.

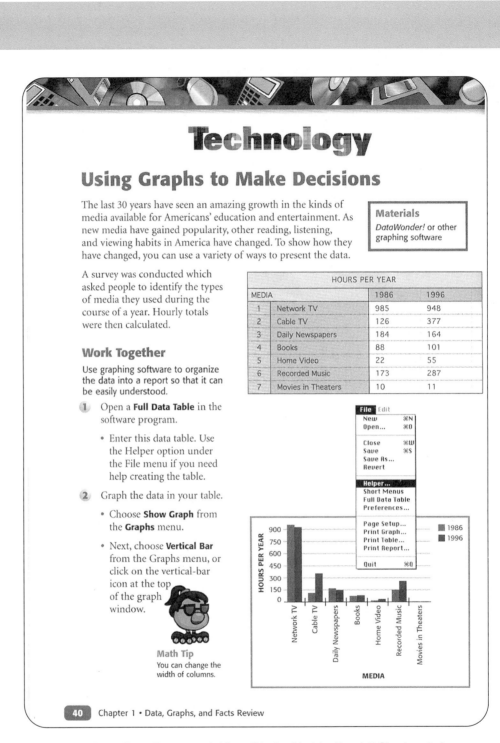

Technology

Using Graphs to Make Decisions

The last 30 years have seen an amazing growth in the kinds of media available for Americans' education and entertainment. As new media have gained popularity, other reading, listening, and viewing habits in America have changed. To show how they have changed, you can use a variety of ways to present the data.

Materials
DataWonder! or other graphing software

A survey was conducted which asked people to identify the types of media they used during the course of a year. Hourly totals were then calculated.

HOURS PER YEAR			
MEDIA		1986	1996
1	Network TV	985	948
2	Cable TV	126	377
3	Daily Newspapers	184	164
4	Books	88	101
5	Home Video	22	55
6	Recorded Music	173	287
7	Movies in Theaters	10	11

Work Together

Use graphing software to organize the data into a report so that it can be easily understood.

1 Open a **Full Data Table** in the software program.

- Enter this data table. Use the Helper option under the File menu if you need help creating the table.

2 Graph the data in your table.

- Choose **Show Graph** from the **Graphs** menu.

- Next, choose **Vertical Bar** from the Graphs menu, or click on the vertical-bar icon at the top of the graph window.

Math Tip
You can change the width of columns.

Figure 4–4 From *Scott Foresman-Addison Wesley Math* by Randall Charles et al., copyright © 1998 by Addison Wesley Longman, Inc. Reprinted by permission.

Math Program

The page shown in Figure 4–4 is from the first chapter of a fifth grade mathematics book that makes use of technology throughout the program. Since this is the first chapter in the book, a number of skills that students are expected to know already are reviewed earlier in this chapter. These skills include organizing data in a number of ways without the assistance of the computer such as using line plots, stem-and-leaf plots, pictographs, line graphs, single- and double-bar graphs, and writing function rules using variables to describe patterns on a table.

Note that in this activity, students are asked to use the graphs to make decisions. On the following page, students are asked to insert the graph in a written report and to respond to questions such as how they could make advertising decisions based upon the media that had shown the greatest increase in the number of hours used and how the scale affects the appearance of the data.

Follow-up activities in this chapter include the use of a mathematics web site (http://www.mathsurf.com) to choose a topic that has data from a period of years and to display the data using a line graph. The web site includes a section for parents and another for teachers as well as a section for students. Other technology in this program includes the use of CD-ROMs for teacher planning, assessment, and interactive lessons as well as the *DataWonder* software that is used in this lesson. Calculators are used frequently as a problem-solving tool to explore patterns, solve multistep problems, and investigate computation strategies.

Most graphing applications give the operator a choice between different types of graphs: bar, column, line, pie, scatter, and so forth. A variety of interesting comparisons can be made using graphs.

Spreadsheets may be used to collect data that can also be displayed graphically, such as data that provide information related to the characteristics of various sports balls. These data, presented in the *Arithmetic Teacher* (November 1990), lend themselves to some interesting explorations. For example, Figure 4–5 illustrates a spreadsheet that shows the characteristics of 10 sports balls and extends this information to a cubic meter of these balls.

Data are entered in columns A–E and simple formulas are entered in columns F, G, and H. Thus, the cost of filling a cubic meter with baseballs (column F) is determined by multiplying the figure in column D by the figure in column E in row 4. The formula is quickly *pasted* into the spreadsheet and applied to all appropriate data in the spreadsheet. Do you see what formulas were used for columns G and H?

An extension of the sports-balls data is shown in Figure 4–6. Here, using the same data, we are able to calculate information about filling our classroom with various balls.

	A	B	C	D	E	F	G	H
1		Approx.	Average	Approx.	Approx.	Cost of balls	Length of 1 cubic	Weight of
2		diameter	weight	cost per	number of balls	to fill	m of balls put	1 cubic m
3	Type of Ball	(cm)	(g)	ball	in 1 cubic m	1 cubic m	end to end (m)	of balls (kg)
4	Baseball	7.6	145	$ 5.00	2200	$11,000	167.2	319
5	Basketball	24	596	$50.00	70	$ 3,500	16.8	41.72
6	Croquet	8.6	340	$ 5.80	1500	$ 8,700	129	510
7	Golf	4.3	46	$ 2.30	12200	$28,060	524.6	561.2
8	Handball	4.8	65	$ 2.95	8800	$25,960	422.4	572
9	Racquetball	5.7	40	$ 1.50	5200	$ 7,800	296.4	208
10	Soccer	22	425	$ 9.95	80	$ 796	17.6	34
11	Softball	9.8	187	$ 5.95	1000	$ 5,950	98	187
12	Table tennis	3.7	2	$ 0.92	19700	$18,124	728.9	39.4
13	Tennis	6.5	57	$ 1.00	3800	$ 3,800	247	216.6
14								

Figure 4–5

	A	B	C	D	E	F	G	H	I
1		Approx.	Approx.	Average	Approx.	Filling our classroom with balls			
2		no. of balls	diameter	weight	cost per	No. of balls	Cost to fill	Length end	Wt. of balls in
3	Type of Ball	in 1 cubic m	(cm)	(g)	ball	in classroom	classroom	to end (km)	classroom (kg)
4	Baseball	2200	7.6	145	$ 5.00	897600	$ 4,488,000	68.2	130152
5	Basketball	70	24	596	$ 50.00	28560	$ 1,428,000	6.9	17021.76
6	Croquet	1500	8.6	340	$ 5.80	612000	$ 3,549,600	52.6	208080
7	Golf	12200	4.3	46	$ 2.30	4977600	$11,448,480	214.0	228969.6
8	Handball	8800	4.8	65	$ 2.95	3590400	$10,591,680	172.3	233376
9	Racquetball	5200	5.7	40	$ 1.50	2121600	$ 3,182,400	120.9	84864
10	Soccer	80	22	425	$ 9.95	32640	$ 324,768	7.2	13872
11	Softball	1000	9.8	187	$ 5.95	408000	$ 2,427,600	40.0	76296
12	Table tennis	19700	3.7	2	$ 0.92	8037600	$ 7,394,592	297.4	16075.2
13	Tennis	3800	6.5	57	$ 1.00	1550400	$ 1,550,400	100.8	88372.8
14									
15	Size of our classroom in cubic m =				408				
16									

Figure 4–6

Key information is put into cell E15 in the spreadsheet. Once the size of the classroom is entered, the information in columns F–I is calculated quickly. Again, it was easy to enter formulas into columns F–I to perform this task. For example, the weight of baseballs to fill the classroom in kilograms is calculated by the formula D4 * F4/1000. D4 and F4 are the cells where the data are located, "*" means to multiply, and "/" means to divide. It is easy to see from the spreadsheet for which of the balls it would require 1 million of the balls to fill the classroom. Questions and discussions emerge when using spreadsheets. They should be pursued.

HyperStudio is a computer application that allows the operator to develop a stack of cards that can be used to display or explain information. *HyperStudio* allows students to use text, pictures drawn by the student, "scanned" pictures or photographs, photographs from digital cameras, pictures, and other graphics found on the Internet, recorded sound, and animation to present information. Direct links to the Internet may be incorporated in a stack. For example, a group of fifth-grade students prepared a report on erosion in a nearby nature area using a *HyperStudio* stack on the computer and projected the cards in the stack on a screen for the rest of the class. In another fifth grade class, students Rachel and Don were paired with kindergarten students Jessica and Richard. Each kindergartner was given a number and worked with the fifth-grader, who helped record the information given by the younger student into a *HyperStudio* stack. The result was a class book featuring the numbers 1 through 20. Figure 4–7 shows selected pages from the number book. If you were to "click" on the button with Richard's name on it you would hear Richard briefly talking about the number 2. Likewise, Jessica talks about the number 11. *HyperStudio* can be effectively used to present and illustrate a variety of mathematics-related material. Encourage the creativity of your students.

The Internet, linking computers together around the world, provides the opportunity for students and teachers to engage in a variety of activities. Access to e-mail, the World Wide Web (WWW), bulletin board services (BBS), mailing lists, and other services is

Figure 4–7

by direct connection from a classroom computer to a service provider. This may require a modem or an established local network. Students and teachers have tremendous amounts of information available to them from a classroom computer connected to the Internet. For example, if you wish to find information about the United States space program you can access the NASA Liftoff to Space Exploration site (http://liftoff.msfc.nasa.gov/). If you want information about lesson plans and resources for teaching mathematics, you may visit the Swarthmore site (http://forum.swarthmore.edu/arithmetic/arith.lessons.html). If you would like a source of mathematical puzzles, you may visit the site developed by the AIMS (Activities that Integrate Math and Science) Educational Foundation (http://www.aimsedu.org/Puzzle/PuzzleList.html).

Resources such as *Classroom Connect* (Housley, 1998), a guide published nine times a year, can provide a rich source of information for teachers wanting to learn more about using the Internet and wanting to have valuable sites identified. For example, from an article by Thomas (1996) comes the description of *WebQuest* activities. These are web-based activities that present a problem or a challenge to students and provide some initial internet links to help the students investigate the problem and propose a solution. Two web sites that are helpful in developing *WebQuest* activities are listed under "Web Sites" at the end of the chapter. One such *WebQuest* activity, developed by teacher Stefanie Riddle, may be found at http://www.linfield.edu/~dcruik/garden.html. In this activity, students are presented the problem of designing a garden, involving budgeting and geometry skills. The links that are suggested include lumber company sites, seed company sites, composting sites, and general gardening sites.

2. *To teach programming.* Learning to write a computer program teaches children to be very careful and to pay attention to details. Some calculators can be programmed, as can all computers. A popular programming language in the mathematics classroom is Logo. Logo was developed at the Massachusetts Institute of Technology by Seymour Papert specifically for children. With it, children can write graphics programs as well as do simple word-processing and other types of programming. Logo provides students with the opportunity to produce intriguing and dynamic geometric designs by directing an onscreen "turtle" to move in various directions for various distances. More will be said about Logo in Chapter 12, Teaching and Learning Geometry. Because of the number of high-quality computer applications, the role of computer programming in schools is decreasing.

3. *For drill and practice.* Much software is written to give children practice in various skills, especially computation. This software is not designed to take the place of teaching but is to be used after the children have already learned the concepts, preferably using physical models. This software is often more fun than the practice exercises in a textbook and involves puzzles, mysteries, and problem solving along with the basic arithmetic operations and a variety of other mathematical topics. High-quality graphics and sound make these activities particularly enjoyable. These activities are available on disk and CD-ROM. Throughout this textbook, we will mention specific software that may be used as a part of the mathematics program.

4. *To simulate real life.* Some software is designed to give students practice with problems that exist in everyday life that are too expensive, time consuming, difficult, or dangerous to re-create in a classroom. These include programs that set up a shop, bank, or stock market and give students a chance to explore the effects of different types of management. For example, *Hot Dog Stand: The Works* by Sunburst Communications challenges students to develop a food concession stand at an arena and try to reach a financial goal by the time a number of events have been held in the arena. Likewise, *DinoPark Tycoon* by MECC provides the chance for students to develop a dinosaur amusement park without going broke. Some simulations involve adventures in the outdoors. They also include programs that give students a chance to create different machines on the screen and run a variety of tests on them.

5. *To give students experience in problem solving, reasoning, and logic.* Many software programs include a wide range of problems for students to solve, from saving the princess from the evil wizard to solving difficult logic problems. Students may build skills in arithmetic, pre-algebra, logical thinking, and word problems as they interact with the software. Many of these programs are so engaging and challenging for the students that they will pay to use them in video arcades and never realize that they are using problem-solving skills. One example of such a piece of software for children ages 6 to 10 is Anno's *Learning Games* by Putnam New Media. Children are engaged in a variety of activities including classification, guess my rule, logic, tangrams, measurement, stories, and eye-hand coordination.

6. *As a tutorial.* This software is designed to teach the students skills and concepts. It is frequently used in conjunction with physical models that the students use simultaneously with the programs. Some of these programs are designed to teach specific math-

ematical skills such as decimals and algebra. The computer is a useful way to individualize instruction. It can determine which skills and concepts a student understands and which need to be repeated or presented in another form.

7. *To aid in spatial visualization.* Computer graphics are a good way to present geometric concepts that are difficult to illustrate in a textbook. For example, the *Geometer's Sketchpad* by Jackiw (1995), and carefully described by Manouchehri et al. (1998), allows middle level students to construct, transform, investigate, and measure figures as well as problem solve. Again, many of the graphic geometric programs are best used along with physical models. Computers can show two- and three-dimensional objects from a variety of different viewpoints and ask children to predict what an object would look like from another viewpoint or after it has been rotated or flipped. As with other types of programs, it is a good idea to use the spatial programs either along with physical models or after the students have had experience rotating and flipping paper or plastic models.

The amount of software available will cause you as a teacher to be discriminating in your choice of software for your classroom or school. What software is worth the expenditure of district funds? To whom do you make software recommendations and on what basis do you make the recommendation? Some individual school districts purchase software through site licenses that allow the district to widely distribute popular and commonly used software. Some individual schools purchase software in packs of 10 units, which provides for distribution throughout the school. Still, the decision about what software to purchase is an important decision. A list of suggestions to use in selecting software follows.

1. Find reviews of the software you are considering purchasing. Avoid "reviews" provided by software distributors or those found in software catalogs. Rather, look for reviews by individuals or organizations with the children's best interest in mind. *Teaching Children Mathematics* and *Mathematics Teaching in the Middle School* are two good sources of software reviews. A web-based educational software review, *SuperKids,* presents reviews of many mathematics software programs. It is found at http://www.superkids.com/aweb/pages/reviews/math/4/sw_sum1.shtml.

2. Attend conferences and workshops where you have the opportunity to learn about software, be introduced to new software, talk to software vendors, and try out various software.

3. Ask other teachers what good software they know about. Teachers who have used computers for some time will know what software is valuable and what software their students enjoy and get the most from.

4. Request software from distributors that you may try out and return within a given amount of time. Thus, you may review the software and return it if it does not meet your needs or does not interest children. Otherwise, you may purchase poor software that you have to keep, using up valuable budget funds.

5. Be sure you know what you want to achieve by purchasing a particular piece of software or what you believe certain software will achieve by its title or a description of it. Then, when you work with it make sure your expectations are met. Be convinced that students will gain from working with your software selection. If you are unsatisfied, do not purchase the software.

Other Technology

Overhead Projectors

The overhead projector is not an example of new technology, but it is very useful in the mathematics classroom. Most commercial mathematics manipulatives that are sold for students also have a matching transparent material that students and teachers can manipulate on the overhead projector. Pattern blocks, Cuisenaire rods, geoboards, and calculators are among the objects that may be used on the overhead projector. This is very useful when a teacher is demonstrating a concept for the students to follow with their own physical models or when a student wishes to explain to other students a new idea that he or she has discovered. Teachers can also make their own transparent materials by cutting them out of colored transparency film or colored plastic report covers. The different colors of plastic are very useful for making attribute materials or other materials where the color of the material is an integral part of the concept being taught. Teachers and students alike will find that it is much easier to manipulate materials on the overhead projector than to draw models on the chalkboard.

Lettering Machines

The lettering machine is a device that will cut out letters, numerals, and other figures for the teacher to use in the classroom. Figures may be cut out of paper, cardboard, felt, railroad board, transparency film, plastic, sandpaper, and a number of other materials. For the mathematics teacher, some of the most useful dies include attribute blocks, pattern blocks, two- and three-dimensional geo-metric models, base-ten blocks, tangrams, pentominoes, fraction pieces, and small figures such as teddy bears and "smiley faces" that can be used as counters. For ex-ample, a primary teacher may make a variety of shapes that he can use on a calendar to illustrate a particular pat-tern that the children are to identify. Teachers find this machine useful for making these manipulatives of lami-nated railroad board or felt rather than purchasing com-mercial materials.

Videotapes and Cameras

Many good videotapes, such as *Donald in Math-emagic Land* and *Powers of Ten,* are available that demonstrate mathematical concepts whose presentation is enhanced by the movement and sound available on video. When looking for videotapes or films to use in the classroom, do not forget that the presentation of mathe-matics can also be enhanced by this medium. Students may want to try their hand at making their own video-tapes to illustrate mathematical concepts that they have discovered.

Slides and Cameras

Still photos and slides are also good for demon-strating mathematical concepts, especially in geom-etry. The NCTM has an excellent set of geometry slides that includes resources for the teacher to use in teaching a number of geometric concepts such as symmetry, tessel-lations, transformations, and other concepts of both two- and three-dimensional geometry. Students may also use a camera to illustrate their own geometry discoveries. Digital cameras provide opportunities for students to take photographs that are immediately transferred from a disk in the camera to a computer and may be used to illustrate a word-processed report or a web site or a *HyperStudio* stack.

Interactive Video, Telecommunications, and Other Newer Technologies

The field of technology is growing rapidly and ed-ucational applications are constantly being devel-oped. Interactive videos, presented on video disks, are used in tutorials and simulations and allow individuals or groups to respond to various situations. They give feed-back and present new situations based on the students' responses. Teachers should look for new products in the field of elementary mathematics as the prices become more competitive. The use of telecommunications was mentioned earlier in conjunction with computers. This is

another area that will become more popular as more schools have the equipment available. Teachers should read journals such as *Teaching Children Mathematics, Mathematics Teaching in the Middle School,* and the many journals in the area of technology to keep abreast of other new developments in technology.

KEY IDEAS

Advances in technology give you the means to elevate your mathematics teaching beyond what can be taught using only paper and pencil. Calculators are recom-mended for school mathematics programs to help de-velop number sense, patterns, operations, graphics, problem solving, and mental computation and estima-tion. Computers may be used as a tool for multimedia presentations, Logo programming, data manipulation, drill and practice, simulations, problem solving, tutori-als, and spatial visualization. The Internet is available for students to find and exchange great quantities of infor-mation. There are other devices that can serve the teacher, including overhead projectors, lettering ma-chines, videotapes, cameras, slides, interactive video, and telecommunications.

DISCUSSION QUESTIONS

1. Reflect on the use of the "calculator" in society today. Here, the term *calculator* is very broad, including such uses as cash registers, gasoline pumps, and hand held calculators. Discuss different businesses and occupations that rely on the calculator.

2. Write a letter to parents to be sent out at the begin-ning of the school year describing how you will be us-ing calculators in your mathematics program.

3. How would you counter the argument that using cal-culators in school is cheating?

4. Develop a spreadsheet using some of the data pre-sented in Figure 4–5 that is appropriate for the class-room in which you are learning how to teach mathe-matics. Discuss with your fellow students what you have found and how you did it.

5. Find more about *HyperStudio* and how it may be used to prepare multimedia presentations in mathematics. You may wish to start at this web site: http://www. hyperstudio.com/main/content.shtml. Share your findings with your class.

6. Log onto the Internet and search for web sites that are useful in teaching mathematics. Find 10 sites not mentioned in this textbook. Share those sites with your fellow students, including why they are useful. You might even want to set up your own homepage with links to these sites.

REFERENCES

Bay, Jennifer M., Ann M. Bledsoe, and Robert E. Reys, "State-ing the Facts: Exploring the United States," *Mathematics Teaching in the Middle School,* 4, no. 1 (September 1998), 8–14.

Bitter, Gary, and Jerald L. Mikesell, *Using the Math Explorer™ Calculator.* Menlo Park, CA: Addison-Wesley, 1990.

Bobis, Janette F., "Using a Calculator to Develop Number Sense," *Arithmetic Teacher,* 38, no. 5 (January 1991), 42–45.

Browning, Christine A., and Dwayne E. Channell, *Explorations: Graphing Calculator Activities for Enriching Middle School Mathematics.* Austin, TX: Texas Instruments, 1997.

Carson, Joan C., and Ruby N. Bostick, *Math Instruction Using Media and Modality Strengths.* Springfield, IL: Charles C. Thomas, 1988.

Christina, Mary Ann, "Building a Teenage Dance Club," *Mathematics Teaching in the Middle School,* 4, no. 1 (September 1998), 26–30.

Edwards, Nancy Tanner, and Gary G. Bitter, "Changing Variables Using Spreadsheet Templates," *Arithmetic Teacher,* 37, no. 2 (October 1989), 40–44.

Fey, James T. (ed.), *Calculators in Mathematics Education.* Reston, VA: NCTM, 1992.

Hembree, Ray, and Donald J. Dessart, "Effects of Hand-Held Calculators in Precollege Mathematics Education: A Meta-Analysis," *Journal of Research in Mathematics Education,* 17, no. 1 (March 1986), 83–99.

Hiatt, Arthur A., "Activities for Calculators," *Arithmetic Teacher,* 34, no. 6 (February 1987), 38–43.

Housley, Kathy (ed.), "Using WebQuests in the K–12 Classroom," *Classroom Connect™,* 3, no. 4 (December 1996–January 1997), 1, 4–6.

_____, *Classroom Connect™.* Torrance, CA: Classroom Connect, Inc., 1998.

Manouchehri, Azita, Mary C. Enderson, and Lyle A. Pugnucco, "Exploring Geometry with Technology," *Mathematics Teaching in the Middle School,* 3, no. 6 (March–April 1998), 436–442.

National Council of Teachers of Mathematics, *Curriculum and Evaluation Standards for School Mathematics.* Reston, VA: NCTM, 1989.

Pagni, David L., "Teaching Mathematics Using Calculators," *Arithmetic Teacher,* 38, no. 5 (January 1991), 58–60.

Roper, Ann, Shirley Hoogeboom, and Judy Goodnow, *Cooperative Problem Solving with Calculators.* Sunnyvale, CA: Creative Publications, 1991.

Ryoti, Don E., "Processing Data," *Arithmetic Teacher,* 34, no. 8 (April 1987), 42–44.

Schielack, Jane F., and Dinah Chancellor. *Uncovering Mathematics with Manipulatives and Calculators: Levels 1, 2 & 3.* Dallas, TX: Texas Instruments, Inc., 1995.

Spiker, Joan, and Ray Kurtz, "Teaching Primary-Grade Mathematics Skills with Calculators," *Arithmetic Teacher,* 34, no. 6 (February 1987), 24–27.

Starkey, Mary Ann, "Calculating First Graders," *Arithmetic Teacher,* 37, no. 2 (October 1989), 6–7.

Taylor, Linda J. C., and Jeri A. Nichols, "Graphing Calculators Aren't Just for High School Students," *Mathematics Teaching in the Middle School,* 1, no. 3 (November–December 1994), 190–96.

Usnick, Virginia E., and Patricia M. Lamphere, "Calculators and Division," *Arithmetic Teacher,* 38, no. 4 (December 1990), 40–43.

Virginia Space Grant Consortium, *The Educator's Guide to the Internet.* Hampton, VA: VSGC, 1994.

Watson, Charles D., and Judy Trowell, "Let Your Fingers Do the Counting," *Arithmetic Teacher,* 36, no. 2 (October 1988), 50–53.

Wheatley, Grayson H., and Douglas H. Clements, "Calculators and Constructivism," *Arithmetic Teacher,* 38, no. 2 (October 1990), 22–23.

Wiebe, James H., "Order of Operations," *Arithmetic Teacher,* 37, no. 3 (November 1989), 36–38.

_____, "Teacher-Made Overhead Manipulatives," *Arithmetic Teacher,* 37, no. 7 (March 1990), 44–46.

Wilgus, Wendy, and Lisa Pizzuto, *Exploring the Basics of Geometry with Cabri.* Austin, TX: Texas Instruments, 1997.

Williams, David E., *Creative Mathematics Teaching with Calculators: Explorations and Investigations.* Sunnyvale, CA: Stokes, 1992.

Williams, Susan E., and George W. Bright, *Investigating Mathematics with Calculators in the Middle Grades: Math Explorer, Explorer Plus.* Austin, TX: Texas Instruments, 1998.

Young, Sharon L., "Ideas," *Arithmetic Teacher,* 38, no. 3 (November 1990), 23–32.

Zollman, Alan., "Low Tech, 198, and the Geometry of the Calculator Keys," *Arithmetic Teacher,* 37, no. 5 (January 1990), 30–33.

Technology

Banta, Milt, Bill Berg, and Heinz Haber, *Donald in Mathmagic Land.* Burbank, CA: Walt Disney Home Video, 1989. (video)

Bogard, Jennabeth, et al., *Hot Dog Stand: The Works.* Pleasantville, NY: Sunburst Communications, Inc., 1996. (software)

Jackiw, Nicholas, *The Geometer's Sketchpad.* Berkeley, CA: Key Curriculum Press, 1995. (software)

MECC, *DinoPark Tycoon.* Minneapolis, MN: MECC, 1994. (software)

Morrison, Philip, Phylis Morrison, and the Office of Charles and Ray Eames, *Powers of Ten.* New York: Scientific American, 1982. (video and book)

Putnam New Media, *Anno's Learning Games.* Reston, VA: Putnam New Media. (software)

Web Sites

http://crux.astr.ua.edu/4000WS/4000WS.html   Bibliographic information on women in science over the past 4000 years.

http://edweb.sdsu.edu/EdWeb Folder/courses/EDTEC596/About WebQuest s.html   This site provides information about developing *WebQuest* activities.

http://edweb.sdsu.edu/webquest/LessonTemplate.html
A *WebQuest* template is provided for those wishing to develop a *WebQuest* activity.

http://forum.swarthmore.edu/arithmetic/arith.lessons.html
Swarthmore College site that is a source of lesson plans for teaching mathematics.

http://liftoff.msfc.nasa.gov/   One of the many valuable NASA sites dedicated to space flights.

http://www.aimsedu.org/Puzzle/PuzzleList.html   Mathematical puzzles are presented on this AIMS site.

http://www.auburn.edu/~churcwb/escher.html   A site dedicated to displaying the art of M. C. Escher.

http://www.census.gov/   Statistics and information from U.S. Census Bureau.

http://www.hyperstudio.com/main/content.shtml   Site of *HyperStudio,* a product that may be used for multimedia presentations.

http://www.linfield.edu/~dcruik/garden.html   An example of a mathematics-based *WebQuest* activity.

http://www.mathsurf.com   A commercial site that challenges students to find and use data on the Internet.

http://www.superkids.com/aweb/pages/reviews/math/4/sw_sum1.shtml   A site that provides reviews of educational software.

Chapter 5

Thinking Mathematically

NCTM Standards

GRADES K–4

Standard 3: Mathematics as Reasoning

In grades K–4, the study of mathematics should emphasize reasoning so that students can—

- Draw logical conclusions about mathematics;
- Use models, known facts, properties, and relationships to explain their thinking;
- Justify their answers and solution processes;
- Use patterns and relationships to analyze mathematical situations;
- Believe that mathematics makes sense.

Standard 4: Mathematical Connections

In grades K–4, the study of mathematics should include opportunities to make connections so that students can—

- Link conceptual and procedural knowledge;
- Relate various representations of concepts or procedures to one another;
- Recognize relationships among different topics in mathematics;
- Use mathematics in other curriculum areas;
- Use mathematics in their daily lives.

Standard 13: Patterns and Relationships

In grades K–4, the mathematics curriculum should include the study of patterns and relationships so that students can—

- Recognize, describe, extend, and create a wide variety of patterns;
- Represent and describe mathematical relationships;
- Explore the use of variables and open sentences to express relationships.

NCTM (1989), pp. 29, 32, 60. Reprinted by permission.

NCTM Standards

GRADES 5–8

Standard 3: Mathematics as Reasoning

In grades 5–8, reasoning shall permeate the mathematics curriculum so that students can—

- Recognize and apply deductive and inductive reasoning;
- Understand and apply reasoning processes, with special attention to spatial reasoning and reasoning with proportions and graphs;
- Make and evaluate mathematical conjectures and arguments;
- Validate their own thinking;
- Appreciate the pervasive use and power of reasoning as a part of mathematics.

Standard 4: Mathematical Connections

In grades 5–8, the mathematics curriculum should include the investigation of mathematical connections so that students can—

- See mathematics as an integrated whole;
- Explore problems and describe results using graphical, numerical, physical, algebraic, and verbal mathematical models or representations;
- Use a mathematical idea to further their understanding of other mathematical ideas;
- Apply mathematical thinking and modeling to solve problems that arise in other disciplines, such as art, music, psychology, science, and business;
- Value the role of mathematics in our culture and society.

NCTM (1989), pp. 81, 84. Reprinted by permission.

You are planning a party for the math club. You are going to let the students make their own ice cream sundaes. You decide to buy chocolate, vanilla, and strawberry ice cream; fudge, caramel, or mint sauce; and nuts or cherries to put on the tops of the sundaes. You tell the students they may have either one or two scoops of ice cream, but the scoops must be the same flavor. They may choose only one sauce and must choose either cherries or nuts but may not have both. List below all the different types of sundaes your students could make following your rules. Remember that math is the study of patterns; this will be a lot easier if you set up and follow a pattern. As you write out your work, be sure to explain all of your thinking. After you solve this problem, ask for some related problems and either solve those problems or trade with a friend and solve her problem.

As you read the following pages, consider these guiding questions:

1. What are four major mathematical thinking processes? Describe activities for students of different ages that would help them develop these processes.
2. What are some materials you might use to assist students in abstracting properties that a group of objects have in common using the multiple embodiment principle?
3. What are the reflexive, symmetric, and transitive properties of relationships and how are these related to order and equivalence relationships?
4. How would you use Venn, Carroll, and tree diagrams to sort and classify attribute materials?

Children attending elementary school today need an emphasis in their mathematics classrooms different from that of 100, 50, or even 20 years ago. The rapid advances in computer technology, the proliferation of inexpensive calculators, the explosion of the amount of data to be dealt with every day, and the ever-increasing rate of change require that children develop new skills. It is no longer sufficient that children develop proficiency in computation and in applying that computation to their day-to-day problems. By the time these children reach adulthood in the twenty-first century, they will be faced with problems that no teacher can foresee. It is crucial, therefore, that these children be taught how to think. Children of different ages think on different levels, but all children are capable of rational thought. Mathematics is an ideal subject in which to develop the thought processes, beginning at a very early age.

The following quotes from two recent reports emphasize the need to drastically change our usual style of mathematics teaching in order to improve the level of reasoning ability of the average American mathematics student. First, in a report approved by the National Science Board entitled *Failing Our Children: Implications of the Third International Mathematics and Science Study* (July 1998), concern over the status of mathematics and science education in the United States, especially at the secondary level, was expressed.

> The Third International Mathematics and Science Study (TIMSS) reports disturbing findings about the performance of U.S. secondary school students in science and mathematics, ranking them well below the international average. Together with an array of related national data, the TIMSS results raise serious concerns about the state of U.S. education.
>
> No nation can afford to tolerate what prevails in American schooling: generally low expectations and low performance in mathematics and science, with only pockets of excellence at a world-class level of achievement. Formal education has traditionally been the path to productive careers, upward mobility, and the joy of lifelong learning. If we do not arm our children with appropriate tools, we fail them.

> It is the conviction of the National Science Board that world-class achievement in science and mathematics education is of critical importance to our Nation's future. In the new global context, a scientifically literate population is vital to the democratic process, a healthy economy, and our quality of life. (http://ustimss.msu.edu/, approved by the National Science Board, July 28, 1998)

The second quotation comes from the National Research Council's publication *Everybody Counts: A Report to the Nation on the Future of Mathematics Education:*

> More than ever before, Americans need to think for a living; more than ever before, they need to think mathematically.... Wake up, America! Your children are at risk. Three of every four Americans stop studying mathematics before completing career or job prerequisites. Most students leave school without sufficient preparation in mathematics to cope either with on-the-job demands for problem solving or with college requirements for mathematical literacy. (1989, pp. 1–2)

To help students strengthen their ability to think mathematically, four major thinking processes are emphasized in this chapter:

- **Observing and inferring** (encouraging children to describe objects both orally and pictorially).
- **Comparing** (asking children to note likenesses and differences).
- **Classifying** (asking children to sort objects on the basis of one or more attributes).
- **Sequencing** (asking children to order elements in a set on the basis of one or more given characteristics).

These processes lead to problem solving and do not require the use of numbers. Gibb and Castaneda (1975) and Mueller (1985) have noted similar processes as necessary for developing a solid understanding of number concepts. These processes should begin before formal work with numbers is introduced and should continue to develop throughout the elementary and middle school years.

Children use mathematical thinking and problem solving frequently in their everyday lives. Ask children to suggest ways that they use these ideas outside of class. Send home notes to parents briefly explaining some of the concepts you are teaching and giving some suggestions for the parents to continue the teaching of those concepts at home. This communication may help prevent complaints from parents wondering when you are going to start mathematics, since the children are not bringing home worksheets full of numbers and the children report that all they do is play with materials during math time.

Some of the ways in which children naturally use the thinking processes at home include observing their surroundings and making predictions about the future, comparing and sorting everyday objects, and following and creating patterns. Enlist the support of parents in building these skills.

You may encourage parents to play a guessing game. Have them ask the children to observe the room and then close their eyes. While the children's eyes are closed, the parents move one object. When the children open their eyes, they try to guess which object was moved.

Parents can play other simple observation games such as "I'm thinking of something . . . ." The parent chooses an object in plain sight and picks one word to describe it, such as its color or shape. The child then tries to guess the object. When the object is guessed, the child chooses a new object.

Several household events can encourage comparing and classifying. Parents should encourage children to set up a classification scheme for putting away their toys or for categorizing favorite books. Children can practice sorting as they put away the silverware and compare teaspoons and tablespoons or as they fold the clothes from the laundry and separate their own clothes from those of their siblings. Children follow simple patterns as they set the table and realize the fork goes on the left of the plate and the spoon and knife go on the right. They note a sequence in the events of the day as they find that in the morning they wake up, go to the bathroom, get dressed, eat breakfast, brush their teeth, and get ready for school. Sequences are also important to older students as they study the patterns in the stages of the moon each month, or in the metamorphosis of a moth. Teachers and parents alike should discuss these events. Teachers should point out the thinking processes that are being learned and the relationship of these processes to problem solving and later to learning number concepts.

In this chapter, we explore some of the ways in which teachers encourage the thinking skills. The emphasis is on assisting children to become creative mathematicians. Children should be encouraged not only to solve problems but also to create them. Teachers should allow children to use their own natural thought processes as often as possible and should aid children in expanding their thinking. This chapter focuses on skills and processes that do not require number concepts. It begins with activities appropriate for very young children but also includes activities challenging for older children and adolescents. We suggest ways to encourage children to look at the relationships between objects and sets and to begin work with formal logic. In Chapter 6, these properties are related to number concepts. In Chapter 7, number processes are expanded to include the processes of joining and separating as addition and subtraction are introduced.

Many of the activities work with sets of objects. These activities may involve the use of commercial materials such as attribute blocks and People Pieces, computer games, or materials collected around the home or con-

structed by the teacher and the students. It is necessary for children to see, manipulate, and construct materials in order to develop solid number readiness concepts.

Developing Concepts

As mentioned earlier, the concepts necessary for a solid foundation upon which to build later number concepts include observing and inferring, comparing, classifying, and sequencing. These concepts develop as children recognize relationships between objects and sets and later as they develop number concepts. These concepts are not exclusive to mathematics but rather are necessary in all subject areas.

Observing and Inferring

To make observations and inferences, children should be encouraged to use all five senses. As children gather information about the world, they should describe what is being observed and inferred. Language is a powerful tool for gathering and disseminating information, so children should be encouraged to talk to each other and to the teacher while they are engaged in these activities. The activities presented here are generally sequenced from simplest to most complex. Grade levels are listed as a general guide. Choose activities that best meet the needs of your students and adapt them as you see fit.

ACTIVITIES

Primary (K–1)

Objective: to develop the ability to observe and describe using the five senses.

1. Choose several objects that are safe to touch, smell, and taste, such as sugar, fruit, crackers, and cookies. Put one object in a clean bag and ask the children to feel the object without looking inside. Have the children describe what they feel. Then let them sniff the object without peeking and describe what they smell. Encourage the children to take a small bite and to describe the taste. Shake the bag and ask the children to describe what they hear. Finally, let the children look at the object and describe what they see. Allow the children to bring in objects to place in the bag.

Objective: to develop inference skills based on the sense of hearing.

2. Have the children close their eyes and listen to familiar sounds, such as a door closing, someone writing on the board with chalk, and a chair that squeaks. Let the

children describe what they hear and make a guess as to what it is. Have them make noises for the other children to guess.

Objective: to develop inference skills based on the sense of touch.

3. Let the children feel several geometric figures placed in a "feely box" and guess what they are. See if they can fit a figure into a frame of the same size and shape without looking. Children may be able to match the shape to the frame without knowing the name of the shape.

Objective: to develop inference skills based on the senses of sight and touch.

4. Outline several familiar objects. Have the children guess which object matches each outline. Give the children the objects to fit onto the outlines to see if their guesses are correct. Let the children make outlines of their own to exchange with each other.

Objective: to distinguish between observations and inferences.

5. Repeat the activity for developing the ability to observe, but let the children guess what the object is at each step. Discuss the difference between observing using the senses and guessing based on observations.

For all of the activities, be sure to discuss with the children the strategies they used to make their guesses. They can learn from each other better ways to make inferences.

ACTIVITIES

Primary–Intermediate (2–5)

Objective: to develop the ability to observe a three-dimensional figure and match it to a two-dimensional model and vice-versa.

1. Using a set of geoblocks, a set of solid wooden blocks of varying shapes and sizes available commercially, or another set of solid figures in which the blocks are different shapes, draw the outline of each face of a block on a sheet of paper. Let children choose from a pile of blocks the block that has all those faces. Have them pick up the block and check each face against the outline to see if it matches (see Figure 5–1).

Objective: to develop the ability to make a sketch from an observation.

2. Using the geoblocks, have the children sketch each face of a block while looking at it. Have the children also sketch each face of a block while feeling the block but not looking at it. Let the children exchange sketches with one another to see if they can select the block that was sketched.

Objective: to describe and recognize three-dimensional geometric figures.

3. Use the geoblocks again. This time, have one child describe a block while another child listens. Let the second child select the block that was described. Change roles so that the selector has a chance to be the describer.

Middle Grades (5–8)

Objective: to continue to develop the ability to draw three-dimensional figures.

1. Using the geoblocks, ask the students to put two or three blocks together to make a structure and then draw each face of the structure as though they were looking at it directly from above and from each of the four sides. They should then exchange drawings and ask other students to reconstruct the original structure by looking at the drawings.

Objective: to strengthen observation skills in nature.

2. Ask children to collect a number of leaves from a variety of trees. Each student should select one leaf and write a description of it. She should in-

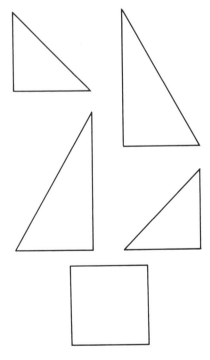

Figure 5–1

clude such features as the vein patterns, the type of leaf edges, size, color, shape, and whether the leaf is single or compound. After each student has written a description, put all the leaves on a bulletin board where they can be seen by everyone. Ask the students to exchange descriptions and attempt to identify each other's leaves.

Experiences such as these in observing, inferring, and describing give children an opportunity to develop and refine many mathematical concepts. Children may use vague or emotional words rather than specific, descriptive words. Children who describe something as *good,* may realize after some of these activities that it is more effective to use words such as *soft, warm,* and *fuzzy.* Let the children discuss which words give better descriptions.

Comparing

Once children learn to observe and describe objects, they should begin to compare two or more objects. Often, children begin to compare objects even before they know the names of the objects. They may say that they want more or fewer even if they do not know the name of what they have. They may be able to tell you what is the same or different about two objects whether or not they know the names of the objects.

Children might enjoy reading or listening to the book *Angus Thought He Was Big.* This gives you a chance to talk about whether children understand that comparisons do not always remain constant. Children themselves may be small when compared to adults but large when compared to a favorite doll. A child may describe a set as having more when it really has fewer but larger objects. Teachers should assist children in developing difficult comparison concepts. Being able to compare individual objects, and later sets of objects, will help children when they are deciding whether 3 is more or less than 5.

ACTIVITIES

Primary (K–2)

Objective: to compare two or more objects using all of the senses.

1. Discuss the terms *alike* and *different* with the children. Then collect a group of objects from the children. Select two objects at random and ask the children to list all of the ways that the objects are alike or different. List their responses on the chalkboard or on a large sheet of paper. Encourage the children to use all of their senses.

2. Play line-up with the children. One child is the leader. The next child in line must name one way in which he or she is like the leader and one way in which he or she is different. Each subsequent child then names one likeness and one difference between himself or herself and the child directly before him or her. After playing the game, ask the children to tell you what *alike* and *different* mean. Encourage them to suggest other objects that they might use to play the same game.

Classifying

After children learn to compare objects, they should begin to categorize, or classify, them. **Classifying** is the process of grouping or sorting objects into classes or categories according to some systematic scheme or principle. The children must use specific properties of the objects to be classified and must make comparisons between objects in order to decide on their proper categories. Students should be encouraged to construct their own categories and not just match objects to labels or categories about which the teacher has decided.

The groups into which objects are sorted are called sets. A **well-defined set** is a collection of objects defined so that given any object, it is possible to determine without question whether or not that object is in the collection. Classification systems also serve as a means to describe an object that is not given. By observing the position in a classification scheme the object would occupy, children can give the properties of the object.

As in other types of mathematical problems, children must find the missing part. This requires that they analyze the structure of the problem much as they will later analyze the structure of a numerical equation. Carpenter (1985) has noted that children naturally attend to the structure of a problem and that expert problem solvers put more emphasis on structure than less capable problem solvers. The activities in this section are designed to help children focus on essential structures or relationships.

Young children should begin by sorting objects that differ in only one way, such as shape or color. Use structured materials such as attribute blocks or People Pieces or use collections of materials found around the home or classroom such as buttons, shells, or baseball cards. **Attribute blocks** are usually made from either wood or plastic and vary in attributes such as color, size, shape, and thickness. Each set of blocks like the one in Fig. 5–2 contains only one block with each possible combination of attributes. For example, a set of blocks with two sizes (large and small), three colors (red, blue, and green), and three shapes (circle, square, and triangle) would have the following 18 pieces:

large, red circle	small, red circle
large, red square	small, red square
large, red triangle	small, red triangle
large, blue circle	small, blue circle
large, blue square	small, blue square
large, blue triangle	small, blue triangle
large, green circle	small, green circle
large, green square	small, green square
large, green triangle	small, green triangle

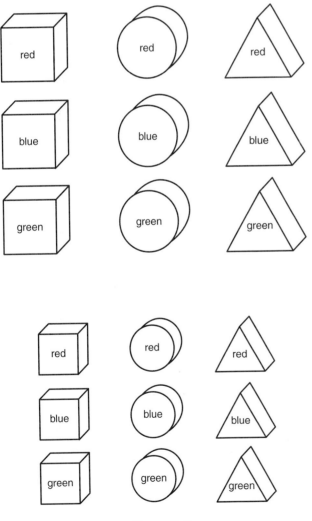

Figure 5–2

Notice the pattern in the listing of pieces. Other sets may have more or fewer shapes, colors, or sizes and may add other variables, such as thickness. You may make a set of attribute shapes of your own by copying the set in Appendix B onto colored construction paper or posterboard or by using the attribute shapes die to punch out pieces of railroad board with a machine such as the Ellison letter machine. These attribute shapes are used for several of the activities in this chapter.

People Pieces is a set of attribute materials consisting of sixteen wooden or plastic tiles with a different person stamped onto each one. The people are of two heights (tall and short), two weights (stout and thin), two colors (red and blue), and two sexes (male and female). List the 16 possible combinations for yourself. Other structured sets you might use include the Animal Tiles from Creative Publications and Zogs from the Addison-Wesley *Explorations 2* book.

The following activities do not require the purchase of any commercial materials.

ACTIVITIES

Primary (K–2)

Objective: to sort materials according to one property.

1. Read *The Button Box* by Margarette Reid and then give the children a set of buttons that are similar except that some are black and some are white. Ask them to sort the buttons into two piles. Encourage them to create their own classification schemes. How many different ways can they sort the buttons?
2. Give the children a large magnet and a group of materials, some of which are made of iron and some of which are not. Ask the children to use the magnet to classify the materials according to whether or not they are attracted by the magnet.
3. Give the children a basin of water and a variety of materials that will not be harmed when they are placed in the water. Ask the children to sort the materials. Put everything that will float in one pile and everything that will not float in another.

Let children collect their own sets of materials and create their own classification schemes. Children may trade materials with each other to see if they all define the sets in the same ways. Encourage them to classify in many different ways and to discuss their methods of classifying with you and with each other.

After the children are proficient at classifying objects into two categories, the activities should be made more dif-

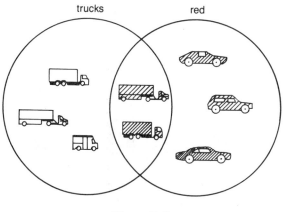

trucks red

Figure 5–3

ficult. You may increase the number of materials to be classified, increase the number of categories into which the materials are grouped, or increase the abstraction of the categories, such as classifying pictures of people as happy or sad rather than as male or female. All of these activities should involve categories that are mutually exclusive.

As children become more mature in their reasoning abilities, they can begin to categorize materials into overlapping categories. For instance, children may group a set of toy vehicles by placing all of the trucks in one group and all of the red vehicles in another. For some children, it will be difficult to decide what to do with the red trucks. The teacher should provide opportunities for the children to construct the concept such that they can overlap the circles as shown in Figure 5–3 and then place the red trucks in the intersection of the two circles. The teacher may need to ask a few leading questions to create disequilibrium in the children. For example, if the children are content placing all of the red trucks in the circle for the trucks, the teacher might ask why they are not in the red circle. The following activities encourage children to use slightly more complicated classification schemes and to create problems as well as solve them.

ACTIVITIES

Primary (1–3)

Objective: to classify using multiple parallel categories.

1. Ask the children to cut out pictures of animals from magazines or newspapers or to draw different animals. Then have them classify the animals in different ways. They might classify them by type of animal, type of food they eat, or according to their natural habitats, such as grassland, forest, and desert.
2. Give the children a set of buttons or toys with a number of properties or attributes. Ask the children to

sort the materials into three categories. See if they can sort the materials into four or more categories. Ask them to tell you the property or properties of each category and how they made their decisions to classify the properties.

Intermediate (3–5)

Objective: to develop the skills of making comparisons in other subject areas

1. In a social studies class when studying different regions of the United States, ask students to make a list comparing and contrasting two regions of the country. One column of the list should contain everything students can think of that is alike about the two regions and the other column, everything that is different between the two. A similar activity could be done when comparing such things as the Revolutionary War and the Civil War, or democracy and theocracy, or President Lincoln and President Washington.
2. Use the book, *The Magic School Bus Inside the Earth* to introduce students to different types of rocks. Ask students to collect rocks in the schoolyard or at home, and bring them into the classroom to make comparisons. Using a list of characteristics of various kinds of rocks, ask students to classify the rocks in various ways.

After the children have set up classification systems, they should be able to abstract properties that a group of objects have in common. **Abstracting** may be thought of as the reverse of classification. Children should be able to look at a set of objects that have been classified and discover the similarity among the elements of the set. They should be able to summarize this similarity in a single statement or rule. Some examples of this type of activity follow.

ACTIVITIES

Primary (1–3)

Objective: to abstract a property of a set.

1. Select a small group of children who are alike in some way; for example, all are wearing tennis shoes, have blonde hair, or are wearing glasses. Do not tell the class how the children are alike. A child who thinks he or she knows the attribute chosen may name a child who has not yet been chosen but who also has the given attribute. When all of the children with the given attribute have been named, the children may guess the attribute. Select one of the children to name a new group of children with a new secret attribute.

Centers Time
ALL TOGETHER

I Spy

I spy something big and square. You can see through it to look outside…

Setting Out
Choose a secret object in the room to describe. Beginning with the words *I spy*, give a list of clues about the object (color, size, what it is used for, general location in the room, for instance).

Along the Way
Raise your hand when you think you can identify my secret object. Call on individuals until someone names your object. When the class has played I Spy several times, some of the children might like to take turns giving the clues.

> I spy something round and red. You use it at recess. It bounces.

STORYBOOK MATH

Caps for Sale
by Esphyr Slobodkina

This story about a peddler and some monkey business leads to some interesting sorting activities.

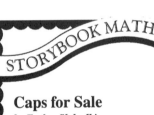

Getting Ready
Make some caps out of construction paper or coffee filters colored with marking pens. Make caps in two sizes, three colors, and three different styles: plain, polka-dotted, and striped.

Setting Out
Let's act out the story as I read it aloud. We can use the caps as props. Choose one child to be the peddler; the rest of the class can be monkeys. They will especially enjoy the mimicry in the story.

Along the Way
Draw special attention to the cap sorting that goes on near the end of the story. *How else could the peddler sort the caps?* Try different ways: by color, size, and style.

Figure 5–4 From Linda Charles et al., *Mathland: Journey Through Mathematics: K.* Mountain View, CA: Creative Publications, 1995. Reprinted by permission.

Math Program

The page shown in Figure 5–4, from a Kindergarten Guidebook, describes a game to play where students must use attributes to describe objects in the classroom. This is part of a unit on making groups in which students find different ways to classify objects and frequently find multiple solutions to problems. Students must use logical reasoning and communicate their comprehension of concepts throughout this unit.

The second part of this page integrates the grouping ideas with the book *Caps for Sale.* Students make caps out of construction paper or coffee filters in two sizes, three colors, and plain, polka-dotted, or striped. After acting out the story, students sort the caps in a variety of different ways.

Each of the eight units in this series uses two major types of activities, Projects and Centers Time. Projects are in-depth explorations lasting approximately one week. Projects in this unit include sorting treasure chests of buttons, shells, and creepy crawlers, and creating and sorting monsters. This page describes an activity from centers time with ideas for integrating math into other traditional centers from the kindergarten class, in this case the book corner, and whole group-games and activities such as this "I Spy" game. Other centers activities include activities from which students can choose at their tables. This program also includes an assessment guide with suggestions on such things as interviews and portfolios, a math tune-up guide for helping students keep skills and mental mathematics abilities sharp, a manipulative kit, a technology package, and family letters for communicating with and involving adults from home.

Venn and Carroll diagrams (see descriptions later in this chapter) are used throughout this unit as children explore a variety of different ways to sort objects ranging from their shoes to the monsters that they create. Students frequently work in small groups as they describe their creatures and discuss the likenesses and differences of their figures. The unit also suggests several ideas for science, social studies, language, and cooking that use the ideas of grouping and classifying. The computer program *The Playroom,* from Broderbund, is also an optional part of the unit.

2. From a set of the attribute shapes from Appendix B, secretly choose an attribute such as small objects. Pick three or four shapes that have the attribute. Let the children guess which of the other shapes belong in the set. After all of the shapes have been chosen, ask the children to identify the attribute they all have in common. Let the children take turns choosing their own sets. Allow the children to make the game more complex by choosing the union or intersection of two or more attributes such as large and red, or small and triangular.

Objective: to identify the attributes of two sets and their intersection.

3. Secretly choose two intersecting attributes from a set of People Pieces, such as male and tall. Set up two overlapping circles, and place one piece of each type in the correct section as shown in Figure 5–5.

   Let the children take turns picking up a piece and guessing in which section the piece belongs. If the child guesses the correct section, leave the piece in that section. If the guess is incorrect, another child may guess. Don't forget that some pieces will not fit into any section. For example, in Figure 5–5, the label for the left circle might be male and the label for the right circle might be tall; short females would not go inside either circle. Continue until all of the pieces are placed correctly. Ask the children to identify the proper labels of each section. Have the children describe the pieces in the intersection. Ask the children how they knew where to place each piece and why some pieces are outside the sets. Discuss and check for understanding.

   If the activity is too difficult, let the children play with nonintersecting circles. If the children are doing well with two intersecting circles, try the activity with three circles. After the children understand the concept of abstracting attributes of intersecting sets, let

them develop their own problems with other attribute materials.

Activities should include a variety of materials. The **multiple embodiment principle,** described by Dienes and Golding (1966), illustrates a given concept in many different forms. The principle helps children to abstract the essence of the concept so that their perception is not based on only one or two specific concrete examples. In looking at only one or two examples, children may be confused by irrelevant features, especially if they occur frequently, and may reject or accept an item as an example of the concept on the basis of some irrelevant feature (Tennyson, 1973; Wilson, 1986). For example, many children believe that a figure is a triangle only if it is an equilateral triangle in the position shown in Figure 5–6a because equilateral triangles in this position are presented frequently in textbooks. The features of congruent sides and a base parallel to the bottom of the page are irrelevant, but they are so common that children believe them to be relevant. The triangles shown in Figure 5–6b may be rejected as triangles if children have not experienced triangles in many forms.

Burger and Shaughnessy (1986) studied the Van Hiele levels of development in geometry (discussed in Chapter 12) and found that when they asked young children to draw a triangle and then asked them to draw another one that was different in some way, the drawings often featured irrelevant attributes and ignored relevant attributes. For example, one child drew an equilateral triangle with one base parallel to the bottom of the page and then rotated it to make "different" triangles, which were pointing right, left, or down. Another "triangle" had

b.

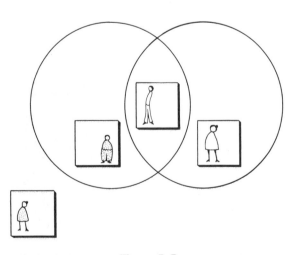

Figure 5–5

Figure 5–6

crooked lines for one side. Congruent triangles were thought to be different and nontriangles were included as triangles.

As children move from classifying to sequencing objects and looking for patterns, the ideas of multiple embodiments, irrelevant features, and negative examples should be continued. Teachers should not only introduce a number of materials but should also encourage children to find examples of their own. To ascertain that the children are abstracting the correct concepts and not focusing on irrelevant details, teachers should take the time to discuss these concepts with the children and check for comprehension.

Sequencing

Children live with sequences and patterns. They may notice patterns in nature such as the symmetry of a leaf or patterns such as the tessellations of tiles on the bathroom floor. To aid young children in recognizing sequences or patterns, form a pattern and ask the children to copy it. Use commercial or teacher-made materials similar to those used for other attribute activities or materials collected by you and the children. Several activities for creating and copying designs are given in Chapter 12.

Have the children look at and copy the provided designs and then play "what comes next?"—in other words, have them extend the pattern by predicting the next object. The following activities focus on completing or extending a definite pattern. Sequencing forms the foundation for children to see the pattern in the counting numbers and to complete counting sequences such as skip-counting or counting backwards. These sequences with numbers will be explored more fully in Chapter 6.

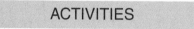

ACTIVITIES

Primary (K–2)

Objective: to recognize and complete a simple pattern.

1. Use a set of materials that differ in only one way, such as a set of beads that are alike except for color. String the beads in a definite pattern such as red, blue, blue, red, blue, blue, red, and so on. Let the children tell you what the pattern is and continue it.
2. Use a set of materials such as wooden or plastic blocks of different shapes and colors to set up a pattern where the materials differ in shape and color. Set up a pattern such as the one shown in Figure 5–7, and ask the children to complete it. Encourage the children to construct other patterns of their own for other children to complete or fill in.

Objective: to recognize and complete the pattern in a two-dimensional array.

3. Use the attribute materials to set up a two-dimensional array such as the one shown in Figure 5–8. Ask the children to find the missing block. After children are proficient at 2-by-2 arrays, extend the arrays to include more blocks. Ask the children to set up arrays for each other. In the beginning, arrays should involve only two attributes, such as color and shape or shape and size. Arrays that use three or more attributes are discussed later in this chapter. Ask the children to discuss the strategies they used to place the shapes in the array.

Relationships

As children compare, classify, and sequence objects, they look at relationships among objects. **Relationships** are rules or agreements that associate one object or concept with another. Mathematics is a collection of relationships among objects or concepts. Children need to have a wide variety of experiences exploring relationships among objects. As children develop more abstractions, the same relationships can be explored on a more abstract level, including using numbers. Two of the most important types of relationships are **order** and **equivalence.**

To understand order and equivalence, the children must first understand three properties of relationships: **reflexive, symmetric,** and **transitive.** Children use the properties of an object in making observations about it, such as that the object is a red circle made of wood and it rolls. To investigate the properties of relationships, the

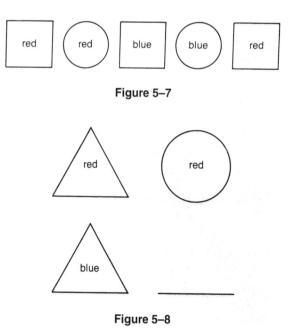

Figure 5–7

Figure 5–8

rule for the relationship and the set of objects upon which the relationship is defined must be clearly stated. For instance, to compare the relative lengths of objects, the relationship "is longer than" should be stated and the set of objects, such as a set of Cuisenaire rods, should be defined.

Three properties of relationships are defined as follows:

1. **Reflexive property.** If A is an element of the set, then A is related to itself.
2. **Symmetric property.** If A and B are both elements of the set and A is related to B, then B is related to A.
3. **Transitive property.** If A, B, and C are all elements of the set and A is related to B and B is related to C, then A is related to C.

Children need not know the names of the properties, but they should have many experiences with relationships and their properties. The following activities facilitate the discussion of a variety of relationships and their properties.

ACTIVITIES

Primary (1–3)

Objective: to explore the properties of relationships.

1. Choose children to act the parts of a grandmother (Mrs. Jensen), a mother (Mrs. Smith), a father (Mr. Smith), a brother (Danny), and a sister (Maureen). Discuss relationships among the family members and ask questions. For example, Mrs. Smith is the mother of Maureen. Is Maureen the mother of Mrs. Smith? Maureen is the sister of Danny. Is Danny the sister of Maureen? If we learn that Mrs. Jensen is Mrs. Smith's mother, then we know that Mrs. Jensen is the mother of Mrs. Smith and that Mrs. Smith is the mother of Maureen. Is Mrs. Jensen the mother of Maureen? Is Maureen the mother of herself?

    Many more family relationships can be discussed, including such ideas as age and height. If Mrs. Jensen is older than Mrs. Smith and Mrs. Smith is older than Maureen, then is Mrs. Jensen older than Maureen?

    Even though young children may use words for family relationships, they may have difficulty exploring the properties of these relationships; they may need to substitute the names of their own family members. Some children may be able to understand the relationships by drawing pictures of their families or by using dolls to represent each person. Others will need to act out the relationships, and still others will not yet be ready to understand the properties, especially those children in the Piagetian preoperational stage.

2. For this activity, a set of Cuisenaire rods may be used. **Cuisenaire rods** are wooden or plastic rods in 10 different colors; they progress in length from 1 to 10 centimeters. Each rod has a cross section of 1 square centimeter. All of the rods 1 centimeter in length are white; the 2-centimeter rods are red, and so on, up to the orange 10-centimeter rods.

Get out a set of Cuisenaire rods and discuss the relationship "is the same color as." Is every rod the same color as itself? If rod A is the same color as rod B, then is rod B the same color as rod A? If rod A is the same color as rod B and rod B is the same color as rod C, then is rod A the same color as rod C?

Now look at the relationship "is longer than" and Figure 5–9. Is rod A longer than itself? If rod A is longer than rod B, then is rod B longer than rod A? If rod A is longer than rod B and rod B is longer than rod C, then is rod A longer than rod C? Because the answer to the first two questions is no, the relationship "is longer than" is not reflexive or symmetric. The answer to the last question was yes; therefore, "is longer than" is transitive.

Intermediate and Middle Grades (4–8)

Objective: to expand the concepts of properties of relationships.

1. Challenge students to find relationships that have certain properties such as a relationship that is reflexive and symmetric but not transitive (is less than five feet away from) or that is not reflexive and not transitive but is symmetric (is the cousin of).
2. For students who have had a great deal of experience with properties of relations, you might ask them to find one or more relations that fit each of the following types:

Property	Reflexive	Symmetric	Transitive
is the same color as	Yes	Yes	Yes
	Yes	Yes	No
	Yes	No	Yes
	Yes	No	No
	No	Yes	Yes
	No	Yes	No
is greater than	No	No	Yes
	No	No	No

On many occasions during the school day, you can discuss relationships between objects or between the children themselves. Encourage the children to ask questions about relationships. Sue is behind John in line. Is John behind Sue? The homework paper is under the book and the book is under the desk. Is the homework paper under the desk?

The reflexive, symmetric, and transitive properties are each independent of the others. It is possible for any of the three properties to be either true or false for any given relationship. Determine for yourself if each property is true or false for these relationships:

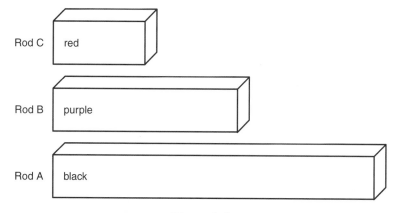

Figure 5–9

"lives next door to" "knows the name of"
"has eaten dinner with" "is congruent to"

Think of other relationships and determine which, if any, of the properties are true for each one.

Relationships that are reflexive, symmetric, and transitive are called **equivalence relationships.** These include such relationships as "is the same age as," "is the same color as," or "is the same shape as." When classifying objects into sets, equivalence relationships are sometimes used.

Equivalence relationships are part of a classification system in which every object belongs in a set and sets do not overlap. The attribute shapes may be sorted into sets using the relationship "is the same shape as." Triangles are in one set, squares in another, and circles in another. Each piece belongs to one and only one set.

An equivalence relationship can be used in exploring properties of numbers. Sets may be sorted using the relationship "has the same number of objects as." All of the sets containing two objects are placed together to aid children in abstracting the concept of the number 2.

The following activities encourage children to form equivalence classes.

eyes as." Choose one child to represent each group. Let the children guess your rule for setting up the classes and suggest other groupings of their own. After the children have abstracted the rules, ask them to share their strategies for solving the problem.

A **strict ordering relationship** is one in which the reflexive and symmetric properties are not true, but the transitive property is true. Consider the relationship "is older than" for the Smith family described earlier. No person is older than himself or herself. If Mrs. Smith is older than Maureen, then Maureen is not older than Mrs. Smith. If Mrs. Jensen is older than Mrs. Smith and Mrs. Smith is older than Maureen, then Mrs. Jensen is older than Maureen. The relationship is transitive only. All members of the family can be ordered from the oldest to the youngest using this relationship.

Strict ordering relationships can also be used with numbers. For example, when the natural numbers are placed in order using the relationship "is less than," you obtain the counting sequence 1, 2, 3, ...

The following activities for ordering do not require the use of numbers.

ACTIVITIES

Primary (K–1)

Objective: to form equivalence classes of structured concrete materials.

1. Using a set of materials such as the attribute shapes, ask the children to form sets using the rule "has the same shape as." Let the children decide on other rules to use. Discuss whether each of the properties is true. Ask the children why the shapes satisfy the rules.

Objective: to abstract the rule used to form equivalence classes.

2. Secretly choose a rule by which to form equivalence classes of students. It may be "has the same color

---

ACTIVITIES

Primary (K–2)

Objective: to order objects using various characteristics of the objects.

1. Give the children a set of baby food jars, each containing a different amount of colored liquid. Let the children order the jars from the one with the least liquid to the one with the most. Include both an empty jar and a full one. Some of the jars may be easy to order, but, in some cases, students may need to compare the jar to a group of two or more jars to determine the exact placement. The activity may be varied by giving the children a number of identical plastic cups and asking

them to pour colored water into the cups so that each cup contains more water than the last one.

2. Read one of the children's books where sizes are compared, such as *The Biggest and Smallest* or *The Longest and Tallest.* Discuss comparing sizes with the children and follow the discussion by playing the game Something Bigger. To play Something Bigger, one child begins by naming a small object. The next child must name an object bigger than the first one. Play continues as long as the children can name something bigger. So that you can check whether the object named is really bigger, you may wish to restrict the play to objects visible in the classroom.

3. Select five or six students and ask them to order themselves according to an attribute of their own choosing. Let the other children in class try to decide what criterion was used for the ordering. The children may select something obvious, such as height, or something less conspicuous, such as the number of pieces of jewelry being worn.

4. Cut out a cartoon strip from the Sunday paper and mount each frame separately on a piece of tagboard. Let the children try to put the cartoon back in its proper order. Choose a cartoon with no reading involved. For a variation, let children draw pictures to tell a story. Ask them to trade pictures with a friend and try to put each other's stories in order. Does everyone agree on the proper order?

5. The computer programs, *Millie's Math House* and *Sammy's Science House,* give the students the opportunity to sequence events in an entertaining electronic format. Both programs ask the students to place various events in some logical order. Students can play these games individually on the computer during math center time or other free time, or if the school has networked versions of these, all the students can be playing the games simultaneously at their own levels during computer time.

After children have experienced activities dealing with relationships among individual objects, they should explore relationships among sets of objects. Equivalence and ordering relations on sets form the basis for understanding number concepts. Children should explore sets to determine if the objects in one set can be placed in one-to-one correspondence with the objects in another set. If there is exactly one element in the second set for each element in the first set and no elements are left over in either set, the two sets are said to be equivalent.

Developing and Practicing Skills

After children have had sufficient experience with the processes of observing, comparing, classifying, and sequencing and have had experience with relationships and

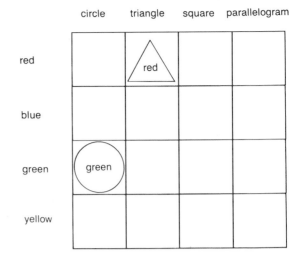

Figure 5–10

their properties, they are ready for more formal activities involving these concepts. Activities in this section require children to use these early concepts to further develop thinking skills. Children are given the opportunity to practice earlier skills and to both solve and create problems. Even though most of the problems do not require the use of numbers, they do require some fairly sophisticated reasoning abilities. In most instances, children are encouraged to use concrete materials to explore teacher-posed problems and to use these materials or to develop new ones to create their own problems. Computers can be used to simulate some of the same types of problems that children may solve with concrete, physical models.

Carroll Diagrams

After children can classify materials easily according to one or two attributes, they may begin to use **Carroll diagrams,** or charts, to classify materials according to two or more attributes. Carroll diagrams are named after the mathematician-author Lewis Carroll. Used to classify materials according to more than one attribute, Carroll diagrams are a good introduction to later work with data tables and multiplication. An example of a Carroll diagram is given in Figure 5–10, which may be used with the attribute shapes.

ACTIVITIES

Primary (K–3)

Objective: to abstract properties using a Carroll diagram.

1. Place about half of the shapes in a Carroll diagram for which the labels are not given, as shown in Figure 5–11. Let the children try to detect your pattern and place the rest of the pieces in the correct places. After

all of the pieces have been correctly positioned, ask the children to tell you what the labels should be. Let them discuss the strategies they used to solve the problem.

2. Divide small groups of children into two teams each. Give each group a set of four People Pieces, such as the tall males. Ask one team to draw a 2-by-2 Carroll diagram for the People Pieces and to label it but not to show the diagram to the other team. (The diagram must be labeled according to the differences in the pieces, in this case the color and weight.) One possible diagram for these pieces is shown in Figure 5–12.

The group with the labeled diagram should then place one piece in the correct place on an unlabeled diagram. The other group must decide where to place the other three pieces and then correctly name the labels for the diagram. Keep track of the number of incorrect guesses as the team places the pieces in the diagram. After one team has correctly placed the pieces and determined the labels, it is that team's turn to make a secret Carroll diagram with another set of four People Pieces.

After students become proficient at solving Carroll diagrams involving two sets of attributes, they should begin to work with diagrams involving three or more sets of properties. Figure 5–13 shows a Carroll diagram for the shape, color, and size of attribute blocks; Figure 5–14 shows a Carroll diagram for the height, weight, sex, and color of People Pieces.

Let the children place the pieces in Carroll diagrams that are already labeled, such as those in Figures 5–13 and 5–14. Explain to the children that they must use all of the labels for each piece.

Let the children make up their own Carroll diagrams and have other students place the pieces in the diagrams. Discuss the construction of the diagrams and the fact that you must use parallel labels, such as male and female, in the same type of position. For instance, male could not

Figure 5–13

Figure 5–11

Figure 5–12

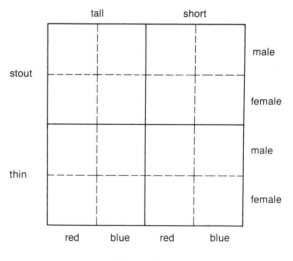

Figure 5–14

label a column if female labeled a row, because you would not be able to find a piece that was both male and female to place in the intersection of that row and column.

The following activities are designed for children who are proficient at filling in and creating Carroll diagrams with three or more sets of labels.

ACTIVITIES

Intermediate (4–6)

Objective: to set up Carroll diagrams involving four sets of characteristics and to abstract properties of sets from their placement in a Carroll diagram.

1. Divide the class into groups of four or five and give each group a set of People Pieces. Ask each group to sketch a Carroll diagram using the People Pieces and showing the color, height, weight, and sex of the characters. Each group should then place the pieces on the table in the order shown on the Carroll diagram.

   After the teacher has checked all the Carroll diagrams to determine if the pieces are in the correct places, each team should turn all but three of the pieces over while leaving them in the same positions. The teams should then trade places with each other and guess what the hidden pieces look like in each other's diagrams. Students should take turns pointing at a hidden piece and giving the color, weight, height, and sex. When a student guesses correctly, the piece should be turned face up and left in that po-

sition. If the guess is incorrect, the piece should be left face down. Once all of the pieces have been correctly identified, the team that has been guessing should draw a Carroll diagram of the set and compare it to the Carroll diagram drawn by the team that created the problem.

2. The same teams used for the activity just described may be used again for this one. Give each team a set of attribute blocks, and ask the teams to devise a Carroll diagram using the shape, size, and color of the blocks, such as in Figure 5–15. Each team should draw the Carroll diagram and place the pieces on the table in the correct places.

   After all of the pieces have been positioned and checked by the teacher, the students should exchange the positions of three of the pieces. Teams may then trade places and attempt to discover which pieces are in the incorrect positions. Each team should draw the Carroll diagram for the set at which they are looking and tell where the pieces should go. The team should then check with the original team to see if the diagram is correct.

3. Students may work individually, in pairs, or in small groups to create their own sets of attribute materials. Students should first decide on a theme for the materials to be made. Themes may arise from special days or seasons, such as valentines, snowmen, pumpkins, or spring flowers. After a theme is chosen, the children should decide on three or four characteristics to vary on their attribute materials. Remind the children that all other attributes must stay the same. For example, a group of children may decide to make hearts for Valentine's Day that differ

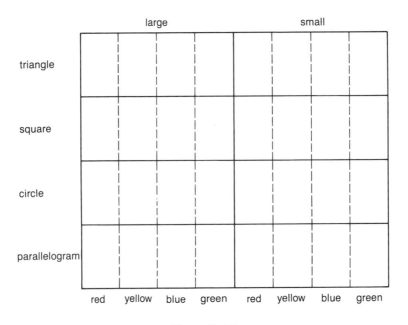

Figure 5–15

in size, color, and arrows. They might have three sizes (small, medium, and large), two colors (pink and red), and with or without arrows. This set of materials would have $3 \times 2 \times 2$, or 12, pieces in order to have one piece of each type. After the children have decided upon the pertinent attributes for the set, they should draw a Carroll diagram to illustrate all the pieces. The diagram in Figure 5–16 is one possibility.

After the diagram is drawn, the children may make the pieces necessary for the set. The pieces may be drawn on index cards or be cut from posterboard. After the set is made, the children may use this set for activities described in this chapter or may develop new activities of their own. Children may exchange sets with each other and draw Carroll diagrams for the other sets.

Tree Diagrams

After the children are comfortable with activities involving Carroll diagrams, they may use other types of diagrams for classifying sets of attribute materials. A **tree diagram** is another useful way of classifying materials. In tree diagrams, the branches at each level indicate the characteristics of a different attribute. For example, to show attribute shapes with two colors and two shapes, you could use the diagram in Figure 5–17. Tree diagrams can be used for sequencing as well as for classifying, and the activities described below involve both concepts. Variations of tree diagrams will be used later for multiplication, prime factorization, and activities involving probability.

Figure 5–16

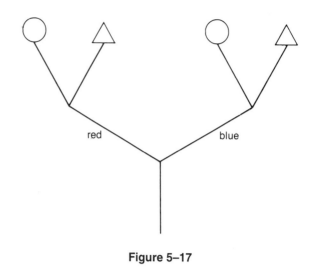

Figure 5–17

ACTIVITIES

Primary (K–3)

Objective: to classify objects using a tree diagram.

1. Draw a tree diagram such as the one in Figure 5–17 and give the children a set of attribute shapes to place on the tree. The children should begin by placing one block at the foot of the tree. Then they should move it to the first branching of tree limbs. The children should decide which branch to take according to the attributes of the piece. They should continue moving the piece upwards, deciding on the proper branch at each intersection. After the first piece is in place, continue by letting other children decide the proper position for the next block. Continue until all of the blocks are in their proper locations or until all of the children have had an opportunity to place a block.

   When children are first learning to use tree diagrams, you should begin with a simple diagram, such as the one in Figure 5–17, and gradually increase the complexity of the task. Ask the children to compare the tree diagram to the Carroll diagram. Use the same set of attribute materials on both diagrams. Encourage the children to create other diagrams for the same or different sets of materials. Discuss the strategies they use to place the materials on the tree.

2. Draw a tree diagram on the floor and make label cards for the branches. The positions of the cards may be changed at the discretion of the children. Use labels such as those shown in Figure 5–18. Ask each child to start at the bottom of the tree and to walk until he or she comes to an intersection. At each intersection, let the child decide which way to go. The child should continue until the end of the last branch.

Ask the children how they decided which way to go at the intersections.

3. Use the tree diagram you have drawn on the floor or one drawn on a large piece of posterboard on a table. Collect small trucks and cars to use with this activity (the children may bring in vehicles for this activity). Using attributes of the vehicles you have, label the intersections on the tree. Try using attributes and their negations, such as red and not red, cars and not cars, and with decals and without decals. Let the children take turns driving the vehicles up the tree, deciding the proper turn to take at each intersection. One such tree diagram is shown in Figure 5–19.

After the children become familiar with the activity, let them decide on other labels and sets of materials to classify using tree diagrams. They may develop their own sets of materials or suggest other activities to use with familiar sets such as People Pieces and attribute blocks.

Older children who have had experience classifying materials on a tree diagram may wish to carry the concepts even further. The following activities are designed to further develop concepts using tree diagrams. If older students have not worked with tree diagrams before, they should first try some of the activities described above.

Figure 5–18

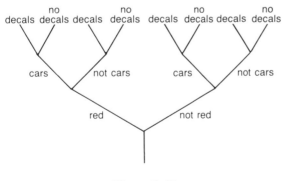

Figure 5–19

ACTIVITIES

Intermediate and Middle Grades (4–8)

Objective: to use a tree diagram to classify objects.

1. Show the children an unlabeled tree diagram on which the pieces have already been placed on the correct limbs, such as in Figure 5–20. Ask the children to tell you what the labels must be.

   After the children have decided on the proper labels, have them label the tree and remove the pieces. Then have them start the pieces at the bottom of the tree and follow them to their correct branches. Discuss with the children the differences between deciding on the labels after the pieces are in place and placing the pieces when the labels are in place.

2. Have the children use a tree diagram to create a set of attribute materials in the same way that they used a Carroll diagram. Ask the children to decide on a theme for a new set of attribute materials and to name three or four categories of properties for these materials. For example, children may decide to create a set of flowers using roses or daisies with three, four, or five leaves and yellow or white petals. This will give them a set of $2 \times 3 \times 2$, or 12, pieces. Ask the children to sketch a tree diagram that would show all the possible pieces, such as the one in Figure 5–21.

   After the tree diagram is drawn, have the children sketch the proper flower at the end of each branch. These sketches may then be transferred to index cards or posterboard so that each piece can be individually manipulated. After the sets are made, children may use them for activities in this section or may make up new activities of their own.

3. Tree diagrams may be used for sequencing if a value is assigned to each branch. The branch on the far left is assigned the highest value and the values decrease as you go to the right. Elements are first sequenced according to the branches on the bottom, and the im-

Figure 5–20

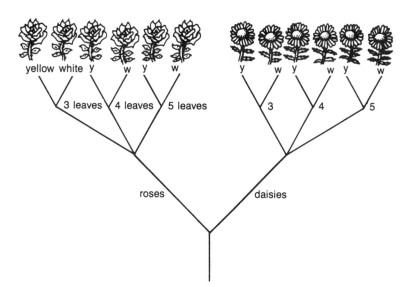

Figure 5–21

portance of the branches decreases as you move up. This may be illustrated by alphabetizing a set of nonsense words. Put each of the following words on a separate index card:

cat	cab	cot	cob	cut	cub
lat	lab	lot	lob	lut	lub
mat	mab	mot	mob	mut	mub

Sketch a tree diagram in which the bottom branches are labeled with the first letters of the words in alphabetical order from left to right, the middle branches are labeled with the second letters in alphabetical order, and the top branches are labeled with the last letters, again in alphabetical order, as shown in Figure 5–22.

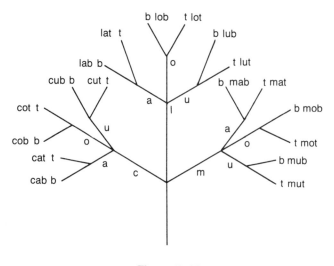

Figure 5–22

Ask the children to take the words and hang them from the proper branches. Then ask the children to tell you what they observe about the order of the words. This activity is helpful for children who have difficulty alphabetizing words when the first few letters of two or more words are the same.

4. When studying binomial nomenclature in science, use a tree diagram to separate kingdoms, phyla, classes, orders, families, genera, and species. Let the students locate the proper position on the tree for a variety of plants and animals. This is a good activity for a bulletin board, as students can draw or find pictures of objects to place on the diagram.

5. Children may use tree diagrams to sequence any set of materials from the greatest to the least. Children may decide to set up an imaginary kingdom with the People Pieces. They may decide that all females are more powerful than males, that the stout ones are more powerful than the thin ones, that the short are more powerful than the tall, and finally that the red are more powerful than the blue. The children should set up a tree diagram such as the one in Figure 5–23 and line up all the People Pieces from the most powerful to the least powerful.

This activity may be done in groups of four or five. Each group may line up the pieces and then show the line-up to another group. The other group should not be shown the original criteria for the line-up or the tree diagram. This other group must then decide on the criteria selected and draw the tree diagram. After the diagram is drawn, ask the original group to determine the accuracy of the drawing. Discuss with the students whether individuals are ever ranked in real life and what types of criteria are used.

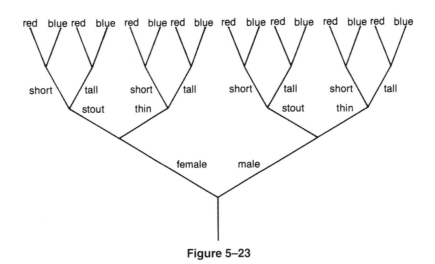

Figure 5–23

As you can see from these activities, skills learned in math class often carry over into other subject areas. Carryover should be encouraged whenever possible. Certainly, in real life, people do not do math for the first 50 minutes of the day, then spelling, and then social studies. These skills must be used together. Encourage the children to find applications for new skills regardless of the subject area.

Venn Diagrams

Another diagram used to classify materials with more than one variable attribute is a **Venn diagram.** Unlike tree or Carroll diagrams, Venn diagrams are not used to give a unique position to each element of a set, but they are useful for classifying by both attributes and the negations of attributes. Young children should begin by using only one or two attributes, while older children may classify using three or even more intersecting categories. Simple intersecting Venn diagrams were introduced earlier in this chapter. A few more examples of Venn diagrams are introduced here for additional practice.

ACTIVITIES

Primary (K–3)

Objective: to classify using Venn diagrams and parallel categories.

1. When you first introduce children to Venn diagrams, use circles with parallel categories, such as colors. Give the children a set of attribute shapes and several large (150-centimeter circumference) loops of yarn or heavy cord. Make three separate circles with the cord and ask the children to put all the red blocks in one circle, all the blue ones in another, and all the yellow ones in another. Do any pieces belong in none of the circles? Ask the children to create other ways to classify the blocks. Discuss their methods of deciding where to place the pieces.

Objective: to form Venn diagrams using two intersecting sets.

2. Ask the children to form two circles of yarn and to put all of the yellow pieces in one loop and all the triangles in another. Let the children discuss what to do with the yellow triangles. Lead them to discover that they can overlap the two loops of yarn and put the yellow triangles inside the section where the loops overlap. This is called the **intersection** of the two sets. Note the intersection of the sets in Figure 5–24.

Let the children suggest other labels for the two circles. Discuss how they know whether or not there will be pieces in the intersection. Will there be any pieces in the intersection if the loops are labeled triangles and squares? If the loops are labeled small and triangles, where would a small green square go?

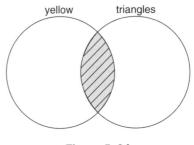

Figure 5–24

3. Using attribute materials such as People Pieces, ask one group of students to draw, secretly, a Venn diagram with two intersecting loops and to add labels to them such as red and male. Form two intersecting loops with the yarn and put one correct piece in each section. Ask children who did not see the Venn diagram to guess where the other pieces should go. After all of the pieces have been placed in the correct sections, ask the children to identify the labels on the secret Venn diagram.

Let a new group of children decide on another diagram. Discuss with the children such things as whether or not all of the pieces go inside the loops. If any pieces do not belong in the loops, do they help you decide on the proper labels for the loops?

Objective: to use the terms *and* and *or* properly when referring to the intersection or union of two sets.

4. Set up two intersecting loops as in the first activity in this group and place the attribute blocks in the proper sections. Using the loops labeled yellow and triangles, ask the children where to find the pieces that are yellow *and* triangles. Note that these pieces are all found in the intersection. Some children may be confused by the word *intersection* and by ending up with a set smaller than either the set of yellow pieces or the set of triangles.

Later, for addition, the children may read "3 + 4" as "3 and 4." These are not the same concepts, even though they use the same familiar word, *and.* Addition is actually based on the concept of union (or), not the concept of intersection (and). **Addition** may be defined as the number of items in the union of two disjoint sets.

Let the children make up several intersecting sets and describe the pieces in the intersection using the word *and.* Be sure to use mutually exclusive attributes such as color and shape or size and thickness. After the children are comfortable using the word *and,* ask them to find the pieces that are yellow or triangles. Note that these are all of the pieces in the union of the two sets. The mathematical use of the word *or* includes those pieces that are yellow *and* triangles.

Give the children several chances to explore the uses of these words with the attribute shapes and in everyday life. Use statements such as "Today we will take attendance *and* say the Pledge of Allegiance before math class" and "Tomorrow we will go to gym *or* music class." Children may wish to discuss whether the promise in your second statement will be broken if you go to gym *and* music tomorrow.

Later, the use of the terms *and* and *or* with Venn diagrams can lead to a more formal study of logic. A **conjunction** (denoted by $p \wedge q$) consists of any two statements joined by *and.* A **disjunction** (denoted by $p \vee q$) consists of any two statements joined by *or.* A **negation** (denoted by $\sim p$) is the statement "it is not true that *p.*" These very basic concepts of formal logic have their beginning in the study of sets.

Objective: to use symbols for union and intersection.

5. After the children are comfortable with the terms *and* and *or* for union and intersection, introduce the symbols for these operations. The symbol $\cup$ is the symbol for **union.** The union of sets *A* and *B* is the set consisting of all the elements in *A or B,* including those in both *A* and *B.* The symbol $\cap$ is the symbol for **intersection.** The intersection of sets *A* and *B* is the set consisting of all elements common to both *A and B.*

Using the same materials used in the previous two activities or attribute materials that the children have created for themselves, let the children begin to work problems such as "Shade the sections in your Venn diagram for yellow objects $\cup$ triangular objects" or "Point to the section for yellow objects $\cap$ triangular objects." Remember that the concepts of union and intersection are more important than the symbols. Don't overemphasize the symbols with young children.

Objective: to form Venn diagrams using negations of attributes.

6. After children can form Venn diagrams with two intersecting loops, try forming Venn diagrams using the negations of the attributes. Put all the pieces that are not male in one section and the pieces that are not red in the other. Ask the children to describe the intersection. Is it the same thing to say "the pieces are not male and not red" as it is to say "the pieces are not male and red"? Where do you find the pieces that are not male or red? Try this activity for yourself. You will find that it is not easy to use the familiar terms *and, or,* and *not* properly in combinations. Note that when you are using the negation of a statement, it is important to identify the universal set. This is the original set of objects under consideration. For example, if your universal set is the set of People Pieces, the red females are not blue and not male, but you do not need to consider red triangles.

After children are familiar with Venn diagrams and the terms and symbols for union and intersection, use Venn diagrams with more than two loops. These diagrams will be difficult for children in the Piagetian preoperational stage, so they are better used with older children. If older children have not had previous experience with Venn diagrams, let them first experience the activities described earlier.

ACTIVITIES

Intermediate (4–6)

Objective: to classify attribute materials according to three intersecting characteristics.

1. Set up a three-loop Venn diagram for the attribute shapes, such as the one shown in Figure 5–25. Ask the children to place the pieces in the proper locations. Are all of the pieces inside the loops? Does each section have more than one piece?

   Completely describe the characteristics of all the pieces in each section. Note that you can tell the color, shape, and size of the pieces in each section if you use the negations of some of the attributes. For example, the pieces in section (a) in Figure 5–25 are red, not squares, and not small. Ask the children to describe the pieces in each section in a similar fashion.

   Encourage the children to create other Venn diagrams using attribute materials they have created. Describe the pieces in each section of the Venn diagrams.

2. Ask a group of children to secretly draw a three-loop Venn diagram. Arrange the yarn into three intersecting loops and ask the children with the secret diagram to place four or five pieces in the correct sections. The children who have not seen the diagram should attempt to place each of the other pieces in a loop by asking the children with the diagram if they have chosen the correct section. After all of the pieces are correctly positioned, the children who placed the pieces should identify the proper labels for the three loops.

In the beginning, use only positive attributes for all three loops and choose attributes so that all sections contain elements of the set. For children who understand the concepts well and really want a challenge, use negations and nonintersecting sets.

Middle Grades (6–8)

Objective: to use intersection of sets to solve everyday problems.

1. Give the students a problem such as the following involving numbers from your classroom. Give students the following three question survey and use the results to make a Venn diagram puzzle such as this one.

   Do you like math? _____

   Do you like to play soccer? _____

   Do you like to read? _____

   The results of the survey showed that 20 people like math, 15 like to play soccer, and 24 like to read. Ten people like to play soccer and also like to read, 12 people like both math and reading, and 8 people like math and like to play soccer. Five people said that they liked all three activities, and 2 people said that they did not like any of the activities. How many people were in the total survey? (Note that the people who liked all three activities were also included in the groups that liked two activities, and these people were included in the groups that liked each individual activity.) Use a Venn diagram such as the one in Figure 5–26 to show your results.

   After solving this problem, students should conduct their own surveys and make their own Venn diagram puzzles.

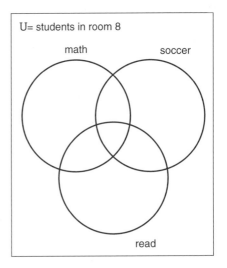

Figure 5–25

Figure 5–26

Objective: to understand the meaning of the complement of a set and to use the symbol for complement.

3. A **complement of a set** consists of all the elements in the universal set that are not elements of the set under consideration. For example, the complement of the triangles in the set of attribute blocks are all the attribute blocks that are not triangles. The children should be familiar with this concept through the use of negations. Two different symbols may be used to denote the complement. The complement of set A may be shown as A' or as $\bar{A}$. This notation is usually read as "the complement of A."

The following activity uses the A' notation. Set up a Venn diagram for the attribute blocks such as the one in Figure 5–27 and label each section as shown.

Ask the children to list the letters designating the sections for various sets and their complements. For example, give the sections for each of the following:

red pieces	red pieces ∩ triangles
(red pieces)′	(red pieces ∩ triangles)′
red pieces ∪ triangles	red pieces′ ∪ triangles′
(red pieces ∪ triangles)′	red pieces′ ∩ triangles′

Which of the above are the same sections? State the characteristics of each of the above sections in words rather than symbols, such as "not red and triangles" is the same as "not red or not triangles." This may be stated formally as "the union of the complements is equal to the complement of the intersections" and "the intersection of the complements is equal to the complement of the union." These are known as **de Morgan's laws.** These concepts are fairly complicated and students will need a great deal of experience working with concrete materials before being able to state the properties abstractly.

The activities using either People Pieces or attribute shapes may also be performed using any set of structured attribute materials, such as those made for the seasons or holidays. Encourage children to use their own sets of materials whenever possible.

Another embodiment of these concepts exists in some computer programs. Three programs that reinforce several of the concepts in this section are *Logical Journey of the Zoombinis, Tabletop Jr.,* and *Escape from the Logic Spiders*. Skills that these develop include identifying, sorting and ordering by attributes (*Logical Journey of the Zoombinis* and *Tabletop Jr.*) and applying logical deductive and conditional reasoning (*Escape from the Logic Spiders*).

Tabletop, Jr. gives primary students an opportunity to develop mathematical concepts of attributes, sorting, statistics, and graphing as they manipulate on-screen materials such as attribute blocks, pizzas, and party hats. The program has 50 challenges with games and puzzles involving such things as putting attribute blocks in Venn diagrams and party hats in Carroll diagrams.

The *Logical Journey of the Zoombinis* was developed for students in grades 4 through middle school. One of the puzzles, Mudball Wall, can be played on-line at http://www.broderbund.com/frames.html?/demo /shockwave. In this game, students try to determine which shape and color of mudballs will move the Zoombinis to safety by determining patterns in a Carroll diagram-type puzzle on three levels of difficulty. Students can play for the highest score on-line as they build their logical reasoning skills. In all, the program contains 12 different puzzles, many based on analyzing attributes of Zoombinis that have 5 choices of eyes, noses, hair, and feet, thus allowing for $5 \times 5 \times 5 \times 5$ or 625 different Zoombinis.

Escape from the Logic Spiders was developed for students a bit older than those who might play the *Logical Journey of the Zoombinis,* although older students might wish to play either game. This game contains 50 activities that require students to answer questions involving logical reasoning with implications and conditional statements. Students must analyze statements involving "and," "or," "some," "all," and "if, then" to avoid the traps set by the logic spiders.

Estimating

Even though the activities described in this chapter often do not require the use of numbers, children should still be asked to estimate and predict. Estimation and prediction skills prove to be invaluable for a wide variety of problem-solving activities, including those involving numbers. The activities in this section describe some ways in which the teacher may encourage the children to estimate and predict.

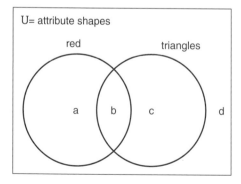

Figure 5–27

ACTIVITIES

Primary (K–3)

Objective: to predict the total set of attribute materials when shown a few.

1. Choose a set of attribute materials the children have not seen before. Put the pieces in a paper bag and take them out one at a time. Ask the children to observe the properties of each piece. After the children have seen three or four pieces, ask them to describe a piece they believe is still in the bag. Remind the children that in this set of attribute pieces, no two pieces are identical but there is one piece for each possible combination of crucial attributes. For example, you may have a set of shapes that are red, blue, and green; large, medium, and small; and circles, triangles, and squares. After the children have seen a large blue square, a medium red triangle, and a small green circle, they may predict that there is still a small green square in the bag. Continue the activity until the children have predicted all the pieces in the set. Ask them how they knew what pieces were still in the bag.

Objective: to predict what the distinguishing characteristics will be in a set of attribute materials.

2. Again, choose a set of attribute materials the children have not seen. Choose attributes that can be distinguished by feel, such as shape, texture, and size. You may wish to make your set from scraps of material. Cut three different shapes using four different types of material, such as silk, felt, cotton, and wool. Paste the materials onto a sheet of cardboard in a Carroll diagram such as the one shown in Figure 5–28.

   Have the children feel three or four of the pieces without looking and predict what pieces will be in the other positions. After they have predicted one other piece, let them feel that piece if they were correct and

then predict another piece. The children may look at the Carroll diagram only after all the pieces have been predicted. Let them discuss their strategies and determine whether or not they could have used any better ones.

Intermediate (4–6)

Objective: to predict the total number of objects in a set.

1. Even though the emphasis in this chapter is on activities that do not require the use of numbers, work with sets and Carroll diagrams is a good introduction to the Cartesian product concept of multiplication. Older children who have worked with attribute materials should not only be able to describe the pieces that should be in an attribute set, but should also be able to predict the total number of pieces in a set after they are aware of all the distinguishing attributes. Again, choose a set of attribute materials the children have not seen.

   Put the pieces in a paper bag and take them out to show the children one at a time. Ask the children to observe the attributes and to guess how many pieces are still in the bag. Encourage the children to draw Carroll or tree diagrams to aid in their predictions.

   After the children have tried predicting a few times, they may be able to give you a formula for determining the total number of pieces in a set of attribute materials. To do so, they must find the number of attributes in each pertinent category and multiply those numbers together. This is the **Cartesian product** concept of multiplication. To find the cardinality of the Cartesian product of two sets, match each element of the first set with each element of the second set. For instance, if a set has four shapes and three sizes, the total number of pieces in the set would be 4×3, or 12, pieces.

Objective: to estimate and use the cardinality of the Cartesian product to find the total number of combinations.

2. Children may wish to find the total number of different combinations for several familiar circumstances. Tell the children stories about events in everyday life that involve Cartesian products, and ask the children to estimate the number of possible combinations. Let the children figure out the exact number using their formula, a tree, or a Carroll diagram after they have estimated. Some ideas for stories follow:
   - Amy received 3 new pairs of pants and 4 new blouses for Christmas. She can wear each of her pants with each blouse. She plans to wear one pair of the pants to school each day with one of the blouses. How many days can Amy go to school wearing a new combination each day? How many different combinations would Amy have if she also received 2 new sweaters, and each sweater goes with each outfit?

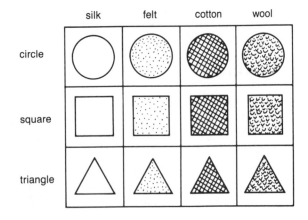

Figure 5–28

- José got a job working in an ice cream parlor. His favorite task is making ice cream sundaes. He likes to make up new combinations. The store has 12 kinds of ice cream, 4 kinds of toppings, and 3 kinds of nuts. How many different sundaes can José make if he puts one dip of ice cream, one topping, and one kind of nut on each sundae?
- Suzanna is in charge of making up names for a new kind of doll. She has decided on 20 good first names, 15 middle names, and 25 last names. How many different names can she make up if each doll gets a first, a middle, and a last name?

Be sure the children estimate before they actually figure out the number of combinations. Many of the children will be surprised at the large number of possibilities. Let the children make up their own stories involving combinations for each other.

Solving and Creating Problems

As you have probably noticed, this chapter contains suggestions for both problem solving and problem creating. Throughout the book, you will see emphasis on the development of children's ability to think. In this section, we present even more ideas for helping children create their own mathematical problems as well as for encouraging them to solve problems created for them.

ACTIVITIES

Primary (K–3)

Objective: to sequence attribute materials according to likenesses and differences.

1. Give the students a set of People Pieces and tell them that the pieces are going to have a parade. The people have strict rules for their parades. They must march in single file. Anyone may lead the parade, but the next person in line must have one attribute the same as the first person and three attributes different. Each person in line must have one attribute the same and three attributes different when compared with the person directly in front of him or her. The only attributes they may use are sex, height, weight, and color.
   - *Understanding the problem.* Each person in the parade matches the person that follows in only one of the four attributes. If only one attribute is the same, the other three will be different. For example, the tall, skinny, blue male could follow the tall, stout, red female because both are tall.

- *Devising a plan.* Try to use all the tall people first, then change to short people (guess and check).
- *Carrying out the plan.* Look for a tall, stout, red female. There are no more, so change the attributes that will be the same for each new piece. Experiment by putting a short, stout, red male next. That works! Continue to add pieces by changing the attributes that are the same.
- *Looking back.* Check to make sure that all of the People Pieces have been used and that each piece is the same in one way and different in three.

To make the activity even more difficult, have the paraders march in a circle so that the first and last people in line also match according to the rules. After the children have tried the parade with the People Pieces, ask them to line up sets they have made using their own rules. They may challenge other students to discover the rules they used and to find one or two pieces out of order.

Objective: to place attribute materials on a network according to a given number of differences among various pieces.

2. Give the children a set of attribute blocks and a network similar to the one in Figure 5–29. The children should play this game in two teams. The play starts with one attribute block placed in the center of the diagram. The first team then places an attribute block adjacent to the first one and scores one point for each difference from the first block in color, shape, or size. Teams alternate placing blocks on the diagram and add the number of different attributes on each turn. If a block has lines connecting it to two or more blocks already in place, that team's score is the total

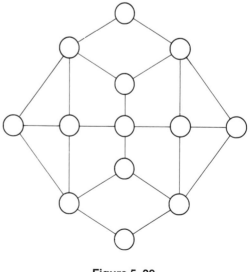

Figure 5–29

number of differences from all the adjoining blocks. Play continues until all of the spaces on the board are filled. The team with the most differences wins.

Students may vary the game by using their own sets of attribute materials. After students have played the game a few times, discuss with them strategies for winning, which should include offensive as well as defensive moves.

3. Network solitaire may be played using a network board similar to the one shown in Figure 5–30. In this diagram, the number of lines between two positions indicates the number of differences there must be between the two connecting attribute blocks. Students may work on this activity alone or in small groups.

The students begin by placing an attribute block anywhere on the diagram and then trying to place other blocks, moving away from the first one according to the number of differences. The activity is complete when all of the spaces on the diagram have been correctly filled with blocks.

Students may check each other or the teacher may check them. As with many problem-solving activities, there are several correct answers. Students may make up networks for each other to solve. Some networks may be impossible, and students should discuss why certain combinations do not work.

Children who have worked with the activities just described and wish for a greater challenge may try some of the following activities. Children who have not tried the previous activities should work through the easier activities before attempting the more difficult ones.

ACTIVITIES

Intermediate and Middle (4–8)

Objective: to place attribute materials in an array according to the number of likenesses and differences between adjoining pieces.

1. This activity is similar to the parade described above. In this case, the People Pieces all wish to move into a 4-by-4 apartment house such as the one in Figure 5–31. The People Pieces are very particular about their neighbors. Each piece can differ in only one attribute from anyone living to the right, to the left, above, or below; its other three attributes must be the same as those of each of its neighbors. As the children work on placing the People Pieces in the array, they may realize that simply using trial and error can become quite frustrating. Remind them that there are other effective problem-solving strategies, such as looking for a pattern.

This activity is also effective with the attribute blocks or other attribute materials. The students may vary the rules so the pieces have two or three differences. Be aware that not all rules are possible, especially with the People Pieces, which only have two choices for each category of differences.

Objective: to choose the correct attribute block with the use of deductive reasoning and questioning.

2. Using a set of attribute blocks, the leader secretly chooses one of the blocks and the rest of the class tries to guess which block it is by questioning the leader. The class may ask only questions of the form, "Does it have any of the attributes of ?" (describing the size, color, and shape of one block).

Figure 5–30

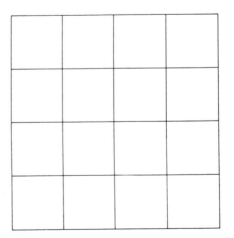

Figure 5–31

Suppose the block is a small red triangle. If someone asks whether the block chosen is small, red, or a triangle, the leader will answer, "Yes, it has at least one of those characteristics." The leader does not tell the class if they guess the secret block. If the block has none of the characteristics guessed, the leader will answer, "No, it does not have any of those characteristics." Play continues until the class is sure which one is the secret block. One person in the class must announce, "I know which block it is." If the rest of the class agrees, then that person may describe the block. If the person is correct, he or she may become the next leader.

After the children have played one or two games, let them discuss the strategies they use. Would they prefer to get a no or a yes answer? How do they eliminate a size, shape, or color?

Objective: to use the properties of isomorphic sets to solve problems involving patterns.

3. Two systems are **isomorphic** if they have the same structure and the same internal set of relationships. Isomorphic sets must be equivalent and the patterns in two isomorphic sets must be the same. The sets shown in Figure 5–32 are isomorphic. The pieces may be put in one-to-one correspondence and they relate to each other in the same way. After the children have worked with simple isomorphic sets, they may work with more detailed sets. Construct a set of attribute materials that are isomorphic to the People Pieces. This means that the pieces must have four sets of distinguishing characteristics with two choices for each.

Make a set of sailboats with purple or green sails, with small or large sails, with a sailor or without, with an anchor or without. After the sailboats are constructed, place the sailboats in a 4-by-4 Carroll diagram next to the People Pieces, which are also in a 4-by-4 Carroll diagram. The diagrams may be similar to the ones shown in Figure 5–33.

Do not put labels on the diagrams. Ask the children to decide on the labels for the Carroll diagram for the People Pieces. Tell the children that the sailboats are isomorphic to the People Pieces and you want them to discover the matching labels for the set of sailboats. For instance, the positions that have males in the diagram for the People Pieces all have purple sails in the diagram for the sailboats. Ask the children to finish the following chart, which asks them to match all the characteristics:

males	purple sails
females	_____
red	_____
blue	_____
tall	_____
short	_____
skinny	_____
stout	_____

After the children have matched the characteristics, ask them to develop their own sets of materials that are isomorphic to either the People Pieces or the attribute blocks. A group of students making up a new set should write down the corresponding characteristics and then turn over each piece of the newly created set so that the characteristics of the set are not visible but the set remains in

Figure 5–32

Figure 5–33

the same Carroll diagram. A group of students who have not seen the new set should then turn the pieces over one at a time and attempt to predict the matching characteristics. Keep track of how many pieces have been turned over before all the characteristics have been identified and matched. The fewer pieces used, the better.

This section gives only a brief idea of the many problems that may be developed using mathematical concepts that often do not involve numbers. Children should be encouraged to develop problems of their own for each other to solve. The classroom should always have a special table or bulletin board that contains problems for the children and a place for the children to suggest new ideas.

Grouping Students for Mathematical Thinking

Many of the activities described in this chapter are best done in a small group or with a partner. While students are solving problems and learning to think mathematically, they need to express their reasoning to other students as well as to the teacher. Young children may work best with only one or two others, while older students might work in slightly larger groups.

Many of the games described that use attribute materials require two teams of students. Each team sets up problems and puzzles and then gives them to the other team to solve. It is helpful if each team has at least two students so they may discuss the strategies and techniques that they are using to solve the puzzle. Teams larger than four students would probably be unwieldy and might not give everyone a chance to fully discuss their thinking processes. This discussion is very useful

not only in helping students learn from each other but also in helping them clarify their own reasoning.

Many of the activities can be presented to the students as a single group initially with time then given for them to work in groups on the solution. The teacher should move from group to group as students are working to monitor student progress and to ask questions that cause the students to think about their solutions. After groups have arrived at one or more solutions, they can gather together as a class to compare the methods they used.

Communicating Learning of Mathematical Thinking Processes

Kindergartners and first graders may communicate much of their reasoning verbally. When the class gets together as one group to discuss processes used, the teacher might assist younger groups in recording their results on an experience chart or graph. Second through fourth graders should record not only the solutions to problems but also the methods that they used. They can trace around attribute blocks and draw pictures of People Pieces to record their solutions to those problems. Middle school students may want to generalize their solutions to specific attribute problems to include general strategies for any similar problems. These might be recorded in students' daily journals or expanded upon to include in a portfolio of the students' best work.

If you have a video camera available, students may want to record some of their work visually. Good problems to videotape include those in which the students themselves are an integral part of the problem, such as making patterns and sets using the attributes of the children in the classroom or discussing relationships as they role play the parents and children in a family.

Encourage children to look for examples of observing and inferring, comparing, classifying, and sequencing at home or to discuss with adults in their lives how these skills are used in their work. Students can discuss their findings with others in the class. You might make a bulletin board to display a list of ways people use these skills at work, such as the librarian's use of the Dewey Decimal System, a store manager's inventory system, or a restaurant manager's method of inferring the amount of hamburger to order each week.

Connecting Learning of Mathematical Thinking

Mrs. Meier's primary class had just finished reading *Frog and Toad Are Friends* by Arnold Lobel. Latisha states that her favorite chapter was "The Lost Button," in which Toad loses a button and Frog's and Toad's other friends keep finding buttons that do not belong to him. Toad's button was big, white, round, thick, and had four holes. His friends found buttons that were small, black, square, thin, and with two holes. Latisha asks if she can write a story about losing one of the sea shells from her collection. She decides to pick one that is small, spiral-shaped, pink, and unbroken. Mrs. Meier suggests that Latisha might want to illustrate her story with pictures of the different types of shells that are featured in the story.

When Julie, Juanita, and Tommy hear the story about Frog and Toad, they decide that they would like to play a game using the buttons in the button box. Julie secretly chooses one of the buttons, and Juanita and Tommy point to different buttons that they think might be the right one. If the button is not right, Julie must give one reason why it is not the right button. For example, if Julie picks a small, square, brown button with four holes when Juanita points to a large, green, square button with four holes, Julie may say, "No, that is not my button because my button is not large." After several guesses, Tommy points to the correct button, and it is his turn to choose the secret button.

Other students in the class chose different activities related to classifying after reading about Toad's button. After sharing their activities with each other, it was evident that all students had made connections between the literature that they were reading and mathematical thinking.

In Ms. Baker's sixth grade, students are studying about leaves in their science class. They are making a leaf notebook with sections for different types of leaves.

Dan decides to classify his leaves as simple or compound. He then subdivides each section into smooth, toothed or lobed types of edges. Each of these is then further subdivided into the type of vein pattern, either pinnate, parallel, or palmate. After the notebook has several types of leaves, Dan decides to make a tree diagram to show the subdivisions. This is added to the table of contents to show the leaves in the notebook visually. Dan can quickly identify the American Basswood leaf as being a simple leaf, with a toothed leaf-edge and a pinnate vein type.

Assessing Learning of Mathematical Thinking

There are many ways in which to assess learning. A paper-and-pencil test is one way to assess learning; however, it may not be the most appropriate method of assessment for young children. Other methods should be used.

As found by Dossey, Mullis, and Jones (1993, p. 2), "On extended constructed-response tasks, which required students to solve problems requiring a greater depth of understanding and then explain, at some length, specific features of their solutions, the average percentage of students producing satisfactory or better responses was 16 percent at grade 4, 8 percent at grade 8, and 9 percent at grade 12." This demonstrates that even though problem solving has been the focus of mathematics teachers for at least the last 25 years, we have a long way to go in helping students become proficient at this. As noted by Lester (1994), "We may have learned quite a lot about how students learn to solve problems and how problem solving can be taught, but we have not learned enough." We must continue to emphasize not only the problem solving, but also the reflection and writing that should accompany it.

As children are solving the problems mentioned in this chapter, the teacher should make regular observations and keep track of them in a log or on a chart. The teacher should make notes of which skills children have mastered and which the children still need to work on. This may be done by using codes on a chart to show the level of mastery for each skill and by keeping anecdotal records for individual children. In addition to watching children work problems, the teacher should note the problems that the children have created. These may be assessed for clarity, appropriateness, and complexity. Children may also aid in the assessment by keeping personal logs noting which tasks they feel confident in doing and which tasks they are challenged by. Children may also mention the other children who have been helpful in explaining certain tasks and who they feel make up good problems. A portfolio containing samples of student work from the beginning, middle, and end of a unit is very useful for both the teacher and the student in noting progress. The form in Figure 5–34 may be included in the portfolio.

The teacher should test the children on certain Piagetian tasks to determine readiness for some of the problems mentioned in this chapter. The children's ability to understand the logic of classification is necessary for many of these problems. This includes testing the children's ability to use additive, hierarchical, and multiple classifications, testing their understanding of class inclusion, and testing their ability to seriate (to arrange in a series).

Additive classification requires children to place objects in categories according to their likenesses and differences. Children should be given a set such as the attribute blocks and asked to group them so that each group is alike in some way. If they can group the blocks according to one criterion, such as shape, they should be asked if there is another way to do it. Preoperational children may use trial and error to group the objects and may not be able to think of more than one or two ways to group them. Concrete operational children will not use trial and

error and will be able to group the objects according to shape, size, and color. Preoperational children need many experiences sorting a variety of objects according to one or two attributes. Concrete operational children are ready to move on to hierarchical classification.

For **hierarchical classification,** it is necessary for children to consider a whole and its parts at the same time. Children must realize that a yellow daisy is both a daisy and a flower. If children are shown eight daisies and two roses and asked if there are more daisies or more flowers, preoperational children will respond that there are more daisies. The children are comparing the daisies to the roses, rather than comparing the daisies to all of the flowers, of which the daisies are one part. Concrete operational children respond correctly.

In **multiple classification,** each item belongs to two or more classes at once. The book *How Many Snails?* by Paul Giganti is a good introduction to multiple classification for young children. To answer the questions raised in the book, children must realize that the objects in the picture belong to more than one category; some of the clouds are also gray and some of the snails also have patterns. Multiple classification may involve

---

Sample
INDIVIDUAL PORTFOLIO RECORD SHEET

Attach this sheet to a sample of a problem you have created or solved either by yourself or in a group. Comment on your strengths and weaknesses and on any other student who may have been helpful in your problem-solving process.

STUDENT COMMENTS

I FEEL I DID WELL WHEN I . . .

I HAD SOME PROBLEMS WHEN I . . .

I AM STILL UNSURE OF . . .

_____ HELPED ME BY . . .

TEACHER'S COMMENTS: (include clarity, appropriateness, complexity, accuracy, persistence, and variety of solutions attempted)

Figure 5–34

solving a matrix problem such as the one in Figure 5–35. The children must notice both that the color is constant in a row and that the shape is constant in a column in order to find the missing piece.

Young preoperational children are often able to solve both two- and three-property matrices but cannot justify their solutions. They appear to solve the problems based on the visual clues. Slightly older preoperational children have more difficulty solving the problems because they try to reason out the answer rather than simply placing the piece that "looks right." They find two-property items easier to work with than three-property items. Concrete operational children can solve both two- and three-property problems and can give you the reasons for the solutions.

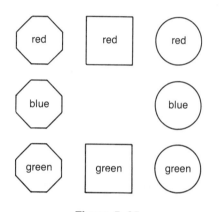

Figure 5–35

Children of all ages can be given matrix problems and encouraged to discuss their solutions. Teachers can judge from the discussions whether the children are thinking *logically* (they can give a reason for their solution) or *graphically* (they simply say that it looks right).

Class inclusion includes being able to distinguish between objects that belong to and objects that are similar to, being able to correctly use the terms *some* and *all*, and being able to distinguish the object that is different. These terms are used extensively in the problems in this chapter, and the teacher needs to determine if the children have a solid understanding of each term before proceeding with the activities.

Seriation is arranging objects in order and must be understood before children can proceed with the activities involving patterns and sequencing. Young preoperational children may be able to distinguish size differences in two objects but are unable to sequence a whole line of objects. Older preoperational children may be able to sequence objects in a line or may be able to put the frames of a cartoon in the correct order but cannot place objects in an array, which requires them to sequence both vertically and horizontally at the same time. Many concrete operational children can sequence two variables simultaneously in an array.

Teachers may see Copeland (1982) or Lowery (1986) for more ideas on both testing and teaching children based on their Piagetian stages. A sample recordkeeping form for use with these Piagetian tasks is shown in Figure 5–36.

Name	Additive Classification	Hierarchical Classification	Multiple Classification	Class Inclusion	Seriation	Comments

Sample Class Assessment Form

Key
N—not begun
B—begun
M—mastered

Figure 5–36 Sample Class Assessment Form

Something for Everyone

The activities described in this chapter are for children with different learning styles and abilities. Children should use materials that suit their strengths and should also explore other modes of learning in order to develop all of their abilities.

For visual learners, seeing and drawing what they are learning is quite helpful. Visual learners enjoy the computer activities that show prenumber concepts such as classification and seriation. They should be encouraged to draw the answers to problems with attribute materials and to create new sets of materials in which they draw the elements they have created. They should make Carroll, tree, and Venn diagrams and add the elements that solve the problems. They may also pose new problems for other children by drawing them.

Tactile/kinesthetic children prefer to solve attribute problems by actually manipulating the materials. If they are working on the computer, they may wish to have a set of concrete materials available to manipulate that match those on the computer screen. They can re-create the problem from the computer with their own pieces. Even without the actual pieces, they enjoy the computer activities if they can move the pieces on the screen with a mouse or other device, although they may prefer Carroll, Venn, and tree diagrams made from string or drawn on a large sheet of posterboard so that they may place the attribute shapes or People Pieces directly on the diagram. They may wish to create new attribute sets from clay or collect household objects for their sets. They may pose problems for other students by creating a model.

Auditory learners wish to solve attribute problems by talking about the problems and their solutions. They prefer written or verbal directions to drawings or models. They prefer writing down "small yellow circle" to drawing a picture of one. They prefer computer programs that contain detailed written directions to pictures and diagrams. They feel more comfortable working with computer programs if they have read or discussed the manual first. They may wish to create problems by writing them or taping them on an audio tape rather than by drawing pictures or making a model. They may need to talk to themselves as they work on difficult problems.

Gifted children should be encouraged to explore topics in greater depth. One good topic is that of formal logic. Children who have a good understanding of the concepts of union and intersection may move from studying those ideas to the concepts of disjunctions and conjunctions. Computer programs such as *The Secret Island of Dr. Quandary* from The Learning Company and *What's My Logic* from Critical Thinking Books and Software, and numerous activity books from companies such as Cuisenaire/Dale Seymour Publications, Carson-Dellosa,

and Creative Publications, include interesting problems and activities designed to teach children to think logically (the addresses are given in Appendix A). Many of the activities can be used by all children, but many others are challenging for even the most gifted students.

Students with a good grasp of logical reasoning will enjoy reading *Anno's Hat Trick* and books from the math game series by Mitsumasa Anno. *Anno's Hat Trick* begins with simple logical reasoning puzzles but the problems soon become challenging even for teachers. Many of the games in the math game series involve such things as using a Carroll diagram to determine how many different outfits can be made by varying hats, shirts, pants, socks, and shoes that each come in five different colors. Gifted children should enjoy the challenge of solving the problems and creating new ones for each other. Don't restrict them to the age levels suggested for the problems. Children should be encouraged to move at their own speed with these activities. Let the children's interests and abilities determine the problems on which they work.

This should also be true for any children having difficulty. There is no reason a 10-year-old should not do activities suggested for the primary grades if the child is more comfortable on that level. The child may simply need more maturation or more experience before he or she is ready for more advanced activities. To determine the cause of the problem, take time to talk to any children having trouble. It could be that the children have not reached the proper level of Piagetian development or that they are not operating in their strongest mode. Children whose strengths lie in holistic or spatial processing may be frustrated trying to work problems in a logical step-by-step sequence. These children may need to see the total picture and then "mess around" with the materials. They may need to be allowed to solve a problem using a method or methods quite different from any the teacher has suggested.

Children who are stronger at linear, sequential processing may be frustrated by a very broad, open-ended problem. They may wish for a very specific problem with a definite sequence of steps to follow. All children should be encouraged to develop their strengths but should also work with children with different strengths in order to develop an appreciation and understanding of other styles. Good problem solvers can choose and use the style best suited to the problem.

KEY IDEAS

The thought processes that children should develop in their mathematics classes are very important. In Chapter 5, we have presented four major thought processes that should be developed beginning even before children learn number concepts and should be continued throughout the elementary and middle grades. Children should observe, compare, classify, and sequence, beginning with a variety of concrete materials such as attribute blocks, People Pieces, or teacher- and student-made collections of objects. Computer programs for developing the concepts can also be quite useful. Later, children should abstract concepts from the work that set a solid foundation for the development of number concepts.

Ideas learned concretely in the primary grades can be formalized and practiced using models such as Carroll, tree, and Venn diagrams. Properties of nonnumerical relationships are useful in later work with numbers. Throughout the activities, children should be encouraged to propose and solve problems. The emphasis should be on levels of thinking that go beyond memorization. The children's own development of thought should be the basis for instruction.

Skills should be informally identified, with a great deal of attention paid to the children's developmental levels. Individual learning styles should also be taken into account when planning lessons.

DISCUSSION QUESTIONS

1. Choose two or three primary mathematics programs and analyze them for their teaching of observing, inferring, comparing, classifying, and sequencing. Using what you know about children's development levels, which program do you think best teaches these skills? Justify your reasoning.

2. Read *How Many Snails? A Counting Book* by Paul Giganti to a six- or seven-year-old child. Ask the child to make up a new page of her own following the pattern of the pages in the book. Analyze the child's work to determine if she understands the principles of additive, hierarchical, and multiple classification.

3. Choose two or three Piagetian tasks and present them to two children in the same grade who have different levels of mathematical proficiency. You may choose tasks from this chapter or find others in books such as *It's the Thought that Counts: A Sourcebook of Mathematics Activities Related to Conservation Abilities* and *Mathematics and the Elementary Teacher.* Based upon the results of the tasks, for what types of mathematical thinking is each child prepared?

4. Play one of the computer games from the reference list and analyze the mathematical reasoning that is required to play the game. If possible, ask a child to play the same game, and compare the reasoning that the child uses in playing the game to your own methods.

REFERENCES

Anno, Mitsumasa, *Anno's Faces.* New York, NY: Philomel, 1989.

————, *Socrates and the Three Little Pigs.* New York, NY: Philomel, 1986.

————, *Anno's Hat Trick.* New York, NY: Philomel, 1985.

————, *Anno's Math Games.* New York, NY: Philomel, 1982.

Atkinson, Sue, *Mathematics with Reason: The Emergent Approach to Primary Maths.* Portsmouth, NH: Heinemann, 1992.

Bamberger, Honi J., Brenda H. Hammond, and Josepha Robles, *LogicTalk Poster Puzzles.* Mountain View, CA: Creative Publications, 1994.

Berenstain, Michael, *Faster, Slower, Higher, Lower.* Racine, WI: Western Publishing, 1991.

Burger, William F., and J. Michael Shaughnessy, "Characterizing the van Hiele Levels of Development in Geometry," *Journal for Research in Mathematics Education,* 17, no. 1 (January 1986), 31–48.

Carpenter, Thomas P., "Research on the Role of Structure in Thinking," *Arithmetic Teacher,* 32, no. 6 (February 1985), 58–60.

Charles, Linda H., *Thinkertasks Jobcards.* Sunnyvale, CA: Creative Publications, 1990 (Series includes Logical Lineups, Crazy Collections and Rebus Rally).

Cole, Joanna, *The Magic School Bus Inside the Earth.* New York, NY: Scholastic, 1987.

Coombs, Betty, and Lalie Harcourt, *Explorations 2.* Don Mills, ON: Addison-Wesley, 1986.

Copeland, Richard W., *Mathematics and the Elementary Teacher,* 4th ed. Englewood Cliffs, NJ: Merrill/Prentice Hall, 1982.

Cruikshank, Douglas E., David L. Fitzgerald, and Linda R. Jensen, *Young Children Learning Mathematics.* Boston: Allyn & Bacon, 1980.

Davidson, Patricia S., *Teaching Activities with Attrilinks.* New Rochelle, NY: Cuisenaire Company of America, 1990.

Dienes, Zoltan P., and E. W. Golding, *Learning Logic. Logical Games.* New York: Herder & Herder, 1966.

Dossey, John A., Ina V. S. Mullis, and C. O. Jones, "Can Students Do Mathematical Problem Solving? Results from Constructed-Response Questions in NAEP's 1992 Mathematics Assessment" (Report No. 23-FR01). Washington, DC: Government Printing Office, 1993.

Downie, Diane, Twila Slesnick, and Jean Kerr Stenmark, *Math for Girls and Other Problem Solvers.* Berkeley, CA: Math/Science Network, Lawrence Hall of Science, University of California, 1981.

Ganeri, Anita, *The Biggest and Smallest.* Hauppauge, NY: Barron's, 1992.

————, *The Fastest and Slowest.* Hauppauge, NY: Barron's, 1992.

————, *The Longest and Tallest.* Hauppauge, NY: Barron's, 1992.

Gibb, Glenadine, and Alberta Castaneda, "Experiences for Young Children," in *Mathematics Learning in Early Childhood.* National Council of Teachers of Mathematics, 37th Yearbook. Reston, VA: NCTM, 1975.

Giganti, Paul, Jr., *How Many Snails? A Counting Book.* New York: Greenwillow, 1988.

Goodnow, Judy, *Cooperative Problem Solving with Attribute Blocks.* Sunnyvale, CA: Creative Publications, 1989.

Graham, Amanda, *Angus Thought He Was Big.* Hicksville, NY: Newbridge Communications, 1991.

Guarino, Deborah, *Is Your Mama a Llama?* New York: Scholastic, 1989.

Hill, Warren, and Ronald Edwards, *Building Thinking Skills.* Pacific Grove, CA: Midwest Publications, 1987.

Holden, Linda, *Thinker Tasks: Critical Thinking Activities.* Mountain View, CA: Creative Publications, 1986.

Holden, Linda, and Ann Roper, *Thinker Games.* Mountain View, CA: Creative Publications, 1987.

Hoogeboom, Shirley, *Animal Attribute Tiles: Activities for Classifying and Sorting.* Mountain View, CA: Creative Publications, 1990.

Hoogeboom, Shirley, and Goodnow, Judy, *Reasoning with Teddy Bear Counters.* Sunnyvale, CA: Creative Publications, 1989.

Hutchins, Pat, *Rosie's Walk.* New York, NY: Scholastic, 1968.

Lester, Frank K., Jr., "Musings about Mathematical Problem-solving Research: 1970–1994," *Journal for Research in Mathematics Education,* 25, no. 6 (December 1994), 660–75.

Lobel, Arnold, *Frog and Toad Are Friends.* New York: HarperCollins, 1970.

Lowery, Lawrence, Carne Barnett, Nancy Dyar, Carol Langbort, Connie Lynch, Evelyn Neufeld, and Walter Smithey, *It's the Thought that Counts: A Sourcebook of Mathematics Activities Related to Conservation Abilities.* Palo Alto, CA: Dale Seymour Publications, 1986.

"Mathematical Thinking (Focus Issue)," *Arithmetic Teacher,* 32, no. 6 (February 1985).

Mueller, Delbert W., "Building a Scope and Sequence for Early Childhood Mathematics," *Arithmetic Teacher,* 33, no. 2 (October 1985), 8–11.

National Council of Teachers of Mathematics, *Curriculum and Evaluation Standards for School Mathematics.* Reston, VA: NCTM, 1989.

National Research Council, *Everybody Counts: A Report to the Nation on the Future of Mathematics Education.* Washington, DC: National Academy Press, 1989.

Nuffield Foundation, *Beginnings.* New York: Wiley, 1967.

Payne, Joseph N., ed., *Mathematics Learning in Early Childhood.* National Council of Teachers of Mathematics, 37th Yearbook. Reston, VA: NCTM, 1975.

Quinn, Robert J., "Developing Conceptual Understanding of Relations and Functions with Attribute Blocks." *Mathematics Teaching in the Middle School,* 3, no. 3 (November–December 1997), 186–190.

Reid, Margarette S., *The Button Box.* New York: Dutton, 1990.

Roper, Ann, *Intermediate Jobcards.* Sunnyvale, CA: Creative Publications, 1989 (Series includes Puzzles with Unifix Cubes).

————, *Primary Jobcards.* Sunnyvale, CA: Creative Publications, 1988 (Series includes: Patterns with Unifix Cubes and Patterns with Learning Links).

Rowan, Thomas E., and Barbara Bourne, *Thinking Like Mathematicians: Putting the K–4 NCTM Standards into Practice.* Portsmouth, NH: Heinemann, 1994.

Sheffield, Linda Jensen, *Intermediate Manipulatives.* Greensboro, NC: Carson-Dellosa, 1994.

Sheffield, Linda Jensen, *Math Manipulatives for the Overhead.* Greensboro, NC: Carson-Dellosa, 1992.

Sheffield, Linda Jensen, *More Math Manipulatives for the Overhead.* Greensboro, NC: Carson-Dellosa, 1993.

Stofac, Valerie J., and Anne Wesely, *Logic Problems for Primary People.* Sunnyvale, CA: Creative Publications, 1987.

Tennyson, Robert D, "Effect of Negative Instances in Concept Acquisition Using a Verbal-Learning Task," *Journal of Educational Psychology,* 64, no. 2 (April 1973), 247–60.

Willcutt, Bob, *Critical and Creative Thinking with Attribute Blocks.* Pacific Grove, CA: Critical Thinking Books and Software, 1998.

Wilson, Patricia S., "Feature Frequency and the Use of Negative Instances in a Geometric Task," *Journal for Research in Mathematics Education,* 17, no. 2 (March 1986), 130–39.

Technology

Baker, Michael, *What's My Logic?* Pacific Grove, CA: Critical Thinking Books and Software, 1990.

————, *Escape from the Logic Spiders.* Pacific Grove, CA: Critical Thinking Books and Software, 1995.

Broderbund, *James Discovers Math.* Novato, CA: Broderbund. (software)

————, *The Tabletop Jr.* Novato, CA: Broderbund. (software)

Burns, Marilyn, *Mathematics: Teaching for Understanding (K to 6).* White Plains, NY: Cuisenaire Company of America, 1992. (three videos and a discussion guide)

Davidson, *Math Blaster Jr.* Torrance, CA: Davidson, 1997. (software)

————, *Math Blaster Mystery: The Great Brain Robbery.* Torrance, CA: Davidson, 1997. (software)

Edmark, *Mighty Math Carnival Countdown.* Orlando, FL: Harcourt Brace, 1996. (software)

————, *Millie's Math House.* Orlando, FL: Harcourt Brace. (software)

————, *Sammy's Science House.* Orlando, FL: Harcourt Brace. (software)

Hancock, Chris, and Scot Osterweil, *Logical Journey of the Zoombinis.* Novato, CA: Broderbund, 1996. (software)

Smith, David A. (producer), *Talking Mathematics: Resource Package for Staff Developers.* Portsmouth, NH: Heinemann, 1996. (seven videotapes and two resource books)

Web Sites

http://ustimss.msu.edu/ *Failing Our Children: Implications of the Third International Mathematics and Science Study.* Approved by the National Science Board, July 28, 1998.

http://www.broderbund.com/frames.html?/demo/shockwave Site for demonstration game from *Logical Journey of the Zoombinis.*

Chapter 6

Attaching Meaning to Numbers

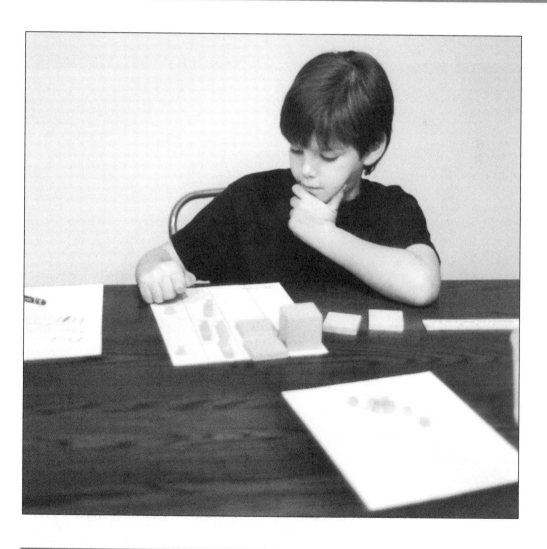

NCTM Standards

GRADES K–4

Standard 5: Estimation

In grades K–4, the curriculum should include estimation so students can—

- Explore estimation strategies;
- Recognize when an estimate is appropriate;
- Determine the reasonableness of results;
- Apply estimation in working with quantities, measurement, computations, and problem solving.

Standard 6: Number Sense and Numeration

In grades K–4, the mathematics curriculum should include whole number concepts and skills so that students can—

- Construct number meanings through real-world experiences and the use of physical materials;
- Understand our numeration system by relating counting, grouping, and place-value concepts;
- Develop number sense;
- Interpret the multiple uses of numbers encountered in the real world.

NCTM (1989), pp. 36, 38. Reprinted by permission.

Think of something you could find 1 million of in your school, home, or community. How will you prove that there are 1 million? Write your plan below for finding 1 million, carry out your plan, and describe your results. As you write out your work, be sure to explain all of your thinking.

As you read the following pages, consider these guiding questions:

1. What are the differences among cardinal, ordinal, and nominal uses of numbers? Describe activities that would help children learn each.

2. How is associating numbers with sets of discrete objects different from associating numbers with measurement? Describe events in everyday life that use numbers in both ways.

3. Why should children learn to recognize small numbers of objects by sight, without counting? How might you help children learn to do this? How can you use combinations and partitioning of sets to help children develop number concepts as you are laying the foundation for addition and subtraction?

4. How could you determine whether a child can conserve numbers and how would you adjust your teaching for a child who does not yet conserve? Describe some common errors that students make as they learn to count and to understand number concepts and place value. How will you use these errors in your lesson planning?

5. What is the difference between rote and rational counting and how should you make use of each?

6. What is the importance of place value to the Hindu-Arabic numeration system, and what is the purpose of teaching about other numeration systems and other bases?

7. Describe proportional and non-proportional materials for teaching place value in base 10 and in other bases. How might you use technology (calculators and computer programs) for these same purposes?

Number concepts begin early in a child's life and extend far beyond being able to count or to recognize numerals. A good foundation in number concepts is crucial in the primary years because it is the basis for much of the work in mathematics throughout the school years and indeed throughout one's life. According to Piaget, children do not acquire number concepts when these concepts are taught to them. They cannot learn arithmetic by internalizing rules or algorithms. They must acquire knowledge by constructing it themselves, not by internalizing it from the environment. Piaget distinguishes between *physical knowledge,* which is present in external objects and includes facts such as weight and color, and *logico-mathematical knowledge,* which consists of relationships that must be constructed by the individual and includes the concept of number. The concept of number takes many years to develop, and children who have mastered number concepts up to 10 may not necessarily have mastered number concepts up to 50 or 100 (Kamii, 1990).

It is almost impossible to live in today's world without encountering numbers. Being able to use and understand numbers is a basic skill that no child or adult can ignore.

Using numbers intelligently is as important, if not more important, than being able to read critically and intelligently. According to the National Research Council:

> Without the ability to understand basic mathematical ideas, one cannot fully comprehend modern writing such as that which appears in the daily newspapers. Numeracy requires more than just familiarity with numbers. To cope confidently with the demands of today's society, one must be able to grasp the implications of mathematical concepts—for example, chance, logic, and graphs—that permeate daily news and routine decisions. Literacy is a moving target, increasing in level with the rising technological demands of society. . . . Mathematical literacy is essential as a foundation for democracy in a technological age. (1989, pp. 7–8)

There are three number concepts with which a child should be familiar: cardinal numbers, ordinal numbers, and the nominal use of numbers. The **cardinal number** of a set tells how many objects are in the set. The **ordinal number** of an object refers to its order in a set, such as first, second, and last; and the **nominal use of a number** is simply the use of a number to name something, such as putting a numeral on a football jersey.

Children encounter these number concepts when very young but often attach little meaning to the numbers they hear or recite. Try this experiment: Close your eyes and think of a tree. Now think of autumn. Think of good-looking. Now think of seventeen. Have you done it? When you thought of a tree did you see a picture in your mind? Did you see pictures for autumn and good-looking? Did you see a picture for "seventeen," or did you see the numeral 17? Why is it that we do not see the letters *g-o-o-d-l-o-o-k-i-n-g,* even though good-looking is a fairly abstract concept, yet we see the numerals for number concepts? Perhaps as children we never truly developed a good foundation in these concepts.

Children should be able to use numbers in their cardinal, ordinal, and nominal senses as well as understand the use of numbers for such measurement ideas as money, time, temperature, length, area, and volume. This chapter contains ideas for using numbers in their cardinal, ordinal, and nominal senses. The measurement chapter includes ideas for those uses of number.

Both parents and teachers should encourage children to use numbers informally whenever possible. You may ask the children to keep a scrapbook of the ways in which numbers are used. You can help the children separate the uses into cardinal, ordinal, nominal, and measurement, with a bulletin board to show the uses the children find.

Encourage children to find the number of objects in a set (the cardinal number). Ask the children to take attendance or the lunch count. Children can help inventory books or count the Cuisenaire rods to make sure none is missing. Parents can ask the children to count the plates, knives, spoons, and forks while setting the table, or to count out prizes for everyone at a party.

Children can use ordinal numbers to find the location of something. Julio can note that he sits in the first row in the fourth seat. This skill can be extended to finding the location of the car in a large parking lot or the location of seats at the circus. Nominal numbers may be noted on the jerseys of the players on the basketball team or used to identify anonymous drawings posted in a display.

Older children can look out for very large numbers. The newspaper reports such things as the national debt or the distance to a newly found star. The *Guinness Book of World Records* reports many interesting facts that the children can challenge each other to discover. They can interview store owners to find how numbers are used to predict future sales.

Children can think of many other interesting projects themselves. Discussion of the uses of numbers should arise naturally throughout the children's day.

As children work with numbers, give them the opportunity to recognize numbers by sight as well as to count. When there are three or four children in a group, the children should be able to look at the group and tell you the number of children in it without stopping to count each child individually. Give the children plenty of opportunities to count larger amounts. Counting can be used for real problems such as those just noted or for contrived problems such as counting the number of times a child can jump rope without missing or the number of stop signs between school and home. Let the children think of other things they would like to count.

Children often have misconceptions when they are learning to count. Here are some examples that typify a child's misunderstanding:

1. If a child sees a group of buttons in a pile and then sees the same buttons spread out, he or she may think that there were fewer buttons when they were piled up.
2. If a child is counting six buttons on the table, the child may point at each of the buttons, but may count to 10 before reaching the last button.
3. A child may miss certain items or recount them, especially when counting items placed in a circle or spread out randomly.
4. If you ask a child to give you three apples, he or she may give you only the third apple counted.

Parents and teachers should be aware of these difficulties as they help children attach meaning to numbers. Many good commercial materials exist, but parents and teachers should also take advantage of materials in the child's environment such as dried beans or peas for counting and coffee stirrers for regrouping. Useful commercial materials include Cuisenaire rods, multibase blocks, chips for trading, abaci, dot cards, interlocking cubes, counters, counting sticks, some computer programs, and calculators. The specific material is not as important as using some physical or visual material to represent the concept. We must realize that 17 is not just the numeral we visualize or just the word we say after 16.

Developing Number Concepts

The concepts that underlie early number ideas include pattern, conservation, one-to-one correspondence, classification, comparison, and sequence. Later number concepts include place value and matching sets to numerals and number words. To understand the difficulties a young child has with number concepts, you must first understand the way a child views the world of numbers.

Very young children do not use nor understand number ideas the way they do terms for objects in their immediate environment, such as dog, mommy, and cup. Around the age of two, they begin to understand the difference between being allowed to have two cookies and being allowed to have only one cookie. At this time, numbers begin to have some meaning for the child.

It is not uncommon for a two- or three-year-old to be able to count to 3 or 4 or even to 10 and beyond and yet not know the meaning of 6. It is up to the teacher or parent to help the child understand the cardinal usage of numbers. The concepts of numbers beyond two or three were not developed until relatively recently in history, and the concept of zero came even later. We should not expect children to learn these ideas automatically. Some children enter kindergarten with an unclear notion of what numbers really are, beyond being words to recite in order.

The following activities are designed to help young children understand early number concepts. They begin on the concrete level with the manipulation of actual objects and the oral discussion of number words. Later, numerals and other written symbols are associated with objects and pictures.

ACTIVITIES

Primary (K–1)

Objective: to develop early number concepts through observations and the use of one-to-one correspondence.

1. Go on a scavenger hunt for the number 2. Have the children hold up their hands and discuss the fact that they each have two hands. If they pick up an object in each hand, how many objects will they be holding? Let the children see how many sets of two items they can find in the classroom. Repeat the activity for other amounts.

2. Play the alike and different game introduced with sets in Chapter 5, only this time make the differences and likenesses be the number of objects on each card. You may have a set of cards such as those pictured in Figure 6–1.

   If you are working on the concept of the number 2, have the child place all of the cards with two objects in the alike pile and those that have more or less than two objects in the different pile. Repeat the game for other amounts.

3. Use the cards from the alike and different game to play several variations. Show the child a set of cards in which all of the cards but one show the same number of objects. Ask the child which card does not belong. If the child responds with a card you do not expect, ask the child the reason for his or her response; the answer may be a legitimate correct response.

   Show the child a set of cards that show the same number of objects. Ask the child to give you another card that shows this number.

Ask the child to sort the cards so that cards in each pile show the same number.

Objective: to reinforce early number concepts on a pictorial, connecting level.

4. Let the children draw pictures of all the body parts they can think of that come in sets of two. Encourage responses that we may not think of immediately, such as elbows and thumbs, as well as the more conventional responses of arms and legs.

Notice that in these activities, the numerals are not introduced. The numbers are discussed orally with the children, and counting is not used. The children learn to associate a number with a set simply by looking at the set, but they can check their answers, obtained by sight, by counting the objects in the sets. After children are comfortable with these activities, add numerals to the activities.

Conservation

For kindergartners, the number concepts up to five should be stressed. Piagetian research has shown that most five-year-olds do not conserve numbers beyond 5. To see if a child can conserve, try the following experiment. Show the child two groups of seven beans each. First, line the groups up so there is an obvious one-to-one correspondence, as in Figure 6–2. Ask the child if the two groups have the same number of objects. If the child says yes, spread the objects apart in one of the groups. Ask the child if the two groups still have the same number of objects or if one group now has more. If the child believes that one group has more objects, this child is not conserving number.

If the child is a nonconserver, try the same activity with smaller numbers of objects. Some children can conserve when there are only three or four objects but are overwhelmed by the visual configuration when there are more. A teacher should judge the readiness of each child

Figure 6–1

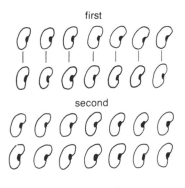

Figure 6–2

individually, however, and not rely on a child's birth date. Some five-year-olds are able to conserve large numbers, and some seven- or eight-year-olds are not able to conserve at all.

Teachers should incorporate the use of dot cards without numerals in their classes with young children. A set of cards with up to five dots in several different configurations, such as the ones in Figure 6–3, can be constructed. Later, cards with numerals may be added to the set so that children may match numerals to dots.

ACTIVITIES

Primary (K–2)

Objective: to develop early number concepts using dot cards.

1. Let the children play a matching game with the cards. Have them sort the cards into piles so that all the cards in one pile have the same number of dots.
2. Play the alike and different game, only this time use the dot cards.
3. Play a game of Go Fish or Old Maid, in which the children try to make books of three cards with the same number of dots.
4. To encourage the problem-finding abilities of children, let them make up their own games with the

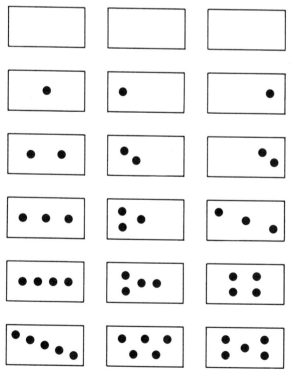

Figure 6–3

cards. Be sure that each child understands the rules before play starts. Let the children change the rules as they go along if everyone playing agrees. Similar games may be played with sets of objects.

Subitizing, the ability to immediately recognize a certain number of objects on sight (usually up to four or five), is an important skill for children to develop as they develop their number sense. Children should have a variety of experiences where they quickly look at a small number of objects and either tell you the number of objects they see, or tell you if the amount is larger or smaller than another amount. Try showing the children a set number of objects, say 10, and then give them several other sets of objects to compare to the first. Ask them if the other sets have more or fewer, or ask them to estimate the amounts in the other sets by comparing to the amount that they know. Let the children discuss how they make their decisions. With experience, children are frequently better than adults at this skill.

The following activities give more suggestions for children to develop their skills at subitizing.

Objective: to develop sight number concepts.

5. Play a magic number game in which small objects are hidden under a box. When the objects are uncovered, the children must tell you how many objects there are. Uncover the objects for only a short while so that the children do not have time to count them. Children should learn to recognize up to four or five objects on sight.
6. To expand sight-number concepts to the semiconcrete level, play the magic number game with the dot cards. Use the cards as flash cards, and have the children tell you the number of dots on a card without counting. You may wish to try this with more dots, although most adults can recognize only about five things without having to count.

   Do not put children into too many testing situations. The activities should be fun for the children and should not always be tests. Go through the cards frequently, reciting the numbers yourself without making the children repeat them. Just let the children see the dots and listen to you say the words.
7. Children's dice and board games often give them the opportunity to use sight numbers. Any game in which a child rolls one or two dice and then moves the number of spaces shown encourages him or her to recognize the number of dots on the dice and then to match the number to moves that are similar to moves on the number line. These games may be played at home and during indoor recess as well as during the mathematics class.

Combinations

As numbers larger than 5 are introduced, the children may begin to see them as combinations of groups of smaller objects. For example, 7 may be seen as 3 and 4 or as 2 and 5. Students should be encouraged to look for patterns in the combinations that add to 7 or any other given number. This grouping should be encouraged because it will greatly facilitate the later learning of addition and subtraction facts. If a child has learned to recognize 8 as 5 and 3, there will be no need to memorize $5 + 3 = 8$ or $8 - 5 = 3$. The child will simply need to learn the symbols $+$, $-$, and $=$; the facts will already be known. The following activities are designed to help children learn larger numbers by partitioning and combining sets.

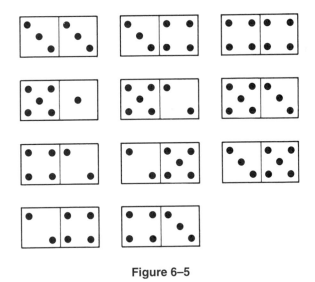

Figure 6–5

Objective: to increase visual number concepts.

3. Using a set of dominoes with up to five dots on each side, let each child sort the dominoes into piles with the same number of total dots. There may be piles such as those in Figure 6–5. The Magic Number game described in #5 of the previous activity set may also be played with dominoes.

ACTIVITIES

Primary (K–3)

Objective: to use partitioning of sets to develop concepts of larger numbers.

1. Make a shake box out of a small box with a partition in the middle. Place 6 to 10 beans in the box (see Figure 6–4).

   Put the lid on the box and shake it. Then remove the lid. Record the number of beans on each side of the partition. For instance, with 7 beans, you may have 6 and 1, 4 and 3, 5 and 2, and so on.
2. Give each child 6 to 10 buttons. Let the children separate the buttons into groups as many ways as possible. For instance, 6 may be 5 and 1, 2 and 4, 3 and 3, and so on. Encourage the children to recognize these amounts without counting, but they may use counting to check the answers, if necessary. Ask the children to record the groups in some orderly fashion and to look for patterns in the groupings.

Zero

Zero is often a difficult concept for children. It is easier to recognize that there are no elephants in the room than it is to realize that there are zero elephants. The idea of "having zero" seems to be a more difficult concept than the idea of "not having any." The following activities are designed to help children learn the concept of zero.

ACTIVITIES

Primary (K–3)

Objective: to introduce the concept of zero concretely.

1. Read the book *Zero is Not Nothing* and let the children name things that they "have zero of" in the classroom. The answers may range from pink elephants to a rug on the floor to sit on.
2. Collect several small empty boxes and put pennies in every box but one. Leave that box empty. Tape the boxes shut. Ask the children to guess which box has zero pennies without peeking inside. If you used cotton balls instead of pennies, could they still guess?

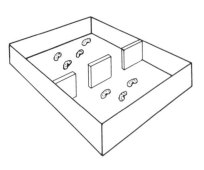

Figure 6–4

3. When you take attendance, talk about the number of children absent. How many are absent if you have perfect attendance? What will happen if zero children enter the room? What if zero children leave?

4. During physical education time or recess, talk about the number of times you jump rope or bounce a ball. Can you jump zero times? Bounce the ball zero times?

5. Play a dice game where each child rolls one die. Put a sticker over the six on the die so one side of each die has zero dots. The child with the larger amount of dots is the winner of the round. Will the child who rolls zero dots ever be the winner?

Objective: to introduce the concept of zero on a semiconcrete level.

6. Add blank cards to either the set of dot cards or the set of picture cards used before. Have the child sort them as before. Tell the child the number of dots on the blank card is zero.

One-to-One Correspondence and Counting

As the number of children attending preschool and watching programs such as "Sesame Street" increases, the number of children entering kindergarten with some ability to count also increases. These children may be counting either **rotely,** just reciting words memorized in order, or **rationally,** with understanding. Some children with the ability to rote count can complete a counting sequence only if they use the "sing-song" pattern that they used in learning to count. Other children chant the counting sequence, becoming progressively faster at repeating the number names. Initially, children develop the ability to count groups of objects, at first pointing and reciting the number names, sometimes skipping numbers, or, at other times, skipping objects. Rational counting occurs when a child can count a set of objects and realizes that the last number name spoken in the counting sequence tells how many objects there are all together—for example, "One, two, three, four, five, six, seven. There are seven buttons." And, when asked again how many objects there are, the child can confidently repeat just the last number name in the sequence, "Seven, there are seven buttons."

The following activities give children a variety of counting experiences based on putting two sets of objects or objects and pictures in one-to-one correspondence. In this way, the children connect the counting numbers to objects and do not just recite them rotely. They learn that each word goes with only one object and that the final word spoken when counting aloud gives the number of objects in the entire set.

Primary (K–1)

Objective: to use one-to-one correspondence and counting to determine the number of objects in a set.

1. Draw and cut out five garages and collect five toy cars or trucks. Tell the children that one vehicle may park in each garage. Randomly set out from one to five garages on the table. Ask the children to match a vehicle to each garage and to count as they make the matches. After the vehicles have been matched to the garages and counted, ask the children to tell you how many vehicles there are altogether. How many garages are there?

   The activity may be varied to use boats and docks or airplanes and hangars. Let the children suggest other things to match. As the children gain the ability to match and count, increase the number of objects to be counted.

2. Using the dot cards from earlier activities and some bingo chips, tell the children to cover each dot on the card with a chip and to count as they make the matches. Ask them how many dots are on each card. Is that the same as the number of chips on the card? Increase the number of dots on the cards when the children are ready.

3. Collect five small cans for flower pots, such as juice cans (be sure there are no sharp edges). Make 15 flowers using pipe cleaners for the stems and construction paper for the petals. Put one to five dots on the outside of each can. Ask the children to match the number of flowers to the number of dots on the can. Let the children count to tell you how many dots and flowers there are. Later, you can increase the numbers of flowers and dots.

In all of these activities, it is fine if children can tell you the numbers without counting; they should not be required to count. After the children are proficient at matching two sets of objects or a set of dots and a set of objects, numerals may be substituted.

Measuring Length

Thus far, the discussion has focused on number as related to sets of discrete or individual objects. Number may also refer to the length of an object, a measurement concept. Number lines, rulers, and Cuisenaire rods depend upon this measurement idea. We also use number in a measurement sense when we say "He is four years old" or "She is three blocks from home." Measurement concepts are discussed in detail later but are mentioned here briefly as they relate to number concepts.

Difficulties arise as children move from associating numbers with sets of discrete objects to associating numbers with lengths. First, children may not understand the number 2 to be two units long; they may understand 2 to be simply two objects. Second, many children do not conserve length. They believe a rod changes in length when its position changes. They have difficulty understanding that 2 is twice as long as 1. To introduce number concepts using measurement, the teacher should first ascertain whether the children can conserve length.

One good model for length is Cuisenaire rods. For young children, Cuisenaire rods may be used to discuss such ideas as longer than, shorter than, and the same length. After discussing these concepts, children who can conserve length may begin to associate the rods with numbers. The children may use the white rod, which is the shortest one, to represent one. Using this white rod to measure, the children may then determine the length of each of the other rods. They will find that if the white rod is 1 unit long, then the red is 2, the light green is 3, the purple is 4, the yellow is 5, the dark green is 6, the black is 7, the brown is 8, the blue is 9, and the orange is 10. Once children have determined these lengths, they should try some of the following activities to reinforce the number concepts.

ACTIVITIES

Primary (K–3)

Objective: to introduce ordering concepts involving length.

1. Make a staircase using one rod of each color. Construct the staircase so that the rod on top is a white rod, the rod on the bottom is orange, and the rods in between are arranged in order of length (see Figure 6–6). What will happen if you put a white rod next to each rod in your staircase?

Objective: to reinforce the concept of equivalent lengths as an introduction to addition.

2. Find the yellow rod. Make trains of rods that are the same length as the yellow rod, such as those shown in Figure 6–7. Have the children record every combination whose length equals the length of the yellow rod, beginning with the colors and later using the numbers to represent the rods.

3. Have one child choose a rod other than the white one and challenge another child to find two rods that will make a train the same length as the first rod. Children

Figure 6–6

Figure 6–7

may determine the number values of their trains after they become proficient at using the colors.

4. Have one child make a train of two rods and challenge another child to find one rod that is the same length as the train. What happens with a train such as brown and black? Let the children play the game for several days before asking them to associate numbers with the rods.

The rods may also be used in an introduction to the **number line.** Construct a number line so that the numbers are one centimeter apart. Mark zero and number the line up to 10 or so, as shown in Figure 6–8.

Give each child a number line in which the numbers are drawn 1 centimeter apart and obtain a transparency of a number line and translucent Cuisenaire rods made

Figure 6–8

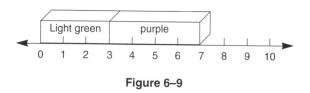

Figure 6–9

for the overhead projector to use yourself. Because children often do not associate the numbers on the number line with lengths, using Cuisenaire rods helps them see that 2 is the distance from 0 (zero) to 2 and not just the point half way between 1 and 3. For this reason, it is important to have 0 (zero) on the number line.

Points to the left of 0 need not be marked at this time, but there should be an arrow pointing to the left from 0 as well as an arrow pointing to the right from the last positive number marked. If the children ask the meaning of the arrows or ask if there are other numbers to the left of 0, answer that the numbers go on forever in both directions.

Decide if the children are ready for a detailed discussion of the concepts of **infinity** or **negative numbers** at this time. If they are, show them that one everyday use of negative numbers is as low-temperature values on the thermometer. Or, let them use a calculator to see what happens if they try to subtract 6 from 4. In general, however, do not introduce a detailed study of negative integers or infinity in the primary grades.

The following activities are designed to introduce the child to the use of the number line.

ACTIVITIES

Primary (K–3)

Objective: to introduce the concept of measurement on the number line.

1. Let the children choose a Cuisenaire rod at random. Place the rod on the number line with the left end of the rod on 0 (zero). Where is the right end? How does this number compare to the value of the rod? Try this with several different rods.
2. Choose two rods to line up on the number line in a train, as shown in Figure 6–9. Place the left end of the first rod on 0 (zero). Can you predict where the right end of the second rod will be?

After working with the Cuisenaire rods on the number line, children should understand the concept of length on the number line and should be able to move on to number-line activities that do not require the use of the rods. The following are examples of other number-line activities.

ACTIVITIES

Primary (K–3)

Objective: to develop number line concepts through body movements.

1. Make a large number line on the floor with masking tape. Make sure the starting point is marked 0 (zero) to show that no steps have been taken at this point. On the number line, mark intervals that are about the size of a child's step (about 25 centimeters). Make sure that each interval is the same size.

   Have the children take turns starting at 0 (zero) and walking a given number of steps. Have them confirm that the point at which they finish corresponds to the number of steps they took. In this way, the number of discrete steps is associated with the distance walked on the number line.
2. Using the 1-centimeter number lines, let the children use their fingers to count a certain number of spaces, beginning at zero. What number is on the point where the children land? Emphasize counting spaces rather than points.

Objective: to practice skills on the number line.

3. Use Freddie the frog with the number line. Let Freddie start at zero and hop a certain number of spaces. Where does he land?

Grouping

Grouping is an important concept in the Hindu-Arabic system of numeration. Many older systems of numeration, such as the Roman and the Egyptian, did not use grouping, and thus they were awkward for writing and manipulating symbols for large numbers. Because place-value is so important in our system of numeration and because grouping is essential to place value, young children should begin grouping even while they are learning the numbers from 1 to 9. They should have experience grouping by twos, threes, fours—all the way to tens—for two good reasons. First, the notion of an exchange point is a key to understanding place value. Second, regrouping using smaller numbers provides valuable practice that is more important to have than waiting until 10 objects have been collected to make an exchange.

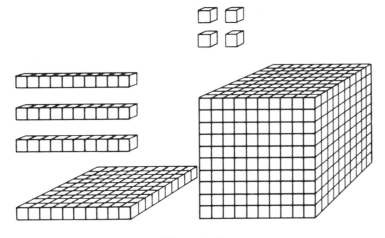

Figure 6–10

There are two basic types of grouping materials: **proportional** and **nonproportional.** Proportional materials are constructed so that if the grouping is by tens, the material that shows 10 is 10 times as large as the material that shows 1 and the material for 100 is 10 times as large as the material for 10, and so forth. Proportional materials include multibase blocks (see Figure 6–10), tongue depressors, coffee stirrers or straws, counting cups and beans, and Cuisenaire cubes, squares, and rods.

Nonproportional materials, such as money, do not show consistent size changes. A dime is not 10 times as large as a penny and a dollar is not 10 times the size of a dime. Nonproportional aids include chip trading, money, and the abacus. Allow children to explore with the proportional grouping materials freely before you begin formal instruction. Let the children discover the size differences and the trades that are possible as they build houses or make designs with the blocks.

The following activities are designed to give children thorough experiences in grouping. This becomes the foundation for later work with place-value.

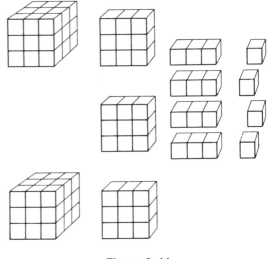

Figure 6–11

ACTIVITIES

Primary (K–3)

Objective: to introduce trading games using proportional materials.

1. **Multibase blocks** are proportional grouping materials that consist of various sizes of wooden or plastic blocks representing the powers of particular grouping points. Multibase blocks are commercially available in sets with grouping points of 2, 3, 4, 5, 6, and 10. A set of blocks with a grouping point of 3 is shown in Figure 6–11. Regardless of the grouping point, the smallest pieces are called units; the remaining pieces are called, in order, longs, flats, and cubes. You may make your own set of multibase blocks using self-adhesive paper (such as Contact paper) printed with a grid approximately 1 centimeter square and railroad board. Cut out units, longs, and flats to match the grouping point desired.

After the children have had an opportunity to play with the materials and to discover the grouping point, give them a handful of units and ask them to make all of the trades possible. For example, the blocks in Figure 6–12a can be traded for the blocks in Figure 6–12b because the blocks represent the same amount of material. If children have difficulty making the exchanges, instruct them to make groups of three units until all units are used and then to exchange each group of three for a long, as shown in Figure 6–13.

Figure 6–12

Figure 6–13

2. After the children have played some grouping games, let them play the Build-a-House game. For this game, children form two families. Each family is trying to build a house before the other. To begin the game, the children agree which city they will live in, Three for One, Four for One, or Five for One, and choose multibase blocks to match the city.

To play, each team rolls one die to determine the paycheck for the week. The dots showing on the die tell the child the number of single units earned that week. Children should trade in single units for a long as soon as possible, trade longs for a flat, and trade flats for a cube. A cube is the house, and a team "wins" as soon as it completes a house.

Children should also play the game in reverse. In this game, they begin with a large cube and try to spend it. The dots showing on the die tell the child the number of single units to spend on that round. In this game, the first team to spend all its money loses.

The second game is usually much more difficult for the children than the Build-a-House game, especially in the beginning. The first move is the most difficult. Having one large cube and needing to spend two units is similar to the problem $1,000 - 2$. Children who realize that they must make several trades before they can spend two units have very good place-value concepts. Discuss with the children the trades that they must make, both as they play the game and after they have finished.

After the children have played the games for a while, ask them to record their plays. How does the game relate to what they are writing down? This activity will give them a good basis for learning addition or subtraction with regrouping.

3. Teachers may construct proportional materials from railroad board or other firm construction material. Figure 6–14 illustrates one such set, with a grouping point of 3, and Figure 6–15 illustrates a set with a grouping point of 4.

Use dot cards with these triangular materials. Place the dot cards face down in a pile in the center of the table. Let the children take turns drawing a card and picking up that many small triangles. Make trades whenever possible. The first team or child to get two large triangles wins.

Repeat the game with squares. Activities suggested for the multibase blocks may also be used with these materials.

4. Another material that the teacher may use is the counting cup and beans. For a grouping point of five, a cup with five beans represents a first grouping, five cups of five in a larger container represent a second grouping, and so forth, as shown in Figure 6–16.

The counting cups and beans may be used to play a store game. A single bean represents a penny, a cup with five beans is a nickel, and five cups of five beans represent a quarter. Put price tags on small objects, such as 37¢ for a hair ribbon and 7¢ for a pencil.

Ask the children to count out individual beans to represent a price and then to make any trades possible. Is the pencil more than a nickel? Is the ribbon less

Figure 6–14

Figure 6–15

Figure 6–16

groups	ones
2	2

Figure 6–17

super–groups	groups	ones
2	2	1

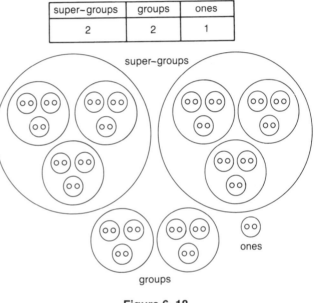

Figure 6–18

than a quarter? Encourage the children to set prices and make up questions of their own. This game may also be played using pennies, nickels, and quarters in place of the beans.

Again, each of the activities described for any of the grouping materials may be used with the counting cups. So far, each grouping activity suggested has focused on only one or two exchanges. Teachers should suggest activities requiring several exchanges and using a variety of grouping points. Discuss with the children why they make the trades that they do.

Objective: to introduce grouping concepts using sets of discrete objects and charts and tallies to keep track of experimentations.

5. Begin with eight buttons. Have the child place them in groups of 3 (***) and record the results on a chart, as shown in Figure 6–17.

Repeat the activity with grouping points of 2 (**), 4 (****), 5 (*****), and 6 (******). Chart the results. Discuss with the children what happens as the grouping point changes.

Repeat the activity but use more buttons, say 25. Put all of the groups of 3 (***) together and label these groups. Next, group together three groups of 3 and label these supergroups. Record the results in a tally box with three sections, such as the one shown in Figure 6–18.

Repeat the activity with other grouping points and starting amounts. Record the results. There may be times when you will need super-supergroups, or more, especially for small grouping points such as 2.

Colored chips are convenient nonproportional teaching aids. They may be purchased commercially or constructed by the teacher.

Objective: to introduce grouping concepts using nonproportional materials.

6. Gather about 120 colored chips. You should have about 40 orange chips, 30 yellow chips, 20 green chips, 20 red chips, and 10 blue chips.

Choose a magic number for trading. Let the children take turns rolling a die and collecting the orange chips. When the magic number is reached, exchange orange chips for yellow chips. For example, if the magic number is 3, three orange chips may be traded for one yellow, three yellows for one green, three greens for one red, and three reds for one blue. Set the goal as either a red or a blue chip. Discuss the children's trades as they play and ask questions such as, "How many more will you need to reach the goal?" or "Who is winning and by how much?"

The chips may be used for the same games as the proportional materials.

After the students have used several different grouping points with the materials, expand the activities to include base-ten activities. Be sure to encourage the children to record their activities as they work and to discuss the strategies they use.

ACTIVITIES

Intermediate and Middle Grades (4–8)

Objective: to compare and contrast different numeration systems.

1. Ask the students to read a book that looks at other numeration systems such as Adler's *Base Five* or *Roman Numerals* or St. John's *How to Count Like a Martian*. Compare and contrast the Hindu-Arabic system with other systems studied. Ask the students to record their findings in a Venn diagram such as the one in Figure 6–19. After students have studied other systems, challenge them to create a system of their own and teach it to others in their group.

Objective: to apply study of other number bases to everyday problems.

2. Encourage students interested in computers to read about binary or hexadecimal numbers and report their findings. Some students might wish to talk to postal workers about the binary code that is used in bar codes to separate items based on zip codes.

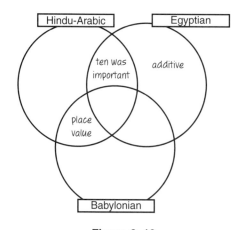

Figure 6–19

Developing and Practicing Number Skills

Once children can orally associate numbers with sets, introduce written numerals. The fact that written numerals are often introduced too early may be one reason we picture numerals instead of sets when we hear a number; therefore, we should be sure children can orally associate the numbers with sets before they are asked to learn written numerals.

Matching Numerals to Sets

Children should be familiar with seeing written numerals before being asked to write them. Numerals are not something children can discover on their own. If we want children to learn Hindu-Arabic numerals, we must teach them.

The following activities are designed to help the child match the numerals from 1 to 5 with sets. These activities may be expanded later to include other numerals as well as the written words for the numbers.

ACTIVITIES

Primary (K–1)

Objective: to match written numerals to sets.

1. Play a Treasure Hunt game. Give each child a numeral and have the child look around the room for sets of objects that match the numeral. For instance, the child with the numeral 3 may find three cars, three pencils, and three chairs in the learning center.
2. Make several sets of cards for different card games similar to Old Maid or Go Fish. The cards should give children a chance to practice matching numerals, sets, and dots, such as those in Figure 6–20.
3. Dominoes with numerals on one side and dots on the other are useful for matching numerals and dots. Children can play dominoes, matching the numerals on the dominoes to corresponding dots.

Objective: to reinforce number concepts.

4. Play riddle games with the children using what they know about numbers. For example, you might give the following clues:

I am less than 10.

I am an even number.

I am more than seven.

What number am I?

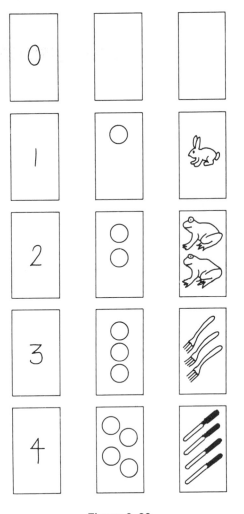

Figure 6–20

As children become more proficient at this game, you might use more complex clues such as:

I am less than the number of toes on one foot.

If you double me, I am less than ten.

I am double an even number.

What number am I?

When a student correctly answers your riddle, that student should choose a new number and make up a riddle with clues for the other students. Students can discuss which riddles have exactly one right answer, which riddles have more than one answer, and which riddles have no right answers. Children can write up their riddles and publish them in the class newsletter or leave them in a learning center for other students to guess.

After children have experience with writing riddles to guess a single number, they can try clues to finding a pair of numbers such as:

I am thinking of two numbers.

My numbers are both even.

My numbers add to 10.

What are my numbers?

Again, students should write riddles for each other and discuss which riddles have 0, 1, or more than one correct answer.

Writing Numerals

After children can match numerals to sets, they can begin to learn to write numerals. Children at this age often do not have good fine motor control and may need to use very large materials in the beginning. The following are a few suggestions for writing numerals with materials other than paper and pencil.

ACTIVITIES

Primary (K–1)

Objective: to use tactile-kinesthetic abilities to write numerals.

1. Cover the bottom of a box lid with sand or salt. Let the children practice writing numerals in the sand. After you check the work, have the children simply shake the box lid to erase their efforts and begin again.
2. Cut large numerals out of sandpaper and let the children run their fingers gently over the numerals. Have them do this blindfolded and try to guess what the numeral is. Then have them draw what they have just felt.

Objective: to reinforce writing numerals.

3. Draw numerals on large squares of posterboard. Use arrows to show the direction to move to write the numerals. Laminate the numerals and let the children copy them with a grease pencil or washable crayon.

Rational Counting

After children have had several ordering experiences such as those described in Chapter 5, are able to associate the numbers from 1 to 5 with sets of objects, and are able to write numerals, they should be ready to order numbers. In this way, counting is developed in a rational, not a rote, manner. It is important for children to realize that three comes after two when they are counting because a set of three has one more object than a set of two, not just because they have heard the numerals recited in that order several times. The activities in Chapter 5 with sets should be repeated with numbers. In summary, these include:

- *Observations and inferences.* By observing a variety of sets of objects, pictures, and dot cards, children learn to associate numbers with sets, first orally, then using the written numerals, and finally using the written number words.
- *Classifications.* The children group together all sets containing the same number of objects. This is a good time for the teacher to determine if children can conserve numbers. If a child realizes that the number of objects in a set stays the same regardless of the configuration, then the child can conserve.
- *Comparisons.* The children use one-to-one correspondence to determine if two sets have the same number or if one set has more or less than another.
- *Sequencing.* The children order sets of objects from those containing the fewest to those containing the most. The increase may be by one object each time but it does not have to be.

The following activities are designed to help children to order numbers rationally. When numbers increase by one each time, the child may begin rational counting. Rational counting should not always begin with one. Children should practice counting beginning with any number. They should count both forwards and backwards. The symbols $>$, $<$, and $=$ may be introduced. Ordinal number concepts should also be developed as children understand the concepts of sequencing.

ACTIVITIES

Primary (K–3)

Objective: to practice rational counting.

1. Children should practice counting several times during the day, whenever the opportunity arises. For example, if you ask the children to set up the chairs for the reading group, observe them to see if they count the number of children in the group and count out the same number of chairs or solve the problem in another way.

   Children can also practice counting on from a given number. If there are already 5 chairs in the circle and they need 8 chairs, ask them to count beginning with 5. As they get more chairs, they can count forward—6, 7, 8. If there are too many chairs in the circle, they can count backward as they remove chairs. If there are 10 chairs and they need only 7,

they can count back from 10 as they take the chairs away—9, 8, 7. The ability to count forward and backward will help them later when they learn addition and subtraction.

2. Children do not always need to count physical objects. They may count the number of days until a special holiday, the number of seconds in the countdown on a microwave oven, or the number of claps of thunder they hear. Again, encourage them to count forward as well as backward, beginning with different numbers. Later they should learn to count by whole numbers other than 1 as well as by fractions and decimals.

Objective: to introduce the concepts *greater than* and *less than.*

3. Make a set of dot cards with numerals on one side and dots on the other. Have the children put the cards in order from the fewest to the most dots. Turn the cards to the numeral side to check. Reverse the process by ordering the numerals and checking on the dot side using one-to-one correspondence. Reinforce the concepts of one less and one greater.

4. An adaptation of the card game War may be played with a deck of cards having from zero to nine dots on a card. When constructing the cards, make four or five cards for each number of dots. The game is played by two or more children. The cards are shuffled, and all are dealt. Each player turns over one card and places it face up on the table. The player with the card showing the most dots wins all the cards on this round. If there is more than one card showing the greatest number of dots, the two players with those cards have a "war." Each of these players then places a card face down on his or her first card and another card face up on top of the second card. The new face-up cards are compared. The player whose card has the most dots wins all the cards in the war as well as any other players' cards on this round. Play continues until one player has all the cards or a time limit expires. If the children question which card has the most dots, they should establish a one-to-one correspondence between the dots to decide.

   The second phase in this game is to use a regular deck of cards or the numerals without the dots. Play continues as before.

5. After the children have had experience with the words *greater than* and *less than,* the symbols may be introduced. A popular idea for introducing the symbols is the use of a "hungry fish" (see Figure 6–21). The fish always wants to eat as much as possible, so its mouth is always open toward the greater amount. The children may use blocks to represent the fish's food. Set up two groups of blocks with between one

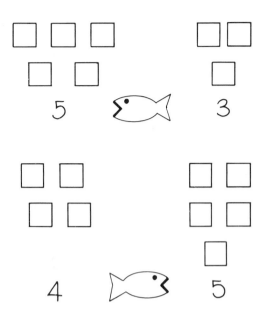

Figure 6–21

and nine blocks in each group and let the children place the corresponding numeral under each set. The children then decide which set is greater, using one-to-one correspondence if necessary, and place the fish between the numerals with its mouth open toward the larger numeral. If the activity is done on paper, the children may trace inside the fish's mouth to keep a permanent record of the larger number. Discuss the terms *greater than* and *less than* as the symbols are introduced.

The symbol for *equals* (=) may be introduced at the same time. The fish cannot decide which group to eat because both are the same size. It keeps its mouth neither wide open nor closed (see Figure 6–22).

After children are comfortable putting numbers in order to count the cardinal number of objects in a set, they may begin to use numbers in an ordinal sense. Ordinal numbers should be used throughout the day just as cardinal numbers should. As children line up for any activities, discuss who is first in line, second, last, and so on.

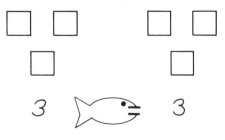

Figure 6–22

Talk about the first thing on the schedule each morning. Let the children suggest other times they use ordinal numbers.

Several computer and calculator activities are designed to help a child with early number concepts. The following examples include programs and activities for both number recognition and counting.

ACTIVITIES

Primary (K–3)

Objective: to use the computer to reinforce matching numerals to pictures of sets of objects.

1. *Sticky Bear Numbers,* available from Optimum Resources, is a program for preschool and kindergarten children. It consists of sets of objects that appear in response to a child's pressing either the space bar or a numeral on the keyboard. The child may make a new set of objects appear by pressing a new numeral or may increase or decrease the set by one by pressing the space bar. For example, by pressing the space bar once, the child makes a train appear. Each additional time the child presses the space bar, another train appears until nine trains are showing on the screen. After nine trains have appeared, the trains disappear one by one as the space bar is pressed until all trains have disappeared. The numeral 0 (zero) then appears on the screen. A numeral accompanies each set shown on the screen. When the space bar is pressed again, new sets of objects appear. Children as young as 18 months old can enjoy the graphics, and older children can begin to associate numerals with sets.

   Other software that you might want to investigate for young children as they learn number concepts includes *James Discovers Math* by Broderbund, *Millie's Math House* from EdMark, *Sunbuddy Math Playhouse* from Sunburst, and *MathKeys* from the Learning Company. Several good new titles are developed every year, so be sure to investigate them as they become available.

Objective: to develop simple programming concepts and to reinforce counting skills.

2. Older children may write programs for younger children, instructing the computer to count by ones, by tens, backwards, etc. Fairly simple programs in BASIC can accomplish this. For example, Program A counts forward by twos beginning at 2 and ending at 40 and Program B counts backward from 50 to 0 by fives.

Program A

10 NEW
20 FOR I = 2 TO 40 STEP 2
30 PRINT I
40 FOR J = 1 TO 500: NEXT J
50 NEXT I
60 END

Program B

10 NEW
20 FOR I = 50 TO 0 STEP −5
30 PRINT I
40 FOR J = 1 TO 500: NEXT J
50 NEXT I
60 END

Even very young children can use a calculator to develop counting skills. As children first learn to count, they may use a calculator to help them keep track of their counting. For example, a child counting a pile of chips can push "+1" on the calculator each time he or she moves a chip. Having finished counting the pile of chips, the child can push "="on the calculator to check if his or her calculator will show the numeral just said.

Children can explore with a calculator to see what happens when they push "+1 = = = =." Later, children may start with any number and then try "+5" or "+2." What happens when you start with a larger number and push "− 2 = = ="? Children may encounter negative numbers doing this. (Calculators work differently, and you may need to explore this with yours before you try this with the children.)

Number Names

After children have learned to match numerals to sets and have learned to count rationally to at least 5, introduce written words for the numerals. Expand many of the same activities used to introduce the numerals to include the number names. In card games, add cards with the number names on them for the children to include in the matches. Mark the number line with the number names as well as with the numerals.

Children's literature is a good source for teaching numerals and number names. Several good children's books introduce numerals and number names. Encourage children to find the number names in stories and to check the pictures to see if the pictures show the correct number of objects.

Children also enjoy finger plays using poems such as "Ten Little Monkeys" and "Five Birds on a Fence," in which they recite the poem and show numbers with their fingers. Children's music also is a good source of ideas for reinforcing counting. Music can be a great memory aid for many children. Librarians and music teachers can help you find excellent children's books, stories, finger plays, and songs.

ACTIVITIES

Primary (K–3)

Objective: to investigate counting in other cultures.

1. Read *Moja Means One* or *Count on Your Fingers African Style* to the students and ask them to compare their own styles of counting to those in the books. Children may wish to read other counting books from around the world and compare them to the more familiar counting books from the United States. If you are fortunate enough to have students who were raised in other cultures or for whom English is not the first language, you might invite the students or their parents to talk to the class about the words and techniques used to count in their native lands.

Place Value

Be certain that children have had many experiences with grouping activities before you formally introduce the numeral 10. It is difficult for young children to understand that 10 represents • • • • • • • • • • objects and not • object. Children may logically assume that if you put a 1 and a 0 (zero) together, you should have 1 plus 0 objects, not 10. Early experience with grouping smaller amounts should help children understand why "ten" is written as 10. The 1 here means one group and the 0 means zero units.

Extensive work on this concept when it is first introduced can help children avoid problems later. Many teachers in the intermediate and middle grades can tell you that place value remains a major difficulty as children learn operations that require regrouping. Even high school students often repeat lessons on addition and subtraction in general math classes because they never fully understood the meaning of place value.

As place value in base-10 is introduced, the previous activities that involved grouping materials in other bases should be expanded to grouping by tens. Children should have extensive experience using both proportional and nonproportional materials to group by tens, hundreds, thousands, and so on. Encourage the children to record the results of their work using such things as place-value charts. The following are some additional activities to be used in base-ten.

Fill the Cube I

You need: 1 Unifix cube with tape on the bottom
1 baggie of popcorn
1 baggie of lentils

1. Estimate: How many kernels of popcorn do you think will fill the cube? Record.

2. Fill the cube with popcorn. Then count the popcorn at least two different ways. Record and explain how you counted.

3. Repeat: Now do it with lentils. Estimate, Count, Record.

4. Write: How did your two counts compare?

Figure 6–23 *Math by All Means: Place Value Grade 2,* by Marilyn Burns. © 1994 Math Solutions Publications. Reproduced with permission.

Math Program

The popcorn activity shown in Figure 6–23 is from a place-value replacement unit for second grade. Replacement units are designed to take the place of a similar unit in any textbook series. In this five- to six-week unit, students have a wide range of experiences to introduce them to large numbers and place value through estimating, counting, looking for patterns in written numbers, relating numeration to money, and working with concrete materials.

This activity occurs about halfway through this replacement unit. It follows lessons in which students have rolled dice to take unit cubes that they trade for tens rods and cubes and a similar lesson in which they roll dice for pennies that are traded for dimes and dollars. These earlier activities give them a concept of place value and trading ones, tens, and hundreds. They have also timed each other as they drew dollar signs for 1 minute and then counted the number of dollar signs they had drawn in at least two ways. In that way, they have had experience counting in different ways before this activity. Note that in this activity, students must estimate both the number of pieces of popcorn and the number of lentils that would fit in a unifix cube. In this way, students are encouraged to discuss how the differences in size between lentils and popcorn would affect the number that fit in a cube. As they do in all parts of this unit, students must then write about their results. The unit has suggestions for assessment that include observations, interviews, and looking at written work. In this activity, teachers are asked to note whether students count by tens as well as by ones (or in other ways such as by twos and by fives), and whether students can estimate and adjust estimates based upon previous knowledge and using proportional reasoning that there must be more lentils than popcorn since the lentils are smaller.

Other parts of this unit involve the use of literature, some of which is written specifically for use with the replacement unit. Other literature, such as *The Popcorn Book* by Tomie dePaola, may also be used with this activity.

Activities in this book include both whole-class lessons and menu activities that occur in pairs or individually. This activity is designed to be done individually, with student responses expected on a variety of levels. This program does not recommend different activities for students on different levels but instead expects students to respond differently to the same activity.

The unit also includes ideas for homework that extend the classroom activities and gives suggestions for ways to communicate with parents.

ACTIVITIES

Primary (1–3)

Objective: to reinforce concretely place value concepts in base-10.

1. With a large box of coffee stirrers or tongue depressors, have a contest to see who can pick up the largest handful of sticks. Have the children group the sticks by tens and secure each group of sticks with a rubber band. If a child has picked up more than 100 sticks, bundle each 10 groups of 10 to form groups of 100. Let the children record results on a chart such as the following:

Bundles of 100	Bundles of 10	Singles

2. Purchase or construct several simple base-ten abaci. Among the most useful are those with 10 beads on each bar, with the first 9 beads of one color and the tenth bead the color of the first 9 beads on the next bar (see Figure 6–24).

   When the children fill up one bar with 10 beads, the color of the tenth bead should remind them to trade in all 10 beads for 1 bead on the next bar. Thus, 10 ones are traded for 1 ten, 10 tens for 1 hundred, and so on. Let the children use the abacus to record results from work with other place value materials.

Objective: to extend sight numbers to amounts between 10 and 20.

3. Use chips placed on a grid such as the one shown in Figure 6–25. You should have a transparent grid for

Figure 6–24

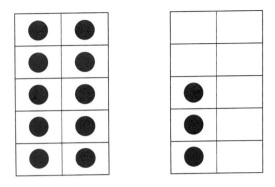

Figure 6–25

the overhead projector, and each student should have a grid of his or her own. You may use the Blackline Masters in Appendix B to make these. Ask the students to explore by placing varying amounts of chips on the grid and determining the total. When children are comfortable finding the total, place a secret amount of chips on the grid and flash it briefly on the overhead projector. Discuss with the students their methods of determining the total.

After the children have had much experience with physical models and with recording base-10 numerals, concepts on the abstract level may be reinforced with materials that use only numerals. These materials may include hundreds charts, place-value charts, Bingo games, flash cards, and playing cards. The following activities are designed to be used after the children have a good concrete understanding of grouping in base-10.

ACTIVITIES

Primary–Intermediate (2–4)

Objective: to explore patterns on a hundreds chart.

1. Make a large hundreds chart out of pegboard, with cup hooks from which to hang numerals (see Figure 6–26). Hang all 100 numerals in their proper places. Let the children discuss the patterns they notice.

   Now turn the cards over so that they are still on the proper hooks but the children cannot see the numerals. Ask a child to guess where the 3 should be and then to check by turning the card over. If the child is correct, leave the numeral showing. If the child is incorrect, turn the card over and let another child guess. Continue by guessing other numbers such as 23 or 30. Let each child have a turn to guess.

Figure 6–26

Figure 6–27

Discuss the patterns as you go along. This activity can also be used with copied hundreds charts and small squares of paper to cover the numerals. (A hundreds chart is included in Appendix B for you to copy.) Let the children remove the square of paper when they guess where the number is.

Discuss the strategies used to find the numbers.

Objective: to provide for practice in forming numerals as they are spoken and to allow for rapid checking of children's responses.

2. Let each child make a place-value chart that includes the hundreds or thousands, depending on the level of practice the child needs. This chart may be made from heavy manila paper by folding up the bottom part of the paper and stapling pockets to hold numeral cards. Label the pockets ones, tens, hundreds, and so on. Let each child make three cards for each numeral from 0 through 9.

Read a numeral you wish the children to form, such as 346 (three hundred forty-six), and let the children form the numeral by placing cards in the correct pockets and then holding the place-value chart up for you to see (see Figure 6–27). Quickly check to see whether or not each child has the correct response. This way, each child can get immediate feedback on

the response and will not practice incorrect techniques. You may also use "magic slates" or individual chalkboards; the children write their responses, hold them up for you to check, and then erase them to prepare for the next problem.

Objective: to provide for practice in recognizing numerals and place values.

3. Use 3-by-5 cards to make a deck of playing cards with values such as:

600	six hundred	6 hundreds
30	thirty	3 tens
4	four	4 ones

These cards may be used in a variety of card games that require the children to make matches, such as Go Fish, Rummy, and Old Maid. After children become proficient with these cards, add others such as 3 tens, 14 ones, and 44; 2 hundreds, 15 tens, 6 ones, and 356. These cards may also be used for games such as Bingo. The Bingo cards should look like regular Bingo cards but with numerals to match the calling cards. The rules are the same as those for regular Bingo.

 Calculators may also be used to reinforce place-value concepts. Let children predict what will show on the display if they press 3×100 or 7×1000. Be careful if you try $3 \times 100 + 5 \times 10 + 7 =$. On a scientific calculator, you will get 357, but on many other calculators you will get 3,057. Children may wish to discuss why this happens and try several examples to test their hypotheses. This is a good time to discuss the order of operations and the use of parentheses.

Some calculators for children such as Speak and Math read a numeral aloud to the child and ask the child to press the correct keys to show the numeral on the display. The calculator then either tells the child that the answer is correct or asks the child to try again. If the second response is also incorrect, the calculator shows the child the correct answer. The games have three levels, beginning with numbers in the hundreds on the first level and going to numbers in the millions with decimals on the third level. The games encourage listening skills as well as reinforce reading and writing of numerals.

Children may also play games such as Go Fish on the calculator. Three or more children may play this game at a time. Play begins with each child putting a secret six-digit number into his or her calculator. All six digits should be different to begin the game. To play, one child asks another for a number, say 6. If the child asked has a 6 in any place, then it is given to the child who asked for it. If the 6 is in the tens place, the child being asked will say, "Take 60." That child will then subtract 60 from his or her number and the other child will add 60 to his or her number.

After the game has progressed, it is possible that the child being asked may have two 6s showing in the number. If this happens, the child must give up only one digit and should choose to give up the 6 in the place with the least value. For example, a child with 236,762 should say, "Take 60" and subtract only 60, not 6,060. Play continues until one player's score goes above six digits, or 1,000,000, or until one player's score goes to zero. The player with the highest score is declared the winner.

Estimating

Often, it is more important for a child to be able to estimate a reasonable response than it is to have an exact answer. Politicians and newspapers may estimate the number of people in a crowd at a rally, or a store manager may estimate the number of pounds of hamburger to have on hand for the big sale, but, in both of these cases, an exact answer may not be necessary or even possible. As we continue to use calculators and computers, estimation skills become even more crucial. Calculators may give an exact answer, but children need to be able to estimate to determine whether that response makes sense. Estimating, therefore, should be a major part of all strands of mathematics.

The following are a few examples of estimating activities related to number concepts.

bers of jelly beans to assist them in making intelligent guesses. Their guessing and their number concepts should improve as the weeks go on.

2. Make a set of large flash cards (about 25 centimeters by 25 centimeters) and put various numbers of bright dots on each one. Doman (1980) uses up to 100 dots on a card for children under the age of four, but most elementary school children (and most adults) have difficulty actually recognizing more than about five dots. Using larger numbers of dots and flashing the cards briefly force the children to use estimation and grouping skills to guess the number of dots on a card. With only a few odd minutes per day of practice, children can become quite accurate in their guesses, and although exact answers are not a goal of estimation activities, a few children may be able to tell you the exact number of dots each time. With this activity, all children should improve visualization skills and develop a better concept of number.

3. Tactile-kinesthetic children are often not given the opportunity to use some of their best abilities. This activity gives tactile-kinesthetic children a chance to shine and helps other children develop tactile skills.

   Children should work in pairs. Let the children put a pile of Cuisenaire rods on the table. One child should close his or her eyes and the other child should select a Cuisenaire rod and place it in the hand of the first child. The first child should put that hand behind his or her back and open his or her eyes. The child with the rod should try to guess the color or length of the rod. Looking at the rods on the table, the child tries to match the rod felt with the rods seen.

   Let the partners change roles and try the activity again. Children are often better at this activity than adults after only a few tries.

Older children can also develop estimation skills with numbers. For these children, the numbers should include thousands and even millions.

ACTIVITIES

Primary (1–3)

Objective: to practice estimating large numbers of concrete objects.

1. Fill a large jar with small objects such as jelly beans. Have a contest to let the children guess how many jelly beans are in the jar. The winner of the week's contest may win a bag of jelly beans. Use another container and another small object the following week. Let children use smaller containers and small num-

ACTIVITIES

Middle Grades (5–8)

Objective: to develop concrete ideas of large numbers.

1. Send the children on a scavenger hunt for 1 million of something. They may decide to look for grains of sand in the sandbox or blades of grass in the yard. This activity will cause them to search for methods other than counting. They may measure 5 milliliters (ml) of sand and count the grains in that amount and then estimate how many milliliters it takes to make 1

million grains, or they may count the blades of grass in 4 square centimeters (cm^2) and estimate the number of square centimeters it takes to make 1 million blades of grass.

2. Children may try to collect 1 million of something, such as bottle caps or twist ties. They must devise a method of keeping track of their collection. They may put 10 caps or ties in a small bag and 10 small bags in a larger bag. Ten bags of 100 may be placed in an even larger bag, and so on. After collecting for awhile, the children may try to predict how long it will take to obtain 1 million of the item and may try to estimate how much space such an amount will occupy.

3. Children can do research to discover the current national debt. They then may determine how high a stack of $1 bills the debt would make or how long a row of $100 bills the debt would make if the bills were laid end to end. Children will probably wish to use a calculator to aid in computations but will discover that the numbers may be larger than what the calculator can display. Then they will need to discuss what to do.

   The children's books *If You Made a Million* (1989) and *How Much Is a Million* (1986) by David M. Schwartz contain some excellent ideas for teaching the concepts of large numbers, money, banking, and interest. They could be used as an introduction to these topics. The book *Innumeracy* (1988) by John Allen Paulos also has several suggestions for estimation topics that would help students (and adults) better understand today's world.

4. Let the children predict how many seconds they have been alive and then use a calculator to check their guesses.

5. Check with a local manufacturer or a restaurant. Ask how many gadgets they produced or hamburgers they sold in the last week. How many would this be per hour? Per month? Per year? If the restaurant is part of a chain, can you estimate how many hamburgers were sold by the entire chain in one year? Use your calculator to assist you.

6. Ask the children to predict how long it would take for all of the children in the school to read a total of 1 million pages in trade books. Ask them to devise a method for keeping track of the number of pages read and for involving all of the students.

7. View the Annenberg video *Animals in Yellowstone.* (Parts of this can also be found on the Annenberg Elementary Assessment video and in the Annenberg Reasoning video. More information can be found at http://www.learner.org/.) Discuss ways in which the students estimated the total number of elk, bison, and pronghorn sheep in Yellowstone National Park. Ask the students to design an experiment to estimate the number of animals or birds in a local park. You may be able to find parents who have the interest and skills to help you with this task. Local conservation societies might also be interested in having the students assist them in some of their work that involves assessing the impact of various projects on the local wildlife.

Work with estimation will probably help children realize a need for rounding numbers. Often, exact answers are not required or even sensible. One cannot tell exactly how many grains of sand there are in a bucket or exactly how many stars are in the sky, but approximate answers involving rounded numbers may be useful.

Number lines may be used for rounding numbers less than 100 to the nearest 10. Children can locate a number such as 47 and determine whether it is closer to the 50 or to the 40. For a number such as 45, determine whether it is more sensible to round up or round down. Base-10 blocks are also useful for rounding numbers. Children may show a number such as 287 with the blocks and then determine whether the amount is closer to 280 or 290 if they are rounding to the nearest 10, or closer to 200 or 300 if they are rounding to the nearest 100. Notice that rules for rounding numbers often do not apply in real life. If 63 students and 3 teachers are going on a field trip in buses with a maximum capacity of 30, finding you need 2 buses when rounded to the nearest whole number will leave 6 people stranded. Use several real-life situations and discuss when it is reasonable to round up and when it makes more sense to round down.

Solving and Creating Problems

As children develop concepts and skills, they should use their problem-solving abilities to construct knowledge for themselves. Many of the activities presented earlier were presented in a problem format. Following are activities to encourage children to seek and define problems as well as to solve them.

ACTIVITIES

Elementary (K–6)

Objective: to reinforce the concepts of greater than and less than and to encourage the development of strategies.

1. The game Guess My Number can be played in several ways. One variation of the game found on many computer programs and on calculators such as Speak and

Math can also be played by two children without a calculator or computer. It involves one player who writes down a secret number from 1 to 100. The second player tries to guess the number with the fewest possible guesses. After each guess, the first player tells the second whether the guess was too high or too low.

- *Understanding the problem.* I need to know that I am trying to guess a number my partner has chosen. This number may be as small as 1 or as large as 100. I will be told if my guesses are too large or too small.
- *Devising a plan.* The number could be even or odd, prime or not prime, but guessing a particular number will not give this information. What I will do, then, is to guess the number 50 and eliminate half of the numbers (eliminate possibilities).
- *Carrying out the plan.* I guess the number 50 and find that I am too high. Therefore, I know the number is from 1 to 49. I have eliminated 51 numbers. Next, I will guess the number 25 and see if I can eliminate more numbers. After six guesses, I discover that my partner's number was 17.
- *Looking back.* I was able to find the number quickly. I did not waste any guesses. I can use this strategy again. I can generalize this process to find that it should never take more than seven guesses to discover a whole number from 1 to 100.

Children can develop several strategies as Guess My Number progresses. They learn that wrong guesses can be valuable. The knowledge that guessing and wrong answers can be quite useful in mathematics is important to a child's willingness to tackle new problems.

One major skill in problem solving is finding a pattern. Working with numbers provides a good opportunity to practice finding patterns. Provide patterns such as 2, 4, 6, 8, —, — or 97, 94, 91, 88, —, —, —. After children understand the process, let them make up patterns for each other and place them in a learning center or copy them for everyone to work. Children may wish to use the constant feature on the calculator as they explore these patterns. An electronic example of this is available at the NCTM *Standards* website (http://standards-e.nctm.org, click e-examples).

After children have worked with patterns of their own, they may be ready for such patterns as Pascal's triangle, Fibonacci numbers, and sequences involving finite differences. For ideas on presenting these topics, see *Teaching Children Mathematics* and *Mathematics Teaching in the Middle School* or the references for this chapter. Encourage children to do further research on their own both with concrete materials and in books.

Study the following:

Pascal's Triangle

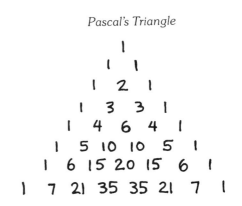

Make a list of the patterns the children find in the table. The patterns may include the following:

- Each number is the sum of the two numbers diagonally above it.
- The sum of the numbers in each row is a power of 2. The first row is just 1, 2^0; the sum of $1 + 1$ in the second row is 2, 2^1; the sum of $1 + 2 + 1$ in the third row is 4, 2^2; and so on.
- Diagonals that intersect in the middle of the triangle are identical, and each of these diagonals has an interesting pattern. The diagonal on the outside is all ones. In the next diagonal, the numbers have a difference of 1. The difference between numbers in a diagonal is equal to the closest number in the next diagonal to the outside.
- Each row is symmetrical.

There are many other patterns as well.

Many interesting activities that relate to the triangle can be found or created. The following are just a few. Children may create more of their own.

ACTIVITIES

Middle Grades (5–8)

Objective: to relate patterns in Pascal's Triangle to everyday life.

1. Flip a penny five times. How many ways can you get five heads? Only one way, right? How many ways can you get one head and four tails? Five ways, right? List them. How many ways can you get two heads and three tails? Three heads and two tails? Four heads and one tail? Five tails? Do you see a pattern? Is it related to Pascal's triangle? Test your hypothesis to see if this pattern holds for flipping coins other numbers of times.

2. How many ways can you select three children for the safety patrol from five volunteers? How is this related to Pascal's triangle?

3. Study the map in Figure 6–28. Danny lives at Main and 1st Street. He has a crush on Maureen, who lives at Grand and 6th Street. Maureen says Danny may visit each afternoon as long as he takes a different path each time. He may travel only north and east and must stay on the labeled streets. For how many afternoons may Danny visit Maureen?

Try to discover how Pascal's triangle is related to each of these activities. Encourage children to make up other patterns by asking themselves such questions as "What would happen if . . . ?" or "What if this were not true?" or "How else may I look at this?"

After working with Pascal's triangle, students might decide to investigate what happens when the odd counting numbers are listed in the same format as Pascal's triangle, as discussed in Chapter 3.

Fibonacci Numbers
Study the following pattern:

1,1,2,3,5,8,13,21,34,55, ...

How was this pattern formed?

As the Italian geometrician Leonardo Fibonacci studied natural objects such as spirals on a pine cone and petals on a flower, he discovered that the number of parts was often a number in this sequence. Let the children go on a scavenger hunt to find natural occurrences of Fibonacci numbers.

Intermediate and middle school children might enjoy videos that make use of patterns such as Pascal's Triangle and the Fibonacci sequence. Three good ones that you might use include *Donald in Mathmagic Land, Math Vantage Unit I: Patterns,* and *The Phantom of the Bell Tower.* Further information on these and other technology and print materials for exploring patterns in more depth is available in the reference list.

The following activity uses Fibonacci numbers. Try to discover how this pattern may help you solve the problem.

ACTIVITIES

Middle Grades (5–8)

Objective: to apply Fibonacci numbers to problem solving.

1. Antonio works at a soda fountain. He mixes milk shakes after school. He makes either regular shakes or extra-large shakes. An extra-large shake is twice the size of a regular shake. How many different ways can Antonio fill shake orders to use the equivalent of 10 regular shakes? For example, Antonio might first make 2 regular shakes and then 4 extra-large shakes, or he could first make 4 extra-large shakes and then 2 regular shakes; these two combinations are considered different. List all the possibilities. Do you see a

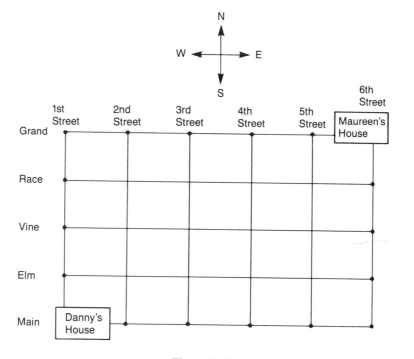

Figure 6–28

relationship to Fibonacci numbers? Try your hypothesis out on different shake orders.

Objectives: to reinforce place-value concepts and to encourage logical thinking.

2. The game Pica-Fermi is an old one, but more recent versions of it may be seen in *Mastermind* and in computer and calculator games. This game is similar to Guess My Number in that it has two players. One player writes down a secret number that the other tries to guess with the least possible number of guesses. This time, the first player may write down a two-, three-, or four-digit number (the number of digits should be agreed upon ahead of time), which the second player tries to guess by naming a number with the number of digits. The first player then tells the guesser the number of correct digits in the wrong place and the number of correct digits in the correct place by saying *pica* for the digits correct and in the wrong place and *fermi* for the digits correct and in the correct place. A sample game follows.

The secret number is 482.

The player guesses	Pica	Fermi
123	1	0
456	0	1
789	0	1
147	1	0
519	0	0
736	0	0
482	0	3

The score is 7 for this round, the number of guesses used to find 482. Try the game yourself with a partner. Discuss the strategies you used.

Objectives: to reinforce concepts of consecutive numbers and to encourage problem-solving strategies.

3. Number Shuffle is played by placing the digits 1–8 in a diagram such as Figure 6–29. No two consecutive digits may be touching horizontally, vertically, or diagonally.

    Encourage students to ask themselves questions such as "Are any positions basically the same because of symmetry?" and "Are any numbers special in terms of consecutive digits?" The last question should prompt the students to place the 1 and the 8 in the two center squares, which is a key to solving this problem.

Objectives: to reinforce place-value, give practice with a calculator, and encourage logical thinking.

4. Challenge the students to make their telephone numbers show on their calculators using only the 1, 0, +, and = keys. No telephone number should require pressing the "+" more than eight times. Many stu-

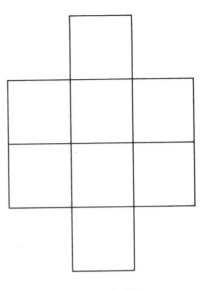

Figure 6–29

dents begin by pressing 1 + 1 + 1 + 1 + 1 . . ., but they should soon realize this will be futile. Others will try 1 000 000 + 1 000 000 + 100 000 . . ., but they should quickly realize that while this may result in the telephone number, the + was pressed more than eight times. Some hints may be needed before the child realizes that he or she may use 1 111 111 + 1 011 111 + ...

Objective: to develop a combination of spatial and numerical problem-solving abilities.

5. Estelle Dickens and Jeffrey Sellon (1981) have developed a set of activities called *Cuisenaire Roddles,* which include games and puzzles for use by one or more children. The children place the Cuisenaire rods on game boards to solve brain teasers or play strategy games that involve such skills as finding number patterns and completing "magic triangles." Children enjoy solving these puzzles and creating puzzles of their own for each other.

Objectives: to encourage historical research, to introduce non-place-value systems of numeration, and to aid in the development of new systems of numeration.

6. Introduce systems of numeration that do not use a base-10 system. Roman numerals may be evaluated in terms of using both an additive and a subtractive system and compared to the Egyptian system, which was strictly additive. The Chinese system, which uses both multiplication and addition, may then be introduced. These systems may be compared to the Babylonian and Mayan systems, which were both place-value systems, although neither used base-ten.

Children may research how our Hindu-Arabic numerals were developed. Encourage children to make up systems of their own and share them with other students. Children may look at the use of binary numbers in computers and perhaps create a tertiary number system, which might be more efficient.

7. Ask your students to read about the lives of female mathematicians who studied number theory and to demonstrate some of their findings. A good place to begin the research is *Women and Numbers: Lives of Women Mathematicians Plus Discovery Activities* by Teri Perl. This book describes their lives in language that is very readable by intermediate and middle grades students; it also suggests a variety of activities that students can do to understand the areas of mathematics that these women explored. For example, after a description of Ada Lovelace is a problem involving triangular numbers. Sonya Kovalevsky's description includes an activity involving prime numbers, Evelyn Boyd Granville's chapter has a problem with Pascal's Triangle, and Fanya Montalvo's has work with Fibonacci numbers. These descriptions give girls good role models of women who found their life's work in the mathematical field, and they also give them an opportunity to expand their mathematical horizons.

For more information on women mathematicians and scientists, see the website 4000 Years of Women in Science at http://crux.astr.ua.edu/4000ws/4000ws.html.

Grouping Students for Learning the Meaning of Numbers

Many of the activities in this chapter can be done by two children working as partners, while others may be done individually or in larger groups. Because the meaning of numbers must be constructed by the children themselves, they must be given time to work with materials and to think about questions that the teacher or other students have asked. It is important to give the students enough time to argue with each other about their work. Group time should be as important as individual time for working on problems and for discussing meanings with the teacher.

The games described in this chapter may be led by the children as well as the teacher. They give the children the opportunity to discuss meanings and understanding without trying to match an answer in a book. Be sure to give children plenty of time to work together on activities to develop grouping concepts. These concepts are crucial to the understanding of place value, and they will take a great deal of time to develop.

Communicating Understanding of the Meaning of Numbers

As students work with a partner and in groups, the discussion that goes on is essential to the development of the concept of number and the idea of place value. Kamii states:

> A characteristic of logico-mathematical knowledge is that there is absolutely nothing arbitrary in it. Two plus two makes four in all cultures. It follows that in the logico-mathematical realm, children *will* arrive at the truth if they debate long enough. They need to talk about their number experiences in everyday life, during games, and as they work with the development of place value concepts. The social interaction that goes on is an important part of the construction of the number concepts. (1990, p. 27)

It is important that the teacher focus on the children's understanding and not try to impose an arbitrary notion of number on the children. The only way the teacher will know what the children understand about numbers is to ask them. The teacher must take the time to listen to the children and to ask them questions that cause them to reach disequilibrium and construct their own concepts of number. In this way, oral communication becomes an integral and necessary part of every lesson.

Older children can communicate their reasoning in written form. They can keep logs about what they have learned and write out their methods of solving different types of problems. They can write down the new concepts they have learned and what areas may still be confusing.

Some of this writing may be expanded into portfolio entries. Students in the middle grades may write a portfolio entry based on their methods of determining the best way to approximate the number of blades of grass on the football field. They might take sample plots of 100 square centimeters each from a number of different parts of the field and explain how this can be used to estimate the number of blades of grass in the whole field. They might explain that parts of the field are bare from overuse and other parts have much thicker grass. They might divide the field into a half-dozen plots with different amounts of grass growth, sample each plot four times, find the average number of blades of grass in each sample, approximate the number of blades of grass in each plot, and total the number of blades of grass from all the plots. Extensions of this activity might include determining the best type of grass seed to replant parts of the field and finding the cost of doing this. Students should suggest other connections and extensions as they work on the problem.

Connecting Number Learning

Mr. Green's primary class is studying Native Americans. They have found that Native Americans used popcorn, and they are reading *The Popcorn Book* by Tomie de Paola. Through this study, they have learned that 1/2 cup of unpopped popcorn will make 12 cups of popped popcorn. They plan to have a popcorn party for their parents and are trying to figure out how much popcorn to buy for this. This will only be a small fraction of the 18.5 billion quarts of popcorn eaten in America each year.

Ms. Paulin's fourth-grade class is investigating the use of numbers in the daily newspaper. Each student has cut out 10 sentences from the paper that make use of numbers. The students are now grouping the sentences according to the numbers in them. They have made a large chart on the wall with the headings 0–9, 10–99, 100–999, 1,000–9,999, and greater than 10,000. So far, the heading with the most sentences under it is greater than 10,000. The students are discussing reasons why there are so many large numbers. They have noticed that there were several articles on the spending habits of citizens of the United States and the federal debt. They are now searching to determine who has found the sentence with the largest number. This is complicated by the fact that some numbers are expressed as numerals and some consist of a combination of numerals and words such as "8 billion."

After the students have completed the task of pasting the numbers on the chart, Ms. Paulin gathers them all on the floor around the chart to discuss their work. Students practice reading some of the numbers in the articles and discuss how large some of them really are. Their homework for the evening is to listen to television or radio for one half-hour and to write down a sentence for every number they hear. These will be sorted and investigated tomorrow according to the type of program that contained the numbers. Students brainstorm questions they would like to investigate, such as "Are there more numbers on the news or more numbers in a sitcom?" and "Are numbers stated in television news programs larger or smaller on average than numbers they found in the newspaper?" These questions are recorded on chart paper for the students to look at after they have collected their data.

Ms. Baker has just finished reading *Counting on Frank* to her sixth-graders. Will comments that the pictures in the book look like a picture book for his little brother. However, Dan says that he likes the numbers in the book. He wonders if they are really true. Ms. Baker is pleased that Dan has mentioned that because she plans to have the students take some of the events in the story and determine if the mathematics is reasonable. She divides the class into pairs and assigns each pair a different "fact" from the book to investigate. After all the groups have reported on their findings, Ms. Baker tells the class that they are going to write their own book for Mr. Meier's primary class to read. Each of the pairs must come up with a new mathematical statement to include in the book. Sabatina is already thinking about a fact based on the number of hairs on her dog. She can hardly wait to get home and have Geraldine help her count hairs on her Dalmatian Gypsy.

Ms. Baker decides that tomorrow would be a good time to introduce the new *Counting on Frank* software that she has just received.

Assessing Number Learning

As in any assessment, begin assessing number learning by looking at goals and objectives. Begin by examining the goals and objectives from the NCTM *Standards,* those set by your state or school district, and those of the textbook series being used. Review standardized tests that the students are required to take. These are often incomplete, however. Many of the conceptual and attitudinal goals and objectives of the teacher and learner are not tested by current standardized tests. Many of these tests are changing, however, to include more conceptual and performance-based items.

Take advantage of the tests provided in the children's textbook for assessing achievement of the objectives of that series. Texts often have pre- and post-tests for the students in the teacher's manual or related materials and practice tests for the students in their own books. Please keep in mind that written tests, especially tests that only look for one right answer, cannot give you all the information that you need about your students.

Your observations of students should provide much additional information. Look for what the child does well and for what the child may be having difficulty with. It is probably more important to look at the child's *processes* than it is to look at the child's *products.* A teacher can learn much more about the child by watching him or her work than by looking at the answers to a test. To aid in keeping track of children's individual work, the teacher should jot down anecdotal records each day. The teacher will probably not be able to observe each child each day but should make a point of seeing each child at least once per week. Ask the children to keep a portfolio of some of their best work, also. They may keep a written log, noting what they have learned and what is still not understood.

When studying number concepts, look for the following as the children manipulate concrete materials:

1. *Conservation.* With young children, be sure to determine whether the child can conserve both number and length.

2. *Counting.* Again, with young children, look for common counting errors. Can the child count rationally? That is, does the child say one number for each object counted or are numbers simply recited in order with no regard for the material being counted? Does the child realize that the sequence of the counting numbers does not change? Does the child understand that objects may be counted in any order? Does the child realize that the number named last when counting refers to the total number of objects in the set and not just to the last object? Can the child start counting with any number or only with 1? Can the child skip count by twos, fives, tens, and so on? Can the child count past the "hard numbers"—for example, 29 to 30, 99 to 100, 999 to 1,000, and so on? Can the child count backward from any number?

3. *Number concepts.* Does the child associate a number with a set of objects or is the number only a word to recite? Does a child recognize amounts up to at least 5 by sight?

4. *Grouping concepts.* Does the child understand trading units for groups and groups for supergroups, and so forth? Can the child record the results of trading?

5. *Place-value concepts.* Does the child understand the meaning of numerals written in standard Hindu-Arabic notation? Can the child model numerals with place value materials such as multibase blocks and chips for trading? Check this understanding by asking the child to count out 25 chips or other small objects. Circle the 5 in 25 and ask the child to show you that many chips. Then circle the 2 in 25 and ask the child to show you how many chips the 2 represents. If the child shows you 2 chips rather than 20, you will know that place-value is not clearly understood. You may wish to view the videotapes by Marilyn Burns (listed in the references) to watch her interviewing children on this concept. You might be surprised at some of the very common misconceptions.

6. *Estimation and approximation concepts.* Can the child use numbers to make reasonable estimates or approximate results?

7. *Problem creating and problem solving.* Can the child use numbers and strategies to create and solve problems?

8. *Uses in everyday life.* Is the child aware of numbers in the world around him or her and can the child use numbers rationally outside of school?

Something for Everyone

Physical models described in this chapter, such as Cuisenaire rods, multibase blocks, chips for trading, bean cups, the abacus, and bundling sticks, are excellent aids for tactile learners, while visual learners may wish to combine these materials with drawings. Auditory learners will wish to discuss what they are doing as they manipulate the objects. Music is an excellent aid for auditory learners, and they will enjoy counting songs and poems.

Students who learn well sequentially and in discrete units often like recipes and rules and tend not to estimate. They see the parts better than the whole. These students can count forward well and prefer discrete materials such as chips to spatial materials such as Cuisenaire rods and multibase blocks when learning number concepts.

Students who tend to be more spatial and holistic see the whole rather than the parts. They may estimate well and see the answer without knowing how they got it. They prefer Cuisenaire rods and multibase blocks to chips or other discrete objects for learning number concepts. They often can count backward better than forward.

Gifted children should be given many opportunities for both problem solving and problem creating. Topics such as Pascal's triangle, Fibonacci numbers, and other numeration systems, such as the Egyptian, Roman, or Babylonian systems, are a good starting point. Gifted students can find a wealth of information and interesting problems in these areas with some research on the Internet or in a good library, in the Ideas section of *Teaching Children Mathematics,* in articles in *Mathematics Teaching in the Middle School,* in the calendar section of the *Mathematics Teacher,* or in the student section of the newsletter of the National Council of Teachers of Mathematics (see Appendix A for the address). Encourage gifted students to make up problems of their own after solving some of these.

Children having difficulty with number concepts should not be rushed to work with numbers on an abstract level. Whether the difficulty is with beginning number concepts, perhaps due to the inability to conserve numbers or to counting misunderstandings, or with later ideas such as place-value, the children need to work with physical models. After the children feel comfortable with the models and seem to have grasped the concepts, be sure to have the children write the numerals with the models still in front of them. For many children, it is very difficult to make the transition from the physical models to the abstract numerals. Do not expect them to be able to remember what you did with the models yesterday if you ask them to work solely with numerals today. The two must be used together.

KEY IDEAS

Work with numbers constitutes a major portion of all elementary and middle school math programs. In this chapter, suggestions for making the most of this work have been presented. It is important that children understand number concepts and not merely recite them in a rote manner. Children should understand the cardinal, ordinal, and nominal uses of numbers. Children should be able to recognize the number of objects in a small set by sight and should be able to use rational counting to solve problems involving numbers.

Physical models such as counters, Cuisenaire rods, multibase blocks, chips for trading, abaci, wooden cubes, and counting sticks should be used extensively. Concrete work should be reinforced with semiconcrete and abstract work using number lines, charts, computers, calculators, and practice activities such as card games and board games devised by the teacher and/or the students themselves.

Because place value is such an important part of our numeration system and an understanding of it is crucial to later work with algorithms, children in kindergarten and first grade should work with grouping and trading such small amounts as those with a grouping point of 3, 4, or 5. This practice should extend to base-ten by the second grade, using both proportional and nonproportional grouping materials. Estimation skills should be practiced frequently. Children should be challenged to create problems involving interesting number patterns as well as to solve them.

Diagnosis of number concepts should be done individually, with a focus on developmental levels and common counting errors in the early grades and misconceptions about place value as the children get older. Provisions should be made for children with different abilities and learning styles.

DISCUSSION QUESTIONS

1. Analyze several of the counting books listed in the references or other favorites of your own. Compare books from different countries. Discuss the use of books from a variety of cultures in an elementary mathematics class. Will the use of different counting systems enhance the class or do you think children will be confused by the different use of numbers? Justify your position.

2. Choose two or three children between the ages of four and nine, and ask them several questions about conservation of numbers, counting, and place value. Analyze any mistakes that they make, and determine whether they can conserve number. Compare any mistakes in counting or place-value concepts to those described in this chapter or those that you see in a video such as the ones by Annenberg, Cathy Richardson, or Marilyn Burns that are listed in the references. Design individualized instruction based upon the results of your observations.

3. Choose and analyze a piece of software designed to help young children learn counting or number concepts. Do you think the software would be a help or a hindrance for a child in the early stages of learning numbers? If possible, watch a young child using the software and interview him or her to determine if new concepts are being developed accurately.

4. Choose a textbook series and examine the sections on place value for grades one through four. What physical models are suggested? How does the development of concepts move from the concrete to the connecting to the abstract level? How much repetition is there from one year of the program to the next? Do concepts build in complexity as the students get older? Compare your results to those of a classmate who has studied another program.

5. Choose a famous number pattern such as Pascal's Triangle, Triangular Numbers, or Fibonacci numbers and research its historical development. What patterns can you find in these numbers that made them so famous? Explore some of the questions that are raised in the history books, and try to find a new pattern that is not mentioned in any of the books. Report on your findings to the class.

REFERENCES

Adler, David A., *Base Five.* New York: Thomas Y. Crowell, 1975.

————, *Roman Numerals.* New York: Thomas Y. Crowell, 1977.

Anno, Mitsumasa, *Anno's Counting House.* New York, NY: Philomel, 1982.

Baroody, Arthur J., "Basic Counting Principles Used by Mentally Retarded Children," *Journal for Research in Mathematics Education,* 17, no. 5 (November 1986), 382–89.

Barta, James, and Diane Schaelling, "Games We Play: Connecting Mathematics and Culture in the Classroom." *Teaching Children Mathematics,* 4, no. 7 (March 1998), 388–93.

Brent, Jan, *The Twelve Days of Christmas.* New York: Putnam, 1990.

Burns, Marilyn, *Mathematics: Assessing Understanding.* New Rochelle, NY: Cuisenaire, 1993.

Carle, Eric, *The Very Hungry Caterpillar.* New York: Putnam, 1969.

Clement, Rod, *Counting on Frank.* Milwaukee, WI: Gareth Stevens, 1991.

Crews, Donald, *Ten Black Dots.* New York: Greenwillow, 1986.

Davidson, Patricia I., Grace K. Galton, and Arlene W. Fair, *Chip Trading Activities.* Arvada, CO: Scott Scientific, 1972.

Dee, Ruby, *Two Ways to Count to Ten.* New York: Holt, 1988.

dePaola, Tomie, *The Popcorn Book.* New York: Holiday, 1978.

Dickens, Estelle, and Jeffrey Sellon, *Cuisenaire Roddles.* New Rochelle, NY: Cuisenaire Co. of America, 1981.

Doman, Glenn, *Teach Your Baby Math.* Philadelphia: The Better Baby Press, 1980.

Dossey, John A., Ina V. S. Mullis, Mary M. Lindquist, and Donald L. Chambers, *The Mathematics Report Card: Are We Measuring Up? Trends and Achievement Based on the 1986 National Assessment.* Princeton, NJ: Educational Testing Service, 1988.

Education Development Center, Inc., *Seeing and Thinking Mathematically in the Middle Grades: The Language of Numbers.* Portsmouth, NH: Heinemann, 1996.

Feelings, Muriel, *Moja Means One: A Swahili Counting Book.* New York: Dial, 1971.

Friedman, Aileen, *The King's Commissioners.* New York, NY: Scholastic, 1994.

Fuson, Karen C., and J. W. Hall, "The Acquisition of Early Number Word Meanings: A Conceptual Analysis and Review," in *The Development of Mathematical Thinking,* ed. H. P. Ginsburg. New York: Academic Press, 1983, pp. 49–107.

Giganti, Paul, Jr., *How Many Snails? A Counting Book.* New York: Greenwillow, 1988.

Ginsburg, Herbert P., *Children's Arithmetic: The Learning Process.* New York: D. Van Nostrand, 1977.

————,"Children's Surprising Knowledge of Arithmetic," *Arithmetic Teacher,* 28, no. 1 (September 1980), 42–44.

Hamm, Diane J., *How Many Feet in the Bed?* New York: Simon and Schuster, 1991.

Hiebert, James, "Children's Thinking," in *Research in Mathematics Education,* Richard J. Shumway, ed. Reston, VA: National Council of Teachers of Mathematics, 1980.

Hulme, Joy, *Sea Squares.* New York: Hyperion, 1991.

Kamii, Constance, "Constructivism and Beginning Arithmetic (K–2)," in *Teaching and Learning Math in the 1990s,* Thomas J. Cooney and Christian Hirsch. eds. Reston, VA: National Council of Teachers of Mathematics, 1990.

Karp, Karen S., and Robert N. Ronau, "Birthdays and the Binary System: A Magical Mixture." *Mathematics Teaching in the Middle School,* 3, no. 1 (September 1997), 6–12.

Leutzinger, Larry P., Edward C. Rathmell, and Tonya D. Urbalsch, "Developing Estimation Skills in the Primary Grades," in *Estimation and Mental Computation,* National Council of Teachers of Mathematics, 1986 Yearbook. Reston, VA: NCTM, 1986.

McIntosh, Alistair, Barbara Reys, and Robert Reys, *Number Sense: Simple Effective Number Sense Experiences.* (Series of four books for grades 1–2, 3–4, 4–6, and 6–8). White Plains, NY: Dale Seymour, 1997.

McKissack, Patricia, *A Million Fish. . . More or Less.* New York: Knopf, 1992.

Merriam, Eve, *12 Ways to Count to 11.* New York: Simon and Schuster, 1993.

National Council of Teachers of Mathematics, *Curriculum and Evaluation Standards for School Mathematics.* Reston, VA: NCTM, 1989.

National Research Council, *Everybody Counts: A Report to the Nation on the Future of Mathematics Education.* Washington, DC: National Academy Press, 1989.

Paulos, John Allen, *Innumeracy: Mathematical Illiteracy and Its Consequences.* New York: Hill and Wang, 1988.

Perl, Teri, *Women and Numbers: Lives of Women Mathematicians plus Discovery Activities.* San Carlos, CA: Wide World Publishing/Tetra, 1993.

Piaget, Jean, *The Child's Concept of Number.* New York: W. W. Norton, 1965.

Pinczes, Elinor J., *One Hundred Hungry Ants.* Boston: Houghton Mifflin, 1993.

Reese, Mary, *Ten in a Bed.* Boston: Little, Brown, 1988.

Roper, Ann, *Cooperative Problem Solving with Unifix Cubes.* Sunnyvale, CA: Creative Publications, 1990.

Roper, Ann, Shirley Hoogeboom, and Judy Goodnow, *Cooperative Problem Solving with Calculators.* Sunnyvale, CA: Creative Publications, 1991.

Schwartz, David M., *How Much Is a Million?* New York: Lothrop, Lee, and Shepard, 1986.

Schwartz, David M., *If You Made a Million.* New York: Lothrop, Lee, and Shepard, 1989.

Schielack, Jane F., and Dinah Chancellor. *Uncovering Mathematics with Manipulatives and Calculators: Levels 1, 2 & 3.* Dallas, TX: Texas Instruments, Inc., 1995.

Scieszka, Jon, and Lane Smith, *Math Curse.* Bergenfield, NJ: Viking, Penguin Books USA, 1995.

Sitomar, Mindel, and Harry Sitomer, *Zero Is Not Nothing.* New York: Thomas Y. Crowell, 1978.

Skemp, Richard R., *The Psychology of Learning Mathematics.* Hillsdale, NJ: Lawrence Erlbaum Associates, 1987.

St. John, Glory, *How to Count Like a Martian.* New York: Henry Z. Walck, 1975.

Stokes, William T., *Notable Numbers.* Los Altos, CA: Covington Middle School, Los Altos School District, 1972.

Taverner, Nixie, *Unifix Structural Material.* North Way, England: Philograph Publications, 1977.

Wahl, John, and Stacey Wahl, *I Can Count the Petals of a Flower.* Reston, VA: National Council of Teachers of Mathematics, 1976.

Watson, Clyde, *Binary Numbers.* New York: Crowell, 1977.

Wilcutt, Robert, Carole Greenes, and Mark Spikell, *Base Ten Activities.* Palo Alto, CA: Creative Publications, 1975.

Williams, Vera B., *Cherries and Cherry Pits.* New York, NY: Mulberry Books, 1986.

Wood, Audrey, and Don Wood, *Piggies.* San Diego: Harcourt Brace Jovanovich, 1991.

Zaslavsky, Claudia, *Count on Your Fingers African Style.* New York: Thomas Y. Crowell, Junior Books, 1980.

Zaslavsky, Claudia, *The Multicultural Math Classroom: Bringing in the World.* Portsmouth, NH: Heinemann, 1996.

Technology

Annenberg/CPB, *Teaching Math: A Video Library, K–4.* Boston, MA: WGBH Educational Foundation, 1995.

————, *Mathematics Assessment: A Video Library, K–12.* Boston, MA: WGBH Educational Foundation, 1995.

Broderbund, *Carmen Sandiego Math Detective.* Novato, CA: Broderbund, 1998. (software)

————, *James Discovers Math.* Novato, CA: Broderbund. (software)

Burns, Marilyn, *Mathematics: Assessing Understanding.* White Plains, NY: Cuisenaire. (Set of 3 videos and discussion guide)

Children's Television Network, *Mathnet Mysteries: The View from the Rear Terrace.* Lincoln, NE: GPN, 1991. (Video Kit)

Creative Wonder, *Counting on Frank.* Minneapolis, MN: The Learning Company. (software)

Davidson, *Math Blaster Jr.* Torrance, CA: Davidson, 1997. (software)

Edmark, *Mighty Math Calculating Crew.* Orlando, FL: Harcourt Brace, 1996. (software)

————, *Mighty Math Carnival Countdown.* Orlando, FL: Harcourt Brace, 1996. (software)

————, *Millie's Math House.* Orlando, FL: Harcourt Brace. (software)

GPN, *Math Vantage: Unit 1: Patterns.* Lincoln, NE: GPN, 1997. (Video and print materials)

HRM, *The Phantom of the Bell Tower.* Pleasantville, NY: Human Relations Media.

MECC, *MathKeys.* Minneapolis, MN: The Learning Company. (software)

Morrison, Philip, Phylis Morrison, and the Office of Charles and Ray Eames, *Powers of Ten.* New York: Scientific American, 1982. (Video and book)

Richardson, Kathy, *A Look at Children's Thinking Video I, Assessment Techniques: Beginning Number Concepts.* Norman, OK: Educational Enrichment, 1990.

————, *A Look at Children's Thinking Video II, Assessment Techniques: Number Combinations and Place Value.* Norman, OK: Educational Enrichment, 1990.

Sunburst, *Sunbuddy Math Playhouse.* Pleasantville, NY: Sunburst. (software)

Walt Disney Company, *Donald in Mathmagic Land.* Burbank, CA: Buena Vista Home Video, 1959.

Web Sites

http://crux.astr.ua.edu/4000ws/4000ws.html   4000 years of women in science.

http://www.learner.org/   The Annenberg/CPB Math and Science Collection.

http://standards-e.nctm.org   NCTM electronic version of the standards.

Chapter 7

Teaching and Learning
Addition and Subtraction

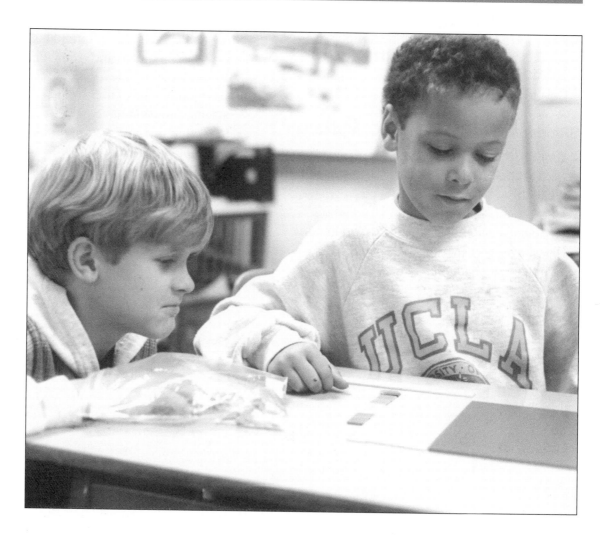

NCTM Standards

GRADES K–4

Standard 7: Concepts of Whole Number Operations

In grades K–4, the mathematics curriculum should include concepts of addition, subtraction, multiplication, and division of whole numbers so that students can—

- Develop meaning for the operations by modeling and discussing a rich variety of problem situations;
- Relate the mathematical language and symbolism of operations to problem situations and informal language;
- Recognize that a wide variety of problem structures can be represented by a single operation;
- Develop operation sense.

Standard 8: Whole Number Computation

In grades K–4, the mathematics curriculum should develop whole number computation so that students can—

- Model, explain, and develop reasonable proficiency with basic facts and algorithms;
- Use a variety of mental computation and estimation techniques;
- Use calculators in appropriate computational situations;
- Select and use computation techniques appropriate to specific problems and determine whether the results are reasonable.

GRADES 5–8

Standard 7: Computation and Estimation

In grades 5–8, the mathematics curriculum should develop the concepts underlying computation and estimation in various contexts so that students can—

- Compute with whole numbers, fractions, decimals, integers, and rational numbers;
- Develop, analyze, and explain procedures for computation and techniques for estimation;
- Develop, analyze, and explain methods for solving proportions;
- Select and use an appropriate method for computing from among mental arithmetic, paper-and-pencil, calculator, and computer methods;
- Use computation, estimation, and proportions to solve problems;
- Use estimation to check the reasonableness of results.

NCTM (1989), pp. 41, 44, 94. Reprinted by permission.

My Math Journal

Copy the addition table in Appendix B and fill it in. Describe all of the patterns that you can find in the table. Include such things as drawing a square around 4, 9, or 16 cells anywhere in the table and looking for sums and differences of the numbers in the cells. As you write your answers, be sure to explain all of your thinking.

As you read the following pages, consider these guiding questions:

1. What is an operation and how does it differ from a specific operation like addition or subtraction?
2. What is the sequence of teaching the concepts and skills of addition and subtraction?
3. What are several embodiments for presenting the concepts of addition and subtraction?
4. What are some different activities to help children memorize the basic addition and subtraction facts?
5. Why should students develop skill in estimating and mental calculating?
6. What are some reasons that students make mistakes in their computation?

Addition and subtraction are widely used in our daily lives. Much of the justification for keeping a strong emphasis on computation in the school curriculum comes from its perceived usefulness. At the market, our purchases are added together. We add and subtract to determine if we have enough money and subtract to determine our change.

Children begin purchasing items early in their lives. Learning to go to the store is a common part of growing up. Role playing various parts in a classroom store is a valuable learning activity.

Computation, on the other hand, is seldom still performed using pencil and paper. Cash registers scan universal price codes and use electronic voices to inform the customer what is being purchased, its cost, and the change due. Gasoline may be purchased by inserting a credit card in a small reader at the pump, activating that particular pump so the customer can fill the automobile tank; the amount of gasoline and its cost are registered in a computer file established for that customer, who will be billed at the end of the month. Even small businesses rely on calculators and computers when determining purchase amounts.

It may be argued that such conveniences undermine the personal interaction of daily life. Still, the efficiency and accuracy of electronic computation is a persuasive argument for its continuing use.

Children growing up in a time of electronic computation will need to be skillful in estimation and mental arithmetic. They will need to know when answers are reasonable and when they are not. They will need to be able to double check purchase lists to assure accuracy and to know what operation is required to determine purchase amounts. They must learn how to comparison shop and how to manipulate numbers to their advantage in the marketplace. Students should be encouraged to make an important decision associated with calculation: whether to use paper and pencil, mental calculation, estimation, or a calculator or computer. This decision is made when a particular calcula-

tion is needed. Students skilled in using a variety of computational techniques have at their command the power and efficiency of mathematics. The instructional program should provide children many opportunities to make decisions regarding which computational technique to employ. This chapter is written to suggest ways in which you may help students think about numbers and create in students the habit of using their heads.

Children begin learning addition and subtraction long before they are introduced to the **basic addition facts,** the whole-number sums from $0 + 0$ to $9 + 9$. First, children develop understanding of everyday relationships. They gain some meaning of whole numbers before they attend school. Through their explorations, youngsters invent informal systems of mathematics. Children use counting procedures to find how many things are in a collection of objects and counting strategies to solve simple word problems.

Your job as a teacher is to determine how children think about numbers. Pose simple word problems and observe how the children solve them. For example, "Sarah has 4 tiles; David gives her 2 more. Now, how many does she have?" The responses can serve as a basis for beginning number work. Perhaps the child **counts all;** that is, counts 1, 2, 3, 4, using fingers to keep track, and then 5, 6, continuing to count fingers, and gives the answer 6 by reporting how many fingers were counted. Perhaps the child **counts on;** that is, says 4, and then 5, 6, counting two more fingers. Perhaps the child uses tiles or beans to count out the answer. Perhaps all counting is done in the child's head with lip movement as the only sign of counting. Perhaps the child visualizes a set of four objects joined with a set of two objects and responds without counting. For children having difficulty, you can provide practice in counting and grouping. You are challenged to build on what children bring to the classroom and provide activities that help children further grow and develop their mathematical thinking and their understanding of the concepts of addition and subtraction.

This work with oral word problems is very important and should precede any written work with number sentences. Students should have extensive work in posing and answering each other's story situations orally and with materials before they ever see an abstract addition or subtraction number sentence. They should use many physical models: attribute blocks, multibase blocks, Cuisenaire rods, beans, and cubes are among the most useful. Other counting objects, like bottle caps, nuts and bolts, buttons, and washers, are ideal for illustrating operations. Calculators and computers help in learning basic arithmetic operations as well. Children beginning to understand the basic operations are active learners.

Developing Addition and Subtraction Concepts

The general concept of an operation serves as a foundation for understanding the concepts of addition and subtraction. The term **operation** refers to a process that involves a change or transformation. The process begins with an object in a particular state of affairs; then an operation occurs that causes a change in the object, resulting in a final state of affairs. Children have many intuitive experiences with operations or transformations. A child's experience in his or her daily life can help provide understanding of a mathematical idea when that experience is tied to a learning activity. For example, a child is sleeping, a parent calls to awaken the child, and soon the child is awake. The initial state of affairs is the child asleep; the final state of affairs is the child awake. What happened in between, being awakened, is the process of transformation from being asleep to being awake.

In her children's book *Footprints and Shadows,* Dodd (1992) artfully describes footprints and shadows that appear and then disappear. In each case there is an example of a transformation, a state of affairs in which a set of footprints or a shadow is displayed and then a new state of affairs in which the footprints and shadows are gone.

These transformations do not appear to be linked with addition, but they are in an important way. To illustrate, a simple machine as a model for the addition process is shown in Figure 7–1. It is a two-dimensional model with an input and an output. The operation or transformation takes place in the center of the machine. What enters at the input is an initial state of affairs, and the output resulting from the operation is the final state of affairs. This process coincides with the child's previous experiences and should be discussed as the mathematical concept is developed.

When this state-operator-state machine is used to model addition, it may appear as in Figure 7–2. In Figure 7–2a, we have a machine similar to those introduced in Chapter 2. It is a single-input machine, sometimes called a function of one variable. It represents a *unary* operation. The join $\square\,\square$ or + 2 is the operator within the

machine. The output is $\square$ + 2. We cannot know the output until we know the input. Therefore, $\square$ stands for a variable.

Figure 7–2b shows a double-input machine, sometimes called a function of two variables. It represents a binary operation. Mathematically, we would write $\square + \triangle$. The two inputs are $\square$ and $\triangle$, and the operator is join or +. In our example, four cubes are in the first input and two cubes are in the second input. The operation is to join the cubes. For either machine, the resulting output is six cubes. Perform the operation of joining objects physically by moving the cubes through the machine, joining them, and moving them to the output. Our introductory work with operations uses the unary operation, but as we look at a model for addition, we employ the binary operation. The binary operation machine more closely resembles addition as it is presented in school.

In the early grades children should be introduced to the concept of an operation and to the concepts of addition and subtraction using physical models. Eventually, we move away from the physical experiences with sets of objects toward the pictorial and abstract. Inputs can be numbers, and operators can be symbols. Children learn that addition renames a pair of numbers with a single equivalent number. For example, the pair (4, 2) is associated with 6 under the operation of addition. Learning how addition works is learning the concept of addition. Learning that 4 + 2 = 6 is learning a basic addition fact.

Each of the following sections, on operations, addition, and subtraction, presents activities for helping students develop concepts. We use the machine model initially but also include other useful models.

Figure 7–1

Figure 7–2

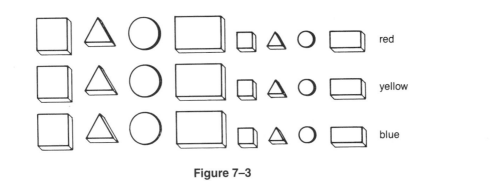

Figure 7–3

Operations

To separate the concept of an operation from the concept of a numerical operation, activities to develop the concept of an operation should use materials that are not models for numbers. For these activities, we use the attribute blocks shown in Figure 7–3.

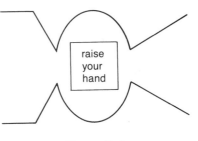

Figure 7–4

ACTIVITIES

Primary (K–3)

Objective: to perform operations on objects.

1. Begin with an introduction to the state-operator-state machine. On the floor, mark a large outline of a machine like that in Figure 7–1, using yarn or masking tape. Do not include the labels. Explain to the children that this special machine usually causes a change to occur. The machine has a starting place called an input and an ending place called an output. The change takes place in the middle.

   Invite a child to help demonstrate the machine. Have her stand in the input. Then ask her to step into the center and to raise one hand over her head. Tell her to step to the output region with her hand still over her head. While she is still in the output, question the class, "How did Marie start in the input? How did Marie end up? What change took place?" Repeat this demonstration several times, inviting other children to move through the machine and to give the operation command.

   Next, put a sign in the center of the machine that says "raise your hand," as in Figure 7–4. Invite several more children to go through the machine and to do what the operator says when they get to the center. Encourage the children to discuss what happens as they pass through the center of the machine.

   To extend this activity, vary the operator. Include face the other way, hold your hands behind your back, start clapping your hands, and hug yourself. At some point, introduce do nothing to show that an operation can result in no difference from the input to the output. This is the first example of what will later be introduced as adding zero to a number.

2. Use the same type of machine that was used in the previous activity. This time, have a child hold an attribute block. The operator should be change color, change shape, or change size. Suppose Rich starts at the input with a large red triangle, and the operator is change color. This means to change only the color and no other attribute. In the center of the machine, let Rich decide how he can perform the operation. He may exchange the large red triangle for a large blue triangle or large yellow triangle. Let the other students comment on the results (see Figure 7–5).

   If the input had been a large, red triangle and the operator had been change shape, the output could have been a large, red square, circle, or rectangle. If the input had been a large, red triangle and the operator had been change size, the output could have been only a small red triangle. Encourage the students to discuss the possible outcomes of various operations.

3. The game Simon Says serves as an example of an operation. The leader may be a student or the teacher. The leader gives commands to the entire class, beginning some with "Simon says." Later the leader can give commands without saying "Simon says."

   The children should follow only commands that are begun with "Simon says"; otherwise, they must sit out the remainder of the game. For example, with the children standing, hands to their sides, the leader commands, "Simon says, 'Touch your nose.' " The children should then reach up and touch their noses

Figure 7–5

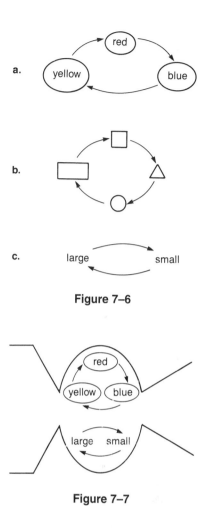

Figure 7–6

Figure 7–7

and remain in that position until another command is given. If the next command is "Put your hand down," no one should respond because the command did not begin with "Simon says." Discuss with the children how this game is like working with the state-operator-state machine. Let them decide when the operation is performed.

The children's position before a command corresponds to the initial state, or input. When a command beginning with "Simon says" is given and the children respond, an operation is performed. The new position of the children is the final state, or output. Giving a command without saying "Simon says" has the same effect as the operator doing nothing.

Objective: to perform an operation on objects to produce a single, unique output.

4. Now draw the machine on the chalkboard, place it on a flannel board, or sketch it on the inside of file folders. The operation for the state-operator-state machine appears in Figure 7–6a. Have the children explore and discuss the operation. For example, the operator in Figure 7–6a means that a red block will change to blue, a blue block will change to yellow, and a yellow block will change to red. Again, only the attribute mentioned will change. Thus, if the input is a small yellow triangle, the output will be a small red triangle. No other block in the set shown in Figure 7–3 will satisfy the given operator.

Other operations for these attribute blocks are shown in Figures 7–6b and c. The operation in 7–6b would cause a small, yellow triangle to change to a small, yellow circle. The operation in 7–6c would cause a small, yellow triangle to change to a large yellow triangle. As students work on these operations ask them to make up operations using variations of those already demonstrated.

Extend this activity by putting two or three operators in the center of the machine as in Figure 7–7.

When an object enters the machine, both operations must be performed. This set of operators would cause a small, yellow circle to change to a large, red circle. You can adjust the complexity of the operators to challenge the children and the children can challenge one another. The common thread throughout these activities is that an operation is taking place, transforming an object from the initial state to the final state.

Addition

Sorting, classifying, and reversibility of thought are necessary for children to understand both addition and subtraction. Sorting and classifying were carefully discussed in Chapters 5 and 6. **Reversibility of thought** occurs when children are able to reverse their thinking process. An example from the Piaget task to check class inclusion is provided here: Suppose you have a set of 10 colored cubes, 7 green and 3 yellow. A child who is observing the cubes is asked if there are more cubes or more green cubes. This question is asked to determine if the child perceives that the total collection of cubes includes the green cubes and is larger than the subset of green cubes. When asked if there are more cubes or more green cubes, children who have not achieved reversibility of thought respond that there are more green cubes. These children are comparing the subset of green cubes with the subset of yellow cubes. When their perception shifts from the whole set (cubes) to the subset (green cubes), they ignore the whole set, the set of cubes, and cannot reverse their thought back to it from the subsets.

The ability to recognize subsets of objects as included in a larger set occurs at about the age of seven. As a result, we sometimes try to teach the concepts of addition and subtraction to children before children can fully comprehend them. Take care to provide a variety of sorting and grouping experiences when the concept of addition is introduced.

A useful early addition experience is to have children respond to number stories. For example, give Missy three oranges and give Loren two. Start with, "Loren has two oranges and Missy gives him three more. How many oranges does Loren have?" Prompt Missy to give Loren her three oranges. Some children will know the answer without counting oranges, while others will need to count. Invite the children to explain how they found the answer.

Along the same lines but subtly different is this story: "Jacob has three computer games and Margo has four computer games. How many do they have together?" Again, invite students to explain how they determined the answer.

The difference between the two number stories is that the first story suggests an operation and the second merely describes a state of affairs. While both stories are useful, the first one provides a somewhat stronger foundation for understanding joining, or combining, the basis of addition.

With encouragement, children can tell number stories of their own, using real or imaginary situations. Telling or writing these stories provides language experience. The final result may be a bulletin board, a class number-stories book, or a HyperStudio stack with number stories.

Colored cubes, beans, bottle caps, color tiles, multibase blocks, Cuisenaire rods, and other counting objects can serve as bases for developing the concept of addition. The operator initially presented is *join* or *combine* (an operator for sets of objects), to prepare children for addition (an operation on number). We use join or combine because we believe these words are easier for children to understand. State-operator-state machines may be used to present the concept of addition, but other models also should be used. Of particular importance is to have children discuss their thinking and the procedures they use to reach solutions. The following activities include various ways to present the addition concept.

ACTIVITIES

Primary (K–3)

Objective: to join objects as a model for addition.

1. Provide the children with individual state-operator-state machines drawn on the insides of file folders, on individual chalkboards, or on paper. Place a large model on the floor with yarn or masking tape. The operator for the machine is join. Let there be two inputs.

   Figure 7–8 shows 3 cubes in one input and 4 cubes in the other input. Take the objects to the center of the machine and join them. Then move them to the output.

   As in an earlier activity, have one child pick up several cubes—6, for example—and move to one of the inputs of the large machine. Then have another child pick up several cubes—4, for example—and move to the other input. Next, have both children move into the center of the machine and join their cubes. Finally, have the children move to the output with their larger collection of cubes.

   Initially, perform this operation without counting the cubes. When the children have joined cubes successfully several times, have them describe how many cubes are in each input and how many cubes result in the output. For example, "6 cubes are in one input, 4 cubes are in the other input, and the output has 10 cubes." Eventually, the children will write number sentences that describe their actions.

2. Once students have mastered the previous operation, extend the activity by introducing problem solving. Set up a machine like that in Figure 7–9 to challenge thinking. The machine in Figure 7–9 shows objects in one input and objects in the output. Challenge the children to find the number of objects missing from the second input. In this case, a group of 5 cubes appears in one of the inputs. Ask the children if they know how many cubes should go in the other input so the number of cubes in the output will be correct. If the children find this question difficult, begin by ask-

Figure 7–8

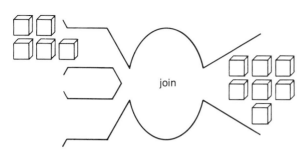

Figure 7–9

ing, "What if we put 1 cube in the other input? Would we get the right number of cubes in the output?" One cube will not produce a large enough output. Next, try 2 cubes, the answer. The problem solving strategy of guess and check is used to solve this problem. This is a manipulative version of the abstract problem 5 + ? = 7. The children should be challenged to make up similar problem situations for members of their group or the whole class.

Vary this activity by using objects such as *Unifix cubes,* multicolored plastic cubes that snap together. Unifix cubes offer children a chance to combine cubes into long sticks or, even better, groups of 10.

Navy beans offer children a chance to work with large collections of objects. The beans can be conveniently grouped into tens as they are put into the input and then combined. Small portion cups serve well for each collection of 10.

Multibase blocks serve as an excellent model for addition. Children who have had earlier exposure to grouping with the multibase blocks can readily combine them and can exchange pieces in the output as in Figure 7–10.

Objective: to use Cuisenaire rods to illustrate addition.

3. Two or more Cuisenaire rods placed end to end form a train. Invite the children to make a train using a light green rod and a yellow rod. Next, have them find an-

other rod that is the same length as the light green and yellow rods combined; they will soon discover the brown rod. Have the children place the brown rod beside the light green-yellow train as in Figure 7–11. Explain that light green plus yellow equals brown.

Ask the children to find another train that is the same length as the brown rod. Expect a variety of answers. Seven two-rod trains are possible if reversals, such as red plus dark green and dark green plus red, are considered different trains. There are also three-rod trains (for example, red plus red plus purple) as well as four-, five-, six-, and seven-rod trains, and there is even an eight-rod train. When the children have discovered the trains, have them say what the trains are.

At this point, numbers are not directly associated with the Cuisenaire rods. Number values will be assigned to the rods later.

Children soon find two-rod trains that are longer than the longest single rod, orange. Here, ask them to make a train using orange plus whatever rod is necessary to equal the length of the original two rods. For example, Figure 7–12 shows a two-rod train, black plus blue, which is equal to orange plus dark green. Other trains may be equal to more than two orange rods; for example, purple plus dark green plus yellow plus black equals orange plus orange plus red.

As children become more proficient at adding rods they produce more complex sums. To shortcut writing the names of all the rods, use the symbols used by the developers of Cuisenaire rods: w (white), r (red), g (light green), p (purple), y (yellow), d (dark green), k (black), n (brown), e (blue), σ (orange).

The first three activities present different embodiments for the concept of addition. Another embodiment begins the transition toward more abstract work. The transition to using symbols should be presented slowly and with concrete models representing the symbolic expressions.

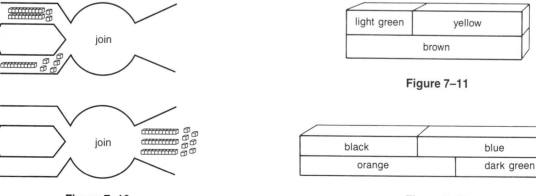

Figure 7–10

Figure 7–11

Figure 7–12

ACTIVITIES

Primary (K–3)

Objective: to introduce the concept of addition using sets of objects.

1. Draw three loops on a large sheet of paper or place them directly on the floor with yarn or masking tape. Place several objects in the top two loops, as in Figure 7–13a. Indicate to the children that they are to combine or join the objects and put them in the third loop. Be sure you introduce the word *combine* or the word *join*.

   Begin the transition from joining objects to adding numbers by asking the children how many objects are in the first loop. In Figure 7–13a, the first loop has 3 objects. The second loop has 4 objects. The loop with the objects combined (Figure 7–13b) has 7 objects. Explain that this diagram shows 3 plus 4 equals 7.

   Let the children develop other examples and invite the children to tell what the various diagrams show. The children read the diagrams at this point rather than actually add the numbers.

   Soon, you can use the symbols for addition. Introduce the symbols in an addition sentence, such as 3 + 4 = 7. Then introduce them in the vertical form:

$$\begin{array}{r} 3 \\ + 4 \\ \hline 7 \end{array}$$

   Help the children read these sentences and become familiar with them.

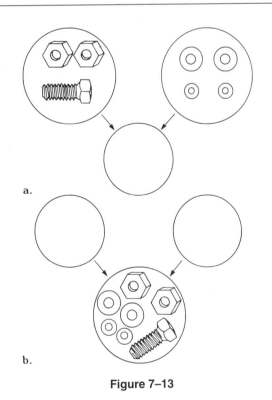

a.

b.

Figure 7–13

ACTIVITIES

Primary (K–3)

Objective: to introduce the symbolism of addition.

1. Review with the children the state-operator-state machine. Using Figure 7–14, ask the children, "How many cubes are there in the first input?" There are 2. "How many are there in the second input?" There are 3. "How many are there in the output?" There are 5 in the output. Summarize, "Then this machine shows us that 2 plus 3 equals 5. It is written 2 + 3 = 5."

   Let the children explore numerous examples of their own until they can easily determine the values illustrated in the machine and easily recognize the symbols of addition.

2. With the Cuisenaire rods, establish a value for the white rod. For example, if the white rod is 1, what is the value of the red rod, the light green rod, the purple rod, and so on? Challenge the children to find the rod values if the white rod has a value of 1. Children may determine these rod values by finding how many white rods it takes to make the red rod (2), the light green rod (3), and the purple rod (4). Be open to other suggestions for determining the rod values. Give children additional experience with the rods to allow them to be at ease in symbolizing the rod values.

   Later, particularly in work with fractions, other rod values will be established. Be careful not to declare 1 the permanent value of white, 2 the permanent value of red, 3 the permanent value of green, and so on. If white equals 1, the train in Figure 7–15 is 4 plus 2 and is equal to 6, or 4 + 2 = 6.

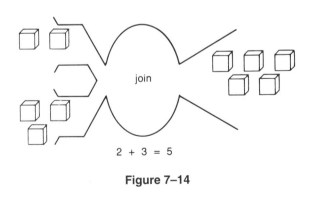

join

2 + 3 = 5

Figure 7–14

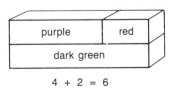

purple	red
dark green	

4 + 2 = 6

Figure 7–15

To this point, we have introduced the concept of addition using several embodiments and the symbols that describe addition. As we continue, we introduce an important property of addition, the commutative property, along with a new embodiment for addition.

ACTIVITIES

Primary (K–3)

Objective: to use dominoes as a model for addition.

1. Use sets of double-six dominoes for this activity. These may be the commercial sets or teacher constructed sets. A set of double-six dominoes consists of 28 dominoes showing all combinations from blank-blank to six-six. To begin, explain that a domino such as the one in Figure 7–16a is read as "3 plus 5." If all of the dots are counted, we can complete the number sentence by supplying the sum, 8; thus, 3 + 5 = 8. If the same domino is picked up differently or rotated, it may be read as "5 plus 3 equals 8," and will appear as in Figure 7–16b.

   Soon, children will pick up a domino, read it as either "3 + 5 = 8" or "5 + 3 = 8," and will know that no matter which way it is read, the sum is still 8. This important characteristic of addition is the **commutative property of addition.** Knowing that order has no effect on the sum reduces the number of addition facts to be remembered.

   When the students can read the dominoes, let them spread the dominoes face down, mix them up, and select them one at a time and explain to other group members or the whole class what they "say." Any domino portion that is blank is read as "zero," meaning that it has zero dots. The domino blank-four is read as "0 plus 4" or "4 plus 0," depending on how it is held. As the children become confident reading dominoes, change to a double-nine set.

   To vary this activity, change the standard domino dot pattern to a more random pattern. This will require that you construct your own dominoes. Thus,

the dot pattern for three may be three dots in a triangular configuration rather than the traditional diagonal line of three dots and four also may be a different pattern as in Figure 7–17. Using different configurations helps children to visualize various dot patterns and to attach number values to those different patterns. Burton, et al., (1993) describes a series of clever domino activities that help develop number sense and operations for kindergarten, first, and second grade students. You are encouraged to consider using them.

The concept of addition has been presented with a model that uses joining or combining sets of objects. While the children were still at the concrete level, number was attached to the operation to assist the children in seeing the relationship between joining objects and adding numbers. We continue by introducing the concept of subtraction in a similar manner.

Subtraction

Teaching the concept of subtraction is much like teaching the concept of addition. The materials, models, and approach are the same. The concept, however, is different. As teachers, we want children to be able to see that subtraction is the inverse of addition. To achieve this, we need to teach subtraction at the same time we teach addition. Subtraction can be fully understood only when children can classify and sort objects by their attributes and achieve reversibility of thought. Children must be able to see the relationship between a collection of objects and a subset of that collection in order to understand subtraction. When a subset is removed from a collection, the idea of subtraction is understood if children realize that returning the subset to the collection restores the collection to its original state. Thus, the student is doing more than merely following the teacher's direction to remove a subset and count the elements in the resulting collection. For the children who cannot yet classify and have not achieved reversibility of thought, you will need to provide additional material, time, and encouragement.

Number stories that introduce children to addition can also introduce children to subtraction. For example, "Cindy has 6 model horses. Trisha takes 2 of the horses

Figure 7–16

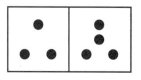

Figure 7–17

to play with. Now, how many horses does Cindy have?" This story, an example of *take away* or *remove,* may be acted out to find the solution.

We begin another story: "Chris has 5 books. Ken has 2 books. How many more books does Chris have than Ken?" Here, the books can be compared and the difference can be determined.

Still another approach is this: "Jack has 3 cookies and Nicole has 7. How many more cookies does Jack need to have as many as Nicole?" This is an example of a *missing addend* approach to subtraction.

Include stories with too much or too little information. For example, "Robert has 4 pencils. Corrie has some pencils. How many more pencils does Corrie have than Robert?" Encourage children to develop their own number stories, and see if other children can solve them. You may place copies of number stories children have written in a learning center for other students to work on. The following activities offer additional ways to teach the concept of subtraction to students.

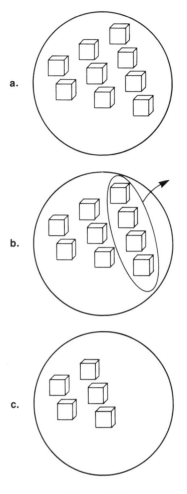

Figure 7–18

ACTIVITIES

Primary (K–3)

Objective: to introduce the concept of subtraction using sets of objects.

1. Draw a loop on a large sheet of paper or use a loop of yarn. Place nine objects in the loop (Figure 7–18a). Then, with yarn or string of a different color, form another loop inside of the first loop, surrounding some of the objects (Figure 7–18b). Ask the children to remove all objects that are inside the smaller loop (Figure 7–18c). Practice this activity a number of times and discuss the results with the children to see if they understand that they have removed some of the objects they had when they started, and that if they returned the objects, the collection of objects would be the same as the original collection.

   Next, ask the children to indicate how many objects there are at each step of the activity. For example, "How many cubes did we start with?" There were 9 cubes. "How many did we take away?" We took away 4 cubes. "How many do we have left?" We have 5 cubes left. "How can we say what we just did in a number sentence?" Nine take away 4 equals 5.

   Children can invent and work out many other examples of the subtraction operation as part of learning about subtraction. This "take away" model is the most direct way to show the meaning of subtraction. It should be used considerably in the beginning stages of learning subtraction.

Objective: to use Cuisenaire rods as a model for subtraction.

2. Have the children place a blue rod in front of them. Then have them put a yellow rod beside the blue rod, with one end even with an end of the blue rod, as in Figure 7–19a.

   Ask the children to find a rod that will form a train with the yellow rod and will make that train as long as the blue rod. You may say, "See if you can find a rod that will go here." as you point to the space at the end of the yellow rod. Children will find that the purple rod will fill the space (Figure 7–19b). Explain that blue minus yellow equals purple.

   Ask, "What is blue minus green?" Have the children place the rods as described above and find the rod to fill the space. Then invite the children to "read" the subtraction sentence that is illustrated.

   The Cuisenaire rods model used here emphasizes the **missing addend concept.** In the abstract version of the missing addends problem $5 + ? = 9$, children ask themselves, "What added to 5 makes 9?"

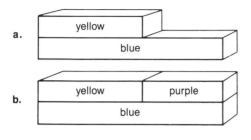

Figure 7–19

With the rods, we are asking, "What added to yellow makes blue?" when solving the problem blue minus yellow equals what?

Objective: to use dominoes to illustrate the concept of subtraction.

3. When dominoes are used for the subtraction concept, the children are encouraged to find the difference between the number of dots on one side of the domino and the number of dots on the other side. Help children make a comparison. "How many more dots are there on one side than the other?" In the case of the two-six or six-two domino, shown in Figure 7–20a, there are four more dots on the six-side.

Let the children discover how to find the difference. Discuss how they found the difference. For example, some children make the comparison by matching the dots on one side of the domino with those on the other side. The dots left over represent the difference. Other children may be more comfortable mentally removing the dots found on the lesser side (2) from the dots found on the greater side (6). Of course, when each side has the same number of dots, as in Figure 7–20b, the difference is zero. How do the children explain this difference?

Children can describe this operation numerically after they learn to make the comparison and find the difference. The number sentence that describes the domino in Figure 7–20a is "6 minus 2 equals 4." Students should be able to pick up any domino and quickly give the number sentence that is shown.

Objective: to symbolize the subtraction concept.

4. Once the language describing subtraction has been introduced and used, the operation can be symbolized. The loops in Figure 7–21 may be used to illustrate the transition from the concrete to the abstract. Children are asked, "How many cubes are in the first loop?" They respond by counting them. There are 7 cubes. "How many cubes are we removing or taking away?" We are removing 2 cubes. "How many cubes are there left?" There are 5 cubes. "We say this using numbers by writing $7 - 2 = 5$."

The transition to the abstract symbols should take place as soon as the children are competent using the loops and using the language that describes the operation they are performing. Practicing subtraction and discussing and recording the results in learning groups will strengthen the children's abilities in subtraction.

5. Activity 2 on page 162 employs the Cuisenaire rods. The language the students are using is "blue minus yellow equals purple," thus the change to numbers is quick. If the white rod equals 1, blue has the value of 9, yellow has the value of 5, and purple has the value of 4. Thus, the number sentence $9 - 5 = 4$ results directly from the sentence using colors.

Again, be cautious by reminding the children, "In this case, the white rod is 1." Later, the value of the white rod may change. Considerable experience is necessary for children to be skilled with the abstract numerical description of the rods.

While presenting the concept of an operation and the concepts of addition and subtraction, take the opportunity to include examples of important properties of these operations. We have already mentioned the commutative property of addition. Note that the join machine, in which one input contains no objects, and the yarn-loop activity, in which no objects are removed, are models of

Figure 7–20

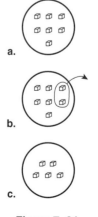

Figure 7–21

the **identity element** for addition and subtraction; that is, any number plus zero or minus zero results in the number you started with. With this background, $6 + 0 = 6$, $0 + 6 = 6$, and $6 - 0 = 6$ will be easy to remember. Allow children to discover that $0 - 6$ (left-hand identity) does not hold for subtraction.

We have already demonstrated the commutative property of addition using dominoes; however, this property can be clearly shown with any of the preceding models. For example, with Cuisenaire rods, the train dark green plus purple can be reconstructed as the train purple plus dark green. Then both can be shown to be equal to orange, as in Figure 7–22. Thus, we have the numerical examples $6 + 4 = 10$ and $4 + 6 = 10$ when the white rod is equal to 1.

Give children the opportunity to discover that in operations with whole numbers, the commutative property does not hold for subtraction. That is, $6 - 4 = 2$, but $4 - 6$ does not have a solution.

Another useful pattern is **adding or subtracting one.** Again, examples from any of the models already presented can illustrate this pattern. After a number of examples, children discover that adding one to a number results in the next number in the counting sequence. For example, $6 + 1 = 7$ and $12 + 1 = 13$. Likewise, children discover that subtracting one from a number results in the previous number in the counting sequence, $9 - 1 = 8$ and $2 - 1 = 1$.

Just as adding zero, using the commutative property of addition, and adding one can help in learning the basic addition facts, the **associative property of addition** can help children as they determine sums such as $9 + 6$. If children are in the habit of making mental groupings of 10, they will likely find that the answer is easier to determine. For example, $9 + 6 = 9 + (1 + 5) = (9 + 1) + 5 = 10 + 5 = 15$. The associative property is shown in $9 + (1 + 5) = (9 + 1) + 5$; how the numbers are grouped to add does not affect the sum.

A good way to show the associative property of addition is to have children place beans or chips on number strips like those in Figure 7–23. For a larger sum, more than two strips may be necessary.

Have the children put beans for the addends on the first and second number strips. Then have them fill up the first strip to complete the ten, using the last beans on the second strip. Here, we see $9 + 6 = 10 + 5 = 15$. This pro-

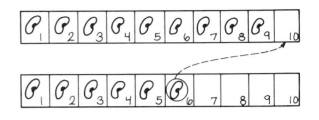

Figure 7–23

cedure will reinforce the groupings of ten that the students made as they were attaching meaning to number.

This is a good procedure to use with problems with three or more addends and with larger problems that require regrouping. Use the associative property to make the learning of certain number combinations easier. Avoid presenting it as simply an abstract property of addition.

The time students spend discussing properties of addition and subtraction is very important to the learning process. After the students understand the concepts of addition and subtraction and are comfortable posing story problems and solving each other's story problems using physical models, they should begin to analyze the operations and discover properties that make it easier to remember the basic facts. The commutative property, the identity element, and the associative property are just a few of the patterns children should discover and discuss. They may notice many patterns of addition and subtraction facts other than the pattern of adding and subtracting one. They may notice that if they know the doubles, they can find the answer to the fact $6 + 7$ by taking the double $6 + 6$ and adding 1 or by taking the double $7 + 7$ and subtracting 1. Encourage the children to keep a written record of the properties and patterns they have discovered. These may all be combined in a class book, bulletin board, or HyperStudio stack for the students to refer to.

Developing and Practicing Addition and Subtraction Skills

Children must learn the skills associated with adding and subtracting. These skills are called the basic facts and algorithms. The **basic addition facts,** of which there are one hundred, are those ranging from $0 + 0$ to $9 + 9$. They are shown in Table 7–1. The **basic subtraction facts,** again numbering one hundred, are those ranging from $18 - 9$ to $0 - 0$. An **algorithm** is any method used to solve a problem; mathematics consists of numerous algorithms for addition and subtraction. As children learn the basic facts and algorithms for addition and subtraction, they can make use of paper-and-pencil procedures, mental arithmetic, calculators, and computers.

Figure 7–22

TABLE 7–1

+	0	1	2	3	4	5	6	7	8	9
0	0	1	2	3	4	5	6	7	8	9
1	1	2	3	4	5	6	7	8	9	10
2	2	3	4	5	6	7	8	9	10	11
3	3	4	5	6	7	8	9	10	11	12
4	4	5	6	7	8	9	10	11	12	13
5	5	6	7	8	9	10	11	12	13	14
6	6	7	8	9	10	11	12	13	14	15
7	7	8	9	10	11	12	13	14	15	16
8	8	9	10	11	12	13	14	15	16	17
9	9	10	11	12	13	14	15	16	17	18

Addend (column header, top) / *Addend* (row header, left side)

Basic Addition and Subtraction Facts

For quick recall, children should be expected to visualize and/or memorize the basic addition and subtraction facts. Begin this memorization when children understand the concepts of addition and subtraction. Your efforts to develop the concepts will pay off as the facts are learned. Because the children have a physical model to which they can refer, they will be able to determine a basic fact temporarily forgotten. They can successfully use a variety of counters, including fingers. They can use Cuisenaire rods, Unifix cubes, number lines, state-operator-state machines, or calculators.

The addition and subtraction facts may be presented almost simultaneously. The join or combine model used with objects is somewhat easier to grasp than the take-away or remove model. We recommend you start first with join, later introducing take away. As the children understand the concepts, they will comfortably work with both addition and subtraction at the same time.

Many math textbooks show relationships between addition and subtraction facts. A family includes several facts, each of which relates the same three numbers through addition or subtraction. One such family follows:

$$8 + 5 = 13$$

$$5 + 8 = 13$$

$$13 - 8 = 5$$

$$13 - 5 = 8$$

Word problems or story problems commonly appear in mathematics textbooks. Those that ask students to compute an immediate answer provide students with an avenue for practicing addition and subtraction skills. For example, in the following word problem, students are asked to find the sum of three numbers: "Crystal has 3 boxes of breakfast cereal at home. Her friends, Jennifer and Megan, each have 2 boxes of cereal at home. How many boxes of cereal do they have altogether?" Students

solve these word problems in a variety of ways. Among methods they may use are counting out loud, counting on their fingers, finding objects to lay out to represent the cereal boxes, drawing pictures, and acting out the word problem. The action students use to find answers is predicated on their understanding the problem, that is, what does the problem ask? what information is given? how am I going to solve this word problem? what operation(s) is called for? does the answer make sense? Students need to be guided through these questions so they may establish a systematic approach to word problems. They find that terms such as *altogether* and *in all* generally refer to addition. Terms such as *are left* and *how many more* suggest using subtraction. Students should be able to differentiate between the meaning of these words and phrases. Because there are exceptions to each word clue students should be aware of how important thoughtful reading is as they solve word problems.

The classroom should contain tools with which to perform simple calculations. The most basic tools for calculating are the many counters already mentioned. When children are first learning the basic addition facts, encourage them to use beans, cubes, bottle caps, nuts and washers, or chips to find the answer. Let them put some objects down, join others with them, and count the result or recognize the answer by sight. Let them use fingers as counters as well. As the work becomes more abstract and the children use paper and pencil or calculators, let them make marks on paper to help reinforce the basic addition facts.

The number line is useful for learning addition facts. For younger children, a walk-on number line provides large motor experiences. Its use in building the concept of number provides familiarity. For older children, a number line on the wall or chalkboard or attached to a desktop is useful. The procedure for use is the same. When children wish to add 8 + 4, they begin at 0 on the number line and take eight steps or move directly to 8 (Figure 7–24a). Next, they take four steps in the same direction along the number line. Where they stop, 12, is the sum of 8 + 4.

Another effective way to use the number line is to have it calibrated in centimeters. Cuisenaire rods may then be placed along the number line to help illustrate that the number line represents a continuous length and not just points where the numbers appear. For example, if the white rod has the value of 1, 8 + 4 may be shown by placing a brown rod followed by a purple rod along the number line beginning at 0 as in Figure 7–24b. The result, 12, is clearly seen.

When students wish to subtract 9 − 5, they again begin at 0 on the walk-on number line and take nine steps or move directly to 9 (Figure 7–24c). Next, they take away by reversing their direction and moving five spaces back, to 4.

With the Cuisenaire rods, a blue rod (representing 9) is placed along the number line, beginning at 0. Then a yellow rod (representing 5) is placed along the blue rod beginning at the point marked 9. The difference, 4, can be seen by reading the number line, as in Figure 7–24d.

Children need careful instruction in working on a number line because they commonly forget to count spaces and instead count marks on the line. The walk-on and Cuisenaire rod number lines provide direct experience in counting spaces.

The calculator is another tool for learning addition facts. It should be used periodically to quickly produce facts that are forgotten or unlearned. Simple four-function (addition, subtraction, multiplication, division), light-activated calculators should be available for classroom use. Calculators speed up computations during games and activities intended to help children memorize basic addition facts. Set up races with basic facts in which some students have calculators and others do not. Students will quickly learn that it is faster to remember $8 + 7$ than it is to push the buttons on the calculator.

Computer games and activities are available to assist children learn and reinforce basic addition and subtraction facts. Oftentimes, a particular piece of software presents more that just computation practice. It may also include work with problem solving, fractions, geometry, measurement, and so on. The activities tend to be fast paced, challenging, colorful, and enjoyable. Examples of such computer activities are *Mighty Math Number Heroes* (Edmark), *How the West Was One + Three × Four* (Sunburst), and *Treasure MathStorm!* (The Learning Company).

The activities that follow are specifically designed for addition but may be used as effectively for subtraction by making simple changes in the materials.

ACTIVITIES

Primary (K–3)

Objective: to help children memorize the basic addition facts.

1. Commercially prepared printed flash cards have been used successfully for many years to help children reinforce basic addition facts. These cards have an addition problem on one side and the same problem with the answer on the other side. One card from a set is shown in Figure 7–25.

   Show children the cards one at a time and ask them to recall the sum. Put aside the sums that the children can quickly recall but return to the stack any sums that they cannot recall. Vary this procedure to involve the whole class, several children and the teacher, several children and an aide, or children

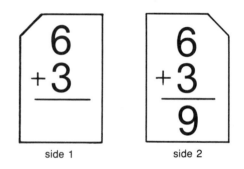

side 1   side 2

Figure 7–25

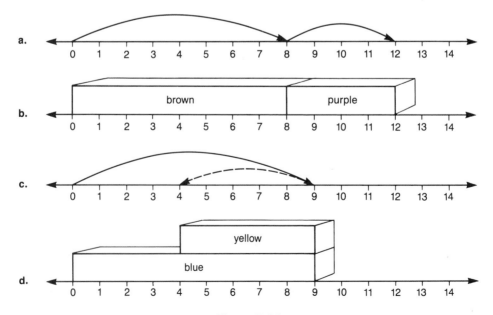

Figure 7–24

showing other children the cards. A major advantage of flash cards is that they are portable and convenient. One disadvantage to flash cards is that they turn many students off to learning basic facts. Students become frustrated if they are not fast enough or if they forget a fact. Be careful not to push a child to the point of frustration by overemphasizing flash cards.

Electronic flash cards are drill activities resembling printed flash cards. They are displayed on preprogrammed calculators or computers. The programs most attractive to children are those on computer software that not only present the problems but also display graphic designs and pictures. Children enjoy graphic presentations and learn basic addition facts as they interact with the computer. At the end of such electronic activities, the children are informed of the number of correct responses they have given. Then they are rewarded or admonished with a final graphic design. Some software games provide friendly competition between students as they try to outdo one another in speed and accuracy.

Certain drill-and-practice programs keep a cumulative record of each child's progress. The chief advantage of using the computer is that it frees the teacher for other important tasks. On the other hand, only one or two children at a time can work at each computer.

Ideally, use both printed and electronic flash cards so that children can practice on problems in several ways.

2. Provide children with frequent practice in mental arithmetic. Because the main focus of learning the basic facts is mental, this type of activity is particularly useful. Limit practice periods to five or ten minutes. Orally present addition facts to children while the children write on a piece of paper or a small individual chalkboard only the answer to the problem. The difficulty of the problems should be determined by the age and experience of the children. Initially, speedy responses are not necessary. Children need an opportunity to practice using their mental faculties.

Ask the children to number from 1 to 5 on their papers. Explain that you are going to give them a problem and they should think of what the answer is and then write the answer down; they should not use their pencils to find the answer. Here are examples of mental exercises: What is 4 plus 7? What is 3 plus 3 plus 2? Answer yes or no; 3 plus 8 is more than 10. Four plus 5 equals 9; what else equals 9? As the children become more proficient, increase the number of questions from 5 to 10, 15, or 20. Expand the questions from just basic facts to other, related mathematical topics, such as place value.

3. **Pic-addition,** short for picture addition, appeals to children. Pic-addition requires construction of activity materials. The first step is to select a picture of an ani-

mal, cartoon character, or athlete that is popular with the children. A fuzzy kitten appeals to some children. A Saturday morning cartoon character appeals to others. An athlete in action attracts the attention of some.

Next, glue the picture to a piece of oaktag or posterboard. Spread the glue thinly over the entire back of the picture. There should be no border (see Figure 7–26a).

In the next step, draw square or rectangular regions with pencil on the back of the oaktag or posterboard holding the picture. Within these regions, draw circular and square frames. With marking pen, write an addition problem in each circular or square frame on the back of the picture. Make sure problems with the same answer, such as $1 + 2$ and $2 + 1$, are placed in different-shaped frames (Figure 7–26b).

Finally, draw regions on the inside of a box lid or on a piece of oaktag to make an answer board. The lines should form regions the same size and shape as those on the back of the picture. Within these regions, draw circular and square frames to match those on the back of the picture. In each circular or square frame, write the answer to the addition problem in the position opposite that of the problem (Figure 7–26c). (When the problem is correctly answered, the problem card is flipped over and the regions are moved to different positions.) Cut the picture apart using the lines on the back to form individual cards.

Have students select one of the individual cards. Instruct them to look at the problem and solve it, then place the card in the answer frame in the region corresponding to the answer, turning the card picture side up. As they complete the solutions, the picture emerges in its entirety.

4. Concentration games are another source of basic fact practice. A popular version is called "peopletration" because children are important participants in the game. Provide 12 large cards (22 centimeters by 30 centimeters) constructed from oaktag or posterboard. Each card should have five problems or answers to problems written on one side and a large alphabet letter, *A* through *L,* on the other side. To assure corresponding sets, the first set of problems and answers on each card should be written with black ink, the second set with red, then blue, green, and purple. Figure 7–27 illustrates two such cards, front and back.

Select 12 children to hold the cards. Give each child one of the cards identified with the large alphabet letters. Have the 12 children stand side by side across the front of the room, holding the cards so the letters face the rest of the class.

Designate which game color to use—green, for example. Instruct one of the other children to select two letters, hoping for a match. For example, a student might say "*C*" and "*H*." Whoever is holding card *C*

a.

b.

5+3	2+0	5+4	2+2
6+3	1+2	1+0	4+1
2+1	0+1	3+3	3+4
5+5	5+2	1+3	4+2
1+1	4+4	3+2	7+3

c.

4	9	2	8
5	1	3	9
7	6	1	3
6	4	7	10
10	5	8	2

Figure 7–26

reads whatever is written in green on the back of the card, in this case, "5 + 2." Whoever is holding card *H* reads whatever is written in green on the back of that card, in this case, "12." Because 5 + 2 does not equal 12, there is no match. Play continues until there is a match. When a match occurs, the two cards are laid down or the children holding them sit down and the game continues. The game is over when all of the cards have been matched.

The conventional concentration game consists of two arrays of cards (10 centimeters by 12 centimeters). Each array contains 16 cards. One side of each card is unmarked. The other side of one array has basic facts such as 2 + 9. The opposite side of the second array has answers such as 11. When an individual points to pairs of cards, the cards are turned over and compared. If the fact and the answer match, the child scores a point and gets another turn. Otherwise, the next player takes a turn. The game ends when all of the cards have been matched.

5. Bingo activities provide opportunities for children to review number facts. **Bugs Bingo** is a popular activity for second- and third-grade students. Two to four players participate. Each group needs three regular dice or dice showing the numerals 1 to 6, as well as about 25 bingo markers (small squares of paper work well) and a Bingo board. The board for this game is shaped like a ladybug, from which the name originates. Figure 7–28 shows one of the game boards and numeral patterns for three others.

Each player puts a marker on the FREE square and then rolls a die. The player with the highest number on the die begins. The first player rolls all three dice

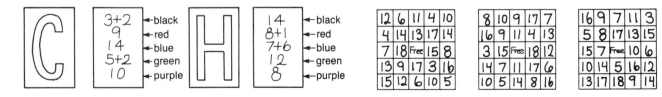

Figure 7–27

Figure 7–28

and adds the number of dots showing. The other players check that the sum is correct.

All players cover that numeral on their boards. Although the numeral may appear more than once on the board, only one numeral is covered at each turn. Once a marker is placed on a numeral, it cannot be moved to another region.

The dice are passed to the next player, and play continues until someone has 5 markers in a row, horizontally, vertically, or diagonally.

If additional boards are needed, they should be made with different numeral patterns. For each board, however, there is one FREE region and there are 24 regions with these numerals:

one each of 4, 5, 6, 15, 16, 17

two each of 7, 8, 9, 12, 13, 14

three each of 10, 11

6. The game Top It uses a deck of cards representing the basic addition facts. Figure 7–29 shows a deck of easy cards and a deck of hard cards. Choose the deck that matches the children's ability levels, or combine the decks into a single deck representing nearly all of the basic addition facts.

The game is for two to four players. Begin play with the stack of cards face down. The first player turns over a card and places it face up, giving the sum. The second, third, and fourth players do the same. The player with the highest sum claims all of the cards played. If any players are tied with high cards, the cards remain in front of the players and those who are tied each draw another card. The player with the highest sum takes all of the cards. The winner of the game is the player with the most cards after all of the cards have been drawn.

This chapter presents a few of the many activities that can be employed to help children practice the basic addition facts. Each activity can be easily adapted to include subtraction practice.

There are also unique opportunities to incorporate literature that focuses on addition and subtraction. It may be in the form of counting forward and backward as in *Dorobō the Dangerous,* written by Vaughan (1995). Crane finds that someone is eating the fish from her pond and children can count along with Crane as she has fewer each day. The story continues as Crane solves her problem and ends as it began with her

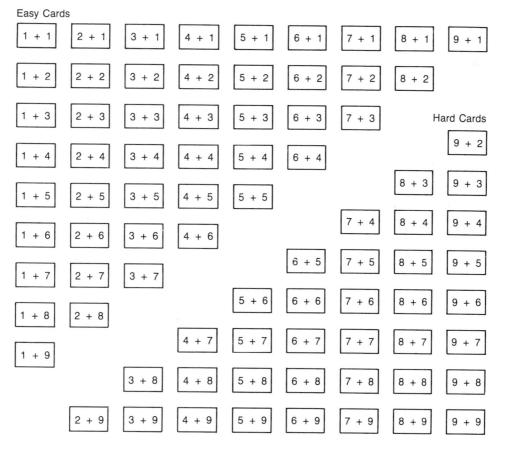

Figure 7–29

counting song. Along the same line are the delightful *Ten, Nine, Eight* by Bang (1983) and *Seven Little Hippos* by Thaler (1991). Both involve counting backward and use well-illustrated themes to do so. The goal is to have children able to accurately and quickly respond to all basic addition and subtraction facts. Other activities and games are listed in the chapter references.

Addition and Subtraction Algorithms

Children progress more rapidly in learning the addition and subtraction algorithms when they already know the basic addition and subtraction facts. As well, modeling addition and subtraction using the base-10 blocks or other physical materials prepares students for learning the algorithms and gives them the opportunity to discuss their work with one another and to write about their work. For example, give the students the base ten blocks and a problem such as: "Jack wants to buy a 39¢ top and a 59¢ airplane. How much will they cost altogether?" Let the children work in small groups to find a solution and have them write down their method using words and symbols. When all the groups are finished, ask each group to share their solution with the whole class. Discuss the pros and cons of each solution. This gives students the opportunity to explore and invent algorithms. Let the students decide which algorithm they prefer and when they no longer need to use the physical models. It is likely that the students will devise some algorithms similar to the standard addition and subtraction algorithms, but be ready for algorithms that are different. The process of inventing algorithms is an important part of learning how and why algorithms work.

In mathematics textbooks, the addition and subtraction algorithms are usually taught sequentially, beginning with the simplest problems, which require no regrouping (carrying or borrowing). The difficulty and complexity increase until multidigit problems with regrouping are presented. However, when students begin multidigit addition and subtraction using physical models, there is no need to separate problems that require regrouping from those that do not. Do not assign page after page of laborious addition and subtraction problems. When children can demonstrate paper-and-pencil algorithms for addition and subtraction, it is time to let them use calculators to speed up computations. Using the calculator is the most efficient procedure for performing an arithmetic operation.

Paper-and-pencil algorithms for addition and subtraction are presented in turn. We begin with the standard and generally most efficient paper-and-pencil algorithm for each operation. Alternative algorithms are then presented. Alternative procedures often serve as teaching algorithms and help to bridge the gap between the concrete and abstract. Sometimes, alternative algorithms are the most efficient paper-and-pencil algorithms for children. It was mentioned above that students sometimes invent algorithms similar to the standard addition and subtraction algorithms. Likewise, they may invent algorithms similar to the alternative algorithms presented below. While in this chapter the standard algorithm is presented first followed by alternative algorithms, it is not suggested that children will invent algorithms in this order. You should not introduce standard algorithms until students have explored, invented, and discussed their own algorithms.

Addition. The standard addition algorithm is generally considered the most efficient paper-and-pencil procedure for adding. The algorithm has been applied to the six problems below, each of which has at least one two-digit addend. The problems are presented in order of difficulty. The first three algorithms involve no regrouping. The others have regrouping in one or more of the place-value positions.

$$
\begin{array}{r} 10 \\ +\ 8 \\ \hline 18 \end{array} \qquad
\begin{array}{r} 34 \\ +10 \\ \hline 44 \end{array} \qquad
\begin{array}{r} 22 \\ +14 \\ \hline 36 \end{array}
$$

$$
\begin{array}{r} {}^{1}19 \\ +\ 2 \\ \hline 21 \end{array} \qquad
\begin{array}{r} {}^{1}37 \\ +28 \\ \hline 65 \end{array} \qquad
\begin{array}{r} {}^{1}63 \\ +59 \\ \hline 122 \end{array}
$$

The first two problems involve adding a number to 10 and adding 10 to a number. Sums involving 10 are important to know because they occur continually during computation. Being able to recognize sums involving 10 and make groupings of 10 while solving problems saves considerable time and energy during computation. The latter three algorithms display the regrouping numeral 1, indicating regrouping has taken place. In these cases, 10 ones have been grouped for one 10. While the algorithm would be simpler without the regrouping numeral, most who use this algorithm include it.

It is important that children understand what happens when regrouping occurs. Work with place value provides this understanding, and children can be taught the standard addition algorithm with little more than a set of multibase arithmetic blocks or a picture of them. Most math texts include illustrations of a counting device and step-by-step procedures for teaching the algorithm that often encourage teachers to use physical materials as models for a textbook algorithm.

For example, Figure 7–30a shows both the numeral representation and the pictorial representation of 22 +

14. The joining of unit cubes and longs (Figure 7–30b) is accompanied by the teacher asking, "How many ones are there?" There are 2 ones plus 4 ones, or 6 ones. The children put the 6 beneath the 2 + 4 and make sure there are as many cubes on the place value board. Next, the teacher asks, "How many tens are there?" There are 2 plus 1, or 3. The children place the 3 beneath the 2 tens + 1 ten and make sure there are as many longs on the place-value board. The transition from the concrete to the abstract should be made as often as necessary for the concepts to make sense to the children.

An algorithm that requires regrouping is only slightly more difficult than one that does not require regrouping when children have the proper foundation, that is, when they have learned about grouping various materials, including the multibase blocks, during the initial study of place-value. When an algorithm requiring regrouping is accompanied by an illustration that reinforces earlier skills, children pick up the process quickly (see Figures 7–31a, b, and c).

The teacher asks, "How many ones are there?" There are 3 ones plus 7 ones, or 10 ones; that is, there is one

group of tens and there are 0 ones. It is important here that the unit cubes be grouped and exchanged for one long, even if just pictorially. "How many units do we have after the exchange?" We have 0. The students write down the 0 beneath the 3 + 7. They record a 1 in the tens column to remind them that they have exchanged 10 ones and now have 1 ten. "How many tens are there?" There are 6 tens plus 5 tens plus 1 ten, or 12 tens; that is, there is one group of 100 (1 hundred) and there are 2 tens. The longs should be put together and exchanged for one flat and two longs. "How many tens do we have after the exchange?" We have 2 tens. The students write down the 2 beneath the 6 + 5. They also record the 1 hundred because they have no more place-value positions in the problem. They check to make sure the multibase blocks show 120.

The addition algorithms for larger numbers are extensions of the above process. They take more time to perform but are not substantively different.

As soon as children can perform the algorithm without physical or pictorial models, they should be encouraged to do so. Math texts provide plenty of practice exercises. Children should practice for several days after they are able to

Figure 7–30

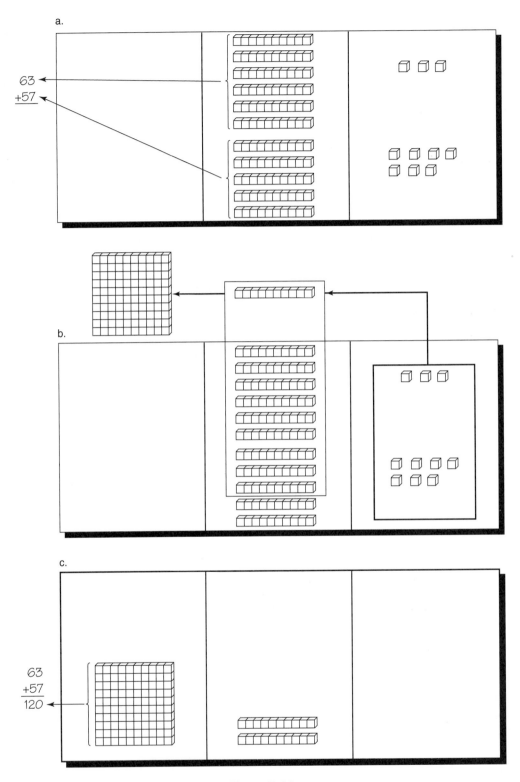

Figure 7–31

perform the algorithm without materials. While there may be 30 problems on a page, 10 to 20 problems will give children the necessary practice. If children continue to have difficulty reaching the correct answer, you should diagnose the difficulty. Assigning more problems to solve is unlikely to be the best strategy. We discuss diagnosing computational errors in the section on assessment.

The following activities differ from those presented earlier. Their primary focus is not physical activities, but alternative ways to present addition algorithms.

ACTIVITIES

Primary (K–3)

Objective: to add columns of three or more numbers.

1. When children are competent with the basic addition facts, challenge them to add three digits. At first, the numbers should be no larger than basic facts, such as $3 + 4 + 8$ or $8 + 1 + 5$. Present the problems in the format the children are used to seeing, most likely the vertical format. When the problems become more difficult, help students develop an algorithm that works for them. A column addition algorithm is shown in row a below.

a.
$$
\begin{array}{ccc}
6 & 6 & \\
7 & 4 & 10 \\
+4 & +7 & +7 \\
\hline
& & 17
\end{array}
$$

b.
$$
\begin{array}{ccc}
6 & 6 & \\
7 & 7 & \rangle 13 \\
+4 & +4 & +4 \\
\hline
& & 17
\end{array}
$$

To approach this problem, find numbers that add to 10 and reorder the problem to put those numbers together. The numbers adding to 10 can then be combined and the final sum calculated. After some practice, most children can group the tens by reordering the problem mentally. They see groups of 10 in the problem and group numbers mentally, shortcutting the algorithm.

A second approach is shown in b. Beginning at the top or bottom of the column, add successive numbers, keeping the intermediate sum in mind until reaching the last number. The last calculation provides the answer to the problem. Let children choose the algorithm they are most comfortable with when adding columns of numbers.

Objective: to use the expanded notation algorithm.

2. **Expanded notation** is a direct outgrowth of work with place value. Children recognize that two flats, four longs, and six small cubes represent $200 + 40 + 6$, or 2 hundreds + 4 tens + 6 ones. An alternative addition algorithm uses this knowledge. The problems below show two solutions using expanded notation. In problem a, no regrouping is necessary. The problem is rewritten from standard into expanded notation. The columns are added and the expanded notation is rewritten into standard notation.

a.
$$
\begin{array}{cc}
63 & 60+3 \\
+24 & +20+4 \\
\hline
& 80+7 = 87
\end{array}
$$

b.
$$
\begin{array}{cc}
58 & 50+8 \\
+29 & +20+9 \\
\hline
& 70+17 = 80+7 = 87
\end{array}
$$

Problem b requires regrouping in the ones column. As in the earlier example, the problem is rewritten from standard into expanded notation. Each column is added. Finally, regrouping takes place as the answer is rewritten into standard notation. The algorithm used with problem b is advantageous because children never lose sight of the numbers they are regrouping. It is important to point out this fact and let the students discuss regrouping.

Objective: to use the loop abacus as a tool in learning the addition algorithm.

3. The abacus is useful as a tool. As children learn about place value, the abacus is handy in teaching the regrouping process. Any time ten counters appear on a given loop, they must be exchanged for one counter on the adjacent loop. Students need to discuss why this exchange is necessary. The regrouping process is demonstrated as we solve a problem on the abacus. In the first frame of Figure 7–32, an abacus is ready to add $746 + 285$. The counters below the holding clips represent 285; the counters above represent 746.

In the second frame, we remove the holding clip in the ones column and exchange ten counters on the ones loop for one counter on the tens loop. We have one counter left in the ones column.

In the third frame, we remove the holding clip in the tens column and exchange ten counters on the tens loop for one counter on the hundreds loop. We have three counters left in the tens column.

In the fourth frame, we remove the holding clip in the hundreds column and exchange ten counters on the hundreds loop for one counter on the thousands loop. We have no counters left in the hundreds column.

In the fifth frame, we see the abacus after all the exchanges have been made.

Objective: to use the partial sums algorithm for addition.

4. Another algorithm that helps children through the process of regrouping or carrying is the **partial sums algorithm.** It may be used whether or not regrouping is necessary. To illustrate this algorithm, note the problem below ($48 + 39$). The first step in the solution is to add the numbers in the ones column, $8 + 9$. The

Figure 7–32

the children to work in groups to determine the solution and record their methods. Discuss the various methods used by the different groups before presenting the standard algorithm. Of course, the concept of subtraction is considerably different. The standard paper-and-pencil algorithm for subtraction relies on children's knowing the basic subtraction facts and being well versed in place-value concepts. You recall that the basic subtraction facts are related to the basic addition facts. Thus, for the addition fact $4 + 7 = 11$, we have the corresponding subtraction facts, $11 - 4 = 7$ and $11 - 7 = 4$. Techniques for helping children memorize these facts were discussed in the section on basic facts.

Six examples of the standard subtraction algorithm are presented below.

$$\begin{array}{r} 18 \\ -10 \\ \hline 8 \end{array} \qquad \begin{array}{r} 44 \\ -34 \\ \hline 10 \end{array} \qquad \begin{array}{r} 36 \\ -22 \\ \hline 14 \end{array}$$

$$\begin{array}{r} {}^{1}2\!\!\!/1 \\ -9 \\ \hline 12 \end{array} \qquad \begin{array}{r} {}^{5}6\!\!\!/5 \\ -37 \\ \hline 28 \end{array} \qquad \begin{array}{r} {}^{2}3\!\!\!/{}^{11}2\!\!\!/2 \\ -63 \\ \hline 259 \end{array}$$

The first three examples involve no regrouping, or borrowing. The last three require that regrouping take place. The first two problems involve subtracting 10 and subtracting so that 10 is the difference. The third problem is solved by applying basic subtraction facts to the ones and tens columns in the problem.

The fourth example necessitates regrouping from the tens place to the ones place. This is shown by crossing out the 2 tens and replacing them with 1 ten. The ones place is increased from 1 to 11, reflecting the exchange of 1 ten for 10 ones. The subtraction is then carried out.

The fifth example is similar to the fourth because there is regrouping from the tens to the ones place. In this case, 6 tens and 5 ones are exchanged for 5 tens and 15 ones.

In the final example, there is regrouping from the tens to the ones place and from the hundreds to the tens place. Thus, 2 tens and 2 ones become 1 ten and 12 ones; then, 3 hundreds and 1 ten become 2 hundreds and 11 tens. The markings have been shown in the procedure as they are used by most who employ this standard algorithm.

When students develop a subtraction algorithm, it is important that they use physical models. At this point, we demonstrate with multibase blocks. The first example is $65 - 37$. Figures 7–33a, b, and c illustrate how to construct the problem using the blocks.

First, attempt to remove 7 small cubes from 5 small cubes. Finding this impossible, perform an exchange (see Figure 7–33b). Trade 1 long for 10 small cubes. Now, from the collection of 15 small cubes, remove 7, leaving 8 small

answer, 17, is the first partial sum and is placed beneath the problem.

$$\begin{array}{r} 48 \\ +39 \\ \hline \end{array} \qquad \begin{array}{r} 48 \\ +39 \\ \hline 17 \end{array} \qquad \begin{array}{r} 48 \\ +39 \\ \hline 17 \\ 70 \end{array} \qquad \begin{array}{r} 48 \\ +39 \\ \hline 17 \\ 70 \\ \hline 87 \end{array}$$

The next step is to add the numbers in the tens column, $40 + 30$, or 4 tens + 3 tens. The result, 70, is the second partial sum and is placed beneath the 17.

Finally, the partial sums are added to arrive at the answer, 87. You may also add the tens first and then the ones using this algorithm. This is very useful for mental computation. Take care with this algorithm to assure that the correct place value positions in the partial sums are maintained.

Subtraction.   Again, for subtraction, give the students a real-life situation such as spending 18¢ out of 25¢ and determining the amount of change they have left. Allow

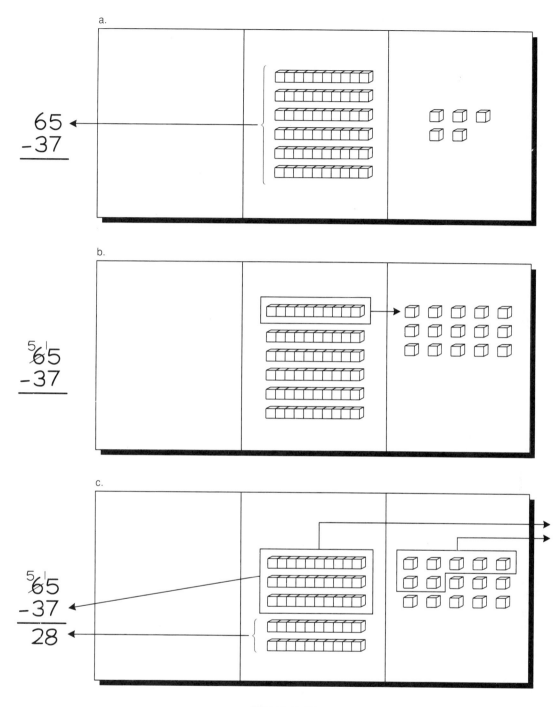

Figure 7–33

cubes. Moving to the tens, remove 3 longs from 5 longs; this leaves 2 longs. Having finished the algorithm, you find the difference is 2 longs and 8 small cubes, or 28 (see Figure 7–33c).

The first few times children encounter subtraction involving regrouping with the multibase blocks, they should use only the blocks. Once the procedure is mastered, use the written algorithm along with the blocks. Finally, as soon as the children are able, use only the written algorithm, bringing the blocks back if there is some difficulty in solving a particular problem. The multibase blocks, or any physical models, clearly show what happens at each step in an algorithm. Once each step is understood and discussed, children should practice the symbolic algorithm.

Children working with physical models or practicing paper and pencil algorithms occasionally discover clever shortcuts or original procedures. Children should be encouraged to create and demonstrate to the class their own algorithms.

As in the case of addition, the activities that follow include alternative algorithms and approaches for subtraction. If some children find an alternative that is superior for them, let them adopt it as their standard algorithm.

ACTIVITIES

Primary (K–3)

Objective: to use the expanded notation algorithm for subtraction.

1. When the **expanded notation algorithm** is used, children see what happens in the process of regrouping, or *borrowing*. The first example below, $43 - 22$, does not require regrouping. Both numbers are rewritten in expanded form. In the ones column, 2 is subtracted from 3, resulting in 1. In the tens column, $40 - 20$ or 4 tens $-$ 2 tens results in 20, or 2 tens. Then $20 + 1$ is rewritten into standard form, 21.

a.
$$
\begin{array}{r}
43 \\
-22 \\
\hline
\end{array}
\quad
\begin{array}{r}
40+3 \\
-(20+2) \\
\hline
20+1 = 21
\end{array}
$$

b.
$$
\begin{array}{r}
43 \\
-27 \\
\hline
\end{array}
\quad
\begin{array}{r}
40+3 \\
-(20+7) \\
\hline
\end{array}
\quad
\begin{array}{r}
30+13 \\
-(20+7) \\
\hline
10+6 = 16
\end{array}
$$

In the second example (b), regrouping is necessary. Children cannot subtract 7 from 3 after the problem is written in expanded form. They must rewrite $40 + 3$ as $30 + 13$. This process regroups 1 ten to 10 ones. Children can subtract 7 from 13, with the result of 6. They may also subtract $30 - 20$ or 3 tens $-$ 2 tens, with the result of 10. Then $10 + 6$ is rewritten into standard form, 16.

You may find it necessary to help children work through several examples of the expanded notation algorithm with concrete objects such as multibase blocks, beansticks, and Cuisenaire rods before you move to symbols. Work first with problems that don't require regrouping, then advance to the more complicated regrouping problems.

Objective: to use the abacus as a model to illustrate the standard subtraction algorithm.

2. Children who have used the abacus when learning place value and addition have the exchanging skills necessary for subtraction. To solve $342 - 164$, be-

Figure 7–34

gin with 342 on the abacus as shown in the first frame of Figure 7–34. As in the second frame, exchange 1 ten for 10 ones, resulting in 12 ones. Then remove 4 ones, as shown in the third frame, resulting in 8 ones. Then exchange 1 hundred for 10 tens as in the fourth frame; there are 2 hundreds and 13 tens remaining. As in the fifth frame, remove 6 tens, leaving 7 tens. Because no further regrouping is necessary, remove 1 hundred, completing the problem. Frame six shows how the abacus looks after 164 has been subtracted from 342. The answer, 178, is easily read.

Objective: to use the "How much more do I add" (HMMDIA) algorithm to subtract.

3. The **"How much more do I add" (HMMDIA) algorithm** is a subtraction algorithm that uses an additive component. We demonstrate with the example on the next page ($168 - 49$). The algorithm consists of

adding to the subtrahend, 49, until you reach the minuend, 168. At each step of this adding process, the number added is recorded. Later, all of the written numbers are added together.

Explain to the children using the example that they will be adding from 49 to 168. Begin with 49. Ask yourself, "How much more do I add to 49 to reach the next group of 10?" The next group of ten is 5 tens, or 50. The answer in this example is 1. Write down the 1 as shown and now think 50 because you have just added one to 49 and gotten 50.

Now ask, "How much more do I add to 50 to reach 100?" In this case, the answer is 50. Write down the 50 as shown and think 100 because you have just added 50 to 50 and gotten 100.

Next, ask, "How much more do I add to 100 to reach 168?" The answer is 68. Write down the 68 as shown. You have reached the number you were adding to, 168, and can stop.

The final step is to add the three numbers that were recorded. The answer to $168 - 49$ is $1 + 50 + 68$, or 119.

You may find it necessary to review this algorithm several times before the process becomes clear. Once you have done this example, give other examples, particularly some that are simpler, such as $25 - 8$. This unusual subtraction algorithm surprises and motivates children.

In this section, we have discussed developing two sets of skills. The first skills were the basic addition and subtraction facts. Children should have fairly immediate recall of these facts. The second skills were the algorithms for addition and subtraction. Current math texts present thorough instruction on how to develop the standard algorithms, and they contain an ample number of problems for practice. Be sure to let students invent and discuss their own algorithms before using those in the text.

Estimating and Mental Calculating

Whether working with pencil and paper or working with calculators and computers, children should develop skill in estimating and mental calculating. To know if an answer seems reasonable, children should estimate the sum or difference either before or after working an algorithm and compare the estimate with the paper-and-pencil results.

Estimating skill should likewise be extended to work with calculators and computers. Trusting that a calculator will provide the correct answer is justified in most cases; however, we should be cautious about the numerals that appear in calculator displays. Incorrect answers are most commonly displayed when the operator instructs the calculator to perform the wrong operation, enters the wrong sequence of numbers and operations, or enters the wrong numbers. Because we cannot predict when those occasions will arise, it is important to have an estimate of the correct answer. Skill in mental calculation means that the child is able to answer number questions in his or her head without relying on paper and pencil or calculator. Facility with mental calculation helps the child perform computations more quickly and demonstrates the child's understanding of the basic arithmetic operations. The following activities are intended to strengthen children's skill in estimating and mental calculation.

ACTIVITIES

Primary (K–3)

Objective: to practice estimation with addition and subtraction.

1. Use a set of double-six or double-nine dominoes. Large-format dominoes work well if this activity is done with the whole class. Constructed from railroad board and approximately 10 cm by 20 cm in size, large-format dominoes, as in Figure 7–35, appeal to students. A complete set of dominoes is displayed in Figure 15–5. To practice estimating with addition, hold a domino before the class for three to five seconds, then ask the children if they believe there are 10 dots, more than 10 dots, or fewer than ten dots on the domino. Let them signal to you that there are 10 dots by putting a hand flat on the table or floor. A hand with thumb up means more than 10; a hand with thumb down means fewer than 10.

   To practice estimating with subtraction, have the children find the difference between the number of dots on one end of a domino and the number of dots on the other end. Have them indicate whether the difference is equal to 3 dots, more than 3 dots, or fewer than 3 dots. They can use the same hand signs as before.

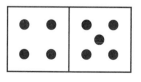

Figure 7–35

Objective: to use the number line to practice mental calculation with addition and subtraction.

2. Use this activity with a wall number line, smaller desk number lines, or a walk-on number line. For addition, begin with an initial jump to the first addend and then explain the next jump, letting the children mentally calculate where the second jump will land. After the children answer, let them perform the second jump. Figure 7–36 shows a number line and the position of a finger after the children have been told to start at 0 and to jump to 8.

    Ask them, "If we make a jump of 6, where do you think we will land?" Let them mentally calculate. Then let them make the jump of 6 to find the answer.

    For subtraction, follow a similar procedure. Let the children make the beginning jump, for example, to 15. Then ask, "If we jump back (subtract) 4, where do you think we will land?" Let them mentally calculate, and then subtract 4 to find the answer. To vary this activity, have the children estimate if the answer will be equal to, more than, or less than a particular number, such as 10, 15, or 20.

Objective: to use numbers that add to 10 for mental addition and subtraction.

3. To begin, use multibase blocks, beans, or Unifix cubes to present combinations of objects that add to 10. For example, 0 + 10, 1 + 9, 2 + 8, and 3 + 7 each equals 10. Have the children estimate the sum of combinations of objects.

Next, present combinations such as 8 + 7 and challenge the children to make a grouping of 10 plus a second number to result in the same amount. As in Figure 7–37, 8 + 7 could be changed to (8 + 2) + 5, then to 10 + 5. Beginning with physical models helps make the grouping to 10 more meaningful and slows the process so most children can successfully participate.

For subtraction, round numbers to 10 for easier calculation. For example, write 12 − 5 on the chalkboard. Explain that sometimes you forget a basic subtraction fact and need a way to figure the answer in your head. One way is to make the larger number a 10 or a 20, whichever is closer. Ask, "Is 12 closer to 10 or 20?" Twelve is closer to 10. Ask, "What do you have to do to 12 to make it 10?" Subtract 2 from 12. Explain, "If you subtract 2 from 10, you must also subtract 2 from 5 so the difference will be the same." Encourage the students to discuss why this is always true. Continue, "What is 5 − 2?" The answer is 3. Summarize, "We have changed 12 − 5 to 10 − 3. What is the answer?" The answer is 7; therefore, 12 − 5 is 7. Review the process several times. The mental process of subtracting or adding to make the larger number (minuend) a multiple of 10 is much quicker than the oral explanation.

The problem 12 − 5 also may be solved by adding 5 to the subtrahend, 5, to reach 10. Then 5 must also be added to 12 to maintain the difference. The new problem becomes 17 − 10. By changing either the minuend or the subtrahend to 10, students may find

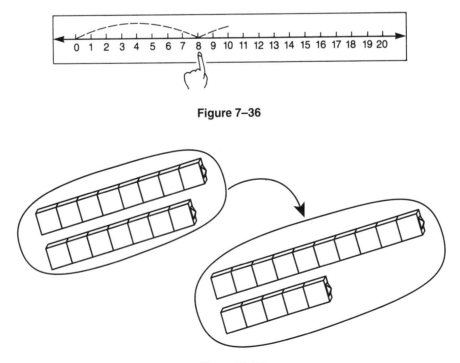

Figure 7–36

Figure 7–37

problems easier to solve. These mental shortcuts are particularly useful when they are performed with larger subtractions in such problems as 36 − 18; the problem may be restated as 38 − 20.

Estimation and mental calculation activities for primary children should be informal and concrete. You can use more formal techniques with older children. The more formal procedures may require children to round numbers to the nearest 10, 100, or 1,000 and to add and subtract numbers that have been rounded to 10, 100, or 1,000.

As you move from topic to topic in the math text you can quickly prepare questions. Mental arithmetic problems should be presented to students three to five days per week, alternating with other warm-up activities. Over time, children will show considerable improvement in their ability to handle mental arithmetic.

ACTIVITIES

Intermediate–Middle Grades (4–8)

Objective: to use estimation to determine if certain purchases can be made.

1. This activity consists of a series of questions that should be answered without calculating on paper. Have students number from 1 to 5 on a sheet of paper. As each question is presented, ask them to estimate the answer by rounding off; then have them record their answer. The questions below ask whether or not certain items can be purchased with a fixed amount of money. You can say, "Answer yes or no. You have $50. Can you buy

- A popcorn popper for $28.95 and a basketball for $24.00?
- An umbrella for $19.99 and a case of apples for $19.99?
- A ring for $37.50 and a chess set for $14.95?
- A radio for $21.89 and some tapes for $29.50?
- Three books for $15.00 each?"

Such questions take little time. Briefly discuss the solutions before going on to another topic. Ask students to explain to the class what they were thinking as they solved a particular problem. One student explained that as she worked on question 1 above, she thought the popcorn popper was about $30.00 and the basketball was about $25.00. The sum of the two items was $55.00. You can't buy that much with $50.00. Other students agreed that they had solved question 1 in the same way. Bill spoke up and said he thought the popper was about $28.00 and he knew the basketball was $24.00. He added the two amounts together and found the sum was $52.00. He agreed that you can't buy both with $50.

Objective: to use historical material to motivate estimation and mental arithmetic.

2. Textbooks from the past (usually available from municipal or college libraries) provide interesting and amusing mental exercises that students enjoy hearing and attempting to solve. One such textbook is Greenleaf's *Intellectual Arithmetic,* published in 1859 (see Figure 7–38). Its formal title is much more impressive: *A Mental Arithmetic, Upon the Inductive Plan; Being an Advanced Intellectual Course, Designed for Schools and Academies.* Examples of the exercises Greenleaf included in his book follow. The page on which each problem can be found is provided in parentheses.

- A farmer sold 6 bushels of wheat, 7 bushels of rye, and 8 bushels of corn; how many bushels did he sell? (p. 12)
- A lady expended for silk 4 dollars, for gloves 1 dollar, and for a bonnet 9 dollars; how many dollars did she expend in all? (p. 12)
- How many are 8 and 9? 8 and 19? 8 and 29? 8 and 39? 8 and 49? 8 and 59? 8 and 69? 8 and 79? 8 and 89? 8 and 99? (p. 15)
- George spent 19 cents for candy and 21 cents for fruit; how much more would he have to spend to make 50 cents? (p. 23)

Objective: to use the calculator to improve addition and subtraction estimation skills.

3. Select two teams of students. Each team may have as few as one member or as many as half of the class. Provide one calculator for each team.

As play begins, one member from Team A says a three-digit number. A player from Team B says another three-digit number. Both players silently write an estimate of the sum of the two numbers. Give a limit of 5 seconds to make estimates.

Then have both players use the calculator to determine the sum. The player whose estimate is closest to the actual sum scores a point for the team. In the case of a tie, both teams earn a point. The next player on each team should name, estimate, and calculate in the next round.

You or the students may suggest other rules, depending on the age and ability of the students. For example, you may stipulate that only two-digit numbers be used or that the number must end in zero or have a zero in the tens place.

The rules for the subtraction activity are similar to those for the addition. One player each from Teams A and B names a three-digit number. Both players then write down their estimate of the difference between the two numbers. They use a calculator to determine the answer. Again, the player whose estimate is closest to the actual difference earns a point for the team. Chil-

A

MENTAL ARITHMETIC,

UPON THE

INDUCTIVE PLAN;

BEING AN

ADVANCED INTELLECTUAL COURSE,

DESIGNED FOR

SCHOOLS AND ACADEMIES.

By BENJAMIN GREENLEAF, A. M.,
AUTHOR OF THE "NATIONAL ARITHMETIC," ETC.

IMPROVED EDITION.

BOSTON:
PUBLISHED BY ROBERT S. DAVIS & CO.
NEW YORK: D. APPLETON & CO., AND MASON BROTHERS
PHILADELPHIA: J. B. LIPPINCOTT & CO.
CHICAGO: KEEN & LEE.
1859.

Figure 7–38

dren who engage in this activity for a while develop estimation strategies that benefit them in the game.

Many calculator activities that call for estimation not only strengthen estimation skills but also improve calculator skill. A sampling of calculator activity books is included in the chapter references.

Solving and Creating Problems

Addition and subtraction are important skills in problem solving. Many problem situations require repeated additions and subtractions. Following are some activities that provide practice in problem solving and cause students to use addition and subtraction.

ACTIVITIES

Primary (K–3)

Objective: to use "magic squares" for problem-solving and computational practice.

1. "Magic squares" have been popular and engaging puzzles for many centuries. A magic square is a square array of numbers that produce the same sum when added along each row, column, and diagonal. For younger children, start with a 3-by-3 frame on the chalkboard or provide children with a worksheet with several such frames. Figure 7–39a shows how the frames look.

   Ask the children to use the numbers 1, 1, 1, 2, 2, 2, 3, 3, 3 and to put one number in each region of the frame. It does not matter how the children decide to place the numbers. Initially, do not attempt to make the square "magic," as the sums of rows, columns, and diagonals are unlikely to be the same. Figure 7–39b shows how one child placed the numbers.

Next, ask the children to add each row and write each sum at the end of the row. Then have them add each column and put each sum at the bottom of the column. Finally, have them add each diagonal and put the sums at the corners.

Talk to the children about some of their answers. Ask, "What is the largest sum you found in your square?" Expect several different answers. The largest would be 9. Ask, "What is the smallest sum you found in your square?" Again, several answers are possible. The smallest would be 3. Ask, "What number do you have the most of?" Six would be the sum found most often.

At the next stage, provide frames and ask the children to put a 1 in each row and to arrange the 1s so that no more than one 1 appears in each column. Ask the children to put a 2 in each row and to arrange the 2s so that no more than one 2 appears in each column. Then have the children put a 3 in each of the empty regions. Figure 7–39c shows one such arrangement.

Again, ask the children to add up each row, column, and diagonal. One of two possible results will occur. All but one diagonal will add to 6, or all rows, columns, and diagonals will add to 6. Discuss what numbers a diagonal needs to add to 6. Invite the children to figure out what numbers to put in the diagonals. Complete the magic square so all of the sums are 6.

Extend magic squares by providing children with a new series of numbers to use in the square. For example, 2, 2, 2, 3, 3, 3, 4, 4, 4 can be used. This time the sum is 9. Challenge the children to put the numbers in the frame to make a magic square. Here is a possible solution using Polya's problem-solving steps.

- *Understanding the problem.* This is just like the problem we solved using 1s, 2s, and 3s, but now we are using three different numbers. The sum will be 9.
- *Devising a plan.* We will try the same plan that worked when we used smaller numbers. We will put a 2 in each row so that no more than one 2 appears in each column. Then we will do the same thing with 3 and 4. We need to make sure both diagonals add to 9 (guess and check).
- *Carrying out the plan.* When we fill in the numbers as we planned, we get a sum of 9 everywhere but in one diagonal, where we get 4 + 4 + 4, or 12. To

get three of the same number that add to 9, the numbers need to be 3. So the diagonal needs to be 3 + 3 + 3. We will exchange the 4s for 3s and see if it works. It does!

- *Looking back.* We'll check again to make sure all the rows and columns and both diagonals add to 9. They do. For both the magic squares we have solved, the second of the three different numbers in the sequence fills one of the diagonals. It was 2 + 2 + 2 in the first magic square and 3 + 3 + 3 in the second magic square. We think it will be 4 + 4 + 4 in a magic square that uses 3, 3, 3, 4 , 4, 4, 5, 5, 5 for its numbers. Let's try it.

Have the children name a number series, using three consecutive numbers three times each. Have the children solve the magic square.

a.

b.

c.

Figure 7–39

CHAPTER 26 · *More About Facts to 18*

PROBLEM OF THE DAY

Answer Key

Lesson 26.1

PROBLEM

Give the sums. Tell how you can use doubles facts and doubles-plus-one.

4	4	5	6
+3	+5	+6	+7

3 + 3 = 6   4 + 4 = 8   5 + 5 = 10   6 + 6 = 12
1 more is 7   1 more is 9   1 more is 11   1 more is 13

SOLUTION

Have children review the doubles facts and then look at the addition problems. Encourage them to take the double of the lesser number and count on by 1.

Lesson 26.2

PROBLEM

Write the sums. Which addition combination does not belong? Tell why.

3	4	5	6
+3	+5	+5	+6
6	9	10	12

4 + 5 = 9 does not belong, because all the other combinations are doubles.

SOLUTION

Have children find the sums. Have children look at the pattern in the combinations and point out that three of them are made with the same two numbers. The combination that does not belong is made with two different numbers.

Lesson 26.3

PROBLEM

In how many different ways can you name 14?
7 + 7 = 14, 8 + 6 = 14, 6 + 8 = 14, 9 + 5 = 14,
5 + 9 = 14, . . .

SOLUTION

Have children begin with the doubles fact and then follow the pattern of adding 1 to the first addend and subtracting 1 from the other addend.

Leson 26.4

PROBLEM

Fred needs 15 inches of tape. He has one piece that is 8 inches long. He has another piece that is 4 inches long. Does he have enough tape?
No; 8 + 4 = 12, and 12 is less than 15.

SOLUTION

Cut three pieces of yarn that are 15 inches, 8 inches, and 4 inches. Have children brainstorm ways to use the yarn to solve the problem. Show children that the two smaller pieces of yarn put together are not as long as the yarn that is 15 inches long. Relate this to the addition sentence.

Figure 7–40   From Math Advantage, Problem of the Day Transparencies, copyright © 1998 by Harcourt Brace & Company, reproduced by permission of the publisher.

Math Program

The page shown in Figure 7–40 shows four Problems of the Day from a first grade math text designed to help students strengthen their mastery of addition facts to 18. These problems are available on a transparency for display at various times during the day. Note that the students are asked to explain their reasoning according to the philosophy of the program that students can better make sense of mathematics through reasoning rather than rules. The Problem of the Day is part of the daily assessment as are Lesson Checks that frequently involve teacher observation of student work using manipulatives. Other assessment options include pretests and other assessment of prior knowledge, performance assessment using interviews and journals, work samples for portfolios, student self-assessment, and more traditional chapter reviews and tests.

In addition to the doubles strategy that is shown in these problems, students learn other strategies such as making ten and counting on, and using patterns to find all the basic facts with a given sum. The tools in this chapter include computer programs, children's literature, linking cubes, egg cartons, card games, counters, tens frames, and calculators. Suggestions in the Teacher's Edition include ideas for Cultural Connections and different modalities and intelligences. The chapter also includes School–Home Connection activities that ask students to do such things as explain to their families ways to use "Make a Ten" to solve an addition problem.

Objective: to construct and solve problems involving addition.

2. Provide the children with a worksheet that contains several frames, each with nine numerals and an empty box at the top. Figure 7–41a illustrates one of these frames.

   Ask the children to choose two numbers in the frame, add them together, and put the answer in the box at the top. Have them do the same thing for each frame on the worksheet. When the worksheet is done, the children will have made problem boxes for other children to solve.

   Have the children exchange worksheets and see if they can find the pair of numbers that have the sum that equals the number on top. Instruct them to circle the two numbers. The children may check their solutions with a calculator. Figure 7–41b shows one solution. With the same set of numbers in a frame, many different problems can be made. It is also possible to have more than one solution for a single problem.

To extend this activity, have the children use subtraction instead of addition. Have them place the difference in the box at the top, with the operation sign on either side. Figure 7–41c shows an example. The circled numerals represent two numbers whose difference equals 13.

To further extend the activity, have the children determine all of the numbers for the frame as well as the solution number and the operation. You will find the problems become more difficult and challenging. Collect the solutions and display them on the bulletin board.

Objective: to use a Bingo activity involving problem solving, addition, and subtraction.

3. **Plus/Minus Bingo** may be played with two players or with the two halves of a class. Each player needs a Plus/Minus Bingo card. The card shown in Figure 7–42a is for a game involving addition; that shown in Figure 7–42b, a game involving subtraction. Each addition card should be a different combination of the same numerals; subtraction cards should be similarly varied. Develop the bingo cards from the sums and differences of numbers found in Groups A and B (see

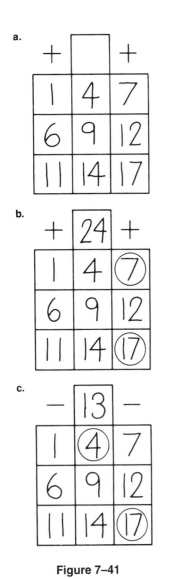

a.

b.

c.

Figure 7–41

a.

PLUS/MINUS BINGO					
63	95	55	71	39	44
35	61	77	99	50	82
91	45	88	67	52	75
86	73	37	53	97	48
57	89	46	80	41	59
43	93	84	42	69	90

b.

PLUS/MINUS BINGO					
21	48	5	57	31	12
3	10	58	23	50	37
43	63	14	54	7	25
20	35	9	65	29	52
61	39	56	16	59	13
45	11	27	67	18	41

c.

GROUP A	GROUP B
69 42 31 24 56 75	11 19 13 15 21 17

Figure 7–42

Figure 7–42c). Select the numerals in Groups A and B to match the level of the children's arithmetic abilities.

In turn, players select one numeral from Group A and one from Group B. The players use calculators or paper and pencil to add the two numbers; then they put a marker (bean or Bingo marker) on the numeral representing the sum. Four markers in a row, column, or diagonal represent a win.

To vary this activity, construct combination cards with some numerals taken from the addition card and some numerals taken from the subtraction card. Play proceeds as described above except players must announce whether they are adding or subtracting at the beginning of each turn. Because of the number of possible answers, let three markers in a row, column, or diagonal represent a win.

ACTIVITIES

Intermediate–Middle Grades (4–8)

Objective: to use "magic squares" for problem solving and computational practice.

1. Begin by challenging the students to complete a 3-by-3 magic square using the numbers 1, 2, 3, 4, 5, 6, 7, 8, 9. The sum for each row, column, and diagonal of that square is 15.

   When that magic square has been solved, ask the students to try another 3-by-3 magic square using the numbers 1, 3, 5, 7, 9, 11, 13, 15, 17. The sum for that magic square is 27. Clever students will be able to use the solution pattern in the first magic square to guide them in solving the second magic square. Figure 7–43a and b show the completed magic squares.

   There are solutions other than the ones shown, representing rotations and reflections of the square. Can you find another solution?

2. To extend work with magic squares, let the students select series of nine digits and try them in 3-by-3 magic squares. Have the students discover sequences that do not work. For example, any nine numbers in an arithmetic sequence can be successfully used in a magic square, but those in a geometric sequence seldom can be used.

   See if students can determine what the sum of each row, column, and diagonal will be. Three times the middle number of a usable nine-number sequence is the sum for the magic square containing that sequence. Encourage students to make up magic square problems for other students.

   Next, present challenge problems, such as a 5-by-5 magic square using the numbers from 1 to 25. The sum here is 65. Unless students discover a solution pattern, this is difficult to solve.

Try a 4-by-4 magic square, using the numbers 1 to 16. The sum is 34. A partially completed 4-by-4 magic square is shown in Figure 7–43c. Sometimes, providing partial solutions is an incentive for students who otherwise might not seek a solution.

Objective: to use problem-solving skills in an addition and subtraction context.

3. The guidelines for this activity are simple. Present to the students a format for addition or subtraction with nine empty regions, as in Figure 7–44a. Explain that the object is to put each of the numbers from 1 to 9 in one of the regions so the correct sum results. Figure 7–44b shows a solution to the problem; Figure 7–44c is a solution to the corresponding subtraction problem.

   A number of solutions are possible for both the addition and the subtraction problem. To encourage students, begin a collection on a bulletin board or chalkboard of the different solutions. Have the students look for patterns to help them find solutions. For example, if the three digits in the sum add to 18, the other digits can be arranged in the addends to solve the problem. On the board, outline an area in which to place nonsolutions. Nonsolutions often provide insight to help solve the problem.

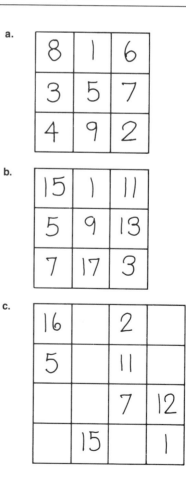

Figure 7–43

a.

b.

c.

Figure 7–44

Grouping Students for Learning Addition and Subtraction

The ways that students are grouped for learning addition and subtraction are not different from the ways that students are grouped for learning multiplication and division. To avoid repetition, we present the grouping discussion for all four basic operations in the Grouping Students section in Chapter 8.

Communicating Learning of Addition and Subtraction

For students to communicate in a variety of ways as they explore the concepts and practice the skills of addition and subtraction is an integral part of learning these topics. The discussion of communication for addition and subtraction does not differ from the same discussion for multiplication and division. To avoid repetition, we again present the discussion on communication in the Communicating section in Chapter 8.

Connecting Learning of Addition and Subtraction

The students in Mr. Thompson's second-grade class were sitting on the carpet as Mr. T, as the children called him, read the poem "Smart" from *Where the Sidewalk Ends* by Shel Silverstein (1974). He began,

"My dad gave me one dollar bill
'Cause I'm his smartest son,
And I swapped it for two shiny quarters
'Cause two is more than one!

As the poem continued, the students chuckled and laughed and made an occasional comment about the coin trading that takes place. The two quarters are traded for three dimes, the three dimes for four nickels, and, finally, the four nickels for five pennies. In the final stanza, the boy's father gets red in the face and shakes his head. Mr. T asked the students to return to their desks and in their math journals explain whether the father was happy (as the boy thought) or sad and why they thought so.

Following this writing activity, Mr. Thompson read *Alexander, Who Used to Be Rich Last Sunday* by Viorst (1978). In this story, Alexander is given a dollar. The story tells how he is parted from his money through a series of events in his life. It is a humorous account of how money disappears. After the story was read, the class discussed the events leading to Alexander losing his dollar. And they were challenged to compare Alexander's plight with that of the son in "Smart." Mr. Thompson asked, "How were the stories alike and how were they different? How did each boy feel at the end of their respective stories? What are other ways that cause money to slip away from us?" Many students participated in the discussion.

The students in Ms. Robinson's fifth-grade class worked together in cooperative groups to prepare a menu for a Thanksgiving dinner. Each group prepared its own menu. After the menus were finished, lists of the ingredients were made and estimates of individual ingredients and the total cost of the food were made. Next, the class took a trip to a local grocery store to price the items that were needed to prepare their menus. When the students returned they wrote about their menus and how the actual cost for the ingredients compared with their estimates.

In Ms. Collin's eighth-grade class the students participated in a holiday extravaganza gift-buying simulation. Each student had up to $250 to spend for five gifts. The students brought department store merchandise catalogs and used them to "purchase" gifts for friends and members of their families. After perusing the catalogs and deciding on their purchases, the students completed a catalog order form, wrote checks to "pay" for their purchases, and balanced their checkbooks.

These activities are intended to involve students in applications of adding and subtracting in a context that helps show how mathematics is connected with a student's daily life. Notice that using the Silverstein poem and the Viorst story helps connect mathematics with literature. There are several excellent sources that suggest how topics in mathematics are integrated with children's literature and how teachers may use children's literature to enrich quantitative and visual thinking. Several are listed in the bibliography at the end of this and other chapters of this book.

This is one way that connections are made between the mathematics that students are learning and other aspects of school and daily life. Another powerful way to make connections is to integrate math with other school subjects. *Math Excursions 2* (Burk, et al., 1991) introduces a set of clever integrated units for primary students. One such unit is "The Popcorn Party," in which students plan and put on a popcorn party for up to 100 people. As students work through the unit, they perform a variety of mathematical tasks and include work in language arts, science, and social studies. For students to see how mathematical connections are made helps them to better understand how mathematics is an integral part of their lives.

Assessing Learning of Addition and Subtraction

Most of the addition and subtraction concepts and skills children learn have been presented by the time children finish the third grade. This is not to say that all children can add and subtract proficiently when they enter the fourth or even fifth grade.

What is a teacher to do in such cases? Individual or small group instruction is necessary. You will need to determine why there is an inability to add or subtract. Is it because the student does not know what addition or subtraction is (concept)? Does the student not know the basic addition or subtraction facts (skill)? Could it be that the student cannot perform an algorithm (skill)? Does the student lack interest because of past failure with addition and subtraction (affect)? Are assignments with too many problems causing discouragement (affect)? Does the student bring to school a negative attitude about school work and achievement (affect)?

There are many ways addition and subtraction learning is assessed. If students are given the opportunity to construct and discuss their own algorithms, then assessment may be based, in part, on the reasoning that went into constructing the algorithm and the validity of the algorithm. Of course, mathematics textbooks and supplemental materials accompanying the textbooks offer options for assessment. Chapter pretests and posttests, mid-chapter checkups, and unit tests are common among math texts. Such tests provide information about how children add and subtract relative to the material contained in the chapter. Have the students collect samples of their work in their math portfolio (see Chapter 15) so progress is documented over the course of a school term.

While testing programs are well established for addition and subtraction, diagnostic teaching techniques are not so well established. Diagnostic procedures require teacher observations of children's daily work to pinpoint the error patterns that lead to low computational success. Teachers need to talk with students and have them discuss their thinking processes. Too often, children who make mistakes are told to redo a problem or to work more problems of the same type, but no one determines the source of the errors. Reworking incorrect problems may reinforce incorrect methods. Discover the cause of the problem to correct the process, not just the result.

Reasons that a child is making mistakes may include

1. *Social, physical, or emotional problems.* Children may be hampered in cognitive skills by noncognitive problems such as a short attention span, hunger, fear of reprisal for getting the incorrect answer or not completing the work, or the desire to be "like everyone else." Ask for information about such children from the parents, previous teachers, or behavior specialists. Those who have worked with a particular youngster in the past may be able to offer advice about how to assist the youngster. Make your own observations. If you are the first to observe this behavior, report your concern to a behavior specialist, resource teacher, or principal. Generally, extra time, care, and patience are necessary to provide the environment in which mathematical growth can take place.

2. *Lack of prerequisite skills or appropriate state of development.* Children may not be ready to learn a particular concept because they have not mastered previous skills or because they have not reached the appropriate developmental stage. Children may not be ready to learn missing addends, the inverse of addition, because they have not yet reached that stage of development and cannot comprehend the reversibility concept.

   By having children explain their thinking as they work, you will be able to pinpoint where their skills fail them. Reteach faulty prerequisite skills to students having difficulty. Give additional time and materials to children who are developmentally unready to learn.

3. *Weak knowledge of basic facts.* This is a common diagnosis. For example, children may know how to perform an addition algorithm but be unable to recall basic addition facts. Children are then frustrated and

unmotivated to even try. You can spot children with a weak command of basic facts by reviewing their paper-and-pencil work, administering fact tests, and listening to them as they explain how they perform operations.

Work with children who need help. Provide activities that assist memorization of basic facts. Also, check to make sure children understand the concept of the operation for which they are practicing skills. The children may need to return to physical materials to build necessary foundations.

4. *Incorrect or incomplete algorithm.* Teacher diagnosis is particularly important in this area. To help diagnose incorrect algorithms, have children show you their work and explain how they arrived at a particular solution. Their thinking is usually revealing. Children tend to make systematic errors. For example, in subtraction, a common error is subtracting the smaller digit from the larger digit regardless of whether it is the minuend or subtrahend. VanLehn (1983) describes many of these faulty procedures, called **bugs.**

Remember, algorithms created by children are very often valid, whereas those memorized by rote may not be valid. Pinpoint the source of the error; have the children reconstruct the algorithm with physical models, and discuss their procedures.

5. *Wrong operation.* Children may use the wrong operation because they have misread the operation sign or because they have chosen the wrong operation in solving a word problem. The latter error is more serious. Continue the work with word problems. Discuss word problems with children having difficulty and encourage them to explain the operation to perform even if they do not work the problem. Practical situations and problems written by the children help children having difficulty understand the appropriate operations to use.

Once children's strengths and weaknesses have been diagnosed, group the children for at least part of their instructional time according to this diagnosis. At other times, let children with strong skills in a particular area help children with weaker skills; use cooperative learning groups; teach the class as a whole group or work with individuals. When grouping, keep the following points in mind:

- *Keep the groups flexible.* Do not group in October and expect to have the same groups in May. Groups should change as skills and concepts change.
- *Avoid labeling children.* Even if they are called eagles and seahawks, children know if the teacher thinks of them as slow and fast.
- *Avoid giving one group busy work while working with another group.* Let groups work independently with materials, games, a computer, the math text, or worksheets, but make sure the tasks are meaningful.
- *Have interesting tasks appropriate to the level of the group.* Each group may have different material, but all materials should be carefully thought out. What may be uninteresting for one group may be just what another group needs.

Your ability to diagnose the cause or causes of difficulty and to remediate the difficulty depends on your own familiarity with mathematics, the learning process, and your students. You will need patience. The students will need support and encouragement.

Children's activities must seem worth doing for them to gain the most. Fourth graders should be convinced that they are not doing only second- or third-grade work. To avoid boredom, try to choose aids or algorithms that are new to the child. Encourage the students to share their own algorithms with others. Construct an algorithm bulletin board to display the students original algorithms. Children who have previously failed may be visual or tactile/kinesthetic learners, so be sure to include experiences for visualizing and manipulating. Allow children to use calculators so that they may learn more advanced mathematics and not always be frustrated by their weaknesses with basic facts. Finally, be willing to set aside the regular textbook assignments that can pile up and, over time, overwhelm the slow, discouraged students.

Something for Everyone

Teaching operations with whole numbers requires attention to various learning modes. The styles of children learning addition and subtraction do not differ appreciably from the styles of children learning multiplication and division. To avoid repetition, we present a complete discussion of learning modes for all four basic operations in the Something for Everyone section at the end of Chapter 8.

KEY IDEAS

Addition and subtraction play prominent roles in our daily lives. Chapter 7 presents ways that the concepts of addition and subtraction may be taught. Children join, take away, and count objects in learning the processes of addition and subtraction. Objects such as cubes, rods, beans, and bottle caps serve the purpose well.

The skills of addition and subtraction require knowing the basic facts. Many activities help children learn the addition and subtraction facts. A variety of paper-and-pencil algorithms may be taught using traditional means.

Calculators and computers play increasingly important roles in addition and subtraction. Estimation and mental calculation need special emphasis as we shift from paper and pencil to electronic computation. It is important for students to decide which computational technique is most appropriate. Students should use oral and written communication skills to learn from one another as well as from the teacher. You should carefully monitor the progress of children as they learn addition and subtraction and adjust instruction according to your diagnosis.

DISCUSSION QUESTIONS

1. Compare the way you learned addition and subtraction, concepts and skills, with the discussion and activities presented in Chapter 7.
2. Select one of the proportional materials presented in Figures 6–14 or 6–15. Construct several pieces of the set and use them as a model in a join machine. Describe how the set you chose can be used to show the concepts of addition and "carrying."
3. Read the section on Basic Addition and Subtraction Facts. Then, consider the table of basic addition facts, Table 7–1, and discuss how you can help children memorize the addition facts by reducing the total number of facts needed to be memorized. You may start by using some of the properties of addition.
4. Develop an alternative algorithm for subtracting 45 − 18, one that is new to you and not mentioned in the text. Describe your algorithm to someone else to see if that person can understand how to perform it.
5. Choose either Silverstein's poem "Smart" or Viorst's story *Alexander, Who Used to Be Rich Last Sunday* and read it. Then, write a letter to either the boy or Alexander and discuss how things might have been made to come out more profitably.

REFERENCES

Abrohms, Alison, *Literature-Based Math Activities: An Integrated Approach.* New York: Scholastic Professional Books, 1992.

Ashlock, Robert B., *Error Patterns in Computation.* Englewood Cliffs, NJ: Merrill/Prentice Hall, 1990.

Bang, Molly, *Ten, Nine, Eight.* New York, NY: Greenwillow Books, 1983.

Braddon, Kathryn L., Nancy J. Hall, and Dale Taylor, *Math through Children's Literature: Making the NCTM Standards Come Alive.* Englewood, CO: Teacher Ideas Press, 1993.

Burk, Donna, Allyn Snider, and Paula Symonds, *Math Excursions 2.* Portsmouth, NH: Heinemann, 1992.

Burns, Marilyn, *Math and Literature (K–3).* Sausalito, CA: Math Solutions Publications, 1992.

Burton, Grace M., Ann Mills, Carolyn Lennon, and Cynthia Parker, *Number Sense and Operations.* Reston, VA: National Council of Teachers of Mathematics, 1993.

Carpenter, Thomas P., James M. Moser, and Thomas A. Romberg, eds., *Addition and Subtraction: A Cognitive Perspective.* Hillsdale, NJ: Lawrence Erlbaum Associates, 1982.

Davidson, Jessica, *Idea Book for Cuisenaire Rods at the Primary Level.* White Plains, NY: Cuisenaire Co. of America, 1977.

Dodd, Anne W., *Footprints and Shadows.* New York: NY: Simon & Schuster Books for Young Readers, 1992.

Driscoll, Mark J., "Estimation and Mental Arithmetic," in *Research Within Reach.* St. Louis: CEMREL, 1979.

————, "Mathematical Problem Solving: Not Just a Matter of Words," in *Research Within Reach.* St. Louis: CEMREL, 1979.

Greenleaf, Benjamin, *A Mental Arithmetic, Upon the Inductive Plan; Being an Advanced Intellectual Course, Designed for Schools and Academies.* Boston: Robert S. Davis, 1859.

Griffiths, Rachel, and Margaret Clyne, *Books You Can Count On.* Portsmouth, NH: Heinemann, 1988.

Immerzeel, George, *Ideas and Activities for Using Calculators in the Classroom.* Dansville, NY: *The Instructor* Publications, 1976.

Jacobs, Russell F., *Problem Solving with the Calculator.* Phoenix: Jacobs, 1977.

Kolakowski, Jane Steffen, *Linking Math with Literature.* Greensboro, NC: Carson-Dellosa, 1992.

Moursund, David, *Calculators in the Classroom: With Applications for Elementary and Middle School Teachers.* New York: John Wiley, 1981.

Reisman, Fredricka K., *Teaching Mathematics.* Prospect Heights, IL: Waveland Press, 1987.

Reys, Robert E., et al., *Keystrokes: Calculator Activities for Young Students.* Worth, IL: Creative Publications, 1979–80.

Satariano, Patricia, *Storytime Mathtime: Math Exploration in Children's Literature.* Palo Alto, CA.: Dale Seymour, 1994.

Schoen, Harold L., and Marilyn J. Zweng, *Estimation and Mental Computation.* Reston, VA: National Council of Teachers of Mathematics, 1986.

Sheffield, Stephanie, *Math and Literature (K–3) Book Two.* Sausalito, CA: Math Solutions Publications, 1995.

Silverstein, Shel, *Where the Sidewalk Ends.* New York: HarperCollins, 1974.

Thaler, Mike, *Seven Little Hippos.* New York, NY: Simon & Schuster Books for Young Readers, 1991.

Thiagarajan, Sivasailan, and Harold D. Stolovitch, *Games with the Pocket Calculator.* Menlo Park, CA: Dymax, 1976.

Thiessen, Diane, and Margaret Matthias, eds., *The Wonderful World of Mathematics.* Reston, VA: National Council of Teachers of Mathematics, 1992.

VanLehn, Kurt, "On the Representation of Procedures in Repair Theory," in *The Development of Mathematical Thinking,* ed. Herbert P. Ginsburg. New York: Academic Press, 1983.

Vaughan, Marcia, *Dorobō the Dangerous.* Morristown, NJ: Silver Burdett Press, 1995.

Viorst, Judith, *Alexander, Who Used to Be Rich Last Sunday.* New York: NY: Aladdin Books, 1978.

Whitin, David J., and Sandra Wilde, *Read Any Good Math Lately?* Portsmouth, NH: Heinemann, 1992.

Technology

Edmark, *Mighty Math Carnival.* Orlando, FL: Harcourt Brace, 1996. (Software)

Edmark, *Mighty Math Number Heroes.* Orlando, FL: Harcourt Brace, 1996. (Software)

The Learning Company, *Treasure MathStorm!* Cambridge, MA: The Learning Company, 1994. (Software)

Sunburst, *How the West Was One + Three × Four.* Pleasantville, NY: Sunburst Communications. (Software)

Tom Snyder Productions, *Fizz & Martina Math Video Kits.* Watertown, MA: Tom Snyder Productions. (Video Kit)

Chapter 8

Teaching and Learning Multiplication and Division

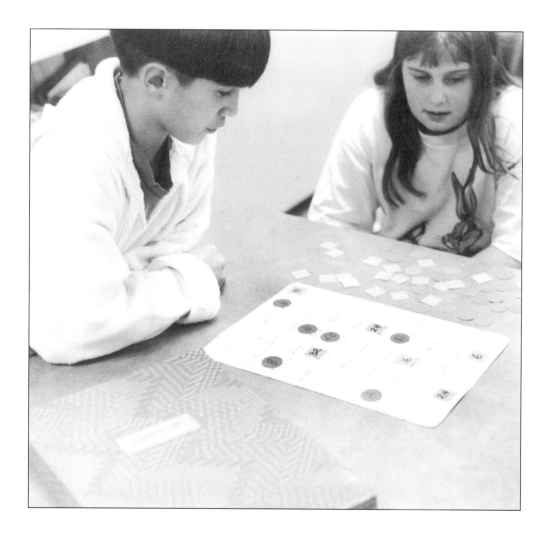

The diagram below shows 13 × 14. How can you use a diagram such as this to mentally multiply any two numbers between 10 and 20? Write a description below that you could use to teach a 10-year old to become proficient at this mental multiplication. Be sure to explain all of your thinking.

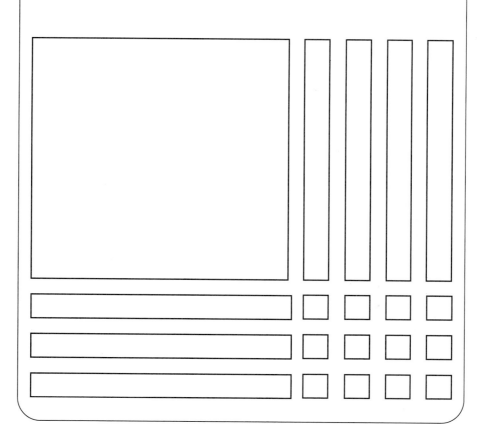

The NCTM *Standards* that refer to multiplication and division, concepts and skills, are the same as those that refer to addition and subtraction, which are listed at the beginning of Chapter 7. You are referred to that list.

As you read the following pages, consider these guiding questions:

1. How are multiplication and division used in activities of daily life?
2. What is the sequence of teaching the concepts and skills of multiplication and division?
3. What are several embodiments for presenting the concepts of multiplication and division?
4. What are some different activities to help children memorize the basic multiplication and division facts?
5. How are the concepts and skills of multiplication and division communicated in the process of learning them?
6. How do you as a teacher diagnose children's errors in performing multiplication and division operations?
7. In what ways do teachers respond to the various learning styles of their students?

Like addition and subtraction, multiplication and division are used extensively in our daily lives. For example, purchasing multiple items such as flashlight batteries, cans of motor oil, bars of soap, bedding flowers, and apples requires multiplication. Filling out tax forms requires some multiplication. Determining how many cookies and brownies are necessary for a group of children requires multiplication or division. Finding out how much you and a friend will each receive when you split baby-sitting money requires division.

Computation, however, is seldom performed with pencil and paper except in school. Calculators or computers do the work, or the computation is performed mentally. The efficiency and accuracy of electronic computation has been a convincing argument for its use. Children growing up in a time of electronic computation need to be skillful estimators and button pushers. They need to know what information a problem is presenting and what operations are required to solve that problem. Again, students should have the opportunity to decide whether to use paper and pencil, mental calculation, estimation, or the calculator or computer.

As with addition and subtraction, teaching multiplication and division begins before children actually start memorizing the basic facts, which are, for multiplication, the whole number products from 0×0 to 9×9. As children informally begin to manipulate objects and count, they learn about relationships and ideas associated with the concept of number. They are also establishing the foundations for learning the concepts of multiplication and division. The activities for learning the concepts of addition and subtraction mentioned in Chapter 7 are necessary for learning the concepts of multiplication and division as well. The skills of adding and subtracting are important prerequisites for performing the multiplication and division algorithms.

Teachers are responsible for determining if children are developing skills that provide a basis for multiplication and division. Word problems help to check children's thinking. For example, "Lori, Julie, and Greg decided to pick clover for a bouquet. Each of them picked two clovers. How many clovers were there all together?" Children with well-developed counting abilities will be able to count out the answer by **counting all,** or using fingers or objects. Some children may **skip count,** that is, count by saying, "two, four, six." Other children may count in their heads. Opportunities to count and skip count should be provided as part of the mathematics program. For children having difficulty, provide practice in grouping objects and counting.

The physical models that help children develop understanding and skill with multiplication and division include attribute materials, multibase blocks, Cuisenaire rods, beans, and cubes. Collections of objects such as bottle caps, shell-shaped macaroni, tiles, and buttons are useful in the early stages of learning about operations. Calculators and computers are helpful tools for learning multiplication and division. Children should be active as they learn about these operations.

Developing Multiplication and Division Concepts

The concept of an operation was carefully developed in Chapter 7. It serves as a supporting concept for all arithmetic operations, including multiplication and division. The idea of an operation as a change or transformation provides a consistent link from one specific operation to another. We introduced addition using real-life situations and a state-operator-state machine, and we introduced subtraction with a concrete take-away model. Thus, we introduce the concepts of multiplication and division using physical models.

Later, we move away from concrete experiences with sets of objects to the pictorial and abstract. Children learn that *multiplication* is renaming a pair of numbers by a single equivalent number. For example, the pair (3, 6) is associated with 18 under the operation of multiplication. Learning how multiplication works is learning the concept of multiplication. Learning that $3 \times 6 = 18$ is learning a basic multiplication fact, a skill that is dealt with later.

In the next two sections, activities to help develop the concepts of multiplication and division are presented.

Multiplication

Sorting, classifying by two or more attributes, and arriving at reversibility of thought are necessary in order for children to understand multiplication and division. Sorting and classifying were presented beginning in Chapter 5. Diagrams were used to assist children using attribute blocks in their sorting. Eventually, children were challenged to show ways of sorting using two attributes simultaneously, such as red and rectangular. **Reversibility of thought** occurs when children construct the knowledge that $2 \times 3 = 6$ also implies that $6 \div 2 = 3$. Achieving reversibility of thought means that children can understand the processes of doing and undoing exemplified in the inverse operations of multiplication and division.

With buttons or cubes, let children construct two groups of three and indicate that there are a total of six as in Figure 8–1a. If, at the same time, the children can begin with a group of six and separate it into two equivalent piles (Figure 8–1b), reversibility of thought is illustrated. Children need a variety of grouping experiences when multiplication and division are being introduced.

Have children continue to respond to number stories as they did while learning addition and subtraction. For example, each of four children is asked to select two poems about pets from those written by the class to put on a bulletin board. As they are about to put them up, the teacher says, "Genny, Ben, Theresa, and Angela have each picked two poems for the board. When they put them up, how many poems will be on the board?" Some children will know the answer without counting. Others will add 2 plus 2 plus 2 plus 2. Still others will count the poems to find the answer. The counting or adding strategies will precede the response, "4 times 2."

The operation presented initially to provide a basis for understanding multiplication joins multiple sets of equal size. Arithmetically, it involves adding several equal numbers to determine a product of two factors. For example, 3×4 may be thought of as three groups of four. The product, 12, can be determined by $4 + 4 + 4$. When first or second grade children participate in the following activity, they tend to count or use repeated addition to determine the answer. Repeated addition is a valuable model for multiplication. It is among the easiest models for young children to understand.

ACTIVITIES

Primary (K–3)

Objective: to use repeated addition as a model for multiplication.

1. Select a favorite flower such as a daffodil and display it. The flower may be real, artificial, or in a photograph. Ask the children how many petals are on a daffodil. If they are unable to tell or do not know, let them count the petals. Respond, "Yes, there are six petals on a daffodil. Here is another daffodil. How many petals are there on two daffodils?" The students may count the additional six petals, they may add 6 plus 6, or they may seem to just know that 2 sixes are 12. Ask, "How many petals would I have if there were three daffodils?" Continue this line of questioning for as long as it is fairly easy for the children to determine an answer. Encourage the children to discuss how they found their answers.

As a variation of this activity, display other flowers with different numbers of petals. The National Council of Teachers of Mathematics has published an attractive book entitled *I Can Count the Petals of a Flower,* by John Wahl and Stacey Wahl. It provides many examples of flowers

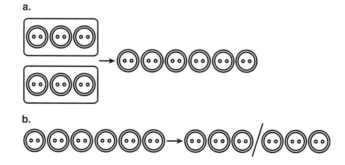

Figure 8–1

with varying numbers of petals. Garden catalogs usually picture many varieties of flowers. The children may have favorite flowers they would like to talk about. Children enjoy not only talking about flowers but also drawing and coloring them. A colorful display can result from a discussion that includes the foundations of multiplication.

2. You may extend the above activity by using materials that are found in small groups. Flashlight batteries are commonly found in groups of two, three, and four. Some pencils are packaged in pairs. Shoes and gloves come in pairs. Tennis balls are usually packaged in threes as in Figure 8–2. Some soaps are found in groups of four. These examples and others that children will name provide opportunities to skip count and use equal addends.

You may also find children's books that suggest counting by various numbers or illustrate objects that come in various sized collections. For example, *How Many Feet in the Bed,* by Hamm (1991) tells a humorous story of a family climbing in bed with father and then climbing out and how the number of feet are counted forward and backward. Another book, *What Comes in 2s, 3s, & 4s?* by Aker (1990) describes and illustrates many common objects that are found in groupings of 2, 3, and 4. Both help to develop the skip counting that is important in learning multiplication and division.

Cartesian products, introduced in Chapter 5, may be models for multiplication. They may be represented by rectangular arrays and intersecting lines. Cartesian products occur when we match, in ordered pairs, all members of one set with all members of another set. For example, let us consider some attribute blocks. Suppose we have three shapes S = {circle, square, triangle} and four textures T = {silk, felt, cotton, wool}. How many possible blocks could be named, each with a different shape and texture? We can make an array with a row for each shape and a column for each texture. This set is

shown in Figure 5–28. Where the attributes intersect, a block can be identified such as {circle, cotton}, {square, silk}, {triangle, felt}, and so on. The three rows and four columns of attributes form a rectangular array of sets that identifies 12 different blocks, designated by one shape and one texture.

ACTIVITIES

Primary (K–3)

Objective: to use rectangular arrays and intersecting lines as models for multiplication.

1. Provide children with objects such as cubes, washers, or tiles. Ask the children to make a row with 5 tiles. Then have them make 2 additional rows, each having 5 tiles (Figure 8–3). Explain to the students that they have made 3 groups of 5 tiles; there are three tiles along one side and 5 tiles along the other. The children can describe their arrangement as "3 by 5." Ask, "How many tiles are there altogether? Count them." There are 15 tiles.

   Now, see if the children can make a 4-by-6 group of tiles. They should have 4 rows with 6 tiles in each row. Some confusion initially may arise with children constructing 6 rows with 4 in each row. Careful explanation and patience will overcome this problem. Soon, the children will be able to construct groups that illustrate any product that is asked for.

2. For children to use intersections as models for multiplication, provide them with 10 pieces of yarn, each about 25 centimeters long. Have the children lay 3 pieces of yarn on their desks side by side as in Figure 8–4a.

   Next, have them lay 4 other pieces on top of the first 3 pieces, crossing the pieces as in Figure 8–4b. Then have the children point to each place where one piece of yarn crosses or intersects another piece of yarn. Let the children find how many intersections there are. Ask, "How many pieces of yarn were laid down first?" There were 3. Ask, "How many were laid down on top of these pieces?" There were 4. Ask, "How many intersections are there?" There are 12.

Figure 8–2

Figure 8–3

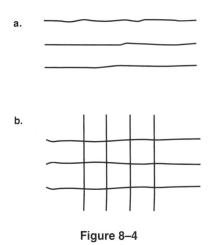

Figure 8–4

Encourage the children to lay out different numbers of pieces of yarn and to record the number of pieces in each direction and the number of intersections. You may wish to have the children glue or tape the yarn onto sheets of paper or to simply draw the pieces of yarn. In cooperative groups or in a whole-class setting, have the children discuss their findings and see if they can find the relationship between the number of horizontal pieces of yarn, the number of vertical pieces of yarn, and the number of intersections.

The array and intersection models may be used later as pictorial models for multiplication. The pictorial array in Figure 8–5a shows a 3-by-6 group, or the product 3 times 6. Figure 8–5b uses intersections to show 3 times 6. Both models work particularly well when children begin to develop skill with basic multiplication facts.

Arrays and intersections are read the same symbolically. In Figure 8–5, the number of rows determines the first factor and the number in each row determines the second factor. The product is determined by counting the number of regions or the number of intersections. Both examples represent 3 times 6 equals 18, or $3 \times 6 = 18$.

Before long, children easily use the symbols for multiplication. Introduce the symbols in a multiplication sentence, $3 \times 6 = 18$, and in the vertical form

$$\begin{array}{r} 6 \\ \times\, 3 \\ \hline 18 \end{array}$$

Help the children read these sentences and become familiar with them.

Children who have had extensive experience with the Cuisenaire rods can extend their work with the rods to show the meaning of multiplication. Capitalizing on the idea of repeated addition, students may begin by finding the value of three light green rods and then finding the single rod that will match this train. Thus, a blue rod is equivalent to three light-green rods.

In the beginning stages of learning how to multiply with the Cuisenaire rods, do not assign number values to the rods. Only when the concept of multiplication has been presented and children are comfortable with the manipulation and language associated with the concept is it time to introduce the symbolism of multiplication. The transition from concrete to abstract requires that the models and symbols be used simultaneously.

ACTIVITIES

Primary (K–3)

Objective: to use Cuisenaire rods to illustrate the concept of multiplication.

1. Cross two rods that are to be multiplied, one on top of the other, as illustrated in Figure 8–6a. Here, we have a purple rod on top of a dark-green rod. It is read from the bottom up, "dark green times purple."

   To perform the multiplication, ask the children to place dark-green rods side by side until the purple rod reaches from one edge of the dark-green rods to the other. This is shown in Figure 8–6b. Then, place the dark-green rods end to end in a train (Figure 8–7). Finally, place two orange rods and a purple rod beside this train to show its value. Thus, dark green times purple equals two orange plus purple.

Objective: to introduce the symbolism of multiplication.

2. With the Cuisenaire rods, establish a value for the white rod (again, be careful not to declare 1 the permanent value of white). If white equals 1, then a tower of yellow and light-green rods is 5 times 3 (yellow times

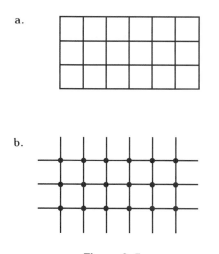

Figure 8–5

light green) and is equal to 15 (orange plus yellow). One effective way to determine the product is to put the rods side by side on centimeter grid paper, outline the rods, and count the number of centimeter squares that are contained in the outline. This technique uses the array model discussed earlier. Additional time and experience with the rods will be needed to allow children to be at ease in symbolizing the rod values.

The concept of multiplication has been presented using several embodiments. Groups containing the same number of objects were joined in some way. Numbers were then attached to the models to assist children in discovering the relationship between joining sets and multiplying numbers. We continue by introducing the concept of division in a similar manner.

Division

Teaching the concept of division is similar to teaching the concept of multiplication. The materials are the same, as is the approach. The concept, however, is different. We believe that if children are taught the con-

cepts of multiplication and division at nearly the same time, the process of learning division becomes easier; the fact that one operation is the inverse of the other can more readily be seen. The operations can be directly compared and the differences noted.

The prerequisites for division are the same as those for multiplication. For the children who cannot yet sort objects by two or more attributes simultaneously and for those who have not achieved reversibility of thought, you must provide additional materials, time, and encouragement.

Division problems typically fall into two categories: measurement problems and partition problems. In a **measurement problem,** the total number of objects is provided along with the number of objects to be put into each group. It is then necessary to find the number of groups that can be made. For example, if there are 15 pieces of paper and each child is given 3 pieces, how many children receive paper? Five children receive paper.

In a **partition problem,** the total number of objects is provided along with the number of groups that are to be made. It is then necessary to find how many objects will go into each group. For example, if there are 15 pieces of paper and 3 children, how many pieces are given each child? The paper is partitioned into 3 sets of 5 pieces. Children should be encouraged to make up problems of their own using real-life situations to help them better understand measurement and partition division.

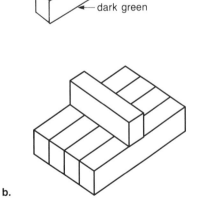

Figure 8–6

ACTIVITIES

Primary (K–3)

Objective: to use objects as a model for division.

1. Begin by reading *The Doorbell Rang* by Hutchins (1986). Mother has baked some cookies that can be shared by two children, but the doorbell rings and another child arrives. That is not a problem because the twelve cookies can still be evenly shared. More children join the party and soon there is just one cookie for each child. The doorbell rings again, and this time it is grandma with a whole tray of cookies. This story lends itself to a discussion of how the cookies can be evenly shared as more children arrive at the party. Physical objects can be used to simu-

Figure 8–7

late the cookies and the sharing can be demonstrated by the students as the discussion proceeds.

A rich extension of this activity is the project described by Burk, et al. (1991). The project, called "Cookies," uses *The Doorbell Rang* and other books about cookies over the course of eight days. Every aspect of the project is carefully outlined and the teacher is given hints about making it successful. The children write story problems, create a drama around the story, make cookies (as props) and serving trays, and then reenact the story. A class story on chart paper is created as the mathematics of *The Doorbell Rang* is examined, followed by individual cookie problems written by the students. The project concludes as children share their story problems.

2. Have the children place brown Cuisenaire rods in front of them. Ask, "How many red rods does it take to make a brown rod?" Let the children experiment to discover that 4 red rods are contained in a brown rod. The result will be similar to the rods in Figure 8–8a.

The division question we have just posed is "brown divided by red equals what?" We found that the answer is 4. If we think of division as the inverse operation to multiplication, we are asking the question "Red times what equals brown?" Here, we do just the opposite of what we did in performing multiplication; we put the brown rod down, lay red rods end to end along the brown rod (Figure 8–8a), and then place the red rods side by side, searching for the rod that equals the width of the red rods, as in Figure 8–8b. It is the purple rod, so $n \div r = p$. If the white rod has the value of 1, then the purple rod has the value of 4.

3. The problem $(\sigma + \sigma + k) \div e$ (orange plus orange plus black divided by blue) is solved by placing the rods together in a train and then finding the number of blue rods it takes to make that same length. It takes 3 blue rods as shown in Figure 8–9.

Had we divided by yellow, we would have found the result to be 5 yellow rods plus a red rod (Figure 8–10). The red rod represents the remainder. It is evaluated by comparing it to the white rod, which has the value of 1. Thus, $(\sigma + \sigma + k) \div y = 5$ remainder 2. Children who have used Cuisenaire rods while learning other number operations will find that division fits well with their other work.

Objective: to practice measurement and partition division using objects.

4. Provide children with a handful of beans. Have them count out twenty-four beans. Tell the students, "Make as many groups of six beans as you can." They will make four groups. This is a measurement problem.

Next, request that the children make six equal groups using the twenty-four beans. Ask, "How many beans are there in each group?" There will be four beans in each group. This is a partition problem.

Give the children plenty of practice using both measurement and partition problems. They should be able to recognize the difference between the two kinds of division and to use materials to illustrate the meaning of each.

Figure 8–8

Figure 8–9

Figure 8–10

Once the language describing division has been introduced, practiced, and discussed, the operation can be symbolized. The transition to the abstract symbols should take place as soon as the children are competent using objects and using the language that describes the operation they are performing.

Activities on pages 198 and 199 employed the Cuisenaire rods. The language the students are using is "brown divided by red equals purple, or 4." The change to number occurs quickly. If the white rod equals 1, brown has the value of 8, red has the value of 2, and purple has the value of 4. Thus, the number sentence $8 \div 2 = 4$ results directly from the sentence using colors. Children need additional experiences with the rods to become proficient using the numerical descriptions of the rods.

In the bean activity on page 199, students had 24 beans and were asked to make as many groups of 6 beans as they could. The children counted them and indicated that there were 24 altogether. Repeat the activity, saying, "We are going to find out how many groups of what size." We are going to find out how many groups of 6. Ask, "How many groups of 6 are there?" There are 4. Explain, "We say this using numbers by writing $24 \div 6 = 4$." The symbols should be written to show the operation.

Earlier, we mentioned that you should take the opportunity to include examples of important properties of the operations being presented. There are some that are important to know when working with multiplication and division. Give the students ample opportunities to discover these properties using physical models. The first of these is the **identity element for multiplication and division.** That is, any number times 1 or divided by 1 results in the number you start with. With this information, $6 \times 1 = 6$, $1 \times 6 = 6$, and $6 \div 1 = 6$ are easy basic facts to remember. Children should discover that $1 \div 6$ (left-hand identity) does not hold for division.

A second important property is the **commutative property of multiplication.** This can be shown using any of the models presented above. For example, with the array of tiles, ask a child to stand in position A as shown in Figure 8–11 and describe the array. In that case, the array would be read 3 by 6, or 3 times 6. There are 18 tiles. Then ask the child to move to position B and describe the array. In this second case, the array should be read 6 by 3, or 6 times 3. The number of tiles stays the same. Students should realize that $3 \times 6 = 18$ and $6 \times 3 = 18$.

Knowing that the order has no effect on the product reduces the number of multiplication facts to be remembered. Children should have the opportunity to discover that the commutative property does not hold for division; that is, $8 \div 4 = 2$, but $4 \div 8$ does not have a whole number solution.

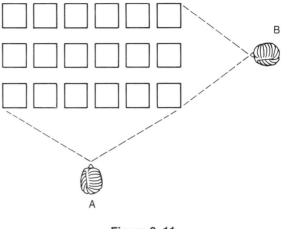

Figure 8–11

A third useful pattern multiplies a number by zero or divides zero by a number. While the results are similar for both of these examples, the ideas are quite different.

Ask the children to make 4 rows of tiles with 3 tiles in each row. They should be able to describe their work as 4 times 3 equals 12. Next, have the children make 4 rows of tiles with 2 tiles in each row and describe the result (4 times 2 equals 8). Then, have them make 4 rows of tiles with 1 tile in each row and describe the result (4 times 1 equals 4). Finally, ask the children to make four rows with zero tiles in each row and describe the result (4 times 0 equals 0).

Have the students experiment with this activity and discuss the results any time zero tiles are put into rows. See if the children can make a generalization regarding the result any time there are zero rows.

Encourage the children to act out these situations and to create situations of their own that involve zero. The children will soon discover that any number times zero is zero. For example, $8 \times 0 = 0$ and $0 \times 5 = 0$.

In division, zero cannot be the divisor. To find how many groups of zero are contained in 24 makes no sense and is *undefined* in mathematics. Thus, $27 \div 0$, $6 \div 0$, and $0 \div 0$ are all undefined. On the other hand, dividing zero by any number is possible. Have the children act out this situation: If there are 0 (zero) pieces of clay and you wish to give each child 3 pieces, how many children will receive clay? The children can decide how this situation is described in division (0 divided by 3 equals 0).

Similarly, describe this situation: If there are 0 pieces of clay and 3 children, how many pieces can be given to each child? Again, the children will see that 0 divided by 3 equals 0. After a number of examples, the children realize that zero divided by any number is zero. Time spent discovering and discussing these properties will make remembering the multiplication and division facts easier.

Developing and Practicing Multiplication and Division Skills

Children need to learn the skills associated with knowing how to multiply and divide. These skills are knowing and working with the basic facts and algorithms. The **basic multiplication facts,** of which there are 100, are those ranging from 0×0 to 9×9. The **basic division facts,** of which there are 90, are those ranging from $81 \div 9$ to $0 \div 1$.

As mentioned earlier, an *algorithm* is any method used to solve a problem; mathematics includes numerous algorithms for multiplication and division. As children learn multiplication and division, they can make use of paper-and-pencil procedures, mental arithmetic, calculators, and computers. We begin our discussion of skills with basic facts and follow with algorithms.

Basic Multiplication and Division Facts

For quick recall, children should be expected to visualize and/or memorize the basic multiplication and division facts. Memorization should begin when children understand the concepts of multiplication and division. Helping children to associate meaning with these operations is rewarded as the facts are learned. With a background in physical models, children will be able to reconstruct a basic fact that they have forgotten. They can use a variety of objects as counters. They may use Cuisenaire rods, intersecting lines, arrays, or calculators.

The multiplication and division facts may be presented almost simultaneously. Typically, elementary mathematics textbooks present multiplication followed by division, with some illustration of how they are related. You may wish to start with the multiplication concept models, and follow shortly by the division concept models. As children understand the concepts, they will work comfortably with both multiplication and division at the same time. Because the multiplication and division facts are closely related, they can be learned together effectively. A family of related facts includes several facts related by the numbers being multiplied and divided. One such family follows:

$$3 \times 6 = 18$$
$$6 \times 3 = 18$$
$$18 \div 3 = 6$$
$$18 \div 6 = 3$$

The classroom should contain tools with which to perform simple calculations. The most basic tools for calculating are the counters mentioned throughout earlier chapters. In the initial stages of learning the multiplication facts, encourage children to use cubes, beans, bottle caps, buttons, or tiles to find the answer by forming the specified number of groups, each containing a given number of objects, such as three groups of five tiles. As the work becomes more abstract and paper and pencil or calculators are used, marks on paper, including intersecting lines, help reinforce basic multiplication facts.

The number line, introduced earlier for addition and subtraction, is useful for multiplication and division. For children with little number-line experience, the walk-on number line is a good place to start. Another alternative is the number line calibrated in centimeters, beside which Cuisenaire rods can be placed. Illustrate multiplication and division using a number line on which you take jumps using your finger or a pencil. When children wish to multiply 3×4, begin at 0 on the number line and take 3 jumps of 4, as in Figure 8–12a. The point at which you stop, 12, is the product of 3 and 4. The number line serves as an example of the repeated addition model for multiplication.

When students wish to divide 14 by 7, explain, "We are going to find how many 7s are contained in 14. Put your finger on your number line at 14." Continue, "We are going to find how many jumps of 7 we can make as we move from 14 to 0. Let's all make one jump of 7 toward 0. Are we at 0 yet? No, so let's make another jump of 7. Are we at 0 yet? Yes, how many jumps did we make?" There were 2 jumps (see Figure 8–12b). Ask, "How many 7s are contained in 14?" There are 2. Summarize, "We can say $14 \div 7 = 2$. Now let's try $12 \div 3$." This is an example of measurement division.

The calculator can play an important role during the learning of multiplication and division facts. It should be used to quickly produce facts that are forgotten, particularly during games and activities intended to help children memorize basic facts. Using the calculator should not replace the memorization of facts. It can, however, assist children by providing immediate feedback and allowing them to continue their activity.

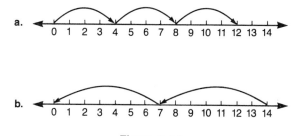

Figure 8–12

Computer games and activities are available to assist children as they learn and reinforce basic multiplication and division facts. In many cases the same software used in reinforcing the basic facts in addition and subtraction also reinforces multiplication and division. Games such as *Calculating Crew* (Edmark) and *Robomath* (MINDPLAY) are designed to strengthen children's abilities in multiplication and division.

You can help children prepare for learning the multiplication and division facts. For example, skip counting forward and backward using various numbers helps children become familiar with the multiples of these numbers. The first 10 multiples of the numbers from 0 to 9 are the basic multiplication facts.

Another way to prepare children for the basic multiplication facts is to have them collect objects and record how many objects there are. For example, put groups of 4 beans in portion cups. Record the number of beans in 1 cup, then 2 cups, 3 cups, and so on, up to 10 cups.

The multiplication table can help children learn the multiplication facts. The table, shown in Table 8–1, has ten rows and ten columns. The multiplication table is read by selecting the first factor from the left side and the second factor from the top. The product of the two factors is found in the table where that row and that column meet. The fact 8×6 is shown in the figure. Use the properties discussed earlier, the identity, zero, and commutative properties, and known facts such as the twos and fives to eliminate all the facts students already know. They will be pleasantly surprised to see how few facts remain to be memorized.

The activities that follow are specifically designed for multiplication. Some are modifications of the activities presented in Chapter 7 for addition. Each activity may be used just as effectively for division by making simple changes in the materials.

TABLE 8–1

X	0	1	2	3	4	5	6	7	8	9
0	0	0	0	0	0	0	0	0	0	0
1	0	1	2	3	4	5	6	7	8	9
2	0	2	4	6	8	10	12	14	16	18
3	0	3	6	9	12	15	18	21	24	27
4	0	4	8	12	16	20	24	28	32	36
5	0	5	10	15	20	25	30	35	40	45
6	0	6	12	18	24	30	36	42	48	54
7	0	7	14	21	28	35	42	49	56	63
8	0	8	16	24	32	40	(48)	56	64	72
9	0	9	18	27	36	45	54	63	72	81

(Factor across the top, Factor down the left side)

ACTIVITIES

Primary (K–3)

Objective: to help children memorize the basic multiplication facts.

1. Commercially prepared printed flash cards have been used successfully for many years to help children reinforce basic multiplication facts. These cards have a multiplication problem on one side and the same problem with the answer on the other side. One card from a set is shown in Figure 8–13a.

   Another useful type of flash card contains the entire multiplication expression and has a sliding paper sleeve. The sleeve may be positioned over any part of the expression for special practice. This type of card helps reinforce the connection between multiplication and division. An example of this card is shown in Figure 8–13b. Show children the cards one at a time and ask them to recall the product. Put aside the products they recalled quickly, but repeat the activity with the products they did not recall. The whole class, small groups, or individuals may be involved, with cards being flashed by the teacher, an aide, or students.

   Electronic flash cards resemble printed flash cards. They are displayed on preprogrammed calculators or computers. The computer records correct responses, reinforces learning with appealing graphics in a game-like setting, provides time limits, and summarizes the results of the drill. A child may practice individually or in friendly competition with another student while the teacher attends to other important tasks.

   Ideally, both printed and electronic flash cards should be used so that children can practice on problems presented in several ways. As with addition and subtraction, be careful not to frustrate children with an overemphasis on flash cards.

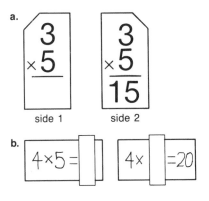

Figure 8–13

2. Provide practice in mental arithmetic. Practice periods should be limited to 5 or 10 minutes. Orally present the multiplication facts to children and have the children write on a piece of paper only the answer to the problem.

An alternative approach is to provide children with numeral cards (0–9) or marking boards and have them hold up the appropriate answer for you to see as in Figure 8–14. Determine the difficulty of the problems based on the age and experience of the students. Initially, speedy responses are not necessary. Students need an opportunity to practice using their minds.

Ask the students to number from 1 to 5 or 10 on their papers. Explain that you are going to give them a problem and they should think of the answer and then write it down. At first, they may need to use their pencils to determine the answer; after a few sessions, they should not. Examples of mental exercises follow: What is 3 times 2? What is 2 times 4 times 3? Yes or no, 4 times 6 is more than 20? Three times 4 equals 12; What else equals 12?

As the students become more proficient, insist that they not use pencils to determine the answer. Increase the number of questions. Expand the questions to include mixed operations. For example, begin with 5, multiply by 3, now add 5.

3. Times Up is a game for two players that helps children learn the multiplication facts. Times Up requires construction of activity materials. First, construct a board with 45 regions, each containing a multiplication expression (see Figure 8–15).

Make two sets of 24 markers, each of a different color—for example, yellow and blue. In each set of markers, there should be one marker with each of the following numerals: 2, 3, 4, 5, 6, 7, 8, 9, 12, 14, 15, 16, 18, 20, 24, 25, 27, 28, 32, and 36. There should be two markers with each of the numerals 10 and 21.

To play this game, each player selects one set of markers and turns them numeral side down, mixing them together. Each player then turns over one marker to determine who will begin the game. The player with the highest number begins.

On each turn, a player turns over one marker, notes the number, and places it on a region of the playing board that corresponds to the number. For example, if a marker with the numeral 6 is drawn, it should be placed on a region containing 2×3 or 3×2. Only one marker may be placed on a region. If the marker cannot be played, it is laid aside face up. Play continues until all of the regions are covered or until no more markers can be placed on the board. The player who has placed the most markers is the winner.

This activity is unusual in that children are given the answer and are expected to find the problem. This allows children to establish a different set of associations with the basic multiplication facts. Competition in this activity is limited to the "luck of the draw." Thus, the opportunity to win is accorded all who play.

4. The game Four-in-a-Row Multiplication is a variation of tic-tac-toe. Two to four students may play. This game requires a game board like the one shown in Figure 8–16 and a pair of dice with the numerals 1 to 6. Blank dice are available on which numerals may be

2 x 9	3 x 5	2 x 1	1 x 7	9 x 3	3 x 2	4 x 2	5 x 4	4 x 6
8 x 3	1 x 3	3 x 7	4 x 9	5 x 2	4 x 8	2 x 6	7 x 3	3 x 4
7 x 4	5 x 5	4 x 4	4 x 1	2 x 2	3 x 9	8 x 2	4 x 3	2 x 5
2 x 3	2 x 7	9 x 4	3 x 6	6 x 4	2 x 4	9 x 2	7 x 2	3 x 3
4 x 7	4 x 5	1 x 5	8 x 4	6 x 3	3 x 8	6 x 2	5 x 3	2 x 8

Figure 8–15

Figure 8–14

1	2	3	4	5	6
2	4	6	8	10	12
3	6	9	12	15	18
4	8	12	16	20	24
5	10	15	20	25	30
6	12	18	24	30	36

Figure 8–16

written, or standard dice may be used for this game. Each player should be supplied with a set of unique markers, 18 each for 2 players, 12 each for 3 players, and 9 each for 4 players.

To start play, each player rolls the pair of dice; the numbers that show are used as factors to form a product. For example, if 3 and 4 are showing, the product is 12. The player with the largest product takes the first turn.

Each player rolls the pair of dice in turn, multiplies the two numbers together, and places a marker on the playing board to cover the product. If the product is already covered, the turn is lost. The winner is the first player to get four markers in a row horizontally, vertically, or diagonally.

To extend this game, dice with the numerals 2 to 7, 3 to 8, or 4 to 9 may be used. For each new pair of dice, a new game board is necessary. For dice with the numerals 2 to 7, the game board contains the numerals 4 to 49. The game board is the section from the multiplication table corresponding to the numbers on the dice.

5. This is a Bingo activity called Multi-Bingo. This game may be played with a small group or the entire class. Each player will need a MULTI bingo card and a number of markers. A sample card is shown in Figure 8–17. Each bingo card has one happy face region (free space) and twenty-four regions with numerals. The numerals are randomly placed in each column. Following are the numerals for each column on the card:

M: 1, 2, 3, 4, 5

U: 6, 7, 8, 9, 10

L: 12, 14, 15, 16, 18

T: 20, 21, 24, 25, 28

I: 30, 32, 35, 36, 42

The leader draws a calling card from a shuffled deck and calls out the letter and multiplication ex-

pression on the card. The calling cards have the following letters and expressions:

M:	1×1,	2×1,	3×1,	4×1,	5×1
U:	2×3,	7×1,	2×4,	3×3,	2×5
L:	2×6,	2×7,	5×3,	4×4,	9×2
T:	4×5,	3×7,	8×3,	5×5,	4×7
I:	6×5,	4×8,	5×7,	6×6,	7×6

Players complete the multiplication and place a marker on the corresponding answer in the appropriate column. The first player to get five markers in a row horizontally, vertically, or diagonally wins the game.

6. This activity, Top It, was introduced earlier to help practice the addition and subtraction facts. Figure 8–18 shows a deck of easy and a deck of hard multiplication cards designed to accommodate the children's skill levels. The decks may be combined into a single deck representing nearly all of the basic multiplication facts.

Begin play with the stack of cards face down. The first player turns over a card and places it face up, giving the product. The second, third, and fourth players do the same. The player with the highest product claims all of the cards played. If any players are tied with high cards, the cards remain in front of the players and those who are tied each draw another card. The player with the highest product takes all of the cards. The winner is the player with the most cards at the end of the game.

This chapter presents a few of the numerous activities that can be used to help children practice the basic multiplication facts. Each activity can be adapted to include division practice. The goal is for the children to be able to accurately and quickly respond to all basic multiplication and division facts. Sources of other activities and games have been included in the references at the end of this chapter.

Although the properties of multiplying by one, the commutative property of multiplication, and multiplying by zero can be helpful in learning the basic multiplication facts, the **associative property of multiplication** can also be helpful for children as they multiply numbers like 4×16. If children rename the larger factor and apply the associative property, the problem can be made easier. For example, 4×16 may be renamed as $4 \times (2 \times 8)$. Using the associative property, the problem may be restated as $(4 \times 2) \times 8$, then 8×8, which is a basic fact and equals 64.

The associative property is shown in $4 \times (2 \times 8) = (4 \times 2) \times 8$; how the numbers are grouped to multiply does not affect the product. As children learn this property, give them repeated simple examples that they can cal-

Figure 8–17

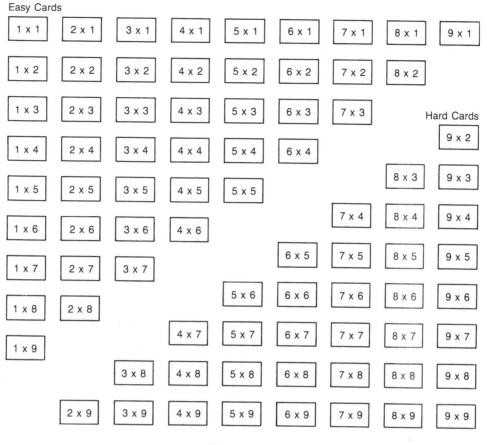

Figure 8–18

culate from memory or with a calculator. These examples should allow them to discover that the product is unchanged regardless of the order in which the numbers are multiplied.

A property that is helpful when mentally multiplying numbers is the **distributive property of multiplication over addition.** For example, when multiplying 7×8, we can think of 8 as $5 + 3$, multiply 7×5 and 7×3, and then add the products. Thus, $7 \times 8 = 7 \times (5 + 3)$, which then equals $(7 \times 5) + (7 \times 3)$, or $35 + 21 = 56$. An illustration using arrays helps children visualize an application of the distributive property. Figure 8–19 shows $7 \times (5 + 3)$. Children can move the dividing line to see that they could use $7 \times (4 + 4)$ or $7 \times (6 + 2)$ as well.

While not very efficient with paper and pencil, the distributive property helps us recall basic facts and simplify the larger problems we do in our heads. Later, students will find knowing the distributive property to be essential as they simplify algebraic expressions. To multiply 8×74 mentally, think $8 \times (70 + 4)$ is $560 + 32$, or 592. Find the product of a larger multiplication problem by adding the products of two smaller problems. There are other variations of the distributive property, such as distributing over subtraction, but the property just described is the

one most widely used. Materials for teaching multiplication, including base ten squares and an addition/multiplication grid, may be found in Appendix B.

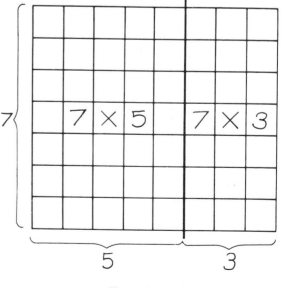

Figure 8–19

Multiplication and Division Algorithms

Children learn the multiplication and division algorithms more rapidly if they already know the basic multiplication and division facts. Further, a firm grasp of addition and subtraction is needed to perform the algorithms efficiently. As with addition and subtraction, modeling multiplication and division using the base ten blocks or other physical models prepares students for learning algorithms and gives them the opportunity to use real-life situations in posing problems, to discuss their work with one another, and to write about their work. The students should be encouraged to construct their own algorithms for multiplication and division before you present those in the book. This gives students the opportunity to explore and invent algorithms. Let the students decide which algorithm they prefer and when they no longer need to use the physical models. It is likely that the students will devise some algorithms similar to the standard multiplication and division algorithms, but be ready for algorithms that are different. The process of inventing algorithms is an important part of learning how and why algorithms work.

In mathematics textbooks, the multiplication and division algorithms are usually taught sequentially, beginning with the simplest problems, those requiring no regrouping (carrying). The difficulty and complexity increases until multidigit problems with regrouping are presented. However, when students begin multidigit multiplication and division using physical models, there is no need to separate problems that require regrouping from those that do not.

We believe children should master the fundamentals of multiplying and dividing, but we caution you about assigning page after page of laborious multiplication and division problems. When children can demonstrate paper-and-pencil algorithms for multiplication and division, it is time to let them use calculators to speed up computations and allow time for higher mental processes and content that could not otherwise be covered. Using the calculator is the most efficient procedure for performing an arithmetic operation.

Paper-and-pencil algorithms for multiplication and division are presented in turn. We begin with the standard, and generally most efficient, paper-and-pencil algorithm for each operation. Alternative algorithms are then presented. Alternative procedures serve as teaching algorithms and help bridge the concrete and abstract. It was mentioned above that students sometimes invent algorithms similar to the standard multiplication and division algorithms. Likewise, they may invent algorithms similar to the alternative algorithms presented below. While in this chapter the standard algorithm is presented first followed by alternative algorithms, it is not suggested that children will invent algorithms in this order. You should

not introduce standard algorithms until students have explored, invented, and discussed their own algorithms.

Multiplication.   The standard paper-and-pencil multiplication algorithm is applied to the six problems below, each of which has at least one two-digit factor.

$$
\begin{array}{cccccc}
12 & 62 & {}^{2}25 & 34 & 43 & {}^{34}38 \\
\times\,3 & \times\,4 & \times\,5 & \times\,10 & \times\,12 & \times\,45 \\
\hline
36 & 248 & 125 & 340 & 86 & {}^{1}190 \\
& & & & {}^{1}43 & 152 \\
& & & & \hline & \hline \\
& & & & 516 & 1{,}710
\end{array}
$$

The first example shows multiplying by a one-digit number with no regrouping. The second problem involves multiplying by a one-digit number with regrouping from the tens to the hundreds place. The third example shows multiplying by a one-digit number with regrouping from the ones to the tens place. Typically, when a single-digit number and a multiple-digit number are multiplied, the multiple-digit number is placed on the top in the standard algorithm, as shown in the first three examples.

The last three examples show multiplying by two-digit numbers. The fourth example shows multiplying by a two-digit number that is a multiple of 10 with no regrouping. The fifth example shows multiplying by a two-digit number with no regrouping. The final example shows multiplying by a two-digit number with regrouping.

In the examples with regrouping from the ones to the tens place the regrouping numeral has been shown. Most who use this algorithm include it. It is important that children understand what happens when regrouping occurs. This is an extension of their work with place value.

Typically, it is at the fourth-grade level that children are introduced to the multiplication and division algorithms. At this time, with a sound foundation of preparation, children can construct the procedures necessary for performing successfully their own or the standard algorithms. Using physical models such as multibase blocks or similar models assists in the effort. Most math texts illustrate the algorithms as they are presented. Teacher's guides suggest that teachers use physical models for a textbook algorithm.

We illustrate using an example stated as a word problem. Miss Jensen's class has completed work on a language arts project. Each student has written two poems and made an illustration of one of the poems. The 26 students believe they have turned in all their work. Just to check, Miss Jensen asks Shelley to count the papers. Because each student used a separate sheet for each part of the project, there should be 3 sheets for each person. Shelley counts 76 papers. Miss Jensen asks the class to verify that 76 is the correct answer.

Figure 8–20 shows a method the class might use to solve the problem 3 × 26 with multibase blocks representing the papers and a place-value board.

In this example, the repeated addition model is used first. What the student sees is 26 + 26 + 26 (see Figure 8–20a). Since there are 26 students and each student should have 3 sheets of paper, three groups of 26 represent the total number of sheets in all. The unit cubes are combined into a group of 10 with 8 remaining. The 10 cubes are exchanged for 1 long (see Figure 8–20b). Then the longs are joined. The result, 7 tens and 8 ones, or 78, is the product of 3 and 26 (see Figure 8–20c).

A second procedure, shown in Figure 8–21, follows the standard paper-and-pencil algorithm. The first step is to multiply 3 × 6. This is illustrated by 3 groups of 6 small cubes. Ten cubes are then exchanged for 1 long (see Figure 8–21a). The next step is to multiply 3 × 20. This is shown by 3 groups of 2 longs. The long from the exchange

Figure 8–20

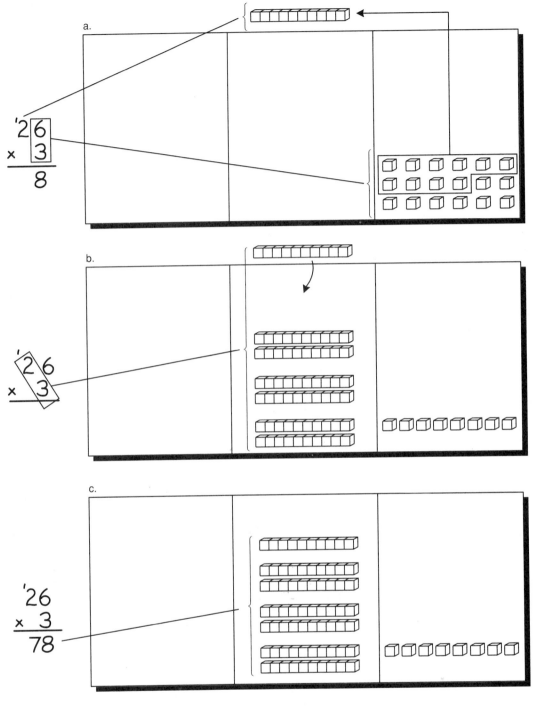

Figure 8–21

above is joined to these 6 longs (see Figure 8–21b). The final result is 7 tens and 8 ones, or 78 (see Figure 8–21c).

Another useful model using the multibase blocks is to organize the blocks into a rectangular arrangement, with each dimension representing one of the factors being multiplied. For example, to multiply 12 × 14, we would construct a rectangular region showing 12 in one dimension and 14 in the other dimension, as in Figure 8–22. The product of 12 and 14 is found by describing the pieces that make up the rectangle, 100 plus 6 tens plus 8 ones (168). For the problem illustrated earlier, 3 × 26, we would construct a rectangle showing 3 in one dimension and 26 in the other dimension, as in Figure 8–23. The final product is found

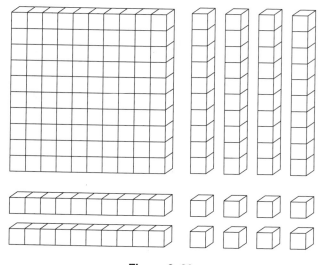

Figure 8–22

by describing the pieces, 6 tens plus 18 ones (60 + 18, or 78). Whether using the repeated addition approach or the standard paper-and-pencil algorithm, the multibase blocks help to show how the algorithm works. A similar material, the algebra blocks, can be used in place of the multibase blocks. The algebra blocks are introduced in some detail in Chapter 14.

Regardless of which procedure is used, the class finds that not all the language arts papers have been turned in. The papers are soon located.

After students have constructed their own algorithms and compared them to those of other students, you may want to introduce the algorithms in the textbook. The multiplication algorithms presented in various math texts tend to be similar and quite easy to follow. The texts provide slow, step-by-step progressions from the easiest to the more difficult multiplication problems. And, texts provide plenty of practice exercises. Children should practice for several days after they are able to perform the algorithm without assistance. It is unnecessary for children to be assigned all of the problems on a textbook page. If children continue to have difficulty accurately completing algorithms, diagnose the difficulty. Assigning additional problems before children's error patterns are corrected is counterproductive. At this point, children need special assistance and perhaps a new ap-

proach to help them learn the algorithms. Once children have learned the algorithms, they need periodic practice to reinforce their skill.

The activities that follow differ from those presented earlier. Their primary focus is not manipulative activities but alternative ways to present multiplication algorithms.

ACTIVITIES

Intermediate (4–6)

Objective: to use a variety of multiplication algorithms.

1. The **expanded notation algorithm** is an outgrowth of the work with place value. Two solutions using expanded notation are shown below. In problem a, no regrouping is necessary to solve 3×23.

   The problem is rewritten from standard into expanded notation. The 3 ones and the 2 tens are each multiplied by 3. Then the expanded notation is rewritten into standard notation.

   In problem b, 4×27 is figured in a similar manner, multiplying the 7 ones and the 2 tens by 4. As the answer is rewritten into standard form, regrouping must occur. The 28 must be expanded to $20 + 8$ and the 20 added to the 80, resulting in $100 + 8$, or 108. The expanded notation algorithm is similar to the standard multiplication algorithm except that regrouping occurs at a different time. The expanded notation algorithm is advantageous because children never lose sight of the numbers they are regrouping.

$$
\begin{array}{cc}
a. & \begin{array}{r} 23 \\ \times\ 3 \\ \hline \end{array} \quad \begin{array}{r} 20+3 \\ \times\qquad 3 \\ \hline 60+9=69 \end{array}
\end{array}
$$

$$
\begin{array}{cc}
b. & \begin{array}{r} 27 \\ \times\ 4 \\ \hline \end{array} \quad \begin{array}{r} 20+7 \\ \times\qquad 4 \\ \hline 80+28= \end{array}
\end{array}
$$

$$
= (80+20)+8 = 100+8 = 108
$$

Figure 8–23

2. Children should have had experience working with the loop abacus. They should know that any time 10 counters appear on a given loop, the counters must be exchanged for 1 counter on the loop immediately to the left. This is demonstrated as we solve 3 × 35 on the abacus. In the first frame of Figure 8–24, an abacus shows 3 × 35.

The clips separate three representations of 35. In the second frame, we remove the holding clips in the ones column and exchange 10 counters on the ones loop for 1 counter on the tens loop. Five counters are left in the ones column.

In the third frame, we remove the holding clips in the tens column and exchange 10 counters on the tens loop for 1 counter on the hundreds loop. No counters are left in the tens column.

The fourth frame illustrates the abacus after all the exchanges have been made. The standard algorithm shows the progression from start to finish.

3. The **partial products algorithm** is another procedure that helps children through the process of regrouping. It may be used whether or not regrouping is necessary. The problem below illustrates the partial products algorithm by multiplying 8 × 57.

Figure 8–24

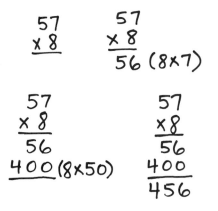

The first step in the solution is to multiply the number in the ones column, 7, by the multiplier, 8. The answer, 56, is the first partial product and is placed beneath the problem.

The next step is to multiply the number in the tens column, 5, by the multiplier, 8. The result, 40 tens, or 400, is placed beneath the 56.

Finally, the partial products are added to arrive at the answer, 456. Take care with this algorithm to ensure that the partial products are written in the correct place-value positions.

The partial products algorithm may be illustrated using physical models. In Figure 8–22, the multibase blocks were used to show 12 × 14. In describing the pieces that make up the rectangular region in Figure 8–22, we found that 12 × 14 was equal to one hundred

plus 6 tens plus 8 ones. The partial products algorithm for 12 × 14 is shown below.

$$
\begin{array}{r}
14 \\
\times\, 12 \\
\hline
8 \quad \}\ \ 8\ \text{ones} \\
20 \quad \} \\
40 \quad \}\ \ 6\ \text{tens} \\
100 \quad \}\ \ 1\ \text{hundred} \\
\hline
168
\end{array}
$$

In this algorithm, we find the same product that we found with the multibase blocks—100 plus 6 tens plus 8 ones. It is important for students to make such connections as they learn mathematics.

Incidentally, the same partial products are found when the horizontal *FOIL* algorithm is used to solve (10 + 2) (10 + 4). This algorithm is presented in Chapter 14, Introducing Algebra.

4. The **lattice algorithm** for multiplication has been around for several hundred years. For each pair of numbers multiplied, a lattice is constructed. The lattice shown first in Figure 8–25 illustrates the problem 68 × 47.

For each place-value position in the factors, a region divided diagonally is provided. Begin by multiplying 4 times 8 and writing the product, 32, in the regions where 4 and 8 intersect. Then multiply 4 times 6 and write the product, 24, where 4 and 6 intersect. Continue by multiplying 7 times 8 and 7 times 6, recording each answer in the appropriate regions.

Finally, beginning at the lower right, add diagonally from right to left (see arrows) to determine the digits in the product of 68 and 47. The answer is read beginning at the upper left, down the left side of the lattice and across the bottom—the answer is 3,196.

This very different algorithm provides a clever approach to long multiplication problems. It can be worked easily with factors of any size.

John Napier, a Scottish mathematician who lived from 1550 to 1617, created a unique multiplication tool for peasant workers who had little education and little knowledge of the basic multiplication combinations. The tool, *Napier's rods,* consisted of a series of rods on which the multiplication tables had been written. A person could carry the rods in a pocket.

The technique of lattice multiplication was used with the rods. Patterns for constructing the rods are shown in Figure 8–26. The first rod is the index rod and contains a vertical listing of factors. The first digit at the top of each rod is another index factor.

Napier's rods resembled the orange Cuisenaire rod in size and shape. We find it easier to use tongue depressors or strips of oaktag to construct the rods.

When multiplying two numbers, lay the appropriate rods side by side next to the index rod. Then add along the diagonals. For example, Figure 8–27 shows how to multiply 5 × 36. The 3 rod and the 6 rod are placed side by side next to the index rod. Move down the index rod to 5. Then add diagonally as we did with lattice multiplication. The result, 180, is read in the same way as a result is read from the lattice.

Children enjoy taking a break to construct and use Napier's rods. See if they can discover how to perform multiplication such as 26 × 365.

Figure 8–27

Figure 8–25

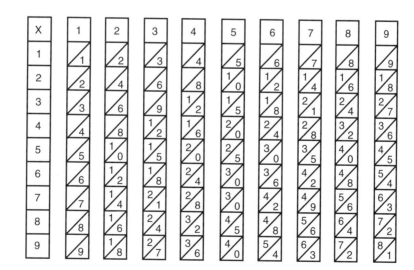

Figure 8–26

Division.   The procedure used to perform division is quite different from that used to perform multiplication. Division does, however, rely heavily on knowledge of multiplication as well as subtraction. Skill with the basic subtraction, multiplication, and division facts is a key to success in performing division algorithms.

Recall that the basic division facts are related to the basic multiplication facts. Thus, for the multiplication fact $3 \times 7 = 21$, we have the corresponding division facts $21 \div 3 = 7$ and $21 \div 7 = 3$. Techniques for helping children memorize these facts were discussed earlier, in the section on basic facts.

When introducing division algorithms, once again, be sure to let students use real-life situations and physical models to construct their own algorithms. Allow plenty of time for students to discuss their results with each other.

Five examples of the standard paper-and-pencil division algorithm are presented below.

The first three examples have one-digit divisors. The first of these has no regrouping, the second has regrouping, and the third has regrouping and a remainder. The last two examples have two-digit divisors; both have regrouping, and the last one has a remainder. The only markings that appear are in the last example, where regrouping was necessary during the first subtraction.

When the division algorithm is presented and discussed, it is important to accompany the instruction initially with physical models. We demonstrate with multibase blocks. The first example is $39 \div 3$. How the problem is presented determines whether children will solve it with measurement or partition division.

In a measurement problem, the total number of objects is provided along with the number of objects to be put into each group. It is then necessary to find the number of groups that can be made. In a partition problem, the total number of objects is provided along with the number of groups to be made. It is then necessary to find how many objects will go into each group.

The first example is stated as a partition problem: We have 39 tomato seeds and 3 planting groups for a science project. How many seeds will each planting group receive? Figure 8–28 shows how to go about solving this problem.

Using the multibase blocks and the place value board, lay out 3 longs and 9 cubes to represent 39, as in Figure 8–28a. Next, separate the pieces into three groups, each of which contains the same number of pieces, as in Figure 8–28b. We find we have 1 long and 3 cubes in each group, or 13 cubes, as in Figure 8–28c. Each planting group will receive 13 seeds.

The example is now stated as a measurement problem: We have 39 tomato seeds. Each student will get 3 seeds for a science project. How many students will get seeds? The solution to this problem requires that the children form groups of 3 cubes and see how many such groups can be made. It is necessary to exchange each long for 10 cubes so the grouping by 3 can be completed. In the end, 13 groups of 3 will be made. Thus, 13 students will get seeds.

While the manipulation is different for each of these problems, the algorithm is the same. How the problem is presented, however, determines how to interpret the result. In the first case, the answer is 13 seeds; in the second case, 13 students.

When regrouping is necessary in the algorithm, as in $132 \div 3$, the partition problem is most appropriate. Suppose a collection of 132 stamps is being divided among 3 children, how many stamps will each child receive? Using the multibase blocks, show 132 by displaying 1 flat, 3 longs, and 2 cubes as in Figure 8–29a.

In order to separate the pieces into 3 groups, exchange the flat for 10 longs and exchange 1 long for 10 cubes as in Figure 8–29b. Then complete the operation by separating the pieces into three groups, as shown in Figure 8–29c. Figure 8–29d shows the final result. Thus, each child will receive 44 stamps. The exchanges, from hundreds to tens and from tens to ones, represent the regrouping in this division problem.

This work with physical models should not last long. Once the students have constructed algorithms and can perform the standard algorithm with manipulatives, encourage them to practice at the abstract level. As in the case of multiplication, the activities presented include alternative algorithms and approaches for division. Some children find that an alternative is superior for them and adopt it as their standard algorithm. It is appropriate for children to create their own algorithms; encourage them to do so.

Figure 8–28

ACTIVITIES

Intermediate (4–6)

Objective: to use various algorithms for division.

1. When the **expanded notation algorithm** is used, children are better able to see what happens in each place value position of the dividend. The problem below shows $96 \div 4$.

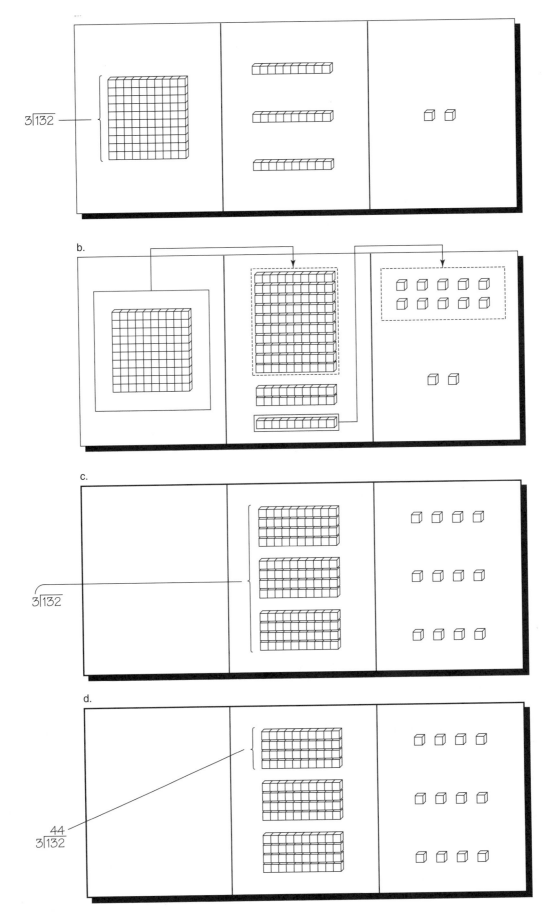

Figure 8–29

The number in the dividend, 96, is rewritten in expanded form. Because 4 does not evenly divide into 90, regrouping is required from the tens to the ones place. Thus, 90 + 6 is regrouped to 80 + 16. Then the 80 is divided by 4 and the 16 is divided by 4, resulting in 20 + 4. Then 20 + 4 is rewritten into standard form, 24.

You may find it necessary to help children work through several examples of the expanded notation algorithm with physical models such as multibase blocks, beans, and Cuisenaire rods while performing the algorithm. Work first with problems that do not require regrouping, such as 48 ÷ 4. With some practice, children should gain understanding of the division process.

2. **Repeated subtraction** may be used as an algorithm. The division problem 48 ÷ 12 may be thought of as asking, "how many 12s are contained in 48?" This is the measurement concept of division. We may solve the problem by seeing how many times 12 may be subtracted from 48. This is illustrated by the problem below. Here, we see that there are four 12s in 48 because it took four subtractions of 12 to reach zero.

$$12\overline{)48} \qquad \begin{array}{r} 48 \\ -12 \ (1) \\ \hline 36 \\ -12 \ (2) \\ \hline 24 \\ -12 \ (3) \\ \hline 12 \\ -12 \ (4) \\ \hline 0 \end{array}$$

It takes many separate subtractions to solve a problem like 48 ÷ 4. It is much more efficient to subtract multiples of 4. The problem below shows that the first subtraction is 10 × 4 and that the second subtraction is 2 × 4. The final result is that 10 + 2, or twelve, 4s are contained in 48. If children had to perform 12 or more subtractions, it is questionable they would maintain much interest. Subtracting using multiples of the divisor helps eliminate this difficulty.

$$4\overline{)48} \qquad \begin{array}{r} 48 \\ -40 \ (10\times4) \\ \hline 8 \\ -8 \ (2\times4) \\ \hline 0 \end{array}$$

3. The **Greenwood,** or **down the side,** algorithm is particularly useful because it helps avoid one of the pitfalls of long division, incorrect estimation of quotient figures.

The Greenwood algorithm incorporates the repeated subtraction idea presented above. The problem below illustrates this algorithm for the division 597 ÷ 27.

The first step is to estimate a multiple of the divisor, 27. In this case, we have estimated 10 × 27. The product 10 × 27, or 270, is subtracted from 597, leaving 327. We again estimate the multiple 10 × 27 in the second step. After subtracting 270 again, 57 remains. Our final estimate is 2 × 27, or 54. Subtracting 54 results in 3. Because 3 is less than the divisor, 3 is the remainder for this problem. We then add 10 + 10 + 2, which results in the quotient figure, 22. Thus, 597 ÷ 27 = 22 r3.

When the partial quotient figures were estimated, the multiples were 10 times the divisor. Using 10 or 100 times the divisor simplifies the estimation. As children gain experience with estimating, they can estimate partial quotients that are close to but less than the dividend.

A variation of the Greenwood algorithm is one in which children put their partial quotients above the dividend in the proper place value position. When all estimates have been made, the final quotient is determined by adding up. The problem below shows how this **pyramid method** works for 597 ÷ 27.

$$\begin{array}{r} 22\ r3 \\ 2 \\ 10 \\ 10 \\ 27\overline{)597} \\ -270 \\ \hline 327 \\ -270 \\ \hline 57 \\ 54 \\ \hline 3 \end{array}$$

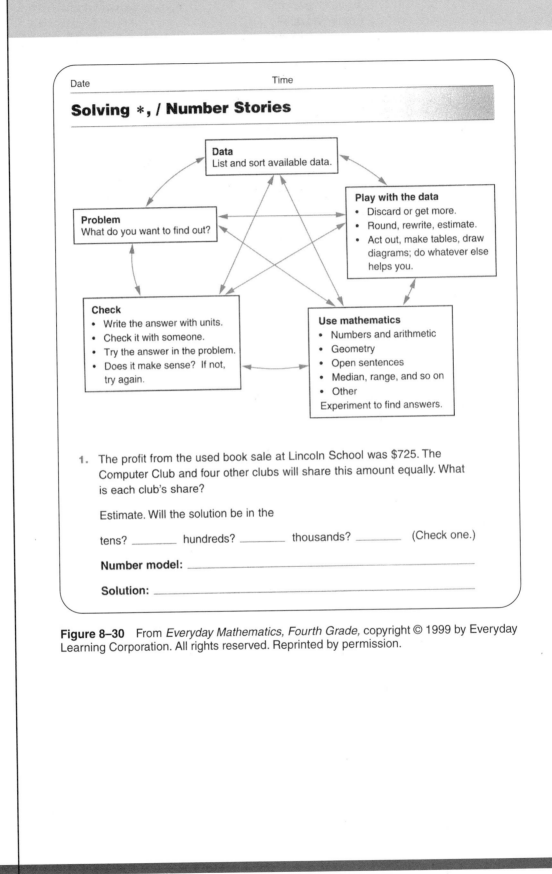

Date _____ Time _____

Solving *, / Number Stories

Data
List and sort available data.

Problem
What do you want to find out?

Play with the data
- Discard or get more.
- Round, rewrite, estimate.
- Act out, make tables, draw diagrams; do whatever else helps you.

Check
- Write the answer with units.
- Check it with someone.
- Try the answer in the problem.
- Does it make sense? If not, try again.

Use mathematics
- Numbers and arithmetic
- Geometry
- Open sentences
- Median, range, and so on
- Other
Experiment to find answers.

1. The profit from the used book sale at Lincoln School was $725. The Computer Club and four other clubs will share this amount equally. What is each club's share?

   Estimate. Will the solution be in the

   tens? _____ hundreds? _____ thousands? _____ (Check one.)

   Number model: _____

   Solution: _____

Figure 8–30 From *Everyday Mathematics, Fourth Grade,* copyright © 1999 by Everyday Learning Corporation. All rights reserved. Reprinted by permission.

Math Program

Figure 8–30 shows a page from a fourth grade student's mathematics journal. In this program, developed under a grant from the National Science Foundation, students have two journals, consumable books linked to the activities in the teacher's manuals that include among other information, summaries of the lessons, reference information, and a glossary. In addition to the journals, students complete a yearlong World Tour project using a *World Tour Book* and a *Student Record Book* using maps and data about countries around the world. Scientific calculators are recommended for these fourth graders primarily for explorations with parentheses and scientific notation.

The problem on this page illustrates the student's use of a problem-solving heuristic for solving number stories. This modeling diagram is used earlier in the program for addition and subtraction problems and is introduced here for multiplication and division number stories. After students solve a variety of number stories involving equal-grouping, scaling, rate, and equal-sharing situations, they are asked to make up their own multiplication and division number stories. Students then trade these stories with a partner for solution and revision.

Later in this unit, on games day, students play a game popular in Japan called *Five Eyes* and a *Division Dash* game to practice their division skills. They also take a 50-facts test and complete activities in the *World Tour Book* using reference books and other materials. In addition to these activities, skills and concepts are practiced regularly through the use of Math Boxes in the journals with review problems, classroom "museums" that use the bulletin board or tables to display topics under discussion, and 5-Minute Math sections designed to strengthen number sense and skills and to develop and solidify mathematical knowledge.

The first estimate is 10, which is placed above the dividend, 597. Then 10×27, or 270, is subtracted from 597. The second estimate also is 10, which is placed above the first estimate. Then 270 is subtracted from 327, leaving 57. The final estimate, 2, is placed above the other two estimates. Then 54 is subtracted from 57, leaving 3, the remainder. The sum of the partial products, $10 + 10 + 2$, is found, with the final result of 22 r3.

When performing the standard division algorithm, four basic steps must be completed, sometimes several times for a given problem. These steps are: (1) estimating the quotient figure, (2) multiplying the partial quotient times the divisor, (3) subtracting the product from the dividend, and (4) checking the difference to make sure it is less than the divisor and, if it is not, revising the quotient figure. Each of these steps provides opportunities for mistakes and frustration.

Hallmarks of the division algorithm are erasure marks on students' papers. Calculators can help students estimate quotient figures. Accord time and patience to children as they develop skill with the division algorithm. Encourage them and provide them with careful teaching and reteaching. Reward their efforts.

In this section, we have discussed developing two sets of skills. The first skills are knowing and working with the basic multiplication and division facts. Children should have a good command of these facts. The second skills are knowing and working with the algorithms for multiplication and division. Current math texts present thorough instruction in developing the standard algorithms and contain an ample number of problems for practice. You are encouraged to employ these instructional sequences.

Estimating and Mental Calculating

Estimation and mental arithmetic play an important role in both paper-and-pencil and calculator computation involving multiplication and division. Students should know if their answers are reasonable. This is done by estimating products or quotients just before or just after working the algorithm or using the calculator, and comparing the estimated results to the calculated results. If the results vary considerably, the students should recalculate the results. The procedure takes just a few moments, and it should develop into a lifelong habit.

Estimating the quotient figure in the standard division algorithm is a skill that challenges many children. For example, below are two division problems that for most fifth graders require estimation. An older student may be able to look at the divisor, realize that $2 \times 64 = 128$, and

estimate the quotient figure in the first example at 1 and the quotient figure in the second example at 2.

$$64\overline{)1279} \qquad 64\overline{)1289}$$

We examine two ways to estimate the quotient figure. The first is to round the divisor up or down, depending on the units digit. The numbers 61 to 64 would be rounded down to 60, while 65 to 69 would be rounded up to 70. In our problem, 64 would be rounded to 60. The guide number, 6, is used to determine the first quotient figure in $1,279 \div 64$. We ask, "How many 6s are contained in 12?" Our estimate is 2. We soon discover that 2 is too large and revise the estimate to 1, which is correct. Using the same procedure for $1,289 \div 64$, we estimate a quotient figure of 2; this one is correct. With this rounding procedure, students should be willing to revise their estimates.

The second way to estimate the quotient figure is to construct a table of multiples of the divisor. Using a calculator, this takes a few moments. The multiples of 64 are:

$1 \times 64 = 64$	$4 \times 64 = 256$	$7 \times 64 = 448$
$2 \times 64 = 128$	$5 \times 64 = 320$	$8 \times 64 = 512$
$3 \times 64 = 192$	$6 \times 64 = 384$	$9 \times 64 = 576$

By examining the dividend of the first problem, the student will realize that 2×64 in the table of multiples is too large, and therefore the estimate must be 1. For the second problem, the estimate 2 is correct because $2 \times 64 = 128$. Not only is the first quotient figure easy to estimate, the other quotient figures in the problem are also easy to estimate.

A variation of this approach is to estimate the entire quotient using the multiples of 64 in combination with the powers of 10. Thus, the first estimated quotient figure is 10, to which you add 9 as you continue the problem. This is similar to the approach used in the Greenwood algorithm discussed earlier.

No single method of estimating quotient figures has been shown to be superior. Encourage the children to construct their own algorithms and let the children select the one they find most comfortable.

ACTIVITIES

Intermediate (4–6)

Objective: to practice estimating multiplication and division.

1. Use a set of double-nine dominoes. The large-format dominoes work well if this activity is done with the

whole class. Hold up a domino for about three seconds. Ask the children if they believe the product of the two sides of the domino is more than, less than, or equal to 40. Let them signal to you that the product is 40 by putting a hand flat on the table or floor. A hand with thumb up means more than 40. A hand with thumb down means less than 40.

For division estimation, put a numeral such as 50 on the chalkboard. Hold up a domino for about three seconds, and have the students find the sum of the two sides and then divide 50 by the sum. Have them indicate whether the quotient is more than, less than, or equal to 5. The students can use the same hand signs as before.

2. On occasion, we need to multiply large numbers or estimate their product in our heads. Sometimes these numbers are powers of 10 or multiples of powers of 10, as in 50×70 or 30×600. Other times, the numbers are not even decades, as in 38×19 or 53×691. In the first case, numbers like 50 and 70 may be multiplied by counting the zeros (there are two) and then multiplying the remaining numbers, 5 and 7. When the result, 35, is rejoined with the two zeros, we have $50 \times 70 = 3,500$.

With 30×600, follow the same procedure. Count the zeros (there are 3) and multiply the remaining numbers, 3 and 6, to get 18. Rejoin the 3 zeros to produce the answer, 18,000.

In the case in which the numbers are not powers of 10 or multiples of powers of 10, use the rounding strategy described in Chapter 3. The numbers are rounded up or down, then multiplied, and then the product is adjusted. For example, with 38×19, round 38 to 40, and round 19 to 20. Then multiply 40×20. The result, 800, is an estimation of the product of 38×19. Because both numbers were rounded up, the estimation is somewhat higher than the actual product of 38×19, which is 722.

For the problem 53×691, round 53 down to 50 and round 691 up to 700. Then compute the product of 50×700, which is 35,000. Because one number was rounded up and one was rounded down, it is more difficult to tell whether our estimation is too high or too low. The actual product of 53×691 is 36,623 and shows us the estimate was low. If both numbers had been rounded down, the estimate would have been below the actual product.

Another type of problem requiring mental calculation is sometimes presented. If 6×49 or 6×51 requires an exact answer, remember that 6×49 is 6 less than 6×50. Without difficulty, we know $6 \times 50 = 300$; six less is 294. Likewise, 6×51 is 6 greater than 6×50, or 306. It is helpful for children to practice multiplying numbers that are even decades, one less, or one greater.

Objective: to use historical material to motivate estimation and mental arithmetic.

3. Chapter 7 presented several mental exercises that appeared in an 1859 text by Greenleaf. Here are mental exercises prescribed by Daniel Fish in *Arithmetical Problems, Oral and Written,* copyrighted in 1874 (see Figure 8–31). Just before he presents 73 mental exercises and 120 written exercises, Fish notes:

Any class or pupil that has gone over the Elementary Rules, in regular course of any textbook on these subjects, should be prepared for test, drill, and review in the examples of this chapter. (p. 47)

Examples of the exercises Fish included in his book follow. The page on which each problem can be found is provided in parentheses.

- $8 \times 9 \div 12 + 3 \times 5 + 10 \div 11 \times 8 + 20 \div 12 + 4 \times 7 - 3 =$ how many? (p. 49)
- A number multiplied by 8, divided by 6, multiplied by 10, and the product increased by 5 equals 45; what is the number? (p. 49)
- A farmer sold a grocer 15 bushels of potatoes at $1 a bushel, and bought 20 pounds of sugar at 15 cents a pound, and 10 pounds of coffee at 30 cents a pound; how many pounds of tea at 75 cents a pound could he buy for what was still due him? (p. 51)
- If it costs $56 for bricks to build a cistern when bricks are worth $8 a thousand, what will it cost for bricks to build it when they are worth $10 a thousand? (p. 52)

Objective: to use the calculator to improve multiplication and division estimation skills.

4. Four to six players and one calculator are needed. One player is *it* for the first round. That player generates a number on the calculator by entering and multiplying four numbers equal to or less than 12, such as $11 \times 8 \times 6 \times 9 = 4,752$. The object of the game is to find numbers that will divide the number generated and then to divide by those numbers, generating new numbers. Play continues until a player correctly announces "prime," indicating that only two factors are left, 1 and the number itself.

Play begins as soon as the initial number is generated. The calculator is passed to the player to the left of the person who is it and continues to the left. The player who is it does not play in that round. The first player divides 4,752 by a number he or she thinks will divide evenly by pressing the divide sign, entering the number, and pressing the equals sign. Neither 1 nor the number itself may be used as a divisor. If the number is correct, the calculator is passed to the next player. If it is incorrect, that is, if the answer is not a whole number, the player restores the previous number, by multiplying

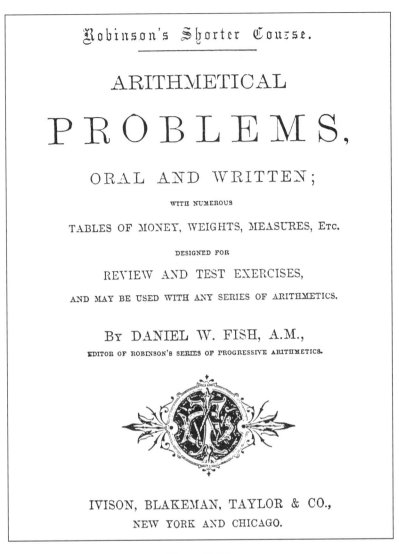

Figure 8–31

by the number used to divide, and passes the calculator to the next player. It may be necessary to round the product to restore the previous number.

For each correct division, a point is scored. The player whose division results in a prime number and who declares "prime" is awarded another point. Each player must either divide or declare "prime." The person correctly declaring "prime" generates a new number. After three rounds, the player with the most points wins.

Solving and Creating Problems

Multiplication and division are important skills in problem solving. These operations are often necessary to help solve problems. For example, in Mr. Edwin's class, the students are constructing a cardboard geodesic dome like the one described in Chapter 12 (see Figure 12–38). The dome radius is to be 125 centimeters. The dome is constructed using triangles of two different sizes; some triangles are equilateral with sides 0.6180 times the dome radius, and the other triangles have one side 0.6180 times the dome radius and two sides 0.5465 times the dome radius. Appliance cartons are available at the local dealer. It takes 15 of the equilateral triangles and 45 of the other triangles to make the dome. How many dishwasher cartons should be requested? Generate discussion about the size of each triangle and the additional information needed in order to request the cartons. Following are more problem situations that require the use of multiplication or division.

ACTIVITIES

Intermediate (4–6)

Objective: to construct and solve problems involving multiplication and division.

1. Provide children with a worksheet that contains several frames, each with nine numerals and an empty box at the top. Figure 8–32a illustrates one of these frames.

   Ask the children to choose any two numbers in the frame, multiply them together, and put the answer in the box at the top. Have them do this for each frame on the worksheet. When this is done, the children will have made problem boxes for other children to solve.

   Have the children exchange the worksheets and see if they can find the pair whose product equals the number on top. Instruct them to circle the two numbers. The children may check their solutions with the calculator.

   Figure 8–32b shows one solution. With the same set of numbers in the frame, many different problems

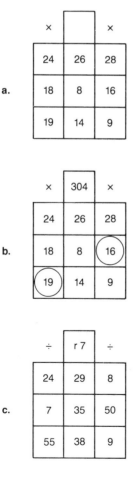

Figure 8–32

can be made. It is also possible to have more than one solution for a single problem.

To extend this activity to division, have the children divide any number in the box by a smaller number in the box and put the remainder in the box at the top. Figure 8–32c shows an example. We solve the problem below:

- *Understanding the problem.* The object here is to divide a larger number by a smaller number to produce a quotient with the remainder 7. The divisor must be greater than 7 because a divisor equal to or smaller than 7 cannot have a remainder of 7.

- *Devising a plan.* We should not use 7 as a divisor because it cannot result in a remainder of 7. Thus, we begin with the smallest possible divisor, 8, and the smallest dividend, 9, and work up through each of the dividends to be sure to try all combinations. After 9, we try these dividends: 24, 29, 35, 38, 50, and then 55 (numbers from the problem). Next, we use 9 as a divisor and work up through the dividends beginning with 24. We make a systematic list, continuing this way until we find the number with a remainder of 7.

  Is it possible that none of the divisions has a remainder of 7? Is it possible that more than one of the divisions have a remainder of 7?

- *Carrying out the plan.* We begin by dividing 24 by 8, 29 by 8, and 35 by 8, finding remainders of 0, 5, and 3. It occurs to us that if we can think of the greatest multiple of the divisor less than the dividend, we can just subtract that multiple from the dividend to get the remainder. For example, we subtract $24 - 24 = 0$, $29 - 24 = 5$, and $35 - 32 = 3$ to find the first three remainders. Going on, we subtract $38 - 32 = 6$, $50 - 48 = 2$, and $55 - 48 = 7$. There is an answer! Is it the only answer? We continue working and find another solution, 55 divided by 24.

- *Looking back.* We take the two number pairs we found, $55 \div 8$ and $55 \div 24$, and divide again to make sure the remainder is 7. It is in both cases. We have satisfied the problem.

Further extend the activity by having the children determine all the numbers for the frame as well as the solution number and operation. The problems will become difficult and challenging. Make a display of problems and solutions.

Objective: to develop a winning strategy.

2. This activity is called **High to Low.** Two players may play. The players mix up double-six dominoes and place them face down on the floor or a table. Each player turns over a domino. The player with the higher product goes first.

Each player draws 10 dominoes, keeping them face down. The first player turns over two dominoes as in Figure 8–33a.

Using each domino to represent a two-digit factor, the player decides which factor each domino will represent. For example, the four-two domino may be used as 42 or, reversed, 24. The three-zero domino may be used as 30 or 3. Once the two factors have been chosen, the player multiplies them together, using paper and pencil or a calculator. The player then puts the product on a scoring sheet similar to the one in Figure 8–33b.

The object is to put the product in one of the spaces so the other products will eventually be in order from highest to lowest. Suppose our first player, Harry, selected 23 and 3 as his two factors. He finds the product is 69 and places it in space number 2 on his scoring sheet as in Figure 8–33b.

The second player, Roberta, turns over two dominoes, selects two factors, multiplies them, and records the answer on her scoring sheet. Because five pairs of dominoes are selected, each player may discard one pair during play. However, the pair must be discarded before the player records the product on the scoring sheet. The player declares that turn a pass. Once a player passes, he or she must play all of the remaining dominoes.

Play continues until all of the spaces on the scoring cards of both players are filled. The players calculate their final scores by marking out any products not in order and adding the remaining products. If all four numbers are in order from highest to lowest, the player doubles the score. The player with the higher score wins.

For division, have the players proceed as above except the two dominoes represent a dividend and a divisor. Have them divide the larger number (dividend) by the smaller (divisor) and put the remainder on the scoring sheet. The other rules, including those for scoring, remain the same.

Objective: to make and use problem tables.

3. This activity serves, in part, as a review of the multiplication and division facts. Begin by putting on the chalkboard, an overhead projector, or worksheets a mixed-up multiplication table with no factors along the left side or across the top. An example is shown in Figure 8–34a.

Explain that all the numbers in the table are in the right place. The students must find the factor that belongs to the left of each row and at the top of each column to make the table correct.

To make this activity more challenging, present a table missing some of the numbers as well as the factors, as shown in Figure 8–34b. Have the children both complete the table and insert the factors.

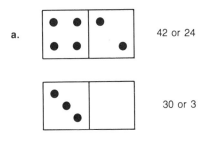

a.   42 or 24

    30 or 3

b.

HIGH	
1.	
2.	69
3.	
4.	
LOW	

Figure 8–33

a.

×					
	15	35	10	25	40
	6	14	4	10	16
	12	28	8	20	32
	18	42	12	30	48
	27	63	18	45	72

b.

×					
	15		10	25	
		14		10	
		28			32
	18		12		
	27				72

Figure 8–34

Notice that the examples use single-digit factors. Extend this activity by introducing numbers each of which is the product of a single-digit factor and a two-digit factor or the product of two two-digit factors. An interesting computer program from Sunburst, *Teasers by Tobbs,* provides a similar activity.

Encourage the children to make up tables of their own to see if they can stump other students. See who can construct the most difficult table puzzle. Display the results on a bulletin board.

Grouping Students for Learning Multiplication and Division

When students are learning the concepts of the basic operations, the activities in which they are engaged lend themselves to either a whole-class setting or cooperative learning groups. You may demonstrate to the whole class, for example, using base ten blocks on the overhead projector, how 13×16 may be illustrated. This provides children the chance to ask questions of the teacher and to clarify their thinking regarding the models being used. When using Cuisenaire rods or objects to illustrate the concept of an operation or the concept of a particular operation, having the students work in groups may be most appropriate. By working in cooperative groups, students will be able to share sometimes scarce materials. As well, a variety of materials may be used simultaneously, in keeping with the principle of multiple embodiment. The conversations among group members as they work together help individuals clarify their thinking and the thinking of others as they construct new concepts and algorithms.

As students learn the skills of the basic operations, the activities in which they are engaged lend themselves, by and large, to cooperative learning group, pair, or individual learning. A cooperative group goal may be to assure that all group members have facility with some or all of the basic facts in addition, subtraction, multiplication, or division. Considerable energy will likely be put forth, and the resulting pride in achieving the "basic facts" goal will be long lasting. When students engage in games and activities, they often are engaged as pairs, threes, or fours. When practicing with the computer or calculator, students will likely work individually or in pairs.

Students who are participating in estimating and mental calculating activities may be organized in any fashion. You may find whole-group instruction efficient for practicing mental arithmetic as you can give instruction, provide examples, and present practice problems. When individuals need or desire special work in estimating and mental calculating, then small group or individual participation may be most appropriate.

Because considerable time is spent developing the basic facts skills in elementary school, you are advised to provide instruction in a variety of group settings to help maintain student interest. The activities suggested in Chapters 7 and 8 provide you with activities that can be adapted to various modes of grouping.

Communicating Learning of Multiplication and Division

Oral and written communication provide ways for children to learn mathematics and thinking processes. Concepts and skills associated with the basic operations can be clarified, as well as illustrated, by children communicating with one another as well as with the teacher. Number stories were mentioned early in the process of developing the concepts of all the basic operations. Oral communication that includes the necessity for children to decide what is being asked, if information is missing, or if a passage or story makes sense, as well as accompanying mental calculation, should be a regular part of instruction.

Stories such as those presented in the Open Court Thinking Story™ books—for example, *Measuring Bowser* (Anderson and Scardamalia, 1985)—are particularly rich in calculations along with practice in logical thinking and problem solving. Another delightful "thinking book" is *Anno's Mysterious Multiplying Jar* (1983). Opportunities for students to listen and respond to stories involving calculating should be plentiful.

The constructivist theory of teaching mathematics discussed in Chapter 2 stresses that students should be asked to share their theories about concepts, that students should be engaged in dialogue with the teacher and with one another, that the teacher should have students elaborate on their initial responses to questions, and that the teacher should ask thoughtful, open-ended questions and encourage students to ask questions of each other. All of these suggestions are intended to develop students' abilities to communicate mathematically.

Students are sometimes asked to keep journals as part of their language arts program. It is just as appropriate to keep a journal in mathematics. The math journal may be kept in the students' individual portfolios (see Chapter 15), along with math assignments, assessment material, and projects. Topics for writing include algorithms that students use to perform various calculations, whether these methods involve paper and pencil, mental calculation, estimation, or the calculator or computer. These journal entries may include the standard algorithms or those devised by individuals. Further, attitudes about mathematics or learning mathematics are appropriate topics for mathematics journals.

Creative stories about number may be episodes written as part of composition practice or as a journal entry. Reading Norton Juster's delightful book *The*

Phantom Tollbooth (1961) will surely inspire students in grades 5–8 to write some wonderfully imaginative stories.

Cooperative and individual writing are appropriate activities for cooperative learning groups. As group members explore a mathematical problem, the group recorder provides a chronicle of the thinking process. These records are then shared with other groups during the "debriefing" time at the end of the activity. Discussion is then invited. Excellent examples of written descriptions of calculations and thinking are presented by Marilyn Burns in her books: *A Collection of Math Lessons from Grades 1 Through 3* (1988), *A Collection of Math Lessons from Grades 3 Through 6* (1987), and *A Collection of Math Lessons from Grades 6 Through 8* (1990).

Connecting Learning of Multiplication and Division

Ms. Roberts gathered her fourth-grade class together in the reading corner and began her lesson by asking what the word *mysterious* means. There were only three students who indicated that they knew for sure what the word means. Carlos responded that mysterious meant something that people could not figure out, like a mystery story. Others joined in and added that mysterious meant something like a robbery or something that was curious. Ms. Roberts asked if it could be about a jar and some math. The students looked puzzled and quickly responded that probably a jar and math were not very mysterious.

Then, Ms. Roberts opened the book *Anno's Mysterious Multiplying Jar* (1983) and began reading, "This story is about one jar and what was inside it." After reading and showing the children the beautiful illustrations on the next two pages, Ms. Roberts continued, "On the sea was 1 island. On the island there were 2 countries. Within each country were 3 mountains. On each mountain there were 4 walled kingdoms." The students were captivated by the story as it continued. Finally, the story came to the lines, "Within each box there were 10 jars. But how many jars were in all the boxes together?"

Ms. Roberts then challenged the students to see if they could figure out how many jars there were. They were to work for 10 minutes in their table groups to get started on the problem and then take the problem home to complete. "That's just like the multiplying that we have been doing," commented Jennifer. Ms. Roberts agreed that that might be a good place to start. The students began their work.

That Jennifer was able to see the connection between her work in multiplication and the challenge set forth in *Anno's Mysterious Multiplying Jar* pleased Ms. Roberts. It also meant that the groups that began working on the problem were likely to devise plans to solve the problem and would soon find the solution.

Mr. Christner's eighth-grade mathematics students welcomed the announcement that they would be viewing a video on Tuesday. The short video, *Powers of Ten* (Eames, 1989), sparked the imagination of the students. This remarkable video shows a series of 42 views of the universe, ranging from 1 billion light years (a square measuring 10^{25} meters on a side) to 0.1 fermi (a square measuring 10^{-16} meters on a side). Each successive view is 10 times narrower than the previous view. Thus, the video begins with a view of space that shows distant galaxies and narrows to eventually show the Milky Way, then the sun and planets, the earth, Lake Michigan, a park in Chicago, a man in the park, the man's hand, a capillary vessel in the man's hand, molecules in a cell in the man's hand, atoms that form the molecular structure in the man's hand, and finally the core of the atom.

To help the students understand the measures, Mr. Christner led a discussion about the meaning of *light year* (the distance that light travels in one year, approximately 6,000,000,000,000 miles), kilometers, meters, millimeters, microns, angstroms, and fermis (the length 10^{-13} centimeters). The students were very impressed with the sizes of the views they had seen in the video. To give the students time to further grasp the information that they had seen and discussed, Mr. Christner made the Morrisons' book, *Powers of Ten* (1982), available for students to look at and read. The book was popular with the students for several weeks.

These activities are intended to involve students in applications of multiplying and dividing in a context that helps show how mathematics is connected with events in their world. Notice that using the Anno story helps connect mathematics and problem solving with literature. *Powers of Ten* set in two media, film and text, help to show clear connections among the elements of the universe. The book may be read and viewed from front to back or from back to front with the same enriching impact.

Another way to make connections is described by the National Research Council in its book *Measuring Up* (1993). In an interesting assessment activity entitled "How Many Buttons?" students are asked to estimate the number of buttons there are in their school. Prior to working on the problem, students have estimated the number of buttons in their class and then carefully counted and recorded their data on a line plot. Using their data and assumptions they must make that arise from questions, the students work in pairs to solve the problem and record their solution strategies, justifying why they chose particular strategies. This activity involves sampling procedures, multiplication and division, graphing, statistics, and use of calculators. For students to see how mathematical connections are made helps them to better understand how mathematics is an integral part of their lives.

Assessing Learning of Multiplication and Division

Learning the basic multiplication and division facts begins in the primary grades, generally in grades 2 and 3. Learning the algorithms for multiplication and division generally begins in earnest in grade 4. That is why the algorithm activities have been focused at the intermediate level.

Not all students who reach or even leave grade 6 can multiply or divide proficiently. What should you as a teacher do when students are not performing at your level of expectation? Use individual or small-group instruction. Determine why there is an inability to multiply or divide. Is it because the student does not know what multiplication or division is (concept)? Does the student not know the basic facts (skill)? Can it be that the student cannot perform an algorithm (skill)? Does the student lack interest because of past failure with multiplication and division (affect)? Are assignments with too many problems causing discouragement (affect)?

There are many ways multiplication and division learning are assessed. As students construct their own algorithms, the opportunity to assess their work arises by questioning the students or reading the descriptions of how they discovered a solution. Math texts include carefully designed testing programs. Virtually every step of the learning process is tested and retested. Students should periodically submit a work sample to be placed in their portfolios. These work samples will document the growth the students are making. Part of the teacher's responsibility is to assure learning takes place at the appropriate developmental level.

In Chapter 7, we discussed several reasons children make mistakes. You may wish to review those reasons for they are the same for children performing multiplication and division. Some children will have difficulty completing algorithms, whether their own or those from the textbook. Your diagnostic skills will be challenged as soon as you enter the classroom. From the time of your first activity and thereafter, there will be children's hands in the air or children lining up by your desk requesting help.

The first comment you may hear is "I don't get it." This means the student does not know what the assignment is, did not listen to your explanation, wants your attention, does not want to try, or is unable to do an algorithm. You must decide what caused the student to say, "I don't get it."

The diagnosis has begun. Generally, you must individually reteach part or all of an algorithm or look at a partially or fully completed algorithm and decide where the student made an error. Most teacher's guides list only the answers to the problems from the student texts. They do not show each step in the algorithm, particularly if the students developed the algorithm. Thus, with only the answer at hand, you must work through the al-

gorithm with which the student is having difficulty to see where the error is.

In a multiplication problem such as 24×54, you may find one or more of these errors: (a) problem miscopied from the text, (b) basic fact error, (c) regrouping was not done, (d) regrouping took place when not needed, (e) student forgot to add the regrouped amount after multiplying, (f) problem not completed, (g) partial products not lined up, and (h) error in adding partial products. Each of these errors is illustrated in problems a–h below. Problem i shows a "standard" algorithm.

a. $\quad^{12}45$ $\quad\underline{\times\ 24}$ $\quad\ 180$ $\quad\underline{\ \ 90\ }$ $\ 1{,}080$	b. $\quad^{1}54$ $\underline{\times\ 24}$ $\ \ 218$ $\underline{\ \ 108\ }$ $1{,}298$	c. $\quad\ 54$ $\underline{\times\ 24}$ $\ \ 206$ $\underline{\ \ 108\ }$ $1{,}286$
d. $\quad^{1}54$ $\underline{\times\ 24}$ $\ \ 216$ $\underline{\ \ 118\ }$ $1{,}396$	e. $\quad^{1}54$ $\underline{\times\ 24}$ $\ \ 206$ $\underline{\ \ 108\ }$ $1{,}286$	f. $\quad^{1}54$ $\underline{\times\ 24}$ $\ \ 216$
g. $\quad^{1}54$ $\underline{\times\ 24}$ $\ \ 216$ $\underline{\ \ 108\ }$ $\ \ 324$	h. $\quad^{1}54$ $\underline{\times\ 24}$ $\ \ 216$ $\underline{\ \ 108\ }$ $1{,}276$	i. $\quad^{1}54$ $\underline{\times\ 24}$ $\ \ 216$ $\underline{\ \ 108\ }$ $1{,}296$

All of this assumes that you and the students are using the same algorithm. For students who use an alternative algorithm or an individually constructed algorithm, there may be other types of errors. It is well worth exploring with the students how they are going about reaching their solutions.

Coping with the "I don't get it" students demands teaching time. Besides diagnosing and correcting students' written errors, students may need to return to physical models to illustrate whatever is not clear from the abstract or pictorial approach. Above all, you must be supportive and encouraging. Let the students know you are working with them for the same ends.

Skillful diagnosis of the cause or causes of students' difficulties requires you to be proficient in mathematics and knowledgeable about children and the learning process. Take advantage of resource people in your school who may be able to assist in diagnosing. Sometimes students need extra time or a new approach for learning basic facts. Sometimes algorithms must be carefully retaught, perhaps using grid paper to emphasize proper alignment of digits as in Figure 8–35.

For students to gain the most from them, activities must seem worth doing. A sixth grader should be convinced that she or he is not doing only fourth- or fifth-grade work. Allow students to use calculators so they

Figure 8–35

may continue to learn other or more advanced mathematics and not always be frustrated by their weaknesses with basic facts. Finally, be willing to set aside certain textbook assignments; assignments can pile up and turn students away from mathematics.

The communication between you and your students, whether it be from conversations or from journal entries, can be the basis for assessing their progress in mathematics. Being a willing and compassionate listener will benefit both you and your students. It may well be that both of you are thinking alike and merely expressing the ideas differently.

Something for Everyone

Teaching operations with whole numbers involves considerable work with abstract symbols. The activities in Chapters 7 and 8 are intended to supplement and enrich the math text. In the mathematics textbook, operations are usually carefully presented using pictorial and abstract modes. Teacher's manuals recommend that teachers use physical models, as well. All of these approaches, the manipulative, pictorial, and abstract, are presented because we know that children tend to learn from the concrete to the abstract.

There are other modes of learning, however, that should be attended to as children learn whole-number operations. Children who learn most effectively in the visual mode should be provided with pictures and encouraged to draw pictures and diagrams as they develop concepts and skills involving operations with whole numbers. Representing operations on the number line and drawing arrays to illustrate multiplication facts may be especially useful for visual learners. The math text can be helpful for these learners as well when attractive illustrations are accompanied by careful instructions, but be aware that children do not always interpret diagrams the way textbook authors intend them to. Ask the children to tell you what they think the drawings mean. Talk about the mathematics that is being presented.

Many computer programs, such as *Math Ideas with Base-Ten Blocks* by Lund (Cuisenaire Co. of America), have effective graphic displays and may be used to reinforce skills in operations with whole numbers as a follow-up to work with the actual manipulative materials. Seeing the graphic display next to the abstract exercise is helpful to visual learners.

Tactile/kinesthetic learners find materials such as colored cubes, base ten blocks, Cuisenaire rods, and abaci useful in learning operations with whole numbers. Tactile learners should see and manipulate physical models of the operations as they are simultaneously writing down the abstract symbols. This manipulation helps them to connect what they are doing to the abstract algorithms they are learning in the books. Be sure that these children understand that the particular material they are using is not important. Encourage them to use several different materials to model the same exercise.

Challenge tactile learners to create their own algorithms for the operations and then test them using physical models to see if their methods will work for all kinds of problems. Let these students teach their algorithms to other students in the class and keep a record of the favorite methods.

Children who learn most effectively in the auditory mode should find it fairly easy to learn basic facts and algorithms by oral means. These children will likely be able to understand oral instructions and suggestions for correcting faulty algorithms more easily than other children. They can sometimes help in explaining adult instructions to other students. They may enjoy listening to tapes or records of songs and poems designed to help children memorize basic facts. They may even make up their own mnemonic devices to remember facts or the steps in an algorithm.

Children who process information linearly and sequentially benefit from an emphasis on following each step in an algorithm. These children can often work comfortably at an abstract level by fifth or sixth grade and may be able to follow the written instructions in the book if accompanied by careful oral directions from the teacher. These children often do well with a traditional approach to instruction, but even these children can benefit from some work with physical models. Although such children may appear to be doing well, they may not have a concrete understanding of what they are doing. They should be encouraged to illustrate each step of an algorithm with physical models such as chips for trading, an abacus, or bundling sticks.

Children who process information holistically or spatially are more apt to visualize an answer without going through a step-by-step process. Even though these children often have a superior number sense, they may not do well in a traditional mathematics program because they have difficulty in memorizing isolated facts or in following an algorithm with several steps.

Such children should be encouraged to explore the relationships among facts both concretely and abstractly. For example, they may be able to find the answer to 6 +

7 because they know the doubles and they know that 6 + 7 is 1 more than 6 + 6 or 1 less than 7 + 7. Some children even hide these abilities because they believe they are cheating if they use the answer to a previous fact to find a new answer instead of memorizing each fact in isolation. Be sure to let such children know that it is good to relate facts. The best mathematicians are those who can find the greatest number of relationships among known ideas and use them to discover new relationships. Children who process information visually should be able to work well with spatial materials such as base-10 blocks and Cuisenaire rods.

Be sure to have children with different learning styles share their methods with each other. All students can benefit by learning to work in different modes and can strengthen their own abilities to learn by being able to choose among a number of different learning strategies.

Promising students should be provided with enriching experiences that extend their thinking abilities. Challenge them with problem-solving activities that use operations with whole numbers (the ones suggested in Chapters 7 and 8 may provide a starting point). Let promising students make up problems for each other and the rest of the class or explore patterns in the addition and multiplication tables or in multidigit algorithms.

Use the pre- or posttests provided in textbooks to assess promising students before you assign work with a given unit. The tests can tell you if there are any gaps in the student's knowledge of the information you are about to present. If the children have already mastered the concepts, provide them with new challenges. Never force the promising students to work every problem on a page when the other children are working only the even exercises; promising students soon learn to hide their talents to avoid boring busywork.

Challenge promising students by exploring algorithms that have been used historically for operations with whole numbers. Children sometimes believe that there is only one right way to work a problem, and they are amazed to find that people in other times or even today in other parts of the world use algorithms quite different from the ones found in American textbooks. Ask the children to explain why these algorithms work. Encourage them to make up other algorithms of their own. After they master operations with whole numbers in base ten, introduce operations in other bases.

Children who have difficulty with operations in base ten may need a slower, more individualized approach. If children do not seem to understand the standard algorithm, try a different method. Children who have trouble with the traditional multiplication algorithm may have more success with a lattice. Children having difficulty dividing may be more successful using the Greenwood method. Or, these students may find success by inventing their own algorithms.

Children having difficulty may need more time to work with physical models. Do not rush them to learn abstract algorithms. Encourage them to write down the algorithm as they manipulate the objects. When the objects are no longer needed, most children give up the objects by themselves because it is faster to write the algorithm without manipulating the objects.

Children's learning styles and abilities should help determine how you present mathematics. Be sensitive to the individual needs of all children with whom you work. Be sure, however, to include enriching and pleasurable activities for all students.

KEY IDEAS

Multiplication and division play important roles in our daily lives. Chapter 8 presents models to help conceptualize multiplication and division. Children exchange sets for objects, count and add, construct arrays, exchange objects for sets, and partition sets in learning the concepts of multiplication and division. Objects such as cubes, rods, beans, and multibase blocks help children learn.

The skills of multiplication and division begin with learning basic facts and continue as children learn various algorithms. A number of activities present ways to help children memorize the basic facts.

A variety of paper-and-pencil algorithms are presented. As well, children are encouraged to construct their own algorithms. Calculators and computers play an increasingly important role in multiplication and division. Estimation and mental calculation become more important as we shift to electronic computation. Children should learn to decide which calculation technique is most appropriate. Continued work on communication skills will improve students' ability to think about multiplication and division.

Carefully diagnose and check the progress of children as they learn multiplication and division. Design instruction to meet the variety of children's learning styles.

DISCUSSION QUESTIONS

1. Select either the concept of multiplication or the concept of division. Discuss how that concept can be presented to a class of second-grade students in a way that leads to conceptual understanding.

2. Compare the array model for multiplication with the Cuisenaire rod model. How are they alike and how are they different? Discuss your ability to teach multiplication using either model.

3. Construct a division basic facts table. How can you help children memorize the basic division facts by

first introducing the families of related facts for multiplication and division?

4. Construct one of the games designed to help students remember the basic multiplication and division facts. Play the game with a classmate or two and discuss the strengths of that game for helping students.

5. Become proficient with multiplication on the Napier's rods. Teach someone else how to multiply 26×365 using the rods. You may need to prepare the other person by showing him or her an easier problem first.

REFERENCES

Aker, Suzanne, *What Comes in 2s, 3s, & 4s?* New York, NY: Simon & Schuster Books for Young Readers, 1990.

Anderson, Valerie, and Marlene Scardamalia, *Measuring Boswer.* LaSalle, IL: Open Court Pub. Co., 1985.

Anno, Masaichiro, and Mitsumasa Anno, *Anno's Mysterious Multiplying Jar.* New York: Philomel Books, 1983.

Burk, Donna, Allyn Snider, and Paula Symonds, *Math Excursions 2: Project-based Mathematics for Second Graders.* Portsmouth, NH: Heinemann, 1991.

Burns, Marilyn, *A Collection of Math Lessons from Grades 3 Through 6.* White Plains, NY: Cuisenaire Co. of America, 1987.

Burns, Marilyn, and Cathy Humphreys, *A Collection of Math Lessons from Grades 6 Through 8.* New Rochelle, NY: Math Solutions, 1990.

Burns, Marilyn, and Barbara Tank, *A Collection of Math Lessons from Grades 1 Through 3.* White Plains, NY: Cuisenaire Co. of America, 1988.

Dienes, Z. P., *The Elements of Mathematics.* New York: Herder & Herder, 1971.

Eames, Charles, *The Films of Charles & Ray Eames* (video-recording). Santa Monica, CA, 1989.

Fish, Daniel W., *Arithmetical Problems, Oral and Written; with Numerous Tables of Money, Weights, Measures, Etc.* New York: Ivison, Blakeman, Taylor & Co., 1874.

Hamm, Diane Johnson, *How Many Feet in the Bed?* New York: NY: Simon & Schuster Books for Young Readers, 1991.

Hutchins, Pat, *The Doorbell Rang.* New York: NY: Mulberry Books, 1986.

Juster, Norton, *The Phantom Tollbooth.* New York: Random House, 1961.

Morrison, Philip, and Phylis Morrison, *Powers of Ten.* New York: Scientific American Library, 1982.

National Research Council, *Measuring Up.* Washington, DC: National Academy Press, 1993.

Reys, Robert E., et al., *Keystrokes: Multiplication and Division.* Palo Alto, CA: Creative Publications, 1979.

Schoen, Harold L., and Marilyn J. Zweng, eds., *Estimation and Mental Computation.* Reston, VA: National Council of Teachers of Mathematics, 1986.

Seymour, Dale, *Developing Skills in Estimation, Book A.* Palo Alto, CA: Dale Seymour, 1981.

Sheffield, Linda Jensen, *Problem Solving in Math, Book D.* New York: Scholastic Book Services, 1982.

Wahl, John, and Stacey Wahl, *I Can Count the Petals of a Flower.* Reston, VA: National Council of Teachers of Mathematics, 1977.

Technology

Eames, Charles, The Films of Charles & Ray Eames. Santa Monica, CA, 1982. (Video)

MINDPLAY, *Robomath.* Tucson, AZ: MINDPLAY. (Software)

O'Brien, Thomas C., *Teasers by Tobbs: Numbers and Operations.* Pleasantville, NY: Sunburst Communications. (Software)

Chapter 9

Attaching Meaning to Rational Numbers

NCTM Standards

GRADES K–4

Standard 12: Fractions and Decimals

In grades K–4, the mathematics curriculum should include fractions and decimals so that students can—

- develop concepts of fractions, mixed numbers, and decimals;
- develop number sense for fractions and decimals;
- use models to explore operations on fractions and decimals;
- apply fractions and decimals to problem situations.

GRADES 5–8

Standard 5: Number and Number Relationships

In grades 5–8, the mathematics curriculum should include the continued development of number and number relationships so that students can—

- understand, represent, and use numbers in a variety of equivalent forms (integer, fraction, decimal, percent, exponential, and scientific notation) in real-world and mathematical problem situations;

- develop number sense for whole numbers, fractions, decimals, integers, and rational numbers;
- understand and apply ratios, proportions, and percents in a wide variety of situations;
- investigate relationships among fractions, decimals, and percents;
- represent numerical relationships in one- and two-dimensional graphs.

Standard 6: Number Systems and Number Theory

In grades 5–8, the mathematics curriculum should include the study of number systems and number theory so that students can—

- understand and appreciate the need for numbers beyond the whole numbers;
- develop and use order relations for whole numbers, fractions, decimals, integers, and rational numbers;
- extend their understanding of whole number operations to fractions, decimals, integers, and rational numbers;
- understand how the basic arithmetic operations are related to one another;
- develop and apply number theory concepts (e.g., primes, factors, and multiples) in real-world and mathematical problem situations.

NCTM (1989), pp. 57, 87, 91. Reprinted by permission.

Divide each geoboard below in half in a different way, using just one rubber band. Sketch where you would place the rubber band on each geoboard to indicate how you would divide it, and then shade one-half. Remember that each half must have the same area but need not be congruent to the other half. A sample has been drawn for you in Figure 9–1.

What methods did you use to divide the geoboards in half? Write a complete description that could be understood by your fellow students.

Figure 9–1

As you read the following pages, consider these guiding questions:

1. How do you distinguish between part-whole, ratio, and division models for common fractions? Describe physical models you could use to illustrate each type.
2. How can you use children's understanding of place value for whole numbers as a basis for introducing decimal fractions?
3. What strategies and physical models might you use to help children understand that there are an infinite number of ways to write equivalent fractions in common and decimal form?
4. Why is it preferable to talk about simplest terms rather than reduced terms, and how might you help children develop this concept?
5. What is the trichotomy principle and how is it related to the density property?
6. What is the difference between a ratio and a proportion and how might you use examples from children's everyday life to help them understand these concepts?
7. What are some common errors students make as they learn concepts of rational numbers and how might you help them correct these misconceptions?

Concepts about rational numbers begin to develop long before children enter school. When children are asked to share a granola bar fairly with a brother or sister, they begin to intuitively grasp the idea of $\frac{1}{2}$. In kindergarten, these intuitive ideas may be introduced more formally but the emphasis should continue to be on situations from the child's life that utilize a variety of concrete materials. Children should realize that rational numbers are very much a part of their everyday lives, and they will need a thorough understanding of them in order to function as intelligent adult consumers.

Ask the children to keep a record of all the times rational numbers are used in their everyday lives. You may be surprised at the large number of uses they find. Create a bulletin board with the uses the children find at home, in newspapers and magazines, and from interviewing people about the uses in their careers. Interviews may reveal such things as the baker using common fractions when preparing recipes or formulas, the bus driver using decimal fractions when buying gas and figuring mileage, the store manager using percents when planning a sale, the car salesperson using percents to figure the commission earned, the nurse using decimal fractions to measure out the medicine to give to a patient, the teacher using percents to figure students' grades, and the government official using percents to determine budgets.

Children themselves must use rational numbers when they cook a meal, sew an apron, measure a garden, build a birdhouse, tip a waiter, or figure the amount they earn for $2\frac{1}{3}$ hours of baby-sitting. The United States' system of money and the metric system of measurement are based on decimal fractions. Conventional measures of length, area, weight, volume, and time make extensive use of common fractions. Sales and sales tax commonly use percents. It is important, therefore, for children to have a solid understanding of all types of rational numbers.

Some people have argued that the proliferation of calculators and the move toward using the metric rather than the conventional system of measure may make it unnecessary to use common fractions, but common fractions will continue to be used to describe such everyday occurrences as eating $\frac{1}{2}$ of an apple, and operations with common fractions must be understood for later work with algebraic fractions, so we present rational numbers in common fraction as well as decimal fraction form.

It is important to remember that common fraction notation and decimal fraction notation are ways of naming the same rational number. The concept of the number is the same regardless of the form in which it is written. Before continuing, we give a formal definition of a rational number.

A **rational number** is one that can be expressed as $\frac{p}{q}$ where p and q are both integers and $q \neq 0$. Rational numbers can be expressed in different ways; they may be written as **common fractions** ($\frac{1}{2}$, $\frac{3}{4}$, . . .); as **decimal fractions,** commonly called decimals (0.5, 0.75, . . .); or as **percents** (50 percent, 75 percent, . . .). Any rational number may be represented by an infinite number of numerals. For example, $\frac{1}{2} = 0.5 = 50$ percent $= \frac{2}{4} = \frac{3}{6} = \frac{4}{8} = \frac{5}{10} =$ . . . . Common fractions may also have several different meanings. They may represent:

1. The part-whole model, where the whole is a unit of measure, a geometric shape, or a set of objects.
2. A ratio between two subsets.
3. Division.

Given the wide range of ways to represent rational numbers and the variety of meanings, it is not surprising that children often are confused when dealing with rational numbers in any form.

Children should use physical models when learning new concepts, and fortunately there are many good materials. Both commercial and teacher-made materials can aid learning of rational number concepts. These materials should be used in the primary grades as children begin to formalize fraction concepts and should also be used in the intermediate and middle school grades, when students learn to operate with common fractions, decimal fractions, and percents. The materials described in this chapter include Fraction Tiles, Fraction Factory, rectangular and circular fraction regions, Decimal Squares, base ten blocks, rulers, number lines, fraction strips, Fraction Bars, colored chips, Cuisenaire rods and arrays. Computer programs, such as Fraction

Attraction and Gears, and calculators are also useful in the development of skills with rational numbers. As children use these materials, ask them to explore, question, discover relationships, and discuss their findings with each other. Learning should be both active and related to the child's world.

Developing Rational Number Concepts

As mentioned in the introduction, rational numbers can be represented in a variety of ways, and the representations may have a variety of meanings. This section begins with a description of several meanings for common fractions and several materials that may be used to develop those meanings. We then compare common fractions to decimal fractions and percents. The section ends with a discussion of equivalent fractions and ordering fractions.

Part-Whole Model for a Common Fraction

The first model for a fraction that children typically encounter in school is the **part-whole model.** In this model, the **denominator** represents the number of parts the whole or unit has been divided into and the **numerator** represents the number of parts currently under consideration. If the unit is a unit of measure such as length, area, or volume, each of the parts must be of equal size, even though they need not be congruent. If the unit consists of discrete objects such as chips or children, the objects need not be the same size. However, when children are first introduced to fractions, it is common to use congruent parts or discrete objects of the same size. The following are examples of activities and materials that can be used to help children develop the part-whole concept of a common fraction using area, length, volume, and discrete objects as the unit.

ACTIVITIES

Primary (K–3)

Objective: to develop the concept of a fraction as part of a region divided into equal-sized pieces.

1. Give each child a number of squares cut out of paper. Ask the children to fold a square in two sections. Unfold the square, and examine the sections. Are they the same size? If the square represents a candy bar to be split among two children, would each child receive the same amount? Compare squares that were folded

in half to those that were not and discuss the differences. Be sure that children understand that when they have half a candy bar, each child must have the same amount of candy. There is no such thing as "the bigger half."

Using another of the squares, ask the children to fold it in half another way. Tell them to color one of the halves and to cut it out to compare the sections. These will probably be similar to the pieces shown in Figures 9–2a and b.

Fold a square as shown in Figure 9–3. Then unfold it and color the two end pieces. Ask the children if the colored pieces are still $\frac{1}{2}$. Let the children cut out the pieces to prove that the two halves do indeed cover the same area.

Challenge the children to find other ways to color $\frac{1}{2}$ of the square. Have them prove the answer by cutting the pieces out and showing that the colored pieces do fill the same area as the noncolored pieces. Figure 9–4 shows other responses that the children may give.

Figure 9–2

Figure 9–3

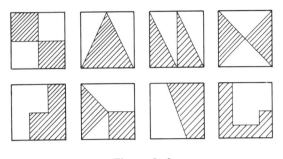

Figure 9–4

After children have shown $\frac{1}{2}$ in many different ways, ask them to repeat the process for other fractions.

2. Use plastic or cardboard regions that have been divided into halves, thirds, and fourths. You may use commercial sets such as Fraction Tiles or Fraction Factory, which are sets made of plastic. A whole square region is one color, and congruent parts are other colors to represent various fractions (available from Creative Publications). Or, using the masters included in the appendix, make your own sets out of colored railroad board or run off copies of the regions onto colored paper and let the children cut out their own sets. It is helpful to have several units of the same color and the halves, thirds, and fourths each of a different color. Your pieces may look like those in Figure 9–5 or Figure 9–6. You may also use the square or circular fraction dies on the Ellison lettering machine to make a set of fraction pieces.

Let the children explore with the materials. Challenge the children to make a complete region using pieces that are all the same color. Ask what each piece is called. Ask how many thirds, fourths, or halves it takes to make a whole region. Count $\frac{1}{3}, \frac{2}{3}, \frac{3}{3}$ or $\frac{1}{4}, \frac{2}{4}, \frac{3}{4}, \frac{4}{4}$ as you make a whole. Let the children predict the number of sixths, eighths, and tenths it will take to make the whole region. Encourage the children to make up their own questions using the pieces. Add pieces of other sizes to the group. Sixths, eighths, and twelfths are good sizes to work with. Notice that you should ask students to make the whole when given a fractional part as well as to find the fraction when given a whole.

Make up word problems using the pieces. Use problems such as: "Mrs. Jensen has a granola bar that she wants to split evenly among her three grandchildren. Show the pieces you would use so that each child gets a piece the same size. What is each piece called?" Let the children make up their own word problems.

3. The fraction one-tenth should receive special attention because of the frequent use of decimal fractions with calculators, computers, and metric measures. With young children, introduce the fractions such

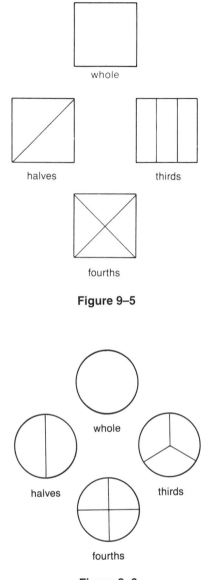

Figure 9–5

Figure 9–6

as halves, thirds, and fourths first because it is easier for such children to divide a unit region into 2, 3, or 4 pieces than it is to divide the region into 10 pieces. The reason is similar to that for teaching children to group by threes and fours before grouping by tens when teaching the concept of place value. When tenths are introduced, you may use commercial materials such as Decimal Squares or base ten blocks or you may make your own materials, similar to those described in the last activity. The decimal patterns in Appendix B can be used for this activity.

The activities described in the previous example may be repeated using tenths. Introduce tenths as common fractions before you introduce them as decimal fractions, since children will be more familiar with the common fraction form after their work with halves, thirds, and fourths. You may also introduce fifths at this time, since children are probably discovering a number of equivalent fractions as they work with the pieces.

Objective: to develop the concept of a common fraction as part of a whole unit of length.

4. Rulers, number lines, fraction strips, and Fraction Bars show fractions based on a unit of length. In each of these, a unit is chosen and then subdivided into equal-sized parts (see Figure 9–7). Fraction Bars (available from Scott Resources) are vinyl strips divided into units, halves, thirds, fourths, fifths, sixths, tenths, and twelfths, with each division printed on a different color of vinyl. The Fraction Bars are all the same length but have different amounts shaded to represent the various fractions. Teachers and students may make similar sets of fraction strips by copying the masters in the appendix onto colored construction paper or railroad board. Again, it is useful to use different colors for each fraction piece. You may also use the masters in the appendix to make fraction number lines. With either the teacher-made fraction strips or the Fraction Bars, the children may repeat the activities described above for the regions.

Fraction Bars come with sets of cards with numerals written on them and Bingo cards with pictures of fractions shown as parts of circular regions.

Children can play several games in which they match the numerals to the bars or the circular regions. The teacher's guides that come with the bars describe a wide variety of activities, and the children can make up others of their own. When numerals for fractions are first introduced, children may have difficulty relating the symbols to the spoken words and concepts with which they are familiar. The written symbols should be introduced only after the children have the concepts and oral language necessary to understand them. Be sure to give students plenty of experiences to understand the written symbols.

After the children have had a number of experiences with the Fraction Bars or the fraction strips, they can draw the corresponding number lines such as the ones shown in Figures 9–8a and b. Later the children will be asked to transfer this skill to using the fraction number lines without the fraction strips or Fraction Bars. Often, textbooks show only work on the number line, and children should be able to use number lines with rational numbers as well as whole numbers.

When the children are comfortable finding fractional parts of various unit lengths, they should study the marks on a conventional ruler and discuss the meaning of the various parts. They may find that some rulers show $\frac{1}{4}$ inch, others show $\frac{1}{8}$ inch, and still others may show $\frac{1}{16}$ inch. Then have children compare English rulers to metric rulers, which show tenths of a centimeter.

Objective: to develop the concept of a fraction as part of a whole unit of volume.

5. Common fractions are often used in everyday life to refer to parts of units other than those for area

Figure 9–7

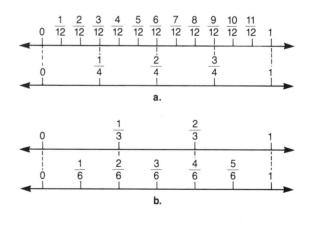

Figure 9–8

or length. These include units of time, weight, mass, money, capacity, and volume. Children should have experience using fractions for all of these measures.

The following are a few ideas for using common fractions to describe parts of a unit of volume. Measuring cups are good for exploring fraction concepts in connection with volume. Children should be given the opportunity to explore pouring water, sand, beans, or rice from one measuring cup into another. Ask the children to predict how many $\frac{1}{2}$ cups it will take to fill a whole cup. Will four $\frac{1}{3}$ cups be more or less than one cup? Is $\frac{1}{2}$ cup more or less than $\frac{1}{3}$ cup? After the prediction, let the children pour to see if they were right. Let the children pose questions to each other. Find simple recipes and let the children do the measuring. Discuss their observations about the fractional parts they have measured.

Objective: to develop the concept of common fractions as part of a set of discrete objects.

6. Often, a common fraction is used to refer to part of a set of discrete objects. A mother may refer to half a dozen eggs, or the teacher may say that $\frac{1}{4}$ of the children may go to the learning center. When a common fraction is used in this way, the denominator refers to the number of equal-sized groups into which the set is divided, and the numerator refers to the number of groups currently under consideration.

Colored cubes, Bingo chips, or even the children themselves are good manipulative materials for this type of fractional representation. A child may start with 12 chips to represent 1 dozen eggs and then discuss what must be done in order to find $\frac{1}{2}$. The separation of the set into two equal parts should be related to earlier work separating regions, lengths, and volumes into two equal parts. After children work with halves, they may find thirds, fourths, sixths, and twelfths of the dozen eggs. Children may then use other units of discrete objects, such as finding $\frac{1}{4}$ of the children in the class or $\frac{1}{3}$ of the books in their desks.

Children may have some difficulty with the fact that fractional parts do not always contain the same number of objects. Half a dozen eggs is not the same number as half the children in the class. Have children compare this to the fact that half of a large circle (or half a large pizza) is not the same size as half of a small circle (or half a small pizza). However, children should realize that half of a dozen eggs is the same number as the other half of the dozen.

Ratio Model for a Common Fraction

The activities just described involve using common fractions to describe a part-whole relationship. Common fractions may also be used to describe a ratio between two sets. In the **ratio model,** the denominator and the numerator each represent the number of parts under consideration. The denominator does not represent the parts of the whole, as in the part-whole model. The numerator and denominator represent subsets that are being compared.

In fact, some young children have difficulty with the part-whole concept because they have difficulty with the class inclusion concept. They want to compare one subset to another subset rather than compare a subset to a whole. They may identify each of the pictures in Figure 9–9 as $\frac{1}{2}$ because they are comparing the one shaded section to the two nonshaded sections.

This is a correct concept of the fraction $\frac{1}{2}$, but only if the fraction is used in a ratio sense. It is true that the shaded section in each picture is $\frac{1}{2}$ the size of the non-shaded section, but because they are looking for a part-whole response and not a ratio response, most textbooks and most standardized tests say the child was wrong in giving the response of $\frac{1}{2}$. Teachers should encourage children to compare the two.

The following activities suggest ways that ratio concepts may be introduced and compared to part-whole models. The activities are suggested for the intermediate grades because that is when ratios are commonly introduced in textbooks. Often, only a few physical models for ratios are included in the textbooks, and you will probably need to supplement children's work in the books. Many younger children may benefit from activities comparing ratio models and part-whole models because the ratio model fits their own intuitive concepts of common fractions.

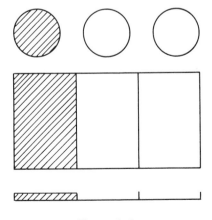

Figure 9–9

ACTIVITIES

Intermediate (4–6)

Objective: to develop the ratio concept of a fraction using objects.

1. Children encounter ratio ideas in everyday life, especially ratios used to describe relationships between discrete objects. The teacher may say that there are two girls for every three boys in a group or there are two cookies for each child at a birthday party.

   Use chips or colored cubes to represent the situations. The chips shown in Figure 9–10 may be used to show that there are two girls for every three boys in the group. Let green chips represent the girls and blue chips represent the boys. Ask the children what part of the whole class is girls. How is the ratio concept of a fraction related to the part-whole concept?

2. Another common use of ratio is with gears. Children may observe gears. In Figure 9–11, note that there are 5 teeth on the small gear and 10 teeth on the large gear.

   You may buy gears from a hardware store, obtain gears from factories (which may give you some of their old ones), or use a commercial set such as TECHNIC™ from Lego. Mark each gear so the children can count the number of turns of each gear. Ask the children to turn the large gear one complete turn and count the number of turns of the small gear. Compare the number of turns to the ratio of the teeth on the large gear to the teeth on the small gear.

   The children should note that the small gear in Figure 9–11 will go around twice while the large gear goes around once. The ratio of the teeth on the large gear to the teeth on the small gear is 10:5, while the ratio of the number of turns of the large gear to the number of turns of the small gear is 1:2.

   Let the children make hypotheses about what will happen with gears of other sizes. Get these gears and test the hypotheses.

Objective: to develop the concept of ratio using length.

3. Cuisenaire rods are a good material to use to represent a common fraction as a ratio between two lengths. Use them with children who have had previous expe-

Figure 9–11

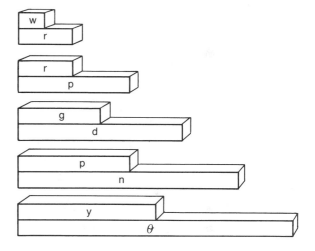

Figure 9–12

rience using the rods. Ask the children to find several pairs of rods for which one rod is half the length of the other. Possibilities are shown in Figure 9–12.

Note that children are comparing the length of one rod to the length of the other and not comparing one rod to the total length of the two. Let the children suggest other fractions to display with the rods such as $\frac{2}{3}$ and $\frac{3}{4}$. Encourage comparing the other rods to the orange rod for the concept of tenths. Being comfortable with finding tenths helps children make the transition to writing decimal fractions.

Ask the children to measure something such as the length of their desk using only orange Cuisenaire rods. They should first estimate and then measure to check how close their estimates are. After measuring the desk in orange rods, ask them to estimate the number of yellow rods to measure the same length. Encourage the students to discuss their estimates in small groups. Observe to see if they realize that it

Figure 9–10

takes twice the number of yellow rods as orange rods, because the yellow rods are half the length of orange rods.

Objective: to develop the concept of ratio using volume.

4. Ask children to try to find examples of ratios used at home. They may notice that salad dressing calls for 1 part vinegar for 5 parts oil or that iced tea mix calls for 1 teaspoon of iced tea mix for 1 cup of water. Bring in ingredients to let the children make the solutions or mixtures at school. Ask questions about the ratios as you mix. If the mixture is 1 part vinegar for 5 parts oil, what part of the total mixture is vinegar? Note that if the ratio is 1:5, the vinegar is $\frac{1}{6}$ of the total because the whole mixture has 6 parts. Have the children compare this work to earlier work with ratios with discrete objects.

Using Common Fractions to Indicate Division

So far, we have discussed two different concepts that may be represented by common fractions, part-whole and ratio. Common fractions may also be used to indicate a division problem. When fractions are used to indicate division, the division problem $5 \div 6$ is shown as $\frac{5}{6}$. The models used may be similar to those used for the partitive division problems with whole numbers in Chapter 8. Therefore, introduce activities using common fractions to indicate division after children have learned to divide with whole numbers and after they understand the part-whole concept of a fraction. The following activities focus on the division concept of common fractions.

ACTIVITIES

Intermediate (3–6)

Objective: to develop the concept of a common fraction representing division using discrete objects.

1. Begin with problems such as $6 \div 2$, which have whole-number answers. Tell the children you have 6 cookies and wish to put them into 2 equal groups. The children may wish to use chips to show that $6 \div 2 = \frac{6}{2} = 3$.

    Ask the children what they would do if you had 7 cookies and wished to put them into 2 equal groups. Again, let the children model this with the chips. They will find that they have one chip left over. Some of the children may decide that they can divide the last cookie in half so that each group will have $3\frac{1}{2}$ cookies. Therefore, $7 \div 2 = \frac{7}{2} = 3\frac{1}{2}$.

These experiences with the division model for common fractions are good for explaining the renaming of improper fractions as mixed numerals. Ask the children to use materials to explain why $\frac{8}{3} = 2\frac{2}{3}$.

Objective: to develop the division concept for common fractions using length.

2. Chips are not a good material to use for many of the division problems involving fractions because they cannot be broken into fractional pieces. Models involving measures of length, area, or volume are often preferable because they can be broken into smaller parts. Using these materials, start with a story situation and let the children discover the answer on their own. Give each of the children some blank 3-by-5 index cards and tell them the 3-inch and the 5-inch sides of the cards represent 3 yards and 5 yards, respectively.

    Tell the children that you have 3 yards of material from which to make puppets for a play. You need to make 4 puppets and wish to use the same amount of material for each one. What part of a yard of material can you use for each puppet? Ask the children to fold the 3-by-5 index cards and measure to find the answer. Many children will be surprised to find that you will have $\frac{3}{4}$ yard of material for each puppet, $3 \div 4 = \frac{3}{4}$ (see Figure 9–13).

    Ask the children to make up a story situation for the problem $5 \div 3$ and to again fold a 3-by-5 card and measure to find the result (see Figure 9–14). Repeat

Figure 9–13

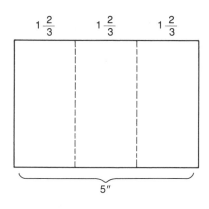

Figure 9–14

the activity with several different measures until the children can generalize that $a \div b = \frac{a}{b}$.

3. After children have had several experiences folding paper to show the division model for a fraction, they can transfer to a number line. Again, begin with the problem 3 ÷ 4. Give each child a number line 3 inches long. Ask the children to divide the number line into 4 equal parts. They will probably find that this is difficult to do unless each unit on the number line is broken into smaller parts.

   Suggest that the children break each unit into 4 equal parts. Ask the children how many small parts there are in 3 units. There are 12. Now ask the children to break the number line into 4 equal parts. The children should discover that each of the parts will be $\frac{3}{4}$ inch long (see Figure 9–15).

   Ask the children to compare this work to the work folding the index cards. Repeat the activity with number lines of different sizes and with different fractions. Ask the children to make up story situations illustrated by their number lines.

Objective: to reinforce the division concept of a common fraction using a variety of measures.

4. Discrete objects and length are not the only models used to show the division concept of a common fraction. Many other units of measure such as time, money, volume, area, and mass may also be used. Make up story situations for other units of measure and let children choose their own methods and materials for solving the problems. Here are a few suggestions:

   • *Money.* Mrs. Jackson has $5 to buy favors for a birthday party. She needs 10 favors and wishes to spend the same amount on each one. What part of a dollar should she spend on each favor?
   • *Time.* The Moyer relay team wishes to run the 1-mile relay in 5 minutes. If the 4 girls on the relay team each run the same distance in the same amount of time, how fast should each girl run her $\frac{1}{4}$ mile?

Figure 9–15

   • *Volume.* The Coleys have a 2-liter bottle of soda. If Amy wants to split the soda evenly into 10 glasses, what part of a liter should she pour into each glass?
   • *Area.* The Sheffields have a 2-acre plot of ground that they wish to plant with corn, tomatoes, and peppers. If they use the same amount of land for each vegetable, how much land will be used for each?

Encourage the children to make up their own situations and trade with each other to solve them.

Decimal Fractions

If you are using a textbook series, decimal fractions may be introduced before, along with, or after common fractions. You will probably wish to follow the textbook guidelines, but there are advantages to introducing decimals earlier because of the use of the decimal in place-value notation, in our money system, in the metric system of measurement, and on calculators and computers, as well as the relative ease of computation with decimal fractions. Conceptually, however, it is probably easier to understand the meaning of halves, thirds, and fourths than it is to understand tenths and hundredths because there are fewer partitions involved. Whenever you decide to introduce common and decimal fractions, be sure the children realize they are simply different notation systems for the same concepts.

We focus here on the use of decimal fractions and percents to represent parts of whole units. Again, a unit may be a set of discrete objects or any unit of measure (length, area, volume, mass, money, or time). Children should have a good concept of tenths before they begin work with written decimal fractions. Work with decimals may begin as soon as children understand the concept of dividing a unit into 10 equal-sized parts.

Because the money system in the United States is based on decimals, children also may be introduced to hundredths at a fairly young age. Most six- or seven-year olds can understand that there are 100 pennies in a dollar and that 1 penny may be written as $.01. This represents $\frac{1}{100}$ of a dollar.

When decimal fractions are introduced, place value for whole numbers should be reviewed. Let the children study the following place-value chart and tell you what happens as you move one place to the right on the chart.

thousands   hundreds   tens   ones   .   __   __

Children should notice that the value of the position on the right is one-tenth of the value of the position directly to the left of it. Ask the children to predict the value of the place to the right of the ones place—that is, the first place after the decimal point. (Note that in countries outside the United States, a comma may be used in place of a decimal point, for example, $1,7 = 1\frac{7}{10}$) Children should realize that this place will have one-tenth the value of the ones place and therefore is the tenths place.

The activities for teaching the concept of a common fraction as part of a whole may be repeated for decimal fractions, beginning with tenths and later expanding to hundredths, thousandths, and so on. The following activities suggest other ways in which decimal fractions may be introduced.

ACTIVITIES

Intermediate (3–6)

Objective: to develop the concept of a decimal fraction using a length, area, or volume model.

1. Take out the white and orange Cuisenaire rods and tell the children that the orange rod represents 1. Ask the children to tell you the value of one of the white rods. Use the decimal notation to represent the value 0.1.

   After the children understand the concept of tenths using the rods, add the orange flats from the Cuisenaire metric blocks and tell the children that the orange flat now represents 1. What is the new value of the orange rod (long)? What is the value of each white rod? What is the value shown by the rods in Figure 9–16 if the flat is 1?

   Ask the children to show 0.45, 0.89, and so on. Let the children make up problems for each other and discuss how they found the answers. After the chil-

dren are proficient at working with both tenths and hundredths, add the orange cube to the set. If the cube is 1, the flat becomes 0.1, the long becomes 0.01, and the white rod becomes 0.001. Repeat the activities with thousandths.

2. After the children have worked with the Cuisenaire metric blocks, they may do the same activities using paper or cardboard models. You may use a commercial set such as Decimal Squares, or make a set out of paper. If you make your own set, a convenient size is 1 square decimeter for a unit. Mark squares with 10 columns for tenths, and mark columns with 10 rows for hundredths (see Figure 9–17). (A master for this square is included in Appendix B.)

   Laminate the decimal squares so that the children may write on them with erasable markers. Make a separate set of cards with various decimal fractions written on them, and ask the children to shade the squares to match the decimal fractions written on the cards. The children may then use the cards to play various games that involve matching the numerals to the pictures, such as Go Fish or Old Maid.

3. Because the metric system is a decimal system, it provides good examples of decimal fractions. Children learning the concept of 0.1 may take strips of paper each 1 decimeter long (or they may use orange Cuisenaire rods) and line them up on a meter stick. Ask, "How many strips of paper or rods does it take to make 1 meter?" Ten. Ask, "How could you express three strips?" 0.3 meter.

   Extend the activity to hundredths by using strips each 1 centimeter long or by using the white Cuisenaire rods. Ask, "What part of a meter is represented by 23 white rods? What part of a meter is represented

Figure 9–16

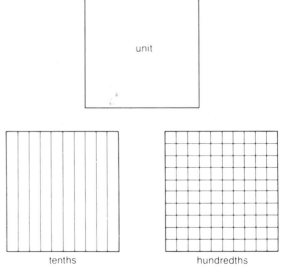

Figure 9–17

by five orange rods and two white rods?" Let the children make up their own questions for each other and discuss their methods of solution. Thousandths may be introduced by using millimeters or by using grams and kilograms or milliliters and liters.

Percent

After children are comfortable using decimal fractions as well as common fractions, introduce them to the concept of *percent*. Percent simply means "per hundred," or "out of 100." A percent may be thought of as a ratio between some number and 100. For example, 18 percent is 18 out of 100. Have children practice writing percents as ratios, common fractions, and decimal fractions. Eighteen out of 100 may be written as $\frac{18}{100}$, 0.18, or 18 percent. Different notations are useful at different times; you might use $\frac{18}{100}$ when writing out the fractional part of a dollar on a bank check, $\frac{9}{50}$ to tell the probability of winning a game, $0.18 to give the price of an apple, or 18 percent to note the discount on a recent purchase.

Note that *percent* and *percentage* are not the same thing. Children (and teachers) often confuse the two. A **percent** indicates a rate, while a **percentage** indicates an amount. For example, if you take out a loan of $500 for one year at 10 percent, the rate is 10 percent, the base is $500, and the $50 you pay in interest is the percentage. The percentage and the base are amounts, and the percent is the ratio between these two amounts.

Materials and activities for introducing percent are similar to those for introducing decimal fractions. You may repeat any of the activities involving hundredths using a percent representation. The following activities give a few additional ideas.

ACTIVITIES

Middle Grades (5–8)

Objective: to develop the concept of percent.

1. The Decimal Squares with 10 rows of 10 squares each may be used again for this activity. Make an overhead transparency of one of the Decimal Squares, and on the overhead projector, let the children watch you shade part of the square red. Ask the children what percent of the square is shaded red.

   A hundreds board without the numbers is also useful for developing the concept of percent. Hang different colored markers on the hooks. For example, if you have 15 green markers on the pegs and 85 red markers, ask the children what percent of the board has green markers and what percent has red markers.

Let children make up different examples for each other. Ask them to compare their answers in common and decimal fractions to their answers in percents.

2. Money is a good tool to use in introducing percent since the United States currency is based on the decimal system. Ask the children to express 18¢ as a percent of 1 dollar. Set up a chart such as the following:

Amount	Percent of 1 Dollar
$0.18	18
$0.26	—
$0.35	—
$0.92	—
$2.96	—

Ask the children to make up other examples for each other and discuss how they found their answers.

Equivalent Fractions

After children understand the concept of a common fraction as part of a unit, they may begin to explore the concept of **equivalent fractions.** Unlike whole numbers, each fraction has an infinite number of symbolic representations. The common fractions that name the same number are called equivalent fractions.

State-operator-state machines may be used to demonstrate this idea. Fraction pieces representing a common fraction in one form are the input and fraction pieces representing the fraction in a different but equivalent form are the output. The following activities include a variety of examples of finding equivalent fractions.

ACTIVITIES

Intermediate (3–6)

Objective: to develop the concept of equivalent fractions.

1. Choose one of the sets of fraction pieces for this activity. The examples here are given for the Fraction Bars. The operator in the state-operator-state machine is "give an equivalent." Use the machines you used earlier for operations with whole numbers.

   Demonstrate the idea first to the whole group before asking the children to work with individual machines. Give the children who will be supplying the input one set of Fraction Bars and the children doing the operation another set of bars. Ask one child to choose a bar such as $\frac{1}{3}$ and place it in the machine. The operators in the machine should then find a bar with an equivalent amount shaded and place the bar in the output (see Figure 9–18). Ask the children to name the

Input

Output

Figure 9–18

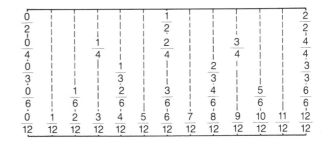

Figure 9–19

amount in the output. Do this for several amounts for which equivalent fractions can be found with the bars.

After the children understand these exchanges, ask them what they would do with a bar such as $\frac{7}{12}$. They will not be able to find a different equivalent amount with the bars. Does that mean that no equivalent amount exists? Lead the children to discuss how they can create new bars to show an equivalent amount such as $\frac{14}{24}$.

After the children have worked with the machine as a whole group, let them work in pairs or individually to find other equivalent fractions. Ask the children to write down all the sets of equivalent fractions they find.

When the children get a list such as $\frac{1}{2} = \frac{2}{4} = \frac{3}{6} = \frac{6}{12}$, ask them if they notice any patterns in the list. They should realize that to convert from one fraction to an equivalent fraction, they can either multiply or divide the numerator and denominator by the same number. Let the children repeat the activity with other materials such as the Fraction Tiles or the fraction strips to see that the same rules are true regardless of the material used.

2. Give each child a strip of adding machine tape 1 foot long. Have the children label the left end of the tape with a 0 and the right end with a 1.

Ask the children to fold the tape in half. Have them now label the left end $\frac{0}{2}$, the middle $\frac{1}{2}$, and the right end $\frac{2}{2}$.

Ask the children to fold the tape in half again and to relabel it. They should now have $\frac{0}{4}, \frac{1}{4}, \frac{2}{4}, \frac{3}{4}$, and $\frac{4}{4}$.

Unfold the tape and label the thirds, and then fold the tape in half again and label the sixths. Fold it in half once more and label the twelfths. The final tape should look like the one in Figure 9–19.

Ask the children to list all the fractions that name the same fold on the tape. Ask them to compare this list to their lists of equivalent fractions from the work with the state-operator-state machines. Ask them how the lists may be extended by continuing to fold the paper. Ask if there is ever an end to the number of equivalent fractions.

After students have worked with the adding machine tape, ask them to place various fractions in the appropriate place on a number line. Stress the importance of the 1 and the 0 on the number line when determining the correct location of each fraction. Where is $\frac{1}{2}$ in relation to $\frac{3}{8}$ or $\frac{4}{3}$? How does this compare to the adding machine tape or fractions on a ruler?

Ordering Fractions

After the children have worked with equivalent fractions, have them use the same materials to order fractions. Following are a few activities for developing the concept of ordering fractions.

ACTIVITIES

Intermediate (4–6)

Objective: to develop the concept of ordering fractions.

1. Use one of the sets of fractional regions such as the pie pieces or the rectangular regions. Ask the children to name two common fractions and to find the corresponding regions. By placing the pieces on top of each other, compare the areas of the two regions to determine which of the fractions is larger.

2. Use the folded adding machine tape that the children have labeled with common fractions. Ask the children to locate $\frac{1}{4}$ and $\frac{1}{2}$ on the tape. Ask the children which is smaller and have them write the answer using the symbol for less than. They should write $\frac{1}{4} < \frac{1}{2}$.

Let the children suggest several other pairs of numbers from the number line and write comparisons using $<$, $=$, or $>$. Are there any pairs of common fractions that cannot be compared using one of these three symbols? Can any pairs be compared using more than one of these symbols? This is called the **trichotomy principle:** Any rational number is greater than, less than, or equal to any other rational number.

After the children have compared pairs of numbers, ask them to compare several numbers at once using $<$. They may write $\frac{1}{12} < \frac{1}{6} < \frac{1}{4} < \frac{1}{3} < \frac{5}{12} < \frac{1}{2} < \frac{7}{12} < \frac{3}{4} < \frac{5}{6} < \frac{11}{12} < 1$. Is it possible to make a longer chain of numbers? Are there any fractions between $\frac{1}{12}$ and $\frac{2}{12}$? The fact that there is always another rational number between any two rational numbers is called the **density property.**

After children have a good concrete understanding of the rational number concepts, develop more abstract skills with the numbers in different forms. Be sure you do not rush the children into this abstract work before they have mastered the ideas concretely. The following section focuses on developing skills with rational numbers written as common fractions, decimal fractions, and percents.

Developing and Practicing Rational Number Skills

The skills associated with rational numbers are renaming equivalent common fractions, reading and writing decimal fractions, converting common fractions to decimal fractions and percents and vice versa, ordering both common and decimal fractions, and using proportions. These skills involve making the transition from work with manipulative materials to abstract work using either mental calculation, paper and pencil, or calculators or computers. We begin with procedures for renaming common fractions.

Renaming Common Fractions

After children can find equivalent fractions using a variety of concrete models, they are ready to discover more abstract procedures for finding equivalent fractions. Children should have made lists of the equivalent fractions that they found using materials and should have generalized the fact that equivalent fractions may be found by multiplying or dividing the numerator and the denominator by the same number. Ask the children to make a list of at least 10 ways to name 1 ($\frac{1}{1}, \frac{2}{2}, \frac{3}{3}, \ldots$). Ask the children what they notice about the numerator and the denominator of each fraction that is equivalent to 1.

Notice that when you have $\frac{a}{b} \times \frac{c}{c}$ or $\frac{a}{b} \div \frac{c}{c}$ you are multiplying by the identity or dividing by the right-hand iden-

tity 1. Multiplying or dividing by the identity does not change the value of the original number. Let the children make up tables with several names for different common fractions, such as $\frac{1}{2}, \frac{1}{3}, \frac{1}{4}, \frac{2}{3}$, and $\frac{3}{4}$.

After children can list several equivalent fractions for any given fraction, have them practice writing fractions in **simplest terms.** We prefer using *simplest terms* or *simplest form* rather than *reduced,* or *lowest, terms,* because some children will think a fraction has gotten smaller when it is reduced even if they have been working with equivalent fractions.

To find fractions in simplest terms, return to the concrete materials you worked with for finding several ways to name a fraction. Tell the children that when you have a list of equivalent fractions, the one in simplest terms has the smallest number in the denominator, and it is not possible to divide both the numerator and the denominator evenly by a whole number greater than 1. It is in simplest terms because it uses the fewest parts.

After working with physical models, challenge students to simplify a fraction abstractly. The children might suggest looking for any numbers that will divide evenly into both the numerator and the denominator and then continue dividing until no more numbers will divide into both. If you are using a calculator such as the Math Explorer, or the TI73 or TI80 experiment by pushing the "simp" button and the "equals" button when the calculator is displaying a common fraction. What happens if you push the "simp" button more than once? Try it for several different fractions and discuss the results (see Figure 9–20).

Children should find the **greatest common factor** (greatest common divisor) of the numerator and denominator to simplify the fraction in one step. If c is the greatest common factor, then dividing both the numerator and the denominator by c gives you a fraction in simplest form.

After children are comfortable with finding equivalent fractions for a given fraction, have them find equivalent fractions with a common denominator for two or more

```
                          +75/100
ANS▶SIMP
                          +15/20
    FACTOR=5
ANS▶SIMP
                             3/4
    FACTOR=5
■
```

Figure 9–20

common fractions. Have children reverse the process used to simplify fractions, that is, have them multiply a fraction by $\frac{a}{a}$ in order to find equivalent fractions. This skill is used in working with addition, subtraction, and division of common fractions, when it is often necessary to write fractions in a form with a common denominator before any operation can be performed. There are several ways to find common fractions with a common denominator, and three of them are discussed here.

ACTIVITIES

Intermediate (3–6)

Objective: to find a common denominator for two common fractions.

1. Sometimes a common denominator is the denominator of one of the common fractions. This is the case for two fractions such as $\frac{1}{2}$ and $\frac{3}{10}$ or $\frac{3}{4}$ and $\frac{5}{16}$. To rename $\frac{1}{2}$ as tenths, the children should first realize that 10 is a multiple of 2. Ask the children what they must multiply by 2 in order to get 10. Since $2 \times 5 = 10$, the numerator must also be multiplied by 5. Therefore, $\frac{1}{2} = \frac{1 \times 5}{2 \times 5} = \frac{5}{10}$. Let the children practice with several pairs of numbers in which one denominator is a multiple of the other before you introduce pairs of common fractions in which this is not the case. Ask students to compare this to the work they did with fraction circles or other concrete fraction pieces. They may wish to use the pieces to discover and/or verify that these fractions are indeed equivalent.

2. Ask the children to find a common denominator for the fractions $\frac{2}{3}$ and $\frac{3}{4}$. First, ask the children to get out their lists of the equivalence classes of these two common fractions. Find examples of equivalent fractions for $\frac{2}{3}$ that have denominators that also appear on the list of equivalent fractions for $\frac{3}{4}$. The children may find denominators of 12, 24, 36, and 48.

   Tell the children that twelfths are the **least common denominator** since 12 is the smallest number that appears as a denominator in both equivalence classes. Therefore, to write $\frac{2}{3}$ and $\frac{3}{4}$ with the least common denominator, the children would write that $\frac{2}{3} = \frac{8}{12}$ and $\frac{3}{4} = \frac{9}{12}$. Let the children find common denominators for other pairs of fractions and discuss their methods.

3. Sometimes it is necessary to find a common denominator for two fractions when one denominator is not a multiple of the other and it is laborious to list equivalence classes until a common denominator appears. Thus, it is often most efficient to use prime factorization to find the **least common multiple** of the two denominators. Remember that prime numbers are those that have exactly two divisors, the number itself and one. The least common multiple is also the least common denominator.

For example, if you wish to add $\frac{5}{12}$ and $\frac{7}{30}$, first find the prime factorization of the two denominators, 12 and 30. $12 = 2 \times 2 \times 3$ and $30 = 2 \times 3 \times 5$. Put these factors into a Venn diagram such as the one in Figure 9–21.

The union of the two sets is the least common denominator, $2 \times 2 \times 3 \times 5$, or 60. (Notice that the intersection of the two sets is the greatest common factor.) Each of the fractions must be written in sixtieths, the least common multiple. Each numerator is multiplied by the number or numbers in the Venn diagram that do not appear in the denominator of that fraction. The numerator of $\frac{5}{12}$ is multiplied by 5, and the numerator of $\frac{7}{30}$ is multiplied by 2. Thus, $\frac{5}{12} = \frac{5}{2 \times 2 \times 3} = \frac{5 \times 5}{2 \times 2 \times 3 \times 5} = \frac{25}{60}$, and $\frac{7}{30} = \frac{7}{2 \times 3 \times 5} = \frac{7 \times 2}{2 \times 3 \times 5 \times 2} = \frac{14}{60}$. Let the children make up other problems for each other and discuss their solutions.

4. For a fraction with a large number in the denominator, children will probably need to use a factor tree to find the prime factors. To make a factor tree, place the number to be factored at the top and choose two factors that when multiplied give you the original number. Continue until all factors are prime numbers. For example, for 48, begin with 6×8 as shown:

$$48 = 2 \times 2 \times 2 \times 2 \times 3$$
$$= 2^4 \times 3$$

Notice that the order in which the factors are found does not matter. You still end up with the same prime factors. This is called the **Fundamental Law of Arithmetic.**

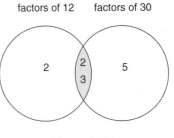

Most textbooks include a chapter on number theory that precedes the unit on operations with common fractions and includes lessons in finding least common multiples and greatest common factors. We also discuss the necessity for finding common denominators in the next chapter when we talk about operations with common fractions.

factors of 12   factors of 30

Figure 9–21

After children understand renaming fractions and can rename fractions in simplest terms and rename two fractions with a common denominator, let them play games that reinforce those skills. Card games, board games, and Bingo are good for this. The following activities are designed to give children practice in renaming common fractions.

ACTIVITIES

Intermediate (3–6)

Objective: to practice finding equivalent fractions.

1. Make a set of cards with fractions on them in both pictorial and numerical form. Make four cards for each of the following fractions: $\frac{1}{6}, \frac{1}{4}, \frac{1}{3}, \frac{1}{2}, \frac{3}{4}, \frac{2}{3}, \frac{5}{6}$, 1. For each fraction, have two pictures depicting the fraction, the fraction itself, and an equivalent fraction. Four sets are shown in Figure 9–22.

   Have the children play a game such as Go Fish. They should try to get four cards with equivalent fractions. A child who gets four equivalent fractions should lay the cards down.

   On each turn, a child should ask, "Do you have any cards showing —?" If the child asked has any of the designated cards, he or she must give them to the asker. If not, the child says, "Go fish." The child who asked then draws a card from the pile. If this card has

the requested fraction, the child may continue asking. If it does not, it is the next child's turn. When all sets of four have been laid down, the child with the most sets is the winner.

After the children become proficient at playing with pictures and numerals, make another set of cards which has just numerals, or encourage the children to make their own cards for the game.

2. Make up Bingo cards with equivalent fractions. The caller's cards may have the following fractions:

B:	$\frac{1}{2}$,	$\frac{4}{5}$,	$\frac{5}{12}$,	$\frac{2}{3}$,	$\frac{3}{4}$,	$\frac{5}{8}$,	$\frac{2}{6}$
I:	$\frac{3}{6}$,	$\frac{4}{5}$,	$\frac{1}{3}$,	$\frac{5}{8}$,	$\frac{5}{6}$,	$\frac{4}{6}$,	$\frac{2}{8}$
N:	$\frac{2}{3}$,	$\frac{2}{9}$,	$\frac{4}{8}$,	$\frac{2}{5}$,	$\frac{3}{5}$,	$\frac{4}{12}$,	$\frac{5}{6}$
G:	$\frac{2}{4}$,	$\frac{10}{12}$,	$\frac{8}{12}$,	$\frac{1}{5}$,	$\frac{2}{3}$,	$\frac{4}{12}$,	$\frac{3}{9}$
O:	$\frac{5}{10}$,	$\frac{5}{15}$,	$\frac{2}{3}$,	$\frac{5}{12}$,	$\frac{1}{4}$,	$\frac{3}{5}$,	$\frac{3}{8}$

One such card is shown in Figure 9–23. Be sure you do not make two cards identical.

When the cards are ready, call the fractions and let the children put markers on the equivalent fractions. The first child to get five in a row wins. Be sure to check the card to make sure the child has covered equivalent fractions.

3. 🖥️ The *Fraction Bars* computer programs by Albert Bennett, Jr., and Albert Bennett, III, available from Scott Resources, are designed to reinforce the concrete work with Fraction Bars. There are seven programs in the series, which begins with basic concepts and proceeds to operations with fractions. All are good for practice after the children have developed the concepts with the concrete materials. Children can practice their skills with equivalent fractions by working with the program on equivalent fractions.

Objective: to determine if two fractions are equivalent.

4. 🖩 After students are competent at finding equivalent fractions, ask them how they would determine if two fractions such as $\frac{18}{24}$ and $\frac{75}{100}$ are equal. The students may try to find a common denominator, which is very

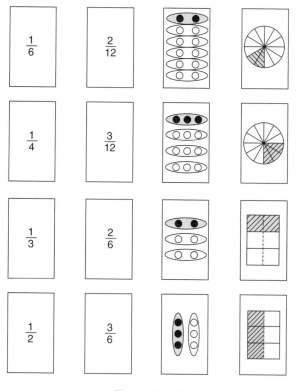

Figure 9–22

B	I	N	G	O
$\frac{3}{6}$	$\frac{8}{10}$	$\frac{6}{10}$	$\frac{1}{4}$	$\frac{6}{16}$
$\frac{9}{12}$	$\frac{3}{9}$	$\frac{1}{3}$	$\frac{1}{2}$	$\frac{10}{24}$
$\frac{4}{6}$	$\frac{1}{2}$	FREE	$\frac{1}{3}$	$\frac{4}{6}$
$\frac{15}{24}$	$\frac{2}{3}$	$\frac{1}{2}$	$\frac{5}{6}$	$\frac{1}{2}$
$\frac{1}{3}$	$\frac{1}{4}$	$\frac{4}{10}$	$\frac{4}{6}$	$\frac{1}{3}$

Figure 9–23

Figure 9–24

time consuming; they may try simplifying both fractions, which in this case would work very well; or they may get out their calculators and divide to determine if both common fractions are equivalent to the same decimal fraction (see Figure 9–24).

Another method that students enjoy is cross multiplying. Ask the students to list several pairs of common fractions that they know are equivalent. They should have fractions in the form $\frac{a}{b} = \frac{c}{d}$. Ask them to multiply $a \times d$ and $b \times c$. Encourage the use of calculators so students may check several pairs without being bogged down by the computations.

After students have cross multiplied with several pairs of equivalent fractions, ask them to compare the findings. Does $a \times d$ always equal $b \times c$? What happens if the original fractions are not equivalent? More advanced students may wish to find out why this works.

Reading and Writing Decimal Fractions

After students understand the concepts of decimal fractions and can extend the place value into hundredths and thousandths, have them practice both reading and writing decimal fractions. Be sure this abstract work is based on a solid concrete foundation. The following activities are designed to give students practice reading and writing decimal fractions.

ACTIVITIES

Intermediate (4–6)

Objective: to practice reading and displaying decimal fractions.

1. Make a set of cards with decimal fractions written in both numerals and words. On one card, write a decimal fraction in words and on another write the same decimal fraction in numerals, such as three hundredths and 0.03. Make about 15 such pairs.

   Let the students use the cards to play the Match Game. Turn all the cards face down on the table in front of the students. The students should take turns turning over a pair of cards. The goal is to get one numeral card and one word card that show the same decimal fraction. If the two cards match, the student gets to keep the cards and takes another turn. If the cards do not match, they are placed face down on the table in their original positions and it is the next person's turn. Play continues until all the cards have been matched. The player with the most matches at the end is the winner.

   Students who still need work on matching the decimal fractions to pictorial representations can play this same game matching pictures and numerals or words. It is helpful in both variations of the game to have an answer key with which to check any matches that the players are not sure of.

2. Ask each student to make a decimal place-value chart. Have each student fold a piece of tagboard or make a pocket chart like the one in Figure 9–25 by folding and stapling a piece of oaktag.

   Give each student two sets of cards with the numerals 0–9 on them. The caller should then read numbers such as thirty-five and four hundred twenty-six thousandths. The players should place the numeral cards in the correct positions and hold the chart up for the caller to check. The teacher or student caller may then quickly check to see which students are correctly displaying the number.

   This activity may be done by the whole class, small groups, or a pair of children working alone. For an-

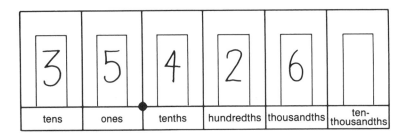

Figure 9–25

other variation of this activity, furnish each child with a calculator and ask the children to put the numbers in the calculator as they are read. You or a caller may then check each calculator display, or the children may compare their displays.

Renaming Common Fractions, Decimal Fractions, and Percents

After children understand the concepts of fractions in common, decimal, and percent form and are proficient at naming equivalent fractions and reading and writing decimal fractions, they are ready to learn to rename fractions as decimals or percents and vice versa. Results from the Fourth National Assessment of Educational Progress show that students have difficulty with this. Only 30 percent of seventh-graders could express 0.9 as a percent and 8 percent as a decimal (Kouba, Brown, Carpenter, Lindquist, Silver, and Swafford, 1988).

Results from the 1996 National Assessment of Educational Progress (NAEP) showed general progress in the United States over earlier mathematics assessments, but improvement is still needed. Results of the Third International Mathematics and Science Study show that middle school students in the United States have difficulty in renaming simple fractions. When presented with a grid of 24 squares and asked to shade $\frac{5}{8}$ of them, only 43 percent of U. S. eighth graders did this correctly. Nearly $\frac{1}{4}$ of the eighth graders shaded in 5 squares rather than the correct 15 squares. By contrast, 92 percent of students in Singapore, 81 percent of Korean students and 80 percent of Japanese students answered this correctly. The international average was 52 percent correct (ENC, 1998). On a similar question from the 1996 National Assessment of Educational Progress, 65 percent of the eighth graders correctly identified 4 shaded squares on a grid of 12 squares as $\frac{1}{3}$ on a multiple choice item where the other choices were $\frac{1}{6}, \frac{1}{5}, \frac{1}{4}, \frac{1}{3}$, or $\frac{1}{2}$ (NCES, 1998, p. 29).

Children who can read a decimal fraction should also be able to write it in common fraction form. Children who can tell you that 0.23 is 23 hundredths should also be able to write it as $\frac{23}{100}$. When they realize that *percent* simply means "per hundred," they can also write it as 23 percent, or 23%. Some fractions must be simplified once they are written in common fraction form, and children should be reminded of that.

Converting a common fraction to a decimal may not be as easy as converting a decimal to a common fraction because just reading a common fraction may not tell you its decimal form. Reminding the children that one meaning for a common fraction is division can help them make the conversion. The common fraction $\frac{5}{6}$ is the same as 5 divided by 6. The division may be done very quickly on the calculator or slightly more laboriously by hand.

Dividing fractions may be the children's first introduction to nonterminating decimals. Children will realize as they divide 5 by 6 that they could go on forever and never reach a point where there is no remainder. Their answer of .8333333 . . . will end in 3 no matter how long they continue the division. Other fractions such as $\frac{1}{2}, \frac{1}{4}, \frac{3}{5}$, and $\frac{7}{10}$ terminate in a few places.

Have students explore converting common fractions to decimal fractions to see if they can predict which common fractions will terminate and which will not. They may need the hint that it will help to first write each fraction in simplest terms and then to factor the denominator into prime factors. Compare the prime factors to the factors of the powers of ten. Using a calculator will help the students explore a greater number of conversions. Lead students to the generalization that whenever the denominator has only 2s and/or 5s as factors, the decimal equivalent will terminate. Otherwise, the common fraction will be equivalent to a repeating decimal. Children who are learning to write computer programs may wish to write a program to convert common fractions to decimals and percents and vice versa.

Note that all rational numbers can be written either as terminating or repeating decimals. Nonrepeating decimals such as the decimal expansion of pi or the square root of 2 or decimals such as 0.101001000100001 . . . are irrational numbers.

After students are comfortable converting decimal fractions to common fractions and common fractions to decimal fractions, they may learn to convert decimal fractions to percents. Begin with decimal fractions in hundredths. These are very easy to convert to percents, since *percent* means per hundred. For example, 0.16 is simply 16 percent (16%).

When students can convert hundredths to percent, ask them to try fractions that are in tenths. They may notice that 0.3 = 0.30 and is therefore equal to 30 percent (30%). (You may need to ask them how many hundredths are equal to 0.3 if they do not notice this on their own.)

After students can convert tenths and hundredths to percents, try other decimal fractions, such as 0.005. Ask the students if this is more or less than 1%. They may need to return to the decimal squares or other pictorial materials to determine that this is $\frac{1}{2}$ of 0.01 and is therefore $\frac{1}{2}$% or 0.5%.

When the students can successfully convert several decimal fractions to percents, ask the students what they notice about the decimal point as they move from a decimal fraction to a percent. Yes, it moves two places to the right. Ask, "How do you convert a percent back to a decimal?" Move the decimal point two places back to the left. If students have a "%" key on their calculators, have them explore its use at this point.

After students can easily convert decimal fractions to percents and vice versa, ask them how they would convert a common fraction to a percent. For most, the easiest method is probably to convert the common fraction to a decimal fraction and then to convert the decimal fraction to a percent. Calculators come in handy when using this method.

The following activities are designed to give students practice in converting decimal fractions, common fractions, and percents.

ACTIVITIES

Middle Grades (5–8)

Objective: to practice converting decimal fractions, common fractions, and percents.

1. The games described earlier for practice with renaming common fractions and with reading and writing decimal fractions may be adapted for practice with renaming decimal fractions, common fractions, and percents. Bingo cards can be made with common fractions on the calling cards and decimal fractions and/or percents on the Bingo cards. Children can play a match game in which they match a card with a common fraction to a card with an equivalent decimal fraction to a card with an equivalent percent. Card games such as Old Maid can also be adapted so that children match these three types of cards.

   Encourage students to create other games of their own to practice making conversions. Keep calculators handy as the children play the games so that the children may check their work.

Ordering Common and Decimal Fractions

After students can find equivalent common fractions and read and write decimal fractions, they are ready to practice ordering both common and decimal fractions. Often, children must determine such things as which of two fractions is greater or whether a given fraction is greater, less than, equal to, or between other fractions. Many children do not have accurate strategies for determining the relative sizes of rational numbers. They may have difficulty because of the infinite number of ways of writing equivalent fractions or because of the denseness of rational numbers. It is difficult for children to realize that there is always another rational number between any two given rational numbers, which is not true for whole numbers.

Children may need to return to some of the work with concrete materials before they begin to practice ordering fractions on an abstract level. The following activities

are designed to give the children practice in ordering both common and decimal fractions. Be sure to discuss strategies with the children as they work. Note that it is not always possible to determine incorrect strategies by simply looking at mistakes on the children's papers.

ACTIVITIES

Intermediate (4–6)

Objective: to practice ordering common and decimal fractions.

1. Ask the children to predict, and then use a concrete material such as the circular regions to determine, which fraction in each of the following pairs is the greater:

$$\frac{1}{2} \qquad \frac{3}{4}$$
$$\frac{2}{3} \qquad \frac{5}{6}$$
$$\frac{3}{8} \qquad \frac{3}{5}$$
$$\frac{3}{8} \qquad \frac{2}{5}$$
$$\frac{1}{3} \qquad \frac{3}{8}$$

   Have the children explain why they made the predictions that they did and tell whether or not they were right. Ask children whose predictions were wrong to explain why the predictions were wrong. Can you tell which is larger by looking only at the numerator or only at the denominator?

   When children can make fairly accurate estimates of the sizes of the fractions, ask them to cross-multiply each pair of fractions the way they did to determine if the two fractions were equivalent and to observe the findings. Ask, "For each pair of common fractions $\frac{a}{b}$ and $\frac{c}{d}$, what is the relationship of the fractions if $ad > bc$? What is the relationship if $ad < bc$?" Cross-multiply with several pairs of fractions and check the results by using concrete materials, converting both fractions to a common denominator or using a calculator to convert both common fractions to decimal fractions. Let the children come up with a generalization. Does the generalization fit their intuitive ideas about ordering fractions?

2. There are computer games designed to give children practice in working with decimals, not only in ordering them but also in performing operations with them. *Get to the Point* by Judah Schwartz, available from Sunburst, consists of three games, one of which is designed to help children order decimals. Children can practice their skills and have fun at the same time.

3. A computer program that students might enjoy using to learn fraction, decimal, and percent

concepts is *Fraction Attraction,* available from Sunburst. In this program, students visit a multimedia amusement park where they engage in four activities designed to build and reinforce concepts of rational numbers. Frac-Track is a racetrack game where horses move around the track based on fractions, decimals, and percents that students choose. In Frac-o-Wheel, varying representations of equivalent fractions are chosen to move a Ferris wheel to load or unload passengers. Whack-a-Frac builds further on the idea of equivalent fractions, and Fuzzy Fracs requires that students understand concepts of ordering and relative size as they attempt to knock down figures in a carnival game in size order.

You also might wish to view the Annenburg middle grades assessment video to watch fifth grade students play a Fraction Track game where students must use equivalent fractions to move game pieces from one side of the game board to the other.

4. The game *Pyramid* can be played by two or more children. The first child must name a common fraction between 0 and 1 and write it on the bottom line of a sheet of paper. This child should then use the calculator to convert the common fraction to a decimal fraction and write the decimal fraction on the same line next to the common fraction. The next child must then name another common fraction that is greater than the first but still less than 1. This common fraction and its decimal fraction equivalent are then written on the next line of the pyramid. Play continues with larger and larger common fractions until the fraction named is not larger than the previous one, until the fraction named is larger than 1, until a time limit is reached, or until the children realize that the game could go on for an infinite number of moves and they tire of it. The beginning of a game is shown below:

$$\frac{1}{2} = 0.5$$

$$\frac{2}{5} = 0.4$$

$$\frac{3}{8} = 0.375$$

$$\frac{1}{3} = 0.333\ldots$$

$$\frac{1}{4} = 0.25 \quad \frac{2}{9} = 0.222\ldots$$

$$\frac{1}{6} = 0.1666\ldots$$

$$\frac{3}{8} = 0.125$$

$$0$$

Children may make the game harder by not allowing denominators that are powers of ten or not allowing unit fractions. To play this game well, some children may need to return to the activities for building the concepts of ordering common and decimal fractions.

Children may explore what happens to a repeating decimal when it is displayed on the calculator, since the calculator obviously cannot show an infinite number of decimal places. Calculators either round or truncate the decimals. When the calculator *truncates* a decimal, it merely cuts off all the decimal places beyond those that it can display. When the calculator *rounds* a decimal, if the first digit beyond the last digit on the display is less than 5, the last digit is not changed. If the first digit beyond the last digit on the display is greater than 5, the last digit is rounded up. If the first digit beyond the last digit on the display is 5, most calculators round up, although the rules vary.

Let the children try a fraction such as $\frac{2}{3}$ to see the response on the calculator. Some calculators will display 0.6666666, and some will display 0.6666667. Ask the children which is more accurate. The calculator function may be compared to a computer that continues to divide until told to stop when converting common fractions to repeating decimals.

Proportions

One of the uses of common fractions is to show a ratio of one part to another part. A **proportion** consists of two equal ratios. If you know that there are 2 girls for every 3 boys in the class and you know the whole class has 10 girls, you may use a proportion to find the total number of boys in the class. Set up the proportion as follows:

$$\frac{2 \text{ girls}}{3 \text{ boys}} = \frac{10 \text{ girls}}{n \text{ boys}}$$

The technique of cross-multiplying works in solving a proportion. In this example, when you cross-multiply, you get $2 \times n = 3 \times 10$. If $2n = 30$, then $n = 15$. The total number of boys in the class is 15.

Children may use proportions to solve problems involving percents and inverse proportions to solve problems involving more complex relationships such as comparing the number of teeth in a gear to the number of rotations it will make. Textbooks for the middle grades give several more examples. However, don't assume that children understand proportions after working these examples abstractly. Proportional reasoning is one of the signs of formal operational thinking, and many adults have difficulty with formal operational thinking. Try some of the following questions yourself (assume letters not mentioned will remain the same):

$\dfrac{a}{b} = \dfrac{c}{d}$ What will happen to *c* if *a* gets larger?

$\dfrac{e}{f} = \dfrac{g}{h}$ What will happen to *h* if *e* gets larger?

$\dfrac{j}{k} = \dfrac{l}{m}$ What will happen to *l* if *k* gets smaller?

Did you have difficulty with any of these? Try to explain your reasoning to a classmate. Do you feel that you could explain proportions well to children? Explaining on an abstract level is difficult. Try returning to concrete examples for your explanations. You may need to substitute numerals for the letters. Now try this one:

The red string is 3 paper clips long. The blue string is 5 paper clips long. If you measure the red string in Bingo chips, you find it is 6 chips long. How many chips will it take to measure the blue string?

Was this any easier? Did you draw a picture or visualize the answer mentally? How does this question compare to the earlier ones? Keep these activities in mind as you introduce proportions to the children. Be sure to include concrete examples to help children develop the concepts. The following activities give a very brief idea of some of the uses for proportions. Be sure to add other ideas of your own.

ACTIVITIES

Middle Grades (5–8)

Objective: to practice using proportions.

1. Proportions are used frequently in children's everyday lives. Give the children some examples of their uses and ask them to make up their own problems using proportions or to collect examples of problems they encounter, say, in the grocery store or while reading the newspaper. The following are a few examples:

- José is baking a birthday cake. The recipe feeds 12 and calls for 3 eggs. José is planning a large party and wants to make a cake for 36 people. How many eggs does he need? Use the ratio $\frac{3}{12} = \frac{n}{36}$ or $\frac{3}{n} = \frac{12}{36}$. Discuss with the children how to set up the proportion. There are two other proportions the children may set up that would be equivalent to these. Can you find them?
- Mrs. Montoya is buying prizes for José's party. The prizes are 3 for $.50. Mrs. Montoya wishes to buy 36 prizes. How much will they cost? How do you decide on the proportions $\frac{3}{\$.50} = \frac{36}{n}$ or $\frac{3}{36} = \frac{\$.50}{n}$?
- Mishon is building a scale model of a car to give José for his birthday. The scale is 5 centimeters per meter. If the model is 30 centimeters long, how long is the car?

$$\frac{5 \text{ centimeters}}{1 \text{ meter}} = \frac{30 \text{ centimeters}}{n \text{ meters}}$$

or

$$\frac{5}{30} = \frac{1}{n}$$

Children may wish to use physical materials to model each of these problems. Be sure to connect the work they are doing concretely to the abstract solution of the equations.

Objective: to practice using proportions to solve percent problems.

2. One method of solving problems involving percents is through the use of the following proportion:

$$\frac{\text{rate}}{100} = \frac{\text{percentage}}{\text{base}}$$

This proportion works regardless of whether the children need to find the rate, the percentage, or the base in a given problem. For example, a store may be having a sale on all its jeans. In one case, the jeans originally cost $20 (base). They have been reduced by $5 (percentage) and you wish to find the percent of the original cost that the reduction represents. Use the proportion $\frac{n}{100} = \frac{\$5}{\$20}$. By cross-multiplying, you find that $\$20 \times n = 100 \times \$5$, or $20n = 500$, or $n = 25$ percent. The jeans are marked down by 25 percent of the original cost.

In another problem, you see a sign that says "20% off everything on this rack." You wish to buy a pair of jeans that were originally $30 and want to find out how much you will save buying them on sale. Again, you can use the proportion to solve the problem. This time, you know the percent and the base and wish to find the percentage. The proportion is $\frac{20}{100} = \frac{\$n}{\$30}$. By cross-multiplying, you find that $20 \times \$30 = \$n \times 100$, or $100n = 600$, or $n = \$6$. You will save $6 on the jeans.

In the third case, the sign says that the jeans have been marked down 40% and that you will save $10 on each pair. What was the original cost of the jeans? This time, you know the percent and the percentage and you wish to find the base. Use the same proportion. The proportion is $\frac{40}{100} = \frac{\$10}{\$n}$. By cross-multiplying, you find that $40 \times \$n = 100 \times \$10$, or $40n = 1,000$, or $n = \$25$. The jeans originally cost $25. The children will find many more examples of ways proportions can be used, not only in their textbooks but also in their own shopping. You may wish to introduce a unit on becoming a wise consumer and ask children to bring in examples of percent problems from their own experiences. The newspaper is a rich source of problems. The children may be surprised to find the number of examples of store sales that do not report the percents correctly. Challenge the children to find examples of misleading or incorrect ads in the paper. They may even wish to inform the store managers of their mistakes.

Ask the children if it makes a difference if the percents are reported as a percent of the original cost or as a percent of the discounted cost. Let the children work several examples to see that it does indeed make a difference. Encourage children to ask questions and explore other aspects of percents. They may even be able to teach their parents and other adults some aspects of becoming wise consumers.

Objective: to practice using proportions with inverse relationships.

3. If children have worked with the gears mentioned earlier in the chapter, they should have noticed that the larger gears with more teeth went around fewer times. If a gear with 10 teeth turned a gear with 5 teeth, the larger gear went around only $\frac{1}{2}$ the number of times that the smaller gear went around. The proportion for the gears is

$$\frac{\text{the number of teeth in the first gear}}{\text{the number of teeth in the second gear}} =$$

$$\frac{\text{the number of turns of the second gear}}{\text{the number of turns of the first gear}}$$

If the larger gear turns 3 times, the proportion is $\frac{10}{5} = \frac{n}{3}$, where n is the number of turns for the smaller gear. By cross-multiplying, you get $10 \times 3 = 5 \times n$, or $30 = 5n$, or $n = 6$. The smaller gear turns 6 times as the larger gear turns 3 times. This works because the number of teeth on one gear multiplied by the number of turns that gear makes is a constant. Therefore, the number of teeth on the first gear times the number of turns of the first gear is equal to the number of teeth on the second gear times the number of turns of the second gear.

The computer program *Gears* by Robert Kimbal and Dave Donoghue, available from Sunburst, gives children the opportunity to collect data on gear rotation through simulation and then to practice solving problems involving this inverse proportion by asking children to select the number of gears and their sizes to match a given problem. Children may also create challenges for each other with the program.

Estimating and Mental Calculating

Test results from the Fourth National Assessment of Educational Progress (Kouba, Brown, Carpenter, Lindquist, Silver, and Swafford, 1988) show that students generally are poor at estimations that involve common or decimal fractions. As we rely more on calculators and computers, estimation and mental calculation skills become increasingly important. The 1992 National Assessment of Educational Progress showed that calculator usage had increased since 1990, and that at grades 8 and 12, students who used a calculator at least weekly had higher mathematics proficiency than their counterparts who never or

hardly ever used a calculator in math class (Dossey, Mullis, Gorman, and Latham, 1994, p. 89). The Third International Mathematics and Science Study showed that 98 percent of eighth graders in the United States reported having a calculator available at home and 59 percent had a computer available. Over 60 percent of the students reported using calculators nearly every day in class (Beaton, et al., 1996, p. 163–164). Children should be encouraged to estimate or calculate mentally in activities involving rational numbers just as they were in whole number activities.

Some of the activities mentioned earlier, such as the Pyramid Game, require that children be able to estimate whether one fraction is larger than another. There are also a number of times when children should be able to accurately calculate an answer mentally. For example, they should know the common fraction equivalents for percents that they encounter every day. Children should have several estimation and mental calculation experiences as they learn rational number skills. The activities presented below give a few more ideas for practicing estimation and mental calculation skills. The activities are listed for a wide range of grade levels because although children should ideally learn to estimate at the same time that they first learn fractions, many children do not. Therefore, the activities may be used with students in the middle grades as well.

ACTIVITIES

Elementary (2–8)

Objective: to develop estimation skills with common fractions.

1. Children should be able to use certain model fractions to compare various amounts. Give children experiences with $\frac{1}{2}$, $\frac{1}{4}$, and $\frac{3}{4}$ so that they may estimate whether other amounts are more or less than these. Begin by letting children estimate when something is half full. Use a glass container and let children pour beans into it until they believe it is half full. After they fill it to what they think is half full, have them empty the beans into another container and again fill the container half full with different beans. Leave these beans in the container and then pour the first amount of beans back into the container. If both estimates were good, the container should be full. Or, measure the total container and the amount poured into it to see how close the amount is to $\frac{1}{2}$ of the container.

After the children can estimate $\frac{1}{2}$ fairly well, pour varying amounts into the container and ask the children if the amounts are more or less than $\frac{1}{2}$. When the children can accurately compare amounts to $\frac{1}{2}$, then repeat the activity with $\frac{1}{4}$ and $\frac{3}{4}$. Older children with more estimation experience may use a liter and estimate amounts in tenths of a liter (deciliters).

2. Ask children to keep a list of the times outside of school that they need to use common or decimal fractions to estimate. They may include some of the following:

- Part of an hour to eat breakfast, take a bath, do homework, and so on.
- Part of a mile or kilometer to walk to a friend's house, the store, or to school.
- Part of a quart or liter of milk drunk for dinner.
- Part of a cake or pie eaten for dessert.
- Part of a pound or kilogram of meat or cheese to buy for lunch.

Children can think of many other examples themselves. Encourage them to share the techniques they use to estimate.

Objective: to practice mental conversion of percents to common fractions.

3. Older students should have experience in converting percents to common fractions mentally because of the widespread use of percents in everyday life. Bring in ads from department store sales and look for the percents that are used. Ask the students to tally how often different percents are used in the ads. They will probably find frequent use of percents that convert to tenths, thirds, fourths, and halves.

4. In many parts of the country, it is common practice to leave a 15 percent tip at a restaurant. Ask the students to determine a method for finding a 15 percent tip based on knowing 10 percent. They will probably tell you that 5 percent is $\frac{1}{2}$ of 10 percent, and therefore, to find 15 percent, you can add 10 percent and 5 percent. Ask students to bring in restaurant receipts and practice finding 15 percent of the total.

Ask the children the benefits of knowing the common fraction equivalents. Discuss how to use proportions to find discounts if you know the common fraction equivalents of the commonly used percents. Ask the children how they convert 20 percent, 30 percent, 40 percent, . . . to common fractions if they know that 10 percent is $\frac{1}{10}$. If 33.3 percent is $\frac{1}{3}$, what is $\frac{2}{3}$? If 25 percent is $\frac{1}{4}$, what is $\frac{3}{4}$? If an item is marked 25 percent off, how can you use the common fraction equivalent to find the discount? Let the children ask similar questions of their own and share their strategies with each other.

Solving and Creating Problems

Throughout this chapter, we have mentioned a number of opportunities for children to solve problems and to create problems of their own, which they will then solve

or which their classmates will solve. Because of the importance of this topic, more ideas for problem solving and problem creating are included here. As with any other topic, problem creating and solving should become the child's natural approach to work with rational numbers.

ACTIVITIES

Intermediate (3–8)

Objective: to explore relationships among common fractions, recognizing that each fraction may be represented in a number of different ways.

1. Pattern blocks are designed so that the areas of many of the blocks are multiples of the areas of other blocks. This makes them well-designed for exploring fractional relationships. The book *Fractions with Pattern Blocks,* by Mathew E. Zullie, available from Creative Publications, suggests many activities for the exploration of these relationships. Many of the activities require that the children use problem solving and higher-level thinking strategies.

Have the children use orange squares, uncolored parallelograms, green triangles, blue rhombuses, red trapezoids, and yellow hexagons for these activities. Ask, "If the yellow hexagon represents 1, what are the values of each of the other pieces?" If the children have difficulty determining the other values, ask, "How many green triangles does it take to cover the yellow hexagon? How many red trapezoids does it take to cover the hexagon? How many triangles does it take to cover the parallelogram?"

Next, challenge the children to find as many examples as they can that show $\frac{1}{3}$ using any number of pattern blocks.

- *Understanding the problem.* I will need to find ways to show $\frac{1}{3}$ using pattern blocks. This means that I should look for single blocks or groups of blocks that can represent the value of 1 (unit). Then I will try to find blocks to represent $\frac{1}{3}$. I will try also to find other ways to make a unit.
- *Devising a plan.* One way I can solve this problem is to take 3 blocks of one shape—for example, 3 orange squares. Then I place them together to form a row. This rectangular row will have the value of 1. Any orange square is $\frac{1}{3}$ of the row. Another way to solve the problem is to look for combinations of blocks that can be placed together into shapes to represent 1. For example, a blue rhombus combined with a green triangle can have the value of 1. Then a green triangle has the value of $\frac{1}{3}$. I will try some of these ways.

- *Carrying out the plan.* I can place 3 of the uncolored parallelograms together to make a shape with the value of 1. One of the parallelograms represents $\frac{1}{3}$ of the unit shape. That works also with 3 green triangles, orange squares, blue rhombuses, red trapezoids, and yellow hexagons.
- I can also use a single red trapezoid as the unit. Then a green triangle represents $\frac{1}{3}$. Another combination representing the value of 1 is 2 red trapezoids. Then a blue rhombus represents $\frac{1}{3}$. If a yellow hexagon and a red trapezoid are combined into a unit, a red trapezoid represents $\frac{1}{3}$. Still another solution is to use 6 green triangles as a unit; then 2 green triangles represent $\frac{1}{3}$. I have found at least ten different ways to show $\frac{1}{3}$ using the pattern blocks.
- Looking back. I need to check to make sure each of the fraction models I made shows the fraction $\frac{1}{3}$. I will then try to generalize my solutions. I can continue to use more blocks to show the unit and try to find other examples in which more than one block is used to show the fraction $\frac{1}{3}$.

Encourage the children to make up questions of their own. Children can make designs to represent the unit and trace the outline. Have them trade outlines and challenge each other to find various fractional amounts of the unit designs. Is there more than one solution for each design? Let the children find out.

2. Earlier in this chapter, we suggested that you have the children explore many ways to show $\frac{1}{2}$ using paper folding and Cuisenaire rods. A similar activity should be repeated using other materials and other fractions.

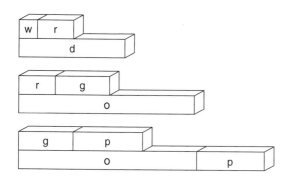

Ask the children to make two trains of Cuisenaire rods such that one train is $\frac{1}{2}$ the length of the other train. This will help the children later when they learn to use the rods to show addition of fractions. Ask the children to use the rods to show other fractional relationships, such as $\frac{2}{3}$, $\frac{3}{4}$, and 0.6.

After the children can find these relationships, tell them that the dark-green rod represents 1 and ask them to find the rod for $\frac{1}{3}$. If the dark-green rod represents 2, which rod is $\frac{1}{3}$? Let the children challenge

each other with problems of their own. Is it always possible to find a rod to represent a given fraction? Why not?

Grouping Students for Learning Rational Number Concepts

Because the concepts of rational numbers and the rules for operations with them frequently are different from the concepts and rules that students have for whole numbers, it is important that students be encouraged to explore these ideas concretely in small groups to encourage open discussion of ideas. When younger students are first discovering the concepts of fractions, they can work in groups of two, three, or more to find ways to divide different amounts of materials equally among the members of the group. For example, three students may be given a large sheet of paper and asked to fold it and then cut along the folds so that each person in the group has the same amount of paper, or four students may be given a bottle of juice or a bag of peanuts to share equally. In each case, discuss the fractional parts that are found and compare the methods used by one group to those used by another.

When students have mastered the concepts of rational numbers, they may work in groups to expand upon these ideas. Ask a group of four to brainstorm everything they know about the fraction $\frac{3}{4}$ or to write equivalent names for $\frac{3}{4}$ in as many ways as possible. They may also list all the ways in which they see rational numbers being used every day.

Communicating Learning of Rational Number Concepts

Payne and Towsley (1990) state that work with fractions and decimals should be mostly oral in grades K–4 and that it should be only oral in grades K–2, using models and realistic problems. Children of this age are not ready for the abstract symbolic notation of fractions. Even in grades 5–8, they recommend that all work begin with concrete models, realistic problems, and oral language. This oral communication of ideas is essential to the development of the concepts of rational numbers. Mack (1990) notes that while students bring a rich informal background to the study of rational numbers through real-life situations, this knowledge is not connected to the abstract symbols and procedures. Indeed, knowledge of rote procedures may actually hinder students in building on prior knowledge. If students try to learn abstract symbols and procedures before they are given a chance to discuss their understanding of rational number concepts

Pieces of Eighths

Jerome wanted to share a pizza with seven friends. He said, "I will cut the pizza into eighths. I will make eight pieces." This picture shows how Jerome's pizza looked when he finished.

1. On the lines below, tell what you think about the way Jerome cut the pizza. Did he cut the pizza into eighths?

   _____

   _____

   _____

2. Show how you would divide the pizza fairly among eight children.

Copyright © 1997 by Kendall/Hunt Publishing Company

Fraction Finale   Unit 18 · Lesson 5 **205**

Figure 9–26 From *Math Trailblazers* Student Guide, Grade One, by TIMS. Copyright © 1997 by Kendall/Hunt Publishing Company. Used with permission.

Math Program

The first-grade page shown in Figure 9–26 is from the Student Guide of *Math Trail-blazers,* an elementary mathematics curriculum project funded by the National Science Foundation and developed as part of the Teaching Integrated Mathematics and Science Project (TIMS). This program is based on the belief that children deserve a challenging mathematics curriculum and that mathematics is best learned through solving many different kinds of problems. Many of the problems involve making connections between the mathematics learned in school and that used in everyday life as seen in this problem.

One of the homework assignments associated with this chapter includes asking students and their families to find and discuss six items at home that come in halves or fourths. Some of the suggestions include crackers, milk (half gallon), and butter (quarter pound sticks). In addition, students fold and color paper shapes as they explore halves, fourths, and eighths.

Notice that even the first graders are expected to write about their mathematical understanding. Reading, writing, and talking are all used in the mathematics classes to help students construct mathematical concepts on a higher level. This is in keeping with the philosophy of the program that children can handle more difficult mathematics and science than is often assumed. In addition to the fraction concepts shown here, the program also includes measurement, data collection, statistics, geometry, ratio, probability, graphing, algebra, and patterns and relationships, all introduced through problem solving and applications.

orally, they may never develop a true understanding of rational numbers.

Children could write about fractions in their daily journals. Younger children might draw or collect pictures of things that represent one-half. This might include a picture of a half-full glass of milk, a drawing of a half-dollar, a clock that shows half past the hour, and a line segment that is $\frac{1}{2}$-inch long. Third- or fourth-grade students might write a journal entry describing how to find $\frac{1}{2}$ or $\frac{1}{3}$ of a set of objects such as 1 dozen eggs, all the students in the class, or all the cookies on a plate.

Connecting Learning of Rational Numbers

Mr. Winkler's primary class has just finished reading *The Doorbell Rang* by Pat Hutchins. In the story, Mom has just finished making a batch of cookies that two children are getting ready to share when the doorbell rings and a third child enters. Just as the three children get ready to share the cookies, a fourth child rings the bell. Before these children can eat, two more children arrive. Each time children arrive in the story, the class has discussed new fractions. They are using a dozen counters to represent the cookies, and they are determining how many cookies each child would get if they had $\frac{1}{2}$, $\frac{1}{3}$, $\frac{1}{4}$, $\frac{1}{6}$ or $\frac{1}{12}$ of the total number of cookies. Mustapha says that this is just like the problems they did with division last month. When Mr. Winkler finishes reading the story, the class decides they would like to act the story out with real cookies. Mr. Winkler agrees to bring in a simple cookie recipe and talk to the cooks in the school cafeteria about using the oven. Each child will talk to their parents about furnishing one of the ingredients for the cookies. Mr. Winkler knows that the recipes will give the students even more work with fractions.

Other children's books that can be used to introduce fraction concepts include *Gator Pie* by Louise Mathews and *Eating Fractions* by Bruce MacMillan. You might also wish to view the *Communication* or *Cookies to Share* videos from Annenburg Video Library to observe a group of fourth graders as they explore fraction and decimal concepts.

Mr. Howsam's seventh- and eighth-grade academic team has entered a statewide competition involving the stock market sponsored by the Economic Council. They have been number one in the district and number five in the state for the last five weeks. They have had many heated discussions about buying and selling stocks that rise or fall fractions of a point. Today, Geraldine enters the team meeting with a long face. Their best stock has fallen 11.25 points, and they know that this big drop will cause their team to drop off the list of the top 10 teams. The academic team spends most of the meeting trying to decide what to do about this stock.

A stock market project designed for middle grades students using real-time data from the New York Stock Exchange is available on-line at http://www.ncsa.uiuc.edu/edu/RSE/RSEyellow/gnb.html.

Assessing Learning of Rational Numbers

As with other concepts, children should be assessed informally as well as formally on their rational number concepts. As children work with concrete materials, keep track of which children demonstrate competence with the rational number concepts and skills and which children are still having difficulty. For additional instruction, group together children having difficulty with the same concepts or skills. Let the other students explore some of the applications of rational numbers.

Dorgan (1994) in a study of three 1992 textbook series for grades 1–5 noted that while textbooks offer opportunities for making connections between pictorial and symbolic representations, there are several areas in which the texts have limited value, including "the development of qualitative reasoning, the building of connections among various modes of representation, and the growth of communication skills" (p. 155). She notes that a student's development of a strong foundation in fraction concepts depends more on the way in which the teacher chooses to use the text than on the text itself.

As you assess children, present problems in a variety of ways, since some children may be able to perform satisfactorily using one model or one type of presentation but not another. Differences are found in performance when children are asked to create their own models for a given rational number rather than to select a model from a number of choices, or when they are asked to write the correct common fraction to match a given picture rather than to select or create a picture to match the fraction. Some children can select the correct model from concrete materials but not from pictures, or can draw a picture but not create a concrete model such as paper folding. Children may select or create the correct model using areas but not using a number line. It is therefore important to present rational number tasks to children using a variety of models and a variety of methods of presentation.

For students in the intermediate grades and beyond, be sure to include portfolio tasks that look at students' concepts of rational numbers. You might ask students to write a detailed description of how they decide on relative size of two different fractions or other rational numbers. They should include diagrams of a variety of different models in their descriptions, such as number lines, area models, volume models, and sets of discrete objects, as well as descriptions of times in everyday life when this concept is important, such as deciding how much stocks have gone up or down as they move from .62 to .75 and estimating which sweater is the best buy if one was $30 and is marked down 25 percent and the other was $33 and is marked down 33 percent.

Some assessment tasks may be paper-and-pencil or calculator tests but others should be individual interviews in order to get the clearest picture of the child's conceptions or misconceptions about rational numbers. Following are some of the common problems that arise as children work with rational numbers.

1. Some children do not realize that in the part-whole model of a fraction, the parts must be of equal size. They may give some of the responses shown in Figure 9–27. Children having difficulty with the part-whole concept should return to work with concrete materials such as paper folding. Have them cut out the regions to show that all halves, thirds, fourths, and so on take up the same amount of area even if they are not congruent.

2. Some children give a ratio answer when a part-whole answer is expected. They may give the responses shown in Figure 9–28.

   This problem is related to difficulty with the Piagetian tasks of class inclusion and reversibility. Children may have difficulty realizing that in the part-

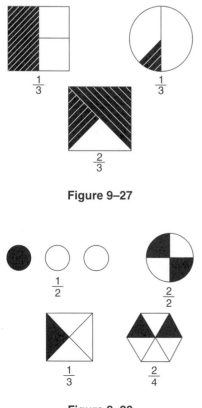

Figure 9–27

Figure 9–28

whole model, the fractional part must be compared back to the whole that includes it; they compare one part to the other parts. Or they may not realize that something divided into two halves will again become one whole when you put the two halves back together. Such children need more experience manipulating concrete models and discussing their meanings before they continue with abstract work with fractions.

3. Some children have difficulty writing a common fraction as a division problem. They think that $\frac{2}{3}$ means $3 \div 2$ rather than the other way around. This misunderstanding is particularly troublesome as children attempt to convert common fractions to decimal fractions.

   Children will also need instruction on which number to put into the calculator first when they divide. Remind them that the numerator is the dividend and the denominator is the divisor. You may also need to return to the concrete models and remind them that the number in the numerator tells you the number you begin with and the number in the denominator tells the number of parts it is being divided into.

4. Some children do not realize that a common fraction is a single number. They think of it as two numbers, one sitting on top of the other. This causes them to work with the numbers separately when they perform operations with common fractions; they may add together numerators and denominators when they attempt to add two common fractions. Work with concrete materials and with renaming common fractions as decimal fractions helps children realize that common fractions represent only one number.

5. Some children have difficulty ordering rational numbers, even unit fractions. They think that $\frac{1}{3}$ is bigger than $\frac{1}{2}$ because 3 is bigger than 2. These children may need to return to work with concrete materials to discover that there is an inverse relationship between the size of the denominator in a unit fraction and the size of the piece that the fraction represents. The activities suggested for estimation should help these children.

   Vance (1986) has found that similar problems arise when children order decimal fractions, especially when the numbers do not contain the same number of decimal places. When ordering .5, .34, and .257, some children decide that .257 is the largest because it uses the most digits or that it is the smallest because it is written in thousandths, which are smaller than tenths or hundredths. Such reasoning would work for the problem above but not for .5 and .678.

   Children having difficulty ordering decimals should return to work with physical models and with estimation. They should work with rewriting decimals so that all the decimal fractions contain the same number of decimal places.

Calculators can be useful here. Vance suggests a calculator game in which the students try to "wipe out" a digit in the calculator display. For example, if the calculator shows 23.9876, wipe out the 7 by subtracting .007. Ask students to see if the same thing happens when they subtract .0007 or .0070.

6. Some students have difficulty understanding that rational numbers are dense. It is hard to understand that with rational numbers there is no next number as there is with whole numbers; there is always another rational number between any two rational numbers. Students who find it hard to give a rational number between $\frac{1}{4}$ and $\frac{2}{4}$ or between 0.1 and 0.2 may need to return to work with concrete materials and with renaming rational numbers. If $\frac{1}{4}$ and $\frac{2}{4}$ are renamed as $\frac{2}{8}$ and $\frac{4}{8}$, or if 0.1 and 0.2 are renamed as 0.10 and 0.20, it is easier for students to find another number between them. The Pyramid Game described earlier also will help students practice finding a rational number between two other rational numbers.

7. Some children understand unit fraction concepts but not concepts of fractions with numerators greater than 1 or concepts of mixed numbers. Children who have a concrete understanding of these concepts may still have difficulty with improper fractions. Such children should return to a variety of models, including concrete regions and the number line, to develop a better understanding of improper fractions.

8. Some students have difficulty converting decimals to percents. They remember that they should move the decimal point two places, but they move it the wrong direction. This is especially true for percents that are less than 1 or greater than 100.

   This problem with the decimal point also arises in writing dollars and cents. A number of adults seem not to realize that when used with a cent sign, the decimal point represents hundredths of a cent. It is tempting to offer the grocer a penny for four oranges when the sign above the oranges reads .25¢ for one orange. Children enjoy looking for mistakes such as this.

   Similar mistakes involving the decimal point arise when children are using a calculator. Be sure children use their estimation skills to determine whether or not their answers make sense. Examples from real life can be useful here. Misplacing the decimal point when solving a real-life problem involving money can be very costly.

9. Some students have difficulty with proportional reasoning. Tasks involving proportions are often difficult on the abstract level, even for adults. Be sure to include concrete work on these concepts and encourage students to discuss their reasoning with each other.

Something for Everyone

Again, we recognize that while children learn in a variety of modes, some children may learn more comfortably in a particular mode, such as visually or auditorily. Because both Chapters 9 and 10 are directed at teaching rational numbers, the specific learning modes associated with rational numbers are discussed at the end of Chapter 10.

KEY IDEAS

Rational numbers in all forms are commonly used in our everyday lives, but research shows that they are generally poorly understood by elementary and middle school students. Chapter 9 presents many ideas for helping students better understand these numbers. Several models for presenting rational numbers in common and in decimal fraction form are shown, including the part-whole, ratio, and division models.

Materials described in this chapter include Fraction Tiles, rectangular and circular fraction regions, Decimal Squares, base ten blocks, number lines, fraction strips, Fraction Bars, colored chips, Cuisenaire rods, and arrays. These concrete materials, as well as pictures, computer programs, calculators, and reinforcement activities, are important to the development and retention of good rational number concepts. Children should explore the meaning of rational numbers written in any form and should be able to read, rename, and order fractions, decimals, and percents.

They should practice estimating and mentally calculating with rational numbers in every form. Problem solving and problem creating should encourage students to delve even deeper into the meanings of rational numbers.

Diagnosis should include looking at children's understanding of the meanings of rational numbers using a variety of concrete and semiconcrete models, not just looking at a child's ability to memorize rotely some poorly understood rules such as how to write equivalent fractions.

DISCUSSION QUESTIONS

1. Analyze two different elementary mathematics textbook series to see how fraction and decimal concepts are introduced. Which concept is introduced first? Are there connections made between fraction and decimal concepts or are these treated as separate topics? Compare your findings to those of a classmate.

2. Describe how you might introduce common fractions using the part-whole model. What physical models might you use? What errors would you expect children to make when first learning these concepts?

How will you help students make the transition from physical models to drawings to abstract concepts?

3. 🖥 Find at least two different computer programs that are designed to help children learn fraction concepts. Analyze each for the clarity of the mathematics presented. If possible, watch a child using at least one of the programs, and interview the child to determine if any learning took place because of using the program.

4. Design a lesson to help children practice the conversion of fractions to equivalent decimals and percents. Be sure to include physical models.

5. Develop an open-ended problem to assess student understanding of proportional reasoning. Be sure that the problem allows students to use different methods of solution and requires them to use higher-level thinking. Include a scoring rubric for your problem.

REFERENCES

Allinger, Glenn D., and Joseph N. Payne, "Estimation and Mental Arithmetic with Percent," in *Estimation and Mental Computation,* National Council of Teachers of Mathematics, 1986 Yearbook. Reston, VA: NCTM, 1986.

Beaton, Albert E., Ina V. S. Mullis, Michael O. Martin, Eugenio J. Gonzalez, Dana L. Kelly, and Teresa A. Smith, *Mathematics Achievement in the Middle School Years: IEA's Third International Mathematics and Science Study.* Chestnut Hill, MA: Boston College TIMSS International Study Center, November 1996.

Behr, Merlyn J., Thomas R. Post, and Ipke Wachsmuth, "Estimation and Children's Concept of Rational Number Size." *Estimation and Mental Computation,* National Council of Teachers of Mathematics, 1986 Yearbook. Reston, VA: NCTM, 1986.

Behr, Merlyn J., et al., "Order and Equivalence of Rational Numbers: A Clinical Teaching Experiment," *Journal for Research in Mathematics Education,* 15, no. 4 (November 1984), 323–341.

Bennett, Albert B., Jr., *Decimal Squares.* Fort Collins, CO: Scott Resources, 1982.

Bennett, Albert B., Jr., and Patricia A. Davidson, *Fraction Bars.* Fort Collins, CO: Scott Resources, 1973.

Bezuk, Nadine, and Kathleen Cramer, "Teaching About Fractions: What, When, and How?" in *New Directions for Elementary School Mathematics,* ed. Paul R. Trafton and Albert P. Shulte. Reston, VA: National Council of Teachers of Mathematics, 1989, pp. 156–167.

Bradford, John, *Everything's Coming Up Fractions with Cuisenaire Rods.* New Rochelle, NY: Cuisenaire Co. of America, 1981.

Carpenter, Thomas P., et al., "Decimals: Results and Implications from National Assessment," *Arithmetic Teacher,* 28, no. 8 (April 1981), 34–37.

Cook, Marci, *Fractions: Try-A-Tile.* Sunnyvale, CA: Creative Publications, 1988.

Dorgan, Karen, "What Textbooks Offer for Instruction in Fraction Concepts," *Teaching Children Mathematics,* 1, no. 3 (November, 1994), 150–155.

Dossey, John A., Ina V. S. Mullis, Mary M. Lindquist, and Donald L. Chambers, *The Mathematics Report Card: Are We Measuring Up? Trends and Achievement Based on the 1986 National Assessment.* Princeton, NJ: Educational Testing Service, 1988.

Dossey, John A., Ina V. S. Mullis, Steven Gorman, Andrew S. Latham, *How School Mathematics Functions: Perspectives from the NAEP 1990 and 1992 Assessments.* Washington, DC: National Center for Educational Statistics, 1994.

Eicholz, Robert E., et al., *Addison-Wesley Mathematics, Book 7.* Menlo Park, CA: Addison-Wesley, 1987, p. 204.

Head, Debby, and Libby Pollett, *Count on Kids, Cluster One: Pattern Blocks Parts and Wholes.* Shelbyville, KY: bby Publications, 1994.

Holden, Linda, *The Fraction Factory.* Sunnyvale, CA: Creative Publications, 1986.

Hutchins, Pat, *The Doorbell Rang.* New York: Greenwillow Books, 1986.

Jenkins, Lee, and Peggy McLean, *Fraction Tiles: A Manipulative Fraction Program.* Hayward, CA: Activity Resources, 1972.

Kouba, Vicky L., Catherine A. Brown, Thomas P. Carpenter, Mary M. Lindquist, Edward A. Silver, and Jane O. Swafford, "Results of the Fourth NAEP Assessment of Mathematics: Number, Operations, and Word Problems." *Arithmetic Teacher,* 35, no. 8 (April 1988), 14–19.

Lichtenberg, Betty K., and Donovan R. Lichtenberg, "Decimals Deserve Distinction," in *Mathematics for the Middle Grades (5–9),* National Council of Teachers of Mathematics, 1982 Yearbook. Reston, VA: NCTM, 1982.

Mack, Nancy K., "Learning Fractions with Understanding: Building on Informal Knowledge," *Journal for Research in Mathematics Education,* 21, no. 1 (January 1990), 16–32.

Mathews, Louise, *Gator Pie.* New York: Dodd, Mead, 1979.

McClain, Kay (ed.), "Not One, but Six Fractions Equivalent to One-Third!" *Mathematics Teaching in the Middle School.* 3, no. 3 (November–December 1997), 213–214.

McMillan, Bruce, *Eating Fractions.* New York: Scholastic, 1991.

National Council of Teachers of Mathematics, *Curriculum and Evaluation Standards for School Mathematics.* Reston, VA: NCTM, 1989.

Payne, Joseph N., and Ann E. Towsley, "Implications of NCTM's *Standards* for Teaching Fractions and Decimals," *Arithmetic Teacher,* 37, no. 8 (April 1990), 23–26.

Post, Thomas R., "Fractions: Results and Implications from National Assessment," *Arithmetic Teacher,* 28, no. 8 (May 1981), 26–31.

Post, Thomas R., Merlyn J. Behr, and Richard Lesh, "Research-Based Observations About Children's Learning of Rational Number Concepts," *Focus on Learning Problems in Mathematics,* 8, no. 1 (Winter 1986), 39–48.

Post, Thomas R., et al., "Order and Equivalence of Rational Numbers: A Cognitive Analysis," *Journal for Research in Mathematics Education,* 16, no. 1 (January 1985), 18–36.

"Rational Numbers (Focus Issue)," *Arithmetic Teacher,* 31, no. 6 (February 1984).

Roper, Ann, and Linda H. Charles, *Fraction Squares Plus Job-cards.* Sunnyvale, CA: Creative Publications, 1990.

Vance, James, "Ordering Decimals and Fractions: A Diagnostic Study," *Focus on Learning Problems in Mathematics,* 8, no. 2 (Spring 1986), 51–59.

Zullie, Mathew E., *Fractions with Pattern Blocks.* Palo Alto, CA: Creative Publications, 1975.

Technology

Annenberg/CPB, *Teaching Math: A Video Library, K–4.* Boston, MA: WGBH Educational Foundation, 1995.

Broderbund, *Math Workshop Deluxe.* Novato, CA: Broderbund, 1998. (Software)

Edmark, *Mighty Math Number Heroes.* Orlando, FL: Harcourt Brace, 1996. (Software)

Eisenhower National Clearinghouse, *Tools for Discussion: Attaining Excellence through TIMSS.* Columbus, OH: Eisenhower National Clearinghouse for Mathematics and Science Education, 1998. (CD-ROM)

Sunburst, *Fraction Attraction.* Pleasantville, NY: Sunburst, 1998. (Software)

—————, *Get to the Point.* Pleasantville, NY: Sunburst, 1998. (Software)

Web Sites

http://www.ncsa.uiuc.edu/edu/RSE/RSEyellow/gnb.html. Interactive stock market project for middle school students available from the National Center for Supercomputing Applications.

National Center for Education Statistics (NCES). *NAEP 1996 Mathematics—Report Card for the Nation and the States: Findings from the National Assessment of Educational Progress.* Washington, DC: U.S. Department of Education Office of Educational Research and Improvement (downloaded from http://nces.ed.gov/naep/96report, September, 1998).

Chapter 10

Teaching and Learning Operations with Rational Numbers

NCTM Standards

GRADES 5–8

Standard 7: Computation and Estimation

In grades 5–8, the mathematics curriculum should develop the concepts underlying computation and estimation in various contexts so that students can—

- Compute with whole numbers, fractions, decimals, integers, and rational numbers;
- Develop, analyze, and explain procedures for computation and techniques for estimation;
- Develop, analyze, and explain methods for solving proportions;
- Select and use an appropriate method for computing from among mental arithmetic, paper and pencil, calculator, and computer methods;
- Use computation, estimation, and proportions to solve problems;
- Use estimation to check the reasonableness of results.

NCTM (1989), p. 94. Reprinted by permission.

My Math Journal

Using only halves, thirds, fourths, sixths, eighths, and twelfths, list at least 15 different ways to make one whole. You may use combinations such as $\frac{1}{2} + \frac{1}{4} + \frac{2}{8}$ as well as $\frac{8}{8}$ or $\frac{3}{3}$. Remember to look for patterns and write your results in an organized list.

How do you know if you have found all the ways possible using only halves, thirds, fourths, sixths, eighths, and twelfths? Use your chart to predict how many total possible ways there are to find combinations equal to one whole. Write a convincing argument that your method will determine all possibilities.

As you read the following pages, consider these guiding questions:

1. What are some of the physical models that can be used to illustrate operations with rational numbers? Choose any equation for adding, subtracting, multiplying, or dividing common fractions, decimal fractions, or percents and illustrate it with a physical model.
2. How are operations with rational numbers used every day? Choose any equation for adding, subtracting, multiplying, or dividing common fractions, decimal fractions, or percents and write a word problem involving a common application that would use that equation to solve it.
3. How do operations with rational numbers compare with operations with whole numbers?
4. Why do rules such as "invert and multiply" work when dividing common fractions?
5. What are some common errors that students make when operating with rational numbers and what might you do to help a student correct these errors?

Operations with rational numbers are generally emphasized in the upper elementary and middle school grades. Operations with decimal fractions may be introduced earlier along with the decimal notation for money or perhaps with measurements in the metric system, but generally math programs wait until fourth or fifth grade to teach rational number operations.

There is some controversy over whether operations with common fractions should be delayed until seventh or eighth grade because of the increased use of decimal fractions and the difficulties many children experience with common fractions, but most textbooks do not delay the instruction that long. Many programs introduce operations with decimal fractions the same year in which they introduce operations with common fractions. That is one of the reasons we do not have separate chapters for common and decimal fractions.

Perhaps more importantly, we do not have these operations in separate chapters because conceptually the two represent the same situations. Children should be able to recognize that if they use three-tenths of a meter of material for a doll's blouse and seven-tenths of a meter of material for a doll's coat, it does not matter if they find the total amount of material by adding $\frac{3}{10} + \frac{7}{10}$ or by adding $0.3 + 0.7$. No matter how it is written, they have used a meter of material.

It is important that operations with rational numbers arise from examples in the "real world." Have children make a list of occasions in which rational numbers are used in their homes or everyday lives. The following are a few suggestions for events or places where rational numbers are used. Ask children to discuss situations in which rational numbers might be used and to make up

story problems using these settings. Have the children add to the list as situations arise.

- Recipes
- Sewing
- Gardening
- Medicine
- Building
- Unit pricing
- Odometer
- Hourly wages
- Track and field events
- Kilowatt hours of electricity
- Stock market
- Scale drawings (architecture, engineering, drafting, surveying, mapmaking, etc.)
- Measurements of all types (time, length, area, volume, money, etc.)
- Probability and statistics
- Graphing

As we discuss the concepts of operations with rational numbers, we frequently draw examples from daily events. You and the children should do the same in your classroom.

Working with physical models continues to be important as children learn to operate with rational numbers. Even children in the seventh and eighth grades are generally concretely operational and cannot fully understand new concepts on an abstract level. Work with physical models helps children construct their knowledge about rational number operations. Continue to use the manipulative materials discussed in Chapter 9 for rational number concepts; these include Fraction Bars, Fraction Tiles, circular and rectangular regions, pattern blocks, Cuisenaire rods, base ten blocks, Decimal Squares, number lines, fraction strips, paper for folding, colored chips, and arrays. Continue to stress calculator skills, especially with decimal fraction operations, and use appropriate computer programs to help the children develop skills with common and decimal fractions and percents.

As children develop understanding and skill in their work with rational numbers, they begin to explore some of the early concepts of operations with these numbers. When they find like denominators for two common fractions, they may notice that when two fractions have like denominators, it is very easy to add them together, to find how much bigger one is than the other, or even to find how many times bigger one is than the other. Encourage and expand on this intuitive understanding of operations with rational numbers as you introduce the operations more formally. Let children continue to question, explore, and discover relationships and algorithms of their own as they expand their knowledge of rational numbers to include operations.

Developing Concepts of Operations with Rational Numbers

After children understand the meaning of rational numbers written as both common and decimal fractions and can rename equivalent fractions, they are ready for operations with rational numbers. Operations with rational numbers should be understood before they are practiced abstractly. Too many students memorize rules such as "invert and multiply" but are not able to explain when or why this should be done. In this section, we concentrate on the meaning of operations with all types of rational numbers.

In the next section, we discuss developing and practicing skills with the operations. Be sure to allow children plenty of time for concept development before you move on to practicing skills. The more time children spend on the concepts, the less time they will need to practice the skills.

Addition of Common Fractions

When you first introduce children to the addition of common fractions, continue to use the physical models they used for learning the concepts of common fractions. Introduce addition using problems that are based on the children's experiences. Use problems that children can solve by exploring familiar materials.

Textbooks generally begin with problems involving common fractions with like denominators and later move to problems with unlike denominators. Children working with concrete materials may not need to separate problems with like from those with unlike denominators, however. If they have worked with renaming fractions concretely in developing concepts of common fractions, the addition and subtraction of common fractions should follow naturally. Following are some examples of situations that may be used to introduce addition of common fractions.

ACTIVITIES

Intermediate (4–6)

Objective: to develop the concept of addition of common fractions with like denominators.

1. Give the children an example of a situation that would require the addition of common fractions, and let them use concrete materials such as the circular or rectangular regions (see Appendix B) to find the answer. A beginning example follows: Danny baked a pie and left it to cool. His sister Maureen came along and cut it into 6 equal pieces. She ate $\frac{1}{6}$ of the pie and gave her friend Suzanna $\frac{1}{6}$ of the pie. How much of the pie did they take altogether?

Let the children manipulate the pieces to show the answer of $\frac{2}{6}$. Then, have the children make up and illustrate other problems of their own. After children have worked several problems using the materials, ask them to write down what they have done. They may initially write 1 sixth + 1 sixth = 2 sixths. After comparing this to earlier work with whole numbers, they may write the equation as $\frac{1}{6} + \frac{1}{6} = \frac{2}{6}$ or

Ask the children to write equations for all their work with the manipulatives. They may have some of the following:

$$\frac{1}{6} + \frac{1}{6} = \frac{2}{6}$$

$$\frac{1}{3} + \frac{1}{3} = \frac{2}{3}$$

$$\frac{1}{4} + \frac{2}{4} = \frac{3}{4}$$

$$\frac{2}{5} + \frac{3}{5} = \frac{5}{5}$$

Ask the children if they notice anything consistent about the problems. Lead them to discuss the fact that in each problem, the denominator remains the same and the numerators are added together. After the children have worked several problems using regions and have recorded the equations, ask them to show the same equations using another material such as the Cuisenaire rods, the number line, or the Fraction Bars. Figure 10–1 shows a few possibilities.

Discuss with the students the fact that the sum remains the same no matter what material is used to illustrate the equations. Ask the students to analyze what is wrong with examples such as $\frac{2}{3} + \frac{1}{3} = \frac{3}{6}$ and $\frac{2}{5} + \frac{1}{5} = \frac{3}{10}$. Ask how they can use the materials to help another child understand why those examples are incorrect. This explanation would make a good daily journal entry.

2. Children sometimes think that whenever you add two fractions, the answer will be less than 1 because that is often the case with the early examples. They need early exposure to problems for which the sum is greater than 1. Again, use examples from the children's

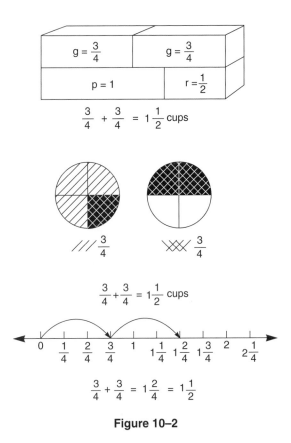

Figure 10–1

Figure 10–2

everyday experiences. For example, for Danny's pie, he used $\frac{3}{4}$ cup of sugar for the crust and $\frac{3}{4}$ cup of sugar for the filling. How much sugar did he use altogether? Again, let the children use any of the familiar manipulatives to find the sum.

Some children may have difficulty when they realize that the answer is larger than 1 cup. Ask them how much larger than 1 cup the sum is. Say, "Yes, you have 1 whole cup and or $\frac{2}{4}$, or $\frac{1}{2}$, of another cup." Figure 10–2 shows some of the possible solutions with the materials.

Again, ask the children to write the equation for the problem. Discuss the fact that $\frac{6}{4}$ and $1\frac{2}{4}$ name the same amount (this should be familiar from the work with equivalent fractions). Let the children suggest other word problems, solve them with the manipulatives, and write the equations. Encourage the children to predict whether the answer to each example will be larger or smaller than 1. After the children have had some practice, let them work the problems mentally, without using the materials or writing the equations.

Some calculators show fractions in common as well as decimal form. Allow the students to use one of these calculators to explore the addition and subtraction of common fractions. What happens when you simplify a fraction or change from a mixed numeral to an improper fraction?

Objective: to develop the concept of addition of common fractions with unlike denominators.

3. After the children have had experience adding common fractions with like denominators, suggest a problem that involves adding fractions with unlike denom-

inators. Again, let the children choose a concrete material with which to solve the problem. Following is one example: After Danny's pie was eaten, he decided to bake a cake. His father said that the cake looked so good that he would like a huge piece. Danny's mom was on a diet, so she wanted only a small piece. Danny cut a piece $\frac{1}{4}$ of the whole cake for his dad and a piece $\frac{1}{8}$ of the cake for his mom. How much of the whole cake did Danny give his parents?

Figure 10–3a shows how the children may demonstrate this with the fraction pieces. Ask the children what they would call the answer. It is difficult to name the answer unless the pieces are all the same size. In Figure 10–3a, you have two pieces, but they are not two-fourths or two-eighths. It is not convenient to say you have one-fourth and one-eighth of the whole cake. Encourage children to draw on their experience with renaming common fractions to suggest that the fourth may be renamed as eighths. The children might exchange the fraction pieces as shown in Figure 10–3b.

Now ask the children to tell you the sum. The two pieces are divided into portions of the same size, eighths, so the sum is three-eighths. Encourage the children to show their work in equation form. Ask the students to share the various ways of writing equations that they have devised. Let them try to use each other's methods and algorithms for a few days and

Figure 10–3

Figure 10–4

discuss the benefits or drawbacks of each type of algorithm. If students have not discovered the conventional algorithm on their own, you might wish to introduce it. Several students may find that it is easiest to work with equations in vertical form, so show the conversion as

$$\frac{1}{4} = \frac{2}{8}$$

$$+\frac{1}{8} = +\frac{1}{8}$$

$$\frac{3}{8}$$

If students prefer another algorithm, do not force them to use the conventional algorithm as long as theirs works and is relatively simple to use and understand.

Let the children suggest other word problems and solve them using other concrete or semiconcrete aids. Some of the problems should involve common fractions that must be renamed with a common denominator. Remind children of their earlier work with renaming fractions. Ask children to write up word problems for each other to leave in the learning center or for you to use on worksheets for the whole class. Encourage children to discuss their methods of solution with each other. If disagreements about the solutions arise, ask questions to lead the children

to discover which solution is correct. They may find that several methods (or none) work. Compare the results to answers obtained using a calculator that shows common fractions (see Figure 10–4).

Objective: to develop the concept of addition of mixed numerals.

4. With mixed numerals as well as with proper fractions, students should develop addition concepts beginning with "real-life" situations. An example follows: Maria needs $1\frac{2}{3}$ yards of material to make a skirt and $1\frac{1}{2}$ yards of material to make a matching jacket. How much material should Maria buy for the outfit?

Again, the children should use the familiar fraction materials to work out the problem. Let the children discuss what to do with the fractions with unlike denominators. Encourage the children to begin by putting the whole sections together and then trading in the parts for amounts shown in sixths, the common denominator. Ask the children what to do with the sixths, since they make more than another whole yard. Encourage the children to write down the equations as they work with the materials to record what they are doing. The children's work with fraction strips may look like that in Figure 10–5.

After the children have added mixed numerals with the aid of one manipulative, encourage them to show the same problem with other manipulatives or pictures. Figure 10–6 shows other possibilities for $1\frac{2}{3} + 1\frac{1}{2}$.

Addition of Decimal Fractions

Depending on the mathematics program you use, you may decide to introduce addition with decimal fractions either before or after addition with common fractions. Many children find addition with decimal fractions easier than addition with common fractions because of their familiarity

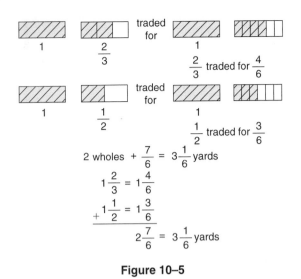

Figure 10–5

with adding amounts of money and the ease of adding decimal fractions on the calculator. As the metric system becomes more popular, even more examples of decimal fractions will be familiar from everyday life. Whether decimal fraction addition is introduced before or after common fraction addition, have students use the same physical models they used to understand the basic concepts of decimal fractions; these include Cuisenaire rods, Decimal Squares, number lines, arrays, and base ten blocks.

If addition of common fractions precedes addition of decimal fractions, have children write equations in both common and decimal fraction form and compare the results. If work with common fractions follows addition of decimal fractions, have children compare the two forms of addition when they learn to compute with common fractions. The activities described for common fraction addition can be repeated with decimal fractions. A few other suggestions follow.

ACTIVITIES

Intermediate (3–6)

Objective: to develop the concept of addition of decimal fractions in tenths using Cuisenaire rods and number lines.

1. As with common fractions, children should begin work with decimal fractions using a situation from everyday life. The following is one example: Amy bought a new odometer for her bike because she wanted to find out how far it was to her friends' homes. She put the odometer on her bike and saw that it was set at zero. After she rode to Maureen's house, the odometer read 0.7 kilometers. Amy rode from there to Ahmad's house and told Ahmad that he lives 0.5 kilometers from Maureen. What did Amy's odometer read when she arrived at Ahmad's?

   Let the children use Cuisenaire rods to show the addition. Let the orange rod represent 1. Which rod shows 0.7? Which rod shows 0.5? Notice that once the children select the black and yellow rods, the addition is shown in the same manner that addition of whole numbers was illustrated.

   Since the sum is more than the orange rod, we know that the odometer will show more than 1 kilometer. Ask the children how they can tell how much more than 1 kilometer will be shown. They should fill in the space next to the orange rod to match the total of the black and yellow rods. The total is an orange rod and a red rod. The red rod is 0.2 of the orange rod, so the odometer must show 1.2 kilometers (see Figure 10–7).

   Let the children suggest other problems of their own and show them with the Cuisenaire rods.

Figure 10–6

Figure 10–7

2. After the children can use the Cuisenaire rods to show problems, they should transfer to the number line. Use a number line with 1 decimeter (10 centimeters) representing one unit. Each centimeter is then 0.1 of the unit. The children can lay the Cuisenaire rods on the number line to show the addition in the same way that they showed addition of whole numbers. When the children use the number line, they can simply read the answer off the number line, as shown in Figure 10–8.

3. After the children work several problems using Cuisenaire rods on the number line, they can show the addition on the number line by simply using arrows, as shown in Figure 10–9.

As children work the problems with any of the models, encourage them to write the algorithms in vertical form near the pictures. After the children have worked several problems, ask them what they notice about the addition algorithm. They should notice that the algorithm for adding decimal fractions is the same as that for adding whole numbers if the decimal points are lined up.

If children have constructed a different algorithm for adding decimals, encourage them to discuss their method. Does their method work if the

decimals have differing place values, as in adding 0.232 and 0.2?

If the children have previously worked with adding common fractions, ask them to write the number sentence for the same exercise in common fraction form next to the number sentence in decimal fraction form, as shown below:

$$\frac{7}{10} \qquad \begin{array}{r} 0.7 \\ + \underline{0.5} \\ 1.2 \end{array}$$
$$+ \frac{5}{10}$$
$$\overline{}$$
$$\frac{12}{10} = 1\frac{2}{10}$$

Ask them to compare the two examples and discuss their findings.

Objective: to develop the concept of addition of decimal fractions in hundredths using base ten blocks, Decimal Squares, and arrays.

4. Children should be familiar with addition of hundredths because of their previous work in learning to add money. They may not relate this to a concrete model, however. Use the flat 10-by-10 base ten block to represent $1. Ask the children how they would show a dime and a penny. They should show you the long and the small cube, respectively. Ask the children to show amounts such as $.23, $.96, and $1.48.

Ask the children to use the blocks to determine Bill's total bill if he orders a hamburger for $1.39, a cola for $.55, and french fries for $.65. The blocks should initially look like those in Figure 10–10.

Have the children make all the trades possible to end up with the least number of separate blocks. After all the trades, the response should appear as in Figure 10–11.

Have the children write the number sentence near the work with the blocks and again allow them to develop their own algorithms for adding decimal fractions. Have they used the traditional vertical algorithm that mirrors addition of whole numbers as long as the decimal points remain in line or have they developed other methods?

Let the children suggest other problems of their own and work them with the blocks. After they have worked several problems with the blocks, have them work a few problems with other materials, such as the Decimal Squares or arrays that use 10-by-10 grid paper. Encourage the children to discuss their methods of solution. They should compare these to other methods, such as calculating mentally, working the example on a calculator, or computing with paper and pencil.

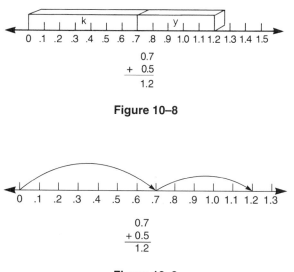

Figure 10–8

$$\begin{array}{r} 0.7 \\ + \underline{0.5} \\ 1.2 \end{array}$$

Figure 10–9

Figure 10–10

Figure 10–11

Objective: to develop the concept of addition of decimal fractions with thousandths.

5. Once children are comfortable working problems involving tenths and hundredths, introduce problems involving thousandths. Following is one example: José is measuring chemicals for an experiment. He has measured 0.125 liter of water and 0.375 liter of oil into the same beaker. How much mixture is in the beaker?

Children may use actual beakers to work out the problem or they may model it using the base ten blocks or the Decimal Squares. If they use base ten blocks, the large cube should represent 1, and the smallest cube should be 0.001. Again, ask the children to write their addition algorithm near the work

with the blocks and to compare this algorithm to the whole number algorithms.

 Children should compare their work with decimal fractions to the algorithm for common fractions if they have had previous work with common fractions. Have children use calculators to compare the work with concrete objects. If you are using calculators that show both decimal and common forms, ask the students to work the problems in both forms and compare the results. Encourage the children to discuss their methods with each other and to estimate results without actually computing them.

Objective: to develop the concept of addition with decimal fractions when some decimals are written in tenths and others are in hundredths or thousandths.

6. Children's main difficulties in adding decimal fractions come when the decimals are not all written to the same decimal place. If children are using the traditional algorithm for adding decimal fractions they may not realize that it is important to keep the decimal points lined up and they may try to write the numerals as shown below:

$$
\begin{array}{r}
0.2 \\
0.03 \\
1 \\
\hline
.06
\end{array}
$$

Ask the children to use one of the concrete models to show the exercise. Using the base ten blocks, with the flat as 1, the materials would look like those in Figure 10–12. Have the children write the number sentence below their work with the blocks. Be sure that they realize the importance of lining up the decimal points and writing all decimal fractions in hundredths. This is a good time to use a calculator to compare the results to paper and pencil computation. Ask the students to try examples such as .5 + .35 + .456 and .500 + .350 + .456. Do they obtain the same result? Ask the children to explain why this is true. If the students have previously added common fractions, ask them to compare this process to converting all common fractions to like denominators before adding.

Subtraction of Common Fractions

When students begin work with subtraction of common fractions, again start with realistic situations. As with whole-number subtraction, problems may involve taking away one amount from another, comparing two amounts, or figuring out how much more is needed. Again, have children use manipulative materials to work out the ex-

amples when you first introduce subtraction of common fractions. Build on previous work with converting common fractions to equivalent fractions with like denominators and work with addition of common fractions.

Because addition and subtraction are inverse operations, you may introduce addition and subtraction of common fractions almost simultaneously. Students in third or fourth grade can generally reverse one operation to develop the other. Therefore, soon after children learn addition of common fractions, they may learn subtraction. Subtraction of mixed numerals may quickly follow addition of mixed numerals.

A few suggestions for teaching the concepts of subtraction of common fractions follow. You and the students should develop other ideas related to the earlier work with addition and the student's experiences outside of school.

ACTIVITIES

Intermediate–Middle Grades (4–7)

Objective: to develop the concept of subtraction of common fractions with like denominators.

1. Suggest a problem such as the following and ask the children to work it using a manipulative such as the circular regions: Emilio had $\frac{3}{4}$ of a pound of cheese. He used $\frac{1}{4}$ of a pound to make macaroni and cheese. How much cheese does Emilio have left? The children's regions should be similar to those in Figure 10–13.

$$
\begin{array}{r}
\frac{3}{4} \\
- \frac{1}{4} \\
\hline
\frac{2}{4} = \frac{1}{2} \text{ pound}
\end{array}
$$

Figure 10–13

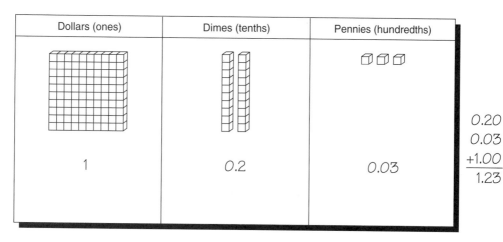

Dollars (ones)	Dimes (tenths)	Pennies (hundredths)
1	0.2	0.03

$$
\begin{array}{r}
0.20 \\
0.03 \\
+1.00 \\
\hline
1.23
\end{array}
$$

Figure 10–12

Ask children to develop their own algorithms for subtracting fractions and to write the algorithm next to the pieces as they work the problem. Compare the various algorithms that the students have constructed and let them decide on the algorithms that they prefer. If they have not developed the traditional algorithm, you may wish to introduce it after they have developed their own understanding of subtraction of common fractions. Let the children suggest other word problems themselves and use other types of materials to work them. They should discuss their methods as they work.

One common mistake that children make when they write word problems for subtraction of common fractions is that they want to subtract a part of the first fraction rather than a part of a whole amount. For example, a child may say, "Jeff had $\frac{1}{2}$ of an apple. Amy ate $\frac{1}{4}$ of what Jeff had. How much does Jeff have left?"

Discuss with the children that $\frac{1}{4}$ of $\frac{1}{2}$ of an apple is only $\frac{1}{8}$ of the whole apple. This is less than $\frac{1}{4}$ of a whole apple. The equation for this problem would be $\frac{1}{2} - (\frac{1}{4} \times \frac{1}{2}) = n$. This is not $\frac{1}{2} - \frac{1}{4}$. Encourage children to show both problems with the manipulatives and to explain their solutions (more is said about problems involving multiplication in the section on multiplication of common fractions).

Objective: to introduce subtraction of fractions with unlike denominators.

2. Use a word problem to introduce subtraction of fractions with unlike denominators. For example, Andreas has $\frac{3}{4}$ of a bushel of apples. Marlo has $\frac{2}{3}$ of a bushel of apples. What part of a bushel more does Andreas have than Marlo?

Notice that this is a comparison type of subtraction problem. Children can use number lines or Fraction Bars to compare the two amounts. If children do not convert the fractions to like denominators, they can tell that $\frac{3}{4}$ is greater than $\frac{2}{3}$ but they will have trouble determining how much greater.

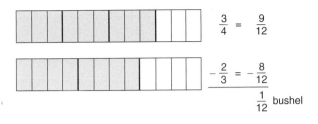

Figure 10–14

Ask the children to always estimate which amount is greater before they begin to subtract and to estimate *about* how much greater that amount is. Compare this to adding $\frac{3}{4}$ and $\frac{2}{3}$. For addition, they first changed both fractions to like denominators. They should do the same when subtracting fractions with unlike denominators. Ask the children to write the algorithms they have developed beside the work with the number line or manipulatives as shown in Figure 10–14 and discuss their strategies of solution.

Objective: to develop the concept of subtraction of mixed numerals.

3. Again, subtraction of mixed numerals should begin with an example from everyday life, such as: Cara has knitted $2\frac{3}{4}$ yards of a scarf. She wants the scarf to be $3\frac{1}{2}$ yards long. How many more yards does she need to knit?

This type of problem, which requires renaming one unit, often is difficult for children. Let the children use materials or a number line. On the number line, have the children show the $2\frac{3}{4}$ yards already completed and add on until they reach the $3\frac{1}{2}$ yards, as shown in Figure 10–15.

Have the children record the algorithm below the materials as they work. Work several problems with mixed numerals with the children, some that require renaming the whole number and some that do not. Have the children use other physical models to demonstrate exchanging the whole number for equivalent parts. Discuss with them the fact that the mathematics

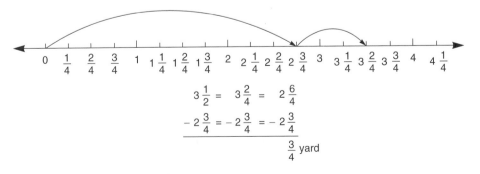

Figure 10–15

remains the same regardless of the concrete materials chosen to illustrate the equations. Figure 10–16 shows an example with pie pieces that some students may use. Other students may begin with $2\frac{3}{4}$ circular pieces and add on fourths until reaching $3\frac{1}{2}$.

Again, encourage the children to estimate or mentally compute several of the examples. Paper-and-pencil computations are not always necessary. Children should compare their various strategies as they work.

Subtraction of Decimal Fractions

Subtraction of decimal fractions may be introduced immediately following addition of decimal fractions. If subtraction of decimal fractions follows subtraction of common fractions, have the children compare the new work with decimal fractions to the previous work with common fractions. Have them write algorithms in both forms and compare the processes and answers. Let them also use calculators for comparison.

If the work with decimal fractions comes first, compare addition and subtraction of decimal fractions with the new work when you introduce addition and subtraction of common fractions. Use the same physical models for both addition and subtraction of decimal fractions. Compare the subtraction algorithms for decimal fractions to the addition algorithms for decimal fractions and the subtraction algorithms for whole numbers. Use the same types of word problems for decimal fractions as you did for subtraction of whole numbers and for subtraction of common fractions. Money and metric measures are good sources of word problems because of the frequent use of decimals in these examples.

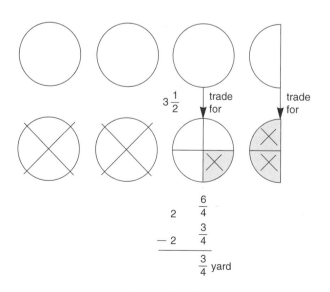

Figure 10–16

The activities for subtraction of common fractions and for addition of decimal fractions can be adapted to subtraction of decimal fractions. A few other ideas follow. You and your students should suggest others.

ACTIVITIES

Intermediate (3–6)

Objective: to develop the concept of subtraction of decimal fractions.

1. Because dealing with money gives children a number of chances to add and subtract using decimals, have the children set up a store or restaurant. Initially, stock the cash register only with dollar bills, dimes, and pennies to reinforce the regrouping the children must do to perform the subtraction algorithm. For example, Ray is told that his bill for lunch comes to $2.57. He hands the cashier $3.00. Have the children make the change either by using the traditional decomposition algorithm or by counting forward from $2.57. Figure 10–17 shows the trades the cashier must make to give Ray his change if the decomposition algorithm is used.

   Counting on from $2.57 has the advantage of helping the children learn to count back change (this seems to be a lost art in many stores). Encourage children to write down an algorithm for the method used. Let children create other algorithms of their own. Because so many stores now use computerized cash registers, encourage children to use calculators to compute the change. A parent or other adult in the community may be willing to come in to explain the use of various machines that aid clerks in making change.

2. Have children play an estimation game that also involves measurement and subtraction of decimal fractions. Make a set of cards that show amounts such as 5 centimeters, 6.2 centimeters, 8.4 centimeters, and 3 centimeters. Place the cards face down on the table.

   Turn over one card and ask a child to draw a line segment approximately the length designated by the card. Then have the child measure the line segment to the nearest tenth of a centimeter (nearest millimeter) and subtract to find how close the length of the line segment is to the length specified on the card. The difference is the child's score for that round. Then turn over a card for the next child and repeat the activity.

   After several rounds, the child with the lowest total is the winner. Children may find the difference on the ruler by comparing the length of the line segment to the length indicated by the card, or they may subtract as shown in Figure 10–18.

Figure 10–17

Figure 10–18

After children have had experience using the rulers, ask them to find the difference mentally, with a calculator, or by writing the subtraction algorithm.

Multiplication of Common Fractions

Too often, children memorize rules for multiplying and dividing common fractions but have very little concept of the meaning behind the rules. If the rule is forgotten, the children cannot reconstruct the algorithm because they have no understanding of the operation. Nor do they know which operation to choose when faced with a word problem involving fractions because they do not associate any real meaning with the operations. They can use a calculator to do the computation for them only if they know what computation is needed.

Unfortunately, this is also a problem for many adults. Ask anyone to give you a word problem that can be solved by $\frac{2}{3} \times \frac{3}{4}$ or $\frac{2}{3} \div \frac{3}{4}$. Perhaps this is a problem for you as well. After reading this section, you should not only be able to write word problems involving multiplication and division of common fractions but should also be able to demonstrate the solutions with a number of manipulatives.

Children usually begin by multiplying a common fraction by a whole number when they are introduced to multiplication of common fractions. This is perhaps the easiest type of problem to understand and to model with the manipulatives. Again, as with the other operations, the children should start with familiar examples and manipulatives or number lines.

The following activities begin with multiplying a common fraction by a whole number and then multiplying a whole number by a common fraction. Finally, we give ideas for multiplying two proper fractions and for multiplying two mixed numerals. If multiplication of decimal fractions has preceded multiplication of common fractions, have the children compare the processes and word problems to note the similarities. The concepts are not new, although the algorithms may be in a different form.

ACTIVITIES

Middle Grades (4–8)

Objective: to develop the concept of multiplying a common fraction by a whole number.

1. Suggest a situation such as the following to the children when they are first learning to multiply common fractions. Ask the children to find the answer using any of the models with which they are familiar from earlier work with addition and subtraction of common fractions. The following example lends itself to being solved by repeated addition, so children who can add common fractions should be able to solve it. The school track is $\frac{3}{8}$ of a mile around. Sandy is on the track team, and she has run around the track three times in practice. How far has Sandy run?

   Figure 10–19 shows some of the ways in which the children may work the problem. Ask them to write the multiplication sentence below their work and to write the answer as a mixed numeral.

   Ask the children to suggest other examples of problems that can be solved by multiplying a common fraction by a whole number and to show the solution with the manipulatives. Have them exchange problems with each other as well as work their own problems. Encourage them to discuss their methods of so-

lution with the author of the problem. If they have solved the problem in different ways, lead them to discover whether or not each solution works.

Objective: to develop the concept of multiplying a whole number by a common fraction.

2. This concept is one with which children should be familiar from earlier work with the concept of a common fraction as part of a set of discrete objects, but review it at this time. Suggest familiar examples such as finding $\frac{2}{3}$ of a dozen eggs, the number of ounces in $\frac{1}{2}$ of a pound, or the number of inches in $\frac{1}{4}$ of a foot. Point out that the word *of* in these examples indicates that the children should multiply. To find $\frac{2}{3}$ of a dozen, have the children multiply $\frac{2}{3} \times 12$. Since there are 16 ounces in a pound, $\frac{1}{2}$ of a pound is $\frac{1}{2} \times 16$, or 8 ounces. Let the children work these exercises using an array of concrete materials such as chips, if necessary, and discuss their thought processes with each other. Figure 10–20 shows $\frac{2}{3} \times 12$.

Objective: to develop the concept of multiplying two proper fractions.

3. Just as arrays can illustrate multiplication of whole numbers and multiplication of a whole number by a common fraction, they can also illustrate multiplication of two common fractions. Again, introduce this multiplication with a "real" situation such as the following: Steve is planting a rectangular garden. He wants $\frac{1}{3}$ of his garden to be flowers. Steve likes roses, so $\frac{1}{2}$ of his flowers will be roses. What part of the total garden will be roses?

   The array in Figure 10–21 represents the garden with $\frac{1}{3}$ planted in flowers and $\frac{1}{2}$ of that part planted in roses. Ask the children to write the corresponding number sentence $\frac{1}{2} \times \frac{1}{3} = \frac{1}{6}$ below the drawing.

   Use several other examples, including ones that do not use unit fractions, and ask the students to show the solutions with arrays. Situations involving measurement, such as cooking, sewing, and building, are good sources of word problems. After the students have worked several examples and written the corresponding number sentences, ask them to

Figure 10–19

Figure 10–20

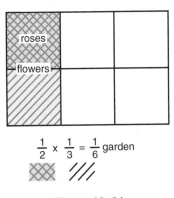

$$\frac{1}{2} \times \frac{1}{3} = \frac{1}{6} \text{ garden}$$

Figure 10–21

compare the sentences to develop a rule for multiplying two common fractions.

After the students realize that they can multiply the numerators and the denominators, ask them if their rule works for multiplying a whole number by a common fraction. Remind children to write the whole number over 1 so that it is in fraction form before they multiply. Encourage the children to solve equations by computing mentally and then comparing their results to the results with the concrete models. They may also use a calculator that displays common fractions to compare results.

4. After the students have used arrays to illustrate multiplication of common fractions, have them use other manipulatives. A few examples follow.

- Fred sees $\frac{3}{4}$ of a pie on the counter. He is hungry, so he eats $\frac{1}{2}$ of the $\frac{3}{4}$ of the pie. How much of a whole pie does Fred eat?

   Notice that Fred is eating $\frac{1}{2}$ of the $\frac{3}{4}$, not of the whole. Figure 10–22 shows the solution. Notice that Fred first cuts each of the fourths into halves; now he has 6 eighths. Then he takes $\frac{1}{2}$ of the 6 remaining pieces, or 3 eighths.

- Rachel is building a scale model of a toy tower. The original tower is $\frac{1}{2}$ of a foot tall. Rachel wants her tower to be $\frac{1}{2}$ of that height. How tall should Rachel build her tower?

Figure 10–22

Use a number line to represent the original tower. Split the number line into halves and mark the height of the original tower. Since the height is 1 space and you cannot divide 1 into halves, divide each space into halves. Look at the number line and realize that the unit is now split into 4 pieces, so each piece is $\frac{1}{4}$. The original tower takes up $\frac{2}{4}$ of the unit (check to make sure $\frac{1}{2} = \frac{2}{4}$). One-half of 2 is 1. The scale model should be $\frac{1}{4}$ of 1 foot tall (see Figure 10–23).

- Brian is making punch. His recipe will serve three people, but Brian needs to serve only two, so he has decided to make $\frac{2}{3}$ of the recipe. The recipe calls for $\frac{1}{2}$ cup of sugar. Brian needs to know how much sugar to use for $\frac{2}{3}$ of the recipe.

   Use Cuisenaire rods to solve the problem (see Figure 10–24). Use the dark-green rod to represent 1 cup of sugar. Why? Can you use any other color rod to represent 1 cup? Try others and see what happens.

   If the dark-green rod is 1 cup, which rod represents the $\frac{1}{2}$ cup of sugar needed for the original recipe? The light-green rod is $\frac{1}{2}$ of the dark-green rod.

   Which rod is $\frac{1}{3}$ of the light-green rod? Which rod(s) represents $\frac{2}{3}$ of the light green rod? Either the red rod or two white rods can be used to represent $\frac{2}{3}$ of the light green rod, but each representation is only $\frac{1}{3}$ of the dark green rod, which represents one cup. Therefore, Brian will need $\frac{1}{3}$ cup of sugar to make $\frac{2}{3}$ of the recipe.

Encourage the children to make up other problems and to discuss their methods of solution. They should realize that the concrete model used does not

Figure 10–23

Figure 10–24

change the answer to the problem. The mathematics remains the same as the materials change.

Objective: to develop the concept of multiplication of mixed numerals.

5. After students are comfortable multiplying two proper fractions, let them encounter situations involving the multiplication of a proper fraction by a mixed numeral or the multiplication of two mixed numerals. One example follows. You and the students should make up other examples of your own.

Raul is looking at a scale drawing of a flower. The scale says the actual flower is $2\frac{1}{2}$ times as large as the drawing. Raul measures the flower in the drawing and sees it is $1\frac{3}{4}$ inches long. How long is the actual flower?

Use a number line to solve the problem, as in Figure 10–25. Measure off $1\frac{3}{4}$ inches twice to show that the actual flower is 2 times as large. Then figure that $\frac{1}{2}$ of $1\frac{3}{4}$ inches is $\frac{7}{8}$ inch and go that much farther on the number line. The real flower must be $4\frac{3}{8}$ inches long.

Again, encourage the students to write the number sentence beneath the materials as they work. Allow students to develop their own algorithms for multiplying mixed numbers. If students try to multiply the whole numbers and then multiply the fractions and add the two parts, use the physical models and the word problems to lead students to discuss why this does not work. This might be a good time to discuss the distributive property by writing the problem as $(2 + \frac{1}{2}) \cdot (1 + \frac{3}{4})$. Some students might prefer an algorithm that tells them this can be solved by $(2 \times 1) + (2 \times \frac{3}{4}) + (\frac{1}{2} \times 1) + (\frac{1}{2} \times \frac{3}{4})$. Other students might discover that they can convert each of the mixed numerals to improper fractions before they multiply, then multiply as they did with proper fractions, and finally convert the answer back to a mixed numeral. Let the children create other problems for each other and solve them using a variety of models, comparing their methods of solution with each other.

Multiplication of Decimal Fractions

If multiplication of decimal fractions follows multiplication of common fractions, children should compare the two by writing number sentences in both forms and comparing the answers. Actual situations that give rise to multiplication of decimal fractions are very similar to those for common fractions. The main difference is that decimal fractions are always tenths, hundredths, or another power of 10. Because multiplying tenths by tenths results in an answer in the hundredths, we do not go beyond multiplying tenths using concrete models. A picture showing 0.52×0.63 must include 10 thousandths and is fairly difficult to draw.

Children multiplying decimal fractions should begin as they did when multiplying common fractions. Give examples of multiplying a whole number times a decimal and then of multiplying a decimal times a whole number. Multiply two decimal fractions later. Adapt the examples given for common fractions to decimal fractions. Have the children again use familiar manipulatives and add other ideas of their own. A few other suggestions follow.

ACTIVITIES

Middle Grades (4–8)

Objective: to develop the concept of multiplying a decimal fraction by a whole number.

1. Money and metric measurement are good contexts for problems involving the multiplication of decimal fractions. Children may begin with the following situation: Kathi has 5 friends coming to her birthday party. She wants to give each friend and herself 0.3 liter of orange juice. How much orange juice will Kathi need so that the 6 children will each get 0.3 liter?

Work this problem as a repeated addition problem. Children who have had previous practice with addition

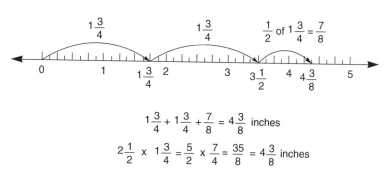

$$1\frac{3}{4} + 1\frac{3}{4} + \frac{7}{8} = 4\frac{3}{8} \text{ inches}$$

$$2\frac{1}{2} \times 1\frac{3}{4} = \frac{5}{2} \times \frac{7}{4} = \frac{35}{8} = 4\frac{3}{8} \text{ inches}$$

Figure 10–25

of decimal fractions should have no difficulty in finding the product. Figure 10–26 shows some possible methods of solving the number sentence 6×0.3.

Have the children record the solution near the picture or materials as they work. Ask the children to compare their work to the addition problem $0.3 + 0.3 + 0.3 + 0.3 + 0.3 + 0.3 = n$. If children have previously multiplied common fractions, ask them also to compare their work to $6 \times \frac{3}{10} = n$.

This is a good time to use a calculator. Ask the students to compare entering $+ .3 = = = = = =$ to entering $.3 + .3 + .3 + .3 + .3 + .3$ and to entering $6 \times .3$. Have them try several examples to see if they always get the same answer with the three methods. Ask them to explain the results using concrete materials.

Encourage the students to suggest and work other word problems, discussing their results with you and each other.

Objective: to develop the concept of multiplying a whole number by a decimal fraction.

2. The following is an example of a problem involving this concept: Jerry has a recipe calling for 5 milliliters of salt. He wants to make only 0.5 of the recipe. How much salt should Jerry use?

Figure 10–27 shows one possible method of solution. Notice that each of the 5 units representing the milliliters is split into 10 equal parts, and, in each case, Jerry takes 5 of the parts.

Again, ask the children to record the number sentence as they work. Let the children suggest and work similar word problems. Encourage them to estimate their answers and to use calculators to compare the results to their concrete work. Ask them to decide if the answer will be larger or smaller than the beginning amount and to explain why this is true.

Objective: to develop the concept of multiplying two decimal fractions.

3. The following is one possible example to use to develop the concept of multiplying two decimal frac-

0.5 x 5 milliliters = 2.5 milliliters

Figure 10–27

tions: Marie is planting a small garden. It is 0.7 meter by 0.8 meter. How many square meters are there in Marie's garden?

Figure 10–28 shows a rectangular array for working this problem. Notice that the garden is less than 1 square meter. Ask the children to predict before working problems such as this whether the answer will be more or less than 1 and to explain their reasoning. In this case, the square meter is broken into hundredths, and the garden takes up 56 of those hundredths. Therefore, the garden covers 0.56 of a square meter.

Use other examples such as the following, which can be shown using string and a meter stick: Amy has a board 0.8 of a meter long. She needs 0.3 of the board for a project. How many meters of board will the project take?

Measure 0.8 meter of string and fold it into 10 equal parts. Take 3 of the parts, and measure that amount.

Ask children to work the following using dimes and pennies: Jeff has $.70. He is feeling generous and wants to give 0.4 of his money to his sister. How much should he give his sister?

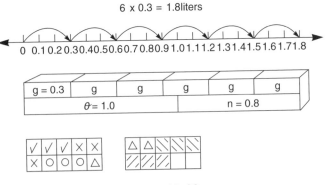

6 x 0.3 = 1.8liters

Figure 10–26

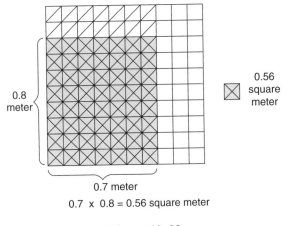

0.7 x 0.8 = 0.56 square meter

Figure 10–28

Jeff can trade in all his money for pennies and then split the pennies into 10 equal piles. He can then give 4 of the piles to his sister.

Work with the children to make up other word problems. Notice that in each case, you need to take one part of the other part and want to know how the final answer relates to a unit. Children will need a great deal of practice with word problems and concrete materials before they become proficient at writing the word problems, but the time spent will pay off well in understanding. If the children have previously worked with multiplication of common fractions, they may also write the problem with common fractions and compare the results, for example, $0.4 \times 0.7 = \frac{4}{10} \times \frac{7}{10} = \frac{28}{100} = 0.28$. After students have worked several problems concretely with decimal fractions, ask them if they can make a generalization about the number of decimal places in the product.

Multiplication with Percent

Many percent problems can be solved as proportions. Another method of solving some problems involving percent is by using the formula $p = r \times b$. This stands for percentage = rate × base. The method is often useful for estimating or computing amounts mentally, such as figuring a 15-percent tip at a restaurant or deciding if you have enough money to buy pants that are 30 percent off the retail price.

The following activities give a few ideas for introducing the concept of multiplying a whole number or decimal fraction by a percent. Because a percent is simply another way of writing a common or decimal fraction, any of the activities described earlier for those forms may be adapted to percents.

Middle Grades (5–8)

Objective: to develop the concept of multiplying a whole number or decimal fraction by a percent.

1. Because *percent* means "per hundred," children should first practice finding percents of multiples of 100. Use the Decimal Squares or base ten blocks to introduce finding percents. Tell the children that you want to leave a 15-percent tip for your dinner. Your bill was $5.00.

   Use the 10-by-10 square from the Decimal Squares or the 10-by-10 flat from the base ten blocks to represent $1.00. You now want to show 15 percent × $5.00. Ask the children to show 15 percent × $1.00. Do this for each of the dollars. How much do you have? Figure 10–29 shows one response. Ask the children to write a number sentence below the work with the squares or the blocks. Encourage the children to suggest and work other problems of their own. After the children have worked several problems with the materials, ask them to rewrite the number sentences using decimals instead of percents and to compare the answers. Use calculators to compute the same problems. If you have a "%" key on the calculator, compare its use to performing the calculation with the amount written in decimal form. Ask the children to practice finding the answers with mental calculation. This is certainly a skill adults frequently need.

2. When amounts are not multiples of 100, the task may not be so easy. Ask the children how they would find 25 percent of 16. Let the children suggest different solutions. They may need to be reminded that a percent is another way of writing a common or decimal

15% x $5.00 = $.75

Figure 10–29

fraction. Discuss the benefits of converting 25 percent to 0.25 and multiplying 0.25×16, or converting 25 percent to $\frac{1}{4}$ and multiplying $\frac{1}{4} \times 16$. Let the children suggest other problems of their own and decide whether to convert to a common fraction or a decimal fraction to find a solution.

In these examples, we were looking for the percentage each time. In the section on developing and practicing skills, we discuss problems involving percentage where the base or the rate needs to be found.

Division of Common Fractions

As mentioned earlier, children and adults often cannot give examples from "real life" of occasions when division of rational numbers is called for. They may vaguely recall that you invert one of the numbers and multiply, but they cannot tell you why this algorithm works or even which number should be inverted. This section focuses on developing the meaning of division of rational numbers and understanding the *invert-and-multiply algorithm*. It introduces an algorithm for division of common fractions that builds on the measurement concept of division and previous work with finding a common denominator. We explore division of common fractions using both measurement and partition division situations, building on previous work with whole numbers. We then use similar situations to explore division of decimal fractions. If children divide decimal fractions before they divide common fractions, have them use this work as a basis for comparison when they begin dividing common fractions.

The following activities begin with the measurement concept of division of common fractions with a whole-number answer and move to fractional or mixed-numeral answers. The partition concept of division of common fractions follows the measurement idea, beginning with whole-number divisors and moving to fractional divisors. Appropriate algorithms are discussed for each type of division.

Middle Grades (5–8)

Objective: to develop the measurement concept of division of common fractions with a whole-number quotient.

1. As with all other operations, begin division of common fractions with an example from the children's lives. The following is one possibility: Brittany has $\frac{1}{2}$ of a quart of orange juice. She wants to pour $\frac{1}{8}$ of a quart into each juice glass. How many juice glasses can Brittany fill?

Ask the children to compare this problem to earlier measurement division problems with whole numbers. A similar whole-number problem might have been: Brittany has 12 quarts of orange juice. She wants to put 3 quarts into each pitcher. How many pitchers can she fill?

Ask the children to first show the problem with whole numbers using materials. Then ask the children to work the problem with fractions. Figure 10–30 shows some possible solutions, using a variety of different familiar manipulatives or pictures.

Notice that in each case, the $\frac{1}{2}$ is exchanged for $\frac{4}{8}$ and the number of $\frac{1}{8}$s in $\frac{1}{2}$ is figured. The algorithm for this may be written as $\frac{1}{2} \div \frac{1}{8} = \frac{4}{8} \div \frac{1}{8} = \frac{4 \div 1}{8 \div 8} = \frac{4 \div 1}{1} = 4 \div 1 = 4$. When the fractions are written with like denominators and the numerators and denominators are divided, the old denominators cancel out and the new denominator is 1. Then divide the numerators the same way you divide whole numbers.

This algorithm appears in an example from a textbook that refers to dividing numerators and denominators as an incorrect algorithm. Such division is actually quite proper and describes well the procedure for working measurement division problems with common fractions. For children familiar with renaming common fractions with like denominators, the method of dividing numerators and denominators is quite similar to the algorithm of multiplying numerators and denominators.

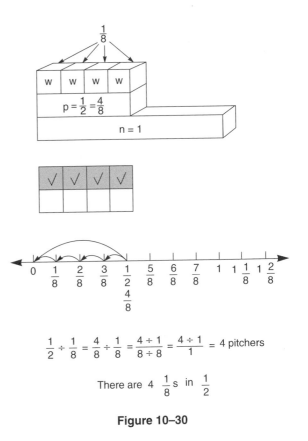

$$\frac{1}{2} \div \frac{1}{8} = \frac{4}{8} \div \frac{1}{8} = \frac{4 \div 1}{8 \div 8} = \frac{4 \div 1}{1} = 4 \text{ pitchers}$$

There are 4 $\frac{1}{8}$s in $\frac{1}{2}$

Figure 10–30

Even though textbooks may not mention this algorithm, children may create it on their own from work with materials. Children easily understand and remember this algorithm after they master algorithms for addition, subtraction, and multiplication of common fractions. We encourage you to use this common-denominator algorithm with your students, and if you decide to teach it in addition to the more traditional invert-and-multiply algorithm, be sure to send a note home to the parents to explain what you are doing and the reason for it.

Other suggestions for measurement situations involving the division of common fractions follow. Discuss the solutions with the children as they work the problems.

Emma works for a cheese packing company. She puts $\frac{3}{4}$ of a pound of Swiss cheese into each party package. Emma has 6 pounds of Swiss cheese. How many party packages can Emma fill (see Figure 10–31)?

Erica is making doll clothes. She needs $\frac{2}{3}$ of a yard of material for each outfit. She has $2\frac{2}{3}$ yards of material. How many outfits can she make (see Figure 10–32)?

Encourage children to make up other problems for each other. Ask the children to write the corresponding number sentences as they work.

Objective: to develop the measurement concept of division of common fractions with a fractional or mixed-number quotient.

2. In the examples given earlier, the quotient was a whole number. Students are often confused when they must divide common fractions that do not have a whole-number quotient. They do not know what to do with the remainder. They may need to be reminded about the algorithm for division of whole numbers that allows them to write the remainder as part of the divisor. For example, the solution to $5 \div 2$ may be written as either 2 with a remainder of 1 or $2\frac{1}{2}$. When written as $2\frac{1}{2}$, the remainder 1 becomes the numerator of a fraction with the divisor 2 as the denominator. Thus, when we say $5 \div 2 = 2\frac{1}{2}$, the remainder 1 is expressed as part of the divisor. In terms of fractions, the problem $5 \div 2$ may be thought of as $\frac{5}{2} = 2\frac{1}{2}$, which is consistent with the division concept of common fractions presented in Chapter 9. This also is the process used when children divide common fractions and the answer is not a whole number, as in the following example.

Danny has to take $\frac{2}{3}$ of a teaspoon of medicine in each dose. The doctor gave him a bottle containing 3 teaspoons of medicine. How many doses can Danny take? Figure 10–33 shows that Danny can take 4 full doses of medicine, and he will then have $\frac{1}{3}$ of a teaspoon of medicine left; that is, $\frac{1}{2}$ of another $\frac{2}{3}$ teaspoon dose of medicine.

Again, we show the common-denominator algorithm for division. Danny has $\frac{9}{3}$ teaspoons of medicine from the doctor and he wants to know how many doses of $\frac{2}{3}$ of a teaspoon each he can make. He can make 4 full doses and $\frac{1}{2}$ of another dose.

Children may wish to try to use a division algorithm similar to that for whole numbers. Study the following:

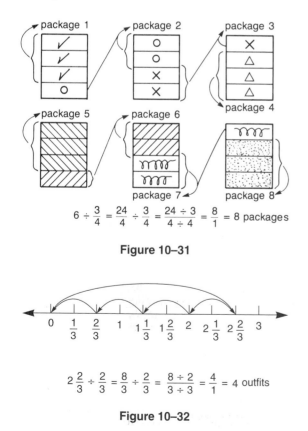

$$6 \div \frac{3}{4} = \frac{24}{4} \div \frac{3}{4} = \frac{24 \div 3}{4 \div 4} = \frac{8}{1} = 8 \text{ packages}$$

Figure 10–31

$$2\frac{2}{3} \div \frac{2}{3} = \frac{8}{3} \div \frac{2}{3} = \frac{8 \div 2}{3 \div 3} = \frac{4}{1} = 4 \text{ outfits}$$

Figure 10–32

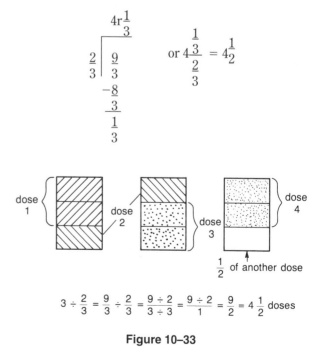

$$3 \div \frac{2}{3} = \frac{9}{3} \div \frac{2}{3} = \frac{9 \div 2}{3 \div 3} = \frac{9 \div 2}{1} = \frac{9}{2} = 4\frac{1}{2} \text{ doses}$$

Figure 10–33

This algorithm will also work.

Encourage the students to suggest other examples and to solve them using the materials and the algorithm of their choice. Ask the students to predict whether the answers will be more or less than 1 before they compute the results. Note that whenever the divisor is larger than the dividend, the quotient will be less than 1. Ask students to discuss their methods of solution. They may use a calculator showing common fractions to compare results.

Objective: to develop the partition concept of division of fractions with whole-number divisors.

3. Recall that division may be shown as either a measurement or a partition concept. In a partition problem, the total and the number of groups are known, and you are asked to find the amount in each group. Children should work a partition problem with whole numbers before they work a corresponding problem with fractions. Here is one suggestion: Neil plans to spend 4 hours on his homework this weekend. He plans to spend equal amounts of time on Saturday and Sunday. How many hours should Neil spend studying each day? Students should recognize this as a partition division problem; they divide the 4 into 2 equal parts to decide that Neil should spend 2 hours studying each day.

After working a problem with whole numbers, try the following: Jack plans to spend $\frac{1}{2}$ hour on his homework this weekend and wants to spend the same amount of time on Saturday and Sunday. How much time should Jack spend on his homework each day?

Figure 10–34 shows different materials used to solve this problem. Ask the children to compare this solution to $\frac{1}{2} \times \frac{1}{2}$. Jack will do $\frac{1}{2} \div 2$ of his homework on each day, or spend $\frac{1}{2}$ of $\frac{1}{2}$ hour.

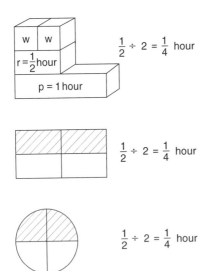

$$\frac{1}{2} \div 2 = \frac{1}{4} \text{ hour}$$

$$\frac{1}{2} \div 2 = \frac{1}{4} \text{ hour}$$

$$\frac{1}{2} \div 2 = \frac{1}{4} \text{ hour}$$

Figure 10–34

Have children make up word problems for other number sentences and compare them to the corresponding multiplication problems. Each problem should be worked with concrete materials, with the number sentences written next to the work.

Following are a few other examples: Compare $\frac{2}{3} \div 3$ to $\frac{1}{3} \times \frac{2}{3}$. Bethany has $\frac{2}{3}$ of a pie. She wants to divide it equally among her two friends and herself. How much of the whole pie should each person get? Each will get $\frac{1}{3}$ of the $\frac{2}{3}$ pie, or $\frac{2}{9}$ of the whole pie.

Compare $\frac{3}{4} \div 5$ to $\frac{1}{5} \times \frac{3}{4}$. Antonio has $\frac{3}{4}$ of a pound of cheese. He wants to make 5 sandwiches and he wants to put the same amount of cheese on each sandwich. How much cheese should he put on each sandwich? Each sandwich should get $\frac{1}{5}$ of $\frac{3}{4}$ of a pound, or $\frac{3}{20}$ of a pound.

After you compare several multiplication and division problems, introduce the children to the invert-and-multiply algorithm for division of common fractions. Discuss why dividing by 3 gives the same answer as multiplying by $\frac{1}{3}$. Compare the results using the invert-and-multiply algorithm to the results using the common-denominator algorithm.

Let the children discuss which method they prefer. Do all children prefer the same algorithm? Does the preferred algorithm depend upon the type of problem being worked? Using the common denominator algorithm fits the measurement problems better, while the invert-and-multiply method matches the partition word problems. As the teacher, you should determine whether the algorithm you prefer is based on the ease of understanding, the ease of use, or simply past familiarity.

The *partition concept of division* of fractions is not difficult to understand as long as the divisor is a whole number, but it can be fairly difficult to explain if the divisor is less than 1. We recommend that you use measurement examples for most of the problems with fractional divisors when students are initially learning to divide fractions. Some of the children may suggest partition word problems with fractional divisors, however, so we present them here. Encourage talented elementary children and middle school students to explore these problems further.

ACTIVITIES

Middle Grades (5–8)

Objective: to develop the partition concept of division of fractions with fractional divisors.

1. Following is a partition word problem for the number sentence $\frac{2}{3} \div \frac{1}{2} = n$: Mr. Washington has $\frac{2}{3}$ of a

ton of grain. It is enough to feed $\frac{1}{2}$ of his herd of cattle. How much grain will it take to feed the whole herd?

Ask the children to compare this to a similar problem with whole numbers, such as: Mr. Ali has 6 tons of grain. This is enough to feed 3 herds of cattle. How much grain will it take to feed one herd of cattle?

Have the children demonstrate how they would solve the problem with whole numbers using manipulatives. Then ask the children to show the fraction problem with the materials. Figure 10–35 shows two possible solutions.

Have the children write the number sentence below the work. Discuss with the children the similarity between solving this problem with the materials and showing $2 \times \frac{2}{3}$ with the materials. Repeat this process with other word problems and other manipulatives. Compare the results to those obtained using a calculator that works with common fractions.

2. Problems in which the divisor is not a unit fraction may pose more difficulties. Challenge the students who are ready to solve a problem such as the following using materials: Evelyn has $\frac{3}{4}$ of a pound of nuts. This is $\frac{2}{3}$ of the original package of nuts. How much did the original package weigh? Write the number sentence $\frac{2}{3} \times n = \frac{3}{4}$ or the sentence $\frac{3}{4} \div \frac{2}{3} = n$.

Children who think of this as a partition division problem may reason this way: "If $\frac{3}{4}$ of a pound is $\frac{2}{3}$ of the package, I should first find $\frac{1}{3}$ of the package and then multiply by 3 to find the whole package. To find

$\frac{1}{3}$ of the package, I need to divide $\frac{3}{4}$ by 2. This tells me that $\frac{1}{3}$ of the original package was $\frac{3}{8}$ of a pound. I should now multiply this by 3, and this tells me that there must have been $\frac{9}{8}$, or $1\frac{1}{8}$ pounds of nuts in the package originally" (see Figure 10–36).

Note that by dividing by 2 and then multiplying by 3, the students have performed the same operation as inverting the $\frac{2}{3}$ and then multiplying by the inverse ($\frac{3}{2}$). The invert-and-multiply algorithm is discussed further in the section on skills. At this point, let the students work several examples using various materials, and encourage them to discuss their solutions.

Division of Decimal Fractions

If division of decimal fractions follows division of common fractions, the students should compare the two algorithms by solving number sentences in both common fraction and decimal fraction form and comparing the two quotients. Word problems and models for the two types of number sentences are essentially the same. Any of the suggestions given earlier for common fractions may be adapted for work with decimal fractions.

Review with children the algorithm for division of whole numbers before you attempt division of decimal fractions. Introduce division of decimal fractions with whole-number divisors first, and then move to divisors with one or two decimal places. A few suggestions for introducing division with decimal fractions follow.

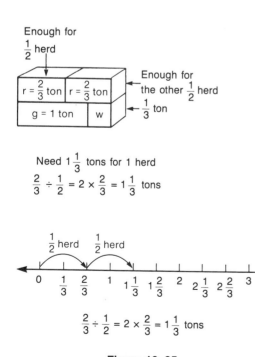

Enough for $\frac{1}{2}$ herd

Enough for the other $\frac{1}{2}$ herd

Need $1\frac{1}{3}$ tons for 1 herd

$\frac{2}{3} \div \frac{1}{2} = 2 \times \frac{2}{3} = 1\frac{1}{3}$ tons

$\frac{1}{2}$ herd $\frac{1}{2}$ herd

$\frac{2}{3} \div \frac{1}{2} = 2 \times \frac{2}{3} = 1\frac{1}{3}$ tons

Figure 10–35

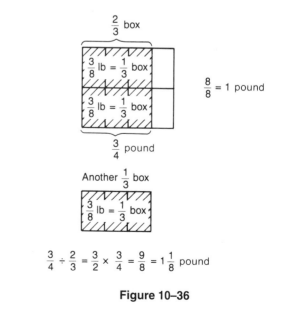

$\frac{2}{3}$ box

$\frac{3}{8}$ lb $= \frac{1}{3}$ box

$\frac{8}{8} = 1$ pound

$\frac{3}{4}$ pound

Another $\frac{1}{2}$ box

$\frac{3}{8}$ lb $= \frac{1}{3}$ box

$\frac{3}{4} \div \frac{2}{3} = \frac{3}{2} \times \frac{3}{4} = \frac{9}{8} = 1\frac{1}{8}$ pound

Figure 10–36

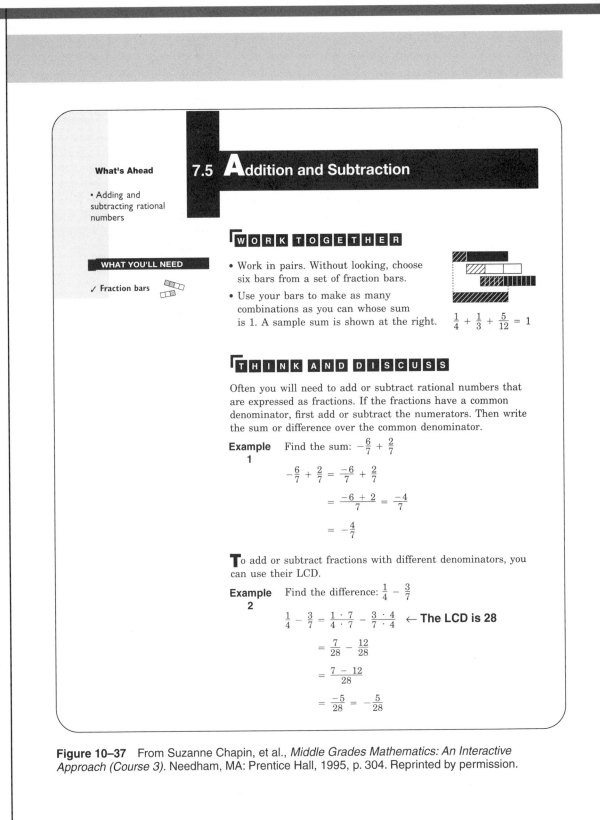

WHAT YOU'LL NEED

✓ Fraction bars

7.5 Addition and Subtraction

WORK TOGETHER

• Work in pairs. Without looking, choose six bars from a set of fraction bars.

• Use your bars to make as many combinations as you can whose sum is 1. A sample sum is shown at the right.

$$\frac{1}{4} + \frac{1}{3} + \frac{5}{12} = 1$$

THINK AND DISCUSS

Often you will need to add or subtract rational numbers that are expressed as fractions. If the fractions have a common denominator, first add or subtract the numerators. Then write the sum or difference over the common denominator.

Example 1 Find the sum: $-\frac{6}{7} + \frac{2}{7}$

$$-\frac{6}{7} + \frac{2}{7} = \frac{-6}{7} + \frac{2}{7}$$

$$= \frac{-6 + 2}{7} = \frac{-4}{7}$$

$$= -\frac{4}{7}$$

To add or subtract fractions with different denominators, you can use their LCD.

Example 2 Find the difference: $\frac{1}{4} - \frac{3}{7}$

$$\frac{1}{4} - \frac{3}{7} = \frac{1 \cdot 7}{4 \cdot 7} - \frac{3 \cdot 4}{7 \cdot 4} \quad \leftarrow \textbf{The LCD is 28}$$

$$= \frac{7}{28} - \frac{12}{28}$$

$$= \frac{7 - 12}{28}$$

$$= \frac{-5}{28} = -\frac{5}{28}$$

Figure 10–37 From Suzanne Chapin, et al., *Middle Grades Mathematics: An Interactive Approach (Course 3)*. Needham, MA: Prentice Hall, 1995, p. 304. Reprinted by permission.

Math Program

The textbook page shown in Figure 10–37 is from Course 3 of a middle grades mathematics program. This would generally be used with eighth-grade students. This page is from a chapter on rational numbers that begins by showing a web at the beginning of the teachers' manual that shows the main topics of the chapter and connections that can be made among the chapters and its applications. These include using exponents and scientific notation in astronomy and biology, using equations with stocks and archaeology, using and comparing rational numbers in sports and physical education and applying operations with rational numbers to electronics and cooking.

Computers and other technology as well as manipulatives are used throughout this series. This chapter recommends the use of the computer programs *Fraction Fuel-Up* by Computer Software, and *Math Blaster Plus* and *Alge-Blaster Plus* by Davidson and Associates. This activity begins with fraction bars to model equations with fractions, applies addition and subtraction to some everyday examples, and then asks students to use both mental math and calculators to find sums and differences of both positive and negative rational numbers. This work follows similar concrete, mental, and calculator work with integers and now extends the operations to rational numbers. The next section of this chapter extends the work to multiplication using arrays and "real-life" applications. Scientific notation using negative exponents, irrational numbers, and algebraic equations that involve rational numbers are also included in this chapter.

This series also includes projects that students work on at home called Backpack Take-Home Activities. One of the activities in this chapter involves using fractions with music and modeling this on a number line. This might be an activity that students develop into a project for their portfolios or that they write about in their journals.

ACTIVITIES

Intermediate (4–7)

Objective: to develop the concept of division of a decimal fraction by a whole number.

1. Metric measures and money are good sources of problems. The following is one suggestion. Encourage children to create other word problems of their own and to discuss their methods of solution.

   Sasha has a board that is 9.3 meters long. She wishes to make a bookshelf with three shelves of equal length from the board. How long should each shelf be?

   Notice that this is a *partition type of division problem*. Model the problem. Cut a piece of string 9.3 meters long and then fold it into 3 equal parts. Ask the children to estimate how long each of the parts is. Will each part be longer than 1 meter? Will each one be longer than 10 meters? About how many meters long is each part? Is each longer or shorter than 3 meters? Ask the children to measure the parts to find the answer to the nearest 0.1 of a meter.

   Ask the students to develop a division algorithm to solve $9.3 \div 3$. Some of the students might use the following form:

$$
\begin{array}{r}
3.1 \\
3\overline{)9.3} \\
\underline{9} \\
3 \\
\underline{3}
\end{array}
$$

Ask the children what should be done with the decimal point. After the children predict that the division algorithm is performed in the same manner as the algorithm for whole numbers, with the decimal point in the quotient directly above the decimal point in the dividend, ask them to work other problems with whole-number divisors using that algorithm and to check the answer by measuring and folding string. Have them use a calculator to see if they get the same results.

Objective: to develop the concept of division of decimal fractions with non-whole-number divisors.

2. After students have had experience dividing with whole-number divisors, give them a problem such as the following: Marta has a lemonade stand. She has made 2.4 liters of lemonade. She wants to sell glasses with 0.3 liter of lemonade in each one. How many glasses can she fill?

   This *measurement type of division problem* can be shown using any of the materials familiar from the work with decimal fractions. Figure 10–38 shows several possibilities. Ask the children to write the number sentence below each example. They may also use a repeated subtraction algorithm to show the measurement idea of division.

   If children have had previous experience with dividing common fractions, ask them to write the number sentence in common fraction form. They may show the problem as $2\frac{4}{10} \div \frac{3}{10} = \frac{24}{10} \div \frac{3}{10} = n$. Using the common-denominator algorithm, this becomes $\frac{24 \div 3}{10 \div 10}$. Since the denominators cancel, the problem is simply $24 \div 3 = 8$. Discuss with the children that this

2.4 ÷ 0.3 = 8 glasses

2.4 ÷ 0.3 = 8 glasses

2.4 ÷ 0.3 = 8 glasses

Figure 10–38

has the same effect as moving the decimal point in both the divisor and the dividend one place to the right.

The children may also use the *division concept of common fractions* to show the problem as $\frac{2.4}{0.3}$. In this form, both the numerator and the denominator may be multiplied by 10 so the divisor will be a whole number. Thus, $\frac{2.4 \times 10}{0.3 \times 10} = \frac{24}{3}$.

This is a good time to use a calculator. Try the problem as $2.4 - .3 - .3 - .3 - .3 - .3 - .3 - .3 - .3$ or $2.4 - .3 = = = = = = = =$. How many glasses of 0.3 liter each can you make? Compare this result to $2.4 \div 0.3$.

After the children have worked several examples and have had an opportunity to create their own division algorithms, you might wish to show them the division algorithm that makes use of the carat to show the movement of the decimal point in both the divisor and the dividend. Ask the children to give you a rule for the number of places that the decimal point should be moved. Be sure the children have experience with divisors and dividends with varying numbers of decimal places so they can generalize that the number of places the decimal point moves in both the divisor and the dividend is equal to the number of decimal places in the divisor. They may need to add decimal places in the dividend to make this work.

Let the children use calculators to check their predictions about moving the decimal points. Using calculators allows them to make predictions and check a much larger number of examples than doing all the calculations with paper and pencil.

Developing and Practicing Skills in Operations with Rational Numbers

After children understand the concepts behind the algorithms for operations with both common and decimal fractions, they can practice their skills with these operations. Do not rush the students into this practice. In many textbooks, one page explains why the algorithms work and then the next page includes thirty or forty exercises for the children to practice the algorithm. It is more beneficial to spend more time on the development of understanding through the use of concrete materials than it is to rush to the abstract algorithms. Children who understand what they are doing often become much more proficient with the algorithms than children who have had a great deal more practice with the algorithms but did not understand the processes they were using.

Because of the proliferation of inexpensive calculators, it is not necessary to spend a great deal of time dividing by a divisor with five or six decimal places or adding two fractions with denominators such as 57 and 34. Very few of us as adults would do those problems with paper and pencil even if the occasion arose for us to work the problems at all. We would work the problems on a calculator. Even fractions with complicated denominators can be easily converted to decimals and the problem worked on a calculator, or the problem can be worked on a calculator that computes with common fractions.

Children should practice simpler problems with paper and pencil, however, and this section is devoted to developing those skills. It is also important that children learn to estimate and calculate mentally with rational numbers. The following section focuses on these skills.

Addition and Subtraction of Common Fractions

After children understand the algorithms for adding and subtracting common fractions, they may practice the two skills together. The activities for reinforcing operations with whole numbers may be adapted to reinforcing the same operations with rational numbers. Children enjoy inventing and playing their own card games, Bingo games, and board games, and they can make the playing cards with number sentences involving addition and subtraction of common fractions. A few other suggestions follow.

ACTIVITIES

Intermediate (4–7)

Objective: to reinforce the skills of adding and subtracting common fractions.

1. Magic Squares, which have the same sum for each row, column, and diagonal, give the children a great deal of practice in both addition and subtraction of fractions. You may fill in as many or as few of the positions of the magic square as you wish, depending on the level of the children. For a real challenge, give the children a blank square and the list of fractions and ask the children to fill in all the spaces so that each row, column, and diagonal has the same sum. Figure 10–39 shows a partially completed square. Discuss with the children the best place to begin and strategies for completing the square. Fraction calculators may be useful here.

2. Children often enjoy using codes and solving puzzles. To solve the riddle in Figure 10–40, children must break the code by completing the addition and subtraction number sentences. Ask the children to make up other codes for each other and trade them.

Magic Sum $1\frac{1}{4}$

Figure 10–39

3. Because computers can individualize work to the level of the children, many computer programs give children practice on the skills they need. The *Fraction Bars Computer Program* series has disks specifically for adding and subtracting common fractions. These disks are good to use as a follow-up to the actual work with the Fraction Bars. Other programs, such as *Fraction Operations* from Tenth Planet, *Fraction Attraction II* from Sunburst, and *Mighty Math Calculating Crew* and *Mighty Math Number Heroes* from Edmark, are designed to give the children more practice with the abstract algorithms. Look for programs that individualize instruction to the needs of the children and explain, not just repeat, the algorithms that the children have missed.

Use these values to solve the following riddle.

$a - \frac{1}{3}$	$b - \frac{2}{3}$	$c - 1$	$d - \frac{1}{4}$
$e - \frac{3}{4}$	$f - 0$	$g - \frac{1}{5}$	$h - \frac{2}{5}$
$i - \frac{3}{5}$	$j - \frac{4}{5}$	$k - \frac{1}{8}$	$l - \frac{3}{8}$
$m - \frac{5}{8}$	$n - \frac{7}{8}$	$o - \frac{1}{10}$	$p - \frac{3}{10}$
$q - \frac{7}{10}$	$r - \frac{9}{10}$	$s - \frac{1}{2}$	$t - 1\frac{1}{2}$
$u - 1\frac{1}{4}$	$v - 1\frac{3}{4}$	$w - 1\frac{1}{3}$	$x - 1\frac{2}{3}$
$y - 1\frac{1}{5}$	$z - 1\frac{3}{5}$		

Why was the elephant wearing blue sneakers?

$$\frac{1}{3} + \frac{1}{3} \qquad 1 - \frac{1}{4} \qquad \frac{1}{4} + \frac{3}{4} \qquad \frac{1}{6} + \frac{1}{6} \qquad \frac{3}{4} + \frac{1}{2} \qquad \frac{1}{4} + \frac{1}{4} \qquad \frac{1}{2} + \frac{1}{4} \qquad\qquad \frac{1}{5} + \frac{1}{5} \qquad 1\frac{1}{5} - \frac{3}{5} \qquad \frac{3}{4} - \frac{1}{4}$$

___ ___ ___ ___ ___ ___ ___ ___ ___ ___

$$\frac{1}{2} + \frac{2}{5} \qquad \frac{7}{8} - \frac{1}{8} \qquad \frac{1}{2} - \frac{1}{4} \qquad\qquad \frac{3}{5} - \frac{1}{2} \qquad 1\frac{1}{8} - \frac{1}{4} \qquad \frac{1}{4} + \frac{1}{2} \qquad \frac{3}{8} + \frac{1}{8}$$

___ ___ ___ ___ ___ ___ ___

$$\frac{2}{3} + \frac{2}{3} \qquad \frac{1}{2} + \frac{1}{4} \qquad 1\frac{1}{10} - \frac{1}{5} \qquad 1\frac{1}{2} - \frac{3}{4} \qquad\qquad 1\frac{1}{2} - \frac{1}{6} \qquad 1\frac{1}{4} - \frac{1}{2} \qquad \frac{3}{4} + \frac{3}{4}$$

___ ___ ___ ___ ___ ___ ___

Figure 10–40

4. The *Math Shop* computer program series available from Scholastic has a number of opportunities for students to practice operations with rational numbers. *Math Shop Spotlight: Fractions and Decimals* has a number of ways for students to practice the addition and subtraction of both common and decimal fractions as students visit various shops to make purchases that require these operations. For example, at the fruit stand, students must decide how many pieces of fruit to buy to meet certain specifications, such as "purchase 20 pieces of fruit that are $\frac{1}{5}$ pears and $\frac{4}{5}$ oranges."

Addition and Subtraction of Decimal Fractions

After children understand the algorithms for addition and subtraction of decimal fractions using the concrete materials, have them begin to practice the algorithms more abstractly. Be sure to make full use of calculators and computers as the children are practicing these skills. Emphasize estimation and mental calculation, because once they leave school, the children will probably be performing more operations either mentally or with a calculator than they will with paper and pencil. A few activities for paper and pencil as well as for calculators and computers follow. Other ideas for estimating and mental calculating are described in that section.

ACTIVITIES

Intermediate (3–6)

Objective: to practice addition and subtraction of decimal fractions.

1. Make up a set of cards for the game Sum of One, as shown in Figure 10–41.

   Children should shuffle the cards and deal them all out to the players. From two to six children may play. At a given signal, each player turns the top card on the dealt stack face up. If any player sees two or more cards that add to one, that player says, "Sum of one." If the player is correct, he or she keeps the cards that add to 1. If players disagree over whether the sum is correct, the children should use a calculator to check. Play continues with every player turning over his or her top card on each turn. The game ends when the designated time period ends or when one player has all the cards. The player with the most cards at the end of

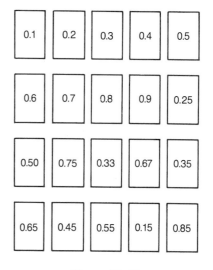

Figure 10–41

the game is the winner. The game may be played with other sums or with differences.

2. Bring in newspaper ads or catalogs from different stores. Make up problems that require the children to add and subtract various amounts using money written as decimal fractions. Ask how much cheaper one item is than another or how much several items would cost all together. Challenge the children to find exactly three items that would have a total cost of $10.00. See if the children can find two items with a difference in price of $.57. Ask the children to make up other problems of their own.

   Encourage mental computation but allow children to use a calculator as they work, if necessary. Let them discuss their strategies for choosing the items and for performing the mental computations.

3. The Target Game allows children to use calculators but requires them to estimate and compute mentally in order to be successful. To play this game, one child begins by displaying a rational number on the calculator. A second child names another rational number as the target, and the third child tries to hit the target by adding to or subtracting from the number currently in the calculator. If the target is hit, the child hitting the target scores 1 point and begins a new game by leaving that number in the display and announcing a new target. The calculator is then passed to the next child, who attempts to hit the new target with addition or subtraction.

   Each time the target is hit, a point is scored and a new target is named. If the target is not hit, the calculator is passed on, and the next player adds to or subtracts from whatever number is currently in the calculator display. A sample game is described on the next page.

Maureen, Esteban, and Marlo are playing. Maureen puts 8.6 into the calculator and Esteban announces a target of 17.2. Marlo is given the calculator and thinks, "If I add 9, I will have 17.6; 17.2 is 0.4 less than that. I will add 0.4 less than 9, or 8.6." Marlo pushes "+ 8.6" and hits the target. She scores 1 point, announces a new target of 12.5, and hands the calculator to Maureen.

Maureen thinks, "12 is 5 less than 17 and 0.2 is 0.3 less than 0.5." She subtracts 5.3, and the calculator shows 11.9. Maureen realizes she did not figure the 0.3 correctly. It is now Esteban's turn, and the target is still 12.5.

Encourage the children to discuss their strategies aloud as they play the game. Strategies should be perfected as play continues. This game may also be played with common fractions, if you have a calculator that can handle them.

4. 🖥 Programs such as the *Decimal Squares Computer Games* by Albert Bennett, Jr., and Albert Bennett, III, available from Creative Publications, build on the children's earlier work with concrete materials. These are good for expanding their understanding as well as for practicing skills. Other programs, such as *Fraction Attraction* and *Get to the Point* by Judah I. Schwartz, available from Sunburst, give more practice with the abstract algorithms. Review software before giving it to the children to be sure it meets their needs.

Multiplication and Division of Common Fractions

After children have a good concrete understanding of multiplication and division of common fractions and can relate the algorithms to both concrete and semi-concrete models, it is time to practice the algorithms more abstractly. As with addition and subtraction, emphasize understanding, not memorization of algorithms. Do not assign 30 or 40 exercises to be worked rotely each night in hopes of building greater proficiency. Be sure children understand any algorithm before they practice it because it is very difficult to "unteach" an incorrectly practiced algorithm. Encourage use of estimation and mental calculation, and teach the use of calculators to solve more difficult problems.

The reinforcement ideas described earlier for whole-number operations or for addition and subtraction of rational numbers may be adapted to multiplication and division of rational numbers. A few additional ideas for extending the algorithms and reinforcing the learning of multiplication and division of common fractions follow.

ACTIVITIES

Middle Grades (5–8)

Objective: to extend the algorithm for multiplying or dividing common fractions by using cancellation.

1. After children have discovered and practiced the multiplication algorithm and the invert-and-multiply algorithm for common fractions, you can help them discover a shortcut for multiplying some fractions. Ask the children to complete the following number sentence and simplify the answer when they are finished:

$$\frac{3}{4} \times \frac{4}{5} = n$$

$$\frac{3}{4} \times \frac{4}{5} = \frac{3 \times 4}{4 \times 5} = \frac{12}{20} = \frac{12 \div 4}{20 \div 4} = \frac{3}{5}$$

Ask the children if there is an easier way to work the problem than to first multiply the 3 and the 5 by 4 and then to divide the 12 and the 20 by 4 to get the 3 and the 5 again. Ask the children to suggest a way to avoid having to multiply both the numerator and the denominator by the same number and then having to simplify the answer. Discuss with the students the relationship between the cancellation process and the use of the right-hand identity for division. Note that in each case you are dividing the numerator and the denominator by the same number; $\frac{a}{a} = 1$, the right-hand identity for division.

Have the children try their suggestions in solving the following problems:

$$\frac{8}{9} \times \frac{9}{15} = n$$

$$\frac{5}{6} \times \frac{7}{5} = n$$

Does the process work for problems such as

$$\frac{4}{5} \times \frac{3}{8} = n$$

$$\frac{2}{3} \times \frac{6}{7} = n$$

Suggest factoring the numerators and denominators before attempting the cancellation. Try to solve the following problem by factoring first:

$$\frac{24}{35} \times \frac{7}{36} = n$$

Let the students suggest other problems and use cancellation before they multiply. Let students use calculators to assist with the larger multiplication problems. In this way, they can explore more examples. (This skill will be very useful in algebra later on.)

Ask the children if they can also use cancellation for division when using the invert and multiply algorithm. Encourage them to explore what happens if they do not invert the divisor before they attempt to cancel.

Objective: to develop the concept of reciprocals.

2. Ask the children to multiply several pairs of common fractions in the form $\frac{a}{b} \times \frac{b}{a}$. They may solve the following problems:

$$\frac{1}{2} \times \frac{2}{1} = n$$

$$\frac{2}{3} \times \frac{3}{2} = n$$

$$\frac{3}{4} \times \frac{4}{3} = n$$

Give the definition of a reciprocal. The *reciprocal* of any number a is the number that you must multiply a by to get 1, the multiplicative identity. Ask the children to find the missing number in each of the following:

$$\frac{5}{6} \times b = \frac{30}{30}$$

$$\frac{7}{8} \times c = \frac{56}{56}$$

$$1\frac{2}{3} \times d = \frac{15}{15}$$

You may need to suggest that the children first write $1\frac{2}{3}$ as an improper fraction. Ask them to give you a rule for finding the reciprocal of any common fraction.

Objective: to develop the meaning of the invert-and-multiply algorithm.

3. After children understand the concept of reciprocals, ask those who seem to grasp the concept well to work a problem involving division of common fractions using a new algorithm. This will reinforce the idea that there are several ways to compute and that the children may choose the method easiest for them. Remind the children that common fractions can be used to represent division: $3 \div 4$ can be shown as $\frac{3}{4}$. Use this idea to show that $\frac{2}{3} \div \frac{4}{5}$ can be written as

$$\frac{\frac{2}{3}}{\frac{4}{5}}$$

How can children solve the number sentence written in this form? Suggest to the children that they multiply the numerator and the denominator by the same number to get a denominator of 1. This renames the fraction with an equivalent fraction and eliminates the messy denominator. (This skill is useful for later work with algebraic fractions.) Notice that it is necessary to multiply both the denominator and the numerator by the reciprocal of the denominator. This has the same effect as inverting the divisor and multiplying the inverted number by the dividend. See the following:

$$\frac{2}{3} \div \frac{4}{5} = \frac{\frac{2}{3}}{\frac{4}{5}} = \frac{\frac{2}{3} \times \frac{5}{4}}{\frac{4}{5} \times \frac{5}{4}} = \frac{\frac{2}{3} \times \frac{5}{4}}{1} = \frac{2}{3} \times \frac{5}{4}$$

Encourage the children to try other examples of their own. Ask them to explain in their own words why the invert-and-multiply algorithm works. This would make a good entry in the student's daily journal.

Multiplication and Division of Decimal Fractions

After children understand the concepts of multiplying and dividing decimal fractions and can relate the abstract algorithms to both concrete and semi-concrete models, they can begin to practice the algorithms more abstractly. Again, we caution you against an overreliance on abstract practice without understanding. Be sure that children understand the concepts and are correctly working the algorithms before they take any practice work home.

We remind you that most adults work problems involving decimal fractions either mentally or with a calculator the majority of the time. This practice will certainly not lessen as our children enter adulthood. Use estimation, mental calculation, and calculators fully as children practice their skills. A few suggestions for practice follow.

ACTIVITIES

Middle Grades (4–8)

Objective: to practice operations with decimal fractions.

1. Ask the students to predict which of the following will have an answer of 2.4 and to explain their predictions.

$$0.2 \times 12 = n$$

$$3.0 \times 0.08 = n$$

$$60 \times 4.0 = n$$
$$0.1 \times 240 = n$$
$$0.24 \times 10 = n$$
$$30.0 \times 8.0 = n$$
$$24.0 \div 10 = n$$
$$240 \div 0.1 = n$$
$$0.24 \div 0.1 = n$$

Ask the students to tell you why they made the predictions they did, and if they were correct. Students may use paper and pencil or a calculator to check, if necessary. Let the students make up other problems for each other.

2. Ask the students to describe the average person in each group of three or four. Tell the children to make several measurements (in meters) of each person in their group. They may measure each person's height; the length of each person's arms, legs, feet, and fingers; the circumference of each person's head, and so on. Avoid any measurements that may embarrass some of the children. After all the measurements are made, ask the children to find the mean of each measurement by totaling the measurements and dividing the total by the number of people in the group. Let the children compare groups to see which group has the smallest or largest mean on certain measures. Use the means to describe an average student. Can you find a student who matches this description? Let the children suggest other problems that involve any of the operations with decimal fractions. Use computer programs to help children practice their skills. The programs mentioned earlier for practicing addition and subtraction of decimal fractions also provide practice for multiplication and division and should be used for these skills as well.

Operations with Percents

Because percents are used so frequently in everyday life, children should develop their skills in this area. After the children understand the meaning of percent using concrete materials and can connect the algorithms to the models, they should practice their skills mentally and with calculators as well as with paper and pencil. Here are a few activities for developing this skill.

ACTIVITIES

Middle Grades (5–8)

Objective: to practice using percents.

1. Earlier, we mentioned using percent in the formula $p = r \times b$. In the earlier discussion, the problems involved knowing the rate and the base and finding the percentage. After mastering those problems, children should also work with problems in which the base or the rate is unknown. Allow children to use a calculator to solve problems such as the following:

   - Juanita bought a coat that was marked $10.00 off. The coat was originally $50.00. What percent was taken off the original price? What percent is the discount of the selling price? Does the discount stay the same? Are the two percents the same? Why not?
   - Fred bought a jacket that was $20.00 off. Fred said he saved 25 percent off the original price. What was the original price?

   Ask the children to make up other problems and to trade the problems with each other. They can use ads from the newspaper as a resource. Children usually prefer solving each other's problems over solving the problems in the book. Discuss what to do with problems that have too much or too little information and the methods used to solve the problems that could be solved.

2. Another common use of percent is to figure the interest on a loan or savings account. Simple interest is figured using the formula $I = prt$; that is, interest = principal $\times$ rate $\times$ time. Ask the students to figure the amount of interest a savings account will pay if it pays simple interest at 5 percent for 2 years on $500.00. Students should take $500.00 $\times$ 5 percent $\times$ 2 to find the interest.

   After students have worked several problems, some of them may wish to explore problems with compound interest or problems with a discount rate rather than simple interest. Children may wish to visit a bank or savings and loan to discuss ways to find the best interest rate on a savings account or on a car loan.

Estimating and Mental Calculating with Rational Number Operations

Throughout the chapter, we have discussed the importance of children using estimation and mental calculation skills. The Second National Assessment of Educational Progress found that only 24 percent of the 13-year-olds tested could correctly choose the number closest to the sum of $\frac{12}{13} + \frac{7}{8}$ from the choices 1, 2, 19, and 21 (Post, 1981). Both 19 and 21 were more popular choices. This demonstrates that most children do not realize that both $\frac{12}{13}$ and $\frac{7}{8}$ are fairly close to 1 and that, therefore, the sum must be almost 2. They are apparently trying to use some misunderstood algorithm that tells them to add either the numerators or the denominators. They probably do not realize that a fraction represents one number to be operated on as one entity and not two numbers, one on top of the other, to be operated on separately. They do not have the necessary understanding of the size of rational numbers. The Fourth National Assessment of Educational Progress found that fewer than 40 percent of the seventh-graders tested could identify the largest and smallest of four fractions, and fewer than 50 percent recognized that $5\frac{1}{4}$ was the same as $5 + \frac{1}{4}$ (Kouba, Brown, Carpenter, Lindquist, Silver, and Swafford, 1988). This basic understanding of the size of rational numbers is crucial to understanding problems that require the use of rational numbers.

Reys and Bestgen (1981) found that students do not perform any better with decimals. Fewer than 30 percent of 13-year-olds could correctly estimate the sum of 95.0 + 865.2 + 1.583 to the nearest power of 10.

It is therefore essential that we help children learn to estimate as well as calculate exactly with rational numbers. We cannot assume that children who can compute accurately with paper and pencil also can estimate. Many children who can correctly compute the product of two rational numbers cannot estimate whether the product will be larger or smaller than 1. The skills of estimation and mental calculation need to be specifically taught. Most children do not automatically transfer skills with paper-and-pencil calculation to mental estimation and calculation. The following activities are designed to help children develop these skills further.

ACTIVITIES

Intermediate–Middle Grades (3–8)

Objective: to develop estimation skills for addition and subtraction of rational numbers.

1. In Chapter 9, we mentioned activities for helping children estimate values of rational numbers by relating them to wholes, halves, and fourths. These skills help the children as they learn to add and subtract fractions. For example, if the children have an exercise such as $1\frac{15}{16} + \frac{12}{23}$, they may think the following way in order to estimate the sum: "$1\frac{15}{16}$ is almost 2. $\frac{12}{23}$ is about $\frac{1}{2}$. Therefore, the sum is about $2\frac{1}{2}$."

A similar activity that relates the problem to money is useful for decimal addition and subtraction because of the children's familiarity with the decimal notation of money. When given a problem such as 2.4876 − 1.98, the children may think, "2.4876 is about $2.50 and 1.98 is about $2.00. Therefore, since $2.50 − $2.00 is $.50, the answer is around 0.5."

Children may wish to use a calculator to see how close the estimates are. Estimates are also a good check on calculator work. Let children suggest other problems for each other to work. After they have worked several examples, children may suggest strategies for refining their estimates. Let them share strategies with each other and decide which ones work best for them.

Objective: to develop estimation skills for multiplication and division of rational numbers.

2. Children are often surprised when they multiply two rational numbers and see that the product is smaller than either of the two factors or when they divide two rational numbers and get a quotient larger than either the dividend or the divisor. These experiences may go against generalizations they have made for whole numbers about the product being larger than either factor or the quotient being smaller than the dividend. Have the children return to the meaning of multiplication and division of rational numbers in order to help them predict the size of the answer to a number sentence involving multiplication or division of rational numbers.

Give the children a word problem such as the following and ask them to tell you whether the scale drawing will be larger or smaller than the original: Jacque is making a scale drawing of his room. He wants the drawing to be 0.1 the size of his room. His room is 3.0 meters by 2.5 meters. How large should the drawing be?

The children should realize that the drawing will be smaller than the room. Ask the children to give you a number sentence for the word problem. Discuss with the children what happens when you take 0.1×3.0. Why is the answer less than 3? Ask the children to tell you the answer without using paper and pencil.

Have the children make up other word problems involving multiplication and predict the answer without using paper and pencil. Let them check using paper and pencil or a calculator if they wish. Encourage children to round mixed numerals to the nearest whole number to estimate their product or to mentally calculate the product of a whole number and a mixed numeral by multiplying the two whole numbers and then multiplying the first whole number times the fraction. For example, $3 \times 2\frac{1}{2} = (3 \times 2) + (3 \times \frac{1}{2})$.

Use word problems for estimation involving division of rational numbers also. Use a problem such as the following, and ask the children if the answer is more than 1 apple: Dan has $\frac{3}{4}$ of a pound of apples. Each apple weighs $\frac{1}{4}$ pound. How many apples does Dan have? Ask the children to write a number sentence for the word problem and to compute the answer mentally. Encourage the children to make up other word problems for each other and to predict the answers before using paper-and-pencil algorithms or a calculator.

Objective: to use estimation skills to correctly place the decimal point in any problem involving operations with decimal fractions.

3. As the use of calculators becomes widespread, children need to become even better at estimating to determine whether or not the answer shown on the calculator is reasonable. One way to practice this skill is to give the children a list of number sentences along with their solutions, only without the decimal points. Ask the children to put the decimal point in the correct place without using paper and pencil or a calculator. Use a list such as the following:

$$6.9 \times 45.0 = 3105$$
$$8.14 \div 0.2 = 407$$
$$0.5 \times 26 = 130$$
$$0.18 \div 0.5 = 36$$
$$3.62 \times 54.789 = 19833618$$

Let students make up other problems on their own.

Objective: to use mental calculations to answer problems involving percents.

4. Because we encounter percents frequently as consumers and often want to figure an amount exactly without using a calculator or paper and pencil, this area is an especially crucial one. Give children experience finding 1 percent and 10 percent of an amount. Ask the children to give you a rule for multiplying by these percents. Let them use calculators to see if the rule always works.

After the children can easily move the decimal point to find 1 percent or 10 percent, ask them for a way to find 5 percent or 15 percent. Good mental calculators might tell you that 5 percent is half of 10 percent and that to get 15 percent you should add 5 percent and 10 percent. Let the children practice finding the exact amount they should leave for a 15 percent tip for meals of varying amounts.

After children can easily find 1 percent, 5 percent, 10 percent, and 15 percent, ask them for an easy way

to find 25 percent, 50 percent, and $33\frac{1}{3}$ percent. The children should know the fraction equivalents of these percents and practice finding $\frac{1}{4}$, $\frac{1}{2}$, and $\frac{1}{3}$ of varying amounts. Bring in sale ads from the paper and ask the children to figure how much they will save on sales of 25 percent, 50 percent, or $33\frac{1}{3}$ percent off.

After children are able to find these percents, ask them for 75 percent, $66\frac{2}{3}$ percent, and 40 percent. Good mental calculators will use 25 percent and/or 50 percent to find 75 percent, $33\frac{1}{3}$ percent to find $66\frac{2}{3}$ percent, and 10 percent and 50 percent to find 40 percent. Given these abilities, the children should be able to either find the exact amount or give a good estimate for any percents they encounter as consumers.

Solving and Creating Problems

Throughout the book, we have emphasized the importance of children both creating their own problems and solving the problems created by others. In this chapter, we have given suggestions for using problem creating and problem solving in teaching operations with rational numbers. Problem creating and solving should be the approaches to learning. Children should learn by asking questions, making mistakes, and finding the answers. Here are a few other suggestions for problems involving rational numbers.

ACTIVITIES

Intermediate–Middle Grades (3–8)

Objective: to use common fractions to describe data collected in an experiment.

1. Ask the children to suggest experiments they can conduct that involve rational numbers. They can use common fractions to describe the number of heads that come up when flipping a coin, the number of spades drawn from a deck of cards, or the number of times a sum of seven is shown when rolling two dice. Conduct one of the experiments 5 times, 10 times, and 100 times. For example, write fractions that represent the number of heads that come up when you flip a coin.

- *Understanding the problem.* If I flip a coin once, the fraction that represents the number of heads is either $\frac{1}{1}$ (one head, no tail out of one flip) or $\frac{0}{1}$ (no head, one tail out of one flip). Now, what I want to do is to flip a coin and see what I get. Each time I flip the coin I can write a new fraction based on one flip, two flips, three flips, and so on. Let's see, if I flip a coin five times I can get 5, 4, 3, 2, 1, or 0 heads. That is one of six fractions. I will need to try.

- *Devising a plan.* I will flip a coin and write a fraction describing the number of heads compared to the number of flips. The denominator will be 1. Then I will flip a coin again and write a different fraction describing the number of heads compared to the number of flips. The denominator will be 2. I will continue to flip the coin, recording a new fraction each time. The denominator will increase by 1 each time I flip the coin (make and use a drawing or model).

- *Carrying out the plan.* On the first flip, I have a head; my fraction is $\frac{1}{1}$. On the second flip, I have a head; my fraction is $\frac{2}{2}$. Next, a tail comes up; my fraction is $\frac{2}{3}$. I continue flipping the coin, and the fractions I get are $\frac{3}{4}, \frac{3}{5}, \frac{4}{6}, \frac{4}{7}, \frac{5}{8}, \frac{5}{9}, \frac{6}{10}$. Now, I want to flip the coin 10 more times to see if I get the same fractions. After that, I will attempt 100 flips.

- *Looking back.* Are all of my fractions written correctly? Do the denominators increase from 1 to 10? (I could write all of the denominators before I ever flip the coin.) Is there any pattern to the numerators? Can I predict the final numerator? Could I write a computer program to simulate the flips so I would not have to do all the work myself? If so, I can repeat the experiment as many times as I want and see if there is a pattern to the results.

Ask the children to describe the fractions they got each time. Which experiment would be the most accurate predictor in the long run? What would happen if they performed the task a thousand or a million times? These activities are a good introduction to teaching probability, which is described in the next chapter.

Objective: to solve problems involving spatial visualization and rational numbers.

2. Use the tangrams in Appendix B for the following activity. Tell the children that all seven pieces together have a value of 1. Ask them to find the value of each shape.

   After the children have determined that the pieces have the values shown in Figure 10–42, ask the children to find the total value of each shape in Figure 10–43. Encourage the children to make other shapes of their own and to challenge each other to find the total values. How many different shapes can they make with the same value? Determine how much more one shape is than another.

Objective: to use decimals and percents to describe data and make predictions.

3. Ask the children to design a survey and collect data on some area of interest to them, such as the food offerings in the cafeteria. Let them list available offerings and suggest others and then ask students to se-

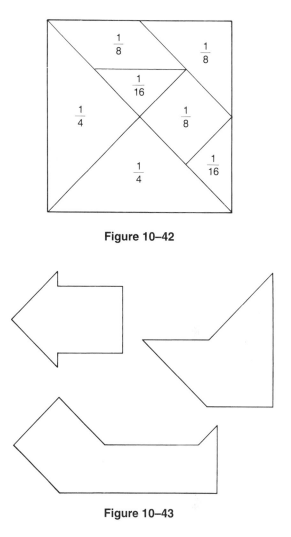

Figure 10–42

Figure 10–43

lect their favorites. When the survey is complete, have the children report the percent of children who chose each offering.

Have the children suggest uses for their data. They may wish to discuss the results with the head of the cafeteria service. Discuss with the children things that must be considered in planning menus, such as cost and nutrition. Have the children interview people from companies that are in charge of planning. How do they make decisions regarding the products or services they offer? The children may even wish to set up a company of their own and to keep records and collect data to plan for the future.

Grouping Students for Learning Rational Number Operations

Several researchers recommend that more time be spent developing the concepts of rational number operations (Hiebert, 1987; and Payne and Towsley, 1990; Mack, 1990).

Students need to work in groups and discuss the concepts that they are constructing using concrete materials. Otherwise, students often have very incomplete or incorrect concepts of operations with rational numbers. They try to apply memorized algorithms to operations with rational numbers, and these algorithms are frequently remembered incorrectly, if at all. Symbols are poorly understood and introduced too early. If the symbols are not understood, and students have attempted to memorize rules rotely, they have nothing to fall back on when their memories fail them. They are not able to judge when they have an incorrect answer from mental estimation, written computation, or a calculator.

To construct correct algorithms, students need to work on real problems using the manipulatives and to discuss their findings with each other. Much of the early work on the development of algorithms should be spent in small cooperative learning groups working on real problems and constructing meaning for each of the operations. For example, to introduce multiplication and division of fractions, you might begin by giving a group a problem such as determining the number of pizzas you need to serve the whole class, if each student wants $\frac{1}{4}$ of a pizza. Let them work with circular fraction pieces to determine the answer. Later determine the number of servings you can get from $3\frac{3}{4}$ pizzas if each serving is $\frac{1}{4}$ of a pizza. Which operations were involved in these problems? Ask the students to write their findings and share them with the entire class. Did each group work the problems in the same way? Which method did they prefer? In this way, the grouping may move from a whole class with the teacher introducing the problem and the students discussing the background knowledge needed to get started, to small groups working cooperatively on the problems, back to the whole class listening to students in different groups explaining their methods of solution.

After the concepts have been constructed, other types of grouping may be used. Practice on the operations may be done in larger groups as students play a game to reinforce the computation skills, or individually as students work on puzzles and problems that require the application of these operations. At times, the teacher may need to work with a small group to remediate any difficulties they may be having, or the teacher may work with the talented students to challenge them to go beyond the explorations of the rest of the class.

Communicating Learning of Rational Number Operations

Like the work with rational number concepts, the work with operations with rational numbers must include a heavy emphasis on verbal communication. The overreliance on rote memorization of symbol manipulation hinders students as they attempt to understand operations with rational numbers. As students work in groups solving problems that involve rational number operations, they should constantly be communicating with each other their understanding of the meaning of the problems. This oral communication frequently helps students make the necessary connections to the concepts they have already learned, such as operations with whole numbers and how they relate to operations with decimal fractions, or the connections between decimal fraction operations and operations with common fractions. When you circulate among the groups as they work on a problem, ask them how this problem relates to earlier ones.

In addition to the oral communication, ask the students to record what they are learning in daily logs and in work for their portfolios. Ask them to look for connections to earlier learning as well as for models that demonstrate what they have learned. Students should make use of concrete materials to exemplify meanings and use pictures in the logs and portfolios to illustrate the written messages.

Connecting Learning of Rational Number Operations

Mr. White's fifth-grade class is investigating the best offers on computer programs that they would like to purchase for their computer lab. They have found three companies that carry the software they want. The first company advertises a total price of $250 with a 10-percent charge for shipping and handling. The second company has a total price of $275 with free shipping and handling and a $25 discount for any purchases over $250. The third company offers the same programs for $300 with a 20 percent discount for schools, and a 5-percent charge for shipping and handling. The students are using the base ten blocks to help determine the best company for the software.

Ms. Willig's eighth-grade class is researching the best way to finance a new automobile. The class has split into teams of three or four, and each team is researching interest rates at different institutions. Jennifer's team has gone to three different car dealers to look at rates if the automobiles are financed at the dealership. Delisa's team has gone to two local banks and is comparing different rates based upon different down payments. Nathan's team has called three credit unions to compare the rates offered there, and Armondo's team is looking into finance companies. When all the data are collected each team will enter the information into a spreadsheet program and graph the results. The class will then analyze the information and make recommendations based on the results. Several students have indicated that they would like to include this information in their portfolios.

Assessing Learning of Rational Number Operations

Use a number of means to assess the children as they add, subtract, multiply, and divide rational numbers. The textbook you use may contain both pre- and post-tests for the rational number chapters. Test the children before beginning a new unit to see which children already understand some of the concepts and which children need to begin at the beginning. If you use a test that pictures concrete materials and uses word problems, you will get a better idea of the children's abilities than if the test has only abstract number sentences for the children to complete. To get a better understanding of the children's levels, add a few questions on the concrete level.

As the children work through the unit, keep anecdotal records of their progress and note any areas of difficulty. Ask the children to explain their thinking processes as they work algorithms or manipulate concrete materials. Tell the children to record the algorithms they create and their solutions to problems in their math journals. They should keep examples of some of their best work in a portfolio.

Lembke and Reys (1994) found that students begin to develop intuitive concepts of percent before formal instruction and that formal instruction tended to make students' concepts of percent less intuitive and more rule-driven, narrowing the variety of strategies that students use to solve percent problems. Be sure in your instruction of percent as well as other types of rational numbers that you build on students' intuitive concepts rather than break them down.

Check the children's written work for any patterns of errors. Some of the common errors children make are listed below. If you see children making any of these mistakes, talk to them about what they were thinking. You will often need to ask the children to return to the concrete models to correct any misunderstandings.

1. In addition and subtraction of common fractions, children add or subtract numerators and denominators.
2. To find like denominators, children add or subtract the same amount from the numerator and the denominator.
3. To multiply common fractions, children cross-multiply; that is, they multiply the numerator of one fraction by the denominator of the other.
4. To cancel when multiplying common fractions, children cancel two numbers from the numerators or two from the denominators.
5. Children cancel when dividing common fractions before they invert and multiply.
6. Children forget to invert when dividing common fractions, or they invert the dividend rather than the divisor.
7. When multiplying mixed numerals, children multiply the whole numbers, multiply the fractions, and then add the products together.
8. When adding or subtracting decimal fractions, children do not line up the decimal points.
9. When multiplying or dividing decimal fractions, children keep the same number of decimal places in the answer as appeared in one of the original numbers.
10. When multiplying or dividing a decimal fraction by a power of 10 or when converting a decimal to a percent or vice versa, children move the decimal point in the wrong direction.

If you see any of these errors, be sure to discuss them with the children. Do not just mark a problem incorrect without any feedback; that does not help the children make the necessary corrections. You will often find in talking to the children that they do not have a clear understanding of rational numbers or their usage in operations. If this is the case, return to the section on concept development in this chapter and use concrete materials with the children. Use word problems and materials that will help guide the children to correct the algorithms for themselves.

Something for Everyone

The physical models discussed in Chapters 9 and 10 should be used by all students initially when learning concepts and operations with rational numbers. Many teachers in the upper elementary grades seem to think that manipulative materials are for only the kindergartners and perhaps the first-graders. They do not believe that older children need these "crutches." Indeed, many of the students in these grades also believe that the manipulatives are "baby stuff."

This is definitely not the case, however. Research has shown repeatedly that manipulatives are helpful for students of any age in learning mathematics and, specifically, in learning rational number concepts (Suydam, 1986). Visual, tactile, and kinesthetic learners need materials to develop a concrete understanding of the concepts. Students with tactile/kinesthetic strengths need to manipulate materials such as region models, base ten blocks, Decimal Squares, Cuisenaire rods, and pattern blocks in order to internalize the concepts discussed in this chapter. They may have difficulty transferring this understanding to paper.

Allow children to devise their own methods of recording what they have learned with the materials. When children are presented with abstract rules or algorithms for such things as finding equivalent fractions, ordering common fractions, or converting a common fraction to a decimal fraction or a percent, be sure they have first modeled the rule with the concrete materials.

If the child is an auditory learner, make sure the child is allowed to explain the rule to you after you explain it. For children who are visual learners, drawing models of the rational numbers is helpful. Make sure children have a variety of models, since some children may understand the concepts for a region model but not for a number-line model. Let these children draw pictures to explain why certain rules work, such as why you can multiply or divide the numerator and the denominator of a common fraction by the same number and not change the value of the fraction. Encourage children to write the algorithm or rule being demonstrated below the picture.

Some children who are able to manipulate symbols abstractly and perform the algorithms correctly may still not understand the meaning of the operations. Therefore, even children who seem to be performing well on an abstract level will benefit from being introduced to the materials.

Make sure to assist students in making the transition from the concrete materials to the abstract algorithms. They will probably not make this transfer automatically. Ask the children to write the algorithms as they manipulate the materials. Do not use the materials one day and expect the children to write the algorithms the next without the materials present. Let each child decide when he or she no longer needs to use the manipulatives. Children are usually good judges as to when the concrete knowledge has become internalized and the manipulation simply slows them down.

Depending on the students' maturational levels and abilities, a few children may only need to see the concepts demonstrated a few times to abstract the necessary information, while others will need to work individually with the materials for a long time as they work through the algorithms. Do not worry about covering all the pages in the textbook as the children learn. You are trying to teach children concepts, not a textbook.

If you find that some children are having difficulty, you may need to use a different concrete model. Some children may not be able to understand a length model such as the Cuisenaire rods or the number line but may be successful with an area model. Some children may not understand the concept of class inclusion or reversibility and may have difficulty with the part-whole model for common fractions. You must have a variety of models available for the children, and you must interview the children individually to determine the best method for teaching each one.

Children who can quickly understand and perform the operations with rational numbers will need more challenging work. Let them demonstrate that they can perform the algorithms correctly, but do not punish them by assigning more exercises from the book.

Many of the problem-solving and problem-creating activities described in this chapter are especially useful for gifted children. Be sure to encourage them to design problems and experiments of their own, but do not always expect them to work alone. They need interaction with their peers and with you. Here are a few other suggestions for avenues of exploration for the gifted students and any others who enjoy a challenge.

ACTIVITIES

Intermediate–Middle Grades (3–8)

Objective: to develop the concept of scientific notation.

1. In scientific notation, a number is written as a value from 1 to 10 multiplied by a power of 10. For example, 3,245,654 can be written as 3.245654×10^6, and 0.000078 can be written as 7.8×10^{-5}.

   Children should explore what happens to the exponent when you multiply and divide powers of 10. For example, $10^5 \times 10^6 = 10^{11}$; and $10^6 \div 10^5 = 10^1$. Ask the children to explain why these statements are true. They may wish to write out all the powers of 10 in expanded form and use the rules they know for multiplying and dividing by powers of 10.

   Ask the children how this knowledge can help them estimate the product or quotient of two numbers written in scientific notation. What happens if you try to add or subtract two numbers written in scientific notation if the powers of 10 are not the same?

   As children explore scientific notation, they can also explore the topic of significant digits. If you have one measurement accurate to four decimal places and another accurate to one decimal place, how many decimal places should you have in the sum, difference, product, or quotient of the two numbers?

Objective: to understand why the invert-and-multiply algorithm works when dividing common fractions.

2. Children should constantly be challenged to discover why rules work, not just how they work. The invert-and-multiply rule for dividing common fractions is just one such example. Earlier in this chapter, we demonstrated this algorithm with numbers using the division concept of a fraction and the multiplicative inverse. Using the following, gifted children could show that this algorithm would work for all rational numbers:

$$\frac{a}{b} \div \frac{c}{d} = \frac{\dfrac{a}{b}}{\dfrac{c}{d}} = \frac{\dfrac{a}{b} \times \dfrac{d}{c}}{\dfrac{c}{d} \times \dfrac{d}{c}}$$

$$= \frac{\dfrac{a}{b} \times \dfrac{d}{c}}{1} = \frac{a}{b} \times \frac{d}{c}$$

Another way to demonstrate the reason that the invert-and-multiply algorithm works is to use the fact that multiplication and division are inverse operations:

$$\frac{a}{b} \div \frac{c}{d} = n$$

Therefore,

$$\frac{c}{d} \times n = \frac{a}{b}$$

To solve for n, multiply both sides of the equation by the reciprocal of $\frac{c}{d}$:

$$\frac{d}{c} \times \frac{c}{d} n = \frac{d}{c} \times \frac{a}{b}$$

Because $\frac{d}{c} \times \frac{c}{d} = 1$, and 1 is the multiplicative identity,

$$n = \frac{d}{c} \times \frac{a}{b}$$

Use the commutative property of multiplication to show that this is the same as:

$$n = \frac{a}{b} \times \frac{d}{c}$$

Ask the children to explain other algorithms for rational numbers. For example, they could use the distributive property to show why, when multiplying two mixed numerals, you cannot just multiply the whole numbers together, multiply the proper fractions together, and then add the two products. Ask them to explain why cancellation works when multiplying or dividing common fractions. Encourage the children to discover and prove other rules for themselves.

Other topics gifted children may be interested in exploring include operations with common fractions in other numeration systems, such as the Egyptian system. Reference books on the history of mathematics and mathematics activity books will give you and the children other ideas.

Many computer programs are designed to individualize instruction based on a child's knowledge and ability. If you have computers available, you should explore the possibilities. In any case, do not try to teach the whole class together from the book. That level of instruction will be inappropriate for most of your students.

KEY IDEAS

Operations with rational numbers are generally introduced in the upper elementary grades and continue to be a major topic of study throughout the rest of elementary and middle school. In spite of their emphasis in the curriculum, operations with rational numbers in any form are generally not well understood by students. In this chapter, we have presented a number of ways to help children understand operations with rational numbers. Concrete materials, computer programs, and calculators are again emphasized for their usefulness in helping students to gain understanding.

Much emphasis is placed on the use of everyday examples and word problems to help children understand when to add, subtract, multiply, or divide common and decimal fractions and percents. The meaning behind rules such as the invert-and-multiply algorithm is described, and alternative algorithms are discussed.

Because so often we need to use common and decimal fractions and percents when we estimate or mentally calculate—for example, in finding a discount at a department store sale or in calculating a tip for a waiter or waitress—these skills are emphasized. Problem creating and problem solving with rational numbers are discussed, including the uses of rational numbers in experiments, data collection, and prediction.

Diagnosis of rational number operations should include data other than just the results of paper-and-pencil tests; include a search for common-error patterns. Individual skills and learning styles should be analyzed when you plan instruction. Challenge each child accordingly.

DISCUSSION QUESTIONS

1. Choose two common fractions such as $\frac{2}{3}$ and $\frac{3}{4}$, and write at least four different number stories using these numbers, each involving at least one of the operations of addition, subtraction, multiplication, and division. Trade problems with a friend, and use physical models, drawings, and equations to illustrate the solutions to each other's problems. Discuss your different methods of solution.

2. Develop an assessment for a fifth, sixth, or seventh grade student on operations with rational numbers, and administer it to a student. Be sure to include application problems as well as computation. Analyze any errors that the student makes. Design a lesson plan based upon the results.

3. Look on the Internet for examples of problems involving operations with rational numbers that are used on a state, national, or international level, such as those from the Third International Mathematics and Science study (http://nces.ed.gov/timss) and the National Assessment of Educational Progress (http://nces.ed.gov/naep). What differences are there between problems given to elementary students and those designed for middle grades students?

Report to the class some of your findings about the proficiency levels of the students tested.

4. Choose one of the pieces of software or one of the videos listed in the references and analyze how you might use it to teach concepts or skills with operations of rational numbers. Prepare a lesson plan using this technology in conjunction with physical models. Be sure to include the assessment that you will use to determine what concepts were learned.

REFERENCES

Behr, Merlyn J., Ipke Wachsmuth, and Thomas R. Post, "Construct a Sum: A Measure of Children's Understanding of Fraction Size," *Journal for Research in Mathematics Education,* 16, no. 2 (March 1985), 120–131.

Bennett, Albert B., Jr., *Decimal Squares.* Fort Collins, CO: Scott Resources, 1982.

Bennett, Albert B., Jr., and Patricia A. Davidson, *Fraction Bars.* Fort Collins, CO: Scott Resources, 1973.

Bezuk, Nadine, and Kathleen Cramer, "Teaching About Fractions: What, When, and How?" in *New Directions for Elementary School Mathematics,* ed. Paul R. Trafton and Albert P. Shulte. Reston, VA: National Council of Teachers of Mathematics, 1989, pp. 156–167.

Bradford, John, *Everything's Coming Up Fractions with Cuisenaire Rods.* New Rochelle, NY: Cuisenaire Co. of America, 1981.

Cole, Joanna, *The Magic School Bus at the Waterworks.* New York: Scholastic, 1986.

Cook, Marci, *Fractions: Try-A-Tile.* Sunnyvale, CA: Creative Publications, 1988.

Dossey, John A., Ina V. S. Mullis, Mary M. Lindquist, and Donald L. Chambers, *The Mathematics Report Card: Are We Measuring Up? Trends and Achievement Based on the 1986 National Assessment.* Princeton, NJ: Educational Testing Service, 1988.

Harnadek, Anita, *Word Problems (Fractions–1, Decimals–1, Percents–1, Percents–2, Mixed Concepts A–1, Mixed Concepts B–1, Mixed Concepts C–1).* Pacific Grove, CA: Midwest Publications, 1980.

Head, Debby, and Libby Pollett. *Count on Kids, Cluster One: Pattern Blocks Parts and Wholes.* Shelbyville, KY: bby Publications, 1994.

Hiebert, James, "Research Report: Decimal Fractions," *Arithmetic Teacher,* 34, no. 7 (March 1987), 22–23.

Holden, Linda, *The Fraction Factory.* Sunnyvale, CA: Creative Publications, 1986.

Jenkins, Lee, and Peggy McLean, *Fraction Tiles: A Manipulative Fraction Program.* Hayward, CA: Activity Resources, 1972.

Kindig, Ann C., "Using Money to Develop Estimation Skills with Decimals," in *Estimation and Mental Computation,* National Council of Teachers of Mathematics, 1986 Yearbook. Reston, VA: NCTM, 1986.

Kouba, Vicky L., Catherine A. Brown, Thomas P. Carpenter, Mary M. Lindquist, Edward A. Silver, and Jane O. Swafford,

"Results of the Fourth NAEP Assessment of Mathematics: Number, Operations, and Word Problems," *Arithmetic Teacher,* 35, no. 8 (April 1988), 14–19.

Lembke, Linda O., and Barbara J. Reys, "The Development of, and Interaction between, Intuitive and School-taught Ideas about Percent," *Journal for Research in Mathematics Education,* 25, no. 3 (May 1994), 237–259.

Mack, Nancy K., "Learning Fractions with Understanding: Building on Informal Knowledge," *Journal for Research in Mathematics Education,* 21, no. 1 (January 1990), 16–32.

McClain, Kay (ed.), "Not One, but Six Fractions Equivalent to One-Third!" *Mathematics Teaching in the Middle School,* 3, no. 3 (November–December 1997), 213–214.

National Council of Teachers of Mathematics, *Curriculum and Evaluation Standards for School Mathematics.* Reston, VA: NCTM, 1989.

Payne, Joseph N., and Ann E. Towsley, "Implications of NCTM's *Standards* for Teaching Fractions and Decimals," *Arithmetic Teacher,* 37, no. 8 (April 1990), 23–26.

Post, Thomas R, "Fractions: Results and Implications from National Assessment," *Arithmetic Teacher,* 28, no. 8 (May 1981), 26–31.

Post, Thomas R., Merlyn J. Behr, and Richard Lesh, "Research-Based Observations About Children's Learning of Rational Number Concepts," *Focus on Learning Problems in Mathematics,* 8, no. 1 (Winter 1986), 39–48.

"Rational Numbers (Focus Issue)," *Arithmetic Teacher,* 31, no. 6 (February 1984).

Reys, Robert E., and Barbara J. Bestgen, "Teaching and Assessing Computational Estimation Skills," *Elementary School Journal,* 82 (November 1981), 117–127.

Robbins, Paul R., and Sharon K. Hauze, *Word Problems with Fractions.* Portland, ME: J. Weston Walch, 1981.

Roper, Ann, and Linda H. Charles, *Fraction Circles Plus Jobcards.* Sunnyvale, CA: Creative Publications (Includes: Adding & Subtracting and Multiplying & Dividing), 1990.

————, *Fraction Squares Plus Jobcards.* Sunnyvale, CA: Creative Publications, 1990.

Sheffield, Linda Jensen, *Problem Solving in Math.* New York: Scholastic Book Services, 1982.

Sheffield, Linda Jensen, *Math Manipulatives for the Overhead.* Greensboro, NC: Carson-Dellosa, 1992.

Sheffield, Linda Jensen, *More Math Manipulatives for the Overhead.* Greensboro, NC: Carson-Dellosa, 1993.

Sheffield, Linda Jensen, *Intermediate Manipulatives.* Greensboro, NC: Carson-Dellosa, 1994.

Suydam, Marilyn N., "Research Report: Manipulative Materials and Achievement," *Arithmetic Teacher,* 33, no. 6 (February 1986), 10, 32.

Thompson, Charles, "Teaching Division of Fractions with Understanding," *Arithmetic Teacher,* 26, no. 5 (January 1979), 24–27.

Vance, James, "Ordering Decimals and Fractions: A Diagnostic Study," *Focus on Learning Problems in Mathematics,* 8, no. 2 (Spring 1986), 51–59.

Vance, James H., "Estimating Decimal Products: An Instructional Sequence," in *Estimation and Mental Computation,*

National Council of Teachers of Mathematics, 1986 Yearbook. Reston, VA: NCTM, 1986.

Williams, Susan E., and George W. Bright, *Investigating Mathematics with Calculators in the Middle Grades.* Austin, TX: Texas Instruments, 1998.

Woodcock, Gary E, "Estimating Fractions: A Picture Is Worth a Thousand Words," in *Estimation and Mental Computation,* National Council of Teachers of Mathematics, 1986 Yearbook. Reston, VA: NCTM, 1986.

Yeager, David Clark, *Story Problems: Fraction, Decimal, Percent.* Palo Alto, CA: Creative Publications, 1983.

Zullie, Mathew E., *Fractions with Pattern Blocks.* Palo Alto, CA: Creative Publications, 1975.

Technology

Annenberg/CPB, *Teaching Math: A Video Library, K–4.* Boston, MA: WGBH Educational Foundation, 1995.

Annenberg/CPB, *Mathematics Assessment: A Video Library, K–12.* Boston, MA: WGBH Educational Foundation, 1995.

Broderbund, *Math Workshop Deluxe.* Novato, CA: Broderbund, 1998. (Software)

Burns, Marilyn, *Mathematics for Middle School.* White Plains, NY: 1989. (series of videos and teacher's guides)

Davidson, *Math Blaster: Episode 1—In Search of Spot.* Torrance, CA: Davidson, 1997. (software)

————, *Math Blaster: Episode 2—Secret of the Lost City.* Torrance, CA: Davidson, 1997. (software)

————, *Mega Math Blaster.* Torrance, CA: Davidson, 1997. (software)

Edmark, *Mighty Math Calculating Crew.* Orlando, FL: Harcourt Brace, 1996. (software)

————, *Mighty Math Number Heroes.* Orlando, FL: Harcourt Brace, 1996. (software)

HRM, *Algebra World CD-ROM.* Pleasantville, NY: Human Relations Media, 1998. (Software)

Scholastic, *Math Shop.* Jefferson City, MO: Scholastic New Media. (Software)

————, *Math Shop Spotlight: Fractions and Decimals I.* Jefferson City, MO: Scholastic New Media. (Software)

Sunburst, *Gears.* Pleasantville, NY: Sunburst. (Software)

————, *Get to the Point.* Sunburst. (Software)

————, *Tenth Planet Explores Math: Number Series Fraction Operations.* Pleasantville, NY: Sunburst. (Software)

————, *Fraction Attraction II.* Pleasantville, NY: Sunburst, 1999. (Software)

Web Sites

http://www.learner.org/   The Annenberg/CPB Math and Science Collection.

http://nces.ed.gov/naep/   National Center for Education Statistics (NCES). *NAEP 1996 Mathematics—Report Card for the Nation and the States: Findings from the National Assessment of Educational Progress.*

http://nces.ed.gov/timss/   National Center for Education Statistics (NCES). *Third International Mathematics and Science Study.*

Chapter 11

Teaching and Learning Probability, Statistics, and Graphing

NCTM Standards

GRADES K–4

Standard 11: Statistics and Probability

In grades K–4, the mathematics curriculum should include experiences with data analysis and probability so that students can—

- Collect, organize, and describe data;
- Construct, read, and interpret displays of data;
- Formulate and solve problems that involve collecting and analyzing data;
- Explore concepts of chance.

GRADES 5–8

Standard 10: Statistics

In grades 5–8, the mathematics curriculum should include exploration of statistics in real-world situations so that students can—

- Systematically collect, organize, and describe data;
- Construct, read, and interpret tables, charts, and graphs;

NCTM (1989), pp. 54, 105, 109. Reprinted by permission.

- Make inferences and convincing arguments that are based on data analysis;
- Develop an appreciation for statistical methods as powerful means for decision making.

STANDARD 11: PROBABILITY

In grades 5–8, the mathematics curriculum should include explorations of probability in real-world situations so that students can—

- Model situations by devising and carrying out experiments or simulations to determine probabilities;
- Model situations by constructing a sample space to determine probabilities;
- Appreciate the power of using a probability model by comparing experimental results with mathematical expectations;
- Make predictions that are based on experimental or theoretical probabilities;
- Develop an appreciation for the pervasive use of probability in the real world.

My Math Journal

Find a partner and a pair of dice and play the following game. Roll both dice and add the two amounts shown together. If the total is odd, you get one point and tally it in the box below. If the total is even, your partner gets a point. The first player to get 10 points is the winner. Keep score below.

GAME ONE

Odd Total	
Even Total	

GAME TWO

Odd Total	
Even Total	

GAME THREE

Odd Total	
Even Total	

Do you think this is a fair game? Explain your reasons for this below.

As you read the following pages, consider these guiding questions:

1. What is the place of probability and statistics in the elementary and middle grades curriculum?
2. What types of graphs might be used to display data, and how do you decide which graph is most appropriate?
3. How might you use technology, including computers and graphing calculators, as students learn to organize, display, and analyze data?
4. What are some common misconceptions students might have as they learn probability, statistics, and graphing concepts, and how might you help them correct these?
5. What are some of the ways that we use probability, statistics, and graphing in other subject areas and in our everyday lives?

It is impossible to pick up a newspaper or listen to the news on television without noticing the extensive use of statistics, probability, and graphs. Computers have made it easier than ever before to handle and report very large amounts of data. Students should be able to understand the statistical reports they will face every day.

Statistics are frequently reported through the use of charts and graphs. Even very young children can make and read simple object, picture, and bar graphs. As children get older, they should learn to read and construct line and circle graphs. They also should learn to plot and read points on a Cartesian coordinate system.

Children should be on the lookout for uses of probability, statistics, and graphs in their everyday lives. We are all familiar with probability from listening to the weather report each day. If there is a 90-percent chance of rain, we do not want to forget to take our umbrellas. If we buy a lottery ticket, we want to know our chances of winning a million dollars. Any type of scientific experiment depends upon the laws of probability. Drugs are tested to determine if the recovery rate improves when the drug is used and to determine if there are any harmful side effects. Businesses use probability for everything from determining the optimum number of check-out lines to quality control on an assembly line. Insurance company officials use probability to set their rates. Wildlife experts tag wild animals and then use probability to determine the number of animals in an area by looking at the ratio of the number of tagged animals spotted to the number of untagged animals spotted.

In many cases, statistics and graphs are used in conjunction with probability. The statistics for a sports player are used to help determine the probability of having a winning team if that player is hired. Statistics are compiled from the results of polls taken to help businesses plan for the future, and probabilities are determined for the success of the business if certain changes are made.

Politicians hire experts in the area of statistics to help them decide the best strategies for winning an election.

An intelligent consumer in today's world must be able to decipher sometimes conflicting sources of information. It is important for children to know some of the fundamental concepts of probability and statistics as well as how to interpret the charts and graphs used to describe those ideas.

Like other topics, probability, statistics, and graphing should be taught using manipulative materials. Children should have numerous chances to perform experiments and collect data to give them practical experience with these topics. Some of the materials include dice, coins, cards, colored cubes, chips, spinners, graph paper, squares, and objects for making concrete graphs.

Children also should make full use of calculators and computers when exploring these topics. Calculators and computers give children the ability to handle more data than they could handle with paper and pencil calculations alone. Graphing calculators allow students to graph various types of information and to explore the effects of changing different variables. Computer programs include those for teaching probability, statistics, and graphing, as well as simulations that give children the opportunity to experiment and make predictions.

Developing Concepts of Probability, Statistics, and Graphing

Since the introduction of the *NCTM Standards* in 1989, probability, statistics, and graphing have received more attention in the elementary and middle grades curriculum. In this chapter, we present a few ideas for teaching some of the basic concepts. Students may wish to explore some of the ideas further on their own. They should find many examples of statistics and graphs in their everyday lives, and they may devise a variety of experiments and surveys to further investigate probability. Do not try to formalize the topics or to teach them on an abstract level. Let the children learn at their own rates on their own levels.

Probability Concepts

Probability can be defined as the measure of likeliness of a particular event occurring. Many of the concepts of probability involve terms the children may hear frequently. These include *impossible, certain, uncertain, likely, equally likely, unlikely, random, sample space, independent, biased, unbiased,* and *random sample.* Children should be given opportunities to become familiar with these terms and their meanings. The following activities may be used to introduce young children to the terminology and to give them a chance to apply the terms to daily events.

ACTIVITIES

Primary (1–3)

Objective: to define and apply the following terms: certain, impossible, uncertain, likely, and unlikely.

1. Discuss with the children events with which they are familiar and ask whether they can be certain that the events will happen. Are there some things you are positive will happen and some you are positive will not happen? Events that we are positive will happen are called **certain,** and events that cannot happen are called **impossible.** At other times, we are **uncertain** whether or not something will happen.

   Give the children a list of statements and ask them to sort them into three piles labeled "Certain," "Uncertain," and "Impossible." Use statements such as the following:

   - Tomorrow, it will rain.
   - Jane will be here every day next week.
   - I will get 100% on my next spelling test.
   - The teacher is older than every child in the room.
   - Tomorrow, we shall all go to the moon.
   - Tonight, the sun will shine brightly at midnight.
   - If I flip a coin, it will land either heads or tails.

   As the children classify the statements, discuss with them the reasons for the classifications. When they have finished, ask them to classify the uncertain statements further as either **likely** or **unlikely.** Will all children agree on whether or not an event is likely? Is it possible for two children to have different answers and for both to be correct? As children discuss these questions, you will get an insight into their conceptions and misconceptions about early probability concepts. When misconceptions appear, lead the children to activities and experiments to help them correct those ideas. Encourage the students to brainstorm a list of synonyms for the terms *certain, impossible, likely* and *unlikely.* Ask them to make their own list of statements to classify into these categories.

   After children have discussed the probability of weather-related events occurring, they may enjoy reading *Cloudy with a Chance of Meatballs* by Barrett (1978) or *It's Raining Cats and Dogs* by Branley (1987). They might wish to write their own stories with impossible events and discuss the humor in commonly heard phrases.

Objective: to develop the concepts of sample space, independent, equally likely, fair, random, unbiased, and biased through use of an experiment and tallies.

2. The **sample space** for a problem consists of all the possible outcomes. The sample space for flipping a coin is heads and tails. Ask the children to predict whether the coin will land with the head or the tail showing if you flip it. Flip the coin and show the children the result. Ask the children to predict the outcomes of several flips of the coin.

   Discuss with the children whether one flip seems to have any influence on the next flip. Events are called **independent** if one event has no effect on another. Give each child a penny and ask the children to make a tally of the heads and the tails out of 10 flips, using the chart in Figure 11–1.

   Tell the children to record the total number of heads and the total number of tails out of the 10 trials. Use calculators to find the total number of heads and the total number of tails for the whole class. Are the totals close to each other? Can you say that heads or tails are more likely?

   If two events have the same probability, then we say that they are **equally likely.** We can say that the coin is a **fair** one if it does not favor either heads or tails. We can also say that heads and tails come up **randomly.** This means that heads and tails have an equal chance of coming up. We may also say that the coin is **unbiased.** It does not favor heads more than tails or vice versa. Use these terms frequently with the children as you perform experiments. Ask the children to define the terms in their own words after they have had a chance to experiment.

   Ask the children if the coin would be **biased** if they dropped it flat on the table instead of flipping it. Would the coin be biased if they flipped a quarter instead of a penny? Would the coin be biased if you flipped a play coin with two heads instead of a head and a tail?

   Children may wish to explore other questions, such as how many times a certain number of heads came up out of 10 flips of a fair coin. Which number of heads was most likely? Which was least likely? What about tails? Let children propose other questions and experiments of their own and help them tally the results.

   Children who are learning to write computer programs can write a simple program to instruct the computer to simulate the flips of a coin and record the results. In this way, the children can collect data on a far greater number of trials. Many calculators also have the capabilities of running simple simulations such as this.

	trials										
	1	2	3	4	5	6	7	8	9	10	total
H											
T											

Figure 11–1

As children get older, they should begin to explore other areas of probability. They may look at events with more than two possible outcomes, and they may begin to use rational numbers to describe probability. The **probability** of an event is

the number of favorable outcomes
the total number of outcomes

If an event is certain, the probability is 1 because all possible outcomes are favorable. If an event is impossible, the probability is 0 because there are no favorable outcomes. All uncertain events have a probability somewhere between 0 and 1. An event with a larger probability is more likely than an event with a smaller probability. The following activities give a few ideas for teaching these concepts to students in the intermediate and middle grades and for expanding on other concepts introduced earlier in the primary grades.

ACTIVITIES

Intermediate–Middle Grades (4–8)

Objective: to develop the concept of assigning a numerical probability to equally likely events.

1. Show the children a spinner with three colors as in Figure 11–2.

   The sample space in this experiment is red, blue, and yellow. Ask the children whether landing on one color is more likely than landing on another color. Spin the spinner a few times to demonstrate that it is a fair spinner; that is, that it does not get stuck on any of the colors. Tell the children that if the spinner is fair, and if each color is equally likely, they can write the probability of landing on any one color as

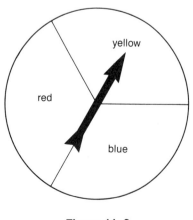

Figure 11–2

the number of favorable outcomes
the total number of outcomes

If you wish to know the probability of getting yellow, the number of favorable outcomes is 1 because there is only one yellow section. The total number of outcomes is 3 because there are three congruent sections altogether. Therefore, the probability of getting yellow is $\frac{1}{3}$.

Ask the children to predict the number of times they could expect to get yellow if they spin the spinner 30 times. Spin the spinner 30 times and record the resulting color each time. How many yellows did you get? Was the actual number close to the prediction?

Ask the children to find the probability of landing on the blue section. What is the probability of landing on the red section? What should you get if you add the probability of the yellow section to the probability of the red section and the probability of the blue section?

Try the experiment using different colors and different numbers of spins. Can you find a formula for predicting the number of times a color will come up? Multiply the probability of the color by the number of spins. Will this always give you the exact number of times the color will come up in the actual experiment? What happens if you add together the probabilities of all the possible outcomes? Will you ever get an answer larger than 1? Ask the children if the spinner would be biased if each child were allowed to turn the spinner so it pointed at her or his favorite color.

2. After the children feel comfortable making predictions with the spinner, try a different material, such as a deck of playing cards. Ask the children to predict the number of times they would draw a black card, a diamond, or a king out of 20 draws. What is the sample space each time? Which is more likely: a black card, a diamond, or a king? Let the children suggest other questions. Discuss with them their strategies and reasoning as they make predictions and perform experiments.

Objective: to distinguish between probable and certain events and between independent and dependent events.

3. Put the name of each child in the class on a 3-by-5 card and put all the names in a box. Predict the number of times a girl's name will be drawn out of a given number of draws when you put the name back in the box after each draw. Can you be certain that your own name will be drawn in 10 draws if the name is replaced after each draw? Can you be certain that a girl's name will be drawn in 10 draws? Can you be certain that a girl's name will be drawn in 100 draws?

   Even though it is very likely that a girl's name will be drawn, you cannot be certain. It is possible to draw only boys' names if the name is replaced after every draw.

Does it make a difference if the name is not replaced after each draw? Some children may wish to research the difference between dependent and independent events.

As mentioned earlier, if events are independent, the outcome of one event has no effect on the outcome of another event. If the first event does affect the next one, the events are said to be **dependent.** Drawing cards with no replacement involves dependent events, while drawing cards with replacement involves independent events. Ask the children to explain why this is true. If you were drawing names of the class members without replacing the name each time, can you be certain that you will eventually draw a girl's name?

Objective: to develop the concept of a random sample.

4. A **random sample** is a sample drawn in such a way that every member of the sample space has an equal chance of being chosen. Random sampling is often used in taking surveys when it is not feasible to survey every possible person or in designing experiments when it is not possible to use every person or event of interest.

Discuss with the children how they might take a random sample of marbles from an opaque bag. Would the sample be random if they were allowed to look into the bag while choosing a marble of a particular color? Would it be random if each child was allowed to choose a marble of his or her favorite color? Would it be random if all of the red marbles were on the top and the blue ones were on the bottom? How could the ideas of random sampling be extended to the activity of taking a random sample of students in the school for a survey?

Put 5 red marbles and 45 blue marbles in an opaque bag. Tell the children you are going to take a random sample of 10 marbles from the bag and use the sample to try to predict the total numbers of red and blue marbles. Let them know that there are a total of 50 marbles and that there are only red and blue marbles. Draw 10 marbles from the bag and record the results. Ensure randomness by replacing the marble each time, blindfolding the person drawing, and shaking up the marbles in the bag.

If you drew 3 red marbles and 7 blue marbles, what would be your prediction for the total numbers of red and blue marbles in the bag? Would you trust your prediction based on the results of only 10 draws? What if you repeated the 10 draws several times?

You and the children can create or find many interesting probability activities as time permits. Some print and electronic sources of activity ideas for the topics in this chapter are listed in the references at the end of the chapter.

Statistics Concepts

Statistics are very often reported using rational numbers. Some of the concepts from statistics are quite abstract and should be reserved for higher grades, but children should be introduced to the basic concepts in the primary grades.

Statistics is the collecting and reporting of data. With all the information collected and reported in the world today, we need to have a way of organizing and describing it so that it is understandable. This collection, tabulation, organization, presentation, and interpretation of data is called **descriptive statistics.** This is the type of statistics most suited for study by elementary students.

The study of statistics and probability is a means of making predictions. The ability to draw inferences and make predictions based on the data collected is studied in **inferential statistics.** Inferential statistics is often not presented until college, but with the proliferation of data and computers in the information age, we are now more likely to see inferential statistics presented in middle and high school. Our focus here, however, is descriptive statistics and ways of presenting the subject to elementary and middle school students.

Tables and graphs are often used to describe the data collected (graphs are discussed in the next section). In addition, there are at least two ideas from the area of statistics you should present to elementary and middle school students; these are the concepts of measures of central tendency and measures of dispersion.

Measures of central tendency are ways of reporting data in the middle. Perhaps the most familiar of these measures is the arithmetic average, or the **mean.** The mean is frequently referred to simply as the **average,** the number found by adding together all the values of interest and dividing by the total number of addends.

Friel (1998) discusses two strategies for helping students visualize the mean: using the "fair-share" model and using the balance model. In the fair-share model, for a problem such as finding the mean number of pets in the class, all the pets are combined and then redistributed so that each student has the same number of pets. In the balance model, the mean is the value about which all the data balances by looking at how far from the mean each student's number of pets is and balancing the sum of the differences.

Another measure of central tendency is the median. The **median** is the value found by listing the values of interest in order from the highest to the lowest and taking the one in the middle if there is an odd number or averaging the two middle scores if there is an even number. The **mode,** another measure of central tendency, is the most frequently reported value.

Measures of dispersion tell you how spread out scores are. The simplest measure of dispersion is the **range,** which is the difference between the highest score and the lowest score. Statisticians use several other measures of dispersion such as standard deviation, but they are generally too complex for children in elementary or middle grades.

A few suggestions for teaching some elementary statistics concepts follow. You may find that your younger students can understand the concepts when they are presented on a concrete level.

ACTIVITIES

Intermediate (2–5)

Objective: to develop the concepts of mode, median, and mean on a concrete level.

1. Tell children the following story and ask them to illustrate it using blocks on a grid as shown in Figure 11–3: Sam practiced his spelling words every day. On Monday he missed 5 words, on Tuesday he missed 1, on Wednesday he missed 3, on Thursday he missed 1, and on Friday he got a perfect score.

   Ask the children if any score showed up more than once. It did; on Tuesday and on Thursday, Sam missed 1 word. Since that is the only score that shows up more than once, that is the mode.

   List the scores from the highest to the lowest: 5, 3, 1, 1, 0. The score in the middle is the median. Therefore, 1 is the median as well as the mode. Are the median and the mode always the same? The children can make up other scores to check their predictions.

   Will the mean be the same? Use the blocks on the grid and the original scores to find the mean number of words Sam missed each day. Given the total number of missed words, figure out how many words would be missed each day if the same number were missed each day. Encourage the children to rearrange the blocks until there are the same number of blocks on each day. The children should be able to rearrange the blocks so that there are 2 blocks on each day.

   Ask the children what would happen if Sam missed 3 words on Thursday instead of 1 word. Now, can they rearrange the blocks so that there are the same number on each day? What should they do with the extra blocks? Can they use rational numbers to answer the question? Could Sam miss an average of 2.4 words per day? Did Sam actually miss 2.4 words on any day? If you read an article that says the average family has 2.2 children, does that mean that any family actually has 2.2 children?

   Let the children keep records of their own test scores or other data of interest and find the mean, median, or mode. They might wish to survey the class to determine the mean, median, and mode for the number of children in each family or the number of pets in each household. After surveys are taken, encourage the children to ask their own questions about the data and to work in groups to come up with answers.

2. Ask each child to draw around one hand on a sheet of paper and to cut out the drawing. Split the class into groups of six to eight, and ask each group to order the hand drawings from the smallest to the largest. The children may need to decide what is meant by the "smallest" hand drawing. Is it the shortest drawing or the one with the least area? Does the hand begin at the wrist and end at the tip of the longest finger?

   Once an ordering scheme is decided upon, ask the children to find the median hand. What is the median if an even number of students are in the group? It should be the average of the two middle hands. To find the average length of two middle hands without measuring, have the students tape the two hands together end to end and then fold the strip in half.

   Are there any hands that seem to be the same size? Is there a mode?

   Suggest that children find the mean hand length by taping the hands together end to end and then folding the strip. For example, if there are 8 children in the group, tape the 8 hands together and then fold the strip of hands in half 3 times to make 8 equal sections. The length of one of those sections should be the mean of the lengths of the children's hands.

   Notice that the mean, median, and mode are found here without measuring. After the children have found these values concretely, ask them to measure the length of each of the hands and to find the mean, median, and mode of the measures. How do these methods compare to the concrete work? Encourage the children to discuss their methods with each other as they are working. Let the children suggest other measures for which they would like to find averages. They might find the average height, shoe size, neck size, and hat size of their group. Is anyone in the group "average"? Does that person have the average size for all the measures?

   Are mean, median, and mode always equally useful? If you have to stock dresses for a department store, would you be more interested in the mean, median or mode? Which does the government use in a census report? (see http://www.census.gov/ for census information)

Sam's spelling words

words missed each day — days of spelling tests

Figure 11–3

Middle Grades (4–8)

Objective: to explore differences in reporting data using the mean, the median, and the mode.

3. The following are the salaries of five professional basketball players: $80,000, $80,000, $100,000, $120,000, and $620,000. The players are complaining about their salaries. They say that the mode of the salaries is $80,000 and that they deserve more money for all the games and practices. The owners claim that the mean salary is $200,000 and that this is plenty for any team. Which side is correct? Is anyone lying? How can you explain the differences in the reports?

   Ask the children to look in newspapers, magazines, and on the Internet for reported averages. Are there any discrepancies in the reports? Are the statistics ever deceiving? Bring in reports for discussion in class. Encourage the children to read any reported statistics critically.

Objective: to use a **line plot** as a quick way to organize numerical data.

4. A *line plot* is a quick way to organize data to show the range and central tendencies, especially if the range is fairly small. It is not a formal graph, but rather is a working graph that can be used in initial data analysis. A line plot is simply a sketch along the horizontal axis in which Xs are used to show the frequency of certain values.

   Ask your students to collect data on some information with a limited number of expected values, such as the number of pets in each household. These data can easily be recorded as students are polled in the classroom. The following line plot shows how students might record the results:

```
      X
X   X
X   X
X   X
X   X  X
X   X  X
X   X  X  X  X              X
0   1  2  3  4  5  6  7  8  9  10
```

   From this line plot, students can quickly see that most of their classmates have no pets or only one pet, while one student has nine pets. This information can then be analyzed further or graphed more formally, if the children wish.

Objective: to use a **stem-and-leaf** plot as a quick way to organize numerical data.

5. A *stem-and-leaf plot* is another quick way to represent the shape of a data set. Unlike the line plot, the stem-and-leaf plot works best for data that span several decades rather than just a few numbers. This plot is most frequently organized by tens and can also be made quickly as data are reported orally. To make this plot, divide each value into tens and units. The tens are the stems of the plot and the units are the leaves. Ask the children to collect data on information that may have values that span several decades. The following plot shows the ages of the people at a family reunion:

```
0 | 2 3 2 5 8
1 | 4 9
2 | 2 0 8 9 5 8
3 | 1 6 9
4 | 5 1 0 9 0 0 6 8
5 | 6 8 9 4
6 | 2 4 2
7 |
8 | 3
```

   From this plot, students can quickly see that there are 5 children under 10, 2 teenagers, and no one in their seventies. As you can see, these data are too spread out to put on a line plot, but they can be neatly organized and analyzed using the stem-and-leaf plot.

Objective: to use a box-and-whiskers plot to aid in the analysis of data.

6. A *box-and-whiskers plot* is another means of looking at data. In this type of graph, you must find the median, as well as the data at the twenty-fifth and seventy-fifth percentiles. If we use the data from the family reunion shown above, we can first find the median by noting that there are 32 people at the reunion and the average of the ages for person #16 and person #17 (when the ages are listed in chronological order) is the median age. In this instance, person #16 is 39 years old, and person #17 is 40. Therefore, the median age is $39\frac{1}{2}$ years old. The median is also the fiftieth percentile. To find the age at the twenty-fifth percentile, we need to find the median age of the first 16 people. This is the average age of person #8 who is 20, and person #9, who is 22. Therefore, the age at the twenty-fifth percentile, the first quartile, is 21. The person at the seventy-fifth percentile is the median of the last 16 people, the average age of person #24 who is 54, and person #25, who is 56 years old. Therefore, the age at the seventy-fifth percentile, the third quartile, is 55.

Name _____ Date _____

1. Your class has been asked by a game company to test their new, exciting chip game, Flip 3 Chips. You will be playing and analyzing the game. The company wants to know whether the game is fair for all players.

Description of Flip 3 Chips

Materials: Three chips
- One chip has an X on one side and a Y on the other side.
- One chip has an X on one side and a Z on the other side.
- One chip has a Y on one side and a Z on the other side.

Small cup

Rules: 1. Shake the chips in the cup and then pour them out.
2. To score, award points by what shows on the chips. It does not matter who flipped the chips.
- Player A gets a point if any two chips match.
- Player B gets a point if all three chips are different.

---

   a. From the description of the game, do you think Flip 3 Chips is a fair game of chance?_____
Explain your answer.

Play the game 20 times. Tally your results below.

Player A (2 chips match)	Player B (no chips match)

   b. From your results, do you think the game is fair?_____ Explain your reasoning.

Figure 11–4   Page 74 from CONNECTED MATHEMATICS PROJECT: HOW LIKELY IS IT, Gr. 6 by Glenda Lappan, James Fey, William Fitzgerald, Susan Friel, and Elizabeth Phillips; Copyright © 1995 by Michigan State University, Glenda Lappan, James Fey, William Fitzgerald, Susan Friel, and Elizabeth Phillips. Reprinted by permission.

Math Program

The page shown in Figure 11–4 is the first page of a four-page unit test on probability in the sixth grade level of *Connected Mathematics,* a mathematics program developed under a grant from the National Science Foundation. In this program, there are eight units each for sixth, seventh, and eighth grades. This unit contains seven two- or three-day investigations, a quiz, two check-ups, a self-assessment and this test. This unit is the students' first introduction to probability in this middle grades program.

Notice that unlike most tests, this one requires that students conduct an experiment, organize the results, and explain their reasoning. On the next page of the test, the teacher sets up a master chart on the board for all students to record their results and students are then asked to compare their own results to the class results. Subsequently, students find the theoretical probability for each part of the original problem and compare that to a related problem as well as to the results from the individual and class experimentation. Explanations are required throughout.

Throughout the unit, the probability is related to rational numbers, geometry, statistics, science, and business. Some of the investigations involve applications of probability to situations such as genetics and contests that are of interest to middle grades students. One section of the book includes an explanation for the teacher of the mathematics underlying the basic principles in the book. In addition to this test, other means of assessment include informal assessment embedded in each investigation, application, connection, and extension questions at the end of each investigation, partner quizzes, notebooks and journals, and a question bank that can be used for homework, reviews, or additional quizzes.

You are now ready to make a box-and-whiskers plot. The right and left sides of the box are the twenty-fifth and seventy-fifth percentiles, and the line in the middle of the box is the median. The two ends of the two whiskers are the ages of the oldest and the youngest person at the reunion, respectively. Can you tell by looking at the plot whether people seem to be bunched in any one age group? Is either of the two extreme ages separated a great deal from the rest of the ages? Encourage students to ask other questions that can be answered by looking at the box-and-whiskers plot.

You may find several other suggestions for handling data in the *Used Numbers* series, which is listed in the reference section.

Objective: to explore box-and-whiskers plots using the list and plot capabilities of a graphing calculator.

7. If your graphing calculator has the capability of creating box-and-whiskers plots, encourage your students to explore this. This might be a good time to join with the science or health teacher in the development of a project that uses some of the statistics and graphing concepts that students are learning. Ask students to collect data such as heart rate from their classmates in a variety of settings such as at rest, after walking for two minutes, and after running for two minutes, and to store these data in three lists on the calculator. After the data are stored, instruct the students to use the calculator to create a box-and-whiskers plot for each of the three sets of data and compare the results. If the calculator has linking capabilities to the computer, this information can be downloaded into the computer for further analysis and for illustrating the reports that are written on the project.

Look at the three box-and-whiskers plots in Figure 11–5. Which one do you think shows students' heart rates at rest, which one shows students' rates after walking for two minutes, and which shows rates

after running? How do you know? Which has the largest range of data? The smallest range? What other information do these graphs show?

Objective: to explore scatter plots using the list and plot capabilities of a graphing calculator.

8. The same data that were used to develop box-and-whisker plots can be used to display scatter plots. The scatter plot in Figure 11–6 shows the student heart rates at rest plotted on the x-axis and the heart rates after running for two minutes plotted on the y-axis.

What relationships do you notice between the rate at rest and the rate after running? What other information can you learn from this graph?

Figure 11–6

You will find several other suggestions for handling data in the books and technology listed in the reference section of this chapter. You may want to attend a workshop on using various types of graphing calculators and computer graphing programs to feel comfortable using some of the new technology.

Graphing Concepts

Unlike probability and statistics, which can be very complex and abstract, the concepts of graphing can be learned as early as kindergarten, and children should graph data frequently in the primary grades. By their very structure, graphs are either concrete or semiconcrete and therefore quite appropriate for elementary school.

Graphs, tables, and charts are often used to display the data collected for descriptive statistics. Children need to learn to read, interpret, and create these displays in order to become intelligent, discriminating consumers. We have already discussed the importance of making a table or chart when solving problems. In this section, we present ideas for teaching graphing using

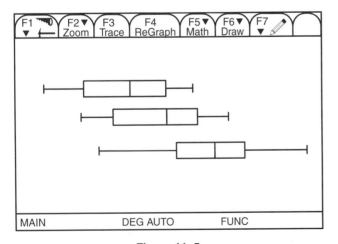

Figure 11–5

concrete objects, pictures, and bar graphs in the primary grades and extending to line, circle, and Cartesian graphs in the intermediate and middle grades.

ACTIVITIES

Primary (K–3)

Objective: to develop the concepts of graphs on a concrete and on a semiconcrete level.

1. You can begin teaching the concept of graphing as early as kindergarten. When graphs are made concretely, it is important to use a system to ensure that each object occupies the same amount of space, so that children are not misled by the differences in the sizes of the objects. The focus should be on the number of objects and not their volume. You might mark off congruent squares upon which to place objects. This keeps the objects lined up, gives each object the same amount of space, and forms a good foundation for later work with bar graphs. Try the following with your class.

   Set up a two-column grid system on the floor (see Figure 11–7). Bring in a large bowl of apples and oranges for the children's snack. Let each child choose one piece of fruit, but ask the children not to eat the fruit yet.

   While the children are holding the fruit, ask if more children have chosen apples or if more have chosen oranges. Let the children discuss ways to find the answer. They may want to walk around the room to count the children with each kind of fruit or they may want the children to sort themselves into two groups before counting.

   After some discussion, ask the children to sort themselves into two groups, one with apples and one with oranges, and then ask the children if they can tell which group is larger without counting. If the sizes of the two groups are similar, they may not be able to tell.

   One of the children may suggest that they line up instead of standing in a group and then look to see which line is longer. This is a good introduction to the squares on the floor. When the children line up, they may not all stand the same distance apart, and therefore, the longer line may not have more children.

   Have the children stand on the squares on the floor. In this way, they are all the same distance apart. Ask the children again if they can tell which group is larger.

   After the children have decided that the longer line represents the most popular fruit, tell them to put the fruit on a napkin on the square on which they are standing and to move away. Now ask the children which is the most popular fruit. Discuss whether it matters if they are standing on the squares or if the

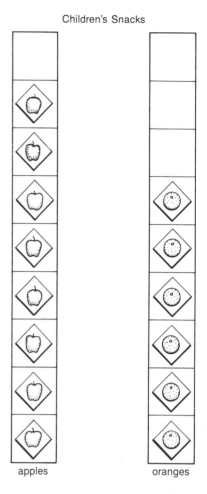

Children's Snacks

apples   oranges

Figure 11–7

fruit alone can represent them. Ask if pictures of the fruit could represent them as well.

Give the children congruent sheets of square paper and ask them to draw a picture of the fruit they chose. (Square Post-It notes are good for this because they can easily be stuck to the blackboard or wall and moved around to answer your questions.) Tape the pictures of the fruit in two horizontal rows, with one row directly beneath the other. Again, discuss which fruit was chosen more often.

To go one step further, tell the children that you want to use just a red square to represent a child who chose an apple and an orange square to represent a child who chose an orange. Give each child a piece of centimeter graph paper (you may copy the master in the appendix) while you demonstrate on large graph paper on the board or on graph paper on the overhead projector. Label the graph and the rows as shown in Figure 11–8, and lead the children to color in the appropriate squares.

Ask the children whether all the graphs they made now give the same information. Which type of graph

Figure 11–8

would be easiest to use if you wanted to print the information in the school paper?

The children can follow up this lesson by suggesting other things to graph, such as eye or hair color or favorite books or pets. Children will be much more involved in lessons on graphing if they are graphing information in which they have a personal interest. Use the information students collect in their graphs as a springboard for more questions. Graphs frequently raise as many questions as they answer. You also might want to explore using a graphing calculator that will make a pictograph.

Objective: to use surveys to collect data and to display the data using graphs.

2. Tell the children to each develop a question with a limited number of answers to ask their classmates or a group of adults. They may have questions such as "What is your favorite subject in school?" or "How many hours a night do you watch TV?" for the students and "Do you think seven-year-olds should get an allowance?" or "Should teachers get higher salaries?" for the adults. Or a child might ask the question of both students and adults and compare the responses. Discuss with the children the importance of selecting a random sample and ask how they would choose one.

After the children have each decided on a question to ask, assist them in devising a tally sheet upon which to record the results. Decide how many people should be surveyed for interesting results. Children with similar questions may wish to team up to be able to question more people.

When the results have been tallied, discuss the best ways to display them. Children asking about favorite pets may make a graph using plastic animals, children asking about favorite sports may draw a picture of each sport for a picture graph, and children asking about allowances may use graph paper to make a bar graph.

Be sure every graph has a title and labels on all the pertinent parts. Encourage the children to make up questions about their graphs for other students to answer.

Even though concrete, picture, and bar graphs should be introduced in the primary grades, children in the intermediate grades should review these types of graphs before moving on to other types. For older children, each picture on a picture graph or each square on a bar

graph may represent more than one object. Children in the intermediate and middle grades should have experience with these graphs as well as line, circle, and Cartesian coordinate graphs and stem-and-leaf plots. Here are several ideas for teaching graphing concepts in the intermediate and middle grades.

ACTIVITIES

Intermediate–Middle Grades (4–8)

Objective: to create and read **picture** and **bar graphs** in which a picture or a bar represents more than one object.

1. Use the results from one of the children's probability experiments as data to be graphed. The children may use their tallies from flipping a coin 100 times. Use a *picture* or *bar graph* to show the results, but let each picture or bar represent 5 flips. Graphs showing 45 heads and 55 tails would look like those in Figure 11–9a and b.

Ask the children how they would graph the same information if each bar or picture represented 10 flips. Discuss how to use a bar or picture. Tell the children to bring to school bar or picture graphs from newspapers or magazines and then discuss what each bar or picture represents in the graph.

Objective: to create and read **line graphs** (frequency polygons).

2. When there is a continued trend from one point to the next, a *line graph* is useful. Line graphs should not be used unless both axes of the graph represent continuous data, such as time and temperature. It is not appropriate to use a line graph to show the numbers of people with different eye colors, for example, because the line between blue and green eyes would have no meaning.

Line graphs can be used in conjunction with subjects other than mathematics. The following activity may be used with a science lesson on plants. You and the children should find several occasions during the day to use their graphing skills.

Plant a fast-growing seed such as a bean seed and graph the plant's height each day after it has sprouted. If the plant is measured in centimeters, it is convenient to use centimeter graph paper to make the line graph. Children may grow the bean plants under several different conditions, such as in a dark closet, on the window sill, with no water, with water every day, and with water once a week. Graph the growth under each condition and discuss the results.

Follow this activity with the computer program *Botanical Gardens* by Robert Kimball and David Donoghue, available from Sunburst, which produces a

Figure 11–9

simulation of growth under different conditions. Students must learn to interpret graphs in order to make hypotheses about the ideal growth conditions.

Find examples of line graphs in newspapers and magazines and discuss whether they are used properly. Encourage children to make up questions for each other that can be answered by looking at graphs. Leave these questions in the learning center or copy them for the class to answer.

Objective: to create and read **circle graphs.**

3. A *circle graph* is used to show information dealing with parts of a whole. The circle represents a whole, and the information being graphed is some fractional part of that whole. When children construct their own graphs, it is helpful if they can use a compass and measure angles. This activity can be used before the children have acquired these skills if you cut out sections of a circle ahead of time.

Tell the children that you are going to make a circle graph to represent their pets. If you have 12 children with pets, cut several circular regions out of different colors of construction paper. Cut each circular region into 12 congruent sections (for a different number of children, adjust the size of the regions accordingly). Select a different color of paper to repre-

sent each type of pet (dogs, cats, etc.). Let each child select a colored region that represents her or his pet and place the region into the circle. Figure 11–10 shows a circle graph for one group of 12 children.

Encourage the children to ask questions about the completed graph. Fractions and percents can be used to describe the sections of the graph if children have studied these topics.

After children have learned to use a compass and protractor, discuss with them the fact that every circle

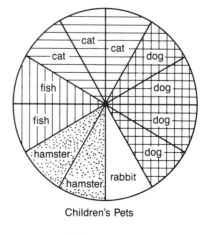

Children's Pets

Figure 11–10

has 360 degrees. Ask how many degrees would show the number of children in the class who have brown eyes. How would they show the number of children that have blue eyes? Let the children find and graph other data. Discuss circle graphs in newspapers and magazines.

If your graphing calculator has the capability of making circle graphs, show the students how to store the information they have collected on their pets in a list, and then use the calculator to graph the data. Several computer programs give you this same capability (see the references for a listing of some). Choose a graphing program on the computer that the students are familiar with, and repeat the same project. Ask students to compare the results of creating a graph by hand, using the graphing calculator, and using a computer program. What are the benefits and the drawbacks of each method?

Objective: to create and read **Cartesian graphs.**

4. *Cartesian graphs* are used for locating positions in two-dimensional space. Children may be introduced to Cartesian coordinates in social studies when they look up a point on a map. Maps generally use a letter and a number to give a location. Ask children to study the map in Figure 11–11 and then tell you where the school, the hospital, and the library are, giving the letter for the horizontal location first and then the number for the vertical location.

Encourage the children to make up other maps of their own. They may make up treasure maps and ask other children to find the secret location of the treasure by moving around on the map using horizontal and vertical locations.

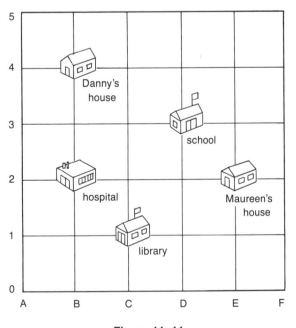

Figure 11–11

The game Battleship is a good follow-up to this activity. Children must guess the coordinates of their opponent's hidden ships in order to sink them.

After students are comfortable using letters and numbers to locate points, introduce them to ordered pairs of numbers, in which the first number gives the x-coordinate and the second number gives the y-coordinate. When older students understand the concept of negative integers, let them use all four quadrants of the Cartesian plane.

Developing Skills in Probability and Graphing

One function of the mathematics curriculum in the elementary and middle grades is to give children a solid foundation in the basic concepts of probability, statistics, and graphing, but most of the skills practice in these areas is reserved for secondary school. However, some additional skills in probability and graphing can be developed before high school, and some ideas for developing these skills follow.

Probability Skills

Probability is a good topic with which to reinforce a student's ability to think systematically. In Chapter 5, we discussed using tree diagrams to find various combinations for attribute materials. Tree diagrams are also quite useful in probability for finding combinations and permutations. The concepts of combinations and permutations are important ones in the area of discrete mathematics and should be explored by elementary and middle school students. The following activities suggest ways to reinforce these skills.

ACTIVITIES

Intermediate–Middle Grades (4–8)

Objective: to use a tree diagram to find combinations and permutations.

1. The topics of combinations and permutations are fundamental to the subject of probability. When we want to know how many ways we can select one number of objects from another number of objects, we are finding the number of **combinations.** The order of the selection does not matter when finding the number of combinations. When we are interested in the order, we are finding the number of **permutations.**

If we flip 2 coins, we may be interested in all the possible combinations of heads and tails we could get. We can list the combinations as 2 heads, 1 head and 1 tail, and 2 tails. Are these combinations equally likely?

A tree diagram is useful for determining the sample space. Make a tree like the one in Figure 11–12, in which the tree gives us the Cartesian product of (H, T) × (H, T) or HH, HT, TH, and TT.

Do you think that the chance of getting 2 heads is the same as the chance of getting 2 tails? Is it the same as the chance of getting 1 head and 1 tail? Remind the students that the probability of getting 1 head and 1 tail is

the number of favorable outcomes
the total number of outcomes

Here, you have 2 favorable outcomes, HT and TH, out of the 4 possible outcomes.

Give the children a penny and a nickel to flip and tell them to record the results of flipping the coins together 20 times. Compile the results from the whole class. Did 2 heads come up as often as 1 head and 1 tail? Does this result match your expectations?

Notice that you are reinforcing the skill of making a table as students record the data from the experiment. You may also ask the children to make a bar graph to show the results of flipping the coins. Does the information on the graph coincide with your expectations based on the tree diagram?

After the children can make a tree diagram to show the possible outcomes from 2 flips of a coin, ask them to expand it to show the outcomes from 3 or more flips. Encourage the children to make up other experiments and to use a tree diagram to find all the possible permutations to predict the outcome before performing the experiment. Can they show other results on a tree, such as the suit of two cards drawn or the numbers shown on the roll of 2 dice? How does this relate to earlier work with tree diagrams and attribute

materials? How can probability be used to discuss the chance of randomly choosing a given attribute piece?

Objective: to extend skills with combinations and permutations.

2. If we want to know the number of different committees of 3 we can form from a group of 5 students, we are looking for the number of combinations. It does not matter who is selected first for the committee. On the other hand, if we are going to pick a chairperson, a secretary, and a treasurer for the committee, we are looking for the number of permutations, because the position of each of the three selections does matter.

Suppose we have 3 children in the group—Danny (D), Maureen (M), and Amy (A)—and wish to select 2 of them. We could select Danny and Maureen; this would be considered the same as selecting Maureen and Danny. Listing all the possibilities, we have: DM, DA, and MA.

Are there any other choices? If we were looking for permutations rather than combinations, then the selection of Maureen and then Danny is considered different from Danny and then Maureen. We must add the following to our list to include all the possible permutations: MD, AD, and AM.

What happens if you are choosing a committee of 3 people out of 5? How many combinations do you have now? Use a tree diagram to help find all the possible permutations. (Remember that for permutations, the order is significant.) Simply list the terms in order from the tree to find all the possible permutations. How can you use a tree diagram to find all the combinations? After you have found the permutations, remove any combinations from your list that have the same elements only in a different order as another combination in the list.

Draw a tree diagram to show all the possible 3-dip ice cream cones if the choices for each dip are vanilla, strawberry, chocolate chip, and rocky road. Assume that it makes a difference which dip is on the top, which is in the middle, and which is on the bottom. What if the order does not make a difference? Will it affect your tree if you do not want any 2 dips that are the same flavor?

If you have calculators with probability functions, explore the use of the keys for finding combinations (nCr) and permutations (nPr). For example, to find the number of combinations possible when you select 3 people for a committee from a total of 5 people, you would push 5 then nCr and then 3 to tell the calculator that the *n* (total number) is 5 and you wish to select 3 (*r*). (Different calculators put these numbers in differently, so be sure to check the one you have.) If the order matters and you are finding permutations, you would choose

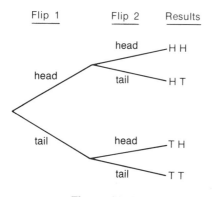

Figure 11–12

nPr instead of nCr. Compare the results you find on the calculator in Figure 11–13 with those from the tree diagram.

Objective: to distinguish between **odds** and **probability.**

3. Children (and adults) are often confused about the difference between odds and probability. As mentioned earlier, the *probability* of an event is

$$\frac{\text{the number of favorable outcomes}}{\text{the total number of outcomes}}$$

The **odds** of an event are

$$\frac{\text{the number of favorable outcomes}}{\text{the number of unfavorable outcomes}}$$

Note that the probability of an event shows the number of favorable outcomes out of the total, similar to the part-whole concept of a fraction discussed in Chapter 9, while the odds compare one part (favorable outcomes) to the other part (unfavorable outcomes) as in the ratio concept of fractions.

For example, with a fair coin, the probability of getting a head is $\frac{1}{2}$, but the odds of getting a head are $\frac{1}{1}$. The total number of outcomes in the sample space is 2 (head or tail), and the total number of unfavorable outcomes is 1 (the tail). If you randomly draw a marble from a bag containing 5 green marbles and 3 red marbles, the probability of getting a green marble is $\frac{5}{8}$, but the odds of getting a green marble are $\frac{5}{3}$. Because the odds of getting a green marble are greater than 1, does that mean you will always choose a green marble?

Ask the children to return to some of the earlier activities for probability and determine the odds as well as the probability of an event. How could you determine the odds if you knew only the probability? Could you determine the probability if you knew only the odds?

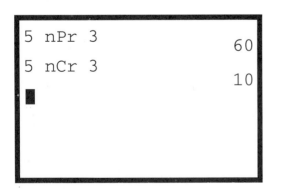

Figure 11–13

Computer programs such as *Graphing* from MECC can list all the possible outcomes of an experiment as well as simulate events such as coin flips thousands of times. Such listings and simulations can be useful as children practice probability skills. Children may also enjoy writing computer programs for simple probability concepts using the random-number generator. Even some calculators contain random-number generators.

Graphing Skills

After children have mastered the basic concepts of graphing and are able to decide on the appropriate graphs to use to display different types of data, they should use graphs in all subject areas whenever they have collected or need to interpret data. Much graphing practice may therefore take place in subject areas other than mathematics. As children construct their own graphs, be sure they clearly label the entire graph as well as all of its pertinent parts, such as the two axes on a line graph or every bar on a bar graph.

Children should practice reading as well as constructing graphs. Children should learn not only to read the data on a graph but also to use the data to solve problems.

After the children have had concrete experiences with a wide variety of graphs, use other computer programs to reinforce graphing concepts. This might be done with the spreadsheet and graphing sections of a program such as Appleworks or Excel, or programs written specifically for graphing such as *Graph Links* and *Data ToolKit* from Harcourt Brace; *Graphers* and *Data Explorer* from Sunburst; or *Tabletop, Jr.* and *Tabletop, Sr.* from Broderbund.

Computer programs allow the children to quickly see the relationships between tables and graphs and to see the effects of editing data and changing variables. This would also be a good time to introduce the program *The Cruncher,* published by Davidson, to intermediate and middles grades students. This program is a good introduction to the use of spreadsheets and can be used to collect, organize, and graph data for student projects such as portfolio entries that are based on the collection and analysis of data on a topic of interest to the students.

In addition to working with computers, children might enjoy the video *Math Vantage: Unit III: Data Analysis* available from GPN. In this series of four 10- to 15-minute programs, middle grades students collect, show, and analyze data and make decisions based upon the data analysis and knowledge of probability. The *Teacher's Guide* and *Student Lessons* add support for teachers who wish to use these lessons.

Teachers might wish to view the *Communication* video from the Annenberg *K–4 Video Library* to see several groups of students during their lessons on data, probability, and statistics. These include a primary class estimating the number of seeds in a pumpkin, a third grade class working in teams to collect data for a bubble gum contest, and a bilingual first grade class analyzing information about ladybugs. In all of these classroom excerpts, students are using a variety of means of representing data in their discussions and writing about mathematical concepts.

Estimating and Mental Calculating

One of the main uses of probability is to predict future events. In fact, the study of probability began in European gambling halls about 300 years ago in analyzing games of chance to better predict their outcomes. These predictions are based on past events and/or mathematical models and are not just random guesses. The field of probability has grown since then, however, and probability is now used to predict everything from next year's corn crop to population growth in the twenty-first century.

Statistics go hand in hand with probability in predicting future events. Statistics are used to analyze the results of polls and experiments. The results of such an analysis affect, for example, what shows are on television next season, who will be the next president of the United States, and which drugs are approved for fighting cancer. Graphs are often used to display and search for trends in these data.

As part of the activities already mentioned in this chapter, you should frequently ask the children to predict outcomes before performing an experiment. The following are a few other suggestions for reinforcing estimation skills.

ACTIVITIES

Elementary–Middle Grades (2–8)

Objective: to use **experimental probability** to predict future events.

1. For some events, such as flipping a coin or drawing a card from a standard deck, we can find a mathematical probability without ever touching a coin or a card. For other events, such as tossing a tack or a paper cup, we must actually perform the experiment before we can accurately predict what will happen. Give each child a paper cup and ask him or her to mark a spot 12 inches above a table from which to drop the cup. The cup should be dropped bottom down, as in Figure 11–14.

   Ask the children to describe the possible outcomes in the sample space. Let each child drop the

cup 20 times and record the numbers of times the cup lands bottom down, top down, and on its side. Let the children predict the number of times it will land in each of those positions for the next 20 tries, for 50 tries, and for 100 tries.

Combine the results from the whole class and make predictions. Do the predictions become more accurate as students collect more data? How close are the predictions?

How do scientists use their experiments to make predictions? You may be able to get a parent or another adult in the community whose career involves using experimental data to make predictions to talk to the children.

Objective: to use **opinion polls** to make predictions.

2. Before the next class election, take an opinion poll to try to predict the results. Do you have to poll everyone in the school to make a prediction? What

Figure 11–14

is an unbiased sample? If everyone in the school votes, will your sample be biased if you poll only sixth-graders? What if you poll only girls? Do some research to learn about the prediction of the winner in the 1948 presidential race between Dewey and Truman.

Objective: to use commercial materials to make predictions.

3. Children enjoy using materials that they see every day to make predictions. It is interesting to determine whether common materials such as bags of pretzels or chips or boxes of raisins always contain the same number of objects. Give each pair of children a small bag of pretzels and ask them to predict the number of pretzels in the bag before opening it. After the predictions are recorded, ask the children to open the bag and count the number of pretzels. Make a graph to show the number of pretzels in each bag. Predict the mean, the median, and the mode. Are these the same? Compute to determine each one. Which would best describe the "average" number of pretzels in a bag? Does the size of the pretzel make a difference? Repeat the activity with another material, for example, raisins or small candies of different colors. With the small candies, you can also predict and determine the most common color. Is the most common or least common color the same for every bag? Make a graph to show your findings and make a list of questions that the class would like to explore further. This activity may take place over a month or so and may include writing to the manufacturer for information on how the product is marketed. How do they use statistics and probability to ensure that every bag has at least some minimum amount of food in it?

Simulations on calculators or simulation games for the computer, such as *Oh, Deer!* and *Lemonade Stand* from MECC, can help children learn to use data to make predictions for the future.

Solving and Creating Problems

Probability, statistics, and graphing offer students a number of excellent opportunities to design and carry out their own experiments. Throughout the chapter, we have discussed the importance of having children make up their own problems and questions. A few additional suggestions for teaching students to create and solve problems in these areas follow.

ACTIVITIES

Elementary–Middle Grades (2–8)

Objective: to use probability to determine the most likely sum of two dice.

1. Make a chart like the one in Figure 11–15a and ask the children to keep a tally of the number of times each total comes up when they roll two dice. Combine the tallies from the whole class. Which total came up the most often? The least often? How would you explain these results?

   Tell the children to use a tree diagram to predict the most common total. Make a tree such as the one in Figure 11–16 to find all the possible permutations of two dice.

   List the ordered pairs at the ends of the branches and find the totals. Make a table, like the one in Figure 11–15b, to show the number of times each total came up. How does this table compare to the actual totals found in your experiment?

   - *Understanding the problem.* Each member of the class has already rolled a pair of dice 2 times, so we have 52 rolls altogether. And, the chart based on our tree diagram shows what would come up most often if everything were perfect. We need to compare the charts to see what is alike and what is different.

     When we rolled the dice, we got 52 answers. Will that make a difference when we compare? We can tell which numbers come up most often and then next most often. Or we can change the numbers to fractions or percents and then compare them.

   - *Devising a plan.* To compare the different numbers that came up most often, we'll make a small table with two rows. In one row, we'll put the percent of times each number came up when we threw the

a.

Totals										
2	3	4	5	6	7	8	9	10	11	12

Which Total Came Up Most Often?

	2	3	4	5	6	7	8	9	10	11	12
Dice	4%	6%	12%	10%	6%	23%	15%	8%	2%	13%	2%
Tree	3%	6%	8%	11%	14%	17%	14%	11%	8%	6%	3%

b.

Figure 11–15

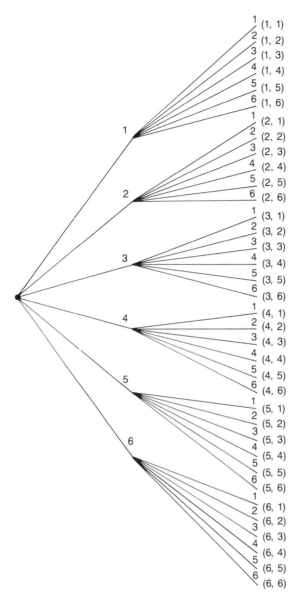

Figure 11–16

dice. In the next row, we'll put the percent of times the number appeared on the tree. Then we can compare the percents (make a systematic list).

- *Carrying out the plan.* We count how many times each number was rolled by the class, and Darlene and Ben use their calculators to find the percent each number represents. We put that information in the table. Then Candy and Jackie calculate the percents from the tree diagram. We put the results in the table, as shown in Figure 11–15.

  Now we can compare the results. The first thing we observe is that the number 7 was rolled most often (23 percent) and also appears on the tree diagram most often (17 percent). Now we can make several other important observations.

- *Looking back.* We were able to find that 7 was the most likely sum of two dice. We found even more information because the table was systematic.

Have the children discuss the other findings from the table. What were the least frequent totals? How many times would you expect to get a total of 7 out of 100 rolls? Would you expect to get a total of 2 very often? Why?

Encourage the children to devise other experiments. Use two spinners, each numbered 1, 2, and 3, or keep track of cards drawn out of two hands that each have cards numbered 1, 2, 3, and 4. Tell children to draw tree diagrams to show all the possible permutations and to use these permutations to predict results for their experiments. How close are the predictions? Encourage students to discuss their strategies as they carry out the experiments.

If you have calculators with a random number generator, experiment with using that to simulate rolling dice, or spinning a spinner, as in Figure 11–17. How do the simulations on the calculator compare with those using actual dice or spinners? Which gave you results closest to those predicted mathematically?

Objective: to use statistics to persuade an audience.

2. Have the children select a problem that directly affects them or the school. This may be a hazardous street in front of the school, lack of appealing food in the cafeteria, or a need for supervised activities after school.

Help the children develop an instrument to collect data to support their case, such as a method of clocking and counting the traffic passing the school, surveys to determine the need for some change in the cafeteria menu, or a method of counting children's after-school activities. Discuss finding a random sampling of times for the traffic count or a random sampling of students and adults to participate in the survey. Discuss the best ways to organize and

Figure 11–17

display the data collected. Help the children present their data to those responsible for making changes, such as members of the traffic bureau or the head cook in the cafeteria.

Claus (1989) reported on a statistics project undertaken by her fourth-grade class. They polled the entire school on cafeteria preferences such as fruit bars versus ice cream and hot versus cold lunches. They presented results to the principal, the PTA, and the school nurse, who used the information to make changes. The use of data collection and statistical interpretation gives students a powerful tool for change.

Objective: to create questions for other children to answer by looking at graphs.

3. Graphs are often presented along with a ready-made list of questions to be answered. Turn the tables by asking the children to write the questions. Tell them that the only rule is that it must be possible to answer the questions using the information found on the graph. Encourage children to think of questions that no one else in the room will think of.

Structure some questions by specifying an operation or operations that must be used in the solution. Play a game like the television show "Jeopardy," in which you give an answer and ask the children to come up with the question. Keep the questions in the learning center for the children to work on later.

Grouping Students for Learning Probability, Statistics, and Graphing

The topics of probability, statistics, and graphing offer a natural opportunity for cooperative learning groups to explore real phenomena in their environments. Russell and Friel (1989) point out that leading elementary textbook series generally present work in data analysis as exercises requiring students to find information on a table or graph that has already been constructed for them. The textbooks rarely ask students to interpret or collect data. They note that the use of real data requires that students select the problems and questions they wish to explore, collect the data, work with a range of different data representations, including those that make use of technology, and learn to analyze data that is frequently "messy," with either too much or too little information that may or may not answer the questions that the students have asked. After the data have been collected and analyzed, students learn to use data not only to answer previous questions, but also to generate new

ones. In their *Used Numbers Project,* Russell and Friel (1989) developed a number of curriculum modules to help K–6 students learn how numbers can be used to describe, interpret, and make predictions about real phenomena. A typical activity begins with the teacher or a student presenting some information to the whole class about an area of interest, such as the average family size in the community. Students then discuss questions that they are interested in exploring and break into small groups to come up with ways to investigate the topic. The teacher circulates to give help as needed, and students can move from whole group, to small group, to individual work in the exploration of the problem. Many of the activities presented in this chapter can be done in this same manner.

Communicating Learning of Probability, Statistics, and Graphing

By the very nature of the topics, this is an excellent area for students to use concrete or visual models to demonstrate findings. Students who have taken a survey to find the answer to a question of interest to the class, can use concrete or visual graphs, tables, or charts to display the information they have found. This is an excellent example of information that should be communicated to a larger audience, not just to classmates. Surveys of interest to the children often pertain to the policy decisions of others, such as the principal, the mayor or the city council, the PTA, your congressperson, or the cafeteria manager. Students should be encouraged to write reports of their findings and conclusions and to illustrate their reports liberally with charts and graphs. They may then present the reports to the appropriate parties. Local newspapers or local cable television companies may be willing to publish or broadcast the results if they are approached by a committee of the students. This is an excellent way to integrate mathematics with other areas of the curriculum such as social studies and language arts and to empower the students at the same time.

When writing reports that make use of charts and graphs, students should learn to make use of graphing programs on the computer and the graphing calculator to illustrate the reports. Reports might be in written form or might be more interactive, using a program such as Microsoft PowerPoint on the computer. Using the graphing capabilities of the calculators and computers not only gives the students a deeper understanding of the data they have collected, but also gives them very practical skills in presenting data that they will use throughout their lives.

Connecting Learning of Probability, Statistics, and Graphing

Mr. Calebreto's second-grade class is studying the weather and discussing how meteorologists make their predictions each day. Mr. Calebreto says that he heard that there is a 50 percent chance of rain tomorrow and asks whether anyone knows what that means. After much discussion, he takes out a coin and says that there is a 50 percent chance of the coin coming up heads. The students have had some experience flipping coins, so they are able to discuss how often heads and tails generally come up for a coin. Mr. Calebreto then flips the coin and announces that it has come up heads. He then asks the students what the chances are of that happening again. Some students think that another head is more likely since the first one and others think it is now time for it to come up tails. Another group of students think that the first flip makes no difference. After a discussion of the coin flip, Mr. Calebreto returns the discussion to the weather and the meaning of a 50 percent chance of rain. The students decide that they should keep track of the predictions each day and keep a chart to see how accurate the predictions are. They will return to the probability discussion each day as they chart both predictions and actual weather conditions.

Mr. Greco's sixth-grade class is studying several double bar graphs that show the percent of males and females in age categories from 0–4 to 80–84. They have noticed that one of the graphs shows a very high percent of people over age 55, another graph shows a much higher percent of males than females, and yet another shows a very large number of both males and females between the ages of 15–19 and 20–24. Mr. Greco has told them that one of the graphs is from a college town, one is from a town with a large retirement community, and one is from a town with a large army base. Students are discussing how they can determine which town is which by looking at the ages and genders shown on the graphs. They decide that it would be interesting to collect data on their own town, make a double bar graph, and compare it to the graphs they are studying. Brittany offers to call City Hall to get the needed information.

Assessing Learning of Probability, Statistics, and Graphing

Most of the assessment in the areas of probability and statistics should be informal. Standardized tests for elementary students may include reading graphs and finding measures of central tendency, but they may not include questions on probability and statistics. This does not mean that probability and statistics are unimportant, however. A good foundation in the basic concepts of these topics will greatly help the students as they progress in school.

Piaget and Inhelder (1975) studied the development of the idea of chance in children and found that children's thinking in this area can be divided into three stages. In the first stage (up until about age 7 or 8), children do not understand the concept of randomness. They look for some hidden order and make predictions based on their own preferences or on the misconception that an outcome should "catch up" to the others. Very unlikely events do not surprise them.

In the second stage (from about age 7 or 8 until about age 11 or 12), a broad understanding of randomness is achieved, but children do not understand the effects of large numbers. Very unlikely events do surprise them and cause them to look for a reason. In the third stage, that of formal reasoning, children understand the effect of large numbers and can assign numerical probabilities.

In a review of a number of studies conducted after the Piaget and Inhelder research, Shulte (1987, p. 32) concluded that "the research indicates that students have some understanding of probability and related topics, that this understanding increases with age and instruction, and that probability can successfully be taught in the elementary school in carefully selected experiments." He recommends that probability be included among the topics presented in elementary school.

Teachers should be aware of some of the misconceptions that students may have about probability as well as about graphing and statistics. The following list gives some of these misconceptions:

1. Students may believe that a mathematical probability should give the exact outcome of an experiment. They may believe that if the probability of getting a head is $\frac{1}{2}$, then they should always get 10 heads out of 20 flips of a coin. Be sure the students have many opportunities to perform experiments to see the differences between mathematical and experimental probabilities.
2. Students may believe that the instrument used in a probability experiment has a memory. They may believe that if they have gotten 5 heads in a row with a coin, then it is more likely that a tail will come up on the next flip. Discuss whether the coin has any memory of what came up on the previous flips. The probability of getting a tail remains the same, no matter what came up previously.
3. Students may hold a bias against or in favor of a particular outcome in an experiment. They may feel that 3 should come up most often on a die because it is their favorite number or that 6 should not come up very often because they do not like it. The activities suggested in this chapter in which the students are

asked to tally a large number of experimental results should be discussed with the students to see if the results match their expectations.

4. Students may expect all outcomes to be equally likely, even if they are not. They may think that a total of 2 on two dice should be just as likely as a total of 7. Students should discuss the activity relating the roll of two dice to the tree diagram described in the problem-solving section of this chapter.

5. Students may wish to overgeneralize from their own experiments or surveys. If they take a poll of all the fifth-graders in their school, they may wish to say that the results would be the same all over the country. Discuss with them what is wrong with such thinking. Making correct inferences from data is a skill that takes time and experience to develop.

6. Students may confuse the different measures of central tendency. They should be given a number of chances to find the mean, the median, and the mode and to discuss which measure is used in the articles they read and which is most appropriate for a given situation.

7. Students may try to use an inappropriate graph to display data. Discuss with them why a line graph is not good for showing favorite colors. Does the line from blue to green have any meaning? What is a more appropriate type of graph?

8. Students may forget to completely label a graph. How can they interpret a graph if some of the labels are missing?

9. Students may use pictures of different sizes on a picture graph, bars of different widths on a bar graph, or spaces of different sizes between numbers on a line graph. How does this affect the interpretation?

When testing students' understanding of these topics, be sure to observe their work during experiments and while they are developing surveys. Do not rely on paper-and-pencil instruments. You may wish to use an instrument such as "How Many Questions?" (Jensen, 1973), which tests a student's ability to ask questions involving graphs rather than his or her ability to answer such questions. This will give you an idea of how well the students understand what graphs may be used for and how creative the students can be in posing questions.

Encourage students to keep records of their work and to write down any questions they have as they progress. Students often are excellent judges of how well they understand the lesson.

Something for Everyone

Many of the topics discussed in this chapter are particularly appropriate for gifted students. Some gifted students may seem to prefer working on abstract problems and may not use concrete materials, even though using these materials may be of benefit to them. Probability and statistics give gifted children an opportunity to be involved with concrete models and simulations that have direct applications in many fields of interest to them, such as future careers in business and the professions.

Gifted students can further explore topics in probability and statistics, such as the counting processes for finding the number of possible outcomes and methods for finding the probability of a statement involving *and* and *or*. Use counting processes to find the number of five-digit zip codes or seven-digit phone numbers. Encourage the students to develop their own rules for finding the number of possible combinations, with or without repetition. How can you determine the number of ways Event A *and* Event B can happen? Is this the same as determining the number of ways Event A *or* Event B can happen?

Compare this work to the work with Venn diagrams using union and intersection (discussed in Chapter 5). Pascal's triangle (which was introduced in Chapter 6) also has interesting applications for finding the number of possible combinations of anything with two possibilities for each move. Encourage children to make connections to earlier learning whenever possible.

Introduce the story, *Socrates and the Three Little Pigs,* by Mori, where Socrates, the philosopher wolf, uses ideas of combinations and permutations to determine the best way to find one pig by itself in one of the five houses in which the pigs live. If your calculators have the capability of finding combinations and permutations, encourage students to explore these functions and to compare them to the mathematics that Socrates uses. Let them investigate problems of their own that use combinations, permutations, or both. Interested students might want to take this further to investigate the uses of combinatorial analysis in computer programming and other everyday problem solving.

Another challenging resource for learning about combinations and permutations is the video and CD-ROM kit, *Major Munchy Interactive: Explorations.* This program starts with a video of four teens trying to win a contest by collecting the six letters in the word Munchy from the Major Munchy cereal company. The kit includes worksheets, transparencies, dice for simulations, and a CD-ROM with further explorations including making frequency distributions, creating histograms, and conducting simulations.

The topic of graphing offers opportunities for learning to suit many varied learning styles. Tactile/kinesthetic children learn well when they have the opportunity to make graphs out of the objects themselves. Visual children can learn well using any type of graph. Graphs suit their style of forming a mental image to fit the data collected. Auditory children enjoy the discussions that accompany collecting data and analyzing the graphs.

Use graphing in conjunction with other subjects, such as science, reading, and social studies, to help children learn those subjects as well. Many of the concepts from this chapter do not need to be a separate unit in mathematics. Use opportunities throughout the school day to help children learn the concepts and their uses in the world surrounding them.

KEY IDEAS

The study of mathematics is changing with the increased use of technology in the world. In this chapter, we discussed three topics that are currently receiving more attention at the elementary and middle school level—probability, statistics, and graphing. We described relationships among these three topics, as well as their integration into other areas of the curriculum.

In the elementary grades, teach these topics concretely, using materials such as dice, coins, cards, colored cubes, chips, spinners, graph paper, squares, and a variety of concrete materials for the graphs. Fully utilize calculators and computers to help children collect and organize large amounts of data. Emphasize helping children understand the concepts rather than encourage rote memorization of terms.

Much of the skill work in probability and statistics will come in the later grades, although children should become fairly skillful at making and reading graphs of all types by the end of elementary school. The topics in this chapter should help children become more skillful at predicting future events. Use these topics as children devise and plan their own experiments or surveys. Assess informally and take into account developmental levels as well as individual learning styles and abilities.

DISCUSSION QUESTIONS

1. Work with a group of middle grades students to design an experiment that involves collecting data to answer a question of local interest. You might want to collect data similar to that collected in a census survey and compare it to the national census (http://www.census.gov/). Use computer software or a graphing calculator to assist in analysis of your data. Present your findings to the class using a computer program such as Microsoft PowerPoint.

2. Ask two or three six- or seven-year-olds and two or three middle grades students to make predictions about the flip of a coin or the roll of a die. Compare their responses. Are the errors in the two groups similar? How would you design a probability lesson for each group of students based upon the results of your questioning?

3. Use one of the Internet sites, activity books, videos, or one of the children's books on probability such as *Do You Wanna Bet?* and design a probability lesson for intermediate students that uses some of the ideas in the book. If possible, use the lesson with children and report on the results. What was the main objective of the lesson, and how did you determine whether most of the students had mastered it? What would you change if you taught the lesson again? What would you be sure to keep?

REFERENCES

Anno, Mitsumasa, *Socrates and the Three Little Pigs.* New York, NY: Philomel, 1986.

Barrett, Gloria, and John Goebel, "The Impact of Graphing Calculators on the Teaching and Learning of Mathematics," in *Teaching and Learning Mathematics in the 1990s,* ed. Thomas J. Cooney, and Christian R. Hirsch. Reston, VA: National Council of Teachers of Mathematics, 1990, pp. 205–211.

Barrett, Judi, *Cloudy with a Chance of Meatballs.* New York: Atheneum, 1978.

Bereska, Carolyn, L. Carey Bolster, Cyrilla H. Bolster, and Richard Scheaffer, *Exploring Statistics in the Elementary Grades.* White Plains, NY: Dale Seymour, 1998.

Bestgen, Barbara J, "Making and Interpreting Graphs and Tables: Results and Implications from National Assessment," *Arithmetic Teacher,* 28, no. 4 (December 1980), pp. 26–29.

Branley, Franklyn M., *It's Raining Cats and Dogs.* Boston: Houghton Mifflin, 1987.

Browning, Christine A., and Dwayne E. Channell, *Explorations: Graphing Calculator Activities for Enriching Middle School Mathematics.* Austin, TX: Texas Instruments, 1997.

Bruni, James V., and Helene J. Silverman, "Developing Concepts in Probability and Statistics—and Much More," *Arithmetic Teacher,* 33, no. 6 (February 1986), pp. 34–37.

Burns, Marilyn, *Math By All Means.* New Rochelle, NY: Cuisenaire Company of America, Inc., 1991.

Burrill, Gail F., Miriam Clifford, and Richard Scheaffer, *Data-Driven Mathematics* (a series of 11 modules on algebra, geometry and advanced mathematics). White Plains, NY: Dale Seymour 1998.

Claus, Allison, "Making Mathematics Come Alive Through a Statistics Project," in *New Directions for Elementary School Mathematics,* ed. Paul R. Trafton and Albert P. Shulte. Reston, VA: National Council of Teachers of Mathematics, 1989, pp. 177–182.

Conference Board of the Mathematical Sciences, *The Mathematical Sciences Curriculum K–12: What Is Still Fundamental and What Is Not?* Washington, DC: CBMS, 1983.

Coombs, Betty, and Lalie Harcourt, *Explorations 1.* Don Mills, ON: Addison-Wesley, 1986, p. 183.

Corwin, Rebecca B., and Susan N. Friel, *Used Numbers: Statistics: Predicting and Sampling.* Palo Alto, CA: Dale Seymour, 1990.

Corwin, Rebecca B., and Susan Jo Russell, *Used Numbers: Measuring: From Paces to Feet.* Palo Alto, CA: Dale Seymour, 1990.

Cushman, Jean, *Do You Wanna Bet?* New York: Clarion Books, 1991.

Dickinson, J. Craig, "Gather, Organize, Display: Mathematics for the Information Society," *Arithmetic Teacher,* 34, no. 4 (December 1986), pp. 12–15.

DiFazio, Martha Hunt, "Graphics Software Side by Side," *Mathematics Teacher,* 83, no. 6 (September 1990), pp. 436–446.

Dossey, John A., Ina V. S. Mullis, Mary M. Lindquist, and Donald L. Chambers, *The Mathematics Report Card: Are We Measuring Up? Trends and Achievement Based on the 1986 National Assessment.* Princeton, NJ: Educational Testing Service, 1988.

Edwards, Nancy Tanner, and Gary G. Bitter, "Teaching Mathematics with Technology: Changing Variables Using Spreadsheet Templates," *Arithmetic Teacher,* 37, no. 2 (October 1989), 40–44.

Edwards, Nancy Tanner, Gary G. Bitter, and Mary M. Hatfield, "Teaching Mathematics with Technology: Data Base and Spreadsheet Templates with Public Domain Software," *Arithmetic Teacher,* 37, no. 8 (April 1990), 52–55.

Friel, Susan N., "Teaching Statistics: What's Average?" in Lorna J. Morrow, (ed.), *The Teaching and Learning of Algorithms in School Mathematics, 1998 Yearbook.* Reston, VA: NCTM, 1998 (208–217).

Friel, Susan N., Janice R. Mokros, and Susan Jo Russell, *Used Numbers: Statistics: Middles, Means and In-Betweens.* Palo Alto, CA: Dale Seymour, 1992.

Hakansson, Joyce (Producer), *The Cruncher.* Torrance, CA: Davidson and Associates, 1994.

Hoogeboom, Shirley, and Judy Goodnow, *Intermediate Probability Jobcards.* Sunnyvale, CA: Creative Publications, 1991.

Jensen, Linda, "The Relationships Among Mathematical Creativity, Numerical Aptitude and Mathematical Achievement." Unpublished doctoral dissertation. Austin, TX: The University of Texas at Austin, 1973.

Jones, Graham A., and Roger Day, *Algebra, Data, and Probability Explorations for Middle School: A Graphics Calculator Approach.* Menlo Park, CA: Dale Seymour, 1998.

Lappan, Glenda, James T. Fey, William M. Fitzgerald, Susan N. Friel, and Elizabeth D. Phillips, *Clever Counting: Combinatorics.* Menlo Park, CA: Dale Seymour, 1998.

—————, *Samples and Populations: Data and Statistics.* Menlo Park, CA: Dale Seymour, 1998.

—————, *Data About Us: Statistics.* Palo Alto, CA: Dale Seymour, 1996.

—————, *How Likely Is It?: Probability.* Palo Alto, CA: Dale Seymour, 1996.

Lovitt, Charles, and Ian Lowe. *Chance and Data Investigations Volume I and II.* Carlton, Victoria, Australia: Curriculum Corporation, 1994.

MacDonell, Alan (ed.), *The Super Source: Probability and Statistics Grades 7–8.* White Plains, NY: Cuisenaire Company of America, Inc., 1998.

Mori, Tuyosi, *Socrates and the Three Little Pigs.* New York: Philomel Books, 1986.

Murphy, Elaine C., *Developing Skills with Tables and Graphs.* Palo Alto, CA: Dale Seymour, 1981.

National Council of Teachers of Mathematics, *Curriculum and Evaluation Standards for School Mathematics.* Reston, VA: NCTM, 1989.

Nuffield Foundation, *Pictorial Representation.* New York: Wiley, 1967.

—————, *Probability and Statistics.* New York: Wiley, 1969.

Piaget, Jean, and Barbel Inhelder, *The Origin of the Idea of Chance in Children.* New York: W. W. Norton, 1975.

Russell, Susan J., and Rebecca B. Corwin, *Statistics: The Shape of the Data.* Palo Alto, CA: Dale Seymour, 1989.

Russell, Susan Jo, and Susan N. Friel, "Collecting and Analyzing Real Data in the Elementary School Classroom," in *New Directions for Elementary School Mathematics.* ed. Paul R. Trafton and Albert P. Shulte. Reston, VA: National Council of Teachers of Mathematics, 1989, pp. 134–148.

Russell, Susan Jo, and Antonia Stone, *Used Numbers: Counting: Ourselves and Our Families.* Palo Alto, CA: Dale Seymour, 1990.

Sandefur, James T., Jr., "Discrete Mathematics: A Unified Approach," in *The Secondary School Mathematics Curriculum,* National Council of Teachers of Mathematics, 1985 Yearbook. Reston, VA: NCTM, 1985.

School Mathematics Study Group, *Probability for the Intermediate Grades.* Stanford, CA: SMSG, Stanford University, 1966.

—————, *Probability for the Primary Grades.* Stanford, CA: SMSG, Stanford University, 1966.

Shielack, Jane F., "Teaching Mathematics with Technology: A Graphing Tool for the Primary Grades," *Arithmetic Teacher,* 38, no. 2 (October 1990), pp. 40–43.

Shulte, Albert P., "Learning Probability Concepts in Elementary School Mathematics," *Arithmetic Teacher,* 34, no. 5 (January 1987), pp. 32–33.

Shulte, Albert P., ed., *Teaching Statistics and Probability,* National Council of Teachers of Mathematics, 1981 Yearbook. Reston, VA: NCTM, 1981.

Shulte, Albert, and Stuart Choate, *What Are My Chances? Books A and B.* Palo Alto, CA: Creative Publications, 1977.

Srivastava, Jane Jonas, *Averages.* New York: Thomas Y. Crowell, 1975.

Srivastava, Jane Jonas, *Statistics.* New York: Thomas Y. Crowell, 1973.

Technology

Broderbund, *Tabletop, Jr.* Novato, CA: Broderbund, 19. (software)

Broderbund, *Tabletop, Sr.* Novato, CA: Broderbund, 19. (software)

Davidson, *The Cruncher.* Torrance, CA: Davidson, 1997. (software)

Edmark, *Mighty Math Number Heroes.* Orlando, FL: Harcourt Brace, 1996. (software)

GPN, *Math Vantage: Unit III: Data Analysis.* Lincoln, NE: GPN, 1997. (video and print materials)

Harcourt Brace, *Data ToolKit.* Orlando, FL: Harcourt Brace, 1996. (software)

Harcourt Brace, *Graph Links Grades 1–6.* Orlando, FL: Harcourt Brace, 1996. (software)

Learning Wave, *Major Munchy Interactive: Explorations in Probability.* Pleasantville, NY: Learning Wave Communications. (video and CD-ROM kit)

Roman, John (Exec. Producer), *Calculator-Based Laboratory Video Workshop.* Dallas, TX: Wholesale Electronic Supply, Inc. Education Division, 1995. (video and book)

Sunburst, *Data Explorer.* Pleasantville, NY: Sunburst Communications. (software)

Sunburst, *Graphers.* Pleasantville, NY: Sunburst Communications. (software)

Web Sites

http://www.census.gov/   United States Census bureau

http://www.mste.uiuc.edu/stat/   K–12 statistics lessons and projects

Chapter 12

Teaching and Learning Geometry

NCTM Standards

GRADES K–4

Standard 9: Geometry and Spatial Sense

In grades K–4, the mathematics curriculum should include two- and three-dimensional geometry so that students can—

- Describe, model, draw, and classify shapes;
- Investigate and predict the results of combining, subdividing, and changing shapes;
- Develop spatial sense;
- Relate geometric ideas to number and measurement ideas;
- Recognize and appreciate geometry in their world.

GRADES 5–8

Standard 12: Geometry

In grades 5–8, the mathematics curriculum should include the study of the geometry of one, two, and three dimensions in a variety of situations so that students can—

- Identify, describe, compare, and classify geometric figures;
- Visualize and represent geometric figures with special attention to developing spatial sense;
- Explore transformations of geometric figures;
- Represent and solve problems using geometric models;
- Understand and apply geometric properties and relationships;
- Develop an appreciation of geometry as a means of describing the physical world.

NCTM (1989), pp. 48, 112. Reprinted by permission.

A pentomino is made by connecting five squares of the same size so that each square shares at least one complete side with another square. Copy two pages of the inch graph paper from Appendix B, cut five squares apart, and try to find all of the possible pentominoes. If you find a shape that can be flipped or rotated to make another shape, it is considered to be the same shape. As you find different shapes, outline them on the graph paper. Work with others in your class to find all 12 pentominoes.

Color each of your 12 pentominoes a different color and cut them out. Try to put all of your pentominoes together in one large rectangle. It is possible to make rectangles that are 3 by 20, 4 by 15, 5 by 12, and 6 by 10. Sketch any of your successes. If you cannot get the large rectangles, try using 6 of the pentominoes to get rectangles that are 3 by 10 or 5 by 6.

As you discuss your work be sure to explain all of your thinking.

As you read the following pages, consider these guiding questions:

1. What implications for teaching and learning geometry come from the van Hieles?
2. How are topology and projective geometry related to students learning Euclidean geometry?
3. How do you sequence the use of geoboards in teaching and learning geometry?
4. What geometry skills are developed as students use *Logo* to discover geometry?
5. How do the activities differ that present the concepts and skills of geometry?
6. What geometry activities can you present that enhance the problem solving skills of students?
7. How are teachers able to connect the learning of geometry with the daily lives of their students?

Most of our buildings and decorations are based on geometric forms. And, much of nature can be described in geometric terms; this accounts, in part, for the origin of geometry. The work of Babylonian astronomers and Egyptian surveyors became the beginnings of mathematics. It is appropriate, then, to help children recognize the geometry that surrounds them.

The environments most familiar to children are those of the home, neighborhood, and school. By and large, the objects in these environments are the products of human effort. The products of nature are evident, as well, and provide rich, intriguing objects of study. Once children are made aware of various shapes and geometric forms, they will find them everywhere. The patterns and forms in nature may not be as obvious but will capture children's interests for long periods of time. Peter Stevens noted in his book *Patterns in Nature* that

> [W]hen we see how the branching of trees resembles the branching of arteries and the branching of rivers, how crystal grains look like soap bubbles and the plates of a tortoise's shell, how the fiddleheads of ferns, stellar galaxies, and water emptying from the bathtub spiral in a similar manner, then we cannot help but wonder why nature uses only a few kindred forms in so many different contexts. Why do meandering snakes, meandering rivers, and loops of string adopt the same pattern, and why do cracks in mud and markings on a giraffe arrange themselves like films in a froth of bubbles? (1974, p. 3)

A children's book that highlights patterns in nature is *Echoes for the Eye: Poems to Celebrate Patterns in Nature,* by Esbensen and Davie (1996), a collection of poems and illustrations of shapes in the natural world. Read the book to students and discuss the images. Children's awareness of geometry in the environment is heightened considerably as teachers focus their attention on various applications of geometry. This awareness also strengthens students' appreciation for and understanding of geometry and helps develop students' spatial sense.

The foundations for learning geometry lie in informal experiences in the elementary and middle school. These experiences should be carefully planned and structured to provide youngsters with a variety of concepts and skills. These concepts and skills serve as a basis for later, more formal work in geometry. That is why it is important to provide extensive, systematic exposure to geometric ideas from kindergarten through grade 8.

Infants explore space initially by thrashing about in a crib or playpen and crawling toward objects or open doors. Children discover that some objects are close, while others are far. They discover that rooms have boundaries, and that sometimes, if a door is left open, the boundaries can be crossed. They discover that certain items belong inside boundaries—for example, father's nose belongs within the boundaries of his face, or the bathtub belongs within the confines of the bathroom.

Children also discover that events occur in a sequence or an order. Early in their lives, they learned that their own crying was often followed by the appearance of a parent, who then attended to their needs. Later, children notice that a stacking toy is put together by putting certain parts in a particular order.

These examples illustrate children's initial experiences in space. They are far removed from school experiences with geometric shapes but nonetheless help show how children discover spatial relationships. Children learn first about the common objects in their environments. Piaget (1967) found that young children view space from a **topological** perspective. For example, shapes are not seen as rigid; they may readily change as they are moved about. Later, children use projective viewpoints as they make the transition to a Euclidean point of view. Shadows provide an example of **projective geometry.** In projective geometry, distances and dimensions are not conserved, but the relative positions of parts of figures and the positions of figures relative to one another are conserved. Employing projective viewpoints helps children, by ages five to seven, to begin to perceive space from a Euclidean point of view, from which they see shapes as rigid—the shapes do not change as they are moved about.

Elementary and middle school geometry plays an important developmental role as children learn geometry. The work of Pierre M. van Hiele and Dieke van Hiele-Geldof has influenced the teaching of geometry in various parts of the world. The van Hieles were Dutch middle-level mathematics teachers who studied the students with whom they worked. As an outgrowth of their research, P. M. van Hiele (1986) and Teppo (1991) described a model of instruction that included three levels through which individuals pass as they learn to work comfortably in the most abstract geometries. Between the levels are learning periods during which the student gains the background for moving to the next level. Each learning period has the same structure. The van Hiele levels are:

- *Level 1: Visual.* Students learn to recognize various shapes globally after repeatedly seeing them as separate objects. Students do not notice the common characteristics of similar figures.
- *Learning Period 1:* Overview of geometric content, exploring content, discussing content with a special focus on language and communication, applying knowledge of content, and developing an overview of the learning.
- *Level 2: Descriptive.* Students observe and manipulate figures, thus determining the properties necessary for identifying various shapes. Measuring is one way students learn the necessary properties.
- *Learning Period 2:* Overview of geometric content, exploring content, discussing content with a special focus on language and communication, applying knowledge of content, and developing an overview of the learning.
- *Level 3: Theoretical.* Students use deduction while working with postulates, theorems, and proof.

Many high school geometry courses begin work at the third level. Burger (1985) noted, however, that many high school students are working at the levels of younger children—Levels 1 and 2. Thus, teachers and students may have difficulty understanding each other. It is important, therefore, for the elementary and middle school mathematics programs to provide informal geometry experiences to help students progress through the first and second levels. The activities suggested in this chapter illustrate the types of geometric experiences necessary to assist students through the early van Hiele levels.

There are many physical models available that enhance the learning environment for geometry. Among those that the authors recommend are pattern blocks, geoblocks, geoboards, mira, paper models, and *Logo* (the computer language of turtle graphics). These and other useful materials are described and illustrated as they are presented in this chapter.

Geometry also serves as an instructional medium in its own right. Geometric models are used to introduce and illustrate a variety of mathematical topics. For example, geometric models are used to illustrate algorithms in Chapters 7 and 8 and geometric models are used to illustrate the concept of fractions in Chapter 9. Visualizing mathematics through models is well established as a teaching method. Materials such as *Math and the Mind's Eye* (Bennett et al., 1987) and *Visual Mathematics* (Bennett and Foreman, 1989, 1990) have been designed for use in grades 4–10 to help students develop their visual thinking. You are encouraged to explore these and other materials that employ geometry to model other mathematical topics.

Developing Geometric Concepts

The concepts upon which geometry is built begin with the simplest figure, the point, and expand to lines, line segments, rays, curves, plane figures, and space figures. We briefly discuss each of these.

The **point,** like all geometric figures, is an abstract idea. A point has no dimensions. It may be thought of as a location in space. For example, the tip of a pencil, the corner of a table, or a dot on a sheet of paper can represent a point.

A **line** is determined by two points and consists of a set of points connecting the two points and continuing endlessly in both directions. Figure 12–1a represents the line AB, defined by the points A and B.

Line segments and **rays** are subsets of a line. Like the line, each is determined by two points. The line segment, however, has two end points and the ray has only one end point. Line segment AB in Figure 12–1b is described by the two points A and B. Ray AB in Figure 12–1c includes end point A and a set of points continuing endlessly beyond point B. The arrowhead indicates the direction of a ray.

Lines, line segments, and rays have one dimension, length. When three or more points are not on the same line, a different kind of geometric figure results. It is a **plane figure,** or a figure in two dimensions. Figures such as *angles* (the union of two rays) and *triangles* (the union of three segments) are plane figures. We now consider curves and other plane figures.

A **curve** is a set of points that can be traced on paper without lifting the pencil. Figure 12–1d shows a simple curve between points A and B. It is **simple** because it does not cross over itself as it is drawn. The curve in Figure 12–1e is not simple because it crosses over itself as it is drawn from point A to point B. These two curves are not closed because they both have end points. When a curve has no end points, it is a **closed curve.** Figure 12–1f illustrates a simple closed curve.

Plane figures that are simple closed curves formed by joining line segments are called **polygons.** A polygon is named by the number of segments joined to make it. There are **triangles** (3 sides), **quadrilaterals** (4 sides), **pentagons** (5 sides), **hexagons** (6 sides), and so on. Figure 12–1g shows several polygons. A common simple closed curve not formed by joining line segments is the **circle.**

The prefixes of the words that name the polygons— **tri, quadri, penta, hexa, octa,** and **deca**—are of Latin or Greek origin and tell the reader how many sides a figure contains. Thus, *tri* means "three;" *quadri,* "four;" *penta,* "five;" *hexa,* "six;" *octa,* "eight;" and *deca,* "ten."

A polygon may have certain properties that provide a more specific description. For example, a **regular figure,** such as a square or an equilateral triangle, has sides

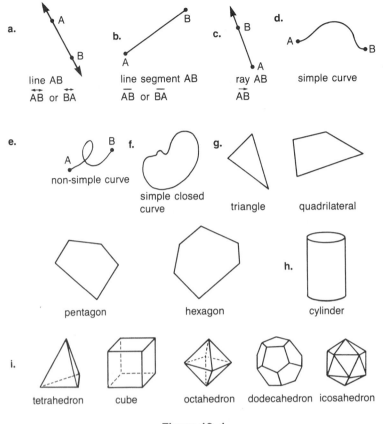

Figure 12–1

that are the same length and angles of the same measure. Having sides that are parallel and having right angles are other descriptive characteristics of plane figures. A **square** is a quadrilateral with all sides the same length and all angles the same size. A **rectangle** is a quadrilateral with opposite sides parallel and the same length and all angles the same size. A **parallelogram** is a quadrilateral with opposite sides parallel and the same length. A **rhombus** is a quadrilateral with opposite sides parallel and all sides the same length. A rhombus is sometimes called a diamond.

A **space figure** is one that does not lie wholly in a plane. A soup can represents one such figure, called a **cylinder,** shown in Figure 12–1h. Other space figures include spheres, pyramids, prisms, and cones. The playground ball serves as a model of a **sphere,** the set of all points in space equidistant from a given point. A **pyramid** is a figure with a base the shape of a polygon and sloping triangular sides that meet at a common vertex. A **prism** is a figure whose ends are congruent polygons and parallel with each other, and whose sides are parallelograms. A **cone** is a figure with a circular base and a curved surface that tapers to a point.

Polyhedrons are space figures that have four or more plane surfaces. **Regular polyhedrons** are those in which each face is a regular polygon of the same size and shape and in which the same number of edges join

at each corner or vertex. There are only five regular polyhedrons: the **tetrahedron** (4 faces), the **cube** (6 faces), the **octahedron** (8 faces), the **dodecahedron** (12 faces), and the **icosahedron** (20 faces). These are shown in Figure 12–1i.

The geometric concepts described above form a major part of the elementary and middle school mathematics textbook presentation of geometry. How these ideas are presented to children is of concern. Suydam (1985, p. 26) noted that "for many children, instruction in geometry in the elementary school revolves around only two points: recognition of shapes and development of vocabulary." She goes on to say that working with physical models and illustrations is valuable in learning geometric ideas. It is these activities that help develop spatial sense and expand the content of geometry. In the NCTM *Standards,* it is noted that:

Spatial sense is an intuitive feel for one's surroundings and the objects in them. To develop spatial sense, children must have many experiences that focus on geometric relationships; the direction, orientation, and perspectives of objects in space; the relative shapes and sizes of figures and objects; and how a change in shape relates to a change in size. . . . When children examine the result of combining two shapes to form a new shape, predict the effect of changing the number of sides of a shape, draw a shape after it has been rotated a quarter or half turn, or explore what happens when the dimensions of a shape are changed, they acquire a deeper understanding of shapes and their properties. (1989, p. 49)

The following development of geometric concepts expands on the elementary or middle school textbook presentation of recognition of shapes and definition of terms. We begin with a description of the views young children have of the world when they enter school, followed by activities that introduce projective geometry, plane figures and their properties, symmetry and motion, and space figures and their properties.

Young Children's Views of the World

The perceptions of children before they are five to seven years old are topological. **Topology** is the study of space concerned with position or location, where length and shape may be altered without affecting a figure's basic property of being open or closed. For example, a five-year-old shown a triangle and asked to make several copies of it may draw several simple closed curves but not necessarily triangles, as in Figure 12–2a. To the child, all of the drawings are the same, because the child perceives that the triangle has only the property of being closed (younger children often draw figures that are not closed). As well, a triangle may be stretched into any closed figure, as in Figure 12–2b (Copeland, 1984, p. 216).

The study of space in which a figure or any enclosed space must remain rigid or unchanged is called **Euclidean geometry.** The historical development of geometry was Euclidean; that is, geometry developed from ideas such as points, lines, and polygons. Some of Piaget's research has implied that children do not develop geometric concepts in a Euclidean manner. Because of their topological perspectives, children need an active, exploratory period when they enter school (1953, p. 75).

In Chapters 5 and 6, relationships among objects and numbers were discussed as the concept of number was developed. Likewise, spatial relationships can be identified as the concepts associated with space are developed. Children who perceive the world from a topological point of view are developing an understanding of four basic relationships:

1. *Is close to* or *is far from;*
2. *Is a part of* or *is not a part of;*
3. *Comes before* or *comes after;*
4. *Is inside of, is outside of,* or *is on.*

During kindergarten and first grade, children develop to the point where they can understand the meaning of Euclidean space. That is, children develop their abilities to reproduce shapes without significantly altering the characteristics of those shapes. For example, in the earlier topological stage, children copy a figure but allow corners to become round and distances to change. At the stage of Euclidean understanding, corners remain corners and distances are unchanged—the figure is considered rigid.

The shift from topological to Euclidean thinking is not sudden. It may occur over a period of two years. Thus, usually between the ages of four and six, children can recognize and name the more common figures: square, triangle, rectangle, circle. Other figures are neither identified nor differentiated from these shapes. For example, the square and other rhombuses may be confused, as may the rectangle and other parallelograms. Even more difficult for children is copying various shapes from blocks or drawings. Children may be able to accurately identify shapes long before they are able to produce their own examples.

During kindergarten and first grade, it is important to continue activities that relate to topological space. The following are typical activities that extend topological ideas.

ACTIVITIES

Primary (K–1)

Objective: to develop and reinforce the concepts of near, far, on, in, under, over, inside, and outside.

1. Developing language in concert with activities is a natural part of teaching. Have children sit in small groups at tables on which numerous objects are placed. Give directions to various children. For example, "Julia, please put the red block as far away from the plastic cup as you can," or "David, please put the short pencil in the tin can." Several children may participate simultaneously. Check the understanding of the language and the concept. Encourage discussion.

2. Draw three regions on the playground or on the floor of the multipurpose room. The regions represent a red base, a green base, and a catchers' region. Select two groups of children: those who attempt to change from the red base to the green base when a whistle is blown and those who begin at the catchers' region. As the children are changing from the red to the green base, the catchers run from their region and tag those who are changing.

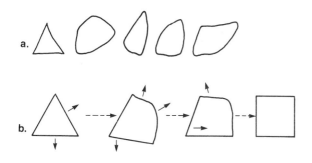

Figure 12–2

The catchers may tag the changers as long as they are outside of both the red and green bases. Once the changers reach the green base, they try to return to the red base. They continue running back and forth between bases as long as possible. Children who are tagged join the catchers. The game is over whenever there are no more children to run between the red and green bases.

Children participating in this activity are concerned about being inside or outside of the various regions. Occasionally during the activity, have the children "freeze." Then instruct, "Raise your hand if you are inside the green region. Raise your hand if you are outside the green region. Raise your hand if you are inside the red region. Raise your hand if you are outside the red region. Raise your hand if you are outside both the red and green regions."

3. Construct the following activity on the playground or on paper. Put drawings such as those in Figure 12–3 on the ground and invite the children to stand *inside* and to see if they can get to the outside by walking. There is one rule: you cannot step over a boundary line.

Students unable to get outside are inside a closed curve. All other students are outside the closed curve or are standing on the curve itself, or the region is not closed. Have the children experiment with several curves until they can easily determine if they are inside or outside a region, or if there is a closed region at all.

A simple curve like that in Figure 12–3a does not divide the plane in which it is drawn. Thus, only one region exists, whereas in Figure 12–3b, two regions exist because the simple closed curve separates the plane into two regions. In Figure 12–3c, there are four regions and the curve itself. The region outside the figure is counted. Figure 12–3d shows one region; Figure 12–3e shows three regions.

If these activities are performed on paper, the children may benefit from coloring each region a different color. Devise variations of this sort of boundary exercise.

4. Another type of boundary activity is the maze. The object of this activity is to see if two children are in the same region. On the playground, the children attempt to walk to one another without walking on or across a boundary. On paper, have children trace the regions with their fingers. The variations and the complexity of these designs are nearly unlimited. Figure 12–4 provides two examples of simple mazes. The children in Figure 12–4a are able to walk to each other because they are in the same region. In Figure 12–4b, the children cannot reach each other because they are in different regions.

5. A third, more complex boundary activity involves having children construct maze puzzles for themselves and other children. Maze puzzles may be constructed by beginning with a simple frame with a door to go in and a door to go out, as in Figure 12–5.

Figure 12–3

Figure 12–4

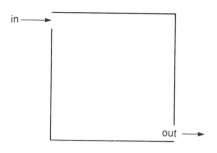

Figure 12–5

To complete the maze, draw lines from any wall. The only rule is that no line can connect one wall with another wall. Steps a, b, and c in Figure 12–6 show how a maze puzzle was constructed. Children are fascinated by the construction of mazes.

Objective: to develop the ability to verbalize about geometric figures and patterns.

6. Encourage children to construct and manipulate space figures. Materials may include tiles, attribute blocks, geoblocks, cubes, cans, empty milk cartons, Unifix cubes, Cuisenaire rods, pattern blocks, parquetry blocks, and clay. **Geoblocks** are pieces of unfinished hardwood, cut into a wide variety of space figures. Allow the children to talk with one another as they work. During that time, circulate and ask individuals, "Tell me what your picture shows. Can you find another shape like this one? How would you describe this piece? How are the buildings the same?"

   Children can learn to be analytical when questions are carefully phrased. For example, "Can you make another house just like the one you have made there? I would like you to try." At the same time, the questions can serve to gather information for the teacher. Be sure to allow children to explain an answer.

Objective: to use visual clues in matching shapes.

7. Encourage children to construct picture jigsaw puzzles. Challenge the students with difficult puzzles, and discuss informally with an individual or a small group how they have gone about putting the puzzle together. It should be evident that strategies are developed as puzzles are completed. Edge pieces are generally put together first, followed by pieces that form distinct images or those that have easily matched colors. Pieces are added to the puzzle when their shapes fit a region that has been surrounded by other pieces. Finally, all other pieces are put into place by the process of elimination.

The preceding activities have been presented to help reinforce the topological ideas of youngsters. They serve as preparation for the following activities, which help introduce children to the Euclidean shapes.

Projective Geometry

As children investigate figures and their properties through shadow geometry, they are being assisted in the transition from a topological perspective of their world to a Euclidean perspective. Piaget (1967, p. 467) noted that "Projective concepts take account, not only of internal topological relationships, but also of the shapes of figures, their relative positions and apparent distances, though always in relation to a specific point of view." Children explore what happens to shapes held in front of a point source of light, such as a slide projector or a bright flashlight. They also explore what happens to shapes held in the sunlight when the sun's rays are nearly parallel. They discover which characteristics of the shapes are maintained under varying conditions. Children need to make observations, sketch the results of their work, and discuss their observations. As a result, children develop a viewpoint that is not part of a topological perspective.

The activities that follow are intended to provide children with experience with projective geometry.

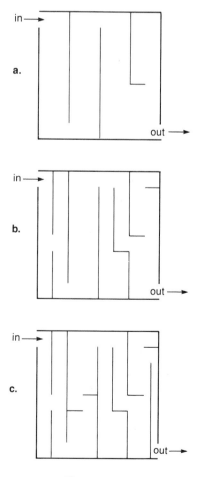

Figure 12–6

ACTIVITIES

Primary (1–3)

Objective: to produce and describe the shadows of squares and other shapes, using the sun as a source of light.

1. Provide pairs of children with square regions such as wooden or plastic geoboards or regions cut from railroad board. Take the children to an area of the playground that has a flat, smooth surface such as blacktop or concrete. Have the children hold the square regions so that shadows are cast on the ground, as in Figure 12–7.

   Encourage the children to move the square regions so that the shadow changes. Be sure both members of a pair have a chance to experiment with shadow-making. After a few minutes, gather the children around you and ask them to talk about the shadows they found as they moved their square regions. If it is difficult for a child to explain the shape of the shadow, have the child illustrate the shadow for the others. Have the children discuss how they were able to make the shapes larger and smaller. See what other observations they have made.

   To make a permanent record of shapes, have one member of each pair of children put a piece of paper on the ground and let the shadow fall on the paper. Have that child draw around the outline of the shadow on the sheet of paper. When each student has had a chance to draw a favorite shape, there will be a collection of interesting drawings that can serve as a source for discussion, sorting, and display.

2. Using the square regions from Activity 1, challenge the children to make the shadow into a square. Ask the students what they had to do to produce a square

shadow. Give the children square regions that have been cut from paper to put on the ground. Have the children use their square regions to make a shadow just large enough to exactly cover the paper square on the ground. Have them make a square smaller than the paper square, then one larger than the paper square. Let the children discuss how they were able to make the shadows different sizes.

   Next, give each pair of children a paper diamond region to put on the ground and ask them to try to make the same shape using the square region. Have them exactly cover the diamond shape, then make diamond shapes smaller and larger than the paper diamond.

   Have the children discover if they can make a triangle or a pentagon shadow using the square region. See if they can make a rectangle or another parallelogram. It will be necessary to provide paper shapes as models for the children to use. Be sure to have the children sketch their results and discuss their findings.

3. Introduce diamond, triangular, and hexagonal regions to see what kinds of shapes their shadows are. Can a diamond shadow be made with a diamond region? Can a square shadow be made? What other shadow shapes can be made? Can a triangular shadow be made with a triangular region? Can square or diamond shadows be made?

   Other shapes should be available with which the children can experiment. Again, outlining the shadows will produce a permanent record of the shadow shapes. Expect the children to make discoveries that you had not thought of, and join in the excitement of such discoveries.

4. Using the outlines that the children drew of shadows cast by square regions, see if the children can find things that are alike and things that are different in the drawings. Encourage the students to count the number of corners and the number of sides of each shadow shape and to compare those numbers. Write down the conclusions made based on these observations.

   Pose problems such as: "Suppose we take one of our shadow drawings and cut it out and glue it to a piece of railroad board cut exactly like the outline. Would it be possible to use that shape to make a shadow that would just match the square region that we started with? How do you think it could be done? Why do you believe that it can't be done?" Let the children perform the experiment to see if they can do this. Have them put their square regions on the ground and see if they can exactly cover the square region with a shadow from the outline region.

Objective: to produce and describe the shadows of squares and other shapes, using a point source of light.

5. Set up a slide or filmstrip projector or use a flashlight so that the light is projected onto a screen or wall. Let

Figure 12–7

the children play in the light by making shadows using their hands or by holding small objects. After this introductory activity, provide the children with square regions and encourage them to explore the different ways that shadows can be produced. Tape paper to the wall and have the children outline the shadows to provide a record of their work that can be displayed on a bulletin board and discussed.

As an extension, introduce other shapes such as triangular, rectangular, and hexagonal regions and let the students find out what their shadows look like. Let the children describe their shadow shapes and explain how various shadows were made.

6. Compare the outline drawings of the shadows of the square regions made using the sun as a source of light with those made using a point source of light. A bulletin board display can have the shadows sorted, with shadows made using the sun on one side and those made using the projector or flashlight on the other side. Can all of the same shadow shapes be made? Do the shapes look similar? For those shadows that are different, would it be possible to make that shape if we tried again using the sun or a point source of light?

To extend this activity, cut out the outline of a shadow of a square region made with a point source of light, glue it to a piece of railroad board cut to exactly the same shape, and see if it is possible to make a shadow that matches the original square region. Are the results of this activity the same as the results obtained using the sun as a source of light?

7. Take a square region and place it on a block or paper cup so that the square region is supported parallel to the floor as in Figure 12–8. Have the children hold a

flashlight above the square region, moving it from side to side, and ask them to observe the shadow that is produced.

What characteristics of the shadow shape are noted? If a sheet of paper is placed beneath the block, an outline of the shadow shape can be drawn. Then direct comparisons can be made between the square region and its shadow, such as comparing the sizes of the corners and the lengths of the sides.

Is it possible to make diamonds or rectangles by moving the light to various positions? As the flashlight is moved higher and lower how does the size of the shadow change? Next, use triangular and rectangular regions and explore their shadows.

The preceding activities in projective geometry have been presented to help children as they make the transition from topological notions to Euclidean notions. You may also wish to examine the activities suggested by Dienes (1967) and Mansfield (1985) in the works listed in the references at the end of the chapter.

Plane Figures and Their Properties

Children's abilities to learn the names and properties of common plane figures, such as triangles, squares, rectangles, circles, parallelograms, rhombuses, hexagons, and so forth, vary considerably within any group of children. Those who are able to observe a shape and then easily find another like it or those who are able to look at a figure and then draw it maintaining the characteristics essential to the figure are ready to proceed with more systematic instruction on Euclidean shapes.

Piaget and Inhelder (1967, p. 43) indicated that the learning of shapes requires two coordinated actions. The first is the physical handling of the shape, being able to run fingers along the boundaries of the shape. The second is the visual perception of the shape itself. It is insufficient for children merely to see drawings or photographs of the shapes. A variety of materials and activities can help to present plane figures to children. Some of these materials and activities are presented below.

Figure 12–8

ACTIVITIES

Primary (K–3)

Objective: to develop tactile understanding of common plane figures.

1. Give children flat shapes to explore. The shapes may be commercially produced, such as attribute blocks, or they may be teacher-constructed from colorful

railroad board. Allow the children time for free play with little or no teacher direction. Perhaps the children will construct houses, people, cars, animals, patterns, or larger shapes.

After having plenty of free time with the shapes, the children will be ready for the teacher to ask a few questions or to compliment them on their work. If someone has constructed a truck, ask several children to construct others just like it. Challenge the children to make an object that is the same except upside down.

If a pattern is made, perhaps it can be extended. Encourage children and ask, "What shapes have you used to make your picture? What would happen if we changed all of the triangles to squares? What would happen if all the pieces were exchanged for larger pieces of the same shape? Let's try it."

2. Construct models of various shapes for the children to handle. One way to construct a model is to bend heavy wire in the shape of a triangle, square, rectangle, circle, parallelogram, rhombus, or hexagon. A touch of solder should hold the ends together. Another way is to glue small doweling to a piece of railroad board. The children can then develop a tactile understanding of the shapes.

Once the children have handled the shapes, encourage them to describe the shapes. Ask, "How many corners does it have? How many sides does it have? What else do you notice?" Ask them to draw a particular shape while looking at and feeling the model. Later, ask them to draw the shapes while only feeling or seeing the models. Finally, ask the children to draw the shapes without either seeing or feeling the models.

Objective: to make patterns using geometric shapes.

3. Parquetry blocks (Figure 12–9) are a unique material to use to learn about plane figures. **Parquetry blocks** are geometric shapes of varying colors and sizes. The first attempt to use them should be in a free-play activity. Then, there are several ways to use the blocks to present shapes.

  • Copy activities include holding up one of the shapes and having children find another block of the same or a different shape. Next, put three or four of the blocks together in a simple design and ask the children to copy the design. It may be copied exactly or with a slight variation, such as with different colors. Finally, put the blocks into a simple design but separate them from each other. Copying this design requires the children to visualize across the separations.

  • Present outlines of parquetry blocks and ask the children to find a piece the same color, shape, and size and place it on the outline. Later, have them match just shape and size. Present more complicated outlines, using designs of two or more blocks, after the children have worked with single blocks.

  • Ask children to make their own outlines for others to fill in either by drawing around the various shapes or by putting all the shapes down and drawing around the entire design. The latter variation produces a challenging puzzle for children to complete.

While our discussion has centered on the parquetry blocks, another learning aid, pattern blocks, works equally well for the activities just mentioned.

Objective: to construct common geometric figures.

4. The **geoboard** is a dynamic aid for use in teaching geometry. It consists of a board 20 to 25 centimeters square with five rows of five escutcheon pins in each row (Figure 12–10). Students can stretch rubber bands around the pins to form various figures. Instructions for constructing a geoboard can be found in Appendix B.

After a period of free play during which the children can discover some of the patterns, shapes, and pictures that can be constructed, direct some copying activities. Construct a particular configuration or shape and show it to the children, asking them to copy it. Initially, construct a line segment, then perhaps combinations of two, three, or more line segments (Figure 12–10). Next, construct simple shapes. Gradually make the shapes more complex and chal-

Figure 12–9

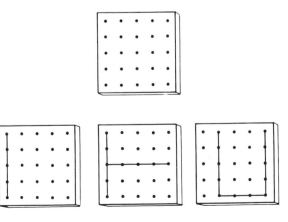

Figure 12–10

lenging, as in Figure 12–11. As soon as the children understand the nature of the copying exercises, allow them to construct shapes for others to copy.

As the children gain experience in recognizing and naming shapes, use the names to describe shapes for the children to construct. Say, for example, "Let's make triangles on our geoboards. If we look at everyone's triangles, can we find some things that are the same? Are there any triangles that are completely different? Who has the biggest triangle? Who has the smallest? Who has the triangle with the most nails inside the rubber band? Who can make a shape that is not a triangle? Now, let's make some squares."

Objective: to discover characteristics of various shapes.

5. **Tessellating** is covering or tiling a region with many pieces of the same shape. Countertops and floors are often tessellated with square pieces. Of the regular Euclidean figures (that is, those with sides of equal length and angles of equal measure), only triangles, squares, and hexagons will completely cover a region without the need for additional pieces to fill in gaps. There are, however, many irregular shapes with which a region may be tessellated. Figure 12–12 shows a tessellation of quadrilaterals. All quadrilaterals will tessellate.

Give children a sheet of paper to serve as a region and numerous pieces of some shape with which to tessellate. Pattern blocks are a handy and colorful material to use in tessellating. Ask the children to cover the paper with a particular shape and to decide which shapes will work. Later, ask them to try to use a combination of two or three shapes to tessellate. Be-

fore they begin, have the children estimate whether or not they can use the shapes to tessellate.

6. Books that feature shapes can help children become aware of how commonplace geometry is in our surroundings. In *Shapes, Shapes, Shapes,* Hoban (1986) invites children to identify a variety of shapes from photographs that they should recognize. *The Button Box* (Reid, 1990) displays a multitude of buttons that illustrate shape and pattern and describes their uses. Bread in a variety of shapes is presented by Morris (1989) in *Bread, Bread, Bread.* This description of bread from many cultures helps children identify many unusual shapes. Grifalconi (1986) tells a story of west Africa in which the shapes of houses are important. *The Village of Round and Square Houses* is a beautifully written and illustrated book about a real place. After reading books such as these to the students and discussing them, leave the books out for the students to peruse on their own.

Objective: to develop the concept of an angle.

7. An **angle** may be thought of as a change in direction along a straight line. On the floor or playground, have children walk along a line that at some point changes direction, however slightly or sharply, as in Figure 12–13a. Discuss with the children that the change in direction forms an angle.

Ask the children if they can think of a figure that has an angle or corner. Children discussing the characteristics of a plane figure will mention the corners or bends that help give the figure its shape. The concept of an angle is being developed at an intuitive level.

Later, more formally define an angle as two rays sharing a common end point. Have children walk along chalk or tape lines that form a zig-zag path. By pointing one arm in the direction in which they have been walking and the other arm in the direction of

Figure 12–11

Figure 12–12

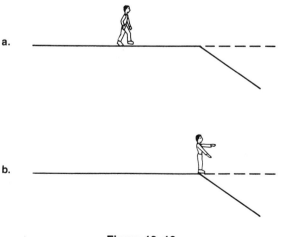

a.

b.

Figure 12–13

change, children can form the angle of change. Figure 12–13b illustrates using the arms.

Then, have the children walk on large polygons. This activity serves as an introduction to one aspect of the computer language *Logo. Logo* activities follow.

Objective: to practice making polygons and discover how their properties may change.

8. Provide the members of a learning group with a 10-foot length of yarn that has been knotted at the ends to form a large loop. First, have two members of the group each hold it with both hands so that 4 vertices are formed, as in Figure 12–14. The other members of the group serve as observers and recorders. The holders pull the yarn taut, producing a quadrilateral, then they explore what happens to the shape as they change the sizes of the angles and the lengths of the sides of the figure. An observer's job is to describe what happens and a recorder's job is to sketch the shape as it changes. Will it be possible to produce a triangle? How about a pentagon? What must be done to make a square, a rectangle, and a parallelogram? When the children have had a chance to discuss their findings and to look at the sketches of the figures, ask them what they can conclude about changing the angles, changing the lengths of the sides, and making other types of geometric figures?

To extend this activity, have a third student hold the yarn so that there are 6 vertices. Now, what different shapes can they make and how does changing the angles and the lengths of the sides affect the appearance of the figure? Does changing the length of the yarn affect the results of this activity? Again, discussion helps children share their observations and their sketches help to verify their conclusions.

Objective: to explore geometric figures using *Logo* activities.

9. *Logo,* the computer language of turtle graphics, provides primary children with a rich source of experiences. *Logo* is available for the most popular computers used in schools. To prepare children to use *Logo,* engage them in a series of noncomputer activities. Following is a brief series of introductory activities.

   a. Find an activity that the children are familiar with. List the individual parts that make up the activity in a series of steps. For example, to put the cat out, we might

   - Call the cat.
   - Does the cat come?
   - If not, go find the cat.
   - When the cat comes, pick it up.
   - Carry the cat to the door.
   - Open the door.
   - Put the cat outside.
   - Shut the door.

   Next, write each step on a separate card. Mix up the cards, and challenge the children to put them back in the correct order. Once the children discover how to do this activity, present a series of cards without first showing the appropriate sequence. Have the children order the steps of the procedure by figuring out the sequence. Procedures besides putting the cat out may include making a peanut butter sandwich, preparing for and taking a bath, and getting ready for bed. Allow the children to make up sequences to challenge one another.

   b. With masking tape or yarn, construct a geometric figure on the floor. It may be a square, a triangle, or a rectangle, at first. Later, make a more complex figure, such as those in Figure 12–15.

   Ask the children to begin by going to any corner and facing an adjacent corner. Have them describe what they are doing as they walk around the boundary of the figure and end up where they started. Limit the descriptions to the use of forward, back, left, and right. It may be helpful to have direction cards that show what is meant by the four commands. Figure 12–16 illustrates what such cards might look like.

   Later, have one child give directions to a second child that will guide the second child in walking the boundary of a figure. The second child should follow the directions exactly.

Figure 12–14

Figure 12–15

Figure 12–16

It will soon be necessary to tell a student how many steps forward or backward to take. For example, "Go forward 12 steps." Agree that such steps are taken by putting one foot directly in front of the other.

Next, give a child a drawing of a figure and instruct the child to give another student commands for making the figure. The teacher or a student can lead the entire class in this activity.

c. Put a blindfold on a child and arrange the desks in a simple maze. Have children carefully give commands that will, if followed, lead the blindfolded child around the desks and out of the maze. Use particular caution to avoid any possibility of injury.

10. Introduce turtle geometry on the computer by putting a small colored sticker on the computer monitor and asking the children to see if they can find the appropriate commands to hide the turtle under the sticker. Encourage the children to estimate the commands before they actually try them. In the beginning, use RIGHT 90 and LEFT 90 to designate the turns but allow the children to experiment with other degrees of turns very soon. The activity with making angles introduced earlier should help students understand how to construct various angles. It will take a little experimentation to determine the size of the turtle steps, as well. Fairly quickly the children will become accomplished at moving the turtle freely around the screen.

To encourage moving the turtle about, put an overhead transparency on the screen with several regions drawn on it. A thin transparency will cling tightly to the screen. Have the children move the turtle from one region to another until it has entered all the regions.

Sketch a simple maze on another transparency and place the transparency on the screen with the turtle in the maze. Challenge the children to get the turtle out of the maze without crossing any boundaries.

From here on, use one or more of several well-written *Logo* manuals. The *Logo* manuals are carefully sequenced. They contain many challenging figures to test children's abilities to use *Logo*. Several of these resources are listed at the end of the chapter.

The activities just presented are intended to give primary children experiences with plane figures to complement work from the mathematics textbook. A number of

activities can be combined to develop a thematic unit about shapes. As a part of her work with kindergarten children, student teacher Nicole Erwert designed a week of shape activities. On **Monday,** each student constructed a shape book with four pages, featuring, in turn, triangles, circles, squares, and rectangles. Then the children looked through magazines for examples of the shapes to cut out and glued on the appropriate page of their book. On **Tuesday,** the students took a shape walk in the school neighborhood, recognizing shapes on buildings, various structures, and in nature. On **Wednesday,** the children constructed a "town" by using common boxes onto which they had glued shapes that they had cut out. All of the buildings were placed on a "street" drawn on a large sheet of butcher paper. On **Thursday,** the students constructed geometric "people" by cutting out shapes and gluing them onto pieces of construction paper as in Figure 12–17. That afternoon a bulletin board was arranged using the geometric people. On **Friday,** a listening activity was introduced. Each student had a worksheet with several triangles, squares, circles, and rectangles drawn on it. Instructions such as "color all of the triangles blue" were given. This quiet

Figure 12–17

Dear Family,

Our class is beginning a mathematics unit called *Flips, Turns, and Area*. The ideas in this unit may be new to you. Your child will learn about special shapes called *tetrominoes*—different arrangements of four squares:

We'll be talking about three ways we can move these shapes—

by sliding: by flipping: and by turning:

We'll work with these ideas using paper cutouts and a computer game called Tumbling Tetrominoes. After we've started the unit, ask your child to explain the game to you.

Being able to visualize how different shapes fit in space is an important geometric skill. It also has a lot of practical aspects. For example, think of how hard it is to get a couch up a stairway and into the living room—it's really a matter of slides, flips, and turns!

Part of this unit is all about discovering *area* as a measure of a flat surface. Look for opportunities at home to talk about area with your child. For example:

> Do you have square tiles covering a floor or bathroom wall? How many squares are there?

> Suppose you make roll-out cookies with your child. This poses a problem of area: How can you place the cookie cutters so that you cover the most area, and have the least amount of dough leftover? Do you have to rotate the cookie cutter to get the best fit?

Have a good time exploring these ideas with your child!

Sincerely,

Figure 12–18 From *Investigations in Number, Data and Space: Flips, Turns, and Area*, by Douglas H. Clements, Susan Jo Russel, Cornelia Tierney, Michael T. Battista & Julie Sarama; Copyright © 1998 by DALE SEYMOUR PUBLICATIONS.

Math Program

The family math page from the third-grade book shown in Figure 12–18 is designed to be sent home at the beginning of this unit entitled *Flips, Turns, and Area.* This page is available in several different languages so that teachers can communicate with parents for whom English is a second language. As you can see from this page, students in this section will be designing tetrominoes and then studying transformations of these shapes as they look at area and tessellation concepts. As part of this unit, students will use an included computer program that is similar to the commercial game Tetris. In this game, however, students attempt to completely cover rectangles with an area of 120 square units. In doing this, students investigate all the factors of 120 and cut out rectangles to determine all the possible 120 square unit rectangles. They then work with paper tetrominoes to try to cover these rectangles.

This *Flips, Turns, and Area* unit is one of 10 units in this third-grade program. It is part of a series for kindergarten through fifth grade entitled *Investigations in Number, Data and Space.* These units could be used as replacement units in conjunction with another program, but they are designed to be a complete, self-contained program. Each unit has a teacher's book, and some contain software, but there are no student books. Students frequently use black-line masters from the teacher's book but are generally involved in active investigations with objects and experiences from their environments. These activities include pair and small-group work, individual tasks, and whole-class discussions. The unit also contains 10-minute math activities designed to be used outside of the regular math period to review concepts that may have been taught at other times during the year. Homework is designed to build on class investigations and is not given every day. Assessment includes Teacher Checkpoints, which are checklists of concepts that teachers should look for as students work, embedded assessment activities that may involve writing and reflections from the students or brief interactions between students and the teacher, and ongoing assessment that includes observations and portfolio or journal work.

This unit includes an investigation of motions with tetrominoes that is designed to last approximately five hours and an investigation of area also designed to last approximately five hours. Each of the sessions in these areas include suggestions for homework and extensions that continue and expand upon the classwork.

activity provided an opportunity for assessment of both shape recognition and listening ability.

Further, center activities were provided throughout the week. Students rotated from centers featuring geoboards on which to construct shapes, building blocks, a game of shape bingo, and shapes used to build patterns.

This was a successful week and raised the shape awareness of the children. They talked about various shapes throughout the day. Next, we turn to activities for older students.

Most of the following activities are intended to support children as they work in the first and second of the van Hiele levels, visual and descriptive. This means the students will continue to analyze the properties of Euclidean figures and will begin to understand the characteristics of the figures in terms of definitions.

ACTIVITIES

Intermediate–Middle Grades (4–8)

Objective: to discover important properties that define a variety of polygons.

1. Periodically designate a bulletin board as a shape board. Attach a label such as "quadrilaterals" and invite the children to put as many different quadrilaterals as they can on the board. After two or three days, have the children describe the ways in which the shapes are different. Thus, the children look at the defining properties of quadrilaterals. Ask the children to classify the quadrilaterals as squares, rhombuses, rectangles, parallelograms, and trapezoids. Which categories overlap? How do the shapes relate? Another time, the board theme may be triangles, then hexagons and octagons.

2. On the overhead projector or chalkboard, display a set of properties of a particular quadrilateral. Reveal the properties one at a time until a student decides a sufficient number of properties have been displayed to identify the shape. That student must then convince the rest of the class that enough characteristics have been given to identify the figure. For example, the following list may be presented.

   - It is a closed figure with 4 straight sides.
   - It has 2 long sides and 2 short sides.
   - The 2 long sides are the same length.
   - The 2 short sides are the same length.
   - One of the angles is larger than one of the other angles.
   - Two angles are the same size.
   - The other 2 angles are the same size.
   - The 2 long sides are parallel.
   - The 2 short sides are parallel.

To vary this activity, have the children develop lists, individually or in small groups, that can be used to challenge the others in the class. They may select particular triangles, quadrilaterals other than the parallelogram described above, or various other polygons.

Objective: to discover the numerous configurations a polygon may have.

3. Challenge the children to find as many different triangles as possible on the geoboard. By different, we mean noncongruent, that is, not the same size and shape. Because of the variety of such figures, it is helpful to structure this activity using the problem-solving skill of simplifying the problem. For example, ask for as many different triangles as can be made using only two adjacent rows on the geoboard (we count 14 such triangles). Before the children begin, have them estimate how many triangles they can make.

   You may wish to simplify the problem even more by asking the students to make triangles on a 2-by-2, 2-by-3, or 2-by-4 arrangement of nails. As the children find the triangles, have them sketch the triangles on a piece of dot paper (see Appendix B) and discuss how they went about finding them. Figure 12–19 shows a few of the possible triangles.

   A little later, ask the children to make as many triangles as possible on a 3-by-3 nail arrangement on the geoboard. Put a rubber band on the geoboard surrounding the 3-by-3 area as a guide. Of course, you may use another arrangement as the basis for constructing triangles.

   Discuss the types of triangles found. There will be **right triangles** (one angle of 90 degrees), **isosceles triangles** (a pair of congruent sides), **acute triangles** (all angles less than 90 degrees), **obtuse triangles** (one angle more than 90 degrees), and **scalene triangles** (no sides of equal length).

   Extend this activity by seeing how many quadrilaterals may be made on a certain part of the geoboard. Be sure to have children estimate before they begin.

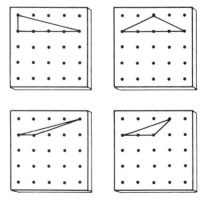

Figure 12–19

We know that 16 noncongruent quadrilaterals can be formed on a 3-by-3 geoboard. How many squares or rectangles or hexagons may be constructed?

As a further extension, have the children use the triangles they constructed on a 3-by-3 area of the geoboard and ask them to produce the triangles on the computer screen using *Logo*. Challenge the children to see if they can use *Logo* to reproduce figures other children have constructed on the geoboard. Encourage children to attempt to make a variety of different polygons, first on the geoboard and then on the screen.

Objective: to use the computer to design geometric figures.

4.   Continue to use *Logo* to strengthen students' abilities to define geometric figures and to develop procedures for complex designs and patterns. A **procedure** is a set of commands that may produce a simple figure or that may combine other procedures to form a more complex figure.

Ask children, as they work individually or in pairs, to develop a procedure for making a *box* with sides of 50 turtle steps. Next, have them make a *flag* using the box procedure. Then, have them make a *windmill* using the flag procedure. Finally, challenge the children to use the windmill procedure to make a *pinwheel*. The results of these four procedures are shown in Figure 12–20 a, b, c, and d. The procedures that may be used to draw these figures are as follows:

The procedures presented above show how the repeat command can be used to replace a set of commands and streamline the procedures. This is a recognition that students should be encouraged to make after the repeat command has been introduced.

Ask children to develop procedures for producing a number of polygons of different sizes. This may involve using variables within the procedures. Variables present an added dimension to working with *Logo*. Challenge the students to use their skills to reproduce materials like the pattern blocks, the attribute blocks, or a "picture" drawn by students on squared paper. As students develop the ability to design figures, they learn valuable information about plane figures.

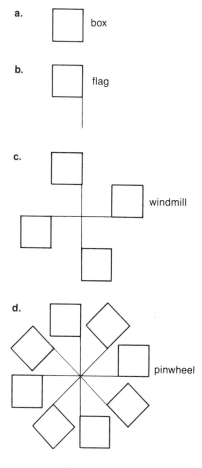

Figure 12–20

Besides using variables as they develop procedures, students will soon be able to use recursion, to employ coordinates to define locations, and to design complex figures. You will find resources for teaching *Logo* in the references at the end of the chapter.

This group of activities for children in the primary, intermediate, and middle grades plays an important role in children's geometric learning. They help define plane figures and their properties in concrete and abstract terms. We now turn to the concepts of symmetry and motion.

Symmetry and Motion

The notions of symmetry and motion are exemplified by patterns in nature and in the art and architecture of human beings. **Symmetry** requires a line or lines about which a figure or design is balanced or a point about which a figure or design is rotated. There is something orderly and pleasant in balance. (**Balance** is the characteristic of a figure that suggests an equality of parts.)

Children often generate symmetrical designs with building materials. Children who have been made aware of the symmetry around them have a fuller appreciation of their environment. Besides, many geometric figures contain fine examples of symmetry, having, in some cases, several lines of symmetry.

ACTIVITIES

Primary (K–3)

Objective: to develop simple symmetrical patterns with objects.

1. Provide the children with Cuisenaire rods, pattern blocks, or parquetry blocks. Encourage them to make designs that they think are pleasant. Compliment the students on their efforts and point out the unique characteristics of the designs. For example, point out those made of materials of the same color, those using pieces of the same shape, and those that have line symmetry. Discuss what it means for a figure to have balance, using one of the children's designs as an example. Have the children look around the room and point to shapes that appear to be the same on both sides.

    Ask the children to make a design with symmetry. You may structure this activity by designating which pieces to use in making a design; for example, using the pattern blocks, have the children take two red pieces, four green pieces, and two orange pieces for their design. Ask the children to sketch the results or to glue colored paper cut into the shapes being used.

2. Provide mirrors with which the children may explore and develop symmetrical patterns. (Inexpensive mirrors are available through school supply catalogs that feature learning aids.) Using Cuisenaire rods, pattern blocks, or parquetry blocks and mirrors, have the children construct symmetrical designs and reaffirm their symmetry.

    Ask the children to make a design using three or four blocks or rods. Then have them place a mirror along one edge of the design, note the reflection, and copy the image in the reflection, placing the copy behind the mirror. Thus, the mirror is lying along the line of symmetry.

    Then ask the children to remove the mirror and to discuss their symmetrical design. Say, for example, "What pattern do you see in your design? If your design were a picture, what would it show? See if you can take the reflected design away, mix up the pieces, and then put the design back the way it was before. Where do you think the line of symmetry is? Check it with the mirror. Can you make a new design and its reflection without using the mirror? Try it. Use your mirror to check to see if your design has symmetry."

    Finally, have the children sketch and color the pattern and its mirror image on a sheet of squared paper. Figure 12–21 illustrates this process.

3. Stretch a rubber band across a geoboard from edge to edge so there is ample space on each side of the rubber band. In the simplest example, the rubber band would be stretched across the center of the geoboard either horizontally or vertically. Construct a figure on one side of the rubber band and challenge the children to construct the image of the figure on the other side. In the beginning, have the children stand a mirror on its edge along the symmetry line and make the image while looking in the mirror. Figure 12–22 provides examples of this activity.

    Let the children make up figures and challenge the rest of the class to construct the mirror image of the figure on the geoboard across the line of symmetry, with or without a mirror. Provide dot paper on which the students may copy their symmetrical geoboard designs. As the students develop proficiency in recreating images, use diagonal lines as lines of symmetry.

Figure 12–21

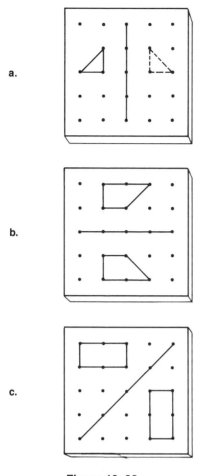

Figure 12–22

Objective: to develop the ability to visualize symmetrical patterns.

4. Ask the children to fold a sheet of paper in half and to cut out some shape from the folded edge. Then have the children open the sheet and observe the symmetrical figure. Provide an opportunity for the children to share their designs.

Next, challenge the class to plan shapes to cut out of folded sheets and to guess what the results will look like. The students may draw what they believe the figures will look like when the paper is unfolded. Then let them cut out the figures and check the results against their estimates.

Another variation of this activity is to punch a hole through the folded sheet with a paper punch. Have the children guess how many holes there will be, then open the sheet to see. Try two holes, then three. Also, try folding the sheet of paper twice and then punching one or more holes through the paper. Add a challenge to this activity by having children guess where the holes will be as well as how many there will be. Display the children's work.

Objective: to identify symmetrical figures.

5. Have the children search through magazines for pictures that have symmetry. Have them cut out those pictures. On a bulletin board, put up the heading "These Pictures Have Symmetry" and the heading "These Pictures Don't Have Symmetry." Have the children classify the pictures they have cut out and place each of them under the appropriate heading.

A variation of this activity is to go on a school or neighborhood walk to look for symmetry in the environment. As examples are found, have two or three children sketch the examples on squared paper. When the walk is over, have the students color the sketches and classify them on the bulletin board.

Another variation of this activity is to provide each child with an object you have cut out from a magazine and then cut in half along its line of symmetry. For example, give children one side of a face, half of a flower in a pot, or half of an orange. Ask the children to paste the half picture onto a piece of drawing paper and to draw the other half of the object using crayons.

Thus far, we have been using line symmetry. With older children, introduce **rotational,** or **point symmetry.** A figure has rotational symmetry if the figure can be rotated about a point in such a way that the resulting figure coincides with the original figure. Thus, the equilateral triangle in Figure 12–23 may be rotated clockwise about point P. In this case, the triangle will coincide with the original triangle three times during one full turn. Each of these positions is shown in Figure 12–23. The first activity that follows presents rotational symmetry.

ACTIVITIES

Intermediate (4–6)

Objective: to introduce the concept of rotational symmetry.

1. Construct a large equilateral triangular shape to serve as a model for rotational symmetry. On the floor, make a masking tape frame in which the triangle fits. Put a

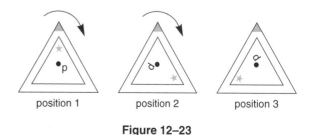

Figure 12–23

small hole through the model at its point of rotation and insert a pencil or a piece of doweling. Make some sort of mark in one corner of the shape to serve as a reference point when the figure is rotated. Put the shape in its frame, and have the class record its position on their paper.

Invite students to carefully rotate the figure clockwise until it again fits the frame. Have the class record the new position.

Have the students rotate the figure again until it once more fits the frame. Have the class record its new position.

The next rotation will put the figure back in its starting position. Ask, "How many different positions are there when we rotate an equilateral triangle?" There are 3 positions. Continue, "We say this figure has rotational symmetry of order 3. What do you think will be the order for the rotational symmetry of a rectangle, a square, or a regular pentagon? Let's try these figures."

You will need to investigate a variety of plane figures before the students will be entirely comfortable with rotational symmetry. As the students catch on, they will be able to think about and draw figures with a specified order of rotational symmetry.

Objective: to introduce the mira as a tool for exploring symmetry.

2. Activities involving the mira are particularly suited to a study of symmetry. A **mira** is a specially designed tool made of red transparent plexiglass that is used in place of a mirror for exploring line symmetry (see Figure 12-24). The mira is superior to a mirror in several ways. In the first place, you can see through the mira, so images are easier to copy. Also, the mira stands by itself and does not need to be held.

An extensive set of activities may be purchased to guide student work (see the references at the end of the chapter).

As with new manipulative aids, the initial activity with the mira should be a period of free play in which the students look for figures and pictures to be checked for symmetry. Provide materials such as pattern blocks, tiles, Cuisenaire rods, and magazine pictures. Encourage students to draw patterns on squared paper and to use the mira to investigate the patterns. Interesting discoveries will result.

3. Have the students consider the letters of the alphabet as shown in Figure 12–25. Ask the students to identify the letters that have at least one line of symmetry and those with more than one line of symmetry. Have the students visually estimate, then have them write down the letters they believe have line symmetry.

Then, have the students use a mirror or a mira to check each letter for symmetry. It is appropriate at this time to see if the students are able to determine if any of the letters have rotational symmetry. That is, can the letter be rotated about a center point in such a way that the letter appears as it normally does before it has been rotated a full turn? For example, the letter *I* has rotational symmetry of order 2.

An extension of this activity involves finding words that have line or rotational symmetry. For example, both TOOT and CHOICE have line symmetry and NOON has rotational symmetry. Is there a word that has both?

4. Let the students explore various materials such as pattern blocks using two mirrors or miras. Suggest to the students that they tape the mirrors at right angles and place blocks at the intersection. Increase and decrease the angle of the mirrors to see what images result. Place the mirrors parallel to each other and observe the image of blocks placed between them.

Try using three mirrors, one lying flat and two at right angles on top. Have the students sketch the images they think will result. Examples of two mirror configurations are shown in Figure 12–26.

Another application of line symmetry and the images that result from using multiple mirrors can be found in computer software. For example, various "works" applications include a word processor, a spreadsheet, a draw program, and a paint program. The latter two programs can be used to draw figures and then produce the mirror (flip) image or rotational image of the shape. Other dynamic geometry programs such as *Geometer's Sketchpad* on a computer or Cabri geometry on a computer or calculator offer even more opportunities for explorations of rotations and symmetry. These exciting graphics features allow students to instantly see the results of using mirrors or rotations.

Figure 12–24

ABCDEFGHIJKLMNOPQRSTUVWXYZ

Figure 12–25

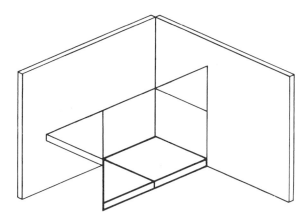

Figure 12–26

Objective: to construct symmetrical figures.

5. Challenge the children by asking them to construct irregular figures on the geoboard. Provide a line of symmetry; this could be a vertical, horizontal, or diagonal line. Have the children construct the reflection of the figure on the opposite side of the line of sym-

metry. Then, let the children check their efforts with the mira or the mirror.

Let the students experiment with lines of symmetry other than those shown in Figure 12–22. See which, if any, other lines can be used to accurately construct reflected images.

If you have a dynamic geometry program available for computers or calculators, encourage the students to explore concepts of geometry using that technology. For example, with the Cabri geometry capabilities on a TI-92 calculator, students might use the following strategies to explore lines of symmetry. If you have not used the TI-92, try to find a teacher or student who has experience with the calculator, or use one of the books from the reference list to help you get started.

Middle Grades (5–8)

Thanks to Vlasta Kokol-Voljč of the University of Maribor in Slovenia for her assistance with this activity.

Objective: to explore symmetry using dynamic geometry.

6. On a TI-92, choose F3 and select 3:Triangle (see Figure 12–27). Construct a small triangle on the middle-left side of the calculator screen (see Figure 12–28). (This triangle will be reflected across the line of symmetry that you are going to construct next.)

Choose F2 and select 4:Line (see Figure 12–29). Construct a line near the center of your screen by pointing to any point near the center and pushing EN-TER. Then use the blue arrow key to move the line where you want it. Push ENTER when the line is in a position that you like (see Figure 12–30). (This line will be used as a line of symmetry. A vertical line might be easiest for students to use, but a diagonal line will make the activity more interesting and will lead to better generalizations.)

Sketch the triangle and the line that are displayed on the calculator screen. Sketch what you think the triangle will look like when it is reflected across the

Figure 12–27

Figure 12–28

Figure 12–29

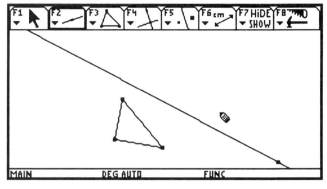

Figure 12–30

line. Check your prediction with a mirror or other reflecting device.

Choose F5 and select 4:Reflection (see Figure 12–31). Using the pointer and the blue arrow key, move the pointer to the triangle and choose "Reflect this triangle" (ENTER). Then move the pointer to the line you just drew and choose "with respect to this line" (ENTER) (see Figure 12–32). Check to see if the calculator screen looks like your drawing. (If the image goes off the screen of the calculator, try using the grabbing hand to move the triangle or the line until

you can see both the line and the image on your screen.)

Observe the position of the reflected triangle. How does the position of the reflected triangle relate to the position of the original triangle in relation to the line?

Repeat this activity with other shapes and other lines of symmetry. Be sure to draw a sketch of your prediction each time (see Figure 12–33).

Once you have mastered using a single line of symmetry, try this activity with two or more lines of symmetry (see Figure 12–34).

Figure 12–31

Figure 12–32

Figure 12–33

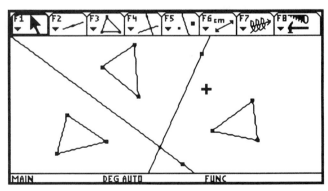

Figure 12–34

Objective: to challenge students with problems involving symmetry.

7. Provide students with three green triangles and three blue diamonds from the set of pattern blocks. Have the students make triangles that measure three inches on a side and have (a) one line of symmetry and no rotational symmetry, (b) two lines of symmetry and no rotational symmetry (no solutions), (c) three lines of symmetry and rotational symmetry of order 3, (d) no lines of symmetry and rotational symmetry of order 3, and (e) no lines of symmetry and no rotational symmetry. Encourage the students to make up similar problems, creating other shapes using four to eight pattern blocks.

Objective: to design tessellations.

8. Tessellations, patterns made by "tiling" a region with shapes, can be produced as simply as placing square tiles or pattern blocks in a region as shown in Figure 12–35a, by combining several shapes in a semi-regular tessellation as in Figure 12–35b, or by creating an Escher-type tessellation in a more artistic arrangement as in Figure 12–35c. In two companion books, Seymour and Britton (1989) and Britton and Britton (1992) have spelled out the nature of tessellations, tessellation art, and the techniques that allow teachers to help students in creating fine examples of tessellations. At the beginning stages, it is suggested that students design their tessellations with paper and pencil.

Colorful and original tessellations result. As the students become more skilled, they may be introduced to *TesselMania!*® (Lee, 1996). This clever computer software introduces the creation of tessellations and allows students to rotate and reflect shapes and to tessellate regions at will. Escher-type tessellations are made simply and quickly in *TesselMania!*®. Color enhances these designs and, when printed, the designs help decorate a classroom.

The activities above provide experiences with the symmetry found in various figures. The activities focus on line and rotational symmetry. These experiences help students not only learn the concept of symmetry but also develop the ability to visualize shapes in the mind's eye. We now turn to space figures.

Space Figures

Up to this point, the activities have dealt principally with plane figures—figures of two dimensions. Like all of us, children live in a three-dimensional world. All of their movements, explorations, and constructions have been in space. The exploration of space is the classic example of early mental growth.

As children continue their growth in geometry, activities with three-dimensional space figures are an important part of this learning. Whenever possible, tap children's environments—the classroom, home,

a.

b.

c.

Figure 12–35

and community. The activities that follow are designed to aid in the development of spatial concepts. Again, activities cannot by themselves teach. Augment them with reading, writing, discussion, examples, and thought.

ACTIVITIES

Primary (K–3)

Objective: to identify and draw two- and three-dimensional objects in the environment.

1. Extend the playground or neighborhood walk mentioned earlier to include a search for three-dimensional figures. On a shape walk, ask students to sketch the shapes they observe. The shapes may be two or three dimensional. Students may draw the shapes of windows, doors, faces of bricks, or fences. Or they may draw the shapes of entire houses, individual bricks, garbage cans, or light posts. It is likely that you will need to discuss how to sketch three-dimensional figures. Have the children share with one another their own techniques. Descriptive stories by the class or individuals may help to conclude an investigation of shapes in the community.
2. Ask the children to bring empty containers from home to serve as a collection of commonly found space figures. Expect containers such as cereal boxes, cans with the tops and bottoms removed, plastic soap containers, and tubes from paper towels or toilet paper. Use these materials as a bulletin board or table display. Classify the various figures by overall shape or the shapes of various faces. Cut the container so it lies flat and the students can examine the pattern of the space figure. In how many different overall shapes are household items packaged?

Objective: to copy and build space figures.

3. Encourage children to use a variety of materials to build space figures. Large blocks and cardboard building bricks along with tiles, geoblocks, Unifix cubes, Cuisenaire rods, and pattern blocks are among those commonly found in primary classrooms. Make a construction and ask the children to copy it.

   A challenging series of work cards accompanies the set of geoblocks. Develop other, similar cards for use with the three-dimensional learning materials.

Objective: to discover characteristics of polyhedrons.

4. Straws and pipe cleaners (or straws of two sizes) can be used to construct polyhedrons. Initially, produce two-dimensional figures. As space figures are investigated, it should become apparent that the faces of all polyhedrons are polygons. Thus, when a cube is constructed, an investigation of its faces yields squares. If a tetrahedron is constructed, an investigation of its faces yields triangles. Encourage children to construct various polyhedrons. Several are shown in Figure 12–36.

   Have the children compare the space figures, noting the number and shapes of the faces, the number of vertices, and any interesting facts about their shapes. Have the children record these findings on a chart and prominently display it.

Encourage the children to construct space figures. As they do so, they develop a sense of how figures fit in space. As children begin to analyze space figures, they prepare the way for a more formal study of objects in space.

ACTIVITIES

Intermediate–Middle Grades (4–8)

Objective: to explore the characteristics of the regular polyhedrons.

1. Among the myriad space figures, there are only five *regular polyhedrons*. A regular polyhedron is one in which all the faces are congruent, all the edges are the same length, and all the angles are the same size. The regular polyhedrons are the tetrahedron (4 faces), hexahedron or cube (6 faces), octahedron (8 faces), dodecahedron (12 faces), and icosahedron (20 faces). They were illustrated in Figure 12–1i.

   Students explore these shapes most effectively when they can hold them, turn them, and note their characteristics. Provide materials and patterns so the students may construct their own set of regular polyhedrons. (See Appendix B for patterns for the five figures.) The patterns may be copied onto heavy paper or oaktag. Have the students cut out the patterns, crease the fold lines with a paper clip, make the folds, and glue the tabs.

Figure 12–36

One systematic investigation of the regular polyhedra is discovering the relationship between the number of faces, the number of edges, and the number of vertices. A table, such as the one shown in Table 12–1, can be used as an effective problem-solving tool to display the information gathered. The table provides a way to systematically organize the information as it is collected.

Have the students handle the tetrahedron. Have them count the number of vertices, or corners, of the tetrahedron. There are 4. Record that number in the table. Next, count the number of faces (4) and record that information. Finally, count the number of edges (6) and record that information. Continue counting vertices, edges, and faces for the other figures.

Once the information has been recorded in the table, challenge the students to look for a relationship between the vertices, edges, and faces of a regular polyhedron. Have them look at the numbers for each of the regular polyhedrons. Give the students time and support as they look for this relationship.

A formula named after the Swiss mathematician Leonhard Euler describes the relationship between the faces, edges, and vertices of polyhedra. The formula states that $V + F - E = 2$; that is, the number of vertices plus the number of faces minus the number of edges equals 2. Many students are capable of finding this relationship.

To extend this activity, see if the students can determine if the relationship discovered for a regular polyhedron holds true for any pyramid or any prism.

Objective: to explore space figures formed by soap films on wire frames.

2. Provide the students with wire somewhat lighter than coat hanger wire; it should be easy to bend and cut the wire. The object is to construct shapes out of the wire that can be used with soapy water to produce various two- and three-dimensional figures. Figure 12–37 shows four possible wire shapes. Encourage the students to create wire shapes with tightly secured corners.

Have the students dip the two-dimensional shapes in a mixture of liquid soap and water (half and half) and record what happens. Let them trade

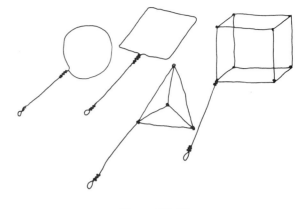

Figure 12–37

their wire shapes and experiment some more. Possible explorations include blowing a bubble with a circular frame and then blowing a bubble with a triangular frame.

See what happens when the three-dimensional frames are dipped in soap and water. What happens when a diagonal is constructed inside a three-dimensional shape that is then dipped in soap and water? Construct shapes that are not polygons, then dip them and blow bubbles or just dip them.

Objective: to combine imagination and knowledge of space figures to create a microworld.

3. Projects using space figures offer motivation for creative learning experiences. One such project was initiated during an introductory class on space figures. As the children and the teacher looked at a set of geoblocks, one child noted that a particular piece looked like an Egyptian pyramid; another student thought that the word *prism* sounded like *prison*. Soon a boy in the class mentioned that it would be exciting to create a city full of shapes. The *geoworld* project was begun. The geoworld was built on a platform of triwall construction board that measured 4 feet by 8 feet. The very first piece of architecture that arose was *tetrahedrons terrace,* a series of connected tetrahedrons. Then came the *cuban embassy,* an idea sparked by surveying atlases for possibilities. The cuban embassy was a large cube. It was surrounded by several cubans,

TABLE 12–1

number of	tetrahedron	cube	octahedron	dodecahedron	icosahedron
vertices	4				
edges	6				
faces	4				

who were represented by smaller cubes with personal characteristics. Many other structures were added to geoworld; when the project had been completed, every member of the class felt a deep sense of pride in the creative work of their peers.

Objective: to construct a geodesic dome.

4. Another project is the construction of a large space figure. Thus, a cube that measures 1 or $1\frac{1}{2}$ meters on a side may be built and used as a quiet place or reading corner. Zilliox and Lowrey (1997) describe their work with sixth graders who constructed a large rhombicosidodecahedron. The great effort and extreme pride in the task illustrate the positive effects of such construction projects. Among the more interesting of all such figures is the geodesic dome, originally conceived by the late Buckminster Fuller. The following steps result in a rather spectacular geodesic dome, whether it has a radius of 10 or 40 inches.

   a. *Make the big decision.* What size dome do you want to build? Decide on the radius desired (half the width at the dome's widest point). Figure 12–38 illustrates what the finished dome will look like.

   b. *Construct the dome using two different sizes of triangles.* The size of each triangle is determined by the size of dome desired. One of the triangles, T1, is equilateral, with each side 0.6180 times the length of the dome radius. The other triangle, T2, has one side equal to the length of a T1 side and two shorter sides, each 0.5465 times the length of the dome radius. Thus, for a dome of radius 10 inches, the T1 triangle has sides 6.2 inches long, and the T2 triangle has one side 6.2 inches long and two sides 5.5 inches long.

Figure 12–38

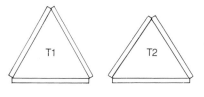

Figure 12–39

   c. *Make a pattern for each triangle.* Figure 12–39 shows one such set of triangles. Note that there is a flap on each side. The flap is used to attach the triangles.

   d. *Using the patterns, make 15 T1 triangles and 45 T2 triangles.* For a 10-inch radius dome, oaktag is suitable material; for a 40-inch radius dome, cardboard appliance cartons are best. It is necessary to lightly crease the fold lines on the flaps.

   e. *Begin construction.* If you use oaktag, use white school glue to attach the triangles. It will take the cooperative effort of several students to put the final pieces in place and hold them while they dry. If you use cardboard, you can use $\frac{1}{4}$-by-20 hexagonal machine nuts ($\frac{3}{4}$ inches long) and bolts with washers to attach the pieces. Follow these four steps: (1) Make six pentagons and five semipentagons from T2 triangles (see Figure 12–40a). (2) Add T1 triangles to the perimeter of one pentagon (see Figure 12–40b). (3) Fill the gaps between triangles with other pentagons (see Figure 12–40c. (4) Add T1 triangles between and below pentagons. Then, add semipentagons at the bottom (see Figure 12–40d).

   As a final touch to the ball-shaped geodesic dome, fill the gaps around the base of the dome and attach the bottom flaps together or to the floor to make the dome more rigid. It is helpful to cut windows and a door into geodesic domes large enough to enter.

During this project, students may wish to send away for a catalog from a company that prefabricates geodesic dome houses or to search for magazine articles about such homes. Some students may investigate some of Buckminster Fuller's other inventions.

Fractal Geometry

Much of the natural world is difficult to describe using common shapes such as triangles, squares, and rectangles. Apart from the human dimension, much of what occurs in nature appears chaotic. The study of chaos is the study of disorder and irregularity. To describe patterns in nature previously deemed chaotic and, thus, indescribable, Benoit Mandelbrot developed a new geometry, called fractal geometry. The study of fractals is an ex-

Figure 12–40

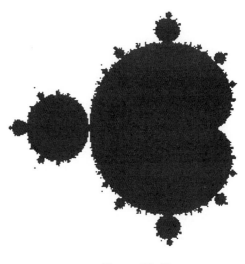

Figure 12–41

ample of a relatively recent discovery in mathematics. Fractal geometry provides ways for scientists who study things that appear to be chaotic in behavior, such as the way veins or arteries branch, to gain greater understanding of those phenomena.

Fractals are used to design computer models of irregular patterns in nature. Mandelbrot invented the name "fractal" to describe the fractional dimension work that he had completed. Gleick (1987, p. 114) noted, "In the end, the word *fractal* came to stand for a way of describing, calculating, and thinking about shapes that are irregular and fragmented, jagged and broken-up shapes from the crystalline curves of snowflakes to the discontinuous dusts of galaxies." A primary characteristic of fractals is self-similarity. This means that if you were to first look at a fractal and become familiar with its shape and then magnify or zoom in on a piece of the original you would find smaller, but similar, shapes to that of the original.

Perhaps the most commonly displayed fractal is the image produced by graphing a Mandelbrot set. A Mandelbrot set is a collection of numbers, from the set of complex numbers. By using computers it can

be determined if a complex number is a part of the Mandelbrot set. If the complex numbers in the Mandelbrot set are graphed, the result is the image in Figure 12–41 (Dewey, 1997). Dewey has a series of computer-generated images of the Mandelbrot set, illustrating the concept of self-similarity. You are encouraged to go to his Web site and view these images: http://www.olympus.net/personal/dewey/mandelbrot.html

Let's look at a fractal that is a useful figure in learning about the nature of fractals. It is the Koch curve or "snowflake." Koch Snowflakes of level or iteration 1, level 2, and level 3 are shown in Figure 12–42 b, c, and d. Notice that the figures are identical in design and different only in detail. This is an example of self-similarity, the characteristic of fractals discussed above. The basic foundation shape for the snowflake, level 0, is an equilateral triangle as in Figure 12–42a.

To construct the first level of the figure, take each side of the triangle and divide it into thirds. Next, using the center third of each side as the base, construct a smaller equilateral triangle projecting from the side of the original triangle. The level 1 snowflake has 12 sides (Figure 12–42b). The level 2 snowflake is constructed by using each of the 12 sides, dividing it into thirds, and constructing smaller equilateral triangles projecting from each side (Figure 12–42c). How many sides does the level 2 snowflake contain?

Besides using fractals to describe patterns in nature such as the shapes of ferns, coastlines, and the growth of trees, fractals have also become an art form. The work of Musgrave (1998) represents fine examples of using fractals as art. You are encouraged to find the Musgrave images on his web site: http://www.seas.gwu.edu/faculty/musgrave/. Another web site is that of Lanius (1998): http://math.rice.edu/~lanius/frac/. It contains a unit on fractals for elementary and middle school students. The activities

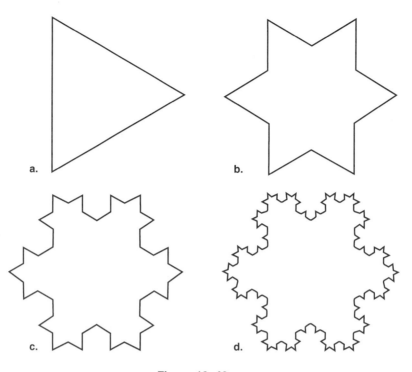

Figure 12–42

below are based on ones described by Lanius. For additional activities you are encouraged to explore her web site.

ACTIVITIES

Intermediate–Middle Grades (4–8)

Objective: to explore the form of the Koch snowflake.

1. Make copies of the triangular grid blackline master (Appendix B) for each student. Begin this activity by having the students color in an equilateral triangle with nine units on a side in the center of the triangular grid as in Figure 12–43a. Challenge the students to locate the three middle units along one side of the triangle and color an equilateral triangle with three units on a side projecting out from the side of the large triangle. Color in the other two three-unit triangles projecting out from the other two sides of the large triangle as in Figure 12–43b. This is the level 1 Koch snowflake. Continue by finding the middle unit along any of the 12 sides of the level 1 snowflake and color the triangle with one unit on a side projecting out from the side. Continue this until there are projections from all 12 sides as in Figure 12–43c. The resulting figure is the level 2 Koch snowflake. Encourage the students to carefully cut

around their figure and glue it to a piece of construction paper.

A variation of this activity is to make copies of the triangular grid blackline master on various colors of construction paper and have the students cut out one triangle with 9 units on a side, three triangles with 3 units on a side, and 12 triangles with 1 unit on a side. Next, have the student glue the large triangle on a sheet of construction paper, followed by gluing the 3-unit triangles to the center of each side of the large triangle, and completed by gluing the 1-unit triangles to the center of each side of the figure.

2. To extend the investigation of the Koch snowflake, suggest to the students that they see what they can discover about the perimeters of the snowflakes as they move from level to level. You may want to look ahead to Chapter 13 for a discussion of measuring length, including perimeter. Use the snowflakes constructed in Activity 1 and determine the perimeters using the side of the small triangle as the unit. A table like that shown in Table 12–2 might be a useful way to help organize the information about perimeters.

How many levels would it take to have a perimeter of at least 200 units? What do you notice about the size of the figure and its perimeter?

Next, consider the area of the Koch snowflake. You may want to look ahead to Chapter 13 for a discussion of measuring area. See what the students can dis-

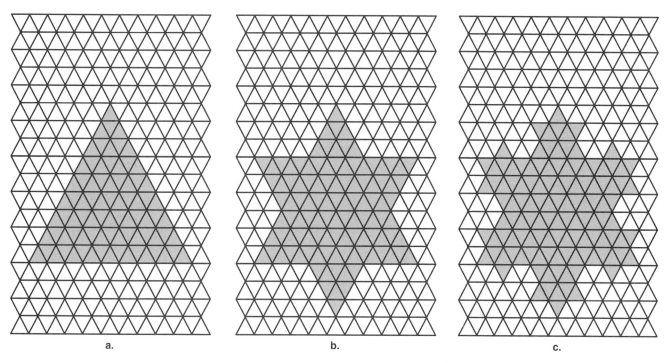

a.   b.   c.

Figure 12–43

cover about the areas of the snowflakes as they move from level to level. Use the snowflakes constructed in Activity 1 and determine the areas using the small triangle as the unit. A table like that shown in Table 12–3 might help organize the information about areas.

How many levels would it take to have an area of at least 150 triangular units? What do you notice about the size of the figure and its area?

3. Another procedure for developing the Koch snowflake is to use a combination of ruler and compass to construct the points of the snowflake (see Constructing Shapes in the next part of Chapter 12). Distribute to the students large sheets of paper on which is found an equilateral triangle of sides 27 centimeters with the middle third of each side missing as shown in Figure 12–44a. First, have the students construct two sides of

an equilateral triangle projecting from the center of each side of the large triangle as in Figure 12–44b. Then have them measure one third of each side of the new figure and construct new triangles in the center of each side, erasing the line in the center third of each side. Continue this procedure for each side of the new figure. The resulting figure is a level 3 Koch snowflake.

4. 🖥️ Students may explore the Koch snowflake using a *Logo* procedure. Long and DeTemple (1996, pp. 1000–1001) provide procedures for drawing the snowflake:

```
TO FRACTAL :LEVEL :SIDE
IF :LEVEL < 1 [FD :SIDE STOP]
FRACTAL :LEVEL − 1:SIDE/3
LT 60
FRACTAL :LEVEL − 1:SIDE/3
RT 120
FRACTAL :LEVEL − 1:SIDE/3
LT 60
FRACTAL :LEVEL − 1:SIDE/3
END

TO FRAC :LEVEL :SIDE
REPEAT 3 [FRACTAL :LEVEL :SIDE RT 120]
END
```

Students are encouraged to discover the different results when the levels and the lengths of sides are entered as variables in running the procedure FRAC. Thus, how do FRAC 3 200 and FRAC 3 100 vary? What interesting designs will result?

TABLE 12–2

Level of Koch snowflake	0	1	2	3	4	5
Perimeter	27	36	?	?	?	?

TABLE 12–3

Level of Koch snowflake	0	1	2	3	4	5
Area	81	108	?	?	?	?

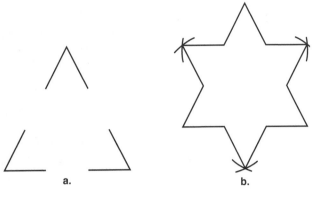

Figure 12–44

This section has focused on how children learn geometric concepts and specific activities to reinforce this learning. The process of learning is developmental; that is, children grow in their abilities to grasp geometric concepts. Children must actively experience geometry. They must be guided in their explorations. Above all, geometry must be a part of the mathematics program. It must be extended far beyond the basal textbook and presented throughout the school year.

Developing and Practicing Geometric Skills

The skills of geometry involve readily identifying, copying, inventing, and constructing figures. Teach the skills in concert with teaching geometric concepts. Developing and practicing skills will, in most cases, follow conceptual development.

Identifying Shapes

The collection of shapes easily identified by primary children varies with the experience and maturity of the children. The most productive activities for shape identification are those in which the child is actively manipulating and discussing figures. A kindergartner or first-grader may call a triangle a rectangle because the names are similar. A second- or third-grader who has used attribute blocks, pattern blocks, and geoboards and who has discussed the figures will seldom misname the triangle. A second- or third-grader may, however, misname a diamond or hexagon. Again, this difficulty can be alleviated through carefully designed experiences.

Primary students should be expected to develop geometric skills at a basic level. Thus, visual skills should include the ability to recognize different figures from a physical model or a picture. Verbal skills should include the ability to associate a name with a given figure. Graphical skills should include the ability to construct a given shape on a geoboard or to sketch the shape. Logical skills

should include the ability to recognize similarities and differences among figures and to conserve the shape of a figure in various positions. Applied skills should include the ability to identify geometric shapes in the environment, in the classroom, and outside the classroom.

At the primary level, children develop skills as a result of extending activities used to develop the concepts. It is important that the teacher provide time, materials, and direction. Pay attention to developing visual, verbal, graphical, logical, and applied skills. Refer to the primary activities suggested earlier for developing geometric concepts.

Intermediate students should be expected to develop skills at a slightly higher level. Thus, visual skills should include the ability to recognize properties of figures, to identify a figure as a part of a larger figure, to recognize a two-dimensional pattern for a three-dimensional figure, to rotate two- and three-dimensional figures, and to orient oneself relative to various figures. Verbal skills should include the ability to describe various properties of a figure. Graphical skills should include the ability to draw a figure from given information and to use given properties of a figure to draw the figure. Logical skills should include the ability to classify figures into different types and to use properties to distinguish figures. Applied skills should include the ability to recognize geometric properties of physical objects and to draw or construct models representing shapes in the environment.

Like children in the primary grades, students in the intermediate and middle grades should learn geometry through physical activities that use a variety of concrete materials. Again, extending the activities intended for conceptual development will provide opportunities to develop skills. The teacher should facilitate activities and discussion during the learning process.

Copying and Inventing Shapes

Copying activities were mentioned earlier in connection with parquetry blocks and geoboards. For students at all levels, copying can be challenging and fun. The complexity of the figures to be copied should vary with the age and experience of the children. Inventing shapes is an outgrowth of copying the shapes formed by teachers and classmates. Asking primary children to find as many four-sided figures as possible challenges them to invent shapes.

Intermediate and middle school students can be challenged with the same problem. The results, however, are likely to be different. How many six- or eight-sided figures can be found? The geoboard is a helpful tool for investigating polygons. Rectangular and isometric dot paper are useful for both sketching and recording shapes. Figure 12–45 illustrates both dot patterns. Both rectangular and isometric dot paper can be found in Appendix B.

 Another tool children may use to invent shapes is *Logo*. Figures may be designed on the computer

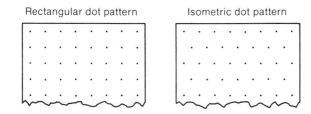

Figure 12–45

and saved on a floppy disk for future access. Using *Logo,* the children can discover more than just what shapes are possible. They must consider the sizes of the exterior and interior angles and the length of each side of the figure. Once they invent a shape, have them describe the shape and make a sketch of it to serve as a challenge to other students and to you.

Constructing Shapes

A skill appropriate at the intermediate and middle school level is that of constructing simple geometric shapes using a compass and straightedge. At this level, the goal is to introduce students to techniques of constructing simple figures. The tools used in constructing figures are inexpensive and readily available. The compass uses the student's pencil as a marking tool, as shown in Figure 12–46. Also pictured is a straightedge; a standard school ruler works fine.

The initial activities should involve copying a given figure. Thus, copying a line segment, an angle, and a circle with a given radius are appropriate. It is expected that the students will have been exposed to terms such as *line, line segment, point, angle, arc, ray, bisector,* and *perpendicular.* Most of these terms will appear in the math book, although words such as *arc* and *bisector* may need to be explained. An **arc** is any part of a circle. A **bisector** is a line that divides an angle or line into two equal parts. **Perpendicular** means to be at a right angle with a line.

ACTIVITIES

Intermediate–Middle Grades (4–8)

Objective: to use a compass and straightedge to construct simple figures.

1. Copy a line segment, AB, onto a line, m (see Figure 12–47a, b, and c).
   a. Place the compass points on A and B.
   b. Mark the length of segment AB onto line m.
   c. Segment A′B′ is the same length as segment AB.
2. Copy an angle, B, onto a given ray (see Figure 12–48a, b, c, d, and e).
   a. With B as the end point, make an arc crossing the rays at points C and A.
   b. Using the same radius and B′ as the end point, make an arc crossing the given ray at point C′.

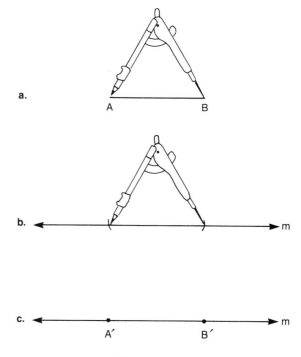

a.

b.

c.

Figure 12–46

Figure 12–47

Figure 12–49

The next three constructions require a somewhat higher level of skill. Instead of copying a given figure, they involve their own unique set of procedures. The first involves constructing the perpendicular bisector of a segment; the second, constructing a triangle from three given line segments; the third, constructing a hexagon inscribed in a circle.

ACTIVITIES

Intermediate–Middle Grades (4–8)

Objective: to use a compass and straightedge to construct a perpendicular bisector and a triangle.

1. Construct the perpendicular bisector of a given line segment, AB (see Figure 12–50 a, b, c, and d).
   a. Using point A as the center, draw an arc.
   b. Using the same radius and point B as the center, draw another arc.
   c. Place the straightedge at the intersections of the two arcs, points X and Y. Draw segment XY.
   d. Segment XY is perpendicular to segment AB and bisects segment AB at point Z.
2. Construct a triangle with sides equal in length to three given line segments, AB, BC, and CA (see Figure 12–51 a, b, c, d, and e).
   a. Draw a line, m. On the line, copy segment AB.
   b. With point B as the center, draw an arc with a radius the same length as segment BC.

Figure 12–48

c. Make A′C′ the same length as AC.
d. Use the straightedge to draw ray B′A′.
e. Angle A′B′C′ is the same size as angle ABC.
3. Construct a circle with a given radius, r (see Figure 12–49 a, b, and c).
   a. Spread the compass points to correspond to the length of the radius, r.
   b. Using the same radius, draw a circle.
   c. The completed circle has a radius equal to r.

Figure 12–50

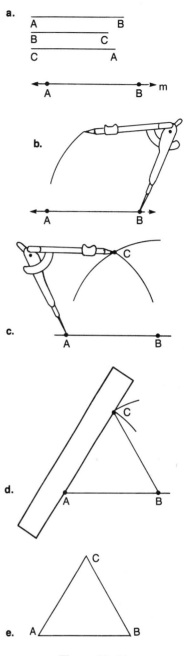

Figure 12–51

c. With point A as the center, draw an arc with a radius the same length as segment CA.

d. Use the straightedge to connect points A and B with the intersection of the two arcs at C.

e. Triangle ABC has sides equal in length to segments AB, BC, and CA.

3. Construct a hexagon inscribed in a circle (see Figure 12–52 a, b, c, and d).

a. Construct a circle with a radius of your choice.

b. Using the same radius, place the point of the compass at any location on the circumference of the circle and draw another circle.

c. Place the point of the compass where the circumference of the second circle intersects with that of the original circle and draw a third circle. Continue around the circumference of the original circle using the points of intersection as centers until a total of seven circles have been drawn.

d. Connect the points of the "star" to form a hexagon inscribed in the original circle. Note that the radius of the circle is also the length of each side of the hexagon. Can you find a simpler way to construct the hexagon?

Figure 12–52

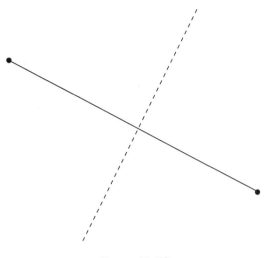

Figure 12–53

The latter construction shows one of the attractive designs that can result from work with constructions. By coloring parts of the design, students can create attractive patterns that can serve as bulletin board or hallway displays. Do you see a way to connect another set of intersections on the figure to produce a second, larger hexagon?

These are but a small sampling of possible constructions using a compass and straightedge; there are many extensions of construction activities. For example, challenge students to use paper folding or to use a mira to construct a perpendicular bisector of a given line or to explore angle bisectors or medians in triangles. Several such activities are presented below.

ACTIVITIES

Intermediate–Middle Grades(4–8)

Objective: to use paper folding to construct a perpendicular bisector of a line segment and an angle bisector.

1. Provide students with one fourth of an $8\frac{1}{2}$-by-11 inch sheet of paper for ease in folding. Have students draw a line segment about 8 centimeters long using pencil and ruler. Invite them to draw the segment in any configuration on the paper. Challenge the students to fold the paper in such a way that a fold on the paper divides the segment in half and is perpendicular to the segment as in Figure 12–53. Have the students discuss

how they made this construction. Perhaps they will suggest that when the two ends of the segment are matched and a crease is made they have found the perpendicular bisector of the segment.

2. On another quarter sheet of paper have the students make an angle using a pencil and a ruler. See if the students can develop a technique to fold the paper so that the fold passes through the vertex of the angle and divides the angle into two equivalent angles. After some practice, it is likely that students will suggest that you must begin at the vertex of the angle and carefully fold so that the rays of the angle coincide with each other in order to produce the angle bisector. It may take several tries for students to perfect this procedure.

Objective: to use paper folding to explore the bisectors of each angle of a triangle.

3. When students have gained experience and skill in folding angle bisectors, ask them what they might expect to find about the fold lines if they were to fold bisectors of each angle of a triangle. In small groups have the recorder write down the suggestions of the group members. Then, have the students try the folds and see what discoveries are made. The recorder should write down the conclusions of the group to use in the follow-up class discussion. Are there conclusions other than the folds will meet at a single point? Will the meeting point always be inside of the triangle? What happens when obtuse or scalene or equilateral or isosceles triangles are used? Would the same thing happen if the medians (the line from a vertex of a triangle through the midpoint of the opposite side) of a triangle were folded instead of the angle bisectors? Encourage speculation and discussion before and after construction.

Objective: to use a mira to construct a perpendicular bisector of a line segment and an angle bisector.

4. Have students draw a line segment about 10–12 centimeters long in any configuration on a sheet of paper.

Challenge the students to use the mira and draw a line that divides the segment in half and is perpendicular to the segment. Have the students discuss how they found where to draw their line. The students should soon discover that all they need to do is reflect the endpoints of the segment onto each other and draw the line along the front edge of the mira. This is shown in Figure 12–54. Discuss why reflecting the endpoints on one another in the mira will cause the segment to be bisected and produce a perpendicular to the segment. Compare the process of folding the perpendicular bisector in Activity 1 on page 366 with the procedure using the mira.

5. On a sheet of paper have students make an angle using a pencil and a ruler. See if the students can develop a technique to draw a line through the vertex of the angle that divides the angle into two equivalent angles. Discuss the suggested techniques. After some practice, it is likely that students will suggest that you must align the front edge of the mira on the vertex and then have one ray of the angle reflect upon the other ray. At this time you can draw the mira line to produce the angle bisector. Have students write in-

structions for a student unfamiliar with the mira describing how to use the mira to bisect an angle.

Objective: to use the mira to explore the bisectors of each angle of a triangle.

6. When students have gained experience and skill in using the mira to construct angle bisectors, ask them what they might expect to find about the angle bisectors of each angle of a triangle. In small groups have the recorder write down the suggestions of the group members. Then, have the students construct the bisectors and see what discoveries are made. The recorder should write down the conclusions of the group to use in the follow-up class discussion. Are there conclusions other than the angle bisectors will meet at a single point? Will the meeting point always be inside of the triangle? What happens when obtuse or scalene or equilateral or isosceles triangles are used? Would the same thing happen if the medians of a triangle were constructed instead of the angle bisectors? Encourage speculation and discussion before and after construction. How does this activity compare with Activity 3 on page 366?

Two other types of "pictures" are used by designers, engineers, and architects. These visual representations are called isometric drawings and orthographic projections or drawings. An **isometric drawing** is a drawing that shows a three-dimensional shape drawn in two dimensions. Figure 12–55a shows an isometric drawing. The angles in an isometric drawing are 60° and 120° to

Figure 12–54

a.

Figure 12–55

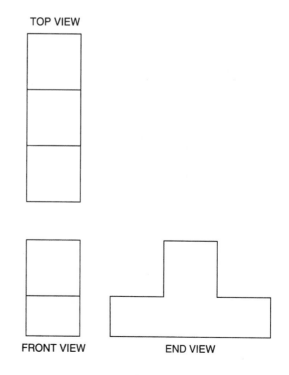

TOP VIEW

FRONT VIEW   END VIEW

b.

represent a perspective view and to reduce distortion; vertical edges remain vertical. An **orthographic projection** is a drawing of three views of an object: a bird's eye view from the top, a view from directly in front, and a view directly from the end (Figure 12–55b). Each of these views correspond to the views shown on the isometric drawing.

ACTIVITIES

Intermediate–Middle Grades (4–8)

Objective: to sketch isometric drawings and orthographic projections from geoblocks.

1. Geoblocks, discussed earlier in this chapter, serve as an excellent aid for developing skill in making isometric and orthographic drawings. Make available to a table group two blocks that have common dimensions and can be combined to make an interesting object (see Figure 12–56a). Then, have the students view the object in such a way that each sees three "sides" of the figure as is shown in Figure 12–56b. Then have each student sketch what the student sees. Drawings may be similar to that shown in Figure 12–43c. Expect some questions about the drawings and some distortion in the drawings as the students begin their work. After the isometric drawings are complete, let the students compare and discuss them. Then have students trade their geoblocks for some from another table and repeat the process to produce another isometric drawing. If there is time, repeat the process, again. Identify the top of the object in the drawing, the front of the object in the drawing, and the end of the object in the drawing. Have the students label their drawings.

2. After the last isometric drawing is completed and labeled from Activity 1, encourage one member of each group to look at one of the objects for which she has an isometric drawing. The view for this observation must be from directly above the object and from the front of the object. Then have the student draw this view. Have the others in the group view and draw the top view. Next, have the students look at the object from directly in front and at eye level and have them sketch the front view. Finally, have the students view the object at eye level directly from the end and sketch the end view. The three views of the object represent the orthographic projection (Figure 12–56). After students have had some experience sketching isometric drawings and orthographic projections, they will be able to identify figures drawn from orthographic projections, will be able to sketch orthographic projections from isometric drawings, and will be able to make accomplished isometric drawings.

Objective: to identify orthographic projections from isometric drawings, draw orthographic projections, and make isometric drawings from orthographic projections.

Ranucci (1973) in the challenging book, *Seeing Shapes,* has a chapter devoted to orthographic and isometric drawings. There are several pages devoted to practicing identifying and drawing shapes. This practice serves as a follow-up to the previous activities. Once the students are confident in their abilities to recognize the drawings and make their own, have them build more complex shapes using the geoblocks and prepare activities that challenge classmates to recognize and draw orthographic projections of their isometric drawings.

Estimating

Throughout the activities presented in this chapter, we have suggested that you encourage children to estimate, asking, for example, "How many squares do you think can be constructed on a geoboard? How many turtle steps do you believe are necessary to hide the turtle under the shape? Which figures do you think have line symmetry? Can you tessellate with a pentagon?" All of these questions relate to estimating.

For those who actively pursue mathematical thinking, estimating is a valuable skill. As related to geometry, estimation involves the ability to reasonably guess how many, to visualize how figures will look before they are constructed, and to estimate the sizes of one-, two-, and three-dimensional figures.

Constantly challenge children to take a moment and estimate before they complete a project, activity, or exercise. After a while, estimating becomes a part of geometric thinking. The entire mathematics curriculum,

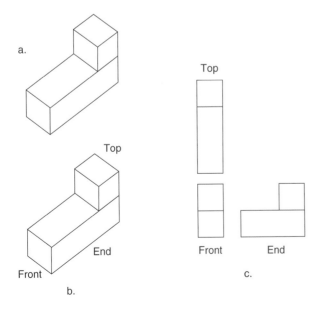

Figure 12–56

then, provides students with practice in estimating. Several activities that reinforce estimation and relate to geometry follow.

ACTIVITIES

Primary (K–3)

Objective: to estimate the sizes and shapes of various figures.

1. On a sheet of paper, draw the outlines of five or six triangles. Use actual cutouts of the shapes to make the outlines. Then put the shapes on one table or counter and the outlines on another. Ask one child to pick up one of the triangles and then move to the edge of the table containing the outlines. Ask another child to look at the triangle being held by the first child and estimate which outline belongs to that shape. Have the child holding the shape put the triangle in the outline to see if it fits. Then ask another child to choose another of the triangular shapes. Continue the activity until all of the shapes have been fitted to outlines.

   Extend this activity by using different shapes. Use squares, rectangles, hexagons, and irregular quadrilaterals. To make the estimating more challenging, use 12 or 14 outlines and two or three different shapes at the same time.

Objective: to estimate and discover the number of noncongruent triangles that can be made on an isometric geoboard.

2. Figure 12–57 shows an isometric geoboard. Begin by asking children to guess how many different triangles can be made using the first two rows of this geoboard. We find that there are twelve different triangles. (One example is shown on the geoboard in Figure 12–57.) Then have the students construct as many triangles as they can.

   Later, have the students guess how many different triangles can be made using three rows of the geoboard. See how many of those triangles the children can construct. It is helpful to provide isometric dot paper for the children to record their findings (see Appendix B). The results make a fine bulletin

board display. This activity can eventually be extended to incorporate the entire geoboard.

Objective: to imagine and describe various space figures from their patterns.

3. Provide the children with patterns for various space figures. Include patterns for a cube, rectangular box, cylinder, cone, and tetrahedron. Have the children describe the figure they believe will result when the pattern is folded. Use dotted lines to indicate how the pattern will be folded. Encourage the children to sketch or find an example of the resulting space figure. Then have some children cut out and fold the figure. Compare the estimates with the final product.

   A variation of this activity is to show the children several household containers such as a cereal box, a paper towel tube, and a cracker box. Have the children sketch the pattern the container would make if it were cut apart and laid out flat. Cut the containers and compare them with the sketches.

It is helpful for children to have the opportunity to mentally visualize shapes. This allows them to gain experience in using the mind's eye as an aid in working with the visual aspects of geometry. We continue with activities for older students.

ACTIVITIES

Intermediate (4–8)

Objective: to visualize and construct a figure of a given size and shape.

1. Provide each student with one or more outlines of figures on oaktag or paper. These figures may be triangles, quadrilaterals, squares, rectangles, pentagons, or hexagons. Also provide construction paper.

   Have each student observe the outline of a figure. Then, using the construction paper, cut out the shape that will fill the outline. Encourage the students to devise ways to determine the appropriate size for the figure they are cutting out. When the figures have been cut out, have the students place them in the outlines and compare the results. Let the students then exchange outlines and try again.

   A variation of this activity is to put one outline on the chalkboard and provide students with construction paper. Have all the students cut out the shape that fits the outline on the board. Again, let students see how well their figures fit the outline.

Objective: to determine the results of a set of *Logo* commands.

Figure 12–57

2. Make a list of several *Logo* commands that will produce a geometric shape or design. Have the children read through the commands and attempt to draw what they believe the results will be. One set of design commands follows:

```
REPEAT 2 [FD 40 RT 90 FD 60 RT 90]
BACK 60
END
```

What do you think the results will be? (see Figure 12–58). Have children act out the commands by walking around the room or on the playground.

Invite individual children to suggest sets of commands and let the other children guess what the results will be. Try the commands on the computer. This particular activity helps children visualize geometric figures by mentally or physically acting out a sequential procedure.

Objective: to estimate and determine the number of squares that can be constructed on geoboards of varying sizes.

3. Have the students estimate how many squares they will be able to construct on a 5 × 5 rectangular geoboard without using any diagonal lines. After the students have guessed, encourage them to begin to systematically estimate and determine how many squares can be made on 2 × 2, 3 × 3, and 4 × 4 rectangular geoboards without using diagonals. The students should find one, five, and fourteen squares, respectively. See if they can use this information to discover how many squares can be made on the 5 × 5 geoboard.

There is a number pattern involving the square numbers (1, 4, 9, 16, . . .) that will show that thirty squares can be made on the 5 × 5 geoboard without using diagonals. How many squares would you expect on a 6 × 6 geoboard? How many on a 10 × 10 geoboard?

Extend this activity by including squares that involve diagonals. Encourage the students to break the problem into subproblems and then combine the results. Be sure to have the students estimate how many squares can be constructed.

Solving and Creating Problems

Just as estimating is an integral part of geometry, so is solving and creating problems. Once learned and practiced, skills in problem solving continue to serve the learner. Many of the activities discussed earlier were presented in a problem format. Following are other useful activities that provide problem-solving experiences.

ACTIVITIES

Primary (K–3)

Objective: to determine patterns for which clues have been given.

1. Make up pattern strips from railroad board, each having approximately 10 squares, 10 by 10 centimeters in size. Place objects on four to six of the squares so that a pattern is suggested. Ask the children to fill in or extend the pattern, depending on which squares have been left blank. For example, in Figure 12–59a the pattern is trapezoid, triangle, triangle, trapezoid, and so on.

The pattern in Figure 12–59b is red triangle, red circle, red square, red diamond, then blue triangle, blue circle, and so on. In Figure 12–59c, the pattern is two rectangles in a horizontal position, two rectangles in a vertical position, circle, two rectangles in a hori-

Figure 12–58

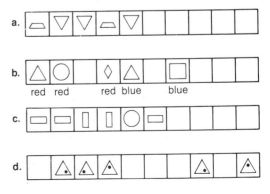

Figure 12–59

zontal position, and so on. Finally, let's consider the pattern in Figure 12–59d.

- *Understanding the problem.* What we need to do to solve this problem is to find shapes to put in the empty regions that fit the pattern already started. The figures that we can see are triangles with dots in them.
- *Devising a plan.* We will begin with the group of three triangles and look for likenesses and differences. If we find what we think is a pattern, we will move to the right along the row and see if the figures fit the pattern we have in mind (look for a pattern).
- *Carrying out the plan.* Because all of the triangles look alike, we look closely at the dots in the triangles. The first triangle has a dot in the lower-right corner. In the next triangle, the dot is in the lower-left corner. In the next triangle, the dot is in the top corner.

    It seems as though the dot is moving from corner to corner. If that is how the pattern works, the very first square should have a triangle with a dot in the top corner. The next three empty squares should have triangles with dots in the lower-right, lower-left, and top corners. The last empty region will have a triangle with a dot in the lower-left corner.

    We have found the pattern. It looks as if either the dots are moving around to the right inside the triangles or the triangles are rotating to the right.

- *Looking back.* When we put all of the triangles and dots in the empty regions, is the pattern of dots the same from the beginning to the end of the row? Yes, it is. The pattern must be correct.

There are many possibilities for patterns such as these. Invite children to make patterns for their classmates to complete. Children can be skillful problem creators.

Objective: to develop spatial visualization using tangram pieces.

2. Tangram pieces were used in Chapter 10 in activities related to fractions. Tangrams offer children the chance to solve puzzles and to engage in creative endeavors, as well. There are seven tangram pieces, as shown in Figure 12–60. All seven may be fitted together to make a square, as in Appendix B.

    Initial activities should include providing frames in which the children fit two or more of the tangram shapes. For example, using an *a* piece and a *d* piece, make the shape shown in Figure 12–61a. The children should be able to put the pieces together and achieve success. Later, use a greater number of pieces and make the shapes more difficult to complete. Ask experienced children to make a shape using all but one *e* piece, as in Figure 12–61b.

Figure 12–60

Figure 12–61

Another enjoyable tangram activity is to construct pictures of animals, people, objects, and houses using all or some of the tangram shapes. Children may fill in frames, construct their own pictures, or develop figures for other children to complete. The waving man in Figure 12–61c is an example of such a creation.

Objective: to use clues to solve mystery shape problems on the geoboard.

3. Provide the children with geoboards. Explain that they will be given clues to the mystery shapes. They should find at least one shape that matches each set of clues. Say, for example, "I am thinking of a shape that has 4 nails on its boundary and 1 nail inside. Can you find it?" Figure 12–62 shows three different shapes that fit the clues; there are others. Once the children have found one solution, encourage them to find others.

   Here are additional clues that describe other shapes. "I am thinking of a shape that has . . . "

   * 4 nails on its boundary and 0 nails inside;
   * 5 nails on its boundary and 0 nails inside;
   * 6 nails on its boundary and 0 nails inside;
   * 10 nails on its boundary and 2 nails inside.

   Once the children are able to find the mystery shapes, ask them to make up clues for shapes that other members of the class can find. Have them put the solutions on rectangular dot paper. Remind the children that often there is more than one shape that matches a set of clues.

Middle Grades (4–8)

Objective: to create dodecagons of the same size using a variety of shapes.

1. Provide students with a set of pattern blocks and an example or two of dodecagons constructed using the blocks. Figure 12–63 shows two such figures. The challenge is to see how many different dodecagons of the same size students can make using the pattern blocks. There are more than 60 different dodecagons of the same size that can be constructed using the pattern blocks.

   Provide outlines of dodecagons on which the students can sketch the pattern blocks used. Let the students color the sketches using the appropriate colors. Then place the figures on a bulletin board as a reference for others who are working on the project.

Objective: to develop visual perception.

2. Exploring pentominoes offers students the opportunity to test their perceptual and creative abilities while problem solving. A **pentomino** is a figure produced by combining five square shapes or cubes of the same size. There is one rule: each square must share at least one complete side with another square in the figure or each cube must share a face with another cube in the figure. Three of 12 possible pentominoes appear in Figure 12–64.

   Pentominoes are two- or three-dimensional, and two pentominoes are considered the same if one is a flip or a rotation of the other. For instance, the pentominoes in Figure 12–65 are considered the same.

   Initially, give students numerous square shapes to explore. Squares of 3 centimeters on a side are ideal. Challenge students to find as many different pen-

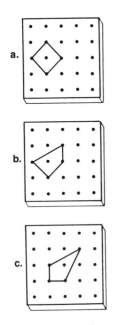

Figure 12–62

Figure 12–63

Figure 12–64

Figure 12–65

tominoes as they can. As they discover the figures, have them shade or color the patterns on a sheet of squared graph paper.

Extend this activity by having students select the pentominoes that they believe can be folded to make a box with an open top. Allow time for students to cut out the pentominoes and to attempt to fold them into boxes. You may continue to extend work with pentominoes by presenting three-dimensional pentominoes with challenging shapes to build. Discovery Toys (1993) has developed a three-dimensional pentomino puzzle set.

3. Another way to investigate pentominoes is to use the small milk containers commonly found in schools. Cut off the top of each container so that the bottom and the four sides are same-sized squares. Then ask the students to see how many of the 12 pentominoes they can make by cutting the cartons along the edges and without cutting any one side completely off. Figure 12–66a shows an example in which a cut was made along each of the four vertical edges and the sides were folded down. Figure 12–66b shows a different pentomino made by cutting along other edges of the milk carton.

4. Once students are comfortable with pentominoes, have them tessellate with various pentominoes. Using only one of the pentomino shapes, is it possible to cover a sheet of paper without leaving gaps? Figure 12–67 illustrates the beginnings of two tessellations.

5. Use pentominoes to further explore symmetry. Have students try to place a mirror or a mira on all or some of the pentominoes so that the reflection is the same as the part of the figure behind the mirror. In other words, do all pentominoes have line symmetry? Identify those that do and those that do not.

6. Have the students consider **hexominoes,** figures constructed using six square shapes. There are considerably more hexominoes than pentominoes. Each of the preceding activities, except the one using the milk container, can easily be done with hexominoes. Use *Logo* to construct pentominoes or hexominoes visually, using turtle graphics.

Objective: to analyze various cubes and determine color patterns.

7. Make available 27 small cubes with dimensions of 2 or 3 centimeters. Have the students construct a large 2-by-2-by-2 cube using these smaller cubes (see Figure 12–68a). Then have the students imagine that the large cube has been painted blue. Encourage the students to make a table to record the number of faces of each smaller cube that are painted blue.

Then present the challenge. Have the students construct a large 3-by-3-by-3 cube using the smaller cubes (see Figure 12–68b). Have them imagine that this cube is painted blue. Ask them to make a table to record the number of smaller cubes with (a) no faces painted blue, (b) exactly one face painted blue, (c) exactly two faces painted blue, and (d) exactly three faces painted blue. Extend the problem by asking the students to construct a 4-by-4-by-4 cube and answer the same four questions regarding the faces painted blue. Here, the table will be especially useful. Then have the students try to construct a 5-by-5-by-5 cube and answer the questions.

For a final, more difficult extension, see if anyone can find the various numbers of blue faces on a 10-by-10-by-10 cube. This last problem may be a question of the week.

Objective: to combine *Logo* procedures to generate other figures.

8. 🖥 When students have had an opportunity to work with *Logo* and can design certain simple shapes, such as a square, a triangle, and a circle, encourage them to solve problems using their

Figure 12–66

Figure 12–67

Figure 12–68

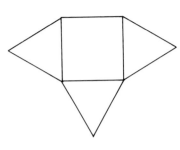

Figure 12–69

skills. Have them construct a shape with each side a specified length in each corner of the computer monitor. Have them make the largest visible square or circle. Challenge the students to construct a large square with a circle inside it and a triangle inside the circle. See if they can construct three shapes side by side that just barely touch each other.

Here is another opportunity for students to develop problems to present to others in the class. When a design or figure has been developed, ask the inventor to sketch the design on a piece of squared paper and post it near the computer as a class challenge. Figure 12–69 shows one such student-generated problem. In addition, *Logo* resources contain many problems for students.

To supplement the many teacher-initiated problem-solving activities, a number of fine games, puzzles, and computer programs have been marketed commercially. Examples of these include the Rubik's Cube, Rubik's Magic, Soma Cube, The Super Egg, What's in the Square, Imagic, Mind's Eye, Perceptual Puzzle Blocks, and computer programs such as *Factory Deluxe, The Factory, The Super Factor, Gears,* and *Building Perspective.*

Using a coordinate system such as that found on maps is a valuable application of geometry. The map can be an imaginary neighborhood or the neighborhood surrounding the school. The sample map shown in Figure 12–70 is the basis for the following activities and questions. Copy it for individual students. Five different, yet related, activities employ the map. These are briefly described below. Expand each activity to match the needs and abilities of the students.

Figure 12–70

ACTIVITIES

Middle Grades (4–8)

Objective: to use a rectangular coordinate system.

1. *Where Is It?* Have the students study the map and answer the following questions:
   - Laura's Gas Station is at the corner of Second and Walnut. Where is Jack's Market?
   - Where is Fire House No. 46?
   - Where is Lincoln School? (Be careful!)
   - Where is Center City Park?

2. *How Far Is It?* Have the students use the map to follow the instructions and answer the questions below:
   - From Tom's Cafe to Fire House No. 32 is 5 blocks by the shortest route. See if you can draw the shortest route.
   - How many different 5-block routes can you find?
   - How many blocks is the shortest route from Alice's Place to Lincoln School?
   - Your bicycle had a flat tire on Sixth Street between Oak and Peach Streets. Give the address of the closest gas station.
   - Suppose you are standing at Third and Walnut and someone from out of town asks how to get to Jack's Market. Tell them how to get there.
   - You are a jogger and you want to jog around the outside of Center City Park for 2.5 kilometers. Every ten blocks equals 1 kilometer. Tell where you begin and finish your jog. Are there different ways to do this?

3. *Location Codes.* Have the students use the map to answer the following questions:
   - Suppose you are part of a group at Doug's place. All of a sudden, one member of the group says, "I know a new way to tell where places are." He goes on, "Laura's Gas Station is (2,1)," and he writes it down. "Sam's Gas Station is (1,4)." Do you see the code?
   - Using the code, where is Jim's house?
   - Using the code, where is the Zoo entrance?
   - What is at (7,1)?
   - What is at (3,2)?

4. *Following Directions.* Have the students use the map to follow the directions below:
   a. Place an "A" at the corner of Fifth and Cherry Streets. The A will represent where you are.
   b. Walk two blocks east, three blocks south, two blocks west, and one block north. Place a "B" at the corner where you have stopped.
   c. Beginning at B, walk one block east, three blocks north, one block east and place a "C" at the corner where you have stopped.

Each die has 3 "East" and 3 "North" Faces.

Figure 12–71

   d. Beginning at C, start out walking south and zig-zag south and west, alternating one block at a time and walking five blocks in all. Place a "D" at the corner where you have stopped.
   e. Beginning at D, walk three blocks west, three blocks north, one block east and place an "E" at your final stopping point (Third and Maple Streets).

5. *A Trip to the Zoo.* Let students play the following game using the map: You and a friend decide to go to the Zoo. You both meet at Doug's place and agree to make the trip in an unusual way. You will need a pair of dice to give directions. (You may use dice like those in Figure 12–71 or regular dice.)

   The faces on the dice give you the directions east and north. East directs you to go one block east, and north directs you to go one block north. (With regular dice, even numbers—2, 4, and 6—direct you to go east and odd numbers—1, 3, and 5—direct you to go north.)

   You and your friend want to see who will get to the Zoo first by rolling the dice and following the directions. Begin now and see who arrives at the Zoo entrance first. If you go directly past City Hall, you get an extra throw.

Children's awareness of geometry in the environment is heightened considerably as you focus attention on various applications of geometry. This awareness also strengthens students' appreciation for and understanding of geometry.

Grouping Students for Learning Geometry

When students engage in learning geometry, a variety of grouping patterns are appropriate. For example, when younger children are learning concepts such as *near, far, on, in,* and so on, you may wish to have the children all together in a discussion corner or in another area of the room. This allows several children to participate simultaneously, allows the students to carry on a discussion, and allows the teacher to observe the work of the children. Other examples of whole-class activities include introductory work on the geoboard, introductory work with *Logo,* constructions of polyhedra models, and projects such as building toothpick bridges or a geodesic dome.

Cooperative learning groups are appropriate for activities in which materials may be shared and for those in which problems are presented. Examples of learning group activities include geoboard problems, tessellations, pentominoes, mirror symmetry, soap films on wire frames, constructing shapes with a compass and straightedge, pattern block challenges, and projects. Roper (1989, 1990) has developed problem solving activities using Pattern Blocks that are intended for use in cooperative learning groups. The focus is to construct shapes with the blocks using instructions that are provided for each member of the group.

Individual or pair learning may best take place when students are exploring the *Logo* environment or making line drawings or coloring patterns. Once children have learned how to make objects by paper folding, folding is done individually.

By and large, the types of activities suggested in this chapter involved the active participation of the children. Such activities tend to be social activities; that is, they are effectively accomplished when children are working together and comparing and discussing their work. Even the skills of geometry are effectively learned as children work side by side informally.

Communicating Learning of Geometry

Description is an important part of communicating in learning geometry. As children observe shapes, discover their properties, develop definitions involving essential characteristics, and draw and construct shapes, their ability to communicate their thoughts is fundamental. For the students, part of the communication process is drawing sketches that illustrate their work. Written communication is used to describe their work and to put into words the shapes and forms with which they are working. Oral communication serves a similar purpose. For example, "In your group today, you are to describe the figure that has been provided. The reporter for your group will present the description orally to the rest of us and we will attempt to sketch the figure from the description. Tomorrow, we will do a similar activity but your group's recorder will write a description that you will share with other groups to see if the members of the other groups can sketch the figure that has been described."

Children enjoy writing and illustrating theme books—for example, a book featuring round objects with pictures and written descriptions of round things found at school and at home. Older students may keep journals of shapes with descriptions of the shapes and where they are found. These journals can spark ideas for creative stories about various shapes. The shape descriptions in Norton Juster's *The Phantom Tollbooth* (1961) will surely inspire writing that includes shapes.

The oral language that children use to describe their movement as they walk around geometric figures made with tape or yarn on the floor becomes the basis for writing *Logo* procedures. The language of the children is translated into the language of *Logo;* likewise, children can read *Logo* procedures and describe them in their own words.

Cooperative and individual writing are appropriate activities for cooperative learning groups. It is a good plan to keep all written material in the individual portfolios for easy access. When a group record has been made, it may be kept in the portfolio of the group record keeper. As group members explore geometric concepts and develop skills, the group recorder provides a chronicle of the thinking process. This chronicle is then shared with other groups during the debriefing time at the end of the activity. Discussion is then invited. Children question one another and seek clarification of the ideas that have been put forth.

Connecting Learning of Geometry

Mr. Grotting's kindergarten children were puzzled when he held out his clenched fist and said that he had something in his hand and he wanted them to guess what it was. The students made several guesses, including a pencil, a coin, a button, a block, and a cracker. Mr. Grotting said no, it was not any of those items. Then he said he would give a clue: the object is round. Quickly, the children again guessed a coin and a button. No, it was not either of those items. Mr. Grotting asked the students about other items that are small and round. A child asked if was a ball. No. Was it a ring? Yes, that was it. It was one of the rings from the dress-up corner. Mr. Grotting then asked if the children could think of anything else that was round, whether big or small. The children named a bicycle wheel, a roller blade wheel, and a car wheel. A few other items were mentioned before it was time for stations.

In the math station in Mr. Grotting's room this week, the children were asked to find pictures or draw pictures of things that are round. When a picture was found or made, the children dictated a sentence about what the round object was to a parent helper who wrote the sentence beneath the picture. After all of the children had had a chance to find round objects, Mr. Grotting and the class described the variety of round things there are. The pictures were sorted by whether the round objects could be found in the classroom or outside of the classroom. All of the pictures were then put together to form a class book entitled "Things That Are Round." The connection between the geometric idea of circle and how the circle is used in the environment became clearer as a result of the focus on round things. Next, a square will be the focus.

Ms. Perkins had a surprise for her seventh-grade class. This day as the students arrived, many brought pictures, including some photographs, of various geometric shapes that they had seen in their community or in magazines. It had begun just as another assignment, but as the students realized how shapes were used in building construction, in framing and outlining, and in vehicles used in transportation, considerable energy was put forth in documenting the shapes. The category of shapes in nature was discovered by several students, and appropriate examples were brought in. Now, the bulletin board was nearly full of pictures and some objects from this impromptu scavenger hunt. Today, Ms. Perkin's surprise was to show a set of high-quality slides she had borrowed from the media center. The slide set, *Geometry in Our World* (Engelhardt, 1987), reinforced the findings of the students. After several of the slides had been shown, Ms. Perkins challenged the students to work in their cooperative groups to make lists of all the different shapes that they had already seen and were likely to see as additional slides were presented. The group discussions were lively. When the group reporters shared with the rest of the class their lists, it became clear that the geometry that the students had been studying surrounded them both in and out of school.

There was not enough time during this day to view all of the slides, so for the next two days, the slides and discussions continued. To culminate this mini-unit each of the student groups selected a particular shape and made a collage of two- and three-dimensional representations of that shape from their environment. One group focused on squares and another group focused on rectangles. Other groups chose circles, triangles, polygons with more than four sides, streets and branches, and decorative patterns. By the end of a week, the classroom was beautifully decorated with the group projects. The connection between geometry and the students' world had been clearly made.

Assessing Learning of Geometry

In assessing geometric learning, consider the objectives. When a school or a district adopts an elementary mathematics textbook series or program, it is, by and large, adopting a collection of objectives. The objectives are found throughout the teacher's manual for each level in the series. The geometry presented in a basal math series is reviewed and assessed at the end of a chapter or section. Chapter tests help in assessing geometric learning but do not tell the whole story.

Activities provide opportunities for observing the actual performance of the children and making additional assessment. Observations are most helpful when teachers make anecdotal records at the time of or shortly after the observation. With the large number of useful geometry activities, there is ample opportunity for teachers to observe and note children's behavior as the children actively engage in learning geometry.

Further, we recommend that the teacher expand on the material presented in the math textbook. Thus, students have a greater opportunity to advance from the first of the van Hiele levels (recognizing shapes) to the second level (establishing relationships between figures and their properties).

Teacher-made tests may provide some assessment of content not found in the math textbook. A test may require paper and pencil, or it may be a task requested by the teacher. Figure 12–72 shows three sample paper-and-pencil test items.

1. Sketch the following on the geoboards below.

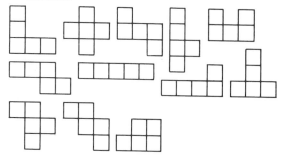

right triangle   hexagon   trapezoid

2. Circle each pentomino that has exactly <u>one</u> line of reflection.

3. Make the following design with *Logo* commands. Use REPEAT and the procedure SQUARE.

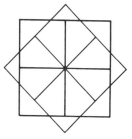

Figure 12–72

The same material can be tested by asking students to construct a particular figure on their geoboards and then to hold the boards up for the teacher to see. Likewise, students can be given pentominoes and asked to use a mirror or a mira to find those figures with exactly one line of symmetry. Another task may be to produce a particular design or figure on the computer using *Logo*. At various times, work completed by the students should be placed in the students' portfolios to use for assessment purposes. Items that might not fit such as a polyhedron model or a geodesic dome could be photographed and the photograph placed in the portfolio.

Assessment is an ongoing task for the teacher. The more information you gather, the better able you will be to fit instruction to the learning styles of your students. Continually monitoring students as they work is among the most important tasks of the teacher.

Something for Everyone

Many of the activities in Chapters 12 and 13 require children to work in visual or in spatial learning modes. Of course, children use other learning modes as they learn the concepts and skills of geometry and measurement. To avoid repetition, the discussion of the learning modes associated with geometry and measurement is presented at the end of Chapter 13.

KEY IDEAS

Geometry abounds in our environment. From nature to architecture, we are continually surrounded by examples of geometry. This chapter presents ways that geometric concepts can be experienced by children. When children enter school, they are in the process of completing a transition from perceiving the world from a topological point of view to perceiving it from a Euclidean point of view. Exhibit geometric figures in many forms and allow children to see, touch, feel, and talk about them.

Textbooks play an important role in defining and illustrating basic geometric figures. Materials such as pattern blocks, geoblocks, tiles, geoboards, mirrors, and *Logo* also serve children as they work at the early van Hiele levels.

There are many fine projects in which classes of children can engage as they learn geometry. The skills of geometry include the ability to name figures and their various properties, the ability to copy figures, and the ability to construct figures. Children should practice visualizing figures. To help assess their progress in learning geometry, observe children as they work.

DISCUSSION QUESTIONS

1. Investigate the geometry of your environment. Select some shops, buildings, or a neighborhood and chronicle all of the examples of shape that you can. Discuss your findings and illustrate them with drawings or photographs.
2. Explain how you might teach students who are visually impaired about polygons and space figures. Design and construct several learning aids that would be appropriate.
3. Construct a geodesic dome with a diameter of 18 inches. Use tag board for the triangles and white school glue to attach the triangles to each other. Decorate the triangles either before or after you attach them. Discuss the value of constructing a geodesic dome in your classroom.
4. Seek out a web site on fractal geometry such as http://math.rice.edu/~lanius/frac/ and investigate the site. From that site link to other sites that feature fractal geometry. Explain to others what you were able to discover from your investigation.
5. Using the discussion about and examples of open-ended problems presented in Chapter 3, design three open-ended problems that focus on geometry, one each at the primary level, elementary level, and middle level.

REFERENCES

Banbury, A. W., S. G. Berman, and H. Erickson, *Investigating Polygons and Polyhedra with Googolplex*. Philadelphia, PA: Arlington-Hews, 1988.

Bartels, Bobbye Hoffman, "Truss(t)ing Triangles," *Mathematics Teaching in the Middle School,* 3, no. 6 (March–April 1998), 394–396.

Battista, M. T., and D. H. Clements, *Exploring Solids and Boxes: 3-D Geometry.* Palo Alto, CA: Dale Seymour, 1995.

Bearden, Donna, Kathleen Martin, and James H. Muller, *The Turtle's Sourcebook.* Reston, VA: Reston Publishing, 1983.

Beaumont, V., R. Curtis, and J. Smart, *How to Teach Perimeter, Area, and Volume.* Reston, VA: National Council of Teachers of Mathematics, 1986.

Bennett, Albert, and Linda Foreman, *Visual Mathematics Course Guide, Vol. I.* Salem, OR: Math Learning Center, 1989.

—————, *Visual Mathematics Course Guide, Vol. II.* Salem, OR: Math Learning Center, 1990.

Bennett, Albert, Eugene Maier, and L. Ted. Nelson, *Math and the Mind's Eye: 1. Seeing Mathematical Relationships.* Salem, OR: Math Learning Center, 1987.

—————, *Math and the Mind's Eye: II. Visualizing Number Concepts.* Salem, OR: Math Learning Center, 1987.

—————, *Math and the Mind's Eye: III. Modeling Whole Numbers.* Salem, OR: Math Learning Center, 1987.

————, *Math and the Mind's Eye: IV. Modeling Rationals.* Salem, OR: Math Learning Center, 1987.

————, *Math and the Mind's Eye: V. Looking at Geometry.* Salem, OR: Math Learning Center, 1987.

Britton, Jill, and Walter Britton, *Teaching Tessellating Art.* Palo Alto, CA: Dale Seymour, 1992.

Browning, Christine A., and Dwayne E. Channel, *Explorations: Graphing Calculator Activities for Enriching Middle School Mathematics.* Austin, TX: Texas Instruments, 1997.

Brummett, M. R., and L. H. Charles, *Geoblocks Jobcards.* Sunnyvale, CA: Creative Publications, 1989.

Burger, William F., "Geometry," *Arithmetic Teacher,* 32, no. 6 (February 1985), 52–56.

Burger, William F., and J. Michael Shaughnessy, "Characterizing the van Hiele Levels of Development in Geometry," *Journal for Research in Mathematics Education,* 17, no. 1 (January 1986), 31–48.

Clements, D. H., S. J. Russell, C. Tierney, M. T. Battista, and J. S. Meredith, *Flips, Turns, and Area: 2-D Geometry.* Palo Alto, CA: Dale Seymour, 1995.

Clithero, Dale, "Learning with Logo 'Instantly'," *Arithmetic Teacher,* 34, no. 5 (January 1987), 12–15.

Copeland, Richard W., *Diagnostic and Learning Activities in Mathematics for Children.* Englewood Cliffs, NJ: Merrill/Prentice Hall, 1974.

Copeland, Richard W., *How Children Learn Mathematics.* Englewood Cliffs, NJ: Merrill/Prentice Hall, 1984.

Cowan, Richard A., "Pentominoes for Fun Learning," *The Arithmetic Teacher,* 24, no. 3 (March 1977), 188–190.

Cruikshank, Douglas E., and John McGovern, "Math Projects Build Skills," *Instructor,* 87, no. 3 (October 1977), 194–198.

Dienes, Z. P., and E. W Golding, *Geometry Through Transformations: 1. Geometry of Distortion.* New York: Herder & Herder, 1967.

Discovery Toys, *Pentominoes.* Martinez, CA: Discovery Toys, Inc., 1993.

Engelhardt, John, ed., *Geometry in Our World* (slide set). Reston, VA: National Council of Teachers of Mathematics, 1987.

Esbensen, Barbara Juster, and Helen K. Davie (illus.), *Echoes for the Eye: Poems to Celebrate Patterns in Nature.* Scranton, PA: HarperCollins, 1996.

Foster, T. E., *Tangram Patterns.* Sunnyvale, CA: Creative Publications, Inc., 1977.

Fouke, George R., *A First Book of Space Form Making.* San Francisco: Western Book Services, 1974.

Fuys, David, "Van Hiele Levels of Thinking in Geometry," *Education and Urban Society,* 17, no. 4 (August 1985), 447–462.

Fuys, David, Dorothy Geddes, and Rosamond Tischler, *The van Hiele Model of Thinking in Geometry Among Adolescents.* [Journal for Research in Mathematics Education, Monograph Number 3] Reston, VA: National Council of Teachers of Mathematics, 1988.

Giganti, Jr., Paul, and Mary Jo Cittadino, "The Art of Tessellation," *Arithmetic Teacher,* 37, no. 7 (March 1990), 6–16.

Gleick, James, *Chaos: Making a New Science.* New York: Viking Penguin, 1987.

Grifalconi, Ann, *The Village of Round and Square Houses.* Boston, MA: Little, Brown, 1986.

Hoban, Tana, *Shapes, Shapes, Shapes.* New York: Greenwillow Books, 1986.

Juraschek, William, "Getting in Touch with Shape," *Arithmetic Teacher,* 37, no. 8 (April 1990), 14–16.

Juster, Norton, *The Phantom Tollbooth.* New York: Random House, 1961.

Kenney, Margaret J., and Stanley J. Bezuska, *Tessellations Using Logo.* Palo Alto, CA: Dale Seymour, 1987.

Kilburn, Dan, and Mark Eckenwiler, *Terrapin Logo for the Macintosh.* Portland, ME: Terrapin Software, 1991.

Laycock, Mary, *Bucky for Beginners.* Hayward, CA: Activity Resources, 1984.

Mandebrot, Benoit B., *The Fractal Geometry of Nature.* New York: W. H. Freeman, 1983.

Mansfield, Helen, "Projective Geometry in the Elementary School," *Arithmetic Teacher,* 32, no. 7 (March 1985), 15–19.

McKim, Robert H. *Thinking Visually.* Belmont, CA: Lifetime Learning Publications, 1980.

Mira Math for Elementary School. Worth, IL: Creative Publications, 1973.

Moore, Margaret L., *LOGO Discoveries.* Palo Alto, CA: Creative Publications, 1984.

————, *Geometry Problems for LOGO Discoveries.* Worth, IL: Creative Publications, 1984.

Morris, Ann, *Bread, Bread, Bread.* New York: Lothrop, Lee & Shepard Books, 1989.

Morris, Janet P., "Investigating Symmetry in the Primary Grades," *The Arithmetic Teacher,* 24, no. 3 (March 1977), 188–190.

National Council of Teachers of Mathematics, *Curriculum and Evaluation Standards for School Mathematics.* Reston, VA: NCTM, 1989.

Onslow, Barry, "Pentominoes Revisited," *Arithmetic Teacher,* 37, no. 9 (May 1990), 5–9.

Piaget, Jean, "How Children Form Mathematical Concepts," *Scientific American,* 189, no. 5 (November 1953), 74–78.

Piaget, Jean, and Barbel Inhelder, *The Child's Conception of Space.* New York: W. W. Norton, 1967.

"Play Dome," *Sunset,* 50, no. 1 (January 1973), 51–53.

Prentice, Gerard, "Flexible Straws," *Arithmetic Teacher,* 37, no. 3 (November 1989), 4–5.

Ranucci, E., *Seeing Shapes.* Worth IL: Creative Publications, 1973.

Rectanus, C., *Math by All Means: Geometry Grade 3.* Sausalito, CA: Math Solutions Publications, 1994.

Reid, Margarette S., *The Button Box.* New York: Dutton Children's Books, 1990.

Roper, Ann, *Cooperative Problem Solving with Pattern Blocks.* Sunnyvale, CA: Creative Publications, 1989.

————, *Cooperative Problem Solving with Pattern Blocks (Primary).* Sunnyvale, CA: Creative Publications, 1990.

————, *Intermediate Jobcards.* Sunnyvale, CA: Creative Publications, 1989.

————, *Kindergarten Jobcards.* Sunnyvale, CA: Creative Publications, 1990.

————, *Primary Jobcards.* Sunnyvale, CA: Creative Publications, 1988.

————, *Starting Out With Pattern Blocks, Tangrams, & Interlocking Cubes.* Sunnyvale, CA: Creative Publications, 1988.

Seymour, Dale, and Jill Britton, *Introduction to Tessellations.* Palo Alto, CA: Dale Seymour, 1989.

Seymour, Dale, and Reuben Schadler, *Creative Constructions.* Worth, IL: Creative Publications, 1974.

Stevens, Peter S., *Patterns in Nature.* Boston: Little, Brown, 1974.

Suydam, Marilyn N., "Forming Geometric Concepts," *Arithmetic Teacher,* 33, no. 2 (October 1985), 26.

Teppo, Anne, "van Hiele Levels of Geometric Thought Revisited," *Mathematics Teacher,* 84, no. 3 (March 1991), 210–221.

van Hiele, Pierre M., *Structure and Insight: A Theory of Mathematics Education.* Orlando, FL: Academic Press, 1986.

Wenninger, Magnus J., *Polyhedron Models for the Classroom.* Reston, VA: National Council of Teachers of Mathematics, 1975.

Wilgus, Wendy, and Lisa Pizzuto, *Exploring the Basics of Geometry with Cabri.* Austin, TX: Texas Instruments, 1997.

Wirszup, Izaak, "Breakthrough in the Psychology of Learning and Teaching Geometry," in *Space and Geometry: Papers from a Research Workshop,* ed. J. Larry Martin, Columbus, OH: ERIC Center for Science, Mathematics Environmental Education, 1976.

Zilliox, Joseph T., and Shannon G. Lowrey, "Many Faces Have I," *Mathematics Teaching in the Middle School,* 3, no. 3 (November–December 1997), 180–183.

Technology

Battista, Michael T., *Shape Makers: Developing Geometric Reasoning with the Geometer's Sketchpad. Triangle and Quadrilateral Activities for Grades 5–8.* Berkeley, CA: Key Curriculum Press, 1998. (software and book)

Burns, Marilyn, *Mathematics with Manipulatives: Geoboards.* White Plains, NY: Cuisenaire Company of America, Inc., 1988. (video and guide)

Davidson, *Geometry Blaster.* Torrance, CA: Davidson, 1997. (software)

Davidson, *Kid Cad.* Torrance, CA: Davidson, 1997. (software)

Davidson, *Math Blaster: Episode 2—Secret of the Lost City.* Torrance, CA: Davidson, 1997. (software)

Edmark, *Mighty Math Calculating Crew.* Orlando, FL: Harcourt Brace, 1996. (software)

Edmark, *Mighty Math Carnival Countdown.* Orlando, FL: Harcourt Brace, 1996. (software)

Edmark, *Mighty Math Cosmic Geometry Grades 6–8.* Orlando, FL: Harcourt Brace, 1996. (software)

Edmark, *Mighty Math Number Heroes.* Orlando, FL: Harcourt Brace, 1996. (software)

Edmark, *Mighty Math Zoo Zillions.* Orlando, FL: Harcourt Brace, 1996. (software)

Sunburst, *Building Perspective.* Pleasantville, NY: Sunburst Communications. (software)

Sunburst, *The Factory.* Pleasantville, NY: Sunburst Communications. (software)

Sunburst, *Factory Deluxe.* Pleasantville, NY: Sunburst Communications. (software)

Sunburst, *Gears.* Pleasantville, NY: Sunburst Communications. (software)

Sunburst, *The Super Factory.* Pleasantville, NY: Sunburst Communications. (software)

Web Sites

http://math.rice.edu/~lanius/frac/   Exceptional site for developing children's understanding of fractals.

http://www.seas.gwu.edu/faculty/musgrave/   A fractal artist, Musgrave exhibits very impressive fractal landscapes.

http://www.olympus.net/personal/dewey/mandelbrot.html This is an easy to understand introduction to the Mandelbrot Set by David Dewey.

http://library.advanced.org/12740/   A site that exhibits beautiful examples of fractals.

Chapter 13

Teaching and Learning Measurement

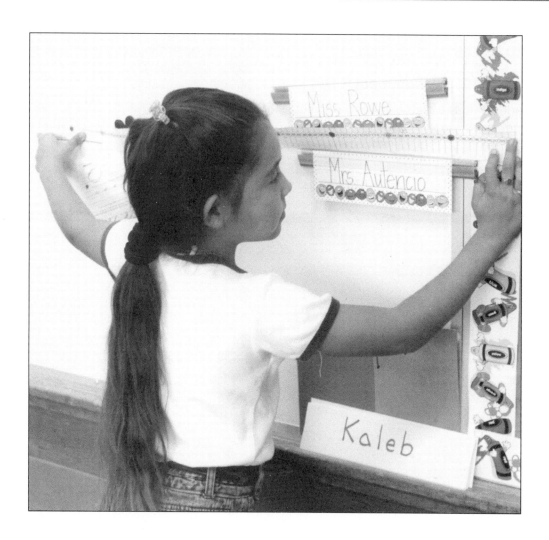

NCTM Standards

GRADES K–4

Standard 10: Measurement

In grades K–4, the mathematics curriculum should include measurement so that students can—

- Understand the attributes of length, capacity, weight, area, volume, time, temperature, and angle;
- Develop the process of measuring and concepts related to units of measurement;
- Make and use estimates of measurement;
- Make and use measurements in problem and everyday situations.

GRADES 5–8

Standard 12: Measurement

In grades 5–8, the mathematics curriculum should include extensive concrete experiences using measurement so that students can—

- Extend their understanding of the process of measurement;
- Estimate, make, and use measurements to describe and compare phenomena;
- Select appropriate units and tools to measure to the degree of accuracy required in a particular situation;
- Understand the structure and use of systems of measurement;
- Extend their understanding of the concepts of perimeter, area, volume, angle measure, capacity, and weight and mass;
- Develop the concepts of rates and other derived and indirect measurements;
- Develop formulas and procedures for determining measures to solve problems.

NCTM (1989), pp. 51, 116. Reprinted by permission.

My Math Journal

Copy the Rectangular Dot Paper in Appendix B and obtain a geoboard. Make all of the polygons you can on the geoboard that have an area of two square units. Remember that you may use triangles and irregular figures as well as rectangles. Record all of your solutions on the dot paper. Compare your findings with your classmates. As you write out your work, be sure to explain all of your thinking.

As you read the following pages, consider these guiding questions:

1. How do the following differ: direct and indirect comparison? arbitrary and standard units? continuous and discrete measurement?
2. What are the concepts related to measurement?
3. What is the nature of activities that help develop measurement skills?
4. How do the activities intended to develop the concept of area and the skill of measuring area compare?
5. What are the tools of measuring?
6. How does estimating fit into teaching and learning of measurement concepts and skills?

Measurement provides quantitative information about certain familiar aspects of our environment. These include length, distance, area, volume, capacity, weight, mass, temperature, time, and angle. Of course, this list is not complete. We know that certain specialized occupations require measures not commonly encountered. For example, surveyors, sailors, and pharmacists may use chain, nautical, and apothecaries' fluid measures, respectively.

In the child's world, it is enough to find out which is biggest, smallest, longest, shortest, fastest, slowest, warmest, or coolest. Children may ask how much or how long when they want to know about measured quantities. Later, youngsters are intrigued by the entries found in publications such as the *Guinness Book of World Records*. A majority of the records reported include some type of measurement.

A world record has little meaning if the units of length, time, or amount are not understood. The basis for establishing understanding is measuring. From measuring springs a sense of quantity relating to the item being measured. A sense of meters and seconds helps put the world record for the women's 1,500-meter run in perspective.

When, in the course of child development, do these ideas begin to be established? Earlier, we mentioned that children flailing about in their cribs explore space. They explore distance as well. Before children talk, they answer the question "How big are you?" by spreading their arms out, indicating to the pleasure of their parents that they are so big. These are the beginnings of children constructing their own meaning of measurement.

From these early beginnings, children compare objects and judge sizes. They order objects by size, weight, length, and duration. They develop an eye for size. "Her cookie is bigger than mine" expresses this visual comparison. In their early experiences, children develop the ability to measure by perception. By the time they enter first grade, they can begin simple measurement activities. Hiebert (1984, pp. 22–23) noted, "Ef-fective instruction should take advantage of what children already know or are able to learn and then relate this knowledge to new concepts that may be more difficult to learn."

Most measurements require tools. Thus, the materials for teaching measurement include the standard measuring instruments. We recommend using rulers, meter sticks, tape measures, trundle wheels, graduated beakers, measuring cups, measuring spoons, pan balances, bathroom scales, thermometers, timers, and protractors. Other useful materials are geoboards, centimeter cubes, Unifix cubes, popsicle sticks, Cuisenaire rods, containers of various sizes, string, and *Logo*. Teachers should collect objects and materials to help children construct measuring concepts.

Providing the opportunity for students to construct their own meaning of measurement involves more than presenting a series of activities or textbook pages. Not only should measurement be introduced, it should also be practiced throughout the school year whenever measuring is needed. You should be alert to measuring situations and encourage the students to measure when the opportunity arises.

Developing Measurement Concepts

The concepts that provide the foundation for measuring skills are those of length and distance, area, weight and mass, time, volume and capacity, temperature, and angle. Angle measure is a concept traditionally developed around age 10, but the utility and popularity of the computer language *Logo* suggests that an earlier introduction to angle measure is appropriate.

By and large, after the concept of measurement has been constructed, children should be provided with a sequence of activities: direct comparison, indirect comparison, arbitrary units, and standard units. Through these activities, children will further refine their concepts of measurement.

Direct comparison means that children take two objects and place them side by side or one on top of the other to discover if they are the same size. This requires that both objects be on surfaces of the same height or in containers of the same diameter.

Using **indirect comparison,** children determine if the sizes of two objects are the same when the objects cannot be directly compared. For example, indirect comparison would be used to find out if a table would fit through a door if the table were not easy to move.

Arbitrary units of measure are used to strengthen a child's understanding of unit. The length of a drinking straw and the area of a floor tile may be used to measure a variety of objects. The transition to **standard units** of measure, those commonly accepted and used throughout the world, follows work with arbitrary units.

The two common standard sets of measuring units are the *metric* and the *conventional systems*. We use the metric system throughout this chapter. Most textbooks for children include sections on both metric and conventional units. The process of measuring is the same regardless of the specific unit being used. You should have little difficulty teaching either metric or conventional units.

As children move through the sequence just described, they begin by using **continuous measurement.** When a piece of string is stretched along the object being measured and then compared with another object or when two objects are directly compared, continuous measurement is used. The measuring tool (string) does not assign a number to the object; rather, it is used to compare lengths.

Later in their work, children begin to use **discrete measurement.** When a pencil is moved along an object to determine the length of the object or a meter stick is used, the type of measurement is discrete. The measuring tool is used repeatedly, or it shows calibrations of a given unit—for example, centimeters. The transition from continuous to discrete measurement is seen in the activities of this chapter.

When teaching measurement, consider children's stages of readiness. Are children ready to learn measurement concepts and skills when they enter kindergarten or first grade? The work of Piaget (1960) suggests that until children have reached certain stages of intellectual development, they will have difficulty measuring successfully. For example, children who are unable to conserve length may believe that a measuring stick changes length as it is moved. Thus, measuring length should be held off until the child is able to conserve length.

More recently, Hiebert found that the absence of conservation did not seem to limit children in learning most measurement concepts. Hiebert (1984, p. 24) noted, "... it appears more productive to involve children in a variety of concrete measuring activities than to wait until they develop certain logical reasoning processes."

The teacher can provide experiences in informal measuring to serve as a foundation for later work. It is important during the primary years to provide activities that form the basis for measurement and to introduce measurement skills, thus allowing children to develop their personal understanding of measurement. Prior to involving children in organized activities, time should be provided for children to play with objects, containers, and water, rice, or sand. This play helps children establish the basis for early measurement activities. The activities that follow provide experiences in visual perception and direct comparison. Indirect comparison, arbitrary units, and standard units are presented in the next section, Developing and Practicing Measurement Skills.

Length and Distance

Length refers to the measure of how long a thing is from end to end. **Distance** is the space between points or objects.

In introducing length, allow children to experience long and short distances. Permit the children to directly compare objects in order to determine which object is taller and which is shorter.

ACTIVITIES

Primary (K–3)

Objective: to experience long and short distances.

1. Ask the children to name something in the classroom that is long. A brief discussion about the meaning of long may be necessary. Children may suggest that these objects are long: a chalkboard, a work table, or the bar on the coat rack.

   Mention that something that is long has great length and ask which has the greatest length, the chalkboard or the work table. The children will use their visual perception to make this judgement. Next, ask the children to name something on the playground that is long and then something that is not found at school that is long. What is the longest thing they can think of, the object with the greatest length?

2. Mark off several long line segments (6 to 8 meters) and several short line segments (2 to 3 meters) on the classroom floor or on the playground with masking tape, yarn, or chalk. Challenge the students to walk along one short line segment, then another short line segment, then a long line segment, and so on, allowing them to find the various long and short line segments. Discuss the meaning of long and short segments as used here. As a variation, provide long and short curves on which the children may walk.

3. Begin by saying that when the students line up for lunch or recess, a line with 4 or fewer students is a short line and one with more than 4 is a long line. In the classroom or on the playground, mark 7 or 8 places at which to line up. Have the children get into long lines. This may result in one long line or several lines with at least 5 students in each one. Then have them get into short lines. Challenge them to get into 1 long line and 3 short lines or 2 long lines and 2 short lines. See if they can form the longest line possible or the shortest lines possible.

4. Provide children with 8 or 10 classroom objects. Each object should be able to stand by itself. Objects may include a cottage cheese container, a can, a jar, a book, and a Cuisenaire rod (see Figure 13–1). Spread the objects out on a table.

Figure 13–1

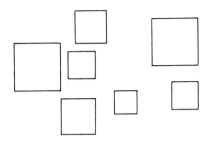

Figure 13–2

Let the children discuss which is the tallest object, then the shortest. Are two objects the same height? Find two objects taller than the cottage cheese container. If the children have some difficulty in visually determining the taller and shorter objects, challenge them to devise a way to determine these objects more easily. Putting the objects side by side is an answer you may expect.

A variation of this activity is to provide objects that do not stand on end: pencil, spoon, eraser, stapler, and so on. To be directly compared, the ends of each pair of objects must be lined up. This task is slightly more difficult than the one above. Again, let the students discuss how the objects can be compared.

5. In each of two bags, place one Cuisenaire rod. The rods should be about the same length, such as dark green and black or brown. Let students take turns reaching into the bags and telling which rod is longer or shorter merely by touch. Reaching into both bags simultaneously may be the most effective procedure, but let the children experiment.

A variation is to put an entire set of 10 rods in one bag and display another set of 10 rods on a table. Have a child reach into the bag, grab a rod, and then choose a rod from the table that is the same length.

Area

The activities above were intended to show how children can be introduced to perceptual and direct measurement of length. The following activities focus on area. **Area** is a measure of the size of a two-dimensional figure, such as a rectangle or a circle.

ACTIVITIES

Primary (K–3)

Objective: to determine the shape with the largest area.

1. Provide children with a collection of square shapes with sides ranging from 4 to 10 centimeters. Arrange the shapes in a random pattern as in Figure 13–2. Ask the children to tell which shape they believe is the largest or has the largest area. To show which one is largest, compare those selected by holding them up against each other. Order the shapes from smallest to largest by comparing them.

Extend this activity by using several rectangles, circles, triangles, and diamonds. Initially, estimate and compare using the same shape. Later, estimate and compare area using different shapes.

2. Have the students draw around one of their feet on a sheet of paper. Put several of the outlines in a cluster. Ask the children, "Whose foot do you think is the largest or has the largest area?" Then compare those selected by holding them up against each other in front of a window. Find out who has the smallest foot in the same way. Ask, "Are there two children who have the same foot size?"

As a variation, repeat the activity but compare hands instead of feet. Then compare hands with feet and determine the largest area. It will be difficult to make the latter comparison; thus, the activity will help children to see a need for other ways to measure area.

Objective: to directly compare areas.

3. Collect several boxlike containers such as a cereal box; half-pint, quart, and half-gallon milk containers; a raisin box; and a crayon box. Trace the faces of these containers onto tagboard and let the children cut them out, as in Figure 13–3.

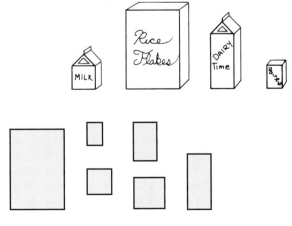

Figure 13–3

Give each child several of the cutout faces. Have the children estimate to determine which of the containers their pieces belong to. Then have them see if the pieces actually fit these containers by holding the pieces against the faces of the boxes.

A variation of this activity is to display the containers and ask the children to cut out a square or rectangular shape the same size as a face of a container. When the shapes have been cut out, have the children compare the cutouts by holding them up against the faces of the containers.

Objective: to determine which of various shapes are larger or smaller than a given shape.

4. Cut a piece of cardboard about the size of the top of a student desk. Hold the piece of cardboard up and ask the children, "Who can name a shape in the room that is bigger than this one? Look around and see if you can find one."

After several shapes, such as the door, a window, and the floor, have been named, ask, "Who can see a shape in the room that is smaller than this shape? Let's name them." Suggestions may include a chair seat, a piece of tablet paper, a book, and a computer disk. As items are mentioned, compare them with the piece of cardboard to reinforce the notion of direct comparison. Periodically, provide a different-sized shape and repeat the process.

Figure 13–4

Weight and Mass

We turn our attention to activities of direct comparison that involve the weight and mass of objects. **Weight** is a measure of the force of gravity acting on an object. **Mass** is the amount of matter in an object.

Figure 13–5

ACTIVITIES

Primary (K–3)

Objective: to determine which object is heavier.

1. Have available several classroom objects such as a pencil, scissors, an eraser, crayons, a small box, an orange Cuisenaire rod, a glue container, and a book. Have children compare the weights of various pairs of these objects and tell which object weighs the most by holding one object in each hand as in Figure 13–4.

Perhaps some items are of equal weight. Have the children compare and recheck pairs until they are able to put the objects in order from lightest to heaviest. Among the objects used should be one or two large objects that are light, such as a paper cup, and small objects that are heavy, such as a rock. This is to help avoid confusing the properties of size and weight.

To extend this activity, use a pan balance to compare the objects mentioned above to confirm or challenge the order determined by feel. Figure 13–5 illustrates one such balance. Do not be surprised to find discrepancies between the order established by holding objects and that established by using a pan balance. Children enjoy experimenting with the balance and various objects found around the room.

Objective: to practice estimating and weighing different materials.

2. Fill several half-pint milk cartons with different materials such as rice, beans, split peas, clay, plaster of paris, and wooden cubes. Seal the cartons and label them by color or letter. Tell the children what the materials are but do not identify the contents of a particular carton. Have the children guess how to order the cartons by weight according to what they contain. Then let the children order the cartons by weight, holding them in their hands and using the pan balance to check their estimates.

Objective: to determine the amount of one material that weighs as much as a selected object.

3. Collect several common objects such as a chalkboard eraser, a can of soup, a container of cleanser, a stapler, and a tape dispenser. Provide a pan balance and a material such as rice, water, clay, or sand.

   Have the children estimate how many small containers of sand it would take to balance the can of soup. Then see how many small containers must be used to balance the soup can, as in Figure 13–6. If the soup can does not balance, have the children increase or decrease the amount of sand in one of the containers. On the chalkboard, record both the estimates and the final results. If the final number of containers is not a whole number, the results should be recorded as, for example, "more than 5 containers but less than 6."

   Repeat this activity using other materials and objects. Be sure to have the children estimate each time they begin.

Time

Time is a measure of the period between two events or the period during which something happens. It is also a precise moment determined by a clock. Introduce time to children by having them directly compare the times of events, establishing whether one event takes more time or less time than another. Events may include twenty

hand claps, a ball bouncing ten times, ice melting under different conditions, and water emptying out of cans with different-sized holes.

ACTIVITIES

Primary (K–3)

Objective: to determine which event among several events takes the most or the least amount of time.

1. Select several events that require a short period of time to complete. Events that may be used include tapping a foot 20 times; sitting in a chair, standing, and sitting again 10 times; hopping on one foot from one side of the classroom to the other; reciting the words to "Row, Row, Row Your Boat"; moving 20 cubes one at a time from one container to another; bouncing a ball 10 times; and pointing to and naming 10 other students.

   Ask the children, "Which of these events can be done the fastest? Let's write on the board those that we think can be done the fastest. Which will be the slowest events? Let's write those down."

   Choose two of the events and begin them at the same time. Record the results. Repeat the process for each pair of the events and determine which event takes the least time and which event takes the most time.

Objective: to investigate the amount of time it takes ice cubes to melt.

2. Fill two equivalent containers with water, one with warm water and the other with cooler water. Leave a third container empty. Let the children see and feel the cups and the water. Explain, "We are going to put an ice cube in each container. Which ice cube do you think will melt first? Let's write our guesses on the board. How many believe the ice cube in this container will melt first?"

   After the guesses are recorded, put the ice cubes in the containers and observe the results. Variations of this activity include using salt water, using very cold and hot water, using varying amounts of water that are the same temperature, and dissolving sugar cubes instead of melting ice.

Objective: to estimate and determine which of several containers empties in the least amount of time.

3. Take several soup cans and puncture three holes in the bottom of each one, using a different-sized nail for each can. Have the children inspect the cans and estimate which they think will empty first, second, third, and so on.

   Using two cans at a time, pour equal amounts of water in each can and observe them (see Figure

Figure 13–6

Figure 13–7

13–7). Repeat this process until the cans have been ordered from fastest to slowest. Similarly, the cans may have different numbers of holes of the same size or different numbers of holes of varying sizes.

Volume and Capacity

The activities above focus on directly comparing events involving the passage of time. The following activities involve volume and capacity. **Volume** is the amount of space contained within a three-dimensional figure. **Capacity** is the amount of space that can be filled.

ACTIVITIES

Primary (K–3)

Objective: to estimate and determine which of several containers holds the greatest amount.

1. Provide the children with several small jars, cans, or plastic containers. For example, you may use a tuna can, a plastic drinking cup, a baby food jar, a soup can, a paper cup, and a peanut butter jar. Have the children estimate which of the containers will hold the least amount, the next to the least amount, and so on, until they have found the container that will hold the greatest amount. Once the estimates have been made, have the children pour rice or water from container to container, checking to see which holds the most. Compare the actual order with the estimated order.

Objective: to determine which containers will hold the same amount of material.

2. Collect 10 or 12 cups and cans of varying sizes. Point out one of the cups and fill it with rice. Have the children estimate which of the other cups will hold the same amount of rice as the first cup.

   Have the children pour the rice from the first cup into the cups they believe have the same volume. Then have them check the cups they thought were too large or too small by pouring the rice into them. In this way, the children can confirm or reject their guesses.

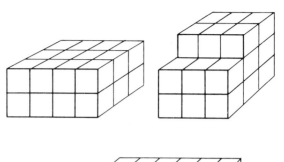

Figure 13–8

Objective: to construct buildings of various shapes using identical numbers of cubes.

3. Provide children with five or six groups of 24 colored cubes. Have them construct a building using the 24 cubes. When they have finished, challenge them to build different buildings using the 24 cubes, as in Figure 13–8. Talk to the children about the shapes of the buildings and whether the different buildings have the same amount of space. If it is unclear that they contain the same space, have the children count the cubes in each building.

Temperature

From activities involving direct comparisons of volume and capacity, we turn to activities dealing with temperature. **Temperature** is a measure of the hotness or coldness of a material.

ACTIVITIES

Primary (K–3)

Objective: to determine relative temperature by feel.

1. Partially fill five sour cream containers with water of varying temperature. Use unheated water, warm tap water, cold tap water, water that has one ice cube in it, and water with five or six ice cubes in it. Label the containers with shapes or colors for identification. Have the children put the containers of water in order from warmest to coldest by putting their hands in the water. Have several small groups of children complete the ordering and compare results.

After the containers of water have been in the classroom for an hour or so, have the children repeat the exercise. Discuss the results with the children.

2. Take the children to the playground and let them work in groups of three or four. Have the children search the play area for four things that feel cool to them and four things that feel warm. The children may find the slide and swing supports to be cool; they may find the asphalt and wooden play apparatus to be warm.

Discuss the findings with the whole group. Ask which was the coolest single object and which was the warmest single object. Talk about what the objects are made of.

3. Arbitrarily group children into groups of six or eight. Have the children in each group shake hands and find the individual with the warmest hand and the individual with the coldest hand. Have those selected form a group and find the child with the warmest hand and the child with the coldest hand. Have those two children circulate among the other children and put their hands against the cheeks of the others.

Ask the children if they know of ways to make their hands warmer. Suggestions may include putting their hands in warm water, rubbing their hands together or rubbing them against their clothing, and clapping their hands. Have the children warm their hands using one of the methods suggested and then have them shake hands again or put their hands against the cheeks of the others.

Angle

The activities above involve children comparing the temperatures of several materials by feeling them. The following activities introduce informally the idea of measuring angles. An **angle** is the space between two rays that share a common end point.

ACTIVITIES

Primary (K–3)

Objective: to estimate and determine the sizes of angles.

1. In Chapter 12, several activities are described in which children investigate geometry using *Logo*. It is necessary for children to experiment with various turns by using commands such as RT 90, RT 30, LT 50, LT 180, and RT 360. At this stage, the children are not measuring angles, but they are developing some initial understanding of angle size. Success with turtle geometry depends on the concept of angle size.

Have children record and label angles of various sizes. Is the angle made with the commands FD 75, BK 75, RT 30, FD 75, and BK 75 the same size as the angle made with FD 75, BK 75, LT 30, FD 75, and BK 75? How are these two angles different?

As children begin to construct simple figures, they will be using exterior angles. An **exterior angle** is the angle between the side of a polygon and the extension of the adjacent side. For example, in order to construct an interior angle of 60° when drawing an equilateral triangle, the procedure makes the turtle turn an exterior angle of 120°, as in Figure 13–9. Children develop skill with exterior angles by designing procedures for drawing a variety of polygons.

2. Trace angles of several sizes on overhead transparencies, putting one angle in the center of each transparency. Place a transparency on the monitor screen so the vertex of the angle is centered on the *Logo* turtle, with one ray in a vertical position as in Figure 13–10. To confirm the alignment of the angle, have the child move the turtle forward and then back to the original position. Realign the angle if necessary.

Have the child estimate the size of the turn necessary to follow the other ray of the angle. Let the child test the estimate by turning the turtle in the appropriate direction and moving forward and then back to produce a second ray. Have the child compare the angle on the transparency with the angle made using *Logo*.

Repeat the activity using various angle sizes. Variations include having the turtle turn left for some angles as well as right and having the turtle begin facing in a different direction rather than toward the top of the screen.

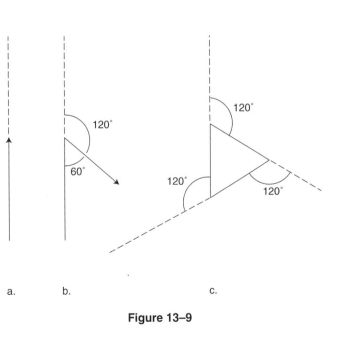

a.   b.   c.

Figure 13–9

Figure 13–10

The activities in this section were presented to serve as examples to reinforce and supplement the math textbook and to provide a foundation on which to build the skills of measuring. Each activity involved direct comparison. You are encouraged to pay attention to the perceptions and observations of children as they begin these measuring tasks. Some of the perceptions will indicate that further direct measurement activities are needed.

Developing and Practicing Measurement Skills

The skills of measurement include using instruments or tools to determine how long, how much, what size, and what temperature. Specifically, the skills of measurement include measuring length, area, weight, time, volume and capacity, temperature, and angle. The skills follow the development of early measurement concepts. Then, consistent practice with the tools of measurement is necessary.

The activities presented in the previous section emphasized direct comparison, the first stage in a four-stage teaching sequence. The remaining stages are indirect comparison, using an arbitrary measuring unit, and using a standard measuring unit. The activities in the following section focus on the latter three stages for each type of measurement described.

Active experiences with measuring provide children with the chance to construct meaning relative to the measurement process. To build understanding of measurement is the focus of the children's active participation. This understanding leads to skill in measuring. Be cautious about telling children how to measure before they have had a chance to experiment.

Measuring Length

When children in the primary grades have had experience using direct measurement of length for a variety of tasks, they should engage in other types of length measurement. Their experiences will provide a basis for constructing knowledge of length as they work through the measurement sections of their textbooks.

Intermediate-level students should have worked with and used length measurement for some time. They will be engaged in estimating with accuracy and measuring with increased precision. The lengths they measure will be longer. They will easily use a variety of standard units of measure. The common metric units of length include centimeter, meter, and kilometer.

As you introduce various units of metric measurement, discuss the prefixes and their meanings. The mathematics textbook will also introduce and explain them. **Milli** means one-thousandth, **centi** means one-hundredth, **deci** means one-tenth, and **kilo** means one thousand. There are several others, but these are among the most commonly used.

Figure 13–11

In most instances of measuring with standard units, instruct children to place the ruler or meter stick along the item being measured, with the end of the ruler or zero lined up with one end of the item being measured, as in Figure 13–11a. Have children then read the spot on the ruler where the other end of the item being measured falls—in this case, 5 centimeters.

If the starting point is not zero, as in Figure 13–11b, make children aware that the *length* is found by either counting the spaces along the item being measured or subtracting the starting point from the end point—in this case, 7 − 2, or 5, centimeters.

ACTIVITIES

Primary (K–3)

Objective: to use indirect measuring to determine length.

1. Cut a piece of adding-machine tape approximately as long as the average height of a child in your class. Put the name of an imaginary child or a character from a story, such as Garfield, on the tape. Attach the adding machine tape to the wall so that one end touches the floor. Have the children estimate whether they are shorter than, taller than, or the same height as Garfield. Record the estimates.

   Then have the children cut strips of adding machine tape to represent their heights. Ask the children to compare their height with that of Garfield. Finally, have the children order their heights by comparing them and taping their paper strips along a classroom or hallway wall.

   Because they will have produced a pictorial representation of class heights, it is useful to describe and discuss their findings and to write down and post these observations beside the paper strips. The observations might include the following:

   - We found that 9 of us are taller than Garfield. There are 15 of us who are shorter than Garfield. Mark and Christine are just as tall as Garfield.

   - The shortest person in the class is Peter. The tallest person in the class is Dana.
   - Five of us thought we were taller than Garfield, but it turned out that 9 of us actually were taller.

   A variation of this activity is to have students lie on pieces of newsprint or butcher paper and have others draw their outlines. Comparisons can then be made as before.

2. On one side of the classroom, arrange six to eight objects of varying lengths. Include items such as a piece of yarn, a piece of chalk, a meter stick, a ruler, a strip of adding-machine tape, and the edge of a desk or table. Next, mark off a length on the chalkboard or bulletin board. Have the children estimate which of the objects are longer and which are shorter than the mark on the board. Have them check their estimates, but with the condition that they cannot move either the objects or the mark on the board.

   A variation of this activity is to provide children with blocks or a similar material and invite one group of children to build a tower on the floor at the front of the room. Invite another group to build a tower on the floor at the back of the room. Challenge the children to estimate which tower is taller. When the estimates have been made, have the children see if they can devise ways to tell which tower is taller without moving the towers.

Objective: to use arbitrary units of measure to determine the lengths of objects.

3. Identify five or six lengths to be measured. For example, you might use the chalk tray, a student desk, a bookcase, a work table, a row of books, and a sink. Provide groups of children with sufficient numbers of different measuring units such as toothpicks, paper clips, straws, tongue depressors, and orange Cuisenaire rods. Have each group measure the lengths of the objects indicated using its particular unit; for example, straws, as in Figure 13–12.

   Have each group record its results. Because it is unlikely that a measurement will be exactly a whole number of units, have the children record the results

Figure 13–12

as, for example, "longer than 6 straws and shorter than 7 straws."

When the measurements have been made, compare the results. Can any conclusions be drawn regarding the number of units used in measuring and the size of the unit? To illustrate the meaning of the above question, have each group put ten of their measuring units end to end and compare the resulting lengths.

4. Announce that a drawing will be held to find three new measuring units. Have all the children write their names on pieces of paper and put the pieces of paper into a container. Draw the name of the child who will provide a *shoe unit*. Draw the name of another child, who will provide a *hand unit*. Draw the name of the third child, who will provide a *thumb unit*.

Have the first child place one foot, with the shoe on, on a piece of tagboard and draw around it. Using

this as a pattern, have the children cut out a number of, say, *Margaret's shoes*. Repeat the process for *Sarah's hand* and *Bob's thumb*. Each of these will be a unit of measure.

 You may wish to begin this activity by reading *How Big is a Foot?* by Myller (1962). In this story a king commissions a carpenter to construct a bed using the king's foot as a measure. The carpenter constructs the bed using his own foot as a measure and a problem arises. The need for standard units of measure will likely become apparent with some discussion. Welchman-Tischler (1992) richly describes how *How Big is a Foot* may be used in a variety of measurement lessons.

For the next two weeks or so, have the children measure the lengths of many objects using these special units. To extend this activity, have the children use only one of the measuring devices and move it along the object being measured, counting the number of times it is used.

5. Another step in measuring with nonstandard units is to provide students opportunities to measure with a variety of nonstandard measuring tapes. Querin (1998, pp. 16–18) describes such activities. Several different tapes such as those shown in Figure 13–13 are available for children to select and use to estimate and measure the length of various objects in the classroom or hallway.

Invite children to design their own nonstandard measuring tapes by drawing repeated pictures or designs on a strip of paper or several strips glued together.

Figure 13–13

Objective: to measure perimeter.

6. Put several large shapes on the floor. The shapes may be drawn on butcher paper or made with masking tape, string, or yarn. Initially, have children walk around the figure and count the number of baby steps or walking steps they take.

    Later, have children use other arbitrary units, such as a piece of dowel or an orange Cuisenaire rod. Eventually, have children use a meter stick or a trundle wheel. A **trundle wheel** is a plastic or wooden disk that is attached to a handle. The circumference of the disk is 1 meter. The trundle wheel is pushed along a line or boundary to determine its length.

    Challenge the students to look for boundaries to measure. Items that lend themselves to boundary work include the outlines of a desktop, a bulletin board or chalkboard, the classroom, a work area, the gymnasium, and the playground.

7. A direct extension of walking around and measuring large floor figures is to use turtle steps in *Logo*. The side of a figure in *Logo* is defined in terms of a particular distance. By virtue of designing a figure, the length of its boundary is determined. Perimeter, then, comes to be viewed as an integral part of each shape.

8. Continued work on the geoboard helps to establish skill in measuring perimeter. Focus activities on counting the units around various figures. After children have gained experience in using geoboards, they are ready to use the diagonal distance between nails in their calculations. Initially, that distance may be known as a little more than 1.

Objective: to use standard units to measure various objects.

9. Have available a large collection of centimeter cubes and eight or ten relatively small objects to measure. Objects may include a book, a pencil, a chalkboard eraser, a sheet of tablet paper, a crayon box, a sneaker, a stapler, a workbook, and a desk. Identify these items with letters, colors, or numerals. Have the children connect the interlocking centimeter cubes until they are as long as the item being measured, as in Figure 13–14.

    Let the children know they are using a unit called a centimeter. Have them count the number of centimeters long each item is and record the length on a piece of paper. Because most items are not a whole number of centimeters long, have the children record the length as, for instance, "more than 7 and less than 8 centimeters."

10. Provide groups of three or four children with pieces of adding-machine tape about 35 centimeters long

Figure 13–14

and several centimeter cubes. Have each group carefully mark along an edge of the paper strip using the centimeter cube as the unit and have them number each mark until they have marked off 30 centimeters. Make sure the children are aware that the first mark is labeled *1* and means the distance from the end of the paper strip.

Challenge the children to use their 30-centimeter ruler to find things in the classroom that measure 4, 10, 13, 19, 22, 27, and 30 centimeters in length. To extend this activity, have the children estimate and measure body parts using their ruler: width and length of hands, length of feet, width of a finger, distance around wrists, and length of smile. Have the students record the estimates and measurements.

11. In the gymnasium or on the playground, mark off six to eight lines using yarn, chalk, or masking tape and label each line with a color or letter. These lines should range from 3 to 10 meters in length and should be placed in a variety of directions.

    Provide groups of two or three children with record sheets with a space to estimate the length of each line and a space to write in the actual measure. Have the children estimate and then measure each of the lines.

    Later, discuss the range of estimates for each line and compare the measured lengths. It may be necessary to go back to the playground and remeasure. To extend this activity, have children find a length between 4 and 6 meters or measure various long objects in the classroom.

These activities have been illustrative of what children in primary grades can do to strengthen their measuring skills. The following activities for intermediate students begin with arbitrary or nonstandard measurement. By this age, the need to practice measuring with direct and indirect comparison has decreased. The following activities focus on the applications and the precision of linear measurements.

ACTIVITIES

Intermediate (4–6)

Objective: to measure lengths using an arbitrary unit.

1. Designate a *measuring unit of the day,* a unit that is easy to provide to students. Possible units might include spaghetti, unsharpened pencils, tongue depressors, and unmarked strips of oaktag. The unit selected may have marks to indicate one-fourth or one-half units.

   As a class, agree on a number of common classroom objects to measure, such as length, width, and height of desks; length and width of the room; length and height of the chalkboard and bulletin board; width and height of the door; and so on. In groups, have the students agree to measure certain of these items. Before the measuring begins, have all of the children estimate the sizes of the objects using the selected unit. Then have the children measure the items to the nearest one-fourth unit and record the measures. To extend this activity, have the children draw or write a description of their classroom using, say, spaghetti units.

2. As a class, select an arbitrary unit with which to measure. For example, the width of a sneaker at its widest part may be the unit. Construct a measuring tape or string based on that unit. Then construct a design on butcher paper and carefully measure it using the sneaker-width unit. Sketch the design on a sheet of notebook paper and indicate the measure of each of its lengths in terms of the new unit, as in Figure 13–15.

   Send the sketch to another class in the school and tell them the measuring unit, the *widest part of a sneaker.* Ask the class to construct the design on their chalkboard or on butcher paper. Then compare the results by putting the two full-sized designs side by side. Discuss any discrepancy between the two designs.

   It is likely that the sizes will differ because of the arbitrary nature of the unit. The need for a standard unit should be evident. Next, create another design using standard units of measure, have another class construct it, and compare the results.

Objective: to estimate and measure with standard units.

3. Begin this activity, entitled The Shape of Me, with a worksheet on which are listed several body parts (see Figure 13–16). Ask the children to estimate in centimeters their head width and length; that is, the distance from one side to the other and from top to bottom. Next, have them estimate their shoulder width. Have them continue until they have estimated all parts. At this point, provide 2-meter lengths of newsprint, kraft paper, or butcher paper to individuals or pairs of children.

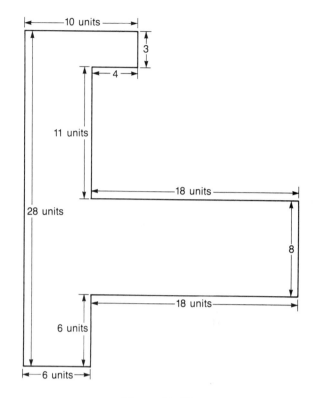

Figure 13–15

Ask the children to construct the body they have estimated using the paper provided. The students should use meter sticks, 30-centimeter rulers, or tapes to construct these figures. Have them complete the figures by dressing them using crayons or marking pens and cutting them out. Display the figures around the room. Finally, have the children measure their body parts and compare the results with their estimates.

4. With the assistance of your class, establish a competition called the Metric Olympics. This series of events will challenge the students to use their estimation and measuring skills. The Metric Olympics consists of six to eight events. These events may include the following:

   - *Sponge throw.* Give students an opportunity to throw each of three sponges as far as they can from behind a line. Lightweight sponges can be thrown 3 to 5 meters. Have the officials mark and measure the length of each toss and record the greatest distance for each participant.
   - *Length guess.* On a classroom or hallway wall, arrange a piece of yarn or string 12 to 15 meters long, as in Figure 13–17. Have each participant estimate the length of the yarn.
   - *Cube toss.* Make two lines 3 meters apart. Have the students stand behind one line and estimate how close to the other line they will be able to toss a

THE SHAPE OF ME

Just for the record let's measure to find out what size we are. But first guess each item below.
Then measure using the materials available. You might like to work with a friend.

		My Guess	The Real Me (Measure)
1. HEAD	Width	_____ cm	_____ cm
	Length	_____ cm	_____ cm
2. SMILE WIDTH		_____ cm	_____ cm
3. HEIGHT (top of head to floor)		_____ cm	_____ cm
4. ARMS (length of each arm from shoulder to fingertip)		_____ cm	_____ cm
5. HAND SPAN (width of palm at widest point when fingers are together)		_____ cm	_____ cm
6. SHOULDER WIDTH		_____ cm	_____ cm
7. LEGS (length from hip to ankle)		_____ cm	_____ cm
8. HIP WIDTH		_____ cm	_____ cm
9. FOOT LENGTH		_____ cm	_____ cm
10. WEIGHT		_____ kg	_____ kg

Figure 13–16

Figure 13–17

cube. They must toss the cube at least 1 meter. The winner of this event is the student whose estimate and performance are closest.

- *Paper plate sail.* Have students sail a paper plate as far as they can from behind a line. Measure the distance in meters using a trundle wheel.

- *Standing long step.* Have students predict how far they can step using one giant step. Have them measure from the starting line to where their heel lands. A variation is to estimate the distance covered in three giant steps. Either way, base the scoring on how close students are to their estimates.

- *String feel.* Seat students and ask them to hold their hands behind their backs. Give each one a piece of string, and ask each child to run both hands over the string behind his or her back and estimate the length of the string. Award students within 5, 10, and 15 centimeters of their estimates 3 points, 2 points, and 1 point, respectively.

Measuring Area

Measuring *area* involves determining how much space there is within a plane figure. In the primary grades, children count units covering or placed inside a figure. At the intermediate level, students can discover the various formulas to calculate area. Both levels require continued manipulation of objects and tools. The common metric units of area include square centimeter, square meter, hectare (equivalent to a square with sides of 100 meters), and square kilometer.

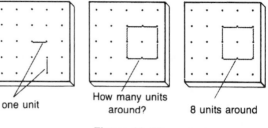

one unit   How many units around?   8 units around

Figure 13–18

ACTIVITIES

Primary (K–3)

Objective: to indirectly measure and compare the areas of objects.

1. Draw several rectangles of various shapes and sizes on butcher paper or on the chalkboard. The largest dimension of any particular rectangle should be about 50 centimeters. Give each rectangle a letter or color for identification. Ask the children to estimate and then determine which rectangle is largest or smallest. Which rectangles are larger than the red one or larger than the red one and smaller than the yellow one?

   Because the children cannot move the rectangles, they must invent a way to compare the sizes of the various shapes. They may cut a piece of paper the size of a given rectangle and compare the paper to other rectangles. To vary this activity, use shapes other than rectangles so children will have the chance to measure squares, triangles, circles, and so on.

   Extend this activity by challenging children to determine the relative area of various classroom items. Ask, for example, "Which is larger, the top of your desk or a pane of glass from the window?" or "Which is smaller, the side of the filing cabinet or the top of the work table?" For each challenge, let the children cut a piece of butcher paper or newsprint the size of one of the items and compare the paper to the other item. The shapes are likely to be different, so additional cutting and rearranging will be necessary.

Objective: to use arbitrary units to measure area.

2. Explore length and area on the geoboard by first designating the units of length and area. For example, designate the distance between two nails in any direction except diagonally as one unit. Then use this unit of length to determine the length of the boundary of a particular figure. Figure 13–18 illustrates this type of activity.

Next, ask children to make a figure with a certain number of units in its boundary. Request, for example, "Make a rectangle with a boundary of eight units."

To measure area, have children count the number of square units within a figure. Designate the smallest square on the geoboard as one square unit. Then inquire, "How many square units can we find in this figure?" Let the children count the number of square units contained in a given figure, as shown in Figure 13–19. As they gain experience, the children can construct squares or rectangles with a given number of square units, demonstrating an initial understanding of area.

There are other ways to determine area, beginning with the area of a triangle. At this point, it becomes necessary to identify a half-unit. A half-unit results from constructing the smallest triangle possible on the geoboard, which is one-half of a square unit. Now, the areas of many other geometric figures can be easily determined. Be sure to match the difficulty of the activity with the ability of the children.

3. On the floor of the classroom or gymnasium or on the playground, design several large (2 to 4 square meters) regular and irregular regions. Some may be squares, rectangles, and trapezoids. Others may be irregular curves, including quadrilaterals and shapes that are not polygons. Have the children estimate the areas of the various figures in terms of floor tiles or other square units designated by the students or teacher.

   Then place the tiles inside the figure and determine its area. Some judgments will be necessary, as not all figures will hold a whole number of square units. It is helpful to have some half-units available to fit into the figure.

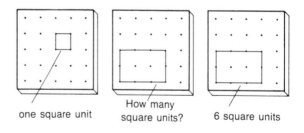

one square unit   How many square units?   6 square units

Figure 13–19

As a variation of this activity, determine how many students can stand within each region. Both of a child's feet must be within the region and all children should be standing comfortably upright. The children can then discover which figures are largest and which are smallest and how all of the figures can be ordered from largest to smallest.

Objective: to use standard units to measure area.

4. Provide groups of three or four children with centimeter cubes and various small square and rectangular regions (8 to 24 square centimeters). Have the children estimate the number of cubes that can be placed in each region. Then have the children fill the region with cubes and count them. Explain that each cube takes up 1 square centimeter of area in the region. The total number of cubes is equivalent to the number of square centimeters in the region. To extend this activity, include regions similar in shape to the region shown in Figure 13–20, irregular polygons, and other closed curves.

5. Have available transparencies of centimeter grids. Also, provide drawings of squares, rectangles, triangles, circles, and hexagons. Later, use drawings of closed curves that are not polygons or circles. Encourage the children to estimate the area of each figure in square centimeters.

Then, lay the centimeter grid over the top of each figure and count the numbers of whole and half square centimeters that fit in the figure. When the figures are less like polygons, it is more difficult to estimate and determine the areas. Introduce the various figures slowly over a period of several days.

Middle Grades (5–8)

Objective: to use arbitrary units to measure area.

1. This activity compares the body surface areas of two students to see which student has the greatest body surface area. Ask for two volunteers to serve as patient subjects. Have the class estimate which of the two has the greatest body surface area. Use toilet paper to carefully wrap each of the students, barely overlapping the tissue. Wrap each leg, then the trunk, then each arm. Finally, lightly wrap the head. Then, even more carefully, unwrap each student and compare the amounts of tissue used. Either count the tissues or place them end to end and compare.

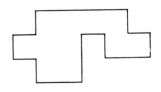

Figure 13–20

2. Procedures to introduce area using the geoboard continue to be valid for upper elementary and middle school students. And, it is helpful for students to be exposed to additional ways to find the areas of triangles and other polygons. For example, the area of a right triangle whose legs have lengths a and b is one-half the area of a rectangle whose sides have lengths a and b. This is illustrated in Figure 13–21a.

The area of any non–right triangle may be found by subdividing the triangle into right triangles by constructing a segment from the vertex to the base. Then, using the previous technique, find the areas of the right triangles and add them together. This is illustrated in Figure 13–21b.

Finally, if the triangle is similar to the one in Figure 13–21c, it may be stretched into a right triangle. The area of the original triangle is the area of the large right triangle minus the area of the right triangle resulting from the stretch, t.

Another method of finding the area of a triangle or the area of an irregular figure is to surround the figure with the smallest rectangle that contains it. Then, find the area of the rectangle and subtract the areas of the newly formed figures. In Figure 13–22, the irregular figure, f, has been surrounded by a square of 9 square units. The areas of the newly formed figures outside f yet inside the square around f total 6 square units. Thus, f has an area of $9 - 6$, or 3, square units. Challenge the students to form as many different shapes as they can on the geoboard with a total area of, say, 3 square units.

The areas of other polygons—parallelograms and trapezoids, for example—may be derived by means similar to those used to find the areas of triangles and

Figure 13–21

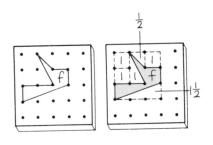

Figure 13–22

irregular figures. This rather brief description is not meant to be complete in terms of the uses of geoboards. A number of fine references are available; some are listed at the end of this chapter.

3. Prepare sheets on which are drawn square grids measuring approximately 2 centimeters on a side or use the 1-inch graph paper from Appendix B. Encourage the children to take any objects that will fit on the grids and trace their outlines. Have the children count the total number of square regions that are partially inside the outline of the object plus the total number of squares that are completely inside the outline.

The hand outlined in Figure 13–23 completely contains 23 squares, plus it partially contains another 26 squares. We can say, then, that the area of the hand outline is greater than 23 square units but less than 49 square units. We can refine our calculation by finding the average of the two numbers, 23 and 49. Thus, the area of the hand is approximately 36 square units.

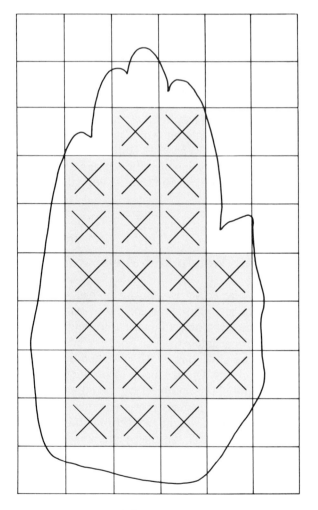

Figure 13–23

Objective: to measure the areas of objects using standard measuring units.

4. The procedure described in Activity 3 above may be repeated using a grid with 1-centimeter squares. The results of measuring should be reported in square centimeters. Similarly, an overhead transparency with a 1-centimeter grid drawn on it may be used. Place the transparency directly on the shape being measured.

The areas of two types of figures can be determined. First are squares and rectangles with dimensions that are whole numbers of centimeters. Second are other polygons with at least two dimensions that are whole numbers of centimeters. These include triangles, quadrilaterals, trapezoids, pentagons, and hexagons. Be sure to have students estimate the area before they find it.

5. This activity utilizes the knowledge students have gained through their use of geoboards. Having made many rectangular regions of varying sizes, students should be able to begin a table that shows the areas of these rectangles (Table 13–1).

Have the students examine the relationships between the lengths, the widths, the products of lengths and widths, and the areas. Once they have discovered that the length times the width equals the area, students are ready to apply that discovery to figures measured with standard measures. Thus, a rectangle with a length of 4 centimeters and a width of 3 centimeters will have an area of 4 by 3, or 12, square centimeters. This finding can be checked using the 1-centimeter transparency grid. The student is now able to measure objects in centimeters or meters and to determine their areas with understanding.

To extend this activity, develop similar tables to show the areas of squares and triangles. From these examples, the formulas for the areas of squares and triangles can be developed.

6. As students develop the facility to determine perimeter and area of a figure, challenge them to use the color tiles to build the shape with the largest area with a perimeter of 20 units. The length of each side of the tile represents one unit and the area of the tile represents

TABLE 13–1   Rectangles on the Geoboard

Length	Width	Length × Width	Square Units
1	1	1	1
2	1	2	2
3	1	3	3
4	1	4	4
2	2	4	4
3	2	6	6
4	2	8	8

one square unit. Encourage the students working in pairs to outline the shapes on grid paper as they construct them with the tiles. When the students have identified the 5-by-5 square as having the greatest area, have them find the figure with the smallest area with a perimeter of 20 units. Let the students draw on the board several possible shapes that have perimeters of 20 units. Perhaps a table would help students "analyze" the relationship between perimeter and area (Table 13–2). You may need to develop an operational definition of what figures can be counted. We would recommend starting with shapes that can be constructed by putting the tiles so that they touch another tile along an entire edge. Touching just at the corners, for example, would not be allowed.

Continue this activity by changing the perimeter to 24, then 28. Have the students write about and then discuss the nature of the shape that contains the greatest area.

Extend this activity by reversing the focus. Now, have the students find the shape with the largest or smallest perimeter given the area. For example, use the area of 24 square units. What is the largest perimeter of a shape with an area of 24 square units? What is the smallest perimeter? Discuss the nature of the shape that has the greatest perimeter. An interesting discussion of the various shapes will ensue.

7. Once students can use various formulas to determine the areas of simple polygons, they are ready to find the areas of large and small regions. Among the large regions are panes of window glass, the tops of tables or desks, the classroom floor or walls, doors, and chalkboards. Small regions include squares, rectangles, triangles, the faces of cereal boxes or milk containers, and the pages of books. In each case, children should use rulers or meter sticks to measure the dimensions of the region and apply the appropriate formula to determine the area.

To vary this activity, ask children to draw particular areas on paper, on the chalkboard, or on the playground. For example, ask them to draw a rectangle of area 6 square meters or a triangle of area 15 square centimeters.

The area formulas that children should have previously discovered include those for *squares* ($A = s \times s$, where s is the length of a side); *rectangles* ($A = l \times w$, where l is the length and w is the width); *triangles* ($A = \frac{1}{2} \times b \times h$, where b is the length of the base and h is the height); and *circles* ($A = \pi \times r^2$, where r is the radius and $\pi = 3.14$).

8. In the previous activity, pi (π) was used in the formula to determine the area of a circle. Rather than giving the students the approximate value of π (3.14), have the students discover the value of pi. Provide groups with four or five jar lids of various sizes and a cloth measuring tape. Two group members will be responsible for carefully measuring the circumference and the diameter of each circular lid. The recorder writes the measurements in a table that lists the names on the jar lid and has spaces to list the circumference and diameter. Another group member has the job of dividing the circumference of each jar lid by the diameter of that lid. The recorder writes the results to two decimal places in the table. When all of the calculations have been made the "calculator" averages the four or five results. The reporter then goes to the board or overhead projector and records the results of her group's work on a summary chart. The results of each group's work will be very close to each other. A final calculation could be the average of the group results. The final number that represents the ratio between the circumference of a circle and its diameter will be between 3.1 and 3.2. This activity should bring meaning to the value of π. Encourage a curious student to see if she can find some historical information about pi.

Measuring Weight and Mass

Remember that *weight* refers to the force of gravity acting on an object, and *mass* is the amount of matter in an object. For any given object on earth, its weight and mass are equal. On a simple balance scale, we simultaneously determine weight and mass when we find that a box balances 124 grams. On the moon or on another body in space, the weight of an object will be different from its weight on earth. The mass, however, remains constant.

We use the term weight in describing the activities in this section. You will see that some activities use the same procedures used to determine mass; namely, the pan balance.

In their work with weight thus far, students have made direct comparisons with objects to determine which are lighter and which are heavier. They have done

TABLE 13–2 Perimeter and Area of Rectangular Shapes

Perimeter	Dimensions	Area
20	1×9	9
20	2×8	16
20	3×7	21
20	4×6	24
20	5×5	25
20	6×4	24
20	7×3	21
20	8×2	16
20	9×1	9

some work with the pan balance. By the time children have completed the primary grades, they should have little difficulty using standard units of weight with either a pan balance or a spring scale. Intermediate grade students need activities that provide practice weighing a variety of objects. Common metric units of mass include the gram and the kilogram.

ACTIVITIES

Primary (K–3)

Objective: to determine which of two objects is heavier using indirect measuring.

1. Place an object, perhaps a full can of soup, on one side of the room and another object, perhaps a book, on the other side. Challenge the children to discover which object is heavier without moving either object to the other side of the room. Have available at least one pan balance. For younger children, suggest finding another object or a material such as clay to use to determine the weight of the can of soup. This intermediate object can then be used to check the weight of the book.

   This activity may be extended by putting four or five objects on each side of the room and having the children order them by weight. All of the checking must be done with intermediate objects.

Objective: to determine the weights of objects using arbitrary measuring units.

2. Use wooden cubes as measuring units. Have available 8 or 10 objects ranging in weight from 10 to 300 grams. The objects may include a chalkboard eraser, a piece of chalk, a pencil, a box of crayons, and a pair of scissors. Ask the students to estimate the weight of each of these objects in terms of the number of wooden cubes it would take to balance the object. Let the children determine how many cubes it actually takes using the pan balance.

   Most objects will not balance a whole number of cubes. In these cases, the weight should be reported as, for example, "more than 12 cubes and fewer than 13."

   You may vary this activity by using different arbitrary units. Paper clips, washers, beans, and pennies will serve the purpose very well.

   Extend this activity by determining the relationships of coin weights. Provide students with one quarter, five dimes, five pennies, and three nickels. The object is to determine the weight of each coin with respect to the other coins. Ask questions such as the following:

- A quarter weighs as much as how many pennies?
- A quarter weighs as much as how many dimes?
- A quarter weighs as much as how many nickels?
- A nickel weighs as much as how many pennies?
- A nickel weighs as much as how many dimes?
- A penny weighs as much as how many dimes?

   Discuss how many pennies weigh as much as two or three quarters. Ask how many dimes weigh as much as three or four nickels, and so on.

Objective: to use standard units to determine the weights of various items.

3. Find 8 or 10 items with weights that range from 10 to 100 grams. Items may include a small school eraser, a pencil, a pair of scissors, a box of paper clips, a piece of chalk, and a cassette tape. Also provide the children with 100 or so centimeter cubes, each of which weighs 1 gram. Let the children estimate the number of centimeter cubes it will take to balance a particular item. Then have them weigh each item using the cubes. Both the estimate and actual weight should be recorded. If it takes 45 centimeter cubes to balance an item, the children should know that the item weighs 45 grams.

   Next, provide 8 to 10 objects that each weigh between 10 and 400 grams. These objects should include items found in the classroom or on the playground. This time, use the set of standard masses that accompany most pan balances. Again, ask the children to estimate the weight of the various objects before the masses are used. A worksheet picturing the objects with space for the estimate and the actual weight may be helpful. Figure 13–24 illustrates part of one such worksheet.

4. Have the children work in groups of three or four. Each group should have access to a pan balance. If there is only one balance, let the groups take turns. Challenge each group to find three objects that each weigh 25 grams or less, three objects that each weigh 50 to 100 grams, three objects that each weigh 150 to 300 grams, and one object that weighs 1 kilogram. Hold the object search in the classroom. Have the students record the objects they find by drawing pictures of them or writing about them. Among the objects students could weigh are containers of water, rice, sand, or beans.

Intermediate (4–6)

Objective: to recognize the need for uniformity when using units of measure.

1. Provide a collection of various sizes of washers or stones. Have the students weigh five objects and record

Figure 13–24

Figure 13–25

the results using the washers, as in Figure 13–25. Objects may include a crayon box, a ruler, a pair of scissors, a textbook, a chalkboard eraser—all objects that would be found in another classroom in the school.

The next step is to give another class the measuring units and the pan balance. Ask them to weigh the same objects that your class weighed and to report back to you on their findings.

Have the students compare the results of the two weighings and discuss why the results were not the same. It is important to realize that measuring units must be uniform, particularly if they are arbitrary units.

Objective: to use standard units to measure weight.

2. Collect four different materials, such as rice, beans, unpopped popcorn, and centimeter cubes. Put each of these materials in a separate bowl. Separate the class into groups of four. Each group will be a team for a prediction contest. Have each team designate a particular member to be a rice grabber, a bean grabber, and so on. Let the rice grabber estimate the weight of rice that she or he can grab using only one hand. The rice grabber should then grab the rice and put it into a plastic sandwich bag. The rest of the team should weigh and record the results. The other grabbers should do the same thing for their particular materials.

Have the teams calculate the total estimated weight for the four items as well as the actual weight. Have them determine the difference between the estimated weight and the actual weight. The team with the lowest difference is the winner.

3. Display a canning or mayonnaise jar full of rice and an intermediate container such as a tuna can. First, have the students estimate the weight of the rice in the jar. Then announce, "We will be trying to find the weight of the rice. But there is a rule: The largest amount of rice that can be weighed is the amount that can be held by the tuna can" (see Figure 13–26).

Have groups of three or four students devise the most efficient plan they can to determine the weight

Figure 13–26

of the rice in the jar. Let each group implement its plan and find the weight of the rice. When all groups have finished, discuss the procedures used and compare the various plans. Also compare the weights that each group derived.

To extend this activity, use a jar of cubes and weigh to determine the number of cubes in the jar. This may involve weighing a sample of the cubes, counting them, and weighing the jar of cubes to find how many such samples are in the jar. Be sure to subtract the weight of the jar from the weight of the jar and the cubes.

4. Provide each group of three or four students with an apple or orange. Have them find the weight of the apple in grams and record it. Have one member of the group take a bite out of the apple. Then weigh the remaining apple and record the weight. Calculate the weight of the bite and record it. Have the group member take another bite, weigh the remaining apple, record the weight, and calculate the weight of the second bite. Continue until the apple has been eaten.

When the children are finished, have them answer questions about the apple: Are all bites the same size? What was the weight of the largest bite? What was the weight of the smallest bite? What was the weight of the average bite? What was the weight of the part of the apple that was eaten? Compare and discuss the results from each group.

Measuring Time

Children develop an understanding of *time* by experiencing events that last varying lengths of time. Younger children who believe that yesterday was a long time ago later come to believe that yesterday was not too long ago when compared with last week. The experiences that these children need include events of various durations. The time it takes the second hand to move from 12 to 12, the time it takes the hour hand to move from 9 to 10, the start of recess to the end, the start of the school day to the end, Monday to Friday, Monday to Monday, the month of February, and the school year are all events that heighten the child's awareness of time.

In the primary grades, the skill of telling time depends on experiences children have had at home and at school.

When children move into the intermediate grades, their abilities to tell time using a clock are more refined.

During the early years in school, students should measure time using various units. These include years, seasons, months, days, hours, minutes, and seconds. The tools used to measure time are the calendar and the clock.

Birthdays and age are important to children and can be used as a starting point for discussing time. Books such as *A Birthday Basket for Tia* by Mora (1992) are also useful in raising awareness of time.

Later, students tell time throughout the school day. Children should have practice with instruments such as a stop watch that can be used to measure time with greater precision than a sweep second hand.

ACTIVITIES

Primary (K–3)

Objective: to measure various events using arbitrary units.

1. Provide the children with 8 soup cans, each of which has a hole punched in the bottom with a nail. Each hole should be a different size. Mark an "S" on one of the cans and use it as a standard. Have the children fill the standard can and one of the other cans, can A, with water while holding fingers over the holes. Let the cans drain together and compare can A with the standard can, telling whether it takes more time for can A to drain, less time for can A to drain, or the same amount of time for both to drain. Continue these comparisons until all cans have been compared with the standard can and rated.

To extend this activity, compare each can with the others and order the entire collection of cans from those that take the least time to empty to those that take the most time.

2. Construct a pendulum using string and a 1- or 2-ounce lead fishing sinker, as in Figure 13–27. As the pendulum swings, have the children practice counting the

Figure 13–27

number of times the sinker crosses a marker at the pendulum's base.

Once they can do this easily, fill one of the cans used as a water clock in the activity above. As the can empties, have the children count the number of pendulum swings. Record this number. Compare the cans based on the number of pendulum swings and again order the cans.

Extend this activity by timing various events by the number of pendulum swings. Using the pendulum, time events such as how long it takes for the children to take their seats and get ready to begin work after recess, to line up for lunch, to wash their hands before lunch, and to clean the floor before going home.

Objective: to use the calendar to measure days, weeks, and months.

3. Have a large, easily displayed calendar with ample regions representing each day. As an introductory activity each morning, discuss that day. Appropriate items for discussion include the date, the weather, important events, what day yesterday was, what date yesterday was, what day tomorrow will be, what date tomorrow will be, how many days it has been since the start of the month, how many days are left in the month, how many weeks it has been since the start of the month, and how many weeks are left in the month. Make notations in the region representing that day; a picture or a word or two will suffice. When a month has been completed, display it as the next month is begun.

Counting days and remembering what happened a day ago, counting weeks and remembering what happened a week ago, and counting months and remembering what happened a month ago will help children develop skill in using the calendar to tell time.

Objective: to use the clock to tell time.

4. Have a clock with hands that are easy to move. A large wooden or plastic clock with gears that allow the hands to move together is commercially available and can be very useful. It is also advantageous to have a real clock with a second hand to help show the passing of seconds and minutes. Each day on a regular schedule, spend three to five minutes setting the clock and having the children determine the time shown by the hands.

At first, show the time on the hour, such as 10 o'clock, 1 o'clock, and 7 o'clock. Soon, introduce time on the half-hour, then on the quarter-hour, five minutes, and one minute. Let the second hand move around and watch the minute hand move one minute.

Later, use a digital clock set at the same time to show the same time on both types of clocks (see Figure 13–28). It is possible that these young people will live in a world that contains only digital clocks and watches.

To extend this activity, challenge the children to play the minute game. Have the children face away from the clock. Then give a command to begin. When they believe a minute has elapsed, they should stand and face the clock. Facing the clock, they can immediately see if they stood before, after, or at the end of one minute. Use this activity for periods of 15, 30, and 45 seconds, as well.

Once the children begin to tell time, they should regularly practice using the clock to time events that take place during school. These events include the periods set aside for reading, mathematics, art, science, and social studies. There are regular times for outside-the-class activities: physical education, lunch, recess, and end of the day. Let children serve as designated timers for a morning or a day, with the responsibility to let the teacher or the class know when certain events are to take place.

Intermediate (4–6)

Objective: to develop timing devices with arbitrary and standard units.

1. There are several ways to develop timers. Using a funnel and sand is one way (see Figure 13–29a). Initially, fill the funnel with sand. The amount of time for the sand to empty out of the funnel becomes an arbitrary unit of time, named *funnel time,* or another name that may have meaning.

Develop another timer by using a candle on which several equally spaced marks have been scratched, as in Figure 13–29b. The amount of time for the candle

Figure 13–28

Figure 13–29

to burn from one mark to another becomes an arbitrary unit of time.

Construct a third timer by tapping or drilling holes in the bottom of a soup can, as in Figure 13–29c. The amount of time for the water to empty out of the can becomes an arbitrary unit.

Once the timers have been constructed, use them to time various events. Events may include how many blocks can be stacked before the sand timer empties, silently reading while the candle timer burns two intervals, and seeing if the entire class can wash and line up for lunch before the water escapes from the can.

Ask the children how they might make arbitrary units into standard units. Try some of the ideas. Calibrate each timer against a clock with a second hand or a stop watch. Perhaps the funnel and sand could be made into a one-minute timer. The candle could time intervals of five minutes. The soup can could be used as a three-minute timer. Each timer can be adjusted to measure time in standard units. Once completed, the timers should be used as a clock or watch would be used to time events.

An extension of this activity is for a class to construct one or two sundials. The sundial proved to be a reliable timepiece for centuries before the advent of mechanical clocks. Designing and building a horizontal sundial requires measuring a series of angles and compensating for the school's location on earth. The finished product is very rewarding. Finding a book that describes the steps necessary to construct a sundial is essential. Winthrop Dolan's *A Choice of Sundials* (1975) is such a book.

Objective: to use standard units to time events in the classroom.

2. As described earlier, the clock in the classroom should be used to time the events of the day. Fourth-graders and some fifth-grade youngsters may have some difficulty using the clock at first if they have not had regular experience telling time. Using both traditional and digital clocks on a regular basis will provide the experience needed by students.

When a period is set aside for sustained silent reading, have the students record the time they begin and the time they finish. Have a student time a recess and report to you when the time is up. Allow the students to earn minutes of special activity time for certain classroom behaviors.

To extend this activity, have the students survey the *Guinness Book of World Records* for some of the many timed events and prepare a collection of the most interesting. Let students collect or draw pictures illustrating these events.

3. Timing events with precision can begin by using the second hand on the clock to determine how much time it takes to clear desks and get ready to go home, or to wash and line up for lunch. To become more precise requires a stopwatch to time these same events to the nearest hundredth of a second. Team relay and individual events in physical education lend themselves to precise timing. Be careful to time events for the interest and motivation afforded by the timing, not to prove that one child is better than another.

A variation of this activity is to have three children, each with a stop watch, time the same event to the nearest hundredth of a second. Compare the results. Ask, "Why are there differences? Did some timers make a mistake? What is the best estimate of the event's time?" Perhaps an average of the three times will give the best estimate. Repeat this activity several times.

4. The topic of time often occurs in children's books. For example, in *Max and Me and the Time Machine* by Greer and Ruddick (1983), Steve and Max are transported back in time and begin an adventure that ends when they are transported back to their clubhouse. When reading this story to a class, a discussion of time and some problems related to time would be appropriate. What is the difference in minutes or seconds between the time the boys thought they were spending back in time (3 hours) and the actual time they spent (3 days)? How many years ago was the year 1250? How could you tell time in the year 1250, before the advent of the modern clock? *The Flight of the Doves* by Macken (1992) provides an opportunity for students to discuss distance and time. A boy and his younger sister run away from their evil uncle in England and set out to find their grandmother in Ireland. The adventure begins. The distances they traveled and the time it took can be the focus of discussion. How do these distances and times compare to distances from the school and time it takes to cover them by various means?

Measuring Volume and Capacity

Remember that *volume* refers to the amount of space contained in a three-dimensional object. Measures of volume include how much space is found in a box, a room, or a jar. Capacity refers to the amount of space that can be filled. Measures of capacity include how much water or rice will fit into a box or jar. Volume and capacity are closely related. A container's capacity is determined by its volume. At the primary level, we have a greater emphasis on capacity. At the intermediate level, we emphasize both volume and capacity.

Children in the primary grades expand their knowledge of volume and capacity through a variety of media. They build with blocks, large and small. They fill a space and find how much water, sand, or rice was used. They also find how many cubes it takes to fill a space. The cubes represent cubic units and provide the basis for the measurement of volume.

Children in the middle grades continue to use containers, filling them with a variety of materials. These experiences serve as a basis for developing formulas for calculating volume. The transition to abstract work depends upon the earlier manipulative activities. Common metric volume units include cubic centimeters, cubic decimeters, and cubic meters. Metric capacity units include the milliliter and the liter.

ACTIVITIES

Primary (K–4)

Objective: to determine the capacities of various containers using indirect measurement.

1. Provide the children with one particular container to use as a pouring container and several others to pour water (or sand) into. Ask the children to identify the containers that they believe can be completely filled when they start with the pouring container completely filled. Put those that the children believe can be filled together and those they believe cannot be filled together. Then have the children actually try to fill the containers to discover which ones can be filled.

   As an extension, provide six clear containers of various shapes and capacities. Without the children present, pour exactly the same amount of rice into each container, as in Figure 13–30.

   Have the children order the containers from those the children believe hold the least to those they believe hold the most. Then, together, pour the rice into a measuring container and let the children discover that all the containers held the same amount of rice. Discuss with the children the apparent differences in the amounts of rice.

2. This activity requires five jars with volumes that range from 500 milliliters to 2 liters and several infant formula bottles (or tuna fish cans) to use as measuring tools. Ask the children to estimate the number of formula bottles of rice it will take to fill each jar. Then have them find the amount of rice that fills the jars. If the amount is not a whole number, it should be noted

as, for example, "more than 8 bottles and less than 9." Encourage the children to record the amount of their estimates and the actual capacities in terms of infant formula bottles. Finally, have the children order the containers by capacity based on the information they have collected.

Objective: to determine the volumes of several containers using standard measures.

3. Find or construct four or five boxes with metric dimensions. The boxes may be constructed by using a pattern similar to the one shown in Figure 13–31. The dimensions should be whole numbers of centimeters like the dimensions of the box shown; it measures 3 by 4 by 2 centimeters.

   Provide the children with centimeter cubes and the boxes. Have them estimate how many cubes they think it will take to fill each box. Then have them carefully stack the cubes in each box to find the actual volume. Explain to the children that the volume of each small cube is 1 cubic centimeter and ask for the volumes of the boxes in cubic centimeters.

   Next, find two or three small boxes that do not have metric dimensions and challenge the children to determine the volumes of the boxes using cubic centimeters. Here, the answers may be stated in terms of, for example, "more than 22 cubic centimeters."

4. This activity requires centimeter cubes and sets of measuring cups and spoons. The cups and spoons should be intended for use in the kitchen and should be calibrated in metric units. Provide the children with 8 to 10 common containers, the capacities of which must be determined using the materials at hand. The containers may include containers for shampoo, milk, syrup, peanut butter, ice cubes, sour cream, detergent, margarine, film, and greeting cards.

   Ask the children which units, those that are stacked or those that are poured, are most appropriate for measuring the capacities of the containers. Have the children estimate the capacity of each

Figure 13–31

Figure 13–30

container and then use the units to find the actual capacity.

Intermediate–Middle Grades (4–6)

Objective: to use water displacement as a way to determine which of several objects has the greatest volume.

1. Construct six balls of clay of varying sizes. Also, find a glass jar with straight sides that will easily hold each ball of clay. A peanut butter jar or a quart canning jar should suffice. Put into the jar enough water to completely cover the largest ball of clay without flowing out of the jar.

   Ask the students if they know how the volume of a ball of clay can be determined. Accept and discuss suggestions. Try reasonable suggestions.

   If displacement is not suggested, have the children attach each ball of clay to the end of a piece of wire. Submerge the balls, one at a time, in the water while the students observe the water level. Discuss how the water level changes depending on the size of the clay. Have the students determine which ball of clay has the greatest volume.

   Extend this activity by using three or four irregular rocks that will fit into a graduated cylinder. Have the students pour water into the cylinder to a level that is clearly marked. Then have them carefully immerse a rock in the water and note the new level of the water. Have them record the difference between the new level and the original level in cubic centimeters; this is the volume of the rock.

Objective: to use arbitrary units to determine the volumes of different containers.

2. For this activity, collect an eye dropper, a spoon of arbitrary size, and three containers of moderate size. The containers may be an infant formula jar, a peanut butter jar, and a mayonnaise jar (see Figure 13–32).

   Ask the students how to determine how many eye droppers of water it takes to fill the large jar. They may suggest using the eye dropper to fill the large jar one drop at a time. Encourage the students to find a method that will take less time and effort. One suggestion may be to discover how many drops of water

it takes to fill the spoon. Next, find how many spoons it takes to fill the formula jar. Then, find how many formula jars it takes to fill the peanut butter jar and how many peanut butter jars it takes to fill the mayonnaise jar. Finally, the volume of the mayonnaise jar can be stated in terms of drops of water.

3. Collect enough bottle caps of the same variety to fill a medium-sized paper bag. Asking for help from the children will speed up this collection. Provide the students with various containers: a soup can; a tuna can; half-pint, pint, and quart milk containers; a shoe box; a cereal box; and a drinking cup. Have the children estimate and then determine the volume of each container in terms of the number of bottle caps. Have them order the collection of containers based on their findings.

   An extension of this activity is to select a second unit, such as small shell-shaped macaroni, and replicate the procedure. The results should prove to be the same. Do all students agree that the results will be the same before the second measure is made?

Objective: to calculate the volumes of various containers using standard measurement.

4. This is similar to Activity 2 above. Ask the students to use an eye dropper to find how many drops of water are in one milliliter. Next, have them determine the number of milliliters of water in a teaspoon and how many teaspoons fill a tablespoon. Then, encourage the students to find how many tablespoons fill a paper cup. With the information they have collected, they should be able to calculate the number of drops of water it takes to fill a teaspoon, a tablespoon, and a paper cup.

   Finally, challenge the students to find the number of liters of water contained in 1 million drops of water. A calculator will be very handy in this activity.

5. Begin by providing the students with small boxes constructed from oaktag. Make three or four boxes with measurements of (a) 2 by 2 by 2 centimeters, (b) 2 by 2 by 3 centimeters, (c) 2 by 3 by 3 centimeters, and (d) 3 by 3 by 3 centimeters. Also provide a large number of centimeter cubes. Have the children find how many cubes can be carefully stacked in each of the containers and record the number of cubes. Have them use a table like the following:

Box	Length	Width	Height	Length × Width × Height	Total No. of Cubes
a	2	2	2	8	8
b	2	2	3	12	12
c	2	3	3	18	18
d	3	3	3	27	27

Figure 13–32

Encourage the students to build "boxes" by stacking centimeter cubes using other dimensions and record their results in the table they have already started. After six or eight examples have been recorded, have the students examine the table for patterns.

Expect a variety of responses, but lead the students to notice the relationship between the product of length, width, and height and the number of cubes counted. The students will be discovering the formula for the volume of a box. The common formula for determining the volume of a rectangular container is $V = l \times w \times h$, where l is the length of the base, w is the width of the base, and h is the height.

6. A **prism** is a figure whose ends are congruent polygons and parallel with each other, and whose sides are parallelograms. The congruent polygons are the bases of the prism. Figure 13–33a shows a triangular prism, whereas Figure 13–33b shows a rectangular prism. Notice how the name of the prism is determined by the shape of its bases. The formula for the volume of any prism may be discovered by first determining the volume of common prisms and using that information to generalize a formula for all prisms. Have students working in groups develop a table that shows the measurements of a square prism, a rectangular prism, and a right triangular prism and challenge them to determine the volume of each figure. The volume of the first two figures may be determined by using the volume formula discussed in Activity 5 above. The volume of the third figure, the right triangular prism, may be determined if the students make the figure into a rectangular or square prism, determine its volume, and then divide the result by 2 (see Figure 13–34). Once the volumes have been found encourage the students to find a common relationship among the dimensions of the prisms and the volumes of the prisms. Have each group discuss its findings and conclusions. Soon, it should be apparent that the area of the base of the prism multiplied by the height of the prism will result in the volume. Be receptive to alternative formulas that result in the correct volumes.

Figure 13–34

7. The purpose of Shroyer and Fitzgerald's unit called *Mouse and Elephant: Measuring Growth* (1986) is to introduce the concepts of area, perimeter, surface area, and volume. The materials used to develop these concepts are tiles and cubes. The entire unit consists of eight activities that take two to three weeks to complete. Students are guided through the problem-oriented unit by the teacher and a number of carefully constructed worksheets that challenge the students to expand their knowledge of area, perimeter, surface area, and volume. The unit is presented in a teacher's guide that is complete, anticipating the needs of a busy teacher and even the expected responses of the students.

Measuring Temperature

Much of what children learn and know about *temperature* comes from their interaction with their environments. When the air is cold, they bundle up. When it is hot, they wear fewer and lighter clothes. In the snow, they shiver. When they are ill, they may feel very warm or they may feel warm yet shiver.

Children's measures of temperature are generally from two sources, the weather and illness. Children hear the measure of the outside temperature daily as they watch television or listen to the radio. When they are ill, their body temperatures are recorded, but weather is by far the more common source of measures of temperature.

Children in the primary grades begin to become aware of temperature as they report the daily weather. Expressions like "It is warm today," "It will be cooler

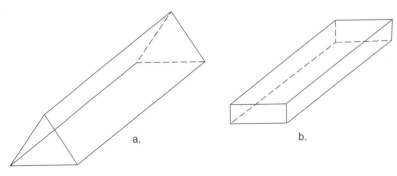

Figure 13–33

tomorrow," and "It is frosty this morning" serve as indicators of temperature. Later, a daily temperature reading may be made and recorded as practice in reading a thermometer.

Students in the middle grades continue to read temperatures and to record and graph the results. There will be work in science that requires reading temperatures, in weather units and in other areas of study. The common metric temperature unit is degrees Celsius. As children are alerted to temperature, they should develop the ability to recognize if various temperatures, such as 20°C, are hot or cold. And, if last night's low temperature was 4°C and today's high was 15°C, children should be able to determine that the difference in temperature from the low to the high temperature was 15°C − 4°C, or 11°C.

ACTIVITIES

Primary (K–3)

Objective: to use indirect measurement to determine temperature.

1. Provide students with thermometer bulbs and tubes from four inexpensive thermometers by removing their backings. About halfway up each thermometer tube, mark a spot with fingernail polish. This mark is a reference point with which to judge the movement of the mercury (see Figure 13–35).

   Ask the children to place the four thermometers in four different locations: (1) in a glass of cold tap water, (2) on a table in the classroom, (3) in a glass of warm tap water, and (4) outside the classroom window. Have the children guess which locations will be the warmest and coolest. Then, using their observations, let the children determine which locations are actually the warmest and coolest.

Figure 13–35

Objective: to use arbitrary units of temperature to measure various materials.

2. Use thermometer bulbs and tubes as in the preceding activity. On each tube, make five equally spaced marks. This may be done by laying the tubes on a piece of lined writing or notebook paper with the bottom of the bulb exactly on one of the lines and then making the five marks.

   Next, indicate six locations in which to check the temperature using the "new" thermometers. These locations may be on a countertop, grasped in the hand of a particular student, in a glass of water, in a sunny spot in the classroom or school, near a light source, and outside the window.

   Have the students record the temperatures they find as they test the various locations. The thermometers should be kept in a location for about five minutes to allow the mercury to stop moving. Because it is unlikely that the temperatures will be exact, the record should show the temperature in a location as, for example, "greater than 3 but less than 4."

   To extend this activity, have the children record the temperature inside the classroom and outside for each hour during a school day. Then let them construct a graph or table to show how the temperatures varied.

Objective: to use standard units to measure temperature.

3. Have the children observe a Celsius thermometer that has been placed in a container of boiling water. *Note: this activity requires you to take special precautions to avoid possible burns from spilled or splashed water.* Ask the children to read the temperature. Next, have the children read the temperature from a thermometer that has been placed in a glass containing chopped ice. (The thermometer should be at room temperature or cooler when it is placed in the ice, not still hot from the boiling water.) Then have the children read the thermometer at room temperature. Finally, check the temperature of the air outside. In each case, have the children write down the temperature they have read from the thermometer.

   It may be necessary to spend a little time explaining how the scale of a thermometer is constructed and how it is read. At first, the temperature may be read as, for example, "more than 95 and less than 100." As the students become more proficient at reading the scales, they will be able to be more precise.

Intermediate (4–6)

Objective: to use standard units to determine temperature.

1. Mount a Celsius thermometer outside the classroom window so that it may be read from inside the room. If this is impossible, find a location outside where the thermometer may be placed. Mount another

thermometer in the room. Have students record the temperature daily at a given time for two weeks. Keep a record on a table labeled for inside and outside temperature or graph the temperatures as in Figure 13–36.

2. Collect five different containers such as a paper cup, a heavy coffee mug, an aluminum cup, a glass measuring cup, and a thermos soup container. Into each one (or one at a time) pour the same amount of boiling water and insert a Celsius thermometer. After one minute, record the temperatures in the containers. Then, at 5-minute intervals, record the temperatures in the containers. After 30 minutes, stop. To complete the activity, graph the results. Then, order the containers from the one that holds the temperature for the longest period of time to the one that holds it for the shortest amount of time.

3. This activity requires three oral Celsius thermometers. Ask for three volunteers. Have the volunteers place the thermometers in their mouths and keep them there for the prescribed amount of time (normally 3 to 5 minutes). Then have them read and record their temperatures.

    Discuss why the temperatures range from 36.5 to 37.5 degrees Celsius and when the children may expect the temperatures to be higher or lower. You may wish to check the temperatures of other students to collect more data. Be sure to thoroughly clean the thermometers before reusing them.

Measuring Angles

Experiences with *Logo* provide young children with the opportunity to use angle measure. With a little practice, children can direct the turtle to turn right or left a specified number. The number represents the degrees of a circle; thus, a complete rotation is 360 degrees. The more children work with turns, the greater their understanding of angle measure. As well, children will experience exterior angles as they write procedures for simple polygons. Apart from this exposure that children in primary grades have to angle measure, most angle measurement is introduced in the middle grades.

The protractor is used to measure angles. Once learned, the skill of measuring angles is fairly easy to maintain. Learning to use a protractor, however, requires careful teaching. Skill in measuring angles should begin with establishing an easily identifiable angle measure, 90 degrees.

ACTIVITIES

Intermediate/Middle Grades (4–8)

Objective: to use a model of 90 degrees to find right angles.

1. The square corner or right angle is easily recognized by children and can be quickly constructed by folding a sheet of paper twice, as in Figure 13–37. Have the students use these models of 90 degrees to check the corners of books, the corners of desks, angles placed on a bulletin board, the corners of a classroom door, and the corners of the chalkboard.

    Next, have students determine if various angles are less than, equal to, or greater than a right angle. Provide the students with 10 angles ranging in size from 70 to 110 degrees. Challenge students to estimate whether each angle is less than a right angle (**acute**), equal to a right angle (90 degrees), or greater than a right angle

Figure 13–37

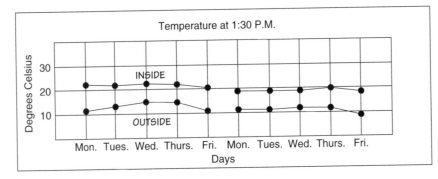

Figure 13–36

(**obtuse**). After the students estimate, have them use the folded right angle to check their estimates.

Objective: to use a protractor to measure angle size.

2. As you introduce the protractor, show students how to place it on the angle so that the vertex of the angle is aligned with the origin of the protractor and one side of the angle, called a **ray,** corresponds to the **referent,** or the 0/180-degrees line of the protractor. Figure 13–38 illustrates a properly placed protractor.

Determining the angle measure requires the student to read the degrees scale, which begins at zero along one of the rays of the angle. In the case of the angle in Figure 13–38, the measure is 60 degrees.

Providing students with explanations and assistance as they begin working with protractors is essential. Provide students with angles to measure. The angles should have rays long enough to accommodate the size of the particular protractor being used. Otherwise, the measuring experience will be frustrating. Angles to measure may be provided on a worksheet or displayed on a bulletin board. If *Logo* is available, it is interesting to measure the angles generated by the turtle to check the accuracy of those angles.

3. In this activity, be sure students have protractors and paper available. Provide the students with five pre-drawn angles. First, have the students estimate the measure of each angle. Then, to provide an opportunity to construct angles using models, have the students measure the angles and construct copies of them adjacent to the originals.

Next, challenge the children to construct angles of given measures without using models. Have them construct the angles in any configuration on the paper to show that they know how to use both the left and the right scales on their protractors.

Objective: to determine the sum of the angle measures of a polygon.

1. This activity begins by challenging the students to see if they can determine the sum of the angle measures of any triangle. Students should use a ruler to draw a large triangle on a sheet of paper. The triangles should vary in shape. Let the students see if they can figure how to determine the sum of the angles of their triangles. Students may choose to use a protractor to measure the angles and then to add the angle measures together. To confirm this sum, students may cut out the triangle and then tear the verticies off of the triangle and position them side by side to verify that 180 degrees is the angle sum of any triangle (see Figure 13–39).

2. Have the students sketch any quadrilateral, any pentagon, any hexagon, any heptagon (7 sides), and any octagon. Ask the students to work with their learning groups to determine the number of degrees in the angle measures of the various polygons that they have sketched and to put the information that they have discovered in a table such as Table 13–3. Let this be a problem of discovery, encouraging the students to devise a way to complete the table. What if you had a polygon of 11 sides, then how many degrees would there be in the angle sum. What about a polygon of 18 sides? Some students may attempt to tear off the verticies of the polygons like they did for the triangle. Some students may use information that they have gained from working with *Logo*. Others may carefully draw the figures and use a protractor to measure the angles. Some may use the information that they

Figure 13–38

TABLE 13–3 Angle Sum of Polygons

Number of Sides	3	4	5	6	7	8	n
Angle Sum	180°						

Figure 13–39

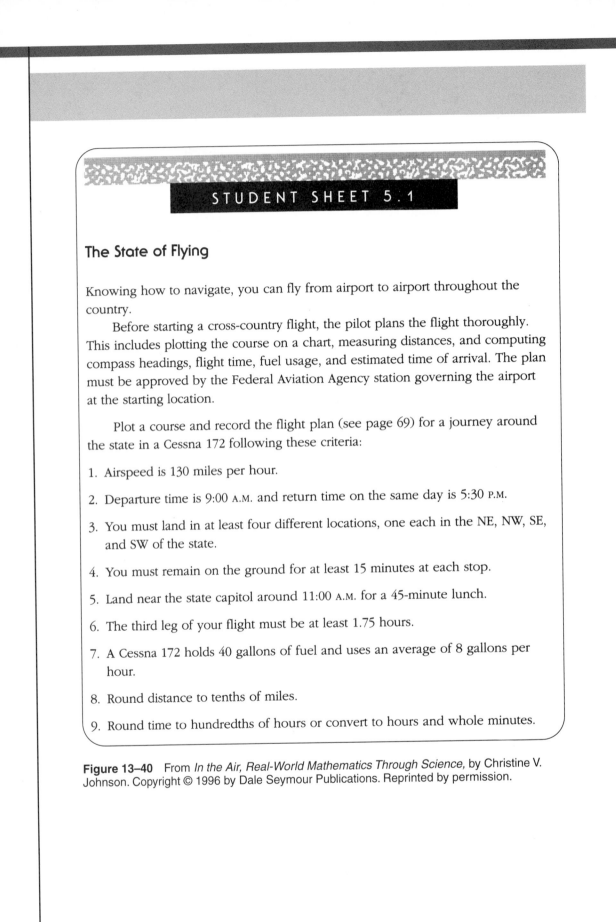

The State of Flying

Knowing how to navigate, you can fly from airport to airport throughout the country.

Before starting a cross-country flight, the pilot plans the flight thoroughly. This includes plotting the course on a chart, measuring distances, and computing compass headings, flight time, fuel usage, and estimated time of arrival. The plan must be approved by the Federal Aviation Agency station governing the airport at the starting location.

Plot a course and record the flight plan (see page 69) for a journey around the state in a Cessna 172 following these criteria:

1. Airspeed is 130 miles per hour.

2. Departure time is 9:00 A.M. and return time on the same day is 5:30 P.M.

3. You must land in at least four different locations, one each in the NE, NW, SE, and SW of the state.

4. You must remain on the ground for at least 15 minutes at each stop.

5. Land near the state capitol around 11:00 A.M. for a 45-minute lunch.

6. The third leg of your flight must be at least 1.75 hours.

7. A Cessna 172 holds 40 gallons of fuel and uses an average of 8 gallons per hour.

8. Round distance to tenths of miles.

9. Round time to hundredths of hours or convert to hours and whole minutes.

Figure 13–40 From *In the Air, Real-World Mathematics Through Science,* by Christine V. Johnson. Copyright © 1996 by Dale Seymour Publications. Reprinted by permission.

Math Program

The activity shown in Figure 13–40 is from a middle-grades instructional module from the Washington MESA (Mathematics, Engineering, Science Achievement) project and published by the Addison-Wesley Publishing Company. These modules may be added to other mathematics and science programs in middle-grades classes. They were designed by a team of writers and teachers working with scientists, mathematicians, and engineers and pilot tested in middle school classrooms to facilitate connections between the classroom and "real-world" mathematics and science.

This activity is taken from a unit entitled *In the Air, Real-World Mathematics Through Science,* which is designed to introduce students to navigation and computing distance, speed, and time. This module involves statistics, measurement, equations, and geometry and is appropriate for pre-algebra students. In this activity, students must plot a course on a state map that meets the criteria set forth in the activity. There are several different ways to meet these criteria, but students must be not only good at reading maps, but must also use a great deal of mathematics in planning the trip. This type of activity would make a good portfolio entry, especially if students expanded on it to add other information such as traveling expenses or did research at the local airport to investigate traveling in a small plane.

In all of the activities in this module, there are several activities to assist in making connections. These include career links, writing links, history links, interest links, and technology links. In the career links are vignettes about the lives of famous people in the aeronautics field, including women and minorities. Assessment is an integral part of instruction and is not a separate section.

This unit also has a family math section in which the family works together to make and time paper airplanes. After constructing the planes, the families must determine how long it would take the plane to fly to school if it were to fly at the same rate. Information is charted and graphed and families must attempt to determine a maximum rate and decide whether flying in a paper airplane would be efficient.

Billstein (1998) describes several activities closely related to the MESA project. His article is about how runways are named after the direction in which they are aligned. Included in the article are activities in measuring angles, plotting compass headings, and determining runway numbers. These activities are sure to stimulate discussion and questions.

gained from determining the angle sum of a triangle. If line segments are drawn from a single vertex to each of the other verticies of a polygon, triangles will be formed. There will be two fewer triangles than there are number of sides in the polygon; thus, a pentagon will have 5 − 2, or 3, triangles formed in its interior. With each triangle having 180 degrees, the angle sum of the pentagon will be 3 × 180, or 540 degrees. A polygon of *n* sides will have $(n − 2)$ 180 degrees for its angle sum.

Objective: to determine if a particular regular polygon will tessellate.

3. Tessellating was introduced in Chapter 12. You may review this concept by having the students discover what angle measurement is important for a regular figure to be able to tessellate. Let the students work with pattern blocks to make tessellations using shapes that are the same. Each group will be able to tessellate with equilateral triangles, squares and hexagons. Are there other pattern blocks that will tessellate? The verticies fit together around a common point in a tessellation. What is the angle measure around that point? (360 degrees) How can we use our information about the angle measures of various polygons to determine if certain regular polygons will tessellate? What would happen if we used two or three or more different regular polygons to tessellate (semiregular tessellation)? For example, with the pattern blocks, two squares, a hexagon, and a triangle will tessellate about a common point (see Figure 13–41). Can this be predicted by what we know about the angle measure needed for a tessellation and the angle measures of those figures?

   If you have dynamic geometry available on either a computer or calculator, try the pattern block activity using the drawing, reflection, and angle measurement capabilities. In this way, students can explore a wide range of regular and irregular figures to determine which ones tessellate and to test their conjectures about why only a few regular figures will work.

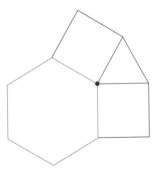

Figure 13–41

The activities presented in the skills section of this chapter give you some idea how extensive measurement is. There are many types and topics of measurement. Types of measurement include direct, indirect, arbitrary, and standard. Topics of measurement include length, area, weight, time, volume, temperature, and angle. Be prepared to use measurement whenever the opportunity arises in the classroom.

Estimating

In no other area of mathematics is estimating more prevalent than in measurement. Once children get in the habit of estimating before they measure, they are better able to determine if their measuring is accurate. Notice that nearly every activity in this chapter has suggested that students estimate before they measure; therefore, no further activities are presented.

As children gain experience in measurement, encourage them to develop a sense of the various units they are using in their measuring tasks. For example, when children are measuring length, they should know that a centimeter is about the width of a thumb, that a meter is about two average steps, and that a kilometer is about a 5- to 10-minute bicycle ride. When children are measuring volume or capacity, they should know that a cubic centimeter is about the size of a bean, that a cubic meter is a space in which they could put their desk and chair, and that a liter is an amount that would fill three or four drinking glasses. Having this sense of measuring units gives the children an important foundation for estimation and measurement.

Solving and Creating Problems

Many of the activities presented in this chapter have been presented in a problem-solving format. That is, students have been challenged to use the skills of problem solving in seeking solutions. We hope you will encourage students to launch into solving a problem without fear of failure or frustration. This requires well-stated problems and considerable teacher support and encouragement. Following are a few examples of activities that provide problem-solving experiences.

ACTIVITIES

Primary (K–3)

Objective: to use estimation and standard measures to solve problems.

1. Present children with five events that require them to use the measurement skills they are learning. Some examples of such events follow:

- Find how much rice it takes to balance a soup can. Tell how much the rice weighs.
- Here is a piece of string. Find an object that is as far from the doorknob as this string is long.
- Here is a sheet of paper. Find a book in the room that is the same size as this piece of paper.
- Find how many centimeter cubes it will take to fill a tuna can. Tell how much all of the cubes weigh in total.
- Use the *Logo* turtle to make a square that has sides of 55 turtle steps. Make two such squares on the screen.

These events are intended for students working in groups of three or four or for the entire class working with the teacher. The size of the class, the amount of help available, and the age and abilities of the youngsters play a role in the organization for this activity. An extension of this activity is presented below as an activity for students in the middle grades.

Objective: to use the pan balance to solve a problem.

2. Provide the children with 8 balls of clay or play dough. They should weigh 5, 10, 15, 20, 25, 30, 35, and 40 grams. Challenge the children to divide the balls of clay among 4 children so that each child will have the same weight of clay. Have the children weigh various combinations of clay balls until they have found pairs that weigh 45 grams. They should match the 5- and 40-gram balls, the 10- and 35-gram balls, and so on. A pair of clay balls on one side of the scales should balance another pair on the other side. As an extension, ask the children to create 4 or 6 clay balls to give to other students to solve. Have the children create the balls without using the standard gram masses; let them use only the pan balance.

Intermediate (4–6)

Objective: to estimate area and volume based on configurations of squares and cubes.

1. On a table or shelf, make arrangements with various numbers of cubes. Challenge the students to find the number of cubes in a pattern without counting. Figure 13–42 shows two such patterns. Allow students to create patterns for the others, including you, to estimate the number of cubes.

   Then, move to estimating larger numbers using patterns shaded on squared paper. Perhaps the first estimates should determine if the pattern has more or less than 25 squares. Next, have the students estimate more precisely how many squares are shown. Figure 13–43 illustrates two such square patterns.

   - *Understanding the problem.* I need to decide how many squares I believe are shaded in the figure on the left.

I cannot count every square. I need to figure out a way to do this so I can do other problems like it.

- *Devising a plan.* I am going to count some of the shaded regions. Then I'll try to fit the regions together in my mind to make a rectangular shape. I'll multiply the length and width to find the answer (make and use a drawing or model and look for a pattern).
- *Carrying out the plan.* In the upper part of the shaded region on the left in Figure 13–43, I see a 3-by-7 rectangle (21 shaded squares). In the bottom part of that shape, I see what is more than another row but not two more rows. I believe there must be a little more than 4-by-7 shaded squares. Thus, I will say there are about 30 shaded squares in the shape. I am interested in knowing how close I am.
- *Looking back.* When I counted the shaded regions, I found 29. My approach for finding the number of shaded regions in that shape was pretty good. I wonder if it will work for the next shape?

An extension of this activity is to use stacks of cubes with the understanding that there are no holes within a figure. These stacks may actually be constructed or they may be pictured. See Figure 13–44a for a picture. As a variation, a top view of the stack may be shown with the number of cubes in each stack indicated, as in Figure 13–44b. Again, encourage the children to estimate how many cubes are contained in the figure.

Objective: to determine when certain vegetables will be ready to harvest.

2. Information for this activity may be easily gathered from garden or seed catalogs or from seed packets. Select two vegetables, such as radishes and beans.

Figure 13–42

Figure 13–43

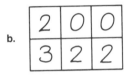

Figure 13–44

Explain to the children that three different kinds of radishes are ready to eat in 22, 25, and 28 days and that three different kinds of beans are ready to be picked in 50, 56, and 68 days.

If the seeds for the radishes are planted on April 20, when could you expect to have ripe radishes? If the bean seeds are planted on June 1, when could you expect to have ripe beans? If you wanted 56-day beans to be ripe on August 20, when should you plan to plant them? If you wanted 25-day radishes to be ripe on May 18, when should you plan to plant them?

This activity may be extended easily by selecting several kinds of vegetables for a garden that should all ripen on a particular day. When should each vegetable be planted? It is necessary to have calendars available for the children to use in seeking solutions to these problems.

Objective: to use estimation and standard measurement on a scavenger hunt.

3. Divide the class into teams of three or four students. Give each team a set of scavenger hunt challenges. Here are a sample of such challenges:
   - Find how many square meters of floor space each person in our classroom has.
   - If there are 100 students in the gym, how many cubic meters does each student have?
   - How many square meters does the school playground have?
   - Find the number of meters you must walk from our classroom to the principal's office and back.
   - Find two pairs of students whose combined weights in kilograms are the same.
   - How many turtle steps (*Logo*) would it take to be 1 meter long?
   - Find the temperature of the oven in degrees Celsius needed to bake a cake.

- Write a problem similar to these for other students to solve.

It is helpful to have a metric tape measure, a trundle wheel, a metric bathroom scale, a computer with *Logo,* and a metric oven thermometer to assist in the above tasks. Give each team three tasks to complete. The winning team is the first to successfully complete its assigned tasks.

Grouping Students for Learning Measurement

Learning measurement is an active process. From the time children first experiment with measurement until they master measuring skills, their work should be active. Thus, much of the work will be done in individual and cooperative learning group settings. Young children will play individually or with a friend or two at the rice (or sand) table, pouring rice from container to container. At this stage, the experience is individual. Later, when a group of four children are given a particular task, such as ordering five containers at the rice table from smallest to largest, cooperative learning will be the focus.

Several types of instruction, such as introductory activities, developing skills in telling time, using the geoboard to find perimeter, and debriefing after a cooperative learning activity, may be best presented in the whole-class setting. These are times when it is either most efficient or most appropriate to use the whole-class setting for sharing and discussion to take place. By and large, the whole-class setting is not used by teachers to tell children how to measure, except to summarize procedures that have come from the students' experiences.

Activities in which children work in small groups provide an opportunity for the children to experiment with measuring and, later, to use standard measuring tools. These small-group settings allow children to discuss with one another their findings, to compare their procedures, and to get feedback from one another regarding the various techniques that they used. As the teacher, you will be busy moving from group to group, monitoring the progress of the students, offering occasional suggestions, and answering questions that all members of the group may have. It is important for the teacher to be a presence without interfering with the interaction of the children. An exception would be when you interrupt a group to encourage the children to return to the task at hand or to modify the behavior of disruptive students. As you read the activities presented in Chapter 13, think about ways in which they can be successfully used in the small-group setting.

Communicating Learning of Measurement

As was the case in learning geometry, description in learning measurement is a focus that should be encouraged. Children should be encouraged to describe what they discovered and to see if others made the same discovery. They should compare and contrast procedures that they used during their activities. They should design instructions for other students to follow. These experiences may involve oral exchanges in which children can question one another and seek clarification. For example, the spokesperson for a small group may report how her group used a strip of adding-machine tape to make a measuring tape and how they found objects in the room that were 10, 20, and 30 centimeters in length. Did other groups use the same procedures? Did they find the same or different objects? What made this task easy or hard?

Another type of important communication is describing specifically how a skill is performed. For example, a child may be asked to describe what he would expect a clock to look like if it showed that it is 10:30 in the morning. This may be a writing task or an oral task. A picture may help the student formulate how he might describe the clock face. Many of the skills involved in measuring include specific procedures that can be the focus of descriptive communication.

A learning-group journal can be used to record the work group members have done in measuring. Headings in such a journal might include "How We Made a Centimeter Ruler," "How to Measure Length," "Comparing Our Estimates with Our Actual Measures," "How to Tell Time, " and "How We Solved the Volume Problem." The group recorder would be responsible for writing the ideas and descriptions of the group members. There should be an opportunity to share these entries with other class members. Individual group members may wish to write their own summaries of a particularly good description that could be included in the student's portfolio.

Connecting Learning of Measurement

Mr. Roberts was excited about the book that he had just purchased at a regional mathematics conference. The book, *Eat Your Math* (Harris and Jones, 1994), described nine food menus to be used on a monthly basis that integrate mathematics with language arts, music, and arts and crafts. Each menu was accompanied with complete instructions for setting up five stations requiring about 20 minutes each to finish. Each station is identified by an activity focused on a particular food and includes a listing of the NCTM *Standards* that are being met by the activity, the materials needed, the directions, and pages for a record book for the entire project.

The Pizza Menu was the project that Mr. Roberts decided to start with. His second/third grade blended classroom would enjoy this project. At the first station, students constructed a "favorite toppings" graph by decorating construction paper triangles and putting them on a large butcher paper graph. At the second station, students estimated the weight of a large store-bought pizza that Mr. Roberts had brought in. Then they recorded their estimates and the actual weight they found by using a scale. Next, the students each cut a piece of string that they thought would go around the pizza and then compared their estimates with the pizza. And, they constructed a graph using the strings to show if their estimates were shorter than, longer than, or almost the same as the circumference of the pizza. At the third station, students used individual-sized cardboard pizzas and traced their circumferences on sheets of one inch grid paper. Then, the students counted the number of square inches to determine the area of the individual pizzas. At the fourth station, students made individual pizzas using English muffin halves and assorted toppings. The pizzas were cooked in a toaster oven. Each student wrote his or her recipe and drew a picture of the pizza. At the fifth station, the students were given paper circles of various sizes and scissors. Their job was to first estimate and then determine by cutting how many pieces of pizza would result if they cut their circular pizza one, two, three, or four times.

After all of the students finished with the stations, Mr. Roberts had the students look at the graphs that were made and discuss what the graphs showed when all of the students' work was considered together. Both the students and Mr. Roberts were excited about how well the pizza project went and they were all eager to work on the Monster Sandwich Menu next month. The connection between mathematics and food was clear as well as the connections between math and language arts and math and arts and crafts.

Ms. Stahl had challenged her sixth- and seventh-grade students to look around their community over the weekend for bridges. She wanted her students to take pictures of the bridges or sketch the sides and tops of any bridges that they found. She knew that there were not many bridges in town but one of the best was a railroad bridge that could be found on the east side of town. She wanted to raise the awareness of the students about the kinds of shapes that were used in bridge building. When the students returned from the weekend, several had sketches of bridges and one student had a photograph of two bridges that she had found. Ms. Stahl provided magazines for the students to look through for pictures of bridges. As the students worked in groups they were asked to find the most common shape in their bridge pictures. In the ensuing discussion, the students noted that triangles were the most common and even if there were rectangles there were diagonal beams that make triangles out of the rectangles.

This investigation was the initiating activity for a 10-day project to culminate in the construction of toothpick bridges. Ms. Stahl was guided in the bridge project by a small publication, *Building Toothpick Bridges* (Pollard, 1985). On the first day of the project, there was a general introduction to bridge building, including some history of bridge development and a description of various types of bridges. On the second day, construction companies of five students were formed with specific roles to play. During the next few days, the bridges were designed and constructed. Finally, at the end of the project, all of the materials used by each group were judged and the bridges were tested to determine their strength. Besides building the bridges, an economy was established and all materials used in the bridge building had to be ordered and purchased and paid for by checks written by the accountant for the group. On the final day, photographs were taken of the bridges and awards were given to bridge companies for a variety of achievements. Then the strength of the bridges in Ms. Stahl's class was tested. The bridge that held the greatest weight held 2,500 grams.

The bridge project provided students the opportunity to connect ideas and skills of math, science, social studies, and art. The project helped the students view their world a bit differently and certainly raised the awareness of the students about bridges in their environment.

Assessing Learning of Measurement

Assessing measurement concepts and skills requires clearly stated objectives. Most likely, the objectives will come from the section or chapter of the math textbook currently being used or from the mathematics program being used. The school district, school, or teacher may be responsible for determining whether the textbook or program objectives adequately represent measurement.

Throughout math textbooks, the teacher is provided with assessment procedures. There are pre-tests for chapters about measurement. There are mid-chapter check-ups to see if the students are understanding the measurement skills presented. There is a review of the measurement chapter content, and there is a chapter test. These assessments provide data regarding student proficiency in measurement. Both content and skills are assessed.

It will be crucial to provide additional assessment techniques for material not presented by the textbook. Measurement is best assessed by observing children

measuring. Many of the activities suggested in this chapter are nearly impossible to include in a basal math textbook. To assess the activities, observe how the children perform various tasks and jot notes about the children's performances. Anecdotal records are an important part of the assessment process.

Assess measurement skills by asking children to make careful measurements. For example, have them cut a piece of string 17 centimeters long, make a rectangle with sides of 6 and 9 centimeters, respectively, or construct a hexagon on the geoboard with an area of 7 square units. Ask children to make a clay ball weighing 35 grams. Have them put 250 milliliters in a container. Ask them to measure an angle of 55 degrees. Have them find how much time elapses between lunch and dismissal time. Ask the children to report the temperature inside and outside the classroom. Your first-hand observations as children perform these tasks will provide you with valuable information regarding the children's measurement abilities. Projects such as recording weather information and using maps to plan a trip involve active and practical uses of measurement and should be part of the assessment of children's ability to measure.

Something for Everyone

Geometry and measurement are good areas for children who may not excel in abstract numerical work in mathematics. These areas are perfect for students who have strengths in the visual and spatial areas. Such children often excel when they are asked to show something on a geoboard or with pattern blocks or to estimate a measurement. They may not be able to give a verbal explanation of what they did, but they can often perform even better than the teacher or the children who are the best students in computation.

Auditory learners may have difficulty in geometry and measurement. They will probably be good at defining geometric terms and stating metric conversions, but they may not be as good at spatial activities unless given a verbal explanation of what to do. They may have difficulty actually drawing figures or finding where to start measuring a given figure. They may be able to talk themselves through some spatial activities by reasoning aloud why two tangrams fit together in a certain way or how the faces of a polyhedron are shaped.

Tactile-kinesthetic learners excel when manipulating the geometry materials and the measuring tools. Most measuring requires some initial investigation with a ruler, a meter stick, a measuring cup, a clock, a thermometer, a protractor, or some other measuring tool. Geometry and measurement are topics that lend themselves to active learning and they are popular with students who perform well in active settings.

Promising students in geometry and measurement may not be the same students who excel in other areas of math. This may be disconcerting for students who are used to being your star math students. They may be embarrassed to realize that they have no idea how tangrams fit together or where the line of symmetry is.

Students with different learning styles may learn from one another when they work in small groups. Try to develop a classroom atmosphere in which students feel free to ask each other for help. Encourage all types of learners to learn from one another. No one learns in strictly one mode, and everyone can improve skills in different areas.

Encourage promising students in geometry and measurement to go further in these areas. Let them combine geometry skills with skills in other subjects (such as art, mechanical drawing, woodworking, metal shop, or home economics) to create new applications for their learning. Students who are adept at tessellating, for example, may wish to study the artwork of Escher and create their own Escher-type drawings. One place to start is at this web site: http://www.auburn.edu/~churcwb/escher.html. The computer program *Shape Up! Deluxe,* available from Sunburst, may motivate student interest in geometry. Students who are good at making scale drawings and at creating three-dimensional models from two-dimensional drawings may wish to make a scale drawing of the classroom and to create a model from a drawing of an ideal classroom.

Another good area for promising students in geometry is that of hypothesizing about geometric relationships. The computer program *The Geometric SuperSupposer* by Schwartz and Yerushalmy, also available from Sunburst, is a good program for such capable students. It helps children explore geometric constructions and hypothesize about such things as the comparative lengths of diagonals of various quadrilaterals or the comparative areas of different types of triangles. In this way, students are encouraged to think like mathematicians—making hypotheses and trying to prove or disprove them. Children may do the same with a compass and straightedge as they learn to make their own constructions.

Another good computer program for promising students is *The Super Factory,* again available from Sunburst. It helps students develop inductive thinking in a visual mode as they design geometric products on a simulated machine assembly line. Programming in *Logo* and exploring using dynamic geometry with such programs as *Geometer's Sketchpad* on a computer or *Cabri Geometry* on a T1-92 are also excellent for students displaying talents in geometric areas.

Students who have difficulty in geometry and measurement may need to be encouraged not to give up. Students may make comments such as, "Tangrams are stupid. I can never do one of those puzzles. Why do we need to do them anyway?" Let these students start with simple tangrams using only two or three pieces or with some of the outlines drawn in and then gradually move on to more difficult puzzles. Be sure to give them tasks at which they can succeed, and let them note their progress.

Discuss with the whole class some of the workers who must have spatial abilities, such as architects, artists, astronauts, construction workers, electricians, engineers, mapmakers, mechanics, plumbers, and surgeons. Above all, make geometry and measurement in the elementary school fun. Create experiences to help students move to the second van Hiele level in order to prepare them for later, more formal work in geometry.

KEY IDEAS

Measuring involves several concepts that need to be constructed by children through a variety of activities. Measuring also involves developing skill in a process that is widely used in our daily lives. Many of the activities presented in this chapter require children to use measurement in the same way they will use measurement outside of school. The teaching sequence suggested using four types of measuring activities: direct comparison, indirect comparison, arbitrary units, and standard units. The topics of measurement include length, area, weight, time, volume, temperature, and angle. Objects used to measure include straws, cubes, and various containers (for arbitrary units) and rulers, balances, clocks, measuring cups, thermometers, and protractors (for standard units).

Developing a sense of measurement units is emphasized. Estimation and problem solving play a prominent role in most of the measurement activities presented. Assessing many of the activities requires you to observe and record how children go about measurement tasks.

DISCUSSION QUESTIONS

1. A variety of measurement concepts have been introduced. After becoming familiar with them—for example, length and distance, weight and mass, time, etc., discuss how you would describe the broader concept of measurement and how you could help students grasp the concept of measurement.

2. Using a geoboard, complete the activities described for the primary and middle grades that focus on area. Then, design five activities of your own that extend those presented. Share the activities with fellow students and help them understand what you have done.

3. Discuss the overriding theme of all of the activities that develop measurement skills. The common elements of

the activities represent the underlying message of teaching measurement.

4. Select a measurement skill such as measuring length, measuring time, or measuring temperature. Write a lesson plan for introducing or reintroducing that skill at grade 3 and at grade 6.

5. Read Billstein's article "You Are Cleared to Land" that is listed in the references for this chapter. Answer the questions that Billstein raises on page 454 of the article. Discuss how this article may be used in a middle-level classroom to interest the students in angle measurement and direction.

REFERENCES

Barson, Alan, *Geoboard Activity Cards (Intermediate)*. Fort Collins, CO: Scott Scientific, 1971.

——————, *Geoboard Activity Cards (Primary)*. Fort Collins, CO: Scott Scientific, 1972.

Billstein, Rick, "You Are Cleared to Land," *Mathematics Teaching in the Middle School,* 3, no. 7 (May 1998), 452–456.

Bitter, Gary G., Jerald L. Mikesell, and Kathryn Maurdeff, *Activities Handbook for Teaching the Metric System*. Boston: Allyn & Bacon, 1976.

Browning, Christine A., and Dwayne E. Channell. *Explorations: Graphing Calculator Activities for Enriching Middle School Mathematics*. Austin, TX: Texas Instruments, 1997.

Dolan, Winthrop W., *A Choice of Sundials*. Brattleboro, VT: S. Greene Press, 1975.

Greer, Gery, and Bob Ruddick, *Max and Me and the Time Machine*. New York: HarperCollins Children's Books, 1983.

Hallamore, Elisabeth, *The Metric Book . . . of Amusing Things to Do*. Woodbury, NY: Barron's Educational Series, 1974.

Harris, Holly, and Sharon Rose Jones, *Eat Your Math*. Corvallis, OR: Callan and Brooks, 1994.

Hiebert, James, "Why Do Some Children Have Trouble Learning Measurement Concepts?" *Arithmetic Teacher,* 31, no. 7 (March 1984), 19–24.

Kaster, Bernice, "The Role of Measurement Applications," *Arithmetic Teacher,* 36, no. 6 (February 1989), 40–46.

Lindquist, Mary Montgomery, "The Measurement Standards," *Arithmetic Teacher,* 36, no. 2 (October 1989), 22–26.

Macken, Walter, *The Flight of the Doves*. New York: Simon & Schuster Books for Young Readers, 1992.

McWhirter, Ross, *The Guinness Book of World Records*. New York: Sterling, 1990.

Mora, Pat, *A Birthday Basket for Tia*. New York: MacMillan, 1992.

Myller, Rolf, *How Big is a Foot?* New York: Atheneum, 1962.

National Council of Teachers of Mathematics, *Curriculum and Evaluation Standards for School Mathematics*. Reston, VA: NCTM, 1989.

Nelson, Doyal, and Robert Reys, eds. *Measurement in School Mathematics*. Reston, VA: National Council of Teachers of Mathematics, 1976.

Piaget, Jean, Barbel Inhelder, and Alina Szemiuska, *The Child's Conception of Geometry*. New York: Basic Books, 1960.

Pollard, Jeanne, *Building Toothpick Bridges*. Palo Alto, CA: Dale Seymour, 1985.

Querin, Tari, "Picture Measuring Tapes," *The Oregon Mathematics Teacher* (May/June 1998), pp. 16–19.

Shaw, Jean, "Mathematical Scavenger Hunts," *Arithmetic Teacher,* 31, no. 7 (March 1984), 9–12.

Shroyer, Janet, and William Fitzgerald, *Mouse and Elephant: Measuring Growth*. Menlo Park, CA: Addison-Wesley, 1986.

Sime, Mary, *A Child's Eye View*. New York: Harper & Row, 1973.

Thompson, Charles S., and John Van deWalle, "Learning About Rules and Measuring," *Arithmetic Teacher,* 32, no. 8 (April 1985), 8–12.

Varma, Ved P., and Phillip Williams, eds. *Piaget, Psychology and Education*. Itasca, IL: F. E. Peacock, 1976.

Welchman-Tischler, Rosamond. *How to Use Children's Literature to Teach Mathematics*. Reston, VA: National Council of Teachers of Mathematics, 1992.

Wilgus, Wendy, and Lisa Pizzuto. *Exploring the Basics of Geometry with Cabri*. Austin, TX: Texas Instruments, 1997.

Technology

Sunburst, *Shape Up! Deluxe*. Pleasantville, NY: Sunburst Communications. (software)

Web Sites

http://www.auburn.edu/~churcwb/escher.html This site presents a gallery of the work of M. C. Escher.

Chapter 14

Introducing Algebra

NCTM Standards

GRADES 5–8

Standard 9: Algebra

In grades 5–8, the mathematics curriculum should include exploration of algebraic concepts and processes so that students can—

- Understand the concepts of variable, expression, and equation;
- Represent situations and number patterns with tables, graphs, verbal rules, and equations and explore the interrelationships of these representations;
- Develop confidence in solving linear equations using concrete, informal, and formal methods;
- Investigate inequalities and nonlinear equations informally;

- Apply algebraic methods to solve a variety of real-world and mathematical problems.

GRADES K–4

Standard 13: Patterns and Relationships

In grades K–4, the mathematics curriculum should include the study of patterns and relationships so that students can—

- Recognize, describe, extend, and create a wide variety of patterns;
- Represent and describe mathematical relationships;
- Explore the use of variables and open sentences to express relationships.

NCTM (1989), p. 102. Reprinted by permission.

Draw an array below that shows $(x + 3)(x + 2)$. Use what you know about arrays for whole numbers and decimals such as 13×12 and 1.3×1.2. Explain how your array shows the product $x^2 + 5x + 6$.

As you read the following pages, consider these guiding questions:

1. What is algebra and why is it important for all students to know?
2. What are some of the algebraic thinking skills and concepts that all elementary students should have to ensure a solid foundation for later algebraic ideas?
3. What are some similarities and differences between operations with whole numbers and operations with integers?
4. How might you model operations with integers using physical materials and examples from children's daily lives?
5. How might graphs on a Cartesian coordinate system be used to give a visual representation of equations and functions?
6. How might graphing calculators and computers be used to facilitate the understanding of translations among words, equations, and graphs?
7. What are some similarities and differences between multiplying whole numbers, fractions, decimals, and factors that include variables? How might you use physical algebra models to illustrate operations with variables?
8. What are some common misconceptions that students learning algebra might have and what might you do to correct these?

One important aspect of teaching middle school mathematics is helping students bridge the gap between the mathematics of elementary school and the mathematics of high school. Frequently, this means helping students make connections between concrete and abstract notions. Algebra is an especially important part of this transition. Through an introduction to algebra, students begin to make the transition from the concrete world of arithmetic to the more formal world of algebra.

We are all familiar with the word *algebra;* most of us probably took an algebra class in high school and perhaps another one in college. How would you define *algebra,* though? Take a few minutes to do this before you move on with your reading.

Algebra is defined in the *Random House Word Menu* as the "theory and practice of arithmetic operations that uses symbols, especially letters, to represent unknown variables in equations" (1992, p. 143). Others define it more simply as generalized arithmetic. In this sense, algebra begins very early in the primary grades as students continue to develop the definition of mathematics in Chapter 1—namely, that mathematics is the science of pattern and order. The informal introduction to algebra in this chapter will continue to build upon the earlier concepts developed through the exploration of patterns. The focus will be on the development of algebraic concepts, with some discussion of practicing skills. The

NCTM *Standards* (1989, p. 71) have called for a decreased emphasis on manipulating symbols, memorizing procedures, and drilling on equation solving when teaching algebra in the middle grades.

An understanding of algebra is increasingly important for success in our technological world, but algebra is frequently neglected in the mathematics curriculum in the United States.

In President Clinton's 1998 *Call to Action for American Education in the 21st Century,* he stated that "All students will master challenging mathematics, including the foundations of algebra and geometry, by the end of 8th grade" (http://www.ed.gov/inits.html#2). An Action Strategy for Improving Achievement in Mathematics and Science from February, 1998, stated that, "In grades 5–8, students should begin to move from mastering the basics of arithmetic to using arithmetic in solving complex problems and learning the foundations of geometry, algebra, probability, and statistics" (http://www.ed.gov/pubs/12TIMSS/SecIV.html).

The Underachieving Curriculum, the report of the Second International Mathematics Study (McKnight, 1987), found that in the United States much of the middle school mathematics curriculum is simply a review of earlier concepts. This is not the case in the rest of the world. For example, nearly one-third of the eighth-grade school year in the United States is spent on fractions, ratio, proportion, and percent, while the Japanese spend only 6 percent of their time on these topics. In the United States, teachers of eighth-grade mathematics report spending about 20 percent of their time teaching algebra, while Japanese teachers spend nearly 37 percent of their time on this topic.

The *Third International Mathematics and Science Study* (Peak, 1996) showed that eighth grade United States students performed at about the international average in algebra (defined as patterns, relations, expressions, and equations), although their performance was below several of the top-scoring countries such as Singapore, Japan, Hong Kong, Korea, the Russian Federation, and the Slovak Republic. This report also showed that topics taught in eighth grade U.S. mathematics classrooms were at a seventh grade level in comparison to other countries. Based on an examination of mathematics textbooks, it was found that especially in nonalgebra classes, there was a preoccupation with arithmetic at the expense of algebra, geometry, and measurement and that even in the algebra classes there was excessive attention to low-level knowledge and skills without sufficient attention to conceptual understanding and complex problem-solving (Silver, 1998, p. 5).

The National Assessment of Educational Progress studies show that students are taking more mathematics courses, but in 1996, 8 percent of 17-year-olds reported that their highest mathematics course taken in high school was general mathematics or prealgebra (http://nces.ed.gov/naep/96report/97986t5.shtml).

Even in high school, students may take a general math course that is another review of elementary school arithmetic. The results are evident from tests such as the Fourth National Assessment of Educational Progress, which showed that only 6 percent of the 17-year-old students in the United States could solve multistep problems, especially if they involved geometry or algebra (Dossey, 1988, p. 16). By 1996, this percent had risen to 7 percent, but was still disturbingly low. (http://nces.ed.gov/naep/96report/97986t2.shtml) Considering the large number of dropouts who left school before taking these tests, the average 17-year-old in the United States probably performs on an even lower level. The achievement of our pre-calculus students is in some cases the lowest in the industrialized world.

The 1996 NAEP study did show some encouraging trends, however. The percent of students who had taken pre-calculus or calculus in high school had risen from 6 percent to 13 percent, and the percent of students whose highest mathematics class in high school was algebra II had risen from 37 percent to 50 percent. (http://nces.ed.gov/naep/96report/97986t5.shtml)

These results led the committee that developed the NCTM *Standards* (1989) to call for an increased emphasis in grades 5–8 on developing an understanding of variables, expressions, and equations, on using a variety of methods to solve linear equations, and on informally investigating inequalities and nonlinear equations. This will also be the emphasis in this chapter. These ideas will be connected to earlier work in grades K–4.

Developing Algebraic Concepts

Patterns and Relationships

In Chapter Five, we discussed early work with patterns and relationships, frequently using examples that did not require the use of numbers. As students build their algebraic thinking skills, these ideas must be expanded to include number patterns and relationships. Beginning in elementary school, students should be asked to generalize patterns and relationships, first in words and later using symbols and algebraic expressions.

One way that this might be done is to build on number stories that are traditionally seen in textbooks. In many cases, these number stories are simply a means to practice skills and algorithms presented in the chapter. For example, a typical skill-oriented number story in a primary math book might say, "Ken has 7 pieces of red candy and 8 pieces of yellow candy. How much candy does he have altogether?" It would be easy to expand this to a more interesting puzzle-type question, such as

"Julia has a bag of candy with only red and yellow candy in it. She has 15 pieces of candy altogether, and there are twice as many pieces of red candy as yellow candy. How many red pieces and how many yellow pieces does Julia have?" Of even more interest for helping students develop a greater understanding of mathematics, especially in the area of patterns and relationships, would be the following question: "Lorena has 15 pieces of candy. Some are red and some are yellow. How many different combinations of red and yellow candy can you find that would give you a total of 15 pieces? How might you convince someone that you have found all the possible combinations?

Several of the activities in this chapter will discuss ways to build from traditional skill-oriented number stories to those that require more complex reasoning and the ability to see patterns and make generalizations. These build on the concept of algebra as generalized arithmetic.

ACTIVITIES

Primary Grades (1–3)

Objective: to identify, describe, and extend patterns involving numerical situations.

1. Read a story involving transportation such as *Curious George Rides a Bicycle,* and ask the children to make a table showing the number of wheels and the number of bicycles such as in Table 14–1.

    Completing the table would be good skill practice, but does not require much complex reasoning. Students might use the constant feature on the calculator to add two each time to complete the second row on the table. To encourage deeper reasoning, ask the children to study the table and describe any patterns they notice. They should fill in the missing numbers on the table and explain how they knew where to put each number.

    After the children have completed the table, ask them to make up a list of questions that could be answered by studying the table. Encourage them to include some questions that would require inferences where the answer is not on the table itself, such as "Would the number 23 appear as the number of

TABLE 14–1

Number of bicycles	1	2		4	5		...	25
Number of wheels	2	4	6			12	...	

TABLE 14–2

Number of tricycles	1	2		4	5		...	25
Number of wheels	3	6	9			18	...	

wheels if the pattern were continued? Why or why not?" Let the children exchange questions with a classmate and try to answer them.

After the children have had experience with the patterns on the table for bicycles, ask them to make a similar chart for tricycles such as Table 14–2.

After the children have completed this chart, comparing it to the chart for the bicycles offers them greater opportunities to search for patterns and make generalizations. Are there any numbers that appear as the number of wheels on the bicycle chart that do not appear on the tricycle chart? Are there any numbers that appear as the number of wheels on the tricycle chart that do not appear on the bicycle chart? How do these numbers compare? What numbers appear on both charts?

Older students might expand this into a study of relatively prime numbers and common multiples. This question could also be expanded to questions such as "I have 25 wheels and they are all on either bicycles or tricycles. How many of each cycle might I have?" Children are often surprised to find that this question has several correct answers. Asking students to develop a method of finding all the combinations of bicycles and tricycles that have a total of 25 wheels gives them an opportunity to use an organized list or another strategy that involves patterns and predictions.

Encourage students who have a good understanding of patterns and generalizations to create other questions of their own such as: "What if we also look at the number of wheels on a car (or a unicycle)? Do we get the same answers to the earlier questions? Why or why not? How many combinations of vehicles are possible for 25 wheels if they can be cars, unicycles, bicycles, or tricycles?"

Objective: to identify, describe, and extend patterns involving money.

2. ⟦📖⟧ A typical number story that you might see in a book shows four dimes and three pennies and asks students to find the total amount of money. To make this problem more interesting and to encourage deeper reasoning, use a book involving money such as *A Chair for My Mother* or *How the Second Grade Got $8,205.50 to Visit the Statue of Liberty,* and then pose a problem that encourages students to look for patterns. One such problem is: "I have 43 cents in my

pocket. I have only dimes and pennies. What coins might I have?" If the children have done the previous problem, they might expect that again there are several correct answers. If children come up with only one possibility, you might suggest that they search for others. Challenge them to find all the possibilities. One of the ways that they might do this is by using a chart such as the following:

Dimes	Pennies	Total
0	43	43¢
1	33	43¢
2	23	43¢
3	13	43¢

After children have analyzed the chart and have made some predictions about the total number of combinations possible, encourage them to ask other related questions. If they have trouble getting started, use some of the question starters suggested in Chapter 3 for encouraging students to dig more deeply into problems such as why, why not, what if, and will that always work? In this case, students might notice that as the number of dimes decreases by 1, the number of pennies increases by 10 and ask if that will always be the case. They can then discuss why that will happen. Other questions students might ask include: What would happen to the number of combinations if there were nickels as well as dimes and pennies? What if there were also quarters? What if there were 48 cents or 97 cents?

What if you know I have 5 coins? What is the least amount of money I might have? What is the greatest amount? How many different combinations of money might I have?

What if I have 5 coins and 33 cents; how many possible combinations of coins might I have? Why is there only one possible combination of coins for this problem?

Encourage students to write their questions and then trade with their friends to solve them. Ask them to discuss the patterns that they noticed and the strategies that they used in their problem solving.

Intermediate and Middle Grades (4–8)

Objective: to identify, describe, and extend patterns and make generalizations using money.

1. Older students also need experience working with money. A typical problem for intermediate students might give them the price of several objects and ask them to find the total price such as: "Dan has decided to buy tops, toy planes, and/or stuffed animals for the school fair. He must spend according to the following prices:

Tops	$ .50 apiece
Toy planes	$ 1.00 apiece
Stuffed animals	$10.00 apiece

If he buys 15 tops, 35 planes, and 50 stuffed animals, how much will he spend?"

A problem that would encourage deeper reasoning and lead to generalizations would be the following: "Latisha has exactly $100 to buy toys for the local children's charity and wants to buy exactly 100 toys. She has decided to buy tops, toy planes, and/or stuffed animals. She must spend according to the following prices:

Tops	$ .50 apiece
Toy planes	$ 1.00 apiece
Stuffed animals	$10.00 apiece

What combinations might she buy?

Notice that this problem required only a slight change from the earlier problem but encourages far more reasoning and generalizations. Ask the students to find more than one answer to this. If they can do that, ask them to find all possible solutions and to convince you that no others are possible. Put these solutions in a chart and look for patterns. What generalizations might be made? What other questions might be asked to further extend this problem?

Objective: to extend and generalize proportional reasoning.

2. Students learning concepts of proportional reasoning might be asked to solve number stories such as "Sue can buy gum at 8 pieces for 3 cents and candy at 5 pieces for 2 cents. How much will it cost to buy 24 pieces of gum and 10 pieces of candy?" A problem that would require deeper reasoning is the following: "Chris and Tyler are pricing small wrapped candy. At the first store, they can get 8 pieces of candy for 3 cents. At the second store, they can get 5 pieces of the same candy for 2 cents. Which store has the better buy?" As students develop a variety of methods for solving the second problem, their understanding of proportional reasoning grows. One student may divide 8 by 3 and 5 by 2 to find the number of pieces of candy per cent. Another may divide 3 by 8 and 2 by 5 to find the number of cents per pieces of candy. Another may find how much of each type of candy could be bought for 6 cents. Yet another may find the price of 40 pieces of candy at each store. For problems such as this, students should be asked to compare and discuss a variety of methods and then asked to generalize their findings to other proportional reasoning problems. Other common proportional reasoning problems involve finding the best paying job per hour when rates are given for varying amounts of time or finding the best car mileage or the best crop yield when given yields and

dimensions of fields. In each of these problems, the same methods used to solve the candy problem can be generalized and discussed in the new setting.

Integers and Their Operations

One topic that is crucial to the understanding of later work in algebra is the study of integers. Fremont (1969, p. 203) stated, "Everything that is done in any future work in algebra will involve using these new numbers and using them with ease. Our start in this area should be unhurried and as meaningful as we can make it." This is as true today as it was over 30 years ago. Students need to understand the meaning of negative numbers and why they function as they do, and not just memorize rules for their operations. It may take longer for students to develop a conceptual understanding of negative numbers than to just memorize the rules, but the goal of operations with integers is understanding, not rule memorization. If you recall the hierarchy of goals in Chapter 3, you will remember that the "doers"—those who can remember rules but do not understand the mathematics—are toward the bottom of the diagram. You want students who understand the mathematics; the calculator knows the rules.

Even young children should be familiar with negative numbers from, for example, scores in games, temperatures, losing or borrowing money, being below sea level, and perhaps reports on the stock market. They may have encountered negative numbers on a number line when they explored what happens if you subtract 5 from 3; the answer is found to the left of zero on the number line. Danny, a first-grader, learned about negative numbers quite well when he borrowed a dollar to buy an action figure and then had to pay it back out of his allowance a week later.

ACTIVITIES

Intermediate Grades (2–4)

Objective: to become acquainted with integers on a number line.

1. Make a large number line on the floor with masking tape, placing zero in the center. Make the numerals to the right of the zero in blue and the numerals to the left of zero in red. Explain to the children that these numerals represent distances in blocks east (blue numerals) and blocks west (red numerals) from City Hall in Anytown, U.S.A. (see Figure 14–1). (You can use landmarks in your own town for this activity.) Place a picture or model of City Hall on zero and place

Figure 14–1

pictures or models of other buildings or landmarks on the red and blue numerals. Pose questions to the students such as "How many blocks is it from school to the zoo?" and "If you start at the library and go five blocks east, where are you?" This activity can later be linked to integers by designating movement toward the east as adding, movement toward the west as subtracting, blue numerals as positive, and red numerals as negative. For example, the question "If the zoo is on the blue five and you go seven blocks west, where are you?" corresponds to the equation $5 - 7 = n$. You would land on the red 2 (-2), which may be the location of the drug store. Encourage the students to make up similar problems for each other. Younger children do not need to worry about writing equations for their situations, but you may wish to ask third- or fourth-graders to begin to use the integer notation. The important thing at this stage is for students to have a concrete understanding of integers.

Objective: to use a calculator to predict patterns involving integers.

2. Give each child a calculator and let him or her explore using the constant feature. You might begin with addition. Start by pressing $3 + 4 = = = =$. Ask the children to explain what is happening. Do they notice that the calculator adds 4 each time they press "equals"? Encourage them to predict the next number before they press "equals." After they are comfortable with addition, try $12 - 3 = = = = =$. Again, ask the children to explain what is occurring. Can they continue to predict the next number when the results are negative? Let the children work with a partner to explore other patterns. Third- and fourth-grade students should be asked to write down any generalizations they can make about adding or subtracting integers.

Middle Grades (5–8)

Objective: to add and multiply integers on a number line.

1. Make a large vertical number line (see Figure 14–2) that resembles a thermometer for the following number-line problems. As with all new concepts, negative numbers should be introduced using con-

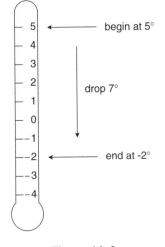

Figure 14–2

cepts with which the children are already familiar. Temperature is an area in which students in many parts of the country have already experienced negative numbers, and therefore, it makes a good model for beginning experiences with integers. This can be used to find the difference in two temperatures such as the difference between 4 degrees and -2 degrees. This difference of 6 degrees corresponds to the equation $4 - (-2) = 6$. The thermometer is also useful when you ask the students to begin at 5 degrees and determine the temperature after a drop of 7 degrees $(5 + (-7) = -2)$. Begin at -4 degrees and determine the temperature after an increase of 8 degrees $(-4 + 8 = 4)$. A future time may be indicated by a positive number and a time in the past by a negative number. If the temperature drops steadily at a rate of 5 degrees per hour and the temperature is now 0 degrees, what will the temperature be in 3 hours? $(3 \times -5 = -15)$ What was the temperature 4 hours ago? $[(-4) \times (-5) = 20]$ Ask the students to make up other questions for each other and to demonstrate solutions on the number line. After the students have worked several problems, ask them if they have discovered any patterns in their work. Keep a written record of the rules the children discover in a prominent place in the classroom. One of the first rules the children should discover is that of the **additive in-**

verse. That is, the sum of any number and its opposite is zero; these opposites are called additive inverses. For example, 1 and −1 are additive inverses because $1 + (-1) = 0$ and $(-1) + 1 = 0$. Rules for operating with integers will be needed all year (and for several years to come) as students work with signed numbers, not only for integers, but also for rational numbers and algebraic expressions.

As with all concepts, it is useful to experience algebraic concepts in a number of different contexts. Another real-life situation involving integers is Danny's experience borrowing money.

Objective: to add, subtract, multiply, and divide integers using discrete objects.

2. Each child will need a handful of Bingo chips of two different colors for the following activities. This example uses blue and red chips. Set up a bank using blue chips for positive amounts ($) and red chips for negative amounts (IOUs). If you earn $2, you take two blue chips. This adds a positive amount to your account. If you owe $3, you take 3 red chips. This adds a negative amount to your account. If you buy a toy for $5, you take away 5 blue chips, thus subtracting a positive amount from your account. If you pay off a debt, you subtract IOUs or red chips, a negative amount, from your account. For example, Danny normally gets an allowance of $1 each week (adding a positive amount). The week he paid off his debt, instead of receiving $1 and adding it to his negative $1 for a net total of zero, his debt of $1 was taken away, again leaving him with a net total of zero. Therefore, subtracting a negative amount had the same outcome as adding a positive amount. Here are some problems to try with the chips.

   a. Julie has $5. She owes Sam $2. What is her net worth? The number sentence is $5 + (-2) =$ _____. She has $5 and adds a $2 IOU. Take 5 blue chips for the positive $5 and 2 red chips for the IOU. Each red chip can be added to a blue chip, its additive inverse, to make $0. When the zeros are taken away, what is left? Three blue chips or a positive $3 (see Figure 14–3).

   b. Jorge owes his dad $6. His father tells Jorge that he will take away $5 of the debt if Jorge rakes the yard. How much will Jorge have or owe after he rakes the yard? The number sentence is $-6 - (-5) =$ _____. He has a $6 debt and his father will

Figure 14–4

take away a $5 debt. Take 6 red chips for the −6. When his father takes away the $5 debt, he will take 5 of the red chips. One red chip is left, signifying a debt to his father of $1 (see Figure 14–4).

   c. What if Jorge decides the following week to again rake the yard when he is only $1 in debt? If his father again agrees to take away a $5 debt, how much will he have or owe? The number sentence is $-1 - (-5) =$ _____. He has a $1 debt and his father will take away a $5 debt. You start with one red chip to signify the $1 debt. Immediately you recognize that you have a problem; you do not have 5 red chips for Jorge's father to take away. You remember that a positive chip and a negative chip add to zero. You decide to add several zeros to the −1. You can add as many zeros as you want without changing the value of the chips, −1. Since you only need 5 red chips for Jorge's father to take away, you decide to add 4 zeros—4 blue chips and 4 red chips. You now have a total of 5 red chips and 4 blue chips. Verify that the chips still have a value of −1. Now you can take away 5 red chips. What is left? The 4 blue chips, signifying a positive $4. Jorge now has $4 (see Figure 14–5).

   d. Marta has $4. She wants to buy a used video game for $9. How much will she owe if she buys the game? The number sentence is $4 - 9 =$ _____. Start with 4 blue chips to signify the $4 she has to begin with. You immediately recognize that to spend $9 you need to take away 9 blue chips and you do not have enough blue chips. Again, you add zeros to your starting amount of 4 blue chips. This time you add 5 zeros—5 red chips and 5 blue chips—to your starting amount of 4 blue chips. At this point, you have 9 blue chips and 5 red chips. You take away the 9 blue chips to pay for the video game, and you are left with 5 red chips, or a debt of $5.

   Ask the students to make up similar problems of their own. After they have worked several problems, they will probably not want to use the chips any more. Encourage the students to just write the equation for the problem and then explain to

Figure 14–3

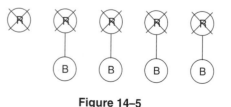

Figure 14–5

each other (and you) how they would go about solving it. Remember that it is the method and not the answer that you are interested in here. After the students have worked several problems, ask them if they notice any patterns. Can they generate any rules? What happens if you subtract a negative number? Is the result always the same as that of adding a positive number? Students will find that this is true. They should also notice that subtracting a positive number has the same result as adding a negative number.

After working several problems involving addition and subtraction of integers, try some problems involving multiplication and division of integers. Again, a time in the future should be represented by a positive number and a time in the past by a negative number. Having a debt of $3 for five weeks in a row can be thought of as $5 \times (-3) = \underline{\hspace{1cm}}$. You would add 3 red chips every week for five weeks. Asking how your finances stood five weeks ago relative to today after this five weeks of debt would be $(-5) \times (-3) = \underline{\hspace{1cm}}$. You would have to start at some representation of zero and take away 3 red chips five times to find the answer.

Because division is the inverse operation of multiplication, the problem $15 \div (-3) = \underline{\hspace{1cm}}$ can be thought of as the inverse of the problem above. When would you have $15 more than you have today if you add a debt of $3 each week? You know that if you continue to add the debt of $3 every week into the future, you will always have less money than you have today. You cannot go into the future; that is, the number of weeks cannot be positive. To have more money when you add a debt every week, you must go into the past. Therefore, $15 \div (-3)$ must equal -5, representing 5 weeks ago. After working several multiplication and division problems with the students, ask them to note any patterns and to generate rules for multiplying and dividing integers. They should notice that multiplying or dividing two negative integers has the same result as multiplying or dividing two positive integers; when multiplying or dividing a positive integer by a negative integer or a negative integer by a positive integer, the result will always be negative.

Objective: to use everyday situations to create integer word problems.

3. Encourage the students to make up several problems of their own using integers. Be on the alert for other types of real-life situations involving positive and negative amounts. You might want to follow the ups and downs of the stock market for experience with posi-

tive and negative rational numbers. Looking at gains and losses of yardage on the football field makes for some interesting problems. What happens if a penalty of 5 yards is taken away (subtracting a negative number)? Does this have the same effect as a gain of 5 yards? Keep the students' problems in the learning center for other students to work on or put them on worksheets and use them instead of the examples in the textbook.

Functions, Variables, Equations, and Inequalities

A **function** is defined as a rule or process that sets up a correspondence between a first set (the **domain**) and a second set (the **range**) such that each element in the first set corresponds with *one and only one* element in the second set. Notice that this is not necessarily a one-to-one correspondence. A statement such as $y = x^2$ is a function of x, but it is not a function of y. For each x, there is one and only one y, but there are 2 x's for each y. For example, for $x = -3$, the only y is 9, but for $y = 9$, there are two possible x's, $x = 3$ and $x = -3$.

In Chapter 7, we used an input-output machine to demonstrate the concept of an operation. In algebra, we build on that concept to further develop the concept of a function. We then relate using the function machine to using tables, equations, and graphs so that students can broaden their concept of a function.

ACTIVITIES

Primary Grades (1–4)

Objective: to develop the concept of a function through the use of an input-output machine.

1. Guess My Rule is played by pairs of students using the input-output machine described in earlier chapters and the attribute blocks. Ask one student to be in charge of placing blocks in the input of the machine and ask the second student to think of a secret rule, such as "change only the color of the block." After the first student places a block in the input of the machine, the second student finds a block that fits his or her rule and places this block in the output of the machine. Try this several times, until the first student can guess the secret rule. Discuss whether more than one output was possible for each input. Ask the students to trade roles and make up a new rule. Was more than one output possible this time?

   After playing the game with attribute blocks, play Guess My Rule with numbers and operations.

Calculators are also useful in this activity. Students may place numeral cards in the input and output. The first student should choose a numeral card to place in the input while the second student decides on a secret rule. Begin with rules that use only one operation. The second student should place the numeral card that shows the result of the operation in the output. Do this several times, until the first student can guess the secret rule. Again, discuss whether more than one output was possible for each input. Ask the children to trade roles and choose another rule. Encourage them to discuss how they determined the rule each time.

Objective: to explore functions on the computer.

2. Use a computer game such as *Jane Plus* from Longman to give students the opportunity to beat the computer at a game of Guess My Rule. In *Jane Plus,* the computer uses stick figures of boys and girls on the screen to indicate a rule such as "add 5" or "multiply by 2." The boys always indicate addition and the girls indicate multiplication. You may use either one or two operations. The game is played in the same manner as Guess My Rule. Because the operations are limited to addition and multiplication, the answer will be a whole number if the input is a whole number. Therefore, this game can be played by younger students. You can also modify the calculator game to restrict the operations in the same way. Other computer programs that ask students to determine the rule for a function include *The King's Rule* and *Teasers by Tobbs,* both by Thomas O'Brien. Another of his problem solving programs, *Puzzle Tanks,* requires that students find the correct amounts of tank trucks to fill or empty tanks to reach a target amount. This program is available for hand-held calculators as well as computers.

Middle Grades (5–8)

Objective: to develop the concept of a function through the use of a function machine and a table.

3. Draw a function machine and a table for recording inputs and outputs as in Figure 14–6 on an overhead

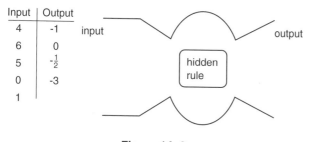

Input	Output
4	-1
6	0
5	$-\frac{1}{2}$
0	-3
1	

Figure 14–6

transparency and put the transparency on the overhead projector for the students to use. Ask one student to write down a secret rule for the function machine on the transparency. Keep the rule hidden.

You may wish to begin with a rule involving only one operation, such as "subtract 7," but the activity becomes much more challenging if you allow more than one operation per rule, such as "subtract 7 and then multiply by 2." The other students will attempt to guess the rule by determining what happens when different numbers are put into the function machine. This is a good activity for using calculators. After the secret function has been written on the function machine and covered, the other students name an input, which is then written on the chart by the student with the secret rule. This student then puts the input into the calculator, performs the function, and records the output on the chart. This continues for several different inputs until the other students are confident that they know the secret rule. To avoid giving away the secret rule too early, when a student believes that he or she knows the rule, that student should predict the output for a given input, but not tell the rule. When most students can predict the output for a given input, ask the first student who predicted the output to tell the rule. If correct, this student is the next one to write a secret function. Figure 14–6 shows the inputs and outputs for the rule "divide by 2 and then subtract 3." Notice that if the game allows division and subtraction, you will frequently have outputs that are integers and other rational numbers, even if all the inputs are whole numbers.

The use of variables is another concept vital to the understanding of algebra. Algebra is often thought of by students as the area of mathematics that uses a lot of letters instead of numbers. These letters, however, are often not very well understood. Today, we generally use the term **variable** to mean a symbol for an element in a replacement set. This frequently does involve using a letter to stand for a number, but letters may also refer to points in geometry such as $\overline{AB} = \overline{BC}$, propositions in logic such as $p \wedge q$, or a matrix in algebra. The symbol used may not even be a letter. For example, $3 + x = 7$, $3 + \square = 7$, and $3 + ? = 7$ all have the same meaning, but the variable changes from x to $\square$ to ?. In this context, students have been studying variables since they began to work with symbols and operations. Primary and intermediate-level teachers should begin to use n or x to acquaint students with the idea of a variable and to help make the bridge to algebra, which formalizes these concepts. It is important that students in the middle grades continue to have many informal experiences with variables and begin to learn more formal symbolization.

Adding and Multiplying

LESSON 1.9
Adding and Multiplying

You will need:
the Lab Gear

ADDITION

Using the Lab Gear, the addition $y + 5$ can be modeled in two ways. You can show two collections of blocks, y and 5. Or you can line up the blocks to get a figure that has length $y + 5$. Both methods are shown here.

1. Sketch this addition both ways, $3x + 2$.

MULTIPLICATION

The multiplication $3 \cdot (2x + 1)$ can be modeled in two ways. One way is to show three collections of $2x + 1$.

As you can see in the figure, $3 \cdot (2x + 1) = 6x + 3$.

The other way is to use the corner piece. First set up the factors (3 and $2x + 1$) on the outside.

Then make a rectangle having those dimensions.

The rectangle represents the product. Again you see that $3 \cdot (2x + 1) = 6x + 3$. This is the familiar *length · width = area* formula for a rectangle.

2. Sketch this multiplication two ways, $2 \cdot (x + 3)$.
 a. Use collections of blocks.
 b. Use the corner piece.

3. What were the length, width, and area of the rectangle in problem 2?

▼ 1.9
Adding and Multiplying

Core Sequence: the whole lesson

Suitable for Homework: 14
(Problems 15-22 could be done at home, using sketches. But it would be better to assign the Pentomino Strips investigation from Lesson 7, the Domino Problem from Lesson 8, or the Word Figures material from Lesson 11 for homework, so the students will have the Lab Gear within reach when working on this lesson.)

What this Lesson is About:
• Lab Gear models for addition and multiplication (when no minus signs are involved)
• Order of operations
• Common algebra mistakes

ADDITION
MULTIPLICATION

*H*ow to model addition and multiplication was implied in previous chapters. Here it is addressed explicitly. Other operations will be discussed in Chapter 2.

*N*otice that there are two approaches: one based on collections of blocks, and another based on a careful rectangular arrangement of the blocks. Neither model works in every situation, and both should be mastered by students.

Figure 14–7 From Anita Wah and Henri Picciotto, *Algebra.* Mountain View, CA: Creative Publications, 1994, p. 27. Reprinted by permission.

Math Program

The page shown in Figure 14–7 involves the students in the use of the Algebra Lab Gear as they learn two ways to model addition and multiplication. The Lab Gear is used throughout this program as students learn to work with equations and inequalities.

This book is based on three "big ideas": (1) students need tools to think with; (2) learning mathematics should be based on solving interesting problems; and (3) students must be involved in their own learning and have experience with ideas in many forms over an extended period of time. Even though the title of this book is *Algebra,* it integrates a great deal of geometry, measurement, number theory, data analysis, and mathematical modeling. This book may be used as a one- or two-year algebra or pre-algebra course or may be used as part of a two-year combined algebra and geometry course if supplemented with other geometry work.

The book suggests a number of projects and research topics that would make good portfolio entries. These require some independent thinking on the part of the students. In addition, at the end of every four lessons, there is a Thinking/Writing lesson in which students must reflect on what they have learned and write a report. Six themes occur throughout the book: dimensions, measurement, making comparisons, growth and change, optimization, and motion. These may draw ideas from real-world problems and give students a chance to explore, develop, and review mathematical concepts. Connections both within mathematics and to other academic subjects are stressed throughout the book. The work with the Algebra Lab Gear is a natural extension of work with base ten blocks. It includes the use of two variables and three dimensions, making it possible to represent such amounts as y^3 and x^2y.

This activity follows a lesson in which students are pricing drapes and determining the best ways to cover windows of a certain size, given a budget within which students must work. They must decide between window-length and full-length drapes for 10 windows and work with a given price per square foot of drapes. The work with the Lab Gear builds on the multiplication concepts that are explored in finding the area of the windows and drapes. Following this lesson with the Lab Gear are lessons on the use of the Lab Gear to factor and to find volume. This is followed by an investigation using polycubes to maximize and minimize volume and surface area. These rich investigations occur throughout the book.

A symbol or variable may stand for one or more numbers, which are called the values of the variable. The term *variable* may be used to mean a symbol that may have *two* or more values during a particular discussion, such as $area = l \cdot w$, thus the concept of variance underlying the term variable. However, a variable may have only one value and students may have difficulty understanding why the c in $5c = 20$ is called a variable when the only amount it can stand for to make this a true statement is 4.

Another difficulty that students may have in working with variables is that they frequently think of a variable as a letter that stands for one particular number. If they see $2s + 5 = 9$ and $2c + 5 = 9$, they think that the s and the c must stand for different numbers. They may believe that it is all right to use l to stand for length and w to stand for width, but you cannot use t to stand for length. The variable t must stand for time, or turkeys, or tubas, or tambourines, but not length or width or dogs.

Students are introduced to variables when they learn simple computer programming languages such as *BASIC,* and they are sometimes confused. Variables may have different forms, and they may be written in several different ways. For example, two versions of a program that accepts the length and width of a rectangle and returns the area of the rectangle are shown below. Two programs may appear different yet perform in the same way when run on a computer.

```
10  PRINT "ENTER LENGTH"
20  INPUT LENGTH
30  PRINT "ENTER WIDTH"
40  INPUT WIDTH
50  PRINT "AREA ="; LENGTH*WIDTH
60  PRINT "WANT TO TRY AGAIN? (Y OR N)"
70  INPUT ANSWER$
80  IF ANSWER$ = "N" THEN 100
90  GOTO 10
100 END
```

```
10  PRINT "ENTER LENGTH"
20  INPUT L
30  PRINT "ENTER WIDTH"
40  INPUT W
50  LET A = L*W
60  PRINT "AREA ="; A
70  PRINT "TRY AGAIN? (Y OR N)"
80  INPUT R$
90  IF R$ = "N" THEN 110
100 GOTO 10
110 END
```

Notice that the variables for length, width, and area are different in each program but do the same work. A variable may be represented by a single letter such as L or by a series of letters such as LENGTH. The variable for the answer, ANSWER$ or R$, is a different type of variable that accepts symbols rather than numbers.

These misconceptions about using variables emphasize the importance of giving students a number of different experiences with variables in the middle grades so that they can build their own concepts. Just as a toddler may not understand that potatoes may be mashed, baked, or french fried and still remain potatoes, students in the middle grades need to experience variables in many different contexts before they begin to understand all the ways variables can be used.

As students learn about variables and their uses, it is a good time to introduce the concepts of Cartesian coordinates and graphing. Since graphing equations is a very important means of visualizing the data being represented, elementary students should be familiar with plotting points on Cartesian coordinates before they need to use them to graph equations. The following activities are designed to familiarize students with this concept.

One area of mathematics in which graphing may be practiced now is graphing equations. This will be a very useful skill later in algebra.

ACTIVITIES

Intermediate Grades (3–5)

Objective: to reinforce the skill of plotting points on a Cartesian coordinate graph.

1. After children have learned to use ordered pairs of numbers to locate points, they may practice by using points to draw a picture. If you put a dot on each of the following points on a Cartesian coordinate system and connect the dots in order, you will make the picture shown in Figure 14–8: (0,6), (3,4), (4,5), (5,4), (8,6), (7,1), (5,2), (4,1), (3,2), (1,1).

   Have the children draw their own pictures and then list the points for the other children to use.

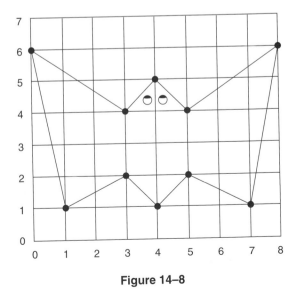

Figure 14–8

Objective: to graph linear equations by plotting points.

2. Use information children may encounter as consumers or in other subjects as a basis for data to be graphed. For example, you may see an advertisement for corn at 15¢ per ear. Tell the children you want to make a graph to help you find the price of any number of ears. Show the children how to make a table that shows the number of ears of corn purchased and the total price. Figure 14–9 shows a table and the corresponding line graph for the data on the corn.

If n stands for the number of ears of corn and T stands for the total price, the equation $T = \$.15n$ can be written to show the relationship between the price and the number of ears of corn. A spreadsheet such as *Cruncher* or *MS Works* might be used to help students make a table of cost per ear versus total cost. Students can experiment with changing a variable such as cost per ear or adding other factors such as the prices of other fruits or vegetables. If corn is 15¢ per ear and lettuce is 90¢ per head, how many different ways could you spend exactly $3 on corn and lettuce? A spreadsheet lets you explore this and many related questions. Articles by Edwards and Bitter (1989) and Edwards, Bitter, and Hatfield (1990) give you some ideas to get started.

Suggest that the children make up other graphs of their own. Can they write the equations for each other's graphs if they have not seen the original data?

Can they add additional pairs to the table by looking at the graph? Ask the children how this work relates to the work with proportions, which were discussed in Chapter 9. Children now have an additional method of solving proportions.

Computer programs such as *Tabletop* from Broderbund, *Cruncher* from Davidson, *Data Toolkit* and *Graph Links* from Harcourt Brace, and *Green Globs and Graphing Equations* by Sharon Dugdale and David Kibbey, available from Sunburst, can give the students additional practice in writing equations and graphing. Graphing calculators are also an excellent tool for the exploration of graphing equations for middle grades students, as in Figure 14–10. Using a graphing calculator, you can very quickly see the effects of raising the price of an ear of corn to 25¢, or you could plot two graphs to determine the number of ears of corn you could buy for $1.35. Students can explore with graphing calculators to determine when and why a slope changes or a graph shifts to the right or left.

Corn	Prices
ears of corn	total price
1	$.15
2	$.30
3	$.45
n	$.15 n

Figure 14–9

a.

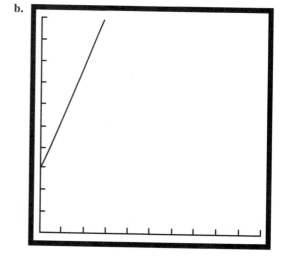

$$Y1 = 2X + 3$$
$$Y2 =$$
$$Y3 =$$
$$Y4 =$$

b.

Figure 14–10

ACTIVITIES

Middle Grades (6–8)

Objective: to use a graphing calculator and Calculator Based Laboratories (CBL™) or Calculator Based Ranger (CBR™) to analyze various types of graphs.

1. Set up a CBL™ or CBR™ attached to a graphing calculator. (If you have never done this, you might want to consult one of the books in the reference list.) Show the students the four graphs in Figure 14–11 and explain that they are going to reproduce the graphs by walking toward or away from the motion detector. Before actually trying this, ask the students to try to determine where to start, how fast to move, and when to stand still. Ask for volunteers to try to match the graphs. If you have an overhead projection screen for the calculator, the class can help the volunteer out by giving suggestions as he or she walks. Discuss the importance of analyzing the slopes and direction of the graphs.

Notice that these graphs plot time on the x-axis and distance on the y-axis. What happens if the y-axis is speed instead of distance? How will that change the shape of the graphs?

Objective: to use variables with functions and graphs.

2. Repeat the activity described earlier with the function machine, using variables instead of the terms *input* and *output* on the chart. The most common variables used are x for the input and y for the output. The function in the previous activity, where the rule was "divide by 2 and then subtract 3," would be written as $y = \frac{x}{2} - 3$. Ask the students to explore whether that is the same as the function $y = \frac{(x-3)}{2}$. How do the graphs differ? Encourage the students to graph several functions, and then ask them if the function graph was always a line. Can they think of a function whose graph would not be a line?

Figure 14–11

Objective: to explore order of operations on different calculators.

3. Use different calculators to determine if you always get the same answer when working out equations. Try equations such as $3 + 4 \times 2 = $ ___ and $2 + 3 \div 4 = $ ___. Discuss with the students the difference between calculators that work the exercise in the order in which you put in the numbers and ones that use algebraic logic. If you have parentheses on your calculator, explore what happens when you use them. When using algebraic logic, you first compute the operations inside parentheses, beginning with the innermost parentheses, then you compute exponents, then you multiply and divide from left to right, and finally you add and subtract from left to right. This is called the **order of operations.**

Students might wish to continue the development of the concept of order of operations by playing *How the West Was One + Three × Four* by Bonnie Seiler.

The order of operations is important to students not only for work with rational numbers, but also for simplifying algebraic expressions and solving equations. An **algebraic expression** is a symbolic form involving constants, variables, operations, and grouping symbols such as parentheses. Two or more algebraic expressions joined by addition or subtraction are called **terms,** and two or more algebraic expressions joined by multiplication or division are called **factors.** If two or more algebraic expressions containing at least one variable are joined by an equal sign, it is called an **algebraic equation.**

The understanding of variables, expressions, and equations is one of the areas on which the NCTM *Standards* recommend an increased emphasis. Again, this understanding should be developed using concrete and pictorial materials. The graphs used above with functions can be expanded to further explore equations.

ACTIVITIES

Middle Grades (5–8)

Objective: to explore the effects of changing amounts in equations using Cartesian graphs.

1. Begin with the equation $y = x$, and make a table of values such as the following:

x	y
2	2
5	5
−1	−1
0	0
$\frac{1}{2}$	

Ask the students to graph this equation using a Cartesian coordinate system. Now try the equation $y = 2x$. Make a table of values and then graph this equation on the same graph. Ask the students to make predictions for the graphs of $y = 3x$ and $y = \frac{1}{2}x$. Make a table of values for these equations and then graph them on the same graph. What do you notice? What happens to the slope as the coefficient of x changes? Encourage the students to ask other questions about the graph, such as what happens if the slope is negative? What if you add some value to the equation as in $y = x + 2$? Is the graph still a line? What has happened to the line?

Objective: to explore the graphs of linear equations using a graphics calculator.

2. Try the previous activity, this time using a graphing calculator. You will not need to begin with the chart of values. Put the calculator in the graph mode and ask for the graph of $y = x$. Then ask for the graphs of $y = 2x$, $y = 3x$, $y = -2x$, and $y = \frac{1}{2}x$ on the same graph. What do you notice? What is the effect of a negative coefficient of x? What happens as the coefficient gets larger? What happens if you add a constant to the equation? Can you make a graph that is nonlinear?

Algebra blocks are another material that can be used for the development of algebra concepts. They give the students a good picture of the concept, are related to earlier concepts learned with whole and rational numbers, and can be manipulated to determine answers to a variety of situations.

Algebra blocks can be purchased commercially, as *Hands On Equations, Algebra Lab Gear, Algeblocks,* or *Algebra Tiles,* or constructed out of railroad board. A master for algebra blocks is included in Appendix B. This set may be used with the large square having dimensions of x by x for an area of x^2, the medium-sized rectangle having dimensions of x by 1 for an area of x, and the small square having dimensions of 1 by 1 for an area of 1. You may change the representations so that the small square has dimensions of y by y for an area of y^2, which would then give the rectangle dimensions of y by x for an area of xy. Changing the values of the squares helps the students realize the variable nature of algebra. As you do the activities in this section, relate the work with the algebra blocks to the earlier work with base ten blocks. Earlier, the large square had dimensions of 10 by 10 for an area of 100, the rectangle had dimensions of 10 by 1 for an area of 10, and the small square had dimensions of 1 by 1 for an area of 1. When we moved to decimals, the large square represented 1, the rectangle 0.1, and the small square 0.01.

Figure 14–12 shows the representation for $3x^2 + 4x + 2$ if the large square is x^2, the rectangle x, and the small square 1. Using the representation in which the small square is y^2, Figure 14–12 represents $3x^2 + 4xy + 2y^2$.

Students should also practice drawing graphs from a story such as a story about Nathan who is late to school and must run to get to school on time. If the students draw a graph with time on the horizontal axis and speed on the vertical axis, the graph will not be the same as one with time on the horizontal axis and distance on the vertical axis. Students in the middle grades should discuss the effects of such things as running at a fast, steady pace; speeding up; slowing down; stopping for traffic; and running at a slow, steady pace on both types of graphs.

ACTIVITIES

Middle Grades (5–8)

Objective: to introduce concrete models for algebraic expressions.

1. Ask the students to each construct a set of algebra blocks using the master from Appendix B. The blocks may be made of either railroad board or laminated construction paper. It is helpful to make one set out of different colored construction paper to represent positive numbers and one set out of red construction paper to represent negative numbers. The *Algebra Tiles for the Overhead Projector* by Howden, available from Cuisenaire Co., have blue x^2s, green xs, and yellow 1s. All of the negatives are red in that set.

Ask the students to use the blocks to show a variety of expressions. Begin by adding positive amounts. You might show $3x^2 + 2x + 5$, $4x^2 + 3x + 2$, and so on. After the students are comfortable with this activity, ask them to show negative amounts as well as positive amounts. Try $3x^2 + (-2x) + (-2)$. This might also be written as $3x^2 - 2x - 2$. After the students can represent amounts using the xs, tell them that they can use any letters to name the dimensions of the rectangles. Let them choose other letters for the dimensions and then tell you what the tiles represent. For example, Figure 14–13 shows $3z^2 - 4zw + 2w^2$ if the dimensions of the large square are z by z and those of the small square are w by w.

Objective: to use algebra blocks to simplify expressions involving additive inverses.

2. Remind students of the rules they developed for additive inverses with integers. Ask them to predict what $x + (-x)$ should be. Work this problem with the blocks. Use the blocks to show zero in a variety of ways. Figure 14–14 shows a few examples.

After the students are comfortable showing zero with the blocks, ask them to put down any combination of blocks, record the blocks they used, and then remove all the zeros. Figure 14–15 shows $3x^2 + (-2x^2) + 2x + (-3x) + 5 + (-2)$. After the zeros are removed, the figure shows $x^2 - x + 3$.

Ask the students to model a number of different algebraic expressions. Let them make up problems for each other that involve the addition and subtraction of expressions. Discuss with them the rules for adding in-

Figure 14–12

Figure 14–13

Figure 14–14

Figure 14–15

tegers and how these rules are related to the addition and subtraction of algebraic expressions or **polynomials,** algebraic expressions built up from constants and variables by adding, subtracting, or multiplying. In a polynomial, a variable cannot appear in a denominator, in an exponent, or within a radical sign.

Objective: to multiply and factor polynomials using algebra blocks.

3. Review with the students the area model for multiplying whole numbers. In Figure 14–16, if the large square is 10 by 10 and the small square is 1 by 1, the picture represents 12 by 13. The area of the large square is 100, the area of the medium rectangle is 10, and the area of the small square is 1. When you add the values, you have $1(100) + 3(10) + 2(10) + 6 = 156$. If the large square is 1.0 by 1.0, the problem becomes $1.2 \times 1.3 = 1.56$. The same principles hold in algebra. If the large square is $x \times x$, the rectangle $x \times 1$, and the small square 1×1. Figure 14–16 now represents $(x + 2)(x + 3)$. The area is now $1(x^2) + 3x + 2x + 6$, or $x^2 + 5x + 6$.

Notice that this model relates to the **FOIL method,** which is frequently taught in algebra classes. **FOIL** is an acronym that stands for "first, outside, inside, and last." For $(x + 2)(x + 3)$, the FOIL method would involve multiplying the *first* terms in the parentheses $(x \bullet x)$, then the *outside* terms $(x \bullet 3)$, then the *inside* terms $(2 \bullet x)$, and, finally, the *last* terms $(2 \bullet 3)$. Locate each of these pairs of terms on the diagram. Try relating this to the multiplying of whole numbers, such as $(10 + 2)(10 + 3)$. Note that the FOIL method is simply an adaptation of the distributive property. Ask students to use the distributive property to show why the FOIL method works.

Have the students model other examples of multiplying polynomials, such as $(x + 3)(x + 4)$ and $(x + 1)(x + 3)$. Encourage them to make up problems for each other. Let one student make a model and ask another student to explain what is being shown.

Figure 14–16

Figure 14–17

After the students have modeled several problems involving the multiplication of two terms with positive amounts, ask them to reverse the operation and try factoring. Start with $x^2 + 5x + 4$ and ask the students to form a rectangle with the pieces. What are the dimensions of the rectangle? These are the **factors** of the polynomial. Figure 14–17 shows the results, $(x + 4)(x + 1)$.

Solving Equations and Inequalities

One very important part of algebra is the solution of equations. Simple equations such as $x + 3 = 5$ might be introduced as early as first grade, but variables such as x are usually not used at this early stage. This type of equation commonly is introduced as an open sentence with an empty box used to denote where the missing number should go. Instead of $x + 3 = 5$, a primary textbook might show $\square + 3 = 5$. To **solve an equation,** you must find replacements for the variables that make the left side of the equation equal to the right side. For example, if you wish to solve the equation $x + 3 = 5$, you must find a value for x that will make this a true statement. In this case, we know the answer is 2, simply because we recognize the addition fact. It is not always that easy to solve an equation, however. The following are a few examples of ways to introduce students to the idea of solving equations. Encourage the students to think of other examples of their own.

ACTIVITIES

Primary Grades (1–3)

Objective: to use everyday situations to introduce the concept of writing and solving equations.

1. Begin the introduction to solving equations using number stories such as the following:

   There were 8 lizards playing in the sunshine. After awhile, some of the lizards decided to crawl under the rock for a nap. Then there were only 5 lizards playing in the sunshine. How many lizards are under the rock?

   The equation for this might be represented as $5 + n = 8$, where n represents the number of lizards under the rock.

   Encourage the children to solve the problem using methods that make sense to them. Some children might decide to draw pictures of the lizards, others might act the problem out with counters, and others might reason through the problem and solve it mentally. After the children have solved the problem, let them share their methods of solution with each other.

   After children are comfortable with simple problems such as these, move on to problems that require more reasoning, such as:

   Laronda saw 18 lizards playing on a rock. Some were brown and some were green. There were twice as many green lizards as brown lizards. How many of each color were there?

   Again, students should select methods of solution that make sense to them. Some students will choose to use physical models for the problem, some might draw pictures, some might use guess and check, and advanced students might try using equations. If b is used for the number of brown lizards, then $2b$ would be the number of green lizards and the equation might be:

$$b + 2b = 18$$

Students might reason that $b + 2b = 3b$ and that if $3b = 18$, then b must be 6. Once the number of brown lizards is found, this number can be doubled or subtracted from 18 to find the number of green lizards. It is not important to teach formal methods of solving abstract equations in the elementary grades; the emphasis should be on making sense of the words and translating them into symbols and equations that represent this sense making.

The references at the end of this chapter list several books for elementary students to give them early practice in algebraic reasoning. Some of these are written for students as young as first grade. If work with algebraic reasoning is begun this early, students should develop a solid basis for later, more formal algebraic work.

Intermediate Grades (3–5)

Objective: to use a balance to introduce the concept of solving equations.

2. For this activity, you will need a pan balance, some inch or 2-centimeter cubes, and a very lightweight paper or opaque plastic bag. (It should be light enough that its presence is not noticeable on the balance. If you cannot find a bag that is light enough, you can hold a screen in front of the balance to hide the secret number of cubes.) Have one student put a secret number of cubes in the bag. This may be named x cubes; or, perhaps, j cubes, if Joanna put the cubes in the bag. Place the bag on the left pan along with two other cubes that can be seen by the students. Now put enough cubes on the right pan to balance the left. Figure 14–18 shows a balance with the bag and 2 cubes on the left pan and 6 cubes on the right pan.

   Ask the students to write an equation describing what they see. They might write $j + 2 = 6$. How can they tell how many cubes are in the bag? It would be easy if the bag were the only thing on the left pan. If they subtract two cubes from the left pan, what must they do to the right pan to keep the balance? Try it.

Figure 14–18

Now you have only the bag on the left pan and four cubes on the right. This can be represented by $j = 4$. Look in the bag to see if you were right.

Ask other children to put different numbers of cubes in the bag and in plain sight on the left pan. Put cubes on the right pan to balance the left side and then determine the number of cubes in the bag. Do you always have to do the same thing to both pans to keep the balance? What if the bag is on the right side? Can you solve the equation $4 = x + 1$ in the same way that you solved the equation $x + 1 = 4$?

Try putting the same number of cubes in two bags along with another number of cubes in plain sight on one pan. What would you do if you saw $2c + 1 = 9$, as in Figure 14–19? If you begin by subtracting 1 cube from each pan, you then have $2c = 8$. Will the pans balance if you subtract 2 from each side? You cannot subtract 2 cubes from the side with the bags unless you open a bag. Can you take half the objects off each side? Yes, you can take off one of the bags and 4 of the cubes. What is left now? Is this the correct answer?

Objective: to use a balance to introduce the concept of inequalities.

3. A balance may also be used to introduce the concept of inequalities. Repeat the activity above, only this time, put one too many cubes on one of the pans. Discuss with the children how you can tell by looking at the balance which side is heavier. Review the use of the greater than and less than signs. Does the balance change when you do the same thing to each side? Again, work the problem until you have only one bag on one of the pans. Ask the students to write the equation for each step. Leave the balance in the learning center so that students can pose different problems for each other.

On the computer, try *Balancing Bear,* available from Sunburst and *Algebra Shop,* available from Scholastic to give students practice with similar ideas.

Figure 14–19

Developing and Practicing Algebraic Skills

Most of the algebra concepts that are developed in the middle grades will not be fully mastered until high school. Some, such as rotely manipulating symbols, memorizing procedures, and drilling on equation solving, are topics that no longer should receive as much attention as before (NCTM, 1989, p. 71). Some topics, however, such as operations with integers, should be practiced and mastered in the middle grades.

ACTIVITIES

Middle Grades (5–8)

Objective: to practice skills in operating with integers.

1. Use a regular deck of playing cards without the jokers and face cards, or make your own deck with 10 red cards (numbered 1 through 10) and 10 black cards (numbered 1 through 10). The black cards are worth positive amounts, and the red cards are worth negative amounts. This is a game best played by four players, but it can be adjusted for other numbers of players by adding more cards. Begin the game by shuffling the cards and dealing five cards face down to each player. Each player then picks up his or her five cards, adds the numbers shown on the cards, and writes down the total number of points. This is the score for round one. On each turn, each player draws one card from the player on the left. If you take a red 5, you must add a negative five to your score. What happens to the player who lost the red five? That person will subtract a negative five. Does this have the same effect as adding a black five? Round two ends when each player has drawn one card from the player on the left. At this point, everyone again adds the points shown on his or her five cards. The score from round two is added to the score from round one. Play continues in the same manner until someone has a score greater in absolute value than 50 or until time is called. The player with the score greatest in absolute value at the end of the game wins.

   Note: An easy way to check that everyone has added correctly on each round is to check the total score for the four players. This should always be zero. Ask the students to explain why this is so. If you are using a different number of players and a different number of cards, determine the sum of all the cards before you begin.

2. Students might enjoy practicing their skills with operations with integers using the computer

program by Bonnie Seiler, *The Great Signed Number Race.* This program builds on a similar program by the same developer, *How the West Was One + Three × Four.* The earlier program gives students the opportunity to construct and solve arithmetic equations as they practice learning order of operations for expressions such as (2 + 3) × 4. In *The Great Signed Number Race,* students work with positive and negative integers and all operations in a race through the Old West.

Objective: to reinforce skills with graphing using the Cartesian coordinate system.

3. The computer program *Green Globs and Graphing Equations,* available from Sunburst, contains several activities that develop skills related to graphing and writing equations. For example, Equation Plotter allows the student to enter an equation from the keyboard. Promptly, the graph of the equation appears on a coordinate grid on the screen. This provides students with an opportunity to explore how equations will appear in graphic form. Activity sheets provided with the software lead students to make various observations. And, teachers and students have the flexibility to experiment on their own.

Another activity is Linear and Quadratic Graphs, in which graphs are displayed on a coordinate grid and students enter equations that match the displayed graphs. Participants may select lines, parabolas, circles, ellipses, and hyperbolas to be displayed. When the students believe they have discovered the appropriate equation, they enter it, and immediately the graph of the equation is plotted on the screen along with the target plot. They may continue entering equations until the graphs match.

Green Globs is an activity that presents 13 "green globs" on the screen in a random fashion. The students attempt to explode all the globs by touching them with the graphs of equations that have been entered from the keyboard. The object is to use the fewest number of equations possible to explode the globs.

Estimating and Mental Calculating

Many algebraic equations can be solved mentally without writing out a lengthy series of equations. Encourage students to work these problems mentally whenever possible. A student should not need paper and pencil to find the solution for $x - 6 = 12$. If exact mental calculation is not possible, ask the students to estimate before working out an equation. Ask for justification for their estimates. For example, for the equation $4x + 920 = 256$, the students may have difficulty determining the exact

answer mentally. One of the first questions they should ask themselves is whether x should be a positive or a negative number. How do you know? Is x greater or less than -100?

Solving and Creating Problems

Using algebra is an excellent way to explore real-life situations. It is not necessary to present these problems in categories, however, such as age problems, money problems, and rate and ratio problems. Many good examples of problems can be found in science books as well as in problem-solving books such as *Problem Solving: A Handbook for Teachers* by Krulik and Rudnick (1987). An example from their book of a problem that could be solved using algebra is the following (p. 103): "In a class election, the winning candidate received three times as many votes as her opponent. If 32 votes were cast, how many votes did the winner receive?"

Some students may try to do the problem using the guess-and-check strategy and may begin by guessing an amount such as 20. When they check whether 20 could be three times the number of votes received by the opponent, they find that this would not be possible. They would then guess to find a number that is a multiple of three and that also fits the other conditions of the problem. Students frequently find after working several problems of this nature using a guess-and-check method that using algebraic notation can be a much more efficient method. For this problem, a student might use a v to represent the number of votes the opponent received. What would represent the number of votes the winner received? Can this number be expressed in terms of v? Yes, it would be $3v$. The equation $v + 3v = 32$ would then represent the voting situation in the class. Students who have worked earlier problems solving equations would realize that this is $4v = 32$, or $v = 8$. When checking their answers, the students should verify that if the loser received 8 votes and the winner 3 times as many, the winner received 24 votes. They find that $8 + 24$ does result in the total of 32 votes in the class. Therefore, the winner received 24 votes. Encourage the students to make up other problems for each other involving algebra. How many different ways can these problems be solved? Can they draw a picture or graph to illustrate the solution?

Use real situations to create other problems in the classroom. You might want to try looking at the stretchiness of a spring. Measure the length of a spring at rest and then measure the length again after hanging a heavy object such as a brick from it. What is the length of the spring now? Can you predict the length if you hang two bricks from it? What about three bricks? Make a graph of the results. What is the shape of the graph? Can you write an equation that would tell you the length of the spring for any given number of bricks? Encourage the students to ask other questions about the situation and explore the answers.

Other situations that are interesting to explore include looking at the distance a toy car travels beyond the end of a ramp compared to the angle on the ramp, the number of times a pendulum swings in 20 seconds compared to the length of the pendulum string, the time it takes water to empty from a paper cup with a hole in the bottom compared to the amount of water in the cup, and the length of time it takes a dropped object to hit the ground compared to the height of the drop. All of these lead to some very interesting physics concepts that can best be explored using very simple algebraic concepts. Encourage the students to carefully set up experiments in which they collect data to be organized in a table and then graphed. After the data are organized in this manner, ask the students to list all of the questions they can think of regarding the experiment. Which of these can be answered based on the data already collected and which need further exploration? Perhaps the science teacher would join you in this project.

Grouping Students for Algebraic Learning

The activities described above that involve experimenting with different physical concepts would best be done in small groups. Three or four students working together can set up the experiment, collect data, and ask and answer a variety of questions about their information. They can also work collaboratively to present their data in an interesting and understandable fashion.

Other activities, such as exploring the effects of changing the constants on the graphs shown on a graphing calculator, would probably best be accomplished by two people working cooperatively. It is difficult for more than two students to work with one graphing calculator, but more students might get together to discuss results.

Other problems might initially be presented to the whole class at once for individual exploration. After students have had an opportunity to explore on their own, they could get together in small groups or as a class to share results.

If you are a middle grades teacher or if you are preparing to become a middle grades teacher, it is likely that one of the issues with which you must deal is whether to track some of the best students into an algebra class in seventh or eighth grade while the other students remain in a different track. Some states, such as California, require that all students take algebra by the end of eighth grade, while many others require that all students take one or two years of algebra in high school. Many programs developed under National Science Foundation grants to implement the NCTM *Standards* integrate algebra, geometry, probability, and statistics and several other concepts through middle and high school.

As you weigh the issues surrounding tracking some students into higher level mathematics, you must look at all the implications of such a move. Does this mean that only some of the students will be exposed to higher-level mathematics by the time they leave school? If students take algebra in place of seventh or eighth grade mathematics, will they miss important geometry, probability, and statistics concepts? If there is no tracking, what other means are in place to ensure that interested students can learn calculus in high school? Which alternative will ensure that higher-level classes such as Advanced Placement Calculus and Advanced Placement Statistics or International Baccalaureate Mathematics Classes will be available to large numbers of students (males and females representing all races and socioeconomic groups) when they reach high school?

Communicating Learning of Algebraic Skills

Students working on projects such as exploring the effects of changing the length of a pendulum string or the angle of a toy car ramp should be encouraged to create different means of presenting their data. They might want to build a model, make a chart, draw a graph, search for equations to describe the graphs, and present questions and answers in written form. Remember that others are interested in the process that they used and not just the results. Several of these projects may make very good exhibits for a math or science fair.

It is interesting to look at results others have presented in such sources as newspapers and magazines. Do they use graphs to illustrate the results? Does the text seem to go along with the graphic information, or are there misleading statements in the article? Students who have struggled with presenting their own results make very good critics of others' information.

Connecting Learning of Algebraic Concepts

Ms. Gonzalez's fourth-grade class has adopted a needy family for Thanksgiving and is planning to buy them some canned goods so they will have a healthy stock of food. Each group is pricing a different type of vegetables and determining the best price. Jennifer's group is looking at corn. They have found 3 12-ounce cans for $1.09 at one store and the same corn at 4 cans for $1.33 at another store. They want to buy 12 cans of the corn and are discussing different ways of determining the best buy.

Lashonda has divided $1.09 by 3 and $1.33 by 4; Greg has divided 3 by $1.09 and 4 by $1.33; Whitney has subtracted $1.09 from $1.33; Millie has multiplied $1.09 by 4 and $1.33 by 3; and Jennifer has made a chart for each and drawn a graph. Each is convinced that he or she has found the best method of solving the problem. Mr. Gonzalez has asked each one to prepare a three-minute presentation of the method of solution, including a description of how this method could be used for any price and any number of cans. These presentations will be made to the whole class and followed by a discussion of how any of these methods could be used.

Ms. Washington is planning a lesson for her seventh-grade class on proportions. She knows how important this concept is for making a bridge between patterns in numerical expressions and the more abstract forms that students will experience in more formal algebra. She is working with Ms. Mazzocca, the science teacher, to make connections to the frequent use of ratios and proportions in the science class. They have begun a list of the science concepts that students will be studying this year that involve these concepts. So far, this list includes mixtures, density, scaling, temperature conversion, speed and acceleration, gravity and other forces, and pitch. They will team teach several of these topics to ensure that the students understand the concepts and do not just rotely apply rules to get the right answers.

Assessing Learning of Algebraic Concepts and Skills

When assessing students' skills in algebra, it is important to remember that the process is at least as important as the answer. Ask the students to explain their reasoning and not just write down numerical answers when working algebraic problems or exercises.

If you use group projects, let the students assess their own work and that of the others in the group. They can list both what they contributed to the project and what they learned from it. They can also list two or three of the most important contributions from the others in the group. Many of these projects make good portfolio entries. Students who have explored some physical phenomena, used charts and graphs to collect and analyze data, made predictions based upon their data, and explored new questions related to this initial information, frequently have developed good problems for inclusion in portfolios.

Some common areas of misunderstanding or difficulty in algebra are listed below. Be on the lookout for these misunderstandings. You might ask students to be on the lookout for them in their own work and in the work of others in the groups in which they are working.

1. A number and a variable placed next to each other should be multiplied, not added. For example, many students think $2a$ means $2 + a$ rather than $2 \times a$. This is understandable, since 54 means $50 + 4$, not 50×4, and $4\frac{1}{2}$ means $4 + \frac{1}{2}$, not $4 \times \frac{1}{2}$.

2. Different variables may stand for the same number, and the same letter in a different equation may stand for a different number. If $2x + 3 = 7$ and $2y + 3 = 7$, both x and y stand for 2. If in one statement $x + 5 = 9$ and in another statement $x + 4 = 0$, x stands for 4 in the first statement and -4 in the second.

3. Translating from a word problem to an equation is also difficult. If there are 4 apples for every orange in the bowl, the situation is not represented by $4a = o$. If a stands for the number of apples and o stands for the number of oranges, ask the students which there are more of in the bowl. The statement tells us there are more apples, 4 times as many as oranges. In the equation $4a = o$, which is larger, a or o? The o must be larger. Does this fit the statement from the word problem? Be on the alert for other incorrect methods of translating a written statement into an equation.

4. It is often easier for students to interpret information in graphical form than in equation form. Be sure to use a geometric or graphical model whenever possible.

5. Tasks given in story form may be easier to understand than tasks given in a purely numerical form. For example, it may be much easier to understand why a negative times a negative is a positive if you use examples involving money and IOUs or temperature than if you simply state the mathematical rule.

6. Some students may believe that every relationship is a linear one. Let them try graphing $y = x^2$ on the calculator or the relationship of the acceleration of a falling object to the distance traveled to see that not all relationships can be graphed with a line.

7. The concept of a variable is a difficult one and students frequently struggle to correctly use symbols, variables, expressions, equations, and inequalities. Give them plenty of experience in defining and illustrating for you the meanings of these terms and symbols.

Something for Everyone

Algebra provides a challenge for students who excel in abstract mathematical work; on the other hand, when physical models are used to illustrate concepts and to reinforce skills, students who have strengths in visual and spatial areas are quite able to grasp the concepts and develop the skills. Because students may be beginning their study of algebra in the early grades, it is important to use a variety of instructional techniques.

Auditory learners will be able to describe and explain algebraic processes. They may, however, have some difficulty in displaying spatially the concepts that are being presented unless clear verbal explanations are provided. In cooperative group activities, students who are auditory learners may be very helpful in describing the problem situations. They will also be very helpful when it comes to writing the results of the experiments and the solutions to the problems.

Those who do well in tactile-kinesthetic situations will succeed when materials such as algebra blocks and balance scales are used to model algebraic equations. Having the chance to move the materials around and discuss the relationship between one configuration and another will help provide the link between the concrete and abstract aspects of algebra.

Students with special talent in mathematics will likely discover algebraic relationships and patterns quickly. Because the work in algebra is at the introductory level, there is plenty of room for these students to excel and move ahead. For example, when using *Green Globs and Graphing Equations,* students will be able to work at several levels and will be able to solve increasingly challenging problems. Talented students can select more difficult problems on which to work. Further, when working with manipulatives, talented students will be able to develop complex examples and solutions. These students should also be helpful when it comes to discussing and explaining concepts and skills in their cooperative work groups.

Those who have difficulty in learning algebra should be encouraged to work with the models that illustrate the concepts. Provide opportunities for them to be successful and to demonstrate to the whole class and to members of their cooperative work group those ideas that they do grasp. Allow these students more time as they begin to learn algebra. Be willing to seek out alternative methods and materials for reteaching concepts and skills that were not immediately learned.

KEY IDEAS

As more states move toward requiring a strong algebra background for all high school students, more and more elementary mathematics programs are including a major strand on algebraic reasoning. In many instances, this means that students are learning to generalize from the patterns that they see and are beginning to symbolize the concepts they have developed concretely. The NCTM *Standards* for Grades 5–8 recommend that increased emphasis be placed on teaching variables, expressions, and equations along with using a variety of methods to solve linear equations and to informally investigate inequalities and nonlinear equations. The presentation of concepts involves using models and simple science activities and is tied to concepts learned in the primary grades. Properties are discovered and invented as students manipulate materials that model topics associated with algebra.

Emphasis is placed on using examples and problems from real-life situations. Thus, students have the opportunity to apply what they have learned to situations that are common in their experiences. Understanding is stressed and encouraged through both oral and written communication. Allowing for a diversity of thought is important at this stage in learning.

Students should have the chance to explore a variety of problem situations that require simple algebraic solutions and to present their own problems based on their experiences. Students are capable of challenging one another in ways that textbooks cannot. Teachers assess student progress by a variety of means, including listening to students as they describe their thinking processes and reading what they have written about their work. There are a number of common misunderstandings that surface as students learn algebra; making students aware of these misunderstandings can allow students to help themselves and to help one another.

DISCUSSION QUESTIONS

1. Set up a debate on the issue of whether all middle grades students should take Algebra I before the end of eighth grade. Look at studies such as the *Third International Mathematics and Science Study* and the *National Assessment of Educational Progress* as you prepare the debate. If possible, look at the November 1998 issue of the NCTM *Mathematics Education Dialogues,* an issue devoted to the discussion of tracking. Interview elementary, middle school, high school, and college mathematics instructors and analyze their responses. Find an Internet site where algebra teaching and learning is being discussed and ask the same questions. Take a position on whether algebra should be a separate course or should be integrated into the rest of the mathematics curriculum, and be prepared to support your position.

2. Analyze the teacher manuals and student books for grades 4 through 8 of a recent mathematics program. What algebra concepts are taught in each? Compare the middle school books to a high school Algebra I textbook. Are there differences in the ways that the material is presented? Are there differences in the topics that are taught? Compare your results to those of a classmate who has analyzed a different series.

3. Choose one of the algebra programs that makes extensive use of physical models such as *Algebra Tiles, Algebra Lab Gear,* or *Algeblocks.*

Learn how to add, subtract, and multiply algebraic expressions using the materials and then teach a middle grades student to do the same thing. Compare the strategies that you and the student use when learning the concepts. How do these strategies compare to learning algebra more abstractly? Which method did you prefer? Which method did the student prefer? You also might want to try this on the computer using a program such as *Computer Interactive Algeblocks* and compare this to learning with the physical models.

4. Talk to middle school teachers and administrators in your area about whether algebra is taught as a separate mathematics class in middle school. If so, is it available to all students? If not, is algebra integrated into every year of middle school mathematics? What do the teachers and administrators see as the benefits and drawbacks of their policies on this issue? How do middle school teachers and administrators discuss the issues with the high school teachers and administrators to ensure smooth transition from one level to the next level?

5. ▢ Choose a middle school mathematics series and compare the algebra part of the series to the recommendations from the *NCTM Standards.* Is algebra covered in the depth recommended by the *Standards?* Is the program conceptually oriented, making use of physical models and everyday applications, or is it more abstract? If possible, compare your series to one of the series developed under a National Science Foundation grant to implement the *NCTM Standards.* (At the middle grades level, these programs include the *Connected Mathematics Project* (CMP), *Math in Context, Middle-School Mathematics through Applications Project* (MMAP), *MathScape,* and *Math Thematics.* More information on all of these can be found at http://www.showmecenter.missouri.edu/.

6. ▢ ▢ Find an algebra (or calculus) book, video, or piece of software that was written for elementary students. (There are several in the reference list.) How do the elementary algebra concepts compare to concepts expected from middle school and high school students? If possible, choose one or more of these materials, design a lesson for primary or intermediate students, and try it out. Compare the algebra learned by these young students to the way you learned algebra. Which method would you prefer as a student? As a teacher? Why?

REFERENCES

Austin, Richard A., and Denisse R. Thompson, "Exploring Algebraic Patterns through Literature," *Mathematics Teaching in the Middle School,* 2, No. 4. (February 1997), 274–291.

Battista, Michael T., and Caroline Van Auken Borrow, "Using Spreadsheets to Promote Algebraic Thinking," *Teaching Children Mathematics,* 4, no. 8 (April 1998), 470–478.

Berman, Barbara, and Fredda Friederwitzer, "Algebra Can Be Elementary . . . When It's Concrete," *Arithmetic Teacher,* 36, no. 8 (April 1989), 21–24.

Brueningsen, Chris, Bill Bower, Linda Antinone, and Elisa Brueningsen, *Real-World Math with the CBL System.* Austin, TX: Texas Instruments, 1994.

Brueningsen, Chris, Elisa Brueningsen, and Bill Bower, *CBR Explorations: Math and Science in Motion: Activities for Middle School.* Austin, TX: Texas Instruments, 1997.

Burmingham, John, *Mr. Gumpy's Outing.* New York: Scholastic Press, 1970.

Burrill, Gail F., Miriam Clifford, and Richard Scheaffer, *Data-Driven Mathematics* (a series of 11 modules on algebra, geometry and advanced mathematics). White Plains, NY: 1998.

Carlson, Ronald J., and Mary Jean Winter. *Algebra Experiments II: Exploring Nonlinear Functions.* Menlo Park, CA: Addison Wesley, 1993.

Charles, Linda H., *Algebra Thinking: First Experiences.* Mountain View, CA: Creative Publications, 1990.

Clark, Anita, *Algebra Activities, K–9.* Lansing, MI: Michigan Council of Teachers of Mathematics, 1990.

Cook, Marcy, *Try-A-Tile: Logic with Algebra.* Mountain View, CA: Creative Publications, 1990.

Coxford, A. F., ed. *The Ideas of Algebra, K–12.* Reston, VA: National Council of Teachers of Mathematics, 1988.

Dossey, John A., Ina V. S. Mullis, Steven Gorman, and Andrew S. Latham, *How School Mathematics Functions: Perspectives from the NAEP 1990 and 1992 Assessments.* Washington, DC: National Center for Education Statistics, 1994.

Dossey, John A., Ina V. S. Mullis, Mary M. Lindquist, and Donald L. Chambers, *The Mathematics Report Card: Are We Measuring Up? Trends and Achievement Based on the 1986 National Assessment.* Princeton, NJ: Educational Testing Service, 1988.

Educational Testing Service, *Algebridge.* Providence, RI: Janson, 1990.

Ferrini-Mundy, Joan, Glenda Lappan, and Elizabeth D. Phillips. "Experiences with Patterning," *Teaching Children Mathematics,* 3, no. 6 (February, 1997), 282–288.

Fremont, Herbert, *How to Teach Mathematics in Secondary Schools.* Philadelphia: W. B. Saunders, 1969.

Fulton, Brad S., and Bill Lombard, *The Pattern and Function Connection.* Millville, CA: Teacher to Teacher Press, 1994.

Glazier, Stephen, *Random House Word Menu.* New York: Random House, 1992.

Goodnow, Judy, *Beginning Algebra Thinking for Grades 5–6.* Oak Lawn, IL: Ideal School Supply, 1994.

Gray, Virginia, *The Write Tool to Teach Algebra.* Berkeley, CA: Key Curriculum Press, 1993.

Greenes, Carole, and Carol Findell. *Algebra Puzzles and Problems* (Series of four books, grades 4–7). Mountain View, CA: Creative Publications, 1998.

Hills, Vernon, *Algeblocks*. Cincinnati, OH: South-Western, 1994.

Hoogeboom, Shirley, and Judy Goodnow. *Beginning Algebra Thinking for Grades 3–4*. Oak Lawn, IL: Ideal School Supply, 1994.

Howden, H, *Algebra Tiles for the Overhead Projector*. New Rochelle, NY: Cuisenaire Co. of America, 1985.

———, "Patterns, Relationships, and Functions," *Arithmetic Teacher* (November, 1989), 18–34.

Jones, Graham A., and Roger Day. *Algebra, Data, and Probability Explorations for Middle School: A Graphics Calculator Approach*. Menlo Park, CA: Dale Seymour, 1998.

Juster, Norton, *The Phantom Tollbooth*. New York: Random House, 1975.

Kalman-Stoveland, Stacy, *Beginning Algebra Thinking for Grades 1–2*. Oak Lawn, IL: Ideal School Supply, 1996.

Krulik, Stephen, and Jesse A. Rudnick, *Problem Solving: A Handbook for Teachers,* 2nd ed. Boston: Allyn & Bacon, 1987.

Lappan, Glenda, James T. Fey, William M. Fitzgerald, Susan N. Friel, and Elizabeth D. Phillips, *Frogs, Fleas, and Painted Cubes: Quadratic Relationships*. Palo Alto, CA: Dale Seymour, 1998.

———, *Growing, Growing, Growing: Exponential Relationships*. Palo Alto, CA: Dale Seymour, 1998.

———, *Say It with Symbols: Algebraic Reasoning*. Palo Alto, CA: Dale Seymour, 1998.

———, *Thinking with Mathematical Models: Representing Relationships*. Palo Alto, CA: Dale Seymour, 1998.

———, *Moving Straight Ahead: Linear Relationships*. Palo Alto, CA: Dale Seymour, 1997.

———, *Variables and Patterns: Introducing Algebra*. Palo Alto, CA: Dale Seymour, 1997.

Lubinski, Cheryl A., and Albert D. Otto. "Literature and Algebraic Reasoning," *Teaching Children Mathematics,* 3, no. 6 (February, 1997), 290–295.

MacDonell, Alan (ed.), *The Super Source: Patterns and Functions Grades 7–8*. White Plains, NY: Cuisenaire Company of America, Inc., 1998.

McKnight, C. C., F. J. Crosswhite, J. A. Dossey, E. Kifer, J. J. O. Swafford, K. J. Travers, and T. J. Cooney, *The Underachieving Curriculum: Assessing U.S. School Mathematics from an International Perspective*. Champaign, IL: Stipes, 1987.

National Council of Teachers of Mathematics, *Curriculum and Evaluation Standards for School Mathematics*. Reston, VA: NCTM, 1989.

———. *Mathematics Education Dialogues,* Reston, VA: NCTM, November, 1998.

Peak, Lois, *Pursuing Excellence: A Study of U.S. Eighth-Grade Mathematics and Science Teaching, Learning, Curriculum, and Achievement in International Context*. Washington, DC: Office of Educational Research and Improvement, U.S. Department of Education, November, 1996.

Picciotto, Henry, *The Algebra Lab Middle School: Exploring Algebra Concepts with Manipulatives*. Worth, IL: Creative Publications, 1990.

Picciotto, Henry, and Anita Wah, *Algebra: Themes, Concepts, and Tools*. Mountain View, CA: Creative, 1994.

Rey, Henry A, *Curious George Rides a Bike*. Boston: Houghton Mifflin, 1952.

Saxelby-Jennings, Jo (ed.), *Algebra Impacts Math Homework: Key Stage One and Two*. Leamington Spa, Warwickshire, England: Scholastic, 1994.

Sherard, Wade H., *Logic Algebra Problems*. Palo Alto, CA: Dale Seymour, 1990.

Silver, Edward, *Improving Mathematics in Middle School: Lessons from TIMSS and Related Research*. Washington, DC: U.S. Department of Education Office of Educational Research and Improvement, 1998.

Sobel, M. A., and E. M. Maletsky, *Teaching Mathematics: A Sourcebook of Aids, Activities, and Strategies,* 2nd ed. Englewood Cliffs, NJ: Prentice Hall, 1988.

Speer, William, David Hayes, and Daniel Brahier, "Becoming Very-Able with Variables," *Teaching Children Mathematics,* 3, no. 6 (February, 1997), 305–308.

Stone, Bob, and Peter Patilla. *Toward Algebra through Structures: Multilink Middle School Mathematics*. Glen Burnie, MD: NES Arnold, 1995.

Texas Instruments, *Getting Started with the CBR*. Austin, TX: Texas Instruments, 1997.

———, *CBL System Experiment Workbook*. Austin, TX: Texas Instruments, 1997.

Van Dyke, Frances, *A Visual Approach to Algebra*. Orangeburg, NY: Dale Seymour, 1998.

Widmer, Connie, and Linda Sheffield, "Modeling Mathematics Concepts Using Physical, Calculator, and Computer Models to Teach Area and Perimeter," *Learning and Leading with Technology,* 25, no. 5 (February, 1998), 32–35.

———, "Putting the Fun into Functions through the Use of Manipulatives, Computers, and Calculators," *School Science and Mathematics,* 94, no. 7 (February, 1998), 350–355.

Willcutt, Robert, *Building Algebraic Thinking with Progressive Patterns: Pattern Blocks, Rods, and Cubes* (series of three books). Pacific Grove, CA: Critical Thinking Press and Software, 1995.

Willoughby, Stephen, "Functions from Kindergarten through Sixth Grade," *Teaching Children Mathematics,* 3, no. 6 (February, 1997), 314–318.

Willoughby, Stephen S., Carl Bereiter, Peter Hilton, and Joseph H. Rubinstein, *Real Math*. La Salle, IL: Open Court, 1991.

Winter, Mary Jean, and Ronald J. Carlson, *Algebra Experiments I: Exploring Linear Functions*. Menlo Park, CA: Addison Wesley, 1993.

Wood, Audrey, *The Napping House*. Orlando, FL: Harcourt, 1984.

Technology

Broderbund, *Tabletop, Sr.* Novato, CA: Broderbund, 19. (software)

Cohen, Don, *Calculus By and For Young People*. Champaign, IL: Don Cohen—The Mathman, 1991. (kit with two videos, book, and worksheets)

Davidson, *The Cruncher.* Torrance, CA: Davidson, 1997. (software)

———, *Alge-Blaster.* Torrance, CA: Davidson, 1997. (software)

Dugdale, Sharon, and David Kibbey, *Green Globs and Graphing Equations.* Pleasantville, NY: Sunburst Communications. (software)

Edmark, *Mighty Math Astro Algebra.* Orlando, FL: Harcourt Brace, 1996. (software)

———, *Millie's Math House.* Orlando, FL: Harcourt Brace. (software)

Edwards, Edgar L., Jr. (ed.), *Algebra for Everyone.* Reston, VA: National Council of Teachers of Mathematics (video, discussion guide, and book), 1990. (software)

GPN, *Math Vantage: Unit I: Patterns.* Lincoln, NE: GPN, 1997. (video and print materials)

———, *Math Vantage: Unit V: The Language of Mathematics.* Lincoln, NE: GPN, 1997. (video and print materials)

Hammer, C., *Algebra Shop.* Jefferson City, MO: Scholastic, 1990. (software)

Harcourt Brace, *Data ToolKit.* Orlando, FL: Harcourt Brace, 1996. (software)

———, *Graph Links Grades 1–6.* Orlando, FL: Harcourt Brace, 1996. (software)

HRM, *Algebra World CD-ROM.* Pleasantville, NY: Human Relations Media, 1998. (software)

Johnson, Anita, *Computer Interactive Algeblocks.* Cincinnati, OH: South-Western, 1996. (software)

Marshall, Gail, and associates, *Balancing Bear.* Pleasantville, NY: Sunburst Communications. (software)

O'Brien, Thomas, *Puzzle Tanks.* Pleasantville, NY: Sunburst Communications. (software available for computer and calculator)

———, *Teasers by Tobbs.* Pleasantville, NY: Sunburst Communications. (software)

———, *The King's Rule.* Pleasantville, NY: Sunburst Communications. (software)

Schwartz, Judah, *What Do You Do with a Broken Calculator?* Pleasantville, NY: Sunburst Communications. (software)

Seiler, Bonnie, *How the West Was One + Three × Four.* Pleasantville, NY: Sunburst Communications. (software)

———, *The Great Signed Number Race.* Pleasantville, NY: Sunburst Communications. (software)

Sunburst, *Bounce.* Pleasantville, NY: Sunburst Communications. (software)

———, *Sequencing Fun!* Pleasantville, NY: Sunburst Communications. (software)

———, *Zap! Around Town.* Pleasantville, NY: Sunburst Communications. (software)

Tenth Planet, *Introduction to Patterns.* Pleasantville, NY: Sunburst Communications. (software)

Web Sites

http://www.ed.gov/inits.html#2   President Clinton's 1998 *Call to Action for American Education in the 21st Century.*

http://www.ed.gov/pubs/12TIMSS/SecIV.html   *An Action Strategy for Improving Achievement in Mathematics and Science,* February 1998.

http://nces.ed.gov/naep/96report/97986t5.shtml   National Assessment of Educational Progress, 1996.

http://www.showmecenter.missouri.edu/   The Show-Me Project: A National Science Foundation project supporting implementation of standards-based middle grades mathematics curricula.

Chapter 15

Organizing for
Mathematics Instruction

NCTM Professional Standards

Standard 4: Tools for Enhancing Discourse

The teacher of mathematics, in order to enhance discourse, should encourage and accept the use of—

- Computers, calculators, and other technology;
- Concrete materials used as models;
- Pictures, diagrams, tables, and graphs;
- Invented and conventional terms and symbols;
- Metaphors, analogies, and stories;
- Written hypotheses, explanations, and arguments;
- Oral presentations and dramatizations.

Standard 5: Learning Environment

The teacher of mathematics should create a learning environment that fosters the development of each student's mathematical power by—

- Providing and structuring the time necessary to explore sound mathematics and grapple with significant ideas and problems;
- Using the physical space and materials in ways that facilitate students' learning of mathematics;
- Providing a context that encourages the development of mathematical skill and proficiency;
- Respecting and valuing students' ideas, ways of thinking, and mathematical dispositions;

and by consistently expecting and encouraging students to—

- Work independently or collaboratively to make sense of mathematics;
- Take intellectual risks by raising questions and formulating conjectures;
- Display a sense of mathematical competence by validating and supporting ideas with mathematical argument.

Standard 6: Analysis of Teaching and Learning

The teacher of mathematics should engage in on-going analysis of teaching and learning by—

- Observing, listening to, and gathering other information about students to assess what they are learning;
- Examining effects of the tasks, discourse, and learning environment on students' mathematical knowledge, skills, and dispositions;

in order to—

- Ensure that every student is learning sound and significant mathematics and is developing a positive disposition toward mathematics;
- Challenge and extend students' ideas;
- Adapt or change activities while teaching;
- Make plans, both short- and long-range;
- Describe and comment on each student's learning to parents and administrators, as well as to the students themselves.

NCTM (1991), pp. 52, 57, 63. Reprinted by permission.

My Math Journal

In the space below, write four or five personal goals for your elementary or middle school mathematics teaching. As you write out your goals, be sure to explain each one and how you expect to accomplish it as a classroom teacher.

As you read the following pages, consider these guiding questions:

1. What considerations should teachers take into account as they plan lessons in mathematics?
2. How does cooperative learning enhance mathematics instruction?
3. What are mathematical projects and how do they differ from textbook learning?
4. In what ways can students' mathematical learning be assessed?
5. What are the characteristics of children with special needs?
6. How would you describe a classroom that would enhance the learning of mathematics?
7. What kinds of learning aids support mathematics instruction?

Teaching mathematics to elementary and middle school students requires you to be knowledgeable in both mathematics and psychology. Equally important is your ability to develop a smooth-running classroom and an environment that is stimulating and attractive. Organizational skills are required. Some individuals are naturally well organized; others need to spend extra time developing the ability to organize their classrooms.

The importance of organization in teaching is a major focus of current writings in mathematics education. The Mathematical Sciences Education Board challenges teachers by noting:

> In reality, no one can *teach* mathematics. Effective teachers are those who can stimulate students to *learn* mathematics. Educational research offers compelling evidence that students learn mathematics well only when they *construct* their own mathematical understanding. To understand what they learn, they must enact for themselves verbs that permeate the mathematics curriculum: "examine," "represent," "transform," "solve," "apply," "prove," "communicate." This happens most readily when students work in groups, engage in discussion, make presentations, and in other ways take charge of their own learning. (1989, pp. 58–59)

The NCTM *Professional Standards for Teaching Mathematics* (1991, p. 22) confirms this challenge by stating: "Because teaching mathematics well is a complex endeavor, it cannot be reduced to a recipe for helping students learn. Instead, good teaching depends on a host of considerations and understandings. Such teaching demands that teachers reason about pedagogy in professionally defensible ways within the particular contexts of their own work." Your work as a teacher will depend on your personal characteristics and preferences, the nature of the students with whom you work, the curriculum, and other factors unique to your teaching situation. These factors will affect how you organize your classroom for mathematics instruction.

In the early stages of your career, preparing to teach, developing timing, spur-of-the-moment activities, and management strategies will consume much of your time. Still, there will be the challenges of integrating subject matter and making connections between mathematics and daily life, using writing and literature to help students communicate about mathematics, engaging in projects, assessing mathematics learning, and working in multiage classrooms. While we cannot offer *the* solution for you in your particular teaching situation, we can provide some guidelines. The more options and alternatives from which you have to choose, the more dynamic your classroom may become. Five aspects of classroom teaching are dealt with in the following pages:

1. Fitting instruction to students' differing needs and styles;
2. Assessing, recording, and reporting students' progress;
3. Students with special needs;
4. Arranging the classroom;
5. Providing learning aids.

Fitting Instruction to Students' Differing Needs and Styles

Both students and teachers have distinct needs and styles of operation in the classroom. Each child's personal learning style is unique to that child. The learning style determines how and when the child discovers relationships, learns to read, and develops the concepts of mathematics.

We have mentioned that students learn in different ways. Some learn best through tactile/kinesthetic experiences; that is, through touching objects and through physical movement. Auditory learners have the ability to listen to others and understand effectively. Those who are visual learners appreciate pictorial models. Students learn in all of these modes simultaneously, but tend to excel in one particular mode.

Then there are students who find learning particularly difficult; they take more time, have less interest, and seem unable to grasp concepts and skills. Likewise, some students are fast learners, enjoy intellectual challenges, and are ready to move ahead. One child may be ill-at-ease, self-conscious, and shy; another child may be at home in the classroom, comfortable with the surroundings and other children. As a consequence, one child may learn slowly and may be dependent on an adult, whereas another child may learn quickly, barely assisted by the teacher.

When 25 or 30 students are brought together for instruction, the combinations of learning styles present a formidable challenge to a teacher. Likewise, your own personal teaching style affects how you teach. Your beliefs, experiences, education, and expectations of students' behavior will cause you to be a certain kind of teacher.

Learning and teaching must be carefully planned. Granted, some of the best learning is spontaneous or incidental, but for long-term, sequential learning to occur in an enriched environment, the teacher must lay the groundwork. You may wish to include students in the planning, to share the learning objectives with the students, and even to encourage the students to lead—all are a part of the learning process.

When you are organizing for mathematics instruction based on sound principles of learning, be sure to consider a variety of different and effective teaching-learning strategies. Other strategies will emerge as thoughtful teachers reflect on how they teach and wish to teach. A particular strategy is a function of the teacher and may be successful only under the conditions experienced by that individual. Be willing to try new approaches.

Planning for Teaching

Excellent teaching occurs, in part, because it is well planned. Teachers are seldom able to spontaneously lead students day after day without pondering, reflecting, deciding, anticipating, and researching. You must be every bit the learner you would expect one of your students to be.

Planning for teaching takes numerous forms. Newcomers to teaching must carefully plan their lessons, often writing a detailed lesson plan so that the teaching situation can be controlled and later analyzed by both the teacher and the cooperating teacher or supervisor. (See Appendix B for a lesson plan outline to assist in planning lessons.) When writing a plan, the student teacher gains skill and confidence in his or her ability to think through the teaching act. Such a plan helps teachers develop a thinking process that eventually frees them from having to write out detailed lesson plans.

Guidelines for designing a lesson plan are presented below. It is assumed the mathematical topic (concept or skill) to be taught has been selected from a math textbook, school district curriculum guide, or a project or unit guide.

Designing a Lesson Plan

I. Research the topic as follows:
  A. Discover various introductory techniques appropriate to the topic.
  B. Select teaching aids and materials that will best illustrate the topic.
  C. Identify various reintroductory methods to aid in mastery of the topic.
II. Consider how you will make this topic (concept or skill) interesting and worthwhile for both you and the students.

III. Plan each individual lesson using the following:
  A. State specific instructional objectives for each lesson in terms of what the students should be able to do when the lesson is completed.
  B. List the mathematical terms that may need to be reviewed or learned by the students.
  C. List your learning aids and materials and explain the part they will play in the presentation of the lesson.
  D. Outline your teaching strategy as follows:
    1. Introduction—What warm-up activity do you have to begin the lesson that will challenge the students' thinking? Exactly what device or technique will you use to motivate this particular lesson? How will you ensure that the students will be interested?
    2. Procedure—How do you plan to succeed in achieving the instructional objectives? Be descriptive. What will the students be doing? What materials will help illustrate the mathematical ideas in the lesson? What problem solving challenges will encourage students to invent solutions? How will the activities be organized? Is this different from the way you taught last time?
    3. Follow-up—Have you planned a game, problem-solving activity, braintwister, discussion, or worksheet? What have you planned and what is its purpose?
  E. State how you will determine if the child has achieved the outcomes stated in the instructional objectives.
IV. Evaluate your teaching performance in light of how the students responded, how you responded, and the relative success of the lesson. What might you do differently the next time you teach this lesson or group of lessons?

By the time you begin full-time teaching, you should be able to plan a week at a time by jotting down topics and key ideas you wish to teach. You will not need to detail every activity but may write out activities that need special planning. Much of the planning, including objectives, activities, grouping, and room arrangement, can be done mentally, but it is sound practice to have the week's plans written out in global terms.

Experienced teachers also must plan. Experience has taught them what to expect, how to react, how to time a lesson, and ways to interest students. Most of the planning done by experienced teachers is done mentally and written in plan books that block out a week at a time. These block plans serve as an important guide throughout the week. Teachers must refine and prepare their teaching to fit the particular group of students with whom they are working. Experienced teachers are aware of their personal teaching styles and adjust their styles to fit the learning styles of their students. Experienced teachers can be a bit more spontaneous and less tied to a fixed lesson plan.

There are times when specific instructional strategies are more appropriate. For example, when a physical model is first introduced to students, free exploration is called for. The teacher behavior is to observe and interact with the students. The class may work as a whole or in small groups. Experience has shown that students must freely interact with the materials before they work with them in a structured situation; otherwise, the students are distracted by the material.

When teachers are concerned about students' skill achievement, they may use more direct instruction. Rosenshine and Stevens (1986) reported that certain teacher behaviors are associated with increased academic achievement on the part of their students. These include beginning a lesson with a short review of previous learning and statement of goals; presenting new material in small steps, with practice after each step; giving clear and detailed instructions and explanations; providing active practice for all students; asking many questions, checking for understanding, and having all students respond; guiding students during initial practice; providing systematic feedback; and providing explicit instruction and practice for seatwork exercises (p. 377).

Throughout the process of planning, teachers must be active learners. They must be current in what is happening in the world because the students will voice their concerns, and teachers should be ready to use students' concerns when they arise and in future lessons. Teachers must also be current in the various subjects for which they are responsible.

To be current in the teaching of mathematics, the teacher may enroll in graduate or in-service courses offered by colleges or school districts. Teachers may attend local, regional, or national meetings held by the National Council of Teachers of Mathematics and other organizations whose purposes include improving mathematics instruction. Another way for teachers to keep current is to become active in state mathematics organizations. Teachers can attend workshops and later help provide workshops for local teachers, students, and parents. Journals such as the *Teaching Children Mathematics, Mathematics Teaching in the Middle School, Learning,* and *Instructor,* along with many of the fine journals published by state mathematics organizations, are rich sources of ideas for teaching mathematics.

Cooperative Learning

Competition. After visiting classrooms to observe, participate with, or teach children, you may begin to develop various concerns. Typical among comments is the following: "I saw the children playing a computation game and the boys were against the girls. The girls always seemed to win, and the teacher constantly praised the girls for being so fast. Competition is useful, isn't it? After all, life outside of school is competitive and students need to learn to compete early to survive." Typical among commercial advertisements is one telling consumers that "Being the best is not everything; it is the only thing." Seldom can one be "the best," but competition is heightened. In the classroom, emphasis on being the best, fastest, or brightest can prove destructive. For every "best" child in a group of 20, 19 feel less able, weaker, or insignificant. Diminishing the worth of children through competition can diminish the worth of the entire group. Employing competition to improve motivation or quality is often ineffective. The students who can win compete, but the others ignore the competition. A firm distinction must be maintained between *being the best* and *doing one's best.* This is not to say that all competitive situations are harmful. Friendly competition sometimes increases friendship and common appreciation among competing individuals or groups.

Cooperating and having a common cause foster personal growth and identification. Mathematics learning should be cooperative. Cooperation involves other people in constructive roles. Students who receive support from other people can see the worth of working together as opposed to working against one another. More productive personal growth results through cooperation than through competition. But cooperation does not just happen; it is learned and requires a teacher who is a model of the cooperative spirit.

Grouping. The nature of young children does not lend itself to extensive group work. Six-year-olds have not fully developed the capacity to work in groups. They do enjoy games involving several other children, but these games should allow them considerable individual freedom. This is the time to introduce whole-class and small-group activities and to carefully guide children through the activities. When whole-class projects are undertaken, the teacher is the catalyst and leader. Likewise, opportunities arise to teach sharing and cooperation by developing small-group projects, such as dramatic play or mathematics activities with a short-term, definite purpose.

Eight-year-olds have developed sufficiently to work in small groups with considerable adult leadership. They are able to understand tasks and to work through them. They are able to respond to the teacher's questions and guidance. They are learning to cooperate without constantly grappling for attention. They are able to assume some leadership in small groups but can rarely lead the entire class. Take care to teach skills of democratic living and to provide time for these skills to be practiced. This is the beginning of a lifelong learning process in group interaction.

Ten-year-olds can effectively work in groups with little adult supervision. At this age, the group tasks and individual responsibilities must be well defined. Those who work well together will be pleased with the group product. Individual students can assume leadership roles and are comfortable leading the whole class.

Grouping students in cooperative learning groups as an alternative to competitive and individualistic learning has emerged in the writings of Johnson and Johnson and others. **Cooperative learning** is an organizational pattern in which students work together in small groups to accomplish academic and collaborative tasks as in Figure 15–1. The proponents of cooperative learning point to the advantages and benefits to students of working together for a common purpose. Johnson and Johnson discuss these advantages:

> Achievement will be higher when learning situations are structured cooperatively rather than competitively or individualistically. Cooperative learning experiences, furthermore, promote greater competencies in critical thinking, more positive attitudes toward the subject areas studied, greater competencies in working collaboratively with others, greater psychological health, and stronger perceptions of the grading system's fairness. The implications of these results for teachers are as follows:

1. Cooperative learning procedures may be used successfully with any type of academic task, although they are most successful when conceptual learning is required.
2. Whenever possible, cooperative groups should be structured so that controversy and academic disagreements among group members are possible and are managed constructively.
3. Students should be encouraged to keep each other on task and to discuss the assigned material in ways that ensure elaborative rehearsal and the use of higher level learning strategies.
4. Students should be encouraged to support each other's efforts to achieve; to regulate each other's task-related efforts; to provide each other with feedback; and to en-

sure that all group members are verbally involved in the learning process.
5. As a rule, cooperative groups should contain low-, medium-, and high-ability students to help promote discussion, peer teaching, and justification of answers.
6. Positive relationships among group members should be encouraged. (1987, p. 40)

There are reference books that provide detailed descriptions of cooperative learning and how to implement cooperative learning in the classroom. There are college-level and in-service courses that help teachers perfect the skills needed to use cooperative learning. But the best way for you to develop the ability to successfully use cooperative learning is to practice it in your own classroom, to evaluate your own progress, and to talk with others who are also using cooperative learning techniques. You are encouraged to use cooperative procedures as one of your options for teaching.

Project Learning. Using projects as the basis for learning mathematics fits very well as individual or group work. A **project** is an activity that takes several days to complete. Projects often have themes and integrate learning mathematics with other school subjects. Project work provides the opportunity for students to invent solutions to problems, to see connections between work in mathematics and problems that arise outside of school, to interact with other students, and to write about and discuss their work. Project teaching and learning provide the chance to use an informal learning environment; your role as a teacher is as an advisor, listener, and coach. You may be working with a group as its members work on their project or you may be working with individuals who have chosen projects of particular interest.

Several projects have been highlighted in the Connecting sections throughout this text. For example, Ms. Collins introduced the holiday extravaganza catalog-buying project to her eighth-grade students (Chapter 7); Mr. Grotting had his kindergarten students involved in a project whose theme was round things (Chapter 12); and Ms. Stahl challenged her sixth- and seventh-grade students to build toothpick bridges (Chapter 13).

We have mentioned several resources for project teaching throughout this text, including resources such as *Math Excursions* (Burk, Snider, and Symonds, 1992), *Eat Your Math* (Harris and Jones, 1994), *Mouse and Elephant: Measuring Growth* (Shroyer and Fitzgerald, 1986), and *Historical Connections in Mathematics* (Reimer and Reimer, 1992). In the catalogs of the suppliers of materials listed in Appendix A, you will find other fine resources for project learning.

Multiage, Multiability Classrooms. In many schools, teachers have children in the same class who may differ

Figure 15–1

in age by two, three, or even four years. Even if the students are all roughly the same age, teachers find that the students' abilities differ widely. In any case, you will need to plan activities that meet the needs of all of your children. They will need to be basic enough that all students can be successful, and at the same time be challenging enough to ensure that the top students learn new mathematical concepts.

In some cases, you will want all students to be involved with the same activities and in other cases, you will need to plan different activities based upon your individual diagnoses. Projects are frequently good ways to involve all students with the same activity and still allow for individual differences. Students may work together in cooperative learning groups to collect data or to solve a problem, and then may work individually on extensions of interest. Verbal students may write about the problem-solving processes used, visual students may draw diagrams, charts, or graphs to illustrate the problem, and tactile-kinesthetic students may build models to demonstrate the ideas. Talented students can investigate related concepts and explore ideas in greater depth while others review basic ideas.

Computers are another good aid in meeting a variety of needs. Several computer programs allow you to place students at different levels and allow students to move ahead at their own pace. Look for programs that have record-keeping capabilities, and allow you to choose or change the level of difficulty and the concepts to be reviewed.

There will also be times, especially when you are working on computation skills, that you will want to group children together to work on particular skills. Be sure that you pre-test the students to determine similar needs. For example, you may find that you have several students who have not yet mastered basic addition facts, while other students have mastered not only all addition and subtraction facts but can add and subtract two-digit numbers mentally. You will want to spend time with the former group with physical models working on basic facts while the latter group goes on to explore other concepts. This is fine; do not feel that all students must work on the same concepts all the time. You should feel free to group children flexibly based upon their needs and their interests and change groups frequently as students' abilities or desires dictate.

Assessing, Recording, and Reporting Students' Progress

Assessment is a multifaceted process. The NCTM defines assessment as ". . . the process of gathering evidence about a student's knowledge of, ability to use, and disposition toward mathematics and of making infer-

ences based on that evidence for a variety of purposes." (NCTM, 1995, p. 3) It involves determining the amount and quality of students' growth, development, and achievement. It involves knowing the objectives of the mathematics program. It requires you to know and understand students. Assessment also includes diagnosing, recording, and reporting students' progress.

Assessment is not an adjunct to the mathematics program. It is an integral part of daily instruction, for you cannot proceed without knowing how the students are performing each day. Assessment begins whenever you first come into contact with students and parents. It occurs every day throughout the school year.

The NCTM *Assessment Standards for School Mathematics* (1995) includes a listing of six standards for an effective assessment system, a complete discussion of each standard, a discussion of the different purposes for which the standards apply, how to implement the standards, and challenges to traditional assessment procedures. In the initial draft of the *Assessment Standards,* the working groups that developed the assessment standards made the following assumptions about assessment:

1. Every student is capable of achieving mathematical power.
2. Evidence about student mathematical performance is needed for a variety of purposes.
3. For each of these various purposes, information needs to be collected from multiple sources using a variety of methods and formats.
4. All evidence about student performance must be considered as a sample of the possible evidence that could have been gathered.
5. Teachers should be the primary assessors of student performance.
6. During their schooling, students should grow in confidence and in their ability to evaluate their own progress and performance. (1993, p. 3)

Based on these assumptions, the assessment standards (1995) listed below provide a framework with which to judge any program of assessment developed by a school district or a school. Following the statement of each standard are a sampling of questions that may be asked to determine how well assessment reflects the particular standard.

Standard 1: The Mathematics Standard

Assessment should reflect the mathematics that all students need to know and be able to do. (p. 11)

- What mathematics is reflected in the assessment?
- What efforts are made to ensure that the mathematics is significant and correct?
- How does the assessment engage students in realistic and worthwhile mathematical activities? (p. 12)

Standard 2: The Learning Standard

Assessment should enhance mathematics learning. (p. 13)

- How does the assessment contribute to each student's learning of mathematics?
- How does the assessment relate to instruction?
- How does the assessment allow students to demonstrate what they know and what they can do in novel situations? (p. 14)

Standard 3: The Equity Standard

Assessment should promote equity. (p. 15)

- What opportunities has each student had to learn the mathematics being assessed?
- How does the assessment provide alternative activities or modes of response that invite each student to engage in the mathematics being assessed?
- How does the design of the assessment enable all students to exhibit what they know and can do? (p. 16)

Standard 4: The Openness Standard

Assessment should be an open process. (p. 17)

- How do students become familiar with the assessment process and with the purposes, performance criteria, and consequences of the assessment?
- How are teachers and students involved in choosing tasks, setting criteria, and interpreting results?
- How is the public involved in the assessment process? (p. 18)

Standard 5: The Inferences Standard

Assessment should promote valid inferences about mathematics learning. (p. 19)

- What evidence about learning does the assessment provide?
- How is professional judgment used in making inferences about learning?
- How sensitive is the assessor to the demands the assessment makes and to unexpected responses? (p. 20)

Standard 6: The Coherent Standard

Assessment should be a coherent process. (p. 21)

- How is professional judgment used to ensure that the various parts of the assessment process form a coherent whole?
- How do students view the connection between instruction and assessment?
- How does the assessment match its purposes with its uses? (p. 22)

Merely reading the assessment standards and questions stated above will not provide enough information to establish a district assessment program or even to judge such a program. The entire *Assessment Standards* document will provide the basis for evaluating an assessment program. As a teacher, you may be involved in helping to establish procedures for assessing the performance of the students at your school or in your district. At that point, you should be challenged to read carefully and understand the full intent of the *Assessment Standards*.

By becoming a dynamic part of mathematics instruction, your assessment program will provide you with more appropriate ways to determine students' progress and a broader base of information on which to judge students' mathematical ability.

Assessing is gathering information using many available techniques. Recording is a way of keeping the information once gathered. Reporting is a way of sharing the data with those most concerned with the children's progress—the children themselves, parents, teachers, and administrators. These three aspects of the assessment process are discussed below.

Assessing Students' Progress

Traditionally, standardized tests and textbook tests have been used as the primary means by which to assess students' mathematical progress. This procedure is limited because standardized and textbook tests provide limited information about children's thinking processes and about the mathematics that children can actually do. Children's thought processes are dynamic; they should be assessed accordingly. Thus, it is important to know about and practice a number of assessment techniques, including observation and questioning, performance-based assessment, diagnostic interviews, teacher-made assessment tasks, writing activities, group problem solving, standardized tests, and textbook tests. Each is discussed in the following paragraphs.

Observation and Questioning. Teacher observation and questioning are among the most valuable methods for assessing the progress of students. Observation should focus on the individual child and the specific mathematical effort in which that child is engaged.

Many aspects of children's behavior are not assessed by tests. These behaviors include attitudes and interests, creative tendencies, and children's abilities to explain their own and other children's mathematical thinking. During discussions, work periods, play time, and instructional time, teachers observing mentally collect information about individual students. This information should then be acted on or written down in the children's mathematics folders, on an annotated class list, or wherever such information is kept. Many of the activities presented in this text are best assessed by teacher observation.

To illustrate assessment observation, we present the following description. Mr. Edwin has presented a problem to the class. There is a large maple tree on the school grounds and each fall it sheds its leaves. How could we figure out how many leaves there are on the tree and what it would cost to rake and dispose of the leaves each year? From that information is it possible to estimate the cost of leaf removal for a small city? Mr. Edwin notices that Darcy and Rob have been carrying out an animated discussion about the problem.

It is apparent that these students are discussing counting or estimating the number of leaves. Darcy is arguing that the easiest way to do that is while the leaves are still on the tree while Rob is arguing that it is better if you wait until they fall from the tree. Rob explains that you must have the leaves in hand in order to count them. Darcy says that is not necessarily so. She draws a picture of a tree and begins to explain how she might be able to estimate the number of leaves by determining the volume of the top of the tree and a sample of that volume.

Mr. Edwin is pleased with the discussion and asks a few questions about the process each student has chosen. He notes that both Darcy and Rob will have a chance to employ their own procedures in the leaf count. He believes that both are developing procedures that have merit.

The above example of observing and questioning is specific to an estimating procedure. Throughout the mathematics program, there are opportunities to question children on every aspect of mathematics. In its booklet, *Assessment Alternatives in Mathematics,* EQUALS and the California Mathematics Council suggest a number of questions that teachers may use to assess children's progress in several aspects of problem solving. For example, in questioning students about problem comprehension, these questions are suggested:

- What is the problem about? What can you tell me about it?
- How would you interpret that?
- Would you please explain that in your own words?
- What do you know about this part?
- Do you need to define or set limits for the problem?
- Is there something that can be eliminated or that is missing?
- What assumptions do you have to make? (p. 24)

Many other questions are presented in this booklet, and the reader is encouraged to build a collection of good questions to use in the classroom. Clearly, the types of questions you ask must be appropriate for the age and developmental level of the children you teach.

Rowan and Robles (1998) present a series of questions and prompts to help teachers promote "the growth of mathematical power" among children. Several classroom vignettes are presented to illustrate how questions and prompts are used to assist the thinking process.

The observing and questioning teacher will gain information about all aspects of children's cognitive growth—language and communication, social awareness, curiosity—not merely mathematical growth. This information will help guide the teacher in planning classroom experiences in a range of subjects. Because teachers make observations every day they are with students, teachers should accept this technique as providing the most consistent and abundant source of information about students.

While accepting observation and questioning as a key assessment technique, you also must accept the need to record the important observations and to collect samples of children's work to serve as written evidence of the observations. Then you will be able to track children's progress, use the information to prepare individual instruction, and accurately report the progress to children and their parents.

Finding time to make and record observations will be a challenge with your already busy schedule. Remembering your observations about a student's mathematics work from among all your daily observations will take practice and concentration, as will remembering to record the information.

Performance-Based Assessment. A number of states, such as Kentucky and Oregon, have opted to substitute alternative assessment, including performance-based assessment, for standardized testing alone. In **performance-based assessment,** students are asked to perform tasks, either individually or in small groups, that require problem solving and higher-level thinking. The tasks are developed by teachers and are aimed at all levels of performance in the elementary and middle school. Frequently, the tasks involve using a variety of concrete materials, are aimed at solving "real-life" problems, and cut across several different subject areas. Tasks are scored according to a scoring rubric that describes various aspects of the student's thinking and communication processes. Students are familiar with the rubric and know what is expected of them as they solve problems. A scoring rubric was illustrated in Chapter 3 in a discussion of problem solving.

Diagnostic Interviews. Diagnostic interviews take place when the teacher meets with individual students and asks them to perform simple tasks or to comment on tasks that are performed for them. Piaget devised many such tasks for use with young children to determine the children's readiness to learn various mathematical topics. The most helpful sets of questions are devised by teachers in their daily interaction with youngsters. Any topic that is taught in the mathematics program may form the basis for diagnostic interviews. You should find out how students are thinking. The best way to do this is to ask them.

Piagetian and similar tasks are carefully described by Richard Copeland (1984) and others. Mary Baratta-Lorton provides extensive diagnostic procedures in her program, *Mathematics Their Way* (1976). References may be found in the chapter references.

Teacher-Made Assessment Tasks.   Teacher-constructed tasks are helpful in assessment when specific information needs to be gathered and other means are either not as good or are not available. The main advantage in constructing your own tasks is the flexibility to choose the format and the specific math content. The chief disadvantage in developing your own assessment tasks is the time that it takes to develop good tasks. The best teacher-made tasks are those that have students solve problems or complete short projects and describe their thinking processes as they work. The quality of the work may be assessed by student-developed assessment criteria (see the Group Problem Solving section that follows) or by using a scoring rubric to assess the quality of the students' responses.

Writing Activities.   Writing activities can help in assessing students' mathematical progress. As they write, students reflect on a variety of topics and feelings and provide both themselves and the teacher with the chance to review their work and their thinking processes. The writing students do may be completed in several contexts. One opportunity for writing occurs when teachers provide questionnaires regarding recent mathematical work. For example, following several days of working with probability events, students were asked (1) to describe the activity that they thought best helped them understand how to determine the probability of an event occurring; (2) to mention one activity that surprised them; and (3) to explain to another person why some games are fair and others are not fair.

Journal writing gives students the chance to express attitudes and feelings about mathematics, as well as demonstrate problem solving skills. Journal entries should be made on a regular basis. It is helpful for you to provide topics about which students can write. Journal "starters" might include the following: (1) Describe what you think about doing math in school. (2) If you could be a number, what number would you be and why? (3) In math, I sometimes wonder about . . . , and (4) draw a cartoon that shows you doing your math homework. You will gain insights about the students as they write down their thoughts about mathematics. You will be better able to serve the needs of individuals as you discover how they are thinking and what they are thinking about.

Writing activities may include describing how a particular problem was solved, how to perform a new algorithm, or how to explain an event. These writing activi-

ties focus on describing a specific skill that requires careful thinking and explanation. For example, students are asked to explain to a classmate why certain figures, such as equilateral triangles, cannot be constructed on a rectangular geoboard.

Another useful writing activity emerges from cooperative learning group work. As a group works on an assignment, problem, or project, the group recorder might be asked to describe how the group decided to complete the assignment or in what ways members of the group praised one another as the work progressed. The written record from group work will have been read to the group and will likely reflect some group editing.

Students appreciate it if teachers respond to their writing. As time permits, comment on a student's writing, jot down questions that arise as you read, or respond to a question raised by a student. Challenge the writer in a written dialogue.

Group Problem Solving.   One way to assess mathematical ability is to assess group work. We have discussed cooperative learning as an organizational procedure that encourages academic and collaborative work, typically surrounding a problem-solving task. To assess group work, you will need to determine how well the assigned problem or task was dealt with. The time following a cooperative activity may be spent as a whole class *debriefing;* that is, discussing the procedures used by each group to solve the problem. The group reporter may orally describe the work or the reporter may read the summary that was part of a writing assignment.

Another effective way to assess group work is to have the students as a class establish the criteria for an individual or a group presenting information to the rest of the class. For example, the following criteria were developed for group presentations for a sixth-grade class working on a "people in the history of mathematics" project.

1. Presenters involve the audience
   a. Students can ask questions both during and after the presentation.
   b. Presenters answer questions directly and completely.
   c. The audience finds the people discussed interesting.
2. Presenters have practiced the presentation
   a. Presentation is made with few pauses and few mistakes.
   b. Presenters are ready when it is their turn.
3. Presenters use pictures, overhead projector, HyperStudio stacks, or other visuals.
   a. Visual aids are used during the presentation.
   b. Visual aids are organized and equipment works.
   c. Visual aids are carefully explained.

4. Presenters know what they are talking about.
   a. It is easy to understand what is being said.
   b. There is enough information about the historic person.
   c. The presenters tell where they found their information.
5. Presenters speak well.
   a. Presenters look at the audience when they talk.
   b. Presenters speak slowly, clearly, and loudly.
   c. Presenters are interested in their historic individual.

After the presentation, an assessment team uses the criteria to determine a score for the presentation.

The outcome of the project represents the collective work of the group. Because of the interdependence of group members in completing the project, the product is seen as the collective work of all group members. By using the techniques discussed above, the value of the project is assessed and insight into the mathematical learning is provided.

An important aspect of group assessment is to determine how well group members worked with one another to complete the task. Did each group member participate? Were ideas readily accepted and discussed? Were members praised for their contributions? Did each group member perform the role assigned to him or her? Were disagreements discussed and resolved in a constructive manner? Did group members feel good about their contribution and the group product? Did group members enjoy working with one another? You may find the answers to these questions by observing groups as they work, listening to the presentations, talking with individuals, and reading journal entries.

Standardized Tests. Standardized achievement tests are among the most controversial of assessment procedures. Standardized, or norm-referenced, tests are typically used for comparing the work of an individual or group with norms established for students in similar age groups or at similar grade levels.

Sometimes, standardized tests help survey students' skill and knowledge in limited aspects of mathematics to provide a basis for evaluating a school district's curriculum. Standardized achievement tests measure knowledge, skills, speed and accuracy, the ability to solve one- or two-step word problems, and vocabulary. Students' scores are reported as percentiles or grade-level equivalents based on national norms.

Teachers should avoid relying heavily on standardized tests as a basis for assessing their students' specific mathematical abilities. Standardized achievement tests tend to be merely approximations of how well particular students in a particular section of the country perform on narrowly defined content. Such tests give little evidence of students' resourcefulness or confidence in attacking new problems. The initial draft of the *Assessment Standards* (1993) that argues for alternative means of assessment states that ". . . the continued use of current tests along with the alternatives is counterproductive to the reform efforts in school mathematics" (p. 221). It is expected that school districts will continue to use standardized texts until alternative assesments are developed.

Textbook Tests. Textbook tests or supplemental tests provided with textbook series have provided one way to assess the textbook learning of students. They may diagnose students' readiness to begin a topic. They sometimes provide a basis for grouping or individual work. They let you know if the students have "mastered" the facts and skills presented in each chapter, partial chapter, or section of the textbook. Teachers have relied heavily on textbook tests in the past.

For a beginning teacher, the use of textbook tests can prove valuable in that they will save considerable time and energy such teachers need for some of the other challenges of first-year teaching. Tests are usually provided in each student's textbook. Parallel forms of the tests are provided in a format that is easy to reproduce for classroom use. Once the test results are compiled, you can begin to reteach topics or provide remedial instruction to individuals or small groups. The teacher's edition of the textbook will guide you to resources available to help students who need additional assistance. In addition, you will probably find that conferencing with or focusing observations on individuals having difficulty will provide you with valuable information about how to help them.

As the reform in mathematics education continues, textbooks themselves will take new and different forms. The assessment of textbook content will begin to mirror the alternative means of assessment discussed in the *Assessment Standards* and in the *Curriculum and Evaluation Standards*. You may expect to see a variety of ways to gather evidence of students' growth in mathematics. The statement above about current tests being counterproductive to reform efforts holds for many textbook tests being used today. As the textbooks change, you also should seize the opportunity to change.

The use of broad-based assessment does not mean that all assessment techniques are used all of the time. Rather, you have available to you alternative techniques that will provide reliable evidence of children's mathematical growth, thought processes, and abilities. You must select the most appropriate technique for the type of task being assessed.

Teachers have a major obligation once data have been gathered by any of the above means. Namely, they must decide what the data mean. The teacher's interpretations of the students' work are crucial in laying the groundwork for further instruction.

One useful function of interpretation is diagnosis. For example, students may be grouped for instruction based on concept or skill deficiencies that show up during assessment procedures. If observation reveals that three students are unable to solve word problems involving selecting the most appropriate operation, then you may wish to design instruction to assist them.

Tallying right and wrong answers is not nearly so important as determining how the child is thinking. It has been said, "Children are not wrong; they merely respond to the stimulus according to their knowledge and development at the particular time when we are checking their progress" (Biggs and MacLean, 1969, p. 191). Teachers should keep this in mind in order to provide students with the encouragement they need to maximize their potential. Most students naturally learn from failure and mistakes. All students should realize that assessment procedures represent another natural step in the learning process.

Recording Students' Progress

During the entire assessment process, organizing the information and work samples gathered is essential. Scores from problem solving, tasks, and tests along with other numerical data should be recorded in a gradebook, a computer database, or a similar repository for quantitative information. The work samples, including qualitative and quantitative material, may be kept in a student portfolio. The mathematics portfolio is a place to collect materials that demonstrate the child's ability to think about, use, and apply mathematics. It includes material that transcends the purely quantitative assessment data (test scores and worksheet or workbook scores). The portfolio will contain a profile of the student's abilities in mathematics in a variety of mediums. The portfolio will contain all work of an individual from which the student's best work may be selected.

For example, materials collected in portfolios by eighth grade mathematics students included the following items:

- Record sheet of all assignments, exams, problem solving activities.
- All daily assignments that had been completed during a progress period.
- The students' mathematics journals used throughout the year.
- Problem-solving challenges that were completed each week.
- Completed project materials and student assessments of the projects.
- Exams and quizzes.

Throughout the year, the teacher and the students reviewed the students' growth and the progress they made. The students were involved in self-assessment. At each progress period, they were guided to review the work in their portfolios and collect each of the following:

1. *Your math self-assessment guide.*
2. *Your completed math record sheet.*
3. *Your favorite work*—On a yellow half-sheet, write a paragraph explaining why this is your favorite work.
4. *Your favorite quotation*—On a sheet of paper, write your favorite quotation from your mathematics journal.
5. *Teacher's choice*—Find the assignment selected by the teacher. On a blue half-sheet, write a paragraph on your feelings about this assignment. Could the teacher have done a better job of explaining how to do it? What were the things that confused you?
6. *Showing growth in mathematical concepts*—Select two papers that show the growth you have made in mathematics this progress period. Use the green half-sheet to explain the concept and how you have improved.
7. *Your favorite problem*—Find your favorite problem that you worked on. On a pink half-sheet tell what it was about the problem that caused you to enjoy it.
8. *Quizzes and exams*—On a white-half sheet write a paragraph on your performance on your quizzes and exams. Have you gone over the problems that you missed?

The students answered several other questions that were on their math assessment guide. These questions asked about the students' class attendance, contribution, participation, effect on the dynamics of the class, effort, honesty, and use of mathematics. At this particular school, students were given a letter grade at the end of each progress period. As part of their self-assessment they were asked to give the grade that they had earned and the reason why. Finally, the students were asked to describe how the mathematics class could be improved.

Whenever the teacher met with parents during the year the portfolios and self-assessment materials served as the basis for discussing the students' progress. Often, the students explained the portfolios and assessment materials to the parents as part of a joint conference.

A number of states are now incorporating portfolios as part of their overall state educational assessment programs from the primary grades through high school. These portfolios contain the summary work of the students as they have progressed through the school systems in that state. These portfolios are assessed by readers at various levels during the students' schooling. The readers may be a combination of parents, teachers, aides, and administrators.

Reporting Students' Progress

Students, parents, and teachers should communicate about the student's growth and progress. The interchange among students, parents, and teachers helps students understand the results of their efforts, helps parents determine their child's mathematical growth and progress, and helps the teacher determine the nature of the child's home environment and the child's perception of the teacher and school. The key to three-way communication is your willingness to share any information you have and any observations you have made.

You should welcome parents to school. The common interest of students, parents, and teachers in the student's growth, development, and school progress should draw them together. The student's and teacher's assessment and the parents' observations should blend together to strengthen the student-parent-teacher partnership. Edge (1998, p. 308) noted that parents have been involved in mathematics classrooms for many years and goes on to highlight two changes: "an increased demand for parental participation in the schooling of their children as well as interaction between parents and schools." So important is the role played by parents that the February 1998 issue of *Teaching Children Mathematics* focused on school-family partnerships. This is a rich resource for suggestions about how and when to involve families in the learning process.

Parents of elementary and middle school students are particularly interested in hearing about their children. Besides quarterly or mid-year conferences, parents should be invited to the classroom to observe the daily routine or specific activities such as mathematics.

Send notes or call parents pointing out a significant event or accomplishment of individuals or small groups of students. A note home need not have a negative connotation. A summary of the past week's activities or of events to come may be distributed to keep parents informed about classroom life. Solicit the help of parents when the parents are known to have particular skills or experiences that can enrich a class. Invite parents to participate.

When reporting the mathematical progress of students, written descriptions along with samples of the student's work are helpful. Sometimes a check sheet of concepts and skills may substitute for the written description. When students have been involved in self-assessment, their views and perceptions add to the sum of information about mathematical progress. At least twice a year, and hopefully more often, students, teachers, and parents should meet face-to-face to discuss the mathematical work and growth of the student. Above all, be open and straightforward in discussing students. Your concerns and those of the parents should be coordinated for the benefit of the children.

Children with Special Needs

In every chapter of this book, we have mentioned children's different learning styles. We have also mentioned children who learn more slowly or more quickly than others. Your own observation of children will confirm these situations.

In addition, there may be children in your classroom with physical or mental handicaps and children qualified for assistance under federal or state guidelines. Resource rooms may be available for special instruction. Because support services are invaluable in meeting the needs of all children, use them to benefit every child in your classroom.

Children with Special Problems

Terms such as *low achievers, emotionally disturbed,* and *culturally deprived* are labels used to describe children who are having difficulties in school. These labels often result in a child's negative performance, both socially and academically. Avoid labeling children. Consider children for both their strengths and weaknesses, as full members of the human family. Children who happen to learn more slowly than others deserve special attention to help them develop mathematical concepts and skills.

Slow learners may be identified by intelligence quotient, achievement, teacher observation, reading ability, readiness level, or other means. They generally fall below an average in one or more of these areas. Slow learners may have many things in common, but each child has a unique set of strengths and weaknesses. Characteristics frequently possessed by slow learners are listed below.

- *Negative self-concept.* Children may come to believe at a very young age that they are stupid. Failure is too easily learned. Many children will not even attempt a task, particularly a new task, because they are afraid of failure.

  Make an effort to ensure success and to look at failure as an acceptable route toward learning. If children view themselves as worthwhile, they are more apt to approach a problem with confidence and have a greater chance of success.

- *Short attention span.* Slow learners often have short attention spans. This may be because problems are too difficult, too long , or uninteresting.

  Children will work for relatively long periods on interesting problems suited to their ability level. They will play in class much longer than they will work. Ensure that children are positively motivated toward appropriate tasks.

- *Specific mathematical disability.* Terms such as *dyscalculia, number blindness,* and *specific minimal brain damage* are used to describe children with specific problems in learning quantitative concepts. There may also be perceptual problems that affect learning spatial concepts. These include difficulties in forming concepts such as position in space (near, far, up, down, left, right), in distinguishing a figure from the surrounding background, and in eye-hand coordination.

Children are easily distracted by extraneous stimuli. Too many problems or pictures on a workbook page, as well as too many objects or people in the classroom, can be distracting. Workbook pages and classroom environments should be relatively plain and simple for children with perceptual problems. Be alert for children with specific mathematical disabilities and seek professional help when problems demand it.

- *Poor self-control.* Some children are explosive, hyperactive, or erratic. They always seem to be in motion. They rarely sit still and often wander aimlessly about the room.

  Some research indicates that poor self-control may be triggered or aggravated by diet. Much research still needs to be done on how diet affects children. Hyperactive children require a structured environment with few extraneous distractions.

- *Language problems.* Children who have difficulty learning mathematics often have language difficulties. In addition, the language of mathematics is often abstract and complex. Children may not understand such common mathematical vocabulary as *up, down, in, out, two,* and *plus.* Even more difficult are phrases such as *divided by* and *divided into.* Children may be unable to read simple directions, equations, or mathematical symbols. They may be unable to communicate concepts they do understand.

Remember to keep conversations with children having language problems as simple as possible. Be alert for any misunderstanding of terms. Develop concepts through physical manipulation and language.

Memory and Application. Studies show that slow and retarded children are capable of learning complex motor and verbal skills. Their retention may be similar to that of younger children of the same mental age. Overlearning may be required to ensure retention.

Allow for practice, drill, and repetition only after a concrete understanding of concepts has been developed. Transfer of learning is difficult for slow and retarded children but may be accomplished if it is incorporated into the lesson. Such children can retain and apply skills when they have transferred and practiced them.

Complex problem solving may be too difficult for slow and retarded children, but they can memorize simple, rote, factual material and they can learn and apply basic facts. Teaching skills such as how to use a calculator, how to be an effective consumer, and other life skills is appropriate.

General Principles of Good Teaching. General principles of good teaching have been mentioned throughout the book and pertain to all children. They are reiterated here because of their significance for children with special problems.

1. All children are ready to learn something. You must determine the level of readiness.
2. Success is important. Carefully sequence learning to ensure several levels of success. Immediate positive feedback is helpful.
3. Self-concept affects success and vice versa. Children must be worthwhile in their own eyes and in the eyes of their peers.
4. Practice is important and should follow the concrete development of concepts. It should be applied in practical situations and should contain provisions for transfer.
5. Be prepared with a variety of teaching strategies. Do not present them all at once, but if one method fails, try another. The child may be capable of mastering the concept, but not in the context in which it was first presented. Several methods of presentation that involve the senses may be needed to meet each child's learning style.
6. Begin work on a concrete level. Move to work on an abstract level only after children understand concepts concretely.
7. Analyze children's mistakes carefully. Children periodically make careless mistakes, but there is often another reason for an error. Look for patterns in children's errors, and discuss their thinking processes to correct mistaken concepts.
8. Learning is different for each child. This book mentions several ways to diagnose and assess individual children. Lessons should be planned according to the diagnoses.

Children with Special Mathematical Talents

Just as children having problems in mathematics need special consideration, so do children with special talents in mathematics. The regular math curriculum may be as unsuited for gifted children as it is for slow children. In 1980, the National Council of Teachers of Mathematics (NCTM) published the *Agenda for Action* that stated: "The student most neglected, in terms of realizing full potential, is the gifted student of mathematics. Outstanding mathematical ability is a precious societal resource, sorely needed to maintain leadership in a technological world" (NCTM, 1980, p. 18). Recognizing that the need for technological leadership is even more critical today, the NCTM, in 1994, appointed a Task Force Report on the Mathematically Promising. This Task Force attempted to broaden the traditional definition of mathematically gifted and talented by defining mathematical promise as a function of ability, motivation, belief, and experience or opportunity. None of the variables are considered to be fixed, but rather are areas that need to be developed so mathematical success might be maximized for an increased number of promising students.

This description recognizes that abilities can be enhanced and developed and acknowledges recent brain-functioning research that documents changes in the brain due to experiences. It also concedes that students are not always motivated to achieve at their highest possible levels and that the popular culture in the United States may even encourage students to disguise their mathematical abilities in order to avoid negative labels such as "nerd" or "geek." Belief in one's ability to succeed and belief in the importance of mathematical success by the students themselves, teachers, peers, and parents are also recognized as important. Lack of such beliefs, especially by females, students of color, students from lower socioeconomic groups, and students for whom English is a second language, are acknowledged as a significant barrier to learning for several students. The importance of the fourth variable, experience or opportunity to learn, is especially evident in international comparisons of mathematics students where research frequently finds that students in the United States are not exposed to the same high level of curriculum as students in several other countries.

Results from the *Third International Mathematics and Science Study* (TIMSS) showed that our best mathematics and science students are not achieving at the level of top students in other countries. There is widespread concern that our expectations for our students are not high enough and that our curriculum is not as challenging as that in other countries. In fourth grade, only 9 percent of the students in mathematics scored above the 90th percentile worldwide. In Singapore, 39 percent of the students scored at this level as did over 20 percent of the fourth graders in Korea and Japan (OERI, 1997, p. 25). By eighth grade, this had dropped to 5 percent of the mathematics students in the United States, while 45 percent of students in Singapore and over 30 percent of students in Korea and Japan were scoring above the 90th percentile (OERI, 1996, p. 26). By the end of secondary school, advanced mathematics and physics students scored significantly below advanced students in other countries.

The right of children to an education suited to their individual needs has prompted some states to legislate special programs for gifted children. Many mathematics educators in the United States are realizing that this is not enough, however. Special gifted programs generally do not focus on mathematics and rarely have teachers who are trained both in mathematics and in understanding the needs of exceptionally bright children. In addition, results from studies such as TIMSS reinforce the fact that the United States cannot afford to focus on a few

students who exhibit special talents in mathematics. Teachers must develop the mathematical talents of all students to their highest levels, and these levels must be higher than those previously reached by only a few.

Whether our most promising mathematics students are in a regular classroom or a special program, there are several things to consider.

Promising mathematics students, of course, are not all alike. They are boys and girls of all races, with all types of other abilities and disabilities, from all areas of the country including the inner-city and rural areas, and they have parents of all educational and economic levels. It has been popular to identify promising students by high intelligence quotients, such as a score of 130 or better. However, this is not a necessary nor a sufficient identifier of promising mathematics students; there are several other characteristics to consider. These characteristics must be nurtured and developed in all children in order to produce the greatest possible number of mathematically talented children. Some of these characteristics are listed below.

- *Creativity.* Many children, from preschool on, have special creative, mathematical talents that are obvious, and all need to have their creativity nurtured. Encourage children to explore, to manipulate, to suggest a variety of solutions to a problem, and to suggest new problems for exploration. Minimize rote memory. Stress flexible thinking.
- *Awareness.* Promising students are often sensitive to and aware of their surroundings. They perceive problems readily and can see patterns and relationships easily. They do not need to have every step of a problem spelled out for them.
- *Nonmathematical abilities.* Although some children have special talents only in mathematics, many children who are mathematically promising are also mentally and emotionally mature. Many mathematically talented children are highly verbal and can express their thought processes. Encourage the students to use verbal, physical, and spatial explanations as well as numerical and algebraic ones.
- *Abstract reasoning abilities.* Talented children may be able to reason at a higher level of abstraction than their age-mates. They may work symbolically with quantitative ideas but may still benefit from manipulation of concrete materials.
- *Transfer ability.* Many promising students can transfer skills learned in one situation to novel, untaught situations. They may apply learning in social situations, when working in other subject areas, at home, and so on. Encourage children to generalize rules and principles and to test the generalizations in new settings.
- *Good memory.* Talented children often have the ability to remember and retain what they have learned. They

do not need as much drill as other children do. Many are bored with repetition and may begin to "turn off" mathematically when asked to repeat things they have already mastered.

- *Curiosity.* Mathematically promising children often display intellectual curiosity. They are reluctant to believe something just because the teacher says it is true. They want to know why it works. They are interested in a wide range of ideas and often explore topics through independent reading. They ask many questions, enjoy solving puzzles, and delight in discovering winning strategies in games. Make available challenging articles, books, puzzles, and games for their use.

Challenging all students, including those performing at the top of the class to perform at a higher level is difficult, but rewarding. It is even threatening to some teachers. Such teachers are sometimes concerned that they will not be able to answer all the children's questions or that the children may be smarter than they are. This may be true but should not necessarily present a problem. Some suggested techniques that are especially appropriate for encouraging and developing mathematically promising children follow:

1. Students need challenging problems. Many of the problem-solving activities suggested in Chapters 3 through 14 are especially appropriate for challenging students to think more deeply about mathematics. Encourage children to create original problems for others to solve. Promising students should enjoy strategy games and complex problems.

2. Children do not need busywork. Because they often finish assignments early, bright students may be asked to do additional problems of the same type. If they can do the initial problems, it is likely that they do not need more practice. Use curriculum compacting to allow them to demonstrate their mastery of low-level work and then let them move on to more challenging tasks.

3. Encourage independent research. Promising students are often capable of independent study and research at a young age. They may even be able to set their own goals and assess their progress. This, of course, does not mean they should always be left alone.

4. Set up a buddy system. Let children work with peers of similar ability so they may challenge each other to ever-higher levels of performance. Children can often communicate with and learn from peers better than from adults.

5. Encourage creative and critical thinking. Avoid forcing children to memorize one method to the exclusion of others. Accept any correct method, and lead children to discover why some methods do not always work. Have the children assess solutions for appropriateness, ease, originality, and the like.

Perhaps you recognized the suggested approaches for teaching for the development of promising students. The same approaches might be used with all children. We mentioned them to alert you to sound practices and to remind you that extra planning is needed to encourage the growth of mathematical talents.

Educators often debate whether programs for gifted children should be enriched or accelerated. Some states have even mandated one type of program. Currently, the trend seems to be toward a third dimension of programs for the development of mathematical abilities—depth and complexity. The *Third International Mathematics and Science Study* characterized the curriculum in the United States as "an inch deep and a mile wide" (OERI, 1996). If, as this study suggests, our curriculum covers too many topics at too low a level, increasing the number of topics or covering them more rapidly will not help students develop the strong mathematical power that is necessary. Instead of racing through topics or adding additional ones, students should develop a deeper understanding of mathematics by asking more complex questions about the topics they are learning. This does not mean, however, that students should not move into traditional high school topics such as algebra and geometry in the middle grades: Quite the contrary. By age 12 or 13, students in many other countries have already explored algebra and geometry on a much deeper level than many secondary students in the United States, and our middle grades students also need to move beyond repetition of elementary mathematics towards a rich exploration of these topics.

A wide range of resources is available electronically, and interesting and stimulating mathematics books, videos, and computer programs should be available either in the classroom or in the library of every school. For the teacher, a professional library, the National Council of Teachers of Mathematics, journals, and activity books are rich sources of good ideas. Students who enjoy competitions should be encouraged to explore their interests through team events such as MATHCOUNTS or through individual entries through their schools or on-line. The reference list has several competitions, programs, and other resources for enriching and deepening mathematics offerings to help increase the number and the mathematical understanding of promising students.

Arranging the Classroom

Classrooms are for children. Classrooms should provide the best physical environment possible for learning. It is possible to have a classroom that is too stimulating, with so many bright pictures and objects that children have difficulty finding a single object or an area in which to

T2. Two boxes of square-shaped cardboard pieces are available to make a larger pattern. There are 4 small squares in each piece.

All pieces in Box 1 look like

All pieces in Box 2 look like

In the required pattern, for every piece from Box 2 there are 2 pieces from Box 1.

    a) If 60 pieces from Box 2 are used in the required pattern, how many pieces will be needed altogether?

Answer: _____

T-2a

    b) What fraction of the small squares in the required pattern will be black?

Answer: _____

Part A

Subject	Item Key	Content Category	Performance Expectation	International Average Percent of Students Responding Correctly		International Difficulty Index
				Upper Grade	Lower Grade	
Mathematics	next page	Proportionality	Solving Problems	22%	16%	699

Figure 15–2 Reprinted with permission from *TIMSS Mathematics Items: Released Set for Population 2 (Seventh and Eighth Grades)*. Copyright 1996 by the International Association for the Evaluation of Educational Achievement, The Hague.

Math Program

The two-box problem is a short-answer free-response question that required students to develop and write their own solutions. The information provided at the bottom of the page under Part A describes how the problem was categorized. Most of the information is straightforward. The "international average" section of the table presents the average percent of students responding (from all countries) at two levels. The upper grade average percent (22%) was for the eighth grade students from 41 countries. The lower grade average percent (16%) was for the seventh grade students from 39 countries. The international difficulty is a statistic describing the relative difficulty of the item based on the performance of students.

All together 102 mathematics items are presented in the document *TIMSS Mathematics Items: Released Set for Population 2 (Seventh and Eighth Grades)* (1996). The document is available in printed format or may be downloaded from the Internet at http://www.csteep.bc.edu/ TIMSS1/Items.html.

Of additional interest may be the test items for the third and fourth grades and the test items for the final year of secondary school. They are found on the same web page as the seventh and eighth grade test items. By reviewing the test items you will be able to capture the mathematical focus and emphasis of the TIMSS study.

work that is not distracting. It is also possible to have a classroom so barren and unchanging that children have little or nothing in which to become interested. It is possible to have a classroom so informal that children do not know what to do or where to go or to have a classroom so formal that children become regimented and repressed. It is a challenge to provide a balanced, comfortable, flexible classroom, so that no matter what activity has been planned, there is space available that lends itself to the activity. Also to be considered are the different learning and teaching styles.

The "two boxes" problem shown in Figure 15–2 is one from the Third International Mathematics and Science Study (TIMSS) seventh and eighth grade item pool. The TIMSS research project was sponsored by the International Association for the Evaluation of Educational Achievement (IEA). The achievement tests, the results of which were reported in Chapter 1, were administered in 1994–95. Following the administration of the test TIMSS kept about one-third of the test items for possible future use and released the remainder of the problems to the mathematics community for its use.

Several basic tenets should be kept in mind in providing the physical learning environment.

1. The physical learning environment provides a support system for the educative process. It is important that the physical environment stimulate learning to complement textbooks, teachers, games, and visual aids.
2. As learning environments improve, so does the learning. That is, there is improvement in mathematical concept and skill development as well as communication.
3. Full use of the learning environment will assist you in teaching every child more fully, so that children receive help from both you and the environment.
4. Classrooms for children should mirror the decisions and interests of the children. Children should have the opportunity to help design parts of their own learning environments. Teachers should also help design the learning space.
5. Children's behavior is affected by their learning environment. Anything that affects behavior also affects learning. The quality of the physical environment must be maintained.
6. Be aware of the physical environment as part of the learning process. An awareness of alternative ways to use space is fundamental.
7. The utility of a classroom depends on the awareness of those who spend time in that classroom. Children and teachers do not need a new building or a new classroom to have a rich learning environment.
8. Consider the human and physical needs of children in designing learning environments. Taylor and Vlastos underscore this belief: "If the child's experiences are a starting point for education, then, by def-

inition, his own language and the culture of his home, neighborhood, and community should be utilized in the educational environment. The classroom and outdoor area should play a vital role in reflecting a child's cultural background and his interests" (1975, p. 24).

These tenets provide the key to developing more effective learning environments: adapting existing classroom space. Aspects of the children's world and their learning of math as described in Chapter 2 are that children (1) have many number experiences, (2) are active, (3) observe relationships, (4) learn mathematics in concert with other subjects, and (5) have feelings that should be considered. These characteristics of children provide the starting point in determining how a specific classroom should be structured.

How can the learning environment be enhanced? Provide bulletin boards that invite a response from children, like that shown in Figure 15–3. Provide bulletin boards that inform, such as one that illustrates a variety of historic mathematical tools. Construct large yarn shapes such as squares, triangles, and pentagons to decorate walls and ceilings. Let the children construct space figures by cutting and folding construction paper. Have tetrahedrons, cubes, prisms, octahedrons, dodecahedrons, icosahedrons, and so forth, hanging from the ceiling or along a wall. Build a geodesic dome that can be used by three or four children as a quiet reading place. Rearrange the student desks and learning centers every so often. Display number lines in various locations and configurations around the room. Most of all, be willing to change the decorations occasionally to provide variety and interest.

Whatever classroom you inherit, you can do much to make it a rich learning environment. Evertson and others offer sound suggestions for setting up the physical environment at the beginning of the school year (1989, pp. 3–14). A complete transformation is not expected immediately. There are limits imposed by the classroom structure, time, money, and other school personnel, but an awareness of the existing potential of each classroom and a sensitivity to the children who will spend so many hours in the classroom should serve you in developing, maintaining, and changing the learning environment.

In a pasture there are donkeys and chickens. All together there are 15 heads and 42 feet. How many donkeys? Chickens?

Figure 15–3

Providing Learning Aids

Although some classes and school districts do not use math textbooks, the predominant learning aid in many classrooms is the math textbook. Whether a hardback book or an expendable workbook, the text will provide a curricular framework for your mathematics program, but as you strive to become a more effective teacher, you will find it necessary to move beyond textbook pages and worksheets. When concepts are to be learned, physical models are needed. When skills are to be sharpened or facts are to be memorized, repetitive games or activities are needed. When independent work is prescribed, activity cards, projects, learning centers, and computer programs are needed. Providing quality learning resources to support a sound program of mathematics instruction is basic to effective teaching.

Acquiring learning aids depends on three factors: (1) the financial resources of the school or district, (2) the energy and creativity of the teachers, and (3) the priorities established by the school or district and its intent in providing a strong mathematics program. The last factor is influenced by the other two.

Knowledgeable teachers and curriculum specialists should serve on advisory committees for developing school- or district-wide guidelines for mathematical instruction. They should make recommendations for the wise expenditure of financial resources to provide the school and classrooms with useful learning aids.

Commercial Materials

Excellent commercial materials are available for use in teaching mathematics in the elementary and middle schools. They include textbooks and workbooks, kits, games, structural materials, activity cards, and computer software. Each is briefly discussed.

Textbooks and Workbooks. For many mathematics programs from kindergarten through high school, textbooks and workbooks provide the foundation on which the program rests. These textual materials are carefully prepared by recognized authorities in mathematics education. A textbook or workbook presents a unified sequence of concepts and topics, which are reintroduced at appropriate intervals throughout the book. Textbooks and workbooks tend to be attractive, colorful, and appealing.

Selecting the mathematics textbook or workbook series is an important task, usually performed by a school district or building textbook committee. Most often, teachers have a number of series from which to choose. This list of acceptable textbooks may be compiled by the state department of education. Several general criteria for selecting textual materials should be considered. One listing of criteria is presented below. A final list of criteria is the responsibility of those who actually choose the mathematics series for a district or school. It is these individuals who have considered the goals of the mathematics program, local priorities, budgetary limitations, and teacher resources.

Here are selected general criteria for choosing mathematics textbooks or workbooks. Does the textbook or workbook

1. encourage active student involvement and investigation and discovery of mathematical ideas?
2. present task-oriented problems at the student's level of understanding and encourage higher levels of thinking?
3. suggest the use of physical models?
4. use correct vocabulary yet avoid wordiness and undue difficulty that may interfere with the student's learning?
5. provide adequate exercises to assist in introducing mathematical concepts and skills?
6. spiral the mathematical ideas so students confront an idea several times in the elementary and middle school years, each time at a slightly more advanced level, but avoiding needless rote repetition?
7. have an accompanying teacher's edition with valuable suggestions for introducing, reinforcing, diagnosing, and reintroducing mathematical concepts and skills?
8. relate mathematical concepts that have common parts, for example, ordering relations with objects (is taller than), numbers (is greater than), and measurement (is longer than)?
9. build mathematical concepts and skills on previously understood concepts and skills?
10. support the learning of basic addition, subtraction, multiplication, and division facts?
11. allow for students to progress at different rates, reflecting individual differences among children?
12. interest students because it is attractive, colorful, and motivating, page after page?

Kits. Commercial kits for use in mathematics learning are typically of three different types. **Kits of diagnostic and learning materials** may contain physical models used to test youngsters relative to their development of prenumber and early number skills; for example, classifying, ordering, corresponding, and counting. Kits are available that provide materials useful in developing an initial understanding of classifying, relationships, number, fractions, and measurement.

Throughout this text, we have spoken of materials available in kits. Unifix and Cuisenaire materials are two such types of manipulatives. It is common to find structural materials in kits. *Explorations* and *Mathematics Their Way,* popular primary-level math programs, employ a wide variety of physical models in kits.

Kits designed to accompany textbook or workbook series provide physical models illustrated or suggested by the teacher's edition of the series. These kits may contain attribute materials, colored rods, counters, or measuring apparatus. This type of kit is a valuable resource, since it allows students to work with concrete materials as they learn mathematical ideas. Similarly, kits with physical models can be specially prepared by distributors for school districts or to meet the recommendations of state departments of education.

The third type of kit is a **skills kit.** The skills kit provides audio cassettes, cards, or games for basic skills practice. These skills may be computation with whole numbers, fractions, geometry, problem solving, or other math topics. The advantage of such materials is that they allow students to work independently or in small groups at their own level, freeing the teacher to work with other students.

The best way to find out what sorts of kits are available is to peruse catalogs from commercial distributors of educational materials. (See Appendix A for a list of suppliers of educational materials.) Exhibits of kits and other materials are found at professional meetings, such as those sponsored by the National Council of Teachers of Mathematics.

When choosing kits for classroom use, carefully review the goals of the mathematics program. The amount of time devoted to kit materials should be determined by the nature of the mathematics program and the particular kits being considered. The convenience of a kit must be weighed against the amount of interest the kit will generate and maintain. If the kit can provide a function not provided by other components of a mathematics program or by classroom materials, it should be considered for possible purchase.

Games. There is a wide selection of games available to reinforce mathematical skills. Card games, race board games, tile games, target games, dice games, table games, word and picture games, and games of probability may help develop skills in recognition of characteristics, counting, recognition of numerals and number patterns, probability, matching, developing strategies, and problem solving. Children are usually motivated by commercial games.

Often, students are unaware of the mathematical value of games. At times, it may be appropriate for you to explain the relationship of a game to a particular skill the students are learning in a nongame context. For example, the popular card game Old Maid helps develop recognition and matching. Once students have played this game, you may help develop the transfer of matching playing cards to matching attribute blocks, parquetry blocks, or tessellation patterns. Be careful, however, not to destroy the students' enjoyment of the game and their motivation for the sake of the mathematics.

Games for classrooms are available from distributors of educational materials, department stores, and toy stores. Select games that fit clearly within the context of the total mathematics program. Sometimes the expense of games may prohibit their purchase. In such cases, teachers are encouraged to construct their own games using materials available in the school. A discussion of constructing games is presented below.

Structural Materials. Structural learning aids are usually designed to help teach particular mathematical concepts and clearly illustrate the concepts for which they were developed. Examples of structural materials are Cuisenaire rods, multibase arithmetic blocks, and attribute blocks. Structural materials help develop concepts of number, properties, place value, and sorting, as well as logical thinking. Sources of structural learning aids appear in Appendix A.

Although sets of structural materials tend to be expensive, they are often the most useful purchases teachers can make to support a sound mathematics program. Shop around for structural materials and purchase materials only when you know the advantages, disadvantages, and uses of the materials. Sales representatives or educational consultants sometimes offer workshops in using certain materials. Take advantage of workshops to learn the full value of materials.

Activity Cards. Activity cards are designed to lead students through developmental sequences that provide guided discovery. Use of activity cards is often associated with classroom learning centers. Activity cards have the advantage of encouraging independent work by students, thus freeing the teacher to work with other students. There are cards for use with attribute blocks, geoboards, pattern blocks, geoblocks, color cubes, and other physical models.

Pictures and diagrams sometimes replace words to direct children to specific activities. The key in considering activity cards for students is the clarity of the instructions. A set of activity cards that children are unable to understand represents a waste of valuable funds.

When considering purchasing activity cards, consider certain general characteristics that the cards should possess. Characteristics of good activity cards are listed below:

1. The questions or activities on an activity card should tend to be open-ended; that is, they should encourage students to give a number of responses to interesting problems.
2. The objectives of an activity card should be clear to the child and the teacher.
3. The wording or directions should be concise and should be presented at the student's reading level.
4. Activity cards should provide some way for students to record their answers or responses.

5. Activity cards should allow for higher levels of thinking than just memorization.
6. Activity cards should be attractive.
7. The cards should make use of the environment—the classroom or outside.
8. The cards should encourage active exploration and manipulation of materials.

Computer Software. Computer software abounds for the educational market. It serves many functions. It provides opportunities for problem solving, direct instruction, skill practice, follow-up instruction for work with physical models such as attribute blocks and Fraction Bars, interaction between student and computer, assessment, and record keeping.

Some of the software available is of high quality in terms of both the way the mathematics is presented and the cleverness of the graphics that accompany the presentation. The future will see a greater number of software programs that are even more sophisticated and useful. New generations of computers introduced into the classroom will allow students more creative applications.

Not all software is equally useful or of the same high quality. You must be a discriminating consumer. Before you make final selections of software for your school or classroom, take the opportunity to examine the content of each program carefully. Use it on your computer. If possible, let students work with it. Test your reactions and those of your students. See if the objectives of the software match the objectives of the mathematics program. Read reviews of the software in journals devoted to computer education. Make sure the software is compatible with your computer. If color plays an important role in a program, the program will be of little use unless you have a color monitor available.

Computer software is available through general educational material catalogs and software distributors and their catalogs. (See Appendix A for a list of suppliers of software.) Once on a mailing list, you will have a source for a great variety of software. Attend workshop sessions at professional meetings to find out more about computer offerings. Check with curriculum specialists to see what they recommend. And ask your colleagues in a school. Those who consistently use software will be able to suggest specific programs and sources.

Teacher-Made Learning Aids

Teachers may wish to construct their own learning aids. By doing so, they save money and at the same time tailor activities to fit their students. All that is required is an interest in such a task and the willingness to devote the time and energy needed to do a quality job. Effective teachers are renowned for these characteristics. Following are some examples of games or activities intended to assist students in practicing and remembering basic facts associated with addition, subtraction, multiplication, division, and fractions. The significance of the games described rests in the adaptability of a single game idea to many useful games that employ the same strategy.

Adapting the Rules or the Action of an Existing Game. Most games that teachers invent are adaptations of existing games they have seen or played. The simplest way to invent games is to modify the rules or the action of one already known. For example, Addition Top It, which we introduced in Chapter 7, is an adaptation of a popular students' card game called War and may be considered merely an addition game. A little more reflection reveals many other potential practice activities. Multiplication Top It was presented in Chapter 8. Then we began to find other uses for Top It.

1. If addition is to be stressed, the cards can be rewritten with series of three or perhaps four addends. Thus, cards may appear in the format in Figure 15–4a.
2. When students are ready for introductory multiplication work, the addition cards may have three, four, or five addends with the same value, as shown in Figure 15–4b.
3. The original instructions did not mention subtraction. Since addition and subtraction facts may be learned in concert, Subtraction Top It is appropriate. Sample cards are shown in Figure 15–4c.
4. Cards with mixed addition and subtraction expressions can be used as practice for both operations. The cards might look like those in Figure 15–4d.
5. If younger children are involved, they can play a similar game using dot patterns instead of addition or subtraction expressions. Figure 15–4e illustrates sample cards.
6. Another way to vary the game is to use numerals, as shown in Figure 15–4f.

The essential action has been retained in each variation shown in Figure 15–4; that is, two cards are drawn, and the larger number takes the smaller. In the case of a tie, another card is picked by both of the players who tied.

The second way to modify a game is to change the rules. One general example will suffice to illustrate changing the rules. Each game discussed above could be constructed so that each numeral or figure is one of two colors, blue or orange. The rules could be altered, so that when both players draw the same color numeral or figure, the larger takes the smaller, but when the two players draw different colors, the smaller takes the larger. Thus, with one rule change, the games assume a different character, although they maintain the goal of providing practice in basic mathematical skills.

Take care to prevent boredom by spacing the uses of variations of the same game and by using only variations

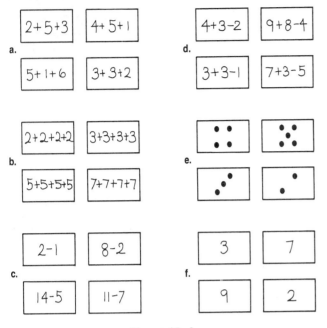

Figure 15–4

appropriate for the practice needed. The multitude of examples listed show how games are invented by modifying the action or the rules of existing games.

Adapting the Rules and the Action. There are times when simultaneously adapting the rules and the action of a game produces an activity quite different from the original. For example, consider three activities involving the creative use of dominoes. First, some description of the dominoes and their construction is appropriate. Although it is quite all right to use commercially produced dominoes for these activities, students are particularly attracted by larger sets, which are easily constructed from railroad board. A set that measures 10 by 20 centimeters is a good size. The complete set of 28 double-six dominoes is shown in Figure 15–5.

Domino Activity 1: Sum

Objective: to score as many points as possible in a single round by adding the numbers of dots on five dominoes.

Materials: dominoes, paper, pencil

Players: 2 to 5

Play:

1. Spread out the dominoes face down.
2. Each player picks one domino, turns it over, and adds the numbers of dots. The player with the highest total plays first.
3. Each player then chooses five of the unexposed dominoes but does not look at them.
4. The first player turns over the five dominoes one at a time. When a domino is turned over, the player adds the numbers of dots, then announces and records the total. The first player continues to turn over the dominoes, announcing and recording each sum.
5. When the first player has finished with all five dominoes, he or she determines the score for the round by adding the five numbers recorded.
6. The next player continues in the same manner, hoping to find a larger total.
7. The player with the highest score wins that particular game. Play continues as before, with different students having the opportunity to win the game. Sample play for one player in one round is shown in Figure 15–6.

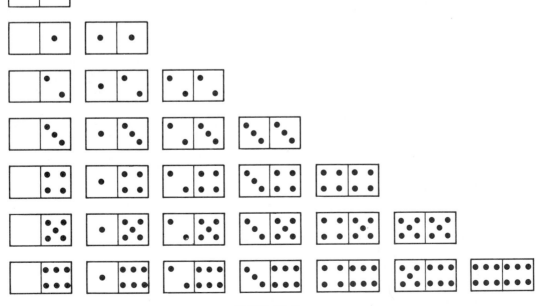

Figure 15–5

Domino Activity 2: Going Down

Objective: to get as close as possible to zero without going below it.

Materials: dominoes, paper, pencil.

Players: 2 to 5.

Play:

1. Spread out the dominoes face down.
2. Each player picks one domino, turns it over, and finds the difference between the number of dots on the two halves. The player with the highest difference plays first. (See Figure 15–7. Player 2 would play first.)
3. Each player then chooses five of the unexposed dominoes but does not look at them. The player must use exactly four of the five dominoes during the round.
4. At the start of play, each player has 10 points.
5. The first player turns over the five dominoes one at a time. When a domino is turned over, the player finds the difference between the numbers on the two halves. The player then subtracts the difference from the starting score of 10 points and records the new score. Because the player may use only four of the five dominoes, he or she must decide which one to discard. The decision whether or not to discard a domino must be made when the difference is determined. Once a domino is used, it may not later be dis-

carded. Likewise, once a domino has been discarded, all of the remaining dominoes must be played.
6. The first player continues until four dominoes have been used, or until the score goes below zero, in which case the player loses the round. Play continues until all players have played.
7. The player closest to zero without going below it wins the round. Sample play for one player in one round is shown in Figure 15–8.

Domino Activity 3: Match

Objective: to collect as many dominoes as possible.

Materials: dominoes

Players: 2

Play:

1. Shuffle the dominoes and stack them face down in the center of the playing area.
2. Each player picks one domino, turns it over, and adds the number of dots. The player with the highest total plays first.
3. The first player declares "Match," picks a domino from the stack, and turns it face up. The second player then picks a domino from the stack and turns it face up.
4. If there is a match, the player declaring match picks up and keeps both dominoes. If no match occurs, the second player picks up both dominoes. A match occurs when the dots on either end of one domino match the dots on either end of the other domino or when the sum of dots on one domino matches the sum of dots on the other domino.
5. Play continues with the second player declaring match. Both players then turn over dominoes to see who will keep the dominoes.
6. Play continues with players alternately declaring match until all the dominoes have been taken.

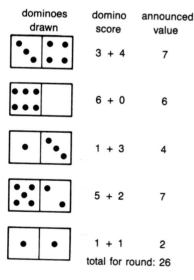

dominoes drawn	domino score	announced value
	3 + 4	7
	6 + 0	6
	1 + 3	4
	5 + 2	7
	1 + 1	2
	total for round:	26

Figure 15–6

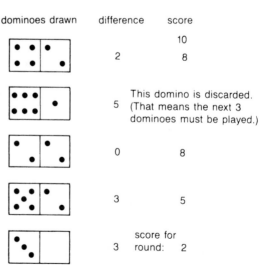

dominoes drawn	difference	score
		10
	2	8
	5	This domino is discarded. (That means the next 3 dominoes must be played.)
	0	8
	3	5
	3	score for round: 2

Figure 15–8

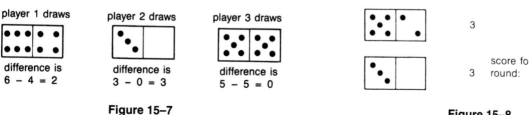

player 1 draws

difference is
6 – 4 = 2

player 2 draws

difference is
3 – 0 = 3

player 3 draws

difference is
5 – 5 = 0

Figure 15–7

7. The player with the greatest number of dominoes wins the game.

As you can see, these domino activities are different from the game of Dominoes. They do, however, represent the creative use of a common material. With additional thought, you should be able to develop some domino activities of your own. How might the dominoes be used with multiplication, fractions, or decimals?

Student-Made Learning Aids

Students are capable of developing and constructing learning aids. We have encouraged you to involve students in inventing problem-solving activities. We also encourage you to challenge students to develop fun games and activities that may be used to reinforce skills. Their first attempts to develop *new* games will most likely involve changing the rules of an existing game. Students may wish to alter games in the ways mentioned earlier for teachers.

After a little practice with games, students will be interested in trying to invent games of their own. One way we have found to generate enthusiasm for inventing games is to announce a games contest. A games contest can be effective if it is preceded by discussion and analysis of the components of various games. Kohl (1974) described six such components in detail: theme, playing board, pieces, decision devices, goals, and teaching the game. Once students know about the structure of games, they will be more effective inventors of games. Cruikshank and Martin (1981) describe how one successful games contest was organized and operated. Whether participating in a games contest, suggesting changes in how games are played, or experimenting with making games, students prove to be imaginative and creative.

Constructing Learning Aids

Once you decide on a sound, usable learning aid, begin construction. Game boards and cards should be attractive and colorful. Children enjoy bright, cheery materials with which to play. These materials can be made with brightly colored railroad board or with colorful lettering and drawings on white railroad board. Pictures cut from magazines, ready-made stickers, or students' drawings sometimes add an extra touch of color that attracts students.

Materials should be durable. Teachers willing to spend the time and effort to produce a long-lasting, durable aid will be rewarded by time saved repairing or remaking the activity. Most teacher-made materials may be protected by covering the board or cards with either plastic laminate or clear contact paper. Both protective materials are readily available at art, hardware, and variety stores. Once covered, front and back, a learning aid will last for months or even years.

The quality of an aid is improved if care is taken when lettering or attaching pictures to the material. Letters and numerals should be easy to read. They may be affixed by hand, such as rub-on letters, or stenciled. Gummed letters or numerals also may be used. Using a lettering machine such as an Ellison to cut out letters, numerals, and teaching aids such as tangrams, pentominoes, fraction pieces, attribute blocks, pattern blocks and base ten blocks can also enhance the quality of your learning aids.

Some activities should have written instructions or should be explained by the teacher. Because an activity with poorly explained rules is of little value, the instructions should be carefully worded to be clear and concise. Pictures or drawings are often useful in explaining the action of a game.

Besides motivating students, learning aids should help reinforce or teach a concept or skill. There should be no question in your mind about what concept or skill is being presented by a learning aid. As well, for nearly every learning aid, consider the potential for adapting it to make another learning aid for teaching mathematics, communication skills, social studies, science, and so on.

Concentration games are among the most versatile. Sixteen to 48 cards may reinforce shapes, number patterns, numeral-number recognition, addition, subtraction, multiplication, division, words with the same beginning sound, homonyms, names and faces, animals and habitats, and so forth. For younger children, fewer cards (8 to 16) should be used and the cards should be laid out in two rows. The simplicity of concentration games makes them practical learning aids.

When you are assigned your first classroom, take the opportunity to go into the room alone and look it over. If it is during the summer, there may be no furniture or the furniture may be in disarray. Imagine how you would like the classroom to look. Imagine children in the room and instruction taking place. Begin to sense how all of the space can be useful. When you leave, let your mind work on how that learning environment will be molded in the months to come into an exciting, alive, dynamic environment for all the children. What a wonderful place it will be in which to learn mathematics!

KEY IDEAS

Fitting mathematics instruction to students' differing needs requires careful planning. Give consideration to both the students' and your own needs and styles. You are encouraged to teach using a variety of approaches.

Assessing mathematics learning involves collecting data through observation and questioning, performance-based assessment, diagnostic interviews, teacher-made assessment tasks, writing activities, group problem solving, standardized tests, and textbook tests. Once collected, assessment data should be used as a basis for further mathematics instruction and discussions with students and parents.

There are a number of students with special needs in most classrooms. Some students need additional help and time as they learn mathematics. Continued work with physical models helps to lay the groundwork for success. Other students have special talent when it comes to mathematics. They, too, need additional time and direction. Exposure to rich resources benefits the mathematically promising student.

The physical environment for learning mathematics should be inviting. It is a special place for students and should reflect their interests as well as those of the teacher. As a part of the learning environment, learning aids provide the framework for the mathematics curriculum. Textbooks, kits, games, structural materials, activity cards, and computers are commonly found in well-established classrooms.

DISCUSSION QUESTIONS

1. Explain the value of developing lesson plans in detail as you begin your student teaching experiences and the value of developing block plans as you begin your teaching career. Describe a situation in which it is important to augment block plans by writing out more complete directions for yourself.

2. Investigate cooperative learning procedures by reading one of the books suggested in the References (Johnson and Johnson, 1987 or Kagan). Discuss when cooperative learning groups are appropriate and when other forms of grouping are appropriate.

3. Select an issue of *Teaching Children Mathematics* or *Mathematics Teaching in the Middle School*. Find an article of interest and prepare a lesson plan to teach the topic suggested in the article. Share your lesson plan with fellow students.

4. Describe the value of various types of assessment techniques: observation and questioning, performance-based, teacher-made, writing, group problem solving, standardized tests, and textbook tests. When is one technique more important or less important?

5. Sketch a classroom with which you are familiar or in which you would like to begin your teaching. Discuss the advantages of the room arrangement with respect to the mathematics teaching style that you envision for yourself and the children that you will be teaching.

REFERENCES

Abruscato, Joseph, "Early Results and Tentative Implications from the Vermont Portfolio Project," *Phi Delta Kappan,* 74, no. 6 (February 1993), 474–477.

Baratta-Lorton, Mary, *Mathematics Their Way.* Menlo Park, CA: Addison-Wesley, 1976.

Barson, Alan, "Task Cards," *Arithmetic Teacher,* 26, no. 2 (October 1978), 53–54.

Biggs, Edith E., and James R. MacLean, *Freedom to Learn.* Reading, MA: Addison-Wesley, 1969.

Burk, Donna, Allyn Snider, and Paula Symonds, *Math Excursions 2.* Portsmouth, NH: Heinemann, 1991.

Burns, Marilyn, "Groups of Four: Solving the Management Problem," *Learning,* 10, no. 2 (September 1981), 46–51.

Charles, Randall, Frank Lester, and Phares O'Daffer, *How to Evaluate Progress in Problem Solving.* Reston, VA: National Council of Teachers of Mathematics, 1987.

Childs, Leigh, and Nancy Adams, *Math Sponges.* San Diego, CA: National Institute for Curriculum Enrichment, 1979.

Coombs, Betty, and Lalie Harcourt, *Explorations 2.* Don Mills, ON: Addison-Wesley, 1986.

Copeland, Richard W., *How Children Learn Mathematics.* Englewood Cliffs, NJ: Merrill/Prentice Hall, 1984.

Cruikshank, Douglas E., and John A. Martin, Jr. "The Mathematical Game Contest," *Arithmetic Teacher,* 28, no. 5 (January 1981), 42–45.

Design Group, *The Way to Play.* New York: Paddington Press, 1975.

Edge, Douglas, "Beyond the Classroom," *Teaching Children Mathematics,* 4, no. 6 (February 1998), 308–309.

Enrichment Mathematics for the Grades, National Council of Teachers of Mathematics, 27th Yearbook. Reston, VA: NCTM, 1963.

EQUALS and California Mathematics Council Assessment Committee, *Assessment Alternatives in Mathematics: An Overview of Assessment Techniques That Promote Learning.* Berkeley, CA: EQUALS, Lawrence Hall of Science, University of California, 1989.

Evertson, Carolyn M., et al., *Classroom Management for Elementary Teachers.* Englewood Cliffs, NJ: Prentice Hall, 1989.

Harris, Holly, and Sharon Rose Jones, *Eat Your Math.* Corvallis, OR: Callan and Brooks, 1994.

The International Association for the Evaluation of Educational Achievement, *TIMSS Mathematics Items, Released Set for Population* 2. Chestnut Hill, MA: Boston College, 1996.

Johnson, David W., and Roger T. Johnson, *Learning Together and Alone: Cooperative, Competitive, and Individualistic Learning.* Englewood Cliffs, NJ: Prentice Hall, 1987.

Johnson, David W., Roger T. Johnson, and Edythe Johnson Holubec, *Circles of Learning: Cooperation in the Classroom.* Edina, MN: Interaction Book Co., 1986.

Kagan, Spencer, *Cooperative Learning.* San Juan Capistrano, CA: Resources for Teachers, Inc. 1992.

Kohl, Herbert R., *Math, Writing and Games.* New York: The New York Book Review, 1974.

Lane County Mathematics Project, *Problem Solving in Mathematics.* Palo Alto, CA: Dale Seymour, 1984.

Moomaw, Vera, et al., *Expanded Mathematics Grades 4–5–6.* Eugene, OR: School District No. 4, Instruction Department, 1967.

National Council of Teachers of Mathematics, *Assessment Standards for School Mathematics.* Reston, VA: NCTM, 1995.

————, *Assessment Standards for School Mathematics* (working draft). Reston, VA: NCTM, 1993.

————, *Professional Standards for Teaching Mathematics.* Reston, VA: NCTM, 1991.

————, *Agenda for Action.* Reston, VA: NCTM, 1980.

National Research Council, *Measuring Up: Prototypes for Mathematics Assessment.* Washington, DC: National Academy Press, 1993.

Office of Educational Research and Improvement (OERI), *Pursuing Excellence: A Study of U.S. Fourth-Grade Mathematics and Science Achievement in International Context.* Washington, DC: OERI, U.S. Department of Education, June 1997.

————, *Pursuing Excellence: A Study of U.S. Eighth-Grade Mathematics and Science Teaching, Learning, Curriculum, and Achievement in International Context.* Washington, DC: OERI, U.S. Department of Education, November 1996.

Peck, Donald M., Stanley M. Jencks, and Michael L. Connell, "Improving Instruction Through Brief Interviews," *Arithmetic Teacher,* 37, no. 3 (November 1989), 15–17.

Peterson, Daniel, *Functional Mathematics for the Mentally Retarded.* Englewood Cliffs, NJ: Merrill/Prentice Hall, 1973.

Reimer, Wilbert, and Luetta Reimer, *Historical Connections in Mathematics.* Fresno, CA: AIMS Educational Foundation, 1992.

Rosenshine, Barak, and Robert Stevens, "Teaching Functions," in *Handbook of Research on Teaching,* ed. Merlin C. Wittrock. Englewood Cliffs, NJ: Merrill/Prentice Hall, 1986.

Ross, Pat O'Connell, *National Excellence: A Case for Developing America's Talent.* Washington, DC: OERI, U.S. Department of Education, October 1993.

Rowan, Thomas E., and Josepha Robles, "Using Questions to Help Children Build Mathematical Power," *Teaching Children Mathematics,* 4, no. 9 (May 1998), 504–509.

Schoen, Harold L., and Marilyn J. Zweng, eds., *Estimation and Mental Computation,* National Council of Teachers of Mathematics, 1986 Yearbook. Reston, VA: NCTM, 1986.

Sheffield, Linda J. (ed.), *Developing Mathematically Promising Students.* Reston, VA: National Council of Teachers of Mathematics, 1999.

Sheffield, Linda J., Jennie Bennett, Manuel Berriozábal, Margaret DeArmond, and Richard Wertheimer, *Report of the NCTM Task Force on the Mathematically Promising.* Reston, VA: National Council of Teachers of Mathematics, December 1995.

Shroyer, Janet, and William Fitzgerald, *Mouse and Elephant: Measuring Growth.* Menlo Park, CA: Addison-Wesley, 1986.

The Slow Learner in Mathematics, National Council of Teachers of Mathematics, 35th Yearbook. Reston, VA: NCTM, 1972.

Taylor, Ann P., and George Vlastos, *School Zone: Learning Environments for Children.* New York: Van Nostrand Reinhold, 1975.

Webb, Norman L., "Assessment for the Mathematics Classroom," in *Assessment in the Mathematics Classroom,* National Council of Teachers of Mathematics, 1993 Yearbook, ed. Norman L. Webb and Arthur F. Coxford. Reston, VA: NCTM, 1993.

Technology

Office of Educational Research and Improvement (OERI) and the National Center for Education Statistics (NCES). *Attaining Excellence: A TIMSS Resource Kit.* Washington, DC: OERI and NCES, 1998.

Web Sites

http://eryx.syr.edu   ERIC database for educational topics.

http://forum.swarthmore.edu/   Comprehensive site for mathematics resources.

http://forum.swarthmore.edu/mathmagic/   Teams of students work together to solve challenging mathematical problems.

http://nces.ed.gov/TIMSS   Report of the Third International Mathematics and Science Study.

http://www.cec.sped.org/ericec/   ERIC Clearinghouse on Disabilities and Gifted Education.

http://www.nctm.org/   Home page of the National Council of Teachers of Mathematics.

http://www.nsta.org   Home page of the National Science Teachers Association.

http://www.shout.net—mathman/   Mathematical resources for talented and motivated children.

http://www.csteep.bc.edu/TIMSS1/Items.html   Location of the released test items from the Third International Mathematics and Science Study.

Sources for Competitions and Other Programs

Following is a list of web sites for some of the agencies that sponsor competitions and other programs for the development of promising mathematics students.

American Mathematics Competitions (American High School Mathematics Examination, American International Mathematics Examination, United States of America Mathematical Olympiad, and American Junior High Mathematics Examination): http://www.unl.edu/amc/

American Regions Mathematics League: http://www.armnmath.org/

Education Program for Gifted Youth (EPGY): Stanford University. http://www-epgy.Stanford.edu/

Institute for the Academic Advancement of Youth Talent Search, John Hopkins University: http://www.jhu.edu/~gifted/ts/

MATHCOUNTS, National Society of Professional Engineers Information Center: http://www.mathcounts.org/

National Engineering Aptitude Search (NEAS+), Tests of Engineering Aptitude, Mathematics, and Science (TEAMS), National Engineering Design Challenge (NEDC), Junior Engineering Technical Society: http://www.asec.org/jets/

National Engineers Week Future City Competition: http://www.eweek.org/

USA Mathematical Talent Search: http://www.nsa.gov:8080/programs/mepp/usamts.html/

Suppliers of Manipulative Materials and Computer Software

Activity Resources Company, Inc.
P.O. Box 4875
Hayward, CA 94540
www.activityresources.com

AIMS Education Foundation
1595 S. Chestnut Ave.
Fresno, CA 93702
http://www.aimsedu.org/

American Educational Products, Inc.
P.O. Box 2121
Fort Collins, CO 80522
http://amep.com/

Apple Computer, Inc.
1 Infinite Loop
Cupertino, CA 95014
http://www.apple.com/

Broderbund Software, Inc.
P.O. Box 6125
Novato, CA 94948-6125
http://www.broderbund.com/education

Carson-Dellosa Publishing Co., Inc.
P.O. Box 35665
Greensboro, NC 27425-5665
http://www.ed-ex.com/c1.html

Classroom Connect
431 Madrid Avenue
Torrance, CA 90501-1430
http://www.classroom.com/

Creative Publications
5623 W. 115th St.
Alsip, IL 60803
http://www.creativepublications.com/

Critical Thinking Books and Software
P.O. Box 448
Pacific Grove, CA 93950
http://www.criticalthinking.com

Cuisenaire Co. of America, Inc.
P.O. Box 5026
White Plains, NY 10602-5026
http://www.cuisenaire.com/

Dale Seymour Publications
P.O. Box 10888
Palo Alto, CA 94303
http://www.aw.com/dsp/

Delta Education
P.O. Box 3000
Nashua, NH 03061-3000
http://www.delta-ed.com/

Didax Educational Resources, Inc.
395 Main Street
Rowley, MA 01969-3785
http://www.didaxinc.com/index.html

Don Cohen - The Mathman
809 Stratford Dr.
Champaign, IL 61821
http://www.shout.net/~mathman

Edmark Corporation
P.O. Box 97021
Redmond, WA 98073
http://www.edmark.com/

Educational Enrichment, Inc.
P.O. Box 1524
Norman, OK 73070
http://www.eeionline.com/eei/

Educational Resources
1550 Executive Drive
Elgin, IL 60121-1900
http://www.edresources.com/homepage.htm

Educational Teaching Aids
620 Lakeview Parkway
Vernon Hills, IL 60061-1838
http://www.etauniverse.com/

ERIC/CSMEE: Clearinghouse for Science,
Mathematics, and Environmental Education
1929 Kenny Road
Columbus, Ohio 43210-1079
http://www.ericse.org/

FASE Productions
4801 Wilshire Blvd.
Suite 215
Los Angeles, CA 90010
http://www.fasenet.org/

GPN
University of Nebraska-Lincoln
P.O. Box 80669
Lincoln, NE 68501-0669
http://gpn.unl.edu/

Hartley Courseware
3451 Dunckel Rd., Suite 200
Lansing, MI 48711
http://www.nol.net/~athel/org/har.html

Heinemann
361 Hanover St.
Portsmouth, NH 03801-3912
http://www.heinemann.com/

Human Relations Media (HRM)
175 Tompkins Ave.
Pleasantville, NY 10570
http://www.absurdmath.inter.net/

Key Curriculum Press
Box 2304
Berkeley, CA 94702-0304
http://www.keypress.com/

Kluwer Academic Publishers
101 Philip Drive
Norwell, MA 02061
http://www.wkap.nl/

Knowledge Adventure, Inc.
1984 Pioneer Ave.
Torrance, CA 90503
http://www.knowledgeadventure.com/home/

Lawrence Erlbaum Associates, Inc.
10 Industrial Avenue
Mahwah, NJ 07430-2262
http://www.erlbaum.com/

University of California, Berkeley
Lawrence Hall of Science #5200
Berkeley, CA 94720-5200
http://www.lhs.berkeley.edu/

The Learning Company
One Athenaeum Street
Cambridge, MA 02142
http://www.learningco.com/

The Math Learning Center
P.O. Box 3226
Salem, OR 97302
http://www.mlc.pdx.edu/

Math Solutions Publications
Marilyn Burns Education Associates
150 Gate 5 Road, Suite 101
Sausalito, CA 94965
http://www.mathsolutions.com/

MindPlay
160 W. Ft. Lowell
Tucson, AZ 85705
http://www.mindplay.com/index.html

National Academy Press
2101 Constitution Ave., NW
Washington, DC 20418
http://www.nap.edu/

National Council of Teachers of Mathematics
1906 Association Drive
Reston, VA 22091
http://www.nctm.org/

National Middle School Association
Corporate Exchange Drive
Suite 370
Columbus, Ohio 43231-1672
http://www.nmsa.org/

Optimum Resource, Inc.
5 Hiltech Lane
Hilton Head, SC 29926
http://www.stickybear.com/

Pierian Spring Software
5200 S. W. Macadam Avenue
Suite 570
Portland, OR 97201
http://www.pierian.com/

Prentice Hall
1 Lake Street
Upper Saddle River, NJ 07458
http://www.phschool.com/

Roger Wagner Publishing, Inc.
1050 Pioneer Way, Suite P
El Cajon, CA 92020
http://www.hyperstudio.com/main/content.shtml

Scholastic News Media
2931 East McCarty St.
Jefferson City, MO 65101
http://www.scholastic.com/

School Science and Mathematics Association
Department of Curriculum and Foundations
Bloomsburg University
400 East Second Street
Bloomsburg, PA 17815-1301
http://www.ssma.org/

Scott Foresman-Addison Wesley
2725 Sand Hill Road
Menlo Park, California 94025
http://www.scottforesman.com/sfaw/
http://www2.awl.com/corp/disciplines/school.html

SRA/McGraw-Hill
220 East Danieldale Rd.
DeSoto, TX 75115-2490
http://www.sra-4kids.com/

Sunburst Communications
101 Castleton Street
P.O. Box 100
Pleasantville, NY 10570-0100
http://www.sunburst.com

Texas Instruments, Inc.
7800 Banner Drive
Dallas, TX 75251
http://www.ti.com/calc/

Third International Mathematics and Science Study
National Center for Education Statistics
555 New Jersey Avenue, NW
Room 400D, Capitol Place
Washington, DC 20208-5574
http://nces.ed.gov/TIMSS/

Tom Snyder Productions
80 Coolidge Hill Road
Watertown, MA 02172-2817
http://www.teachtsp.com/

Tricon
2150 Enterprise Dr.
Mt. Pleasant, MI 48858
http://www.triconpub.com/

Appendix B

Blackline Masters

Permission is granted by the publisher to reproduce the forms on pages 482–513.

Attribute Shapes

Dot Cards

Ten Frame

Ten Frames

Base Five Patterns

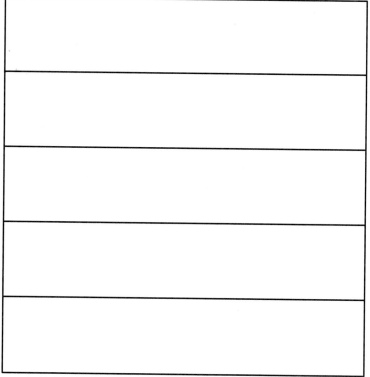

Base Five Patterns

Base Ten Patterns (Decimal Patterns)

Base Ten Patterns (Decimal Patterns)

Base Ten Patterns (Decimal Patterns)

Hundreds Chart

1	2	3	4	5	6	7	8	9	10
11	12	13	14	15	16	17	18	19	20
21	22	23	24	25	26	27	28	29	30
31	32	33	34	35	36	37	38	39	40
41	42	43	44	45	46	47	48	49	50
51	52	53	54	55	56	57	58	59	60
61	62	63	64	65	66	67	68	69	70
71	72	73	74	75	76	77	78	79	80
81	82	83	84	85	86	87	88	89	90
91	92	93	94	95	96	97	98	99	100

Blank Hundreds Chart

Table for Addition or Multiplication

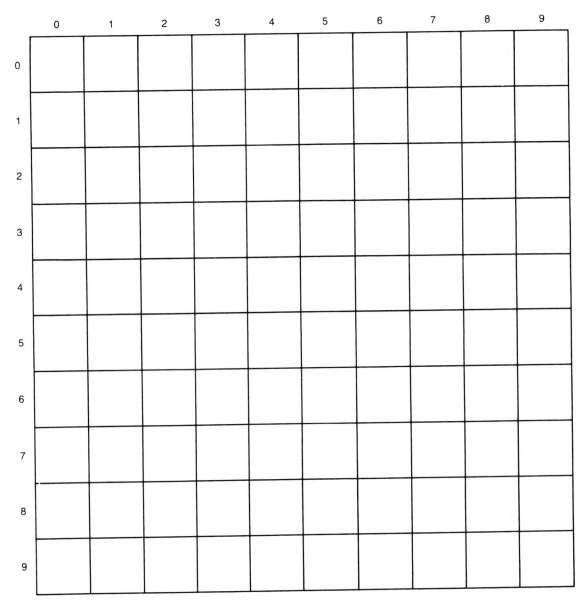

Centimeter Graph Paper

Inch Graph Paper

Circular Fraction Patterns

Rectangular Fraction Patterns

one unit

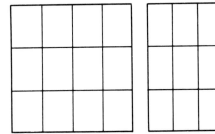

Fraction Strips

1

$\frac{1}{2}$	$\frac{1}{2}$

$\frac{1}{3}$	$\frac{1}{3}$	$\frac{1}{3}$

$\frac{1}{4}$	$\frac{1}{4}$	$\frac{1}{4}$	$\frac{1}{4}$

$\frac{1}{6}$	$\frac{1}{6}$	$\frac{1}{6}$	$\frac{1}{6}$	$\frac{1}{6}$	$\frac{1}{6}$

$\frac{1}{8}$	$\frac{1}{8}$	$\frac{1}{8}$	$\frac{1}{8}$	$\frac{1}{8}$	$\frac{1}{8}$	$\frac{1}{8}$	$\frac{1}{8}$

$\frac{1}{12}$	$\frac{1}{12}$	$\frac{1}{12}$	$\frac{1}{12}$	$\frac{1}{12}$	$\frac{1}{12}$	$\frac{1}{12}$	$\frac{1}{12}$	$\frac{1}{12}$	$\frac{1}{12}$	$\frac{1}{12}$	$\frac{1}{12}$

$\frac{1}{24}$	$\frac{1}{24}$	$\frac{1}{24}$	$\frac{1}{24}$	$\frac{1}{24}$	$\frac{1}{24}$	$\frac{1}{24}$	$\frac{1}{24}$	$\frac{1}{24}$	$\frac{1}{24}$	$\frac{1}{24}$	$\frac{1}{24}$	$\frac{1}{24}$	$\frac{1}{24}$	$\frac{1}{24}$	$\frac{1}{24}$	$\frac{1}{24}$	$\frac{1}{24}$	$\frac{1}{24}$	$\frac{1}{24}$	$\frac{1}{24}$	$\frac{1}{24}$	$\frac{1}{24}$	$\frac{1}{24}$

How to Make a Geoboard

You need: One 8″ × 8″ piece of $\frac{3}{8}''$ plywood

Twenty-five $\frac{5}{8}''$ escutcheon pins (#16 cr #18)

One straight and accurate ruler

One pencil

One hammer

Some fine sandpaper

Step 1: Use the sandpaper to smooth the edges of your board.

Step 2: Carefully measure and lightly mark on your board five evenly spaced rows and columns. Where each intersection occurs, drive a nail. Each row and column is $1\frac{3}{4}''$ from the next row and column. The border is $\frac{1}{2}''$.

Step 3: Pound the nails into the board at the intersections of the rows and columns. Be sure the nails are in the straightest rows possible. Constantly line them up by sighting along the rows of escutcheon pins.

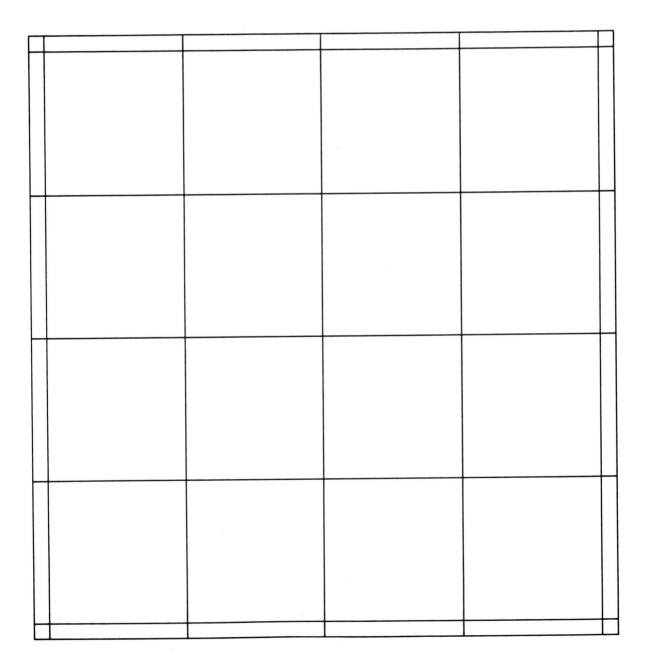

Geoboard Dot Paper

Name:

Rectangular Dot Paper

Isometric Dot Paper

Triangular Dot Paper

Triangular Grid Paper

Tangram Pattern

Regular Polyhedrons

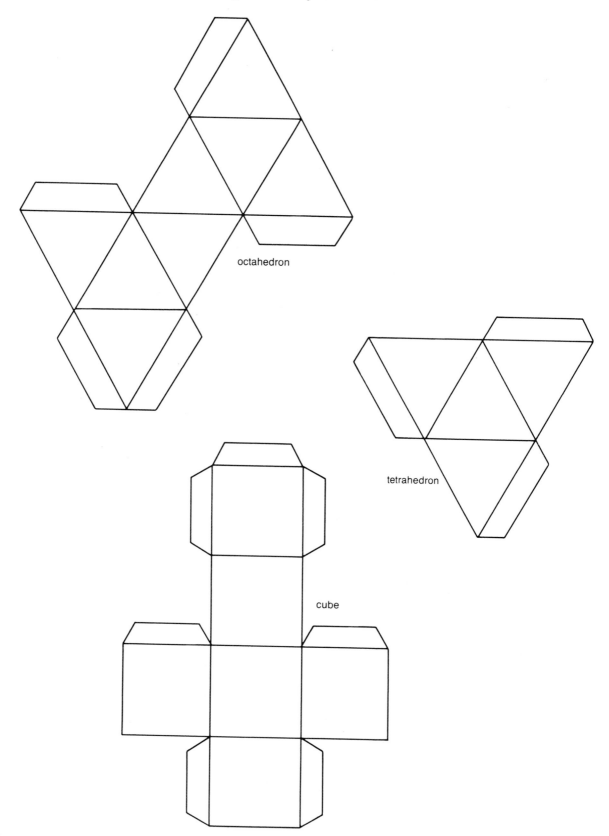

octahedron

tetrahedron

cube

Regular Polyhedrons

icosahedron

Regular Polyhedrons

dodecahedron

Algebra Blocks

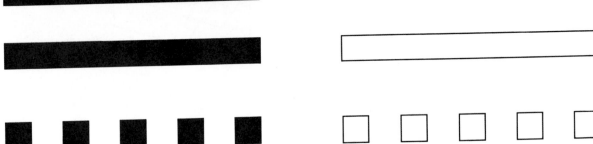

Large Coordinate Grid

Small Coordinate Grids

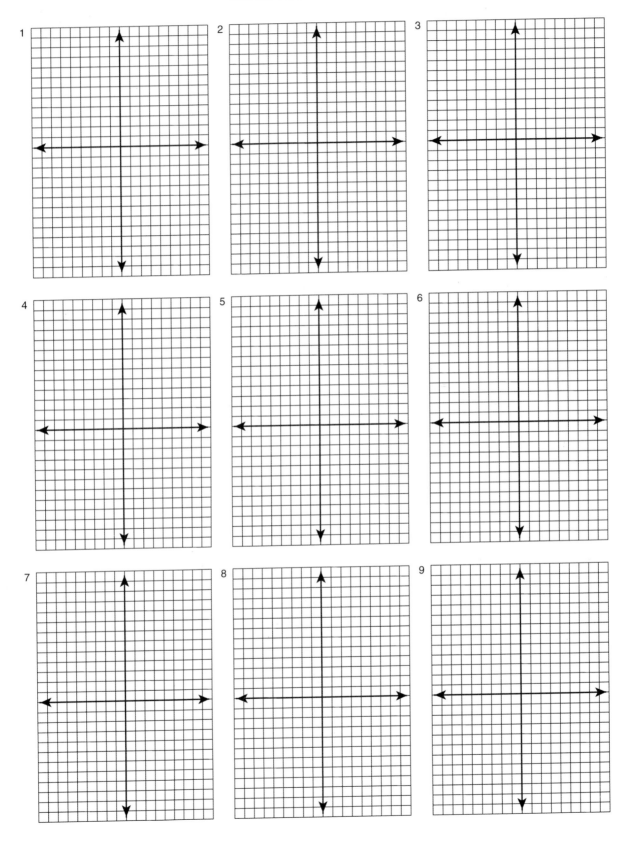

Lesson Plan Outline

NAME_____ DATE _____

GRADE LEVEL _____ SUBJECT_____ TIME _____

INSTRUCTIONAL OBJECTIVES: (The student will be able to . . .)

TERMS or VOCABULARY:

LEARNING MATERIALS or AIDS:

TEACHING STRATEGY:

- Introductory Activity:

- Meeting the Objective (Instructional Input, Modeling, Adapting for Special Students):

- Practice (Guided and Independent):

- Closure:

ASSESSMENT: (How will you know if the objectives were achieved?)

LESSON EVALUATION: (After you have taught the lesson describe how you believe it went.)

Index